The Christian Life

COLLEGE TEXTS IN THEOLOGY

General Editor

Francis L. B. Cunningham, O.P.,
S.T.Lr., S.T.D.

BASIC

God and His Creation

The Christian Life

Christ, and His Sacraments

SUBSIDIARY

Toward Marriage in Christ

THEOLOGY

A Basic Synthesis for the College

The Christian Life

Edited by

Francis L. B. Cunningham,
S.T.Lr., S.T.D.
of the Order of Preachers

The Priory Press ● *Dubuque, Iowa*

Revisores Ordinis: Joannes J. McDonald, O.P., S.T.M., Fredericus E. Klueg,
O.P., S.T.Lr., S.T.D. Imprimi potest: Joannes E Marr, O.P., S.T.M.,
Prior Provincialis. Nihil obstat: Fredericus E. Klueg,
O.P., S.T.Lr., S.T.D., Censor. Imprimatur:
✠Leo Binz, Archiepiscopus Dubuquensis
festum S. Rosae a Lima, O.P.
die 30a Augusti 1959

Third Printing

Library of Congress Card No. 59–15306

Dedicated

to the memory of the late

POPE PIUS XII

champion

of an educated laity

ACKNOWLEDGMENTS

To the Confraternity of Christian Doctrine we express our gratitude for their permission to use their version of Sacred Scripture and the translations of certain papal encyclicals. Unless otherwise noted, however, all translations from ecclesiastical documents, from the Fathers and from St. Thomas are original, inspired more by the necessity to make them meaningful in English than by slavish adherence to the original.

More than any of the other volumes of this series, *The Christian Life* has been the result of extensive collaboration; no doubt something of evenness and uniformity of style has thereby been sacrificed, but the practical gains realized by this exchange and interaction have been so considerable that the editor has neither excuse nor regret, even though he must in all cases accept whatever of blame, literary or doctrinal, is leveled against these joint efforts. It was, typographically, impossible to give due credit to the various individuals on the title page for their several efforts. The writers will here be individually listed, and I am sure their charity will forgive so inadequate a recompense from one so heavily obligated. But it should be understood, on the other hand, that no one person has been responsible for any single chapter, and that most chapters have benefitted from the talents of many collaborators.

Once again a benign justice, a debt of gratitude, fortunately impels me publicly to thank my colleagues of St. Rose Priory.

The chief collaborators on this text, however, whose indefatigable, experienced and invaluable assistance have alone made so extensive a work possible, have been the following:

J. E. Bidwill, O.P., S.T.Lr.
St. Mary's College
Winona, Minn.

D. K. O'Rourke, O.P., S.T.Lr., J.C.D.
Mt. St. Bernard Seminary
Dubuque, Iowa

T. C. Donlan, O.P., S.T.Lr., S.T.D.
Dominican House of Theology
Dubuque, Iowa

J. S. Reidy, O.P., S.T.Lr., Ph.D.
Pontifical Faculty of Philosophy
River Forest, Ill.

C. D. Fandal, O.P., S.T.Lr., S.T.L.
University of Dallas
Dallas, Texas

J. G. Roxburgh, O.P., Ph.L.
Rosary College (St. Clara's)
Sinsinawa, Wisc.

R. B. O'Riley, O.P., Ph.B.
St. Rose Priory
Dubuque, Iowa

M. R. Scullion, O.P., S.T.Lr., Ph.D.
Dominican House of Studies
River Forest, Ill.

The considerable past and present college experience of the above fathers, most of whom have taught theology for years at the collegiate level, has been a most valuable aid in selecting and in disposing of material, in practical emphases, in developing approaches, etc. Other college teachers and administrators have contributed notably to the final product by their helpful suggestions, emendations, revisions and recommendations; unfortunately their very number precludes individual mention. But special thanks must be given to the following, who by their writings and efforts have contributed significantly to this volume:

R. J. Aumann, O.P., S.T.Lr., Ph.L., S.T.D.
De Paul University
Chicago, Ill.

J. T. Bonée, O.P., S.T.Lr., Ph.Laur.
Pontifical Faculty of Philosophy
River Forest, Ill.

C. J. D. Corcoran, O.P., S.T.Lr., Ph.Laur.
Spiritual Institute
River Forest, Ill.

J. W. Curran, O.P., S.T.P., S.T.D.
Xavier College
Chicago, Ill.

T. V. Flynn, O.P., S.T.Lr., Ph.D.
Loras College
Dubuque, Iowa

W. B. Mahoney, O.P., S.T.Lr., Ph.D.
Albertus Magnus Lyceum for Natural Science
River Forest, Ill.

THE EDITOR

vii

TO THE STUDENT

One of the most fascinating objects in this wide wide world of ours is a small piece of silvered glass: a mirror. Pick one up for yourself and see. For there are few things that interest us more than our own selves: what we are and where we come from, where we are going and what we may be. This is only natural, of course; ours is a curious mind, and the closest object for our scrutiny lies right at hand. It can be overdone, it frequently is. Yet the ancient admonition "Know thyself" possesses as much validity in our atomic age as it had in the garden of delights.

Know thyself. Few commands will be more readily accepted and acted upon as this. But its dangers are only too obvious. "No man is a just judge in his own cause," warns another equally ancient bit of distilled wisdom. One's own view of the face in the charming mirror does not necessarily reflect the view that others possess. The injunction can only be truly fulfilled if we can establish objective standards, principles and norms by which to judge ourselves and our actions, and only if we use them with scrupulous honesty. In the powerful glare of Klieg lights the mirrored face appears in its harsh reality, stripped of make-up and illusion, laid naked to essential beauty or ugliness. It may not be a pretty sight, but no advantage is gained, in any case, by turning off the lights or using a mirror with a painted image.

This book is your mirror. You can look into it and see yourself truly; you can know yourself. It is a mirror brilliantly illuminated, for its lights are the light of reason (man's participation of the light of the divine intellect) and the light of faith, that brighter, more realistic light which enables us to see all things as they truly are, as they are in the sight of God. It is a realistic mirror, for it reflects man—you—in his essential relationships: to God, first of all; to other men; to himself. It is a vast mirror, for it images the whole field, natural and supernatural, of human action, man's all but infinite possibilities in all their bewildering variety, his paths of ultimate triumph—and the byways, detours and exodus of defeat. It is a mirror of deep perspective, which peers beneath the veneer of reality to the essential and the absolute.

Here you can know yourself. You, the college student, whose precise vocation at the present moment is the acquisition of knowledge. But that means an honest look: a peering into the mirror, not a casual glance. There is a tremendous amount of material in this volume to be assimilated, to be read over carefully and correlated with what you already know and with reality itself. Sincere effort, hard work, real study—these are prerequisite for any advance in knowledge, and especially in self-knowledge. Remember you deceive only yourself if you peek instead of peer: the aged actress who sees in her mirror the sensational ingénue of bygone days is no worse a fool, no greater a self-deceiver. For here are the divine principles and practical norms of successful human living for all the multiple areas of our activity. Here are the guide-posts and directives to keep one on the straight path which leads to our only true home, where resides in eternal bliss the family of God.

Know thyself. Use the tools of knowledge earnestly and effectively; no other knowledge you will ever acquire can have such far-reaching effects for now and forever. And above all put this knowledge to work. Theology was never meant to remain locked up in the ivory casket of the mind. What is the use of looking in any mirror, after all, if you do not intend to do something about what you see there?

They said it could be done, they said *anybody* could do it: for the Father, the Son and the Spirit have promised their divine assistance to anyone willing to make the effort.

Francis L. B. Cunningham, o.p., s.t.lr., s.t.d.
General Editor, COLLEGE TEXTS IN THEOLOGY

CONTENTS

CHAPTER THREE

The Passions of Man

CHAPTER FOUR

Habits and Virtues

CHAPTER FIVE

Sin

CHAPTER SIX

Law

CHAPTER SEVEN

Divine Grace

CHAPTER EIGHT

Faith: Beginnings of Eternal Life

CHAPTER NINE

Hope: The Assurance of God

CHAPTER TEN

Charity: Divine Friendship

CHAPTER ELEVEN

Prudence

CHAPTER TWELVE

Justice

CHAPTER THIRTEEN

Religion

CHAPTER FOURTEEN

The Social Virtues

CHAPTER FIFTEEN

Fortitude

CHAPTER SIXTEEN

Temperance

CHAPTER SEVENTEEN

Christian Specialization and Perfection

GENERAL BIBLIOGRAPHY

As with the other volumes of this basic series of college texts in theology, the bibliography recommend works in English, more or less easily available, which clarify the doctrine of this volume by way of simplification, difference of approach, amplification, application of principles, etc. No attempt has been made to make this bibliography exhaustive or critical, but what is included is judged capable of assisting the student in one way or another. At the end of each chapter is appended a Bibliographical Note which contains the specific references to books and periodicals of special value for the material treated in that chapter. Here the references have been limited to general works in moral theology or basic sources.

The first and most fundamental of these bibliographical items is the English *Summa*, generally available in the three volume edition published by Benziger Brothers, Inc. It is one of the basic sources for *The Christian Life*, being adhered to scrupulously with regard both to doctrinal content and order; frequent references to it will be made throughout the book, and the specific questions treated in any chapter are indicated in its Bibliographical Note.

Many commentaries on the *Summa* are found in most libraries. Some treat the matter at hand in highly technical language and will be especially useful to those who seek a more scientific knowledge of a subject. Among these commentaries we can list the abbreviated *Handbook of Moral Theology* by Dominic M. Prümmer, O.P. (New York: P. J. Kennedy and Sons, 1957); *Preface to Happiness* by E. F. Smith, O.P., and L. H. Ryan, O.P. (New York: Benziger Bros. Inc., 1950); two volumes of the Fides series edited by A. M. Henry, O.P.— Volume III, *Man and His Happiness*, and volume IV, *The Virtues and States of Life* (Chicago: Fides, 1956); the two volume *Moral Theology* by Charles J. Callan, O.P., and John A. McHugh, O.P. (New York: Joseph F. Wagner, 1958); and Francis J. Connell, C.SS.R., *Outlines of Moral Theology* (Milwaukee: Bruce, 1953).

Definitions of theological terms will be found in T. Pègues, O.P., *Catechism of the "Summa Theologica"* (Westminster, Md.: The Newman Press, 1950). To this should be added the other two volumes of COLLEGE TEXTS IN THEOLOGY: *God and His Creation* by William B. Murphy, O.P., *et al.* and *Christ, and His Sacraments*, by Thomas C. Donlan, O.P., *et al.* (Dubuque: The Priory Press, 1958), whose explanations of terms and doctrinal points will be often referred to in the present text.

Other commentaries render theological teaching in a more simplified and popular style. Chief among these is *A Companion to the Summa* by Walter Farrell, O.P., Volumes II and III (New York: Sheed and Ward, 1953), noted for its timely and lively examples. Popular works which treat of moral theology and may be consulted as collateral sources are: *The Meaning of Man* by Jean Mouroux (New York: Sheed and Ward, 1948), a valuable and remarkable work; *The Christian Virtues* by Charles E. Sheedy, C.S.C., (Notre Dame, Ind: University of Notre Dame Press, 1949); another work by Jean Mouroux entitled *The Christian Experience* (New York: Sheed and Ward, 1954), which discusses how the Christian can see things as Christ saw them, react to them as he reacted, and love for the reasons he proposed; and a series of pamphlets called "Theology for the Layman" published by The Holy Name Society, 141 East 65th Street, New York City. (References to this series at the end of the individual chapters will be abbreviated *TFTL*).

Since theology not only teaches truth but also proposes that this truth be employed by each Christian in his spiritual life, this bibliography would not be complete unless works which apply the present doctrine to Christian perfection were listed. Among the more important we can name Abbot Columba Marmion, O.S.B., *Christ the Life of the Soul* (St. Louis: Herder, 1935); *The Mystical Evolution* by John G. Arintero, O.P. (St. Louis: Herder, 1949), which gives the principles for progress in holiness; *Christian Perfection and Con-*

templation by Reginald Garrigou-Lagrange, O.P. (St. Louis: Herder, 1937); and "Christianus" in *The Collected Works of Abbot Vonier* (Westminster, Md.: The Newman Press, 1952), a broad outline of the ideal of Catholic living in an imperfect world.

In recent years the Popes have spoken authoritatively and meaningfully about the needs of the Christian family and social justice. Students who wish to be advised of contemporary Catholic thought on marriage, virtue, education, society, politics and many other questions of morality can fulfill this desire by consulting *The Mind of Pius XII,* edited by Robert C. Pollock (New York: Crown Publishers Inc., 1958), and *The Pope Speaks* (Chicago: Pantheon, 1957).

Of course, no student should take up the study of theology without a copy of the Bible close at hand. Dogmatic definitions made by the Church throughout the centuries will be found in *The Sources of Catholic Dogma* (St. Louis: Herder, 1957).

Periodicals which contain articles pertinent to all the above categories are subscribed to by most libraries. Essays concerning the repercussions of this doctrine on daily spiritual life can be found in *Cross and Crown, The Life of the Spirit, Spiritual Life* and *Worship,* which adds a great deal of material on the liturgical life. Two periodicals will be valuable for their technical treatment of specific topics: *The Thomist* and *Theological Studies.* Articles which will be an aid to harmonious family living can be read in *Liguorian, The Grail, Altar and Home* and *Integrity* (a magazine which has, unfortunately, ceased publication, but whose back issues are preserved by most libraries). Finally, we can name *The Catholic Mind* and *The Pope Speaks,* both of which provide translations of current pronouncements made by the pope.

INTRODUCTION

The Creator says to Adam:

I have set thee in the midst of the world, that thou mayst the more easily behold and see all that is therein. I created thee a being neither heavenly nor earthly, neither mortal nor immortal only, that thou mightest be free to shape and to overcome thyself. Thou mayst sink into a beast, and be borne anew to the divine likeness. The brutes bring from their mothers' body what they carry with them as long as they live; the higher spirits are from the beginning, or soon after, what they will be for ever. To thee alone is given a growth and de-development depending on thine own free will. Thou bearest in thee the germs of a universal life.

In these words from his *Speech on the Dignity of Man*, the great Renaissance genius, Pico della Mirandola, sets before our eyes a truly lofty conception of mankind, one which derives from the noblest Greco-Roman tradition. But still loftier, and infinitely more profound, is the deceptively simple statement with which another genius introduces this second part of theology. "Man, as Damascene states,[1] is said to be made to God's image insofar as this image implies 'an intelligent being endowed with free will and self-movement.' Therefore, now that we have treated of the exemplar, God, and of those things which came forth from the power of God in accordance with his will, what remains for us to consider is his image, man, inasmuch as he too is the principle of his actions, in possessing free will and power over his works."[2]

---

[1] *On the True Faith*, Bk. II, Chap. 12.

[2] St. Thomas, *Summa*, II, Prologue. It should be noted that the division of this second part of the *Summa* into two (I-II and II-II) is one made for the sake of convenience by certain editors because of the length of the material; it has no formal *ratio* whatsoever.

At once a new perspective and new human vistas are opened up for us. Great as is the dignity of man, as Mirandola so justly remarked, magnificent as are his possibilities of self-development, he is not the measure of reality, nor can his potentialities be defined by the self-circumscribing limits of his innate capacities, however noble they be. The excellent philosophical definition of man as *rational animal* must yield to the more realistic concept of theology, the more nobly human because the more divine: *man is the image of God.* Here is the leitmotiv for our study of this singular creature of God.

"The proper study of mankind," said Alexander Pope, "is man"—an apt summary of the spirit of his age of rationalism. All of Christian tradition protests against this mockery of the true state of things; divine revelation contradicts it outright; a just philosophy recoils from so limited an approach to reality. That distilled wisdom of Catholicism which is theology knows one subject and one subject only: God. But theology first considers God as he is the cause of all things and their exemplar; in this vision it considers all of reality, which is more true in divine thought than when seen directly in itself. Now the theologian turns to study God as he is the end and perfecting goal of creatures in their return to him from whom they first came forth; in particular he will study the creature who alone holds the reins of his own conduct: man.

"Moral theology," then, completes the preceding treatise on God, for it shows forth all the implications of the fact that man proceeds from God as his image, and thus brings to a new perfection our knowledge of divine being. God is viewed from this new aspect as the goal of all, and this is a comprehension of ultimate reality which at the same time produces a divinely true picture of man. In consequence, only in this new theological vision is found that necessary wisdom, at once speculative and eminently practical, which will direct man, amidst his temporal and spiritual responsibilities, in a single unified movement towards eternal life.

Here lies one of St. Thomas' greatest contributions to theology, one most strikingly original and perennially significant.[3] Other theo-

---

[3]Cf. Thomas Deman, O.P., *Aux Origines de la Théologie Morale* (Montréal: Institut d'Études Médiévales, 1951).

logians before him had considered the material on the virtues, but only as appendages to the treatise on Christ; and they had considered the study of man's last end, but only as an introduction to the treatise on the last things. Under the higher viewpoint of God as final cause, St. Thomas was able intellectually to organize man's multifarious activity into an integral and organic whole, rigorously scientific yet theologically vital; he was able to synthesize the data of revelation and tradition, the teachings of even the pagan philosophers and moralists, the facts both of natural and supernatural reality, into a unified complex of theological wisdom. Here divine truth and grace inform, elevate and perfect natural truth and nature itself, much as the soul in union with the body so informs it as to bring it to heights and perfections not native to matter. Man can do no more, can never do better.

This magnificent synthesis, however—which introduced moral considerations in their necessary, rightful and organic place in theology, preserving at the same time its unity of object and distinctive method—was little appreciated by later theologians. Modern manuals of moral theology provide, to be sure, authoritative solutions for cases of conscience, but according to a heterogeneous collection of rules and usually under the aspect of duty and obligations. Perspective is lacking; and breadth. And the unity vitalized by principles, the wholeness of approach and of organic integration—all this has been attenuated, if not wholly lost.

In this volume we shall, as far as possible, adopt this point of view of the Angelic Doctor, utilize his methods, follow his order. This theological contemplation of the image of the Trinity looks toward the realization of man's possibilities in full measure through his free fashioning and perfecting of his divine resemblance. Hence it begins with the contemplation of man's end, that to which man must tend in his return to God, final cause of all. This is the key to an understanding of the multiplicity of human actions and of their principles, and the keystone as well as the foundation of all further investigations. From this examination follows naturally the considerations of the means to that end—of those acts by which man, with the aid of God, attains his perfecting imaging of the Trinity in his final happiness. This consideration of means is both general (a study of sources of human acts) and particular: a study of individual human acts in their existential reality, as they occur in concrete situations.

The general study of human acts considers them in themselves, in their internal principles (virtues and vices), and in the extrinsic principles (law and grace) of these acts. Our theological interest in man's concrete actions and particular situations embraces both those which are common to all men and the specialized situations, the "states of life," in which certain men may be placed by God. For its part, the study of particular and individual human actions is traditionally organized under the aegis of the three theological and four cardinal virtues; distinguished according to their matter or object, these virtues subsume, under their general and humanistic control, the multifarious activity of God's image. Thus they encourage an organized consideration of the complex dynanism of human behavior.

The theology of God as final cause, therefore—which is the theology of man in his relationship to God, object of his return, and thus in his relationships to other men and to himself—will follow the order indicated on the following pages.

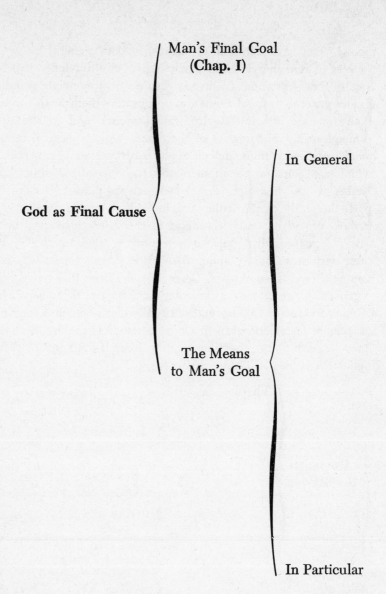

Man's Final Goal
(Chap. I)

God as Final Cause

In General

The Means
to Man's Goal

In Particular

Human Acts
- Proper to Man **(Chap. II)**
- Passions **(Chap. III)**

The Principles of Human Acts
- Intrinsic
  - Habits and Virtues **(Chap. IV)**
  - Sin and Vice **(Chap. V)**
- Extrinsic
  - Law **(Chap. VI)**
  - Grace **(Chap. VII)**

Common to All Men
- Theological Virtues
  - Faith **(Chap. VIII)**
  - Hope **(Chap. IX)**
  - Charity **(Chap. X)**
- Cardinal Virtues
  - Prudence **(Chap. XI)**
  - Justice
    - In Itself **(Chap. XII)**
    - Religion **(Chap. XIII)**
    - Social Virtues **(Chap. XIV)**
  - Fortitude **(Chap. XV)**
  - Temperance **(Chap. XVI)**

Specializations **(Chap. XVII)**

CHAPTER ONE

Man's High Destiny

The proper subject matter of this volume is God himself as he is the end to which man tends. Insofar, therefore, as man by his free and controlled action proceeding from intelligence and will images God, moral theology initiates a study of human dynamism, that is to say, a study of our actions, as human beings, in relation to the divinity.

The first point of our inquiry, in consequence, will be to determine what human actions are in their relationship to God.

1. What Is Human Action?

What is characteristic of human action precisely as it is human? Man shares many activities in common with the lower creation of which he is lord: falling downward like stones, growing larger like trees, digesting food, dying. But these acts are not characteristically human; hence we call them **acts of man**. Truly *human* action encompasses those actions which proceed from a man's deliberate will; these are actions which are performed by man precisely as man, since they proceed from his characteristically human faculties of reason and will.

When man *chooses* a certain college, *decides* what field he will major in, *elects* a class president, he acts as a man. What is typical of such **human action?**

A. Human Actions Are Always for an End

Man can know the truth of things because his intellect is a power ordained to the true as to its proper object. Every action that proceeds from a potency (i.e., the power to act in a certain way) is caused by that potency in accordance with the nature of its own object. The object of the will, which is the source and determinant of actions that are properly human, is the *good.* Just as the eye, if it sees, must see color, so the will, if it acts, must act for the good. But for the will the good is one and the same thing as the end or goal; because it is suitable and desirable, the good moves the will to action, and under this aspect receives the name of **end,** *that on account of which the will acts,* the final cause. Since in every human action man acts for a good, he must also act for an end.

Every action, however, even non-human action, is in some way for an end. What is typical about human action for an end? *It is conscious, self-determining action for an end,* action over which man has mastery. Whereas lower creatures are moved by another to an end—whether blindly, like the tree which thrusts its roots toward water; or instinctively, like the robin which gathers straw to build a nest—man freely chooses to pursue an end: he moves himself to this goal. By his reason he knows the good formally as an end for him; by an act of the will following this judgment of reason, he freely chooses it. Consequently, human action is typically, characteristically, action for an end: *to act consciously for an end is proper to man.*

Hence it is clear that the principle of human acts, insofar as they are human, is the end, goal or purpose. If no good, real or apparent, is known by reason, no human action is performed; if the good proposed by reason as an end is rejected by the will, no further human action follows. Moreover, as principle of human action and termination of the will's intention in acting, the end determines what kind of action the will puts forth or elects—good if the end is morally good, evil if it is morally evil. Acting for an end, then, constitutes man a *moral* being; human acts are the same thing as moral acts, and thus moral action also receives its specification from its end.

Do we have here the ultimate explanation and determination of human activity? Surely not just any goal or good accounts for the complexity and diversity so characteristic of human actions. Experience—one's own, the testimony of history, the common consent of mankind—points to the fact that there is some *ultimate* end which gives meaning and direction to this variety and multiplicity. We shall have to explore this important key to human behavior in detail.

B. Man Acts for an Ultimate End

You buy a ticket to a baseball game. Why? Either because the highest goal of your life has been to own a baseball ticket or for some other reason, such as to get into the ball park. Like all your actions, the purchase of a baseball ticket is either an end chosen for its own sake or a stepping stone to some further goal. But stepping stones must lead somewhere, to some final destination. In the last analysis, there must be some end sought for itself alone, not ordered to any other goal.

The reason for this lies in the fact that an infinite series of intermediate ends is impossible. Just as all motion must have one supreme beginning if there is to be any motion at all, so all human action must have an ultimate end of there is to be any action at all. An intermediate goal can be the explanation of an action performed here and now, or of a particular series of actions; but of its nature, as intermediate, it itself demands explanation in terms of the goal it is ordered to. Since the whole reason for acting is to achieve a desired goal, an infinite number of subordinated goals could never explain why man acted in the first place. No one begins a series of actions if these actions lead nowhere.

Thus, if there were no last end, man would desire nothing, neither would his action ever be terminated, nor his intention ever find rest. *In every human action, therefore, man acts for an ultimate end.* This last end has (at least in the estimation of the one acting) the nature of a perfect good, desirable for its own sake, and all his many intermediate ends are subordinated and ordained to it as the imperfect good to the perfect good.

From the fact that there is a final goal for all human actions, we conclude:

1. **There is only one ultimate goal for any man.** "No man can serve two masters; for either he will hate the one and love the other, or else he will stand by the one and despise the other" (Matt. 6:24). From his last end man takes his entire rule of life; this is necessarily one, for otherwise man would be led into conflicting and contradictory activities and finally to no human action at all. Furthermore, since everything desires its own perfection, what man desires as his ultimate end is *that good which is his perfection and fulfillment,* such a fulfillment that nothing is left besides it for man to desire. This would not be possible, however, if there were some other good or end required for his perfection.

2. **Whatever man wills he wills for an ultimate goal.** Whatever man desires, he desires under the aspect of good. If it is not his perfect good, his ultimate goal, he must necessarily desire it as tending to the perfect good. Thus, intermediate goals (becoming a priest; robbing a bank) are chosen because of their relationship to a final goal (eternal salvation; acquisition of wealth).

This does not mean, however, that in his every human action man always expressly intends (*actual* intention) the last end; in this life it is impossible to be always thinking of the last end. A *virtual* intention suffices—that is to say, an intention which was formed in the past regarding the end and never retracted, but here and now influences the act a person is performing. While walking to church on Sunday, for example, one does not need to be thinking of his ultimate goal at every step.

3. **The last end of all men is happiness.** As St. Augustine points out, all men are agreed on at least this one point: they all desire the ultimate goal which is happiness.[1] Divided they may be on all else, but men, no matter what prejudices color their lives, are unified by their common pursuit of happiness. For each of Adam's children desires the fulfillment of his own perfection—it is this, we have seen, that is man's final goal—and happiness means just such a fulfillment. No such unanimity, however, is found among men with respect to the object which will bring them happiness. Over the course of centuries men have pursued the will-o'-the-wisps of riches, of power, of pleasure—and still do today. For men's goals are as diverse as their personalities are divergent. The man of truly Christian virtue, however, desires as his last end that good which is his most perfect fulfillment: God himself.

4. **Man alone has happiness for his ultimate goal.** If we speak of man's last end as the *object* which brings happiness, then the ultimate goal of all creatures, including man, is the same; for God, who created all things, made all things for himself. But men and angels are unique in that they alone are able to *possess God.* Irrational creatures attain God as their end, on the other hand, only by sharing a certain likeness of him, simply by existing or living or knowing.

Since possession of the ultimate end constitutes happiness, only man, of all the creatures on earth, can ever be happy.

From these last considerations arise two vital questions concerning man's ultimate goal: *first,* in what **object** does man's happiness truly consist? As we have seen, there is wide variance of opinion on this important point among men outside the fold of Christ. We shall, through reason enlightened by faith, show that man's true objective goal is, in truth, God himself (**Section 2**). *Secondly,* what is the nature of human happiness? The determination of this question will disclose the action on man's part that constitutes his **subjective** happiness—the fulfillment of his perfection through the possession of God—and the properties which flow from it (**Section 3**).

[1]Cf. *On the Trinity,* Bk. XIII, Chap. 3.

2. Where Does Man's Happiness Lie?

Four hundred years before Christ, the great Greek philosopher, Aristotle, pointed out our present problem and the practical necessity and utility of its solution:

> If there is some end to the things we do which we desire for its own sake (everything else being desired for the sake of this); and if we do not desire everything for the sake of something else (for at that rate the process would go on to infinity, and thus our desire would be empty and vain); then it is manifest that this must be the good, and the chief good. Will not the knowledge of it, then, have a great influence on life? Shall we not, like archers who have a mark to aim at, be more likely to hit upon what is necessary? If so, we must try, at least in outline, to determine what it is. . . .[2]

With the philosopher, the theologian sees the necessity and the usefulness of this inquiry. Indeed, all men at one time or another, implicitly or explicitly, have looked at reality and asked: *why? where lies my happiness?* From reason and from faith we acquire a double answer: 1) the object which will make man happy can be found in no created good; 2) God alone is the object of human happiness.

A. Man's Happiness Is Found in No Created Good

In the beginning God blessed man and said to him: " 'Be fruitful and multiply: fill the earth and subdue it. Have dominion over the fish of the sea, the birds of the air, the cattle and all the animals that crawl on the earth.' God also said, 'See, I give you every seed-bearing plant on the earth and every tree which has seed-bearing fruit to be your food. . . . ,' and so it was. God saw all that he had made was very good" (Gen. 1:28-30). But despite their wonderful variety, none of these good things, no created thing, can bring perfect happiness to him who images God. We can see this more clearly if we examine each of the classes of created goods which man can possess; they may be outlined as follows:

[2]*Nicomachean Ethics*, Bk. I, Chap. 1.

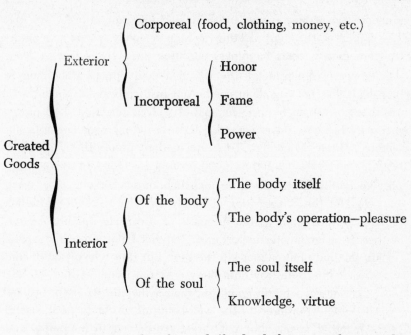

1. **Riches,** whether they be real (food, clothing, penthouse, television sets) or artificial (money) are only *useful* goods; of their nature they are means to some goal, never the ultimate goal itself. Natural riches are used to sustain life or contribute to "gracious living"; money is only a means to procure these natural riches. Furthermore, these external goods often cause evil and cannot supply every good. Poor King Midas, whose every touch turned things to gold, nearly starved to death: wealth, natural or artificial, is no guarantee of wisdom, or health, or virtue.

2. **Honors** are only signs and attestations on the part of others of an excellence in the person who is honored. Thus the excellence is a greater good than the honor bestowed, which exists, in any case, in the person paying honor, not in the one honored.

3. **Reputation** (fame or glory), even when justified by true worth, is not the object of man's happiness. Like honors, fame depends on the estimation of other men and presupposes excellence already possessed. Moreover, the judgment of men is only too frequently

erroneous, awarding praise to those entirely unworthy of it. And fame is one of the most fleeting of human goods—where are Saturday's heroes?—whereas happiness perdures.

4. **Power** is the principle by which a man directs other men to their goal; it is not a goal in itself. And history bears abundant witness that power can be used for evil as well as for good: "All power corrupts," Lord Acton remarked, "and absolute power corrupts absolutely." Hitler, Mussolini, Tojo, are modern proofs that happiness, the supreme goal and perfect good, cannot be found in power.[3]

5. **No bodily** good can bring man happiness.

1) Not the *conservation* of bodily life. For the soul, on which the body depends as the principle of life itself and life's activities, is of far greater importance: "Do not be afraid of those who kill the body but cannot kill the soul. But rather be afraid of him who is able to destroy both body and soul in hell" (Matt. 10:28).

2) Not good bodily *qualities*, such as health, strength, beauty. All these are ordered to the well-being of the body itself, useful as material means, but not directly ordained to happiness and imperfect as compared with spiritual goods. The leper, Joseph Damien, reached perfect happiness. Health of mind is better than health of body, strength of will better than strength of arm, the beauty of virtue better than bodily beauty.

3) Not *pleasure*. Bodily pleasure is delight in the things of the senses, following upon the possession of sensible goods. Sensible good is not perfect good, cannot completely satisfy man's hunger for perfect fulfillment; pleasure in sensible good is a thing of the too fleeting moment, "gone, alas! like our loves too soon"; and bodily pleasures man shares with the animals, whereas happiness is uniquely his alone.

[3]As St. Thomas points out, there are four general reasons why happiness cannot be found in any external good: 1) happiness, man's supreme good, is incompatible with evil; exterior goods can be found both in evil and in good men; 2) happiness satisfies every need: but after acquiring any one of these goods, man may still lack many goods that are necessary for him; 3) as the perfect good, happiness can bring no evil: yet any of the four external goods may bring evil to its possessor; 4) man is ordained to happiness through intrinsic principles: external goods are rather the result of external causes and in many cases simply of good fortune. Cf. *Summa*, I-II, q. 2, a. 5.

6. **Goods of the soul** cannot provide happiness. The human soul is not its own happiness, for the object of happiness is the perfect good and the soul is made perfect by its habits and acts. Nor can the powers and habits of the soul of themselves be its perfect good, since these are in potency to further perfection by their acts. There is no act of the soul (despite the fact that the soul's acts bring perfection and goodness to habits, powers and the soul itself) which is the final object of happiness. For man through his will tends to the perfect and universal good. Human actions, on the contrary, are always particular, no matter how noble they be. Even man's highest acts—of knowledge, of love, of virtue—are particular goods incapable of satisfying the infinite longing of the will. These are not man's *objective* happiness, but the *subjective* means by which he possesses the object of his happiness.

From this detailed examination of created goods we can conclude, on the basis of reason alone, that none of them can provide that perfect completion and fulfillment for which man's whole being yearns. Nor—even if it were possible for one man to possess all these goods simultaneously—can the sum total of all created goods bring happiness. Each of these goods, taken singly, is intrinsically imperfect and limited; taken collectively, the total remains imperfect and limited. The will seeks goodness itself, unlimited, universal, perfect; man can find no final satisfaction or rest in the imperfect goods of his universe.

B. God Alone Is the Object of Man's Happiness

(1) *The Datum of Reason*

Happiness is the perfect good, one which brings the appetite to complete rest; otherwise, if there still remains something to be desired, it would not be the ultimate end. But the object of the will, which is man's appetite, is the universal good, just as the object of the intellect is universal truth. It is clear from this that nothing can bring man's will to rest except the universal good. This universal good is not found in any creature (for every creature merely shares in goodness) but only in God. Hence God alone can satisfy the will of man, and therefore he alone is the object of man's happiness.[4]

[4]St. Thomas, *Summa*, I-II, q. 2, a. 8.

All of creation comes forth from God and is utterly dependent upon him for its whole being; all of creation moves toward God, impelled from the depths of its being by an urge toward him who is its end. In his own way, as an intellectual being, man shares in this vast aspiration toward otherness, toward that beyond and outside himself in which alone he finds perfection and fulfillment. Aristotle recognized that man is called by his very nature to God, and that thus his work in creation is an essential response to this call: so he plays his predestined part in the drama of created being. But this is no guarantee that man will achieve the object of his desire. Reason can tell us this alone: *if* man is to have happiness, then it can only consist in the possession of *the good*. Reason cannot assure us that such happiness is realizable, nor can it tell us what this possession of God would be like were it possible.

(2) The Teaching of Faith

What man cannot know by his native powers of understanding God reveals to him. "Keep me, O God, for in you I take refuge," exclaims the psalmist. "I say to the Lord, 'My Lord are you. Apart from you I have no good'" (Ps. 15:1-2). This was the secret of Israel: that the Lord was their allotted portion and their cup (Ps. 15:5). In the beginning man had walked with God in the cool of the evening of paradise. The inheritance basely squandered by Adam, man's union with God, became the portion of the chosen people. Slowly God teaches his elect that happiness consists in the communion of man with God despite all obstacles and sufferings: total abandonment to God is the lesson Abraham learns through faith; Yahweh, in the historic struggles of his people, appears as their sole salvation; in their alliance with him (so the nation learns gradually and not without defection) resides their happiness, and the happiness of each individual Jew; amidst his sufferings Job teaches the further lesson that human happiness cannot remain earthly—and the final preparation of the chosen for the coming of the Messias consists in the revelation that man's happiness is only to be found in his response to the love of God: "Wisdom instructs her children and admonishes those who seek her. He who loves her loves life; those who seek her out win her favor. He who holds her fast inherits glory . . ." (Sir. 4:11-13); "and the faithful shall abide with him in love: because grace and mercy are with his chosen ones" (Wisd. 3:9).

Christ comes. And he comes to fulfill the promises: the theme of all his teachings will be entrance into the kingdom, into the happiness which is a participation of the very goodness of God in intimate association with him. "Rejoice in this," he insists, "that your names are written in heaven" (Luke 10:20). In this supernal happiness, St. Paul points out, "God will be all in all" (I Cor. 15:28), "and so we shall ever be with the Lord" (Thess. 4:17). And St. John does not hesitate to say that "he who abides in the doctrine, he has both the Father and the Son" (II John 10); for he had previously recorded his Master's astonishing words: "Now this is everlasting life, that they may know thee, the only true God, and him who thou hast sent" (John 17:3).

By his own infallible word, God himself instructs us that he himself is our ultimate goal. This is the high destiny of man: the everlasting possession of the absolute, supreme and universal good who is God. Asured by divine faith of this reality—that God himself truly is attainable by man as the object of his ultimate happiness—we must ask this necessary question: what is man's subjective happiness? In other words, how does man attain God, the object of his happiness?

3. WHAT IS MAN'S HAPPINESS?

That God is truly, not only in the abstract but concretely, the object of man's happiness is clear, but this is not enough. Diamonds exist, but a woman is not happy in that fact alone; happiness comes only when she possesses a diamond, when she knows it is hers and can display it on her finger. Nor does the mere existence of God as his ultimate goal bring happiness to man; only when he possesses the universal good is his search for happiness terminated. This means that man has somehow reached out and made that ultimate goal his own, so that happiness is found within himself.

How does man possess God? What is the essence of happiness? Of all of the things of which perfect happiness is comprised, which is the one that primarily and essentially constitutes man's happiness, so as to be the source of all the other qualities that happiness possesses?

Revelation alone could possibly propose an answer to this question —an answer summarily expressed in Moses' demand to see God's glory: "If therefore I have found favor in thy sight, show me thy face, that I may know thee . . ." (Ex. 33:13). For God in himself, not as related to creatures, is the object of man's happiness. But the light of reason can clarify the conditions presupposed to man's happiness: the kind of activity from man's point of view which is the possession of happiness, and the requirements for that happiness.

A. The Requisites for Man's Happiness

(1) Personal Activity

The first point reason makes is that happiness must truly belong to man; it must necessarily be *personal*, something *he* acquires, that *he* possesses. The pantheistic absorption into the divine substance which is the goal of so many eastern philosophies and religions does violence to man's very nature. The oblivion of nirvana effaces the image of God in man, because it is precisely as the principle of his own activity that man imitates God. No, man *himself* must attain his own destiny, or he cannot fulfill the needs of his nature and thus realize his perfection. His happiness, then, will be something really his, something proportioned to his limitations as a created being. Consequently, man's happiness, like man himself, must be a created good.

The second mark reached by reason is that the essence of happiness must be an activity of the soul. Every being acquires perfection in direct proportion to the realization of its potentialities; the potential acrobat reaches perfection through practice, the student through study. Thus, only man's own activity, an activity of the soul, will accomplish his goal. But not every activity of man's soul can fulfill the task; his sensitive activities, the powers to see and hear and touch, are inadequate because they attain sensible objects and God is spiritual, an intelligible object. Hence, the task of possessing God belongs either to the intellect or the will.

The will, however, cannot produce the kind of activity which is necessary. It can move other human powers to grasp an object, it can rejoice in the possession of that object, but it can never reach out and actually take hold of an object. The task, then, of possessing happiness must be an operation of the intellect, for man's intellect can know universals and it is the universal good that he pursues. Furthermore, man's highest operation is that of his speculative intellect. This power contemplates truth for its own sake, and its ultimate object is divine truth, the highest intelligible good. Hence his happiness must consist principally in an operation of the speculative intellect, an operation we call *contemplation*. In short, reason most logically concludes that man's subjective happiness—his completion, his fulfillment, his perfection—will consist in the highest operation of his highest power.

(2) The Contemplation Which Is Happiness

Of course, indiscriminate contemplation will not suffice. Man can know and contemplate philosophical truths, truths garnered from sense experience, but this knowledge is an imperfect contemplation of God: "We see now through a mirror in an obscure manner . . ." (I Cor. 13:12). Even a direct knowledge of the angels would be insufficient; angelic beauty is only a participated beauty, a lovely but pale reflection incapable of leading man to a perfect knowledge of God.

Yet in some way man must possess God by intellectual means. Reason itself apprises us of this irrefutable fact. Among the ancients, both Plato and Aristotle gained some degree of insight into this fact, but neither of them was able to discover God as man's goal. For Plato, ultimate happiness consists in man's complete and loving surrender of self to the abstract idea of the good and the beautiful. The flaw in this teaching lies in Plato's uncertainty as to whether this abstract idea of goodness and beauty is God himself or something distinct from him. Aristotle, whose teaching on so many difficult philosophical questions has endured for centuries, indicates that some sort of union with the divine is ultimately needed for happiness. His doctrine about the nature of God, however, is so brief that it cannot serve as a guide in this most fundamental of all moral questions. Thus the teaching of the two philosophers who represent the highest attainment of reason unaided by revelation fails to solve the most important question about man's destiny.

What, then, is the answer? How does man contemplate God? Although it is objectively possible for unaided reason to arrive at the solution, since human intelligence is open to all being, *de facto* it has never been done by reason independently of the guidance offered by revelation. The solution is suggested by the fact that **man naturally desires the vision of God.**[5]

"Rational animal" may be the definition of man, but it certainly does not exhaust the dimensions of his grandeur; a dimension that may be called the most profound mystery of man's spirit: his desire to *see* God. Unsatisfied with the knowledge of God's existence known from created things, man aspires to a knowledge of the divine essence itself, a desire which is simultaneously a thirst for happiness. For perfect happiness requires perfect knowledge, and perfect knowledge of God cannot be obtained through mirror-images or shadows or any created intermediary whatsoever. Only the *vision* of the divine essence can satisfy man.

Man's intelligence is capable of embracing all being. From this capacity there arises in the will a desire to possess a knowledge of the essences of all being. Most especially, man longs to know the essence of uncreated being, which is to know God *in himself*. The existence of such a desire shows that God makes man for God; it indicates that man, although limited, seeks perfection in the illimitable, and that, although contingent, he yearns for the absolute. The contemplation of God which is man's happiness will thus be found only in a direct and intuitive vision of God in himself.

[5] For a brief survey of this problem, cf. Jerome Wilms, O.P., *Divine Friendship* (Dubuque: The Priory Press, 1958), 1-5.

This is a fact verifiable by unaided reason; it is a philosophical conclusion. But it leaves unanswered the great question: can man *see* God, can man really have a *vision* of God? Certainly man's natural powers are not capable of this kind of knowledge of God, because it is essentially *above and beyond nature*. This is **supernatural** knowledge, similar to the knowledge God has of himself. Consequently, there is no guarantee that man's merely natural desire for the vision of God will ever be realized. It is a desire that can be fulfilled only by the free gift of God; a gift not demanded by nature, not owed to nature, and infinitely beyond the powers of nature. The existence of such a desire indicates the truth that man, made in God's image, can be raised to the divine level, that his mind is basically "capable of divinity." But this radical capacity can be fulfilled only if God through a wholly gratutious and supernatural gift, gives man this vision of himself which will make man happy far beyond the intrinsic limits of human possibility.

(3) The Vision of God

Man *will* see God, *will* enjoy the vision of the divine essence, *will* know the divine nature by a face to face vision. This is the testimony of God's own word: "When he appears," says St. John, "we shall be like him, for we shall see him just as he is" (I John 3:2). St. Paul is even more explicit: "We see now in a mirror in an obscure manner, but then face to face. Now I know in part, but then I shall know even as I am known" (I Cor. 13:12). Instead of a natural knowledge of God through images and examples, by ideas and abstract concepts, by reasoning processes, which is like reflections seen "in a mirror," we will see God directly in himself. Instead of the shadowy knowledge gained through supernatural faith, which is "obscure," we will see God clearly. Instead of these imperfect ways of knowing God, we will actually *see* him "just as he is" in himself, with the impact and the immediacy and the intimacy of a "face to face" vision. This will be as revealing to us as his knowledge of us is to him; we shall know even as we are known, in the fulness of divine knowledge and divine love.

The Church does not hesitate to propose this testimony of Scripture by defining that the souls of the blessed "see the divine essence by an intuitive and face to face vision, without the mediation of any creature . . . ; the divine essence is manifested to them plainly, clearly and openly."[6] Therefore, faith impels us to conclude that man sees God as his end by an intuitive vision of God in himself, a direct and immediate knowledge independent of any created idea or thing. In this act his perfect happiness is achieved.[7]

(4) The Significance of the Beatific Vision

God's power alone can actualize a knowledge of God which is of so intimate and superhuman a nature. Seeing God face to face is something *essentially* **supernatural,** accomplished by the special gift of God which is the consummation and perfection of grace, and which the Church calls the "light of glory."[8]

This incomparable "light" is a supernatural habit permanently perfecting, elevating and strengthening the intellect of the blessed in heaven. By it man is made capable of seeing the very essence of God. This vision is something essentially supernatural, like grace itself; it is not supernatural only because of the way it is produced or because of its direction to an end above all natural powers. That is to say, the beatific vision is somethng above and beyond nature, something which does not flow from nature, something which is in no way owed to nature. From God's viewpoint, a viewpoint which transcends the whole order of created being, this beatific vision is a participation of something which is proper to God alone. It is so far superior to all of nature, so perfectly and completely supernatural, that it is connatural only to the Godhead.

Revelation assures us of this participation: ". . . he has granted us the very great and precious promises, so that through them you may become partakers of the divine nature" (II Pet. 1:4). Thus, while it is obvious that we will never see God as perfectly as he sees him-

---

[6]Benedict XII, constitution *Benedictus Deus* (January 29, 1336); Denz. 530.

[7]Cf. Donlan, *et al., Christ, and His Sacraments* (Dubuque: The Priory Press, 1958), 589-92.

[8]Cf. the condemnation by the Council of Vienne of those who deny the necessity of the light of glory; Denz. 475.

self, nonetheless we will see him, and in this beatifying vision which unites us to God, we will achieve that fullest of perfections, the high destiny for which we were created.

To attain a good so far beyond his own powers, man must be raised, even in this life, to the supernatural order. He must have something added to his nature, and that something we call grace.

Man has no facility or tendency of his own to reach out for the supernatural. But he does have a passive capacity to receive the actions of God. We call this passive capacity an *obediential* potency, something which makes nature obedient to the influence of God. The supernatural order itself is something properly divine, and the grace given to man so that he may be lifted up to a supernatural sphere of activity is something wholly gratuitious, a gift of God's benevolence. Grace is the seed planted in this life which flowers through human actions into glory in the beatific vision.

B. The Qualities of Happiness Possessed

The abstract consideration of initiative vision as the essence of subjective happiness may make eternal joy seem a rather cold and bleak prospect. But if we consider it realistically as an activity of man, the whole concept regains warmth and attractiveness. Then it is seen to be a consummation in the life of God himself at the highest level of human possibility; the satisfaction of the deepest aspirations of the human spirit; a sharing of the eternal glory of the Son of God; the consummate perfecting of the image of the Trinity. From this most intimate "seizure" of God by contemplative union flow all the gifts which make man totally, supremely, eternally happy.

(1) Qualities in the Soul

We have already discussed the role of the intellect in the possession of happiness. Now we turn to those qualities of happiness which accrue to the will.

1. **Joy.** "The kingdom of God is not meat and drink," exclaims St. Paul, "but justice and peace and joy in the Holy Ghost" (Rom.

14:17), and St. Augustine adds that happiness is "joy in truth."[9] Supreme spiritual delight is caused by the actual possession of the ultimate goal, for then the will rests in perfect contentment in the intellect's perfect possession of God's glory, of supreme and sovereign good.

2. **Possession.** St. Paul speaks of this life as a race, at the end of which there will be a prize for the winner—happiness. "So run," he says, "as to obtain it" (I Cor. 9:24). The actual grasp of happiness, complete possession, the security of never losing God—"I held him, and I will not let him go" (Cant. 3:4)—and of being freed forever from the fear of damnation: all this belongs to the will. The faith of this life, which is an act of the intellect, becomes the act of vision in heaven. The love found in this life which is an act of the will, becomes joy in heaven. Similarly, the will's desire for happiness which hope fosters on earth is fulfilled in heaven through possession.

3. **Sinlessness.** "Blessed are the clean of heart, for they shall see God" (Matt. 5:8). These words of Christ are echoed by St. Paul: "Follow peace with all men, and holiness; without which no man shall see God" (Heb. 12:14). Thus, although sinlessness in this life leads to happiness, happiness in heaven will lead to sinlessness. The blessed in heaven are sinless because sin, the greatest evil, is excluded by the perfect good. Furthermore, even the possibility of sinning will be excluded, for the intellect sees God as the perfect universal good, and so cannot propose to the will a particular good contrary to God.

B. Qualities of the Body

"For the corruptible body must put on incorruption, and this mortal body must put on immortality" (I Cor. 15:33). It is a fact that sense images cannot adequately represent the divine essence which, in heaven, will be united to the intellect in a purely spiritual way. From this it is clear that bodily immortality will not be an essential addition to eternal happiness. Nonetheless, the reunion of

[9]*Confessions*, Bk. X, Chap. 23.

body and soul will add accidentally to the essential happiness of heaven. Man is not by nature a separated substance; hence, the soul is more perfect in its nature when joined with the body, and from the very happiness of the soul the body and the bodily senses will receive a certain overflow. Moreover, Benedict XII says: ". . . on the day of judgment all men with their bodies will make themselves ready to give an account of their own deeds before the tribunal of Christ. . . ."[10] Hence, since body and soul were partners in the working out of salvation, both deserve a reward: glory for the soul, and a share in that glory for the body.

We can summarize the qualities of glorified bodies in this way: ". . . neither shall they be able to die anymore, for they are equal to the angels, and are sons of God, being sons of the resurrection" (Luke 20:36). Thus the glorified bodies of the just will be: 1) **impassible**—free from injury, physical defects, corruption; 2) **subtle**—being dominated absolutely by the soul, making it independent of material needs; 3) **agile**—moving with the speed of thought; and 4) will possess **clarity**—a translucence similar to that of Christ at his transfiguration.

Exterior goods, like the acts of nutrition and generation, will cease to be needed; physical organs, although remaining intact, will no longer function. After all, these goods are necessary for sustaining animal life and propagating the race, and the glorified body is a spiritual body, not needing food and drink and bodily pleasures. Indeed, the very lack of bodily goods in heaven gives emphasis to the fact that in this life the body is the means used by the higher faculties to reach out for their goal.

C. The Companionship of Friends

If there were but one soul enjoying God it would be happy, even though it would have no neighbor to love. But if a neighbor were there, love of him would follow from the perfect love of God. Therefore, friendship is, as it were, concomitant with perfect happiness.[11]

[10]*Op. cit.*, Denz. 530.
[11]St. Thomas, *Summa*, I-II, q. 4, a. 8.

Thus St. Thomas beautifully explains the *social* aspect of perfect happiness. It is an accidental requirement for *personal* happiness, since we will no longer have to help friends or sacrifice for them—the test of friendship in this life. But no matter how great and essential the personal gift of salvation may be, "the end of all gifts of God is that we may be united among ourselves with a unity similar to the unity obtaining between the Father and the Son";[12] for Christ prayed: "that all may be one, even as thou, Father, in me and I in thee. . . . And the glory thou hast given me, I have given to them, that they may be one, even as we are one" (John 17:21-22).

Eternal life will perfect the unification, in knowledge and love, of the Mystical Body of Christ; it is the beatitude of a fraternal society. A self-centered possession of God is out of the question. God is glorified when man is made happy, when the product of God's creative power returns to rest in his vision. But since there are many men, untold millions who are called to give glory to God, the more who respond, the greater God's glory will be. Hence man, even in this life, must search his heart to discover every means he can to work for the happiness of others.

4. THE ATTAINMENT OF HAPPINESS

The threads of all the conclusions reached thus far are drawn together in this final section of our study. Here, two basic but momentous questions concretize the soul's demand for happiness: is happiness *possible?* *by what means* can it be attained?

A. The Possibility of Happiness

(1) Can Happiness Be Attained?

The vision of God is within the grasp of man, for Christ has promised: "He who does the will of my Father in heaven shall enter the kingdom of heaven" (Matt. 7:21). The whole purpose of his

---

[12]St. Thomas, *Commentary on St. John*, Chap. 17.

passion and death was to bring men to God: "We are free to enter the Holies [heaven], in virtue of the blood of Christ" (Heb. 10:19).

We·know that man's ultimate goal is the perfect universal good. But man is able to possess this goal, the highest good, *if* God elevates his natural powers; for his intellect can apprehend the universal and perfect good and his will can desire it. Hence man can attain happiness, but only insofar as his powers of knowledge and love are realized—through God's supernatural grace.

(2) Is Happiness Attained in the Same Degree by All?

"In my Father's house there are many mansions" (John 14:2). The ultimate goal of man is, of course, one: the one sovereign good who is God. But there are many mansions in God's kingdom, one man more perfectly sharing in the vision of God than another. There are two reasons for this:

1) the created intellect cannot, of itself, see God; rather, the power of vision has to be added by divine grace. This power is called the "light of glory." Hence the intellect which has more of the light of glory will see God to a greater degree.

2) the capacity of each man for happiness varies with the degree of grace and charity in his soul: he who has charity to a greater degree will participate more fully in the light of glory; for greater charity means greater desire, and greater desire means a greater disposition to receive the light of glory.

(3) Can Happiness Be Attained in This Life?

Because ignorance and error attack the intellect, weakness and malice the will, passion the appetites, and hunger, thirst and death the body, *perfect* happiness can never be found on earth, for perfect happiness excludes every evil.

But men can achieve an *imperfect* happiness in this life, a beginning and foretaste of eternal happiness; this will consist in the supernatural knowledge and love of God, exemplified by a life of virtue, which brings man closer to God. In the midst of trials and misfortune, such a man is a friend of God. And from this friendship flows joy, peace of conscience, tranquility of soul and the hope of eternal life—all of which are of far more worth than anything the world has to offer.

(4) Can Perfect Happiness Be Lost?

Perhaps the most consoling thing about man's eternal goal is that it will be eternal and can never be lost. This fact is based on the testimony of Sacred Scripture: "And this is the promise that he has given us, the life everlasting" (I John 2:25); it is also the teaching of the Church: "the same vision and enjoyment, without any interruption or departure of the aforesaid vision and enjoyment, exist continually and will continue even up to the last judgment, and from then even unto eternity."[13]

Reason also gives several causes for the stability of perfect happiness:

    1) any loss of happiness would be an evil, causing sadness of soul that such a good was not possessed;

    2) God, the object of happiness, is infinite and eternal, and hence happiness is also eternal;

    3) the will can never be satisfied completely by any other good, and thus the will can never turn away from its happiness;

    4) happiness is lost when God punishes those who sin. But in the vision of God the blessed cannot sin, because they cannot apply their wills to evil. Nor would God ever deprive man of the beatific vision.

B. The Means to Happiness

(1) The Necessity of God's Assistance

Sacred Scripture asserts that the vision of God is beyond the natural powers of man: "Eye has not seen, nor ear heard, nor has it entered into the heart of man what things God has prepared for those

---

[13]Benedict XII, *op. cit.;* Denz. 530.

who love him" (I Cor. 2:19). Furthermore, the Church has condemned those who say that ultimate beatitude can be reached by natural perfection.[14] The reason is easy to see: God is supernatural; therefore no creature, human or angelic, can attain God by his natural powers.

Nature, however, has not left man completely destitute, for it has provided him with a passive power—the obediential potency—which, through the gift of grace, enables him to be raised to the supernatural level.

Even angels are powerless to bring us to the perfect knowledge of God. They too were created and no creature can give to another perfect knowledge of the uncreated; this is a power belonging to God alone.

(2) The Necessity of Man's Action for Happiness

The Scriptures are replete with warnings to men that they must do good works in order to be saved. "If you know these things, blessed shall you be if you do them" (John 13:17); "so faith, too, unless it has works, is dead in itself" (Jas. 2:17)—these are just two examples. The Church has also defined against the Protestants that good works are necessary: "If anyone shall say that the just ought not to expect any hope for an eternal recompense from God through the merit of Jesus Christ for the good works which have been performed in God, if they doing well and in keeping the divine commandments they persevere to the end; let him be anathema."[15]

We must do our part to attain happiness: it is, we have seen, our personal goal, the major business of every man born of woman. God alone is by nature happy and possesses happiness from all eternity. Not having happiness, man must tend toward it. This he does by meritorious good works, which rectify his will and dispose him for happiness. All of the rest of this volume will be devoted to the general and particular means by which man works through his actions and with God's assistance to realize his destiny.

[14]Council of Vienne; Denz. 474.
[15]Council of Trent, Sess. VI, *Decree on Justification*, Can. 26; Denz. 836.

5. Summary and Conclusion

In all his human acts man acts for an end, and indeed for a final end, which we call happiness. The true objective happiness of man cannot consist in any created good, but is found only in God, the uncreated good. Happiness as it is attained by men consists essentially in an act of the speculative intellect, elevated by the light of glory, by which they see the essence of God.

Acts of the will necessarily follow upon the intellect's vision of God: joy, possession, sinlessness. Happiness is accidentally increased by the reunion of soul and body, and by the companionship of friends.

God in his great mercy makes happiness possible for all men, although some may be happier than others by reason of a greater participation in the happiness of God. Perfect happiness, however, is not a thing of this earth, it is the eternal enjoyment of the kingdom of heaven. But once happiness is achieved, it can never be lost, for the blessed soul can sin no more. Since it is supernatural, happiness cannot be attained by natural powers; since it is the personal goal of every man, his own good works are necessary to attain it.

The following are a few of the many practical conclusions which flow naturally from this doctrine on man's ultimate goal.

1. Christ brought us knowledge of the way to perfect happiness— a sharing in God's own life. Because each man is immensely more precious to him than the beauty of the stars, he wants all men to know of the things God has prepared for those who love him. To insure that his supernatural truth will be made available, he told his apostles to "go into the whole world and preach the gospel to every creature" (Mark 16:15). "He who hears you," he said, "hears me" (Luke 10:10). The Church is still carrying out his commands today, both in our land and in remote lands, bringing the "good news" of the right direction to perfect happiness, peace and unending joy. It is a task and a duty every Catholic, in his own way, must share.

2. "You see how vast the distance from heaven to earth? But let us rather begin from below. Do you not see how far it is from hell to the earth? And then from this earth to the heavens? And from the

heavens above us to the higher heaven beyond? And from there to the angels, to the archangels, to the heavenly powers, to the royal throne itself? Above this immense intervening void he has raised our nature—even to the very summit. Consider how low it was, and whither it has ascended. For it was not possible to descend lower than man had descended, or to go higher than Christ had now raised it."[16]

3. "The Holy See's work in favor of peace and international concord . . . seems to be as thorny as it is difficult. Its difficulty lies in this: that the fundamental conceptions of justice and love which make for individual happiness and the nobility of common social life have in many respects fallen into oblivion or contempt by a false process of thought and action which humanizes what is divine and divinizes what is human."[17]

4. "God 'from one man . . . has created the whole human race and made them live all over the face of the earth, determining their appointed times and the boundaries of their lands; that they should seek God' (Acts 7:26-27).

"A marvelous vision, which makes us see the human race in the unity of one common origin in God 'one God and Father of all, who is above all, and through all, and in us all' (Eph. 4:6); in the unity of nature which in every man is equally composed of material body and spiritual, immortal soul; in the unity of the immediate end and mission in the world; in the unity of dwelling place, the earth, of whose resources all men can by natural right avail themselves, to sustain and develop life; in the unity of the supernatural end, God himself, to whom all should tend; in the unity of means to secure that end."[18]

[16]St. John Chrysostom, *On the Ascension of Our Lord Jesus Christ.*
[17]Pope Pius XII, greeting to the new Italian Ambassador, December 7, 1939.
[18]Pius XII, encyclical *Summi Pontificatus,* October 20, 1939.

BIBLIOGRAPHICAL NOTE

St. Thomas' formal treatment of the doctrine on man's final end can be found in the *Summa*, I-II, Questions I to V inclusive. A technical consideration of an important particular aspect of this doctrine is "St. Thomas' Argument from the Natural Deside in the *De Beatitudine*," has been written by Cornelius Wilham, O.P., *Irish Theological Quarterly*, XXIII (1956), 367-379. Other articles which are more popular in style are: "Knowledge of Our End," by L. Lallement in *Life of the Spirit*, XII (1957), 228-32; and "Natural Beatitude and the Future Life," by William R. O'Connor in *Theological Studies*, XI (1950), 221-239.

Written in a popular vein is *Man and Eternity* by C. Lattey, S.J. (London: Burns, Oates and Washbourne, Ltd., 1937),and a brief study is the pamphlet, *The Happy Ending*, by Raymond Smith, O.P. (*TFTL*-25). Other short articles of interest and value are "The Testing of Angels and Man," by F. J. Sheed in *Theology and Sanity* (New York: Sheed and Ward, 1946), 140-155; and "Man and His Destiny," by C. C. Martindale, S.J., in *The Teaching of the Catholic Church*, edited by G. D. Smith (New York: Macmillan, 1949), I, 186-319. A much deeper and more technical study is *Man's Last End* by J. Buckley, S.J., (St. Louis: Herder, 1949). *Happiness and Contemplation* by Josef Pieper (London: Faber and Faber, 1958) offers especially valuable insights and is highly recommended.

Steps to Happiness: Human Acts

1. INTRODUCTION

Having recognized that God himself is man's end, the true and universal good for which he was made and by which his perfection as the image of the Trinity is realized, the theologian now must consider the acts by which, with the aid of God, man attains his final happiness. All the rest of moral theology, in fact, will be concerned with human actions and how they lead man to his eternal happiness or turn him away from it. Its first area of inquiry will embrace the general principles of human acts: human acts in themselves (Chapter Two); the passions of man (Chapter Three); the internal principles of human acts: virtues (Chapter Four) and vices (Chapter Five); and the extrinsic principles of these acts: law (Chapter Six) and grace (Chapter Seven). The remaining chapters of this volume will constitute the second area of investigation, the study of particular human actions, of specific virtues.

Like a pilgrim the Christian must daily progress in the ascent of that high mountain on which is built the abiding City of God. God already dwells within him by grace, and through charity each of his acts becomes a step forward in his journey toward God and eternal glory. Aware of this higher divine life within, of his supernatural destiny, man recognizes that his action yet remains his, yet remains human. Grace does not overthrow the natural structure of the human act but builds upon it, elevates and perfects it. To understand these necessary tools for the making of man's happiness, then, to realize precisely how they are related to his ultimate end, the theologian must first analyze the moral organism of human action at the natural level. While he takes what he can from revelation and the teaching of the Church, he will have no hesitation in using the tools of moral philosophy; indeed, these will be indispensable in achieving that clarity and perception, of perennial value, which characterize St. Thomas' scientific treatise on human acts. This is a preparatory but fundamental study of man's action in his progress to eternity.

For the theologian as for the philosopher, this study presents two problems. The first concerns the psychological structure of the human act, its physical nature, so to speak: what it is, and how it operates. Then there is the moral aspect of human action to determine, its moral value of good or evil, how it is constituted, what its implications are. So our investigation of human acts will follow the plan which appears on the opposite page.

2. The Voluntary and Involuntary

A. The Nature of Voluntary Actions

A human action, we have seen, is one which proceeds from a *deliberate* will. Only those actions which fall under the dominion of the will are properly called human. Other actions performed by men, such as those of the vegetative powers or those done without advertence, are called acts of man. A human act is essentially and by definition *voluntary* (from the Latin word, *voluntas*, for the will).

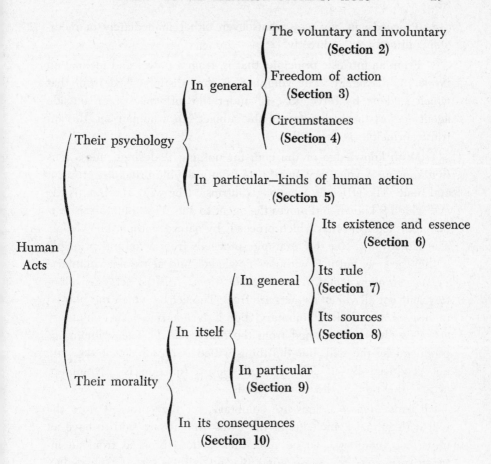

The **voluntary** is defined by Aristotle as *"that which proceeds from an intrinsic principle with knowledge of the end."*[1] This important definition demands close analysis if we are truly to understand these means, human actions, for obtaining our goal.

1. **That which** refers to anything which proceeds from an intrinsic principle. This may be an act, the omission of an act, or the effect produced by an act or omission.

[1]*Nicomachean Ethics*, Bk. III, Chap. 1.

2. **Proceeds:** in any way whatsoever, either immediately or mediately, directly or indirectly.

3. **From an intrinsic principle,** that is, from a power and inclination *proper* to the agent. The voluntary is thus distinguished from that which is done by **force,** that is, under the influence of an outside agent *against* the inclination of the subject. In a human act, this intrinsic principle is the will.

4. **With knowledge of the end,** for nothing is desired unless it is first known. A voluntary agent acts from a double principle, efficient and final. The efficient principle is intrinsic (the will), the final is the end which is known and moves the agent to act. The voluntary is thus distinguished from that which proceeds by nature, without knowledge. The growth of a tree, for example, proceeds from a natural principle within the tree, but it is without knowledge, and hence not voluntary.

The voluntary is not the same as freedom. All free acts are voluntary, but not all voluntary acts are free. The act by which the blessed in heaven see God is voluntary, but it is not free. The voluntary action is also distinguished from the *thing willed.* The voluntary is produced by the will, but the thing willed is the object of the will, not produced by it. The farmer's desire for rain is a voluntary action, the rain is the thing willed.

All truly *human* actions are voluntary, for they proceed from the will with formal knowledge of the end. Animals are said to have an imperfect voluntary. To be sure, their actions proceed from an intrinsic principle, the sense appetite, and with a sort of knowledge; but since their knowledge is limited to the senses, it is only an imperfect and material knowledge of the end. Their actions, therefore, are voluntary only in a very imperfect sense.

B. The Kinds of Voluntary Action

(1) The Voluntary in Relation to Knowledge

In relation to the knowledge so requisite for a voluntary action, the voluntary can be divided as follows:

$$
\text{Voluntary}
\begin{cases}
\text{imperfect} \\
\\
\text{perfect}
\begin{cases}
\text{free}
\begin{cases}
\text{perfectly} \\
\\
\text{imperfectly}
\end{cases} \\
\\
\text{necessary}
\end{cases}
\end{cases}
$$

The *imperfect* voluntary is that which proceeds from imperfect, material knowledge of the end. Indeliberate movements of the sense appetites in man and the actions of animals are of this kind. The *perfect* voluntary is that which proceeds from perfect, that is, formal knowledge of the end precisely as the goal or purpose for acting. This kind of voluntary belongs only to intellectual beings. When it proceeds from a judgment of reason which appraises an action or objective neither as absolutely bad nor as absolutely good, the will is not necessarily moved to act; the voluntary action, should it take place, is *free,* for the will can act in a contrary manner. But when the will is so determined that it cannot act otherwise, the voluntary is *necessary.* The blessed in heaven necessarily love God (how could they do otherwise?); man in all his human acts necessarily seeks happiness.

The free voluntary, however, can be more or less perfect. It is *imperfectly* free when it proceeds from imperfect deliberation and consent, such as the action of a man half asleep or greatly distracted; but the voluntary is *perfectly* free when it proceeds from full deliberation and consent.

(2) *The Voluntary in Relation to the Will*

But since the will as well as the intellect is a principle of voluntary action, the voluntary can also be divided according to the manner in which it proceeds from the will.

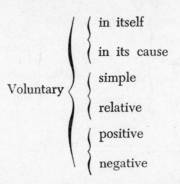

Voluntary
- in itself
- in its cause
- simple
- relative
- positive
- negative

1) The voluntary in *itself* is that which the will directly intends, either as an end or as a means to an end; e.g., a man
deliberately intends to get drunk. The voluntary *in its cause*
is present when the will immediately intends the cause, but not
the effect which flows from it, even though it is foreseen (at
least in a vague way) that the effect will take place once the
cause is placed. For example, a man may foresee that if he gets
drunk he will quarrel, although he has no intention of provoking
a quarrel. He gets drunk (voluntary in itself) and his drunkenness is the cause of a quarrel (voluntary in its cause).

2) The *simple* voluntary is that which the will here and now
wills, whether it be with reluctance or not. The *relative* voluntary, contrariwise, is that which the will would like to do,
which it would do if circumstances were different, but here
and now does not do.

The man held up at the point of a gun voluntarily surrenders
his wallet, as voluntarily as he puts his contribution in the
Sunday collection, however, reluctantly. Yet he would like to
keep his money; if the circumstances were different, if there
were no robber with a gun in his ribs, he would keep his money.
The keeping of his money is a *relative* voluntary (relative to other
circumstances he would act otherwise), the surrender of his
money is a *simple* voluntary, even though partly opposed to his
will. The notion of the simple voluntary is very important, for
even though a man performs an action reluctantly he is still responsible for it.

3) The *positive* voluntary is that which is done by placing an act of the will, either of volition (I will) or of unwillingness (I will not).

The *negative* voluntary, in contrast, proceeds without a will-act, it is an omission.

Take, for example, a Sunday morning. One man says, "I will go to Mass." This is a positive voluntary, because he has placed a will-act. His neighbor says, "I will not go to Mass." This is also a positive voluntary because a will-act has been made, even though expressed negatively—an unwillingness. But a third party down the street simply decides to go golfing, knowing that it is Sunday and that he has an obligation to attend Mass and that he cannot do both, yet without making any positive act of his will to get out of going to Mass. The omission of Mass is a *negative* voluntary.

It should be noted that every negative voluntary is an omission, but not every omission a negative voluntary, for a man may make a positive will-act, e.g., not to go to Mass. An omission, then, can truly exist without any act willing the omission. Nevertheless, it always presupposes some act which is the cause or the occasion of the omission. In the example, the will to go golfing is the cause of omitting Mass. A negative voluntary is thus voluntary in its cause. For an omission to be sinful, however, there must be an obligation to perform some act, and the person must be aware of the obligation and able to fulfill it, but does not do so.

C. Impediments to the Voluntary

By no means are all of our actions perfectly voluntary. Some are less voluntary, others completely involuntary. An involuntary action, by definition, is the direct opposite of the voluntary: it is that which is done without knowledge and contrary to the inclination of the will.

There are two elements to the voluntary, knowledge of the end and the inclination of the will. On the part of either of these two elements the voluntary may be impeded. These impediments to the voluntary are four: violence and fear (which impede the inclination of the will) and concupiscence and ignorance (which impede knowledge). We shall consider each of these in detail.

(1) Violence

Violence is a *physical motion imposed from without, which is contrary to the will's inclination and without the co-operation of the one acted on.* Three elements are included in the definition of violence: 1) that it proceeds from an extrinsic principle; 2) that the effect produced is caused exclusively by the outside force, and in no way attributed to the one who suffers the violence; and 3) that it is opposed to the inclination of the will, which does not remain passive but actively resists.

What effect does violence have on the voluntary? The voluntary is an act of the will, either elicited or commanded. An *elicited* act of the will is one which proceeds immediately from the will itself (such as love or desire); a *commanded* act of the will is one which proceeds from some other power, but under the command of the will (such as to walk, to run, to speak).

The will cannot suffer violence with regard to its elicited acts. The voluntary is from an intrinsic principle, violence from an extrinsic principle. An act cannot proceed totally from an outside force and at the same time be from a principle within; it cannot be at the same time in conformity with the inclination of the will and contrary to that inclination. The interior, or elicited, act of the will can, then, *never* be forced.[2] Neither man, nor devil, nor angel—not even God— can force man against his will. True, God can and does move man's will, but he cannot force it, for that would be a contradiction.

The will can suffer violence, however, with regard to its commanded acts, for the exterior members can be impeded from following out the command of the will. A man may be made to walk

[2]St. Anselm, *On Free Will*, Chap. 6, points out: "No one can unwillingly will something, because he cannot will while not willing to will."

against his will, he may be unwillingly confined to prison. But he cannot be forced to *want* to do these things.

From these points it follows that violence causes an action to be completely **involuntary**, because it is directly opposed to the voluntary. Thus it is clear that:

1) all the elicited acts of the will are voluntary;

2) the commanded acts that are caused totally by violence are completely involuntary;

3) if the person suffering violence does not resist but gives consent, the action is not completely involuntary, but is simply voluntary, relatively involuntary.

(2) Fear

Fear is *a disturbance of the mind caused by an imminent evil.* Fear is of two kinds, antecedent and concomitant:

1) *Antecedent* fear is that which precedes the action and causes it; the action is done *out* of fear. The victim of a robbery gives his money to the robber because of fear.

2) *Concomitant* fear is that which accompanies an action, but is not the cause of it; in fact, it would deter, rather than cause an action. The action is done *with* fear and in spite of fear. The robber takes another's money while fearful of being caught. He robs, not because he is afraid, but despite his fear.

Antecedent fear causes an action which is simply voluntary, relatively involuntary. It is simply voluntary because, in the concrete circumstances, the will actually places the act; here and now, in our example, the man wills to surrender his money to the robber. The act is relatively involuntary, because, abstracting from the circumstances, the man would will to keep his money.[3] If, however, the fear is so great that it destroys the power of deliberation, the act is completely involuntary, for the consequent action is not a human act.

Concomitant fear does not destroy or diminish the voluntary; an action done with fear remains perfectly voluntary and free. The will

---

[3] Although this is true in the majority of cases, the relative involuntary is not always necessarily present. For a man to refrain from sin because of the fear of hell does not necessarily mean that he would sin if there were no hell.

is so strong in its resolution to commit the act that fear is overcome. From these conclusions we draw the following corollaries:

1) Fear does not completely excuse from sin (unless the use of reason is taken away), for the act done out of fear is simply voluntary. But fear lessens culpability, because the act is less voluntary and less free.

2) Grave fear does not excuse from actions which are intrinsically evil. To deny the faith, even under the threat of death, would be seriously sinful.

3) Grave fear excuses from actions contrary to purely positive law. A man would be excused from Mass on Sunday if his life were threatened by his attending. Positive law would still be binding, however, even under grave fear, if the contrary action were in contempt of religion or of the common good. A soldier would be obliged to keep his post in battle despite his fear of death.

Contracts entered into under grave fear are valid, but rescindible, that is, they can be justly cancelled. Certain contracts, however, which by positive law require perfect freedom, are invalid if entered into out of fear, e.g., marriage, religious profession.[4]

(3) Concupiscence

Concupiscence, in its wide sense, is the privation of rectitude in the sense appetite as a result of original sin. In its strict sense, which we use in this context, it is *the desire of the sense appetite for a sensible good.* It is either antecedent or consequent.

1) *Antecedent* concupiscence precedes the consent of the will and entices the will to pursue a sensible good. The aroma of a broiling steak may so stir the sense appetite that you order one for dinner.

2) *Consequent* concupiscence follows an act of the will; the sense appetite is deliberately aroused by the will. A man can, in anticipation, deliberately arouse his imagination and stir his appetite for a delectable dinner.

[4]Cf. the Code of Canon Law, Can. 1307, §3, 1087, §1 and §2.

Antecedent concupiscence increases the voluntariness of an action. The voluntary is intensified, at least on the part of the inclination of the will, because the will is more inclined to pursue a sensible object which is presented as more desirable. Concupiscence exaggerates the goodness of the sensible object and overlooks whatever is evil in it, thus making it more attractive and desirable. Nevertheless—an important qualification—the freedom of the act is diminished, because the judgment of reason is clouded. And if concupiscence is so vehement that it takes away the use of reason, the action which it causes is neither voluntary nor involuntary, since it is not a human act at all.

Consequent concupiscence, it is obvious, increases the voluntary, because the will, by its own choice, intensifies its act by deliberately arousing the sense appetite.

Habit influences the voluntary in much the same way as intecedent concupiscence; we will discuss this point in the chapter on habits and virtues.

(4) Ignorance

Ignorance is *lack of due knowledge in a capable subject.* It differs from nescience, which is the mere absence of knowledge, e.g., in an infant. Ignorance is the lack of *due knowledge,* that is, knowledge that a person is obliged to have, as the doctor is obliged to possess medical knowledge.

Ignorance is divided as follows:

Ignorance
- on the part of the object
  - of fact
  - of law
- on the part of the subject
  - invincible
  - vincible
- in relation to the will
  - antecedent
  - consequent
  - concomitant

1. **In relation to its object,** ignorance is either ignorance *of the law* or *of the fact.* Ignorance of the law is present when one does not know the existence of a law, or its meaning, e.g., ignorance of the law of fasting on an ember day. When one is ignorant of a concrete fact determining the application of a law, there is ignorance of fact. A man may know the universal law of fasting on ember days, but does not know that today is an ember day.

2. **In relation to the person who is ignorant,** ignorance is either *vincible* or *invincible.* Vincible ignorance is that which can be overcome by ordinary diligence. It is voluntary. Invincible ignorance is that which cannot be overcome by ordinary diligence, e.g., idolatrous pagans who have never heard of the true God may be invincibly ignorant. Such ignorance **is involuntary.**

3. **In relation to the will,** ignorance is *antecedent, concomitant* or *consequent.*

Antecedent ignorance is that which precedes any act of the will—that is, it is *not willed*—and yet it is the cause of doing an act which would not be done knowingly. A hunter shoots a man, thinking he is shooting a deer.

Concomitant ignorance, although it precedes the act of the will, is not the cause of the action which follows, for that action would be performed even with knowledge, e.g., a man, thinking a deer is in his rifle sights, shoots his enemy, whom he would have shot even if he had known.

Consequent ignorance follows the act of the will, that is, it is ignorance which is in some way willed. Such ignorance may be either direct or indirect.

1) Directly willed ignorance is present when one wills deliberately to be ignorant, so that he may feel free to act. This is called *affected* ignorance. E.g., a man may refuse to look at a calendar to see if it is Friday, so that he may feel free to eat meat.

2) Indirectly willed ignorance results from negligence. It is light or grave, depending on the matter and on the degree of negligence.

These distinctions having been made, we can see the effect of ignorance on the voluntariness of human action.

1) **Antecedent ignorance causes an involuntary.** An act of this kind is performed out of invincible ignorance and is contrary to the inclination of the will. If knowledge were present, the act would not have been performed.

2) **Concomitant ignorance has no moral effect on the act; it causes a non-voluntary.** A non-voluntary is an act which is done out of ignorance, but is not contrary to the habitual inclination of the will. The act is not voluntary, because it proceeds from invincible ignorance; it is not involuntary, because it is not against the will's inclination, inasmuch as the act would have been done even wth knowledge.

3) **Consequent ignorance causes a simple voluntary,** because it is vincible, willed ignorance. *Affected* (direct) ignorance **increases the voluntary,** or at least is a sign of the intensity of the will in the pursuit of its object. Such ignorance is merely a subterfuge which gives the will freedom of action.[5] *Indirect* ignorance, however, **diminishes the voluntary,** inasmuch as the act is in some respect involuntary, since it would not have been done with full knowledge. The voluntary is diminished in the degree that the ignorance is invincible and inculpable. For example, a doctor who out of ignorance gave a patient harmful medicine would be responsible, but not as responsible as if he had done it knowingly.

3. The Freedom of Human Action

Voluntariness is the essential characteristic of human action, but the voluntary may be either necessary or free. Of its very nature the

[5] It is presumed that a person who would act out of affected ignorance would act the same way even if he had knowledge. But if knowledge would have deterred his action, then affected ignorance diminishes the voluntary.

will, if it acts, necessarily seeks the *universal* good, the end in which man's happiness is to be found, its own ultimate and perfect fulfillment; once in possession of that good—God himself clearly seen in the beatific vision—the will is necessitated to the act of loving God. But between the first stretching out to infinite good and its ultimate possesson there lies the vast arena of particular goods, which serve either as means or obstacles in attaining that good. None of these lesser goods satisfies the will's appetite for the infinite, and in relation to these objects the will wields dominion over its own action. Here, in this field of multifarious activity, *the voluntary and the free are absolutely synonymous.*

In considering the general characteristics of human acts, therefore, this question of human freedom demands discussion. And since the will is a *passive* power, undetermined and potential with respect to its object,[6] the problem is twofold: 1) what moves the will to action, and 2) in what manner is it so moved?

A. The Movement of the Will

We have seen that good is the object of the will, and that the good moves the will in the order of *final* causality. But since the will is in potency to its operation, its motion must also be attributed to an *efficient* cause. What moves the will to its act?

The source of the will's movement must be found either within man—the intellect, the sense appetite, the will itself; or extrinsic to him: the heavenly bodies, God. Whatever the source, the movement will be one of two kinds, for the will is in potency to its acts in two ways:

1) as to the **exercise** of its act—it can act or not act (e.g., a man may read or not read);

2) as to **specification**—it can act for this or that object; e.g., having decided to read, a man has a choice of any of several books.

---

[6]It would be well here for the student to review what has already been studied concerning the will. Cf. *God and His Creation*, 447-457.

With these notions in hand, we can consider each of the possible movers or efficient causes of the will-act.

(1) The Intellect as Mover

The intellect does not move the will to the exercise of its act; quite the contrary, the will moves the intellect and all the other powers of the soul. The will is directed to the universal end and the common good, whereas the other powers are directed to particular ends and goods. And the end is the principle of all action. Hence the will, in moving to the universal end, moves the other powers to their particular ends, for the particular ends are included in the universal end. The will is like a general who commands the particular acts of his subordinates for the common good of the whole army.

But the intellect moves the will *as to specification* of its act. The object by itself cannot move the will—it must first be known. The will, however, is not a cognitive but an appetitive power; it depends absolutely on the intellect to apprehend and present its object. In this way the intellect specifies the will by presenting its object to it.

(2) The Sense Appetite as Mover

"But everyone is tempted by being drawn away and enticed by his own passion" (Jas. 1:14). Thus God's word expresses the fact that the sense appetite can also move the will, but in an indirect way, as to specification.

Any object which is apprehended as good can move the will. When passion, the motion of the sense appetite, is aroused, it can influence the intellect to apprehend the object as good—something the intellect might not do if it were not affected by passion. For example, murder appears good to a man in a fit of anger, a judgment he would never make while he was calm.

In such a case, therefore, the sense appetite moves the will *indirectly* to its object by influencing the judgment of the practical intellect.

(3) The Will as Mover

The will moves itself to the exercise of those acts which are concerned with the means. The end is the principle, the starting point of action. Once the will is in act toward the end, it can move itself to the willing of the means. Just as the intellect from knowledge of principles can move itself to conclusions, so the will from the intention of the end can move itself to the willing of the means.

That the will moves itself is no contradiction of the axiom that a thing cannot be in potency and act at one and the same time. The will does not move itself to its first volition of the end, but is rather moved by it. But once it is in act, the will can move itself to the other acts dealing with the means. To say that the will moves itself to certain of its acts, then, does not imply that the will is its own *first* mover, but a secondary and proximate mover.

(4) The Exterior Mover

The will is exteriorly moved in the order of *specification* by an extrinsic object apprehended by the intellect. But also in the order of *exercise* the will needs an exterior mover which moves the will efficiently. The will is not always in act; by its nature it is in potency to act. Whatever is in potency to its act must be moved to that act by something which itself is already in act. Otherwise, a thing would be in potency and act at the same time, which is contradictory. Consequently, **the first movement of the will toward the end depends on some mover outside the will.**

When the will moves itself to certain acts which deal with the means, it is necessarily presupposed that the will is already in act by its volition or willing of the end. Since there cannot be an infinite series of ends, the first volition of the end must come from an extrinsic cause. This is true, not only with reference to the very last end of life, but also with regard to the relative last end of any series of actions. The student studies in order to pass his examinations in order to earn a degree. If earning a degree is not referred to a superior end, it is the last end of this series of actions. Since the student at some time began to will the end, a degree, this volition must depend on an exterior mover.

(5) *The Corporeal World as Mover*

What is this exterior mover of the will? Some have thought that the heavenly bodies, the sun, the moon and the stars, have a direct influence on man's actions. This is not an outmoded superstition of the pagan past; there are many devotees of astrology in our own day who firmly believe that their fate is decided by the stars.

But neither the heavenly bodies, nor atmospheric conditions, nor any object in the material universe can move the will to its act directly. No body can so act on an immaterial thing. The will, being a spiritual faculty which does not reside in a corporeal organ, cannot be moved directly to act by any cosmic power.

But the will can be moved *indirectly* by bodies *as to specification*. The sense appetites, residing as they do in corporeal organs and having material objects, can be influenced by corporeal agents. The sense appetites, however, indirectly move the will by proposing an object which the intellect presents to the will as a good to be pursued or an evil to be avoided.

A moonlight night, for example, is an invitation to a stroll; a bitter wind will move a man to the comfort of a warm shelter, a sweltering day will influence him to go to the beach.

(6) *God, the Will's Mover*

There is no doubt that God can move the will as its object. The intellect can apprehend God as good, and so the will can desire him. But far more than this, God also moves the will to the *exercise* of its act. The will, we have seen, needs an exterior mover, and that mover can be none other than God. The intrinsic motion of anything can be caused only by that agent which is the cause of the nature of a thing. A thing operates according to its nature; the source of the activity must be traced to that which caused the nature. The growth of a flower, for example, can be caused from without only by the agent which made the flower to be what it is. Any other action from outside is violence.

Now God alone is the cause of the human will. The will is a spiritual faculty which comes into being at the same time as the soul. The soul, however, is immediately created by God. As God is the only cause of the soul, he is the only cause of the will. Further, the will has an inclination to universal good, which cannot be given to it by any particular cause, but only by the universal cause, God.

Every act of the will depends on God as exterior mover. As to the first volition of the end, the will is completely in potency and is moved to that volition by God, not by itself. As to the means, the will moves itself, but is at the same time moved by God. No motion, even self-motion, escapes the universal causality of God. God moves the will as first and universal mover, the will moves itself to the means as a secondary and proximate mover.

B. The Manner of the Will's Movement

(1) The Natural Movement of the Will

A stone naturally obeys the law of gravity: throw it into the air and it will invariably fall to the ground. A tree naturally grows upward. A bird flies naturally. All things perform actions which are natural to them, acts which belong to them by their very nature. Man is part of created nature, and therefore some of his will-acts are natural, that is, they are not free. Just as man's knowledge starts from naturally known principles, so man's free actions must be from principles naturally willed. In all things, nature is first. Man's will, therefore, is naturally, necessarily moved to certain objects.

1. The will naturally desires good in general. Good is the will's object, and just like every power the will has a natural inclination to its object, as sight is ordered to color, hearing to sound, etc.

2. The will naturally inclines to the last end, or happiness in general. The end is the principle of action. Just as speculative first prin-

ciples are naturally known by the intellect, the practical first principle is naturally desired.

3. The will also naturally desires the good of the other powers of the soul, and of the whole man, such as knowledge of truth, preservation of life, etc.[7]

(2) How the Object Moves the Will

No particular object can move the will to the *exercise* of its act by necessity. Every will-act presupposes an act of the intellect. But it is in man's power not to think of the object. Consequently, he does not have to will that object; his will is free.

Nor can any particular object move the will necessarily *as to specification.* The object of the will is good; but any particular good can be apprehended under the aspect of non-good, and therefore can be rejected by the will. The universal good is the only perfect good; particular goods are limited, lacking in some perfection that can be found only in the universal good. All particular goods, therefore, have some aspect of non-good about them. Viewed as good, they attract the will; as non-good, they are repugnant to it. The will, therefore, is free to choose or reject any particular good. Limited objects cannot necessitate a power of unlimited capacity.

Thus so far as specification is concerned, the will is necessarily moved only by good in general and by the last end. These objects represent the perfect good, and have no aspect of non-good by which the will would be free to turn aside from them. Yet the will enjoys freedom of exercise in regard to these objects, for the will is able to refrain from acting. But once it acts, the will cannot help but act for good in general and the last end.

The will has neither freedom of exercise nor of specification in regard to God clearly seen in the beatific vision. God, the universal

---

[7]These things, by their nature, are good. But they can be apprehended as evil through some accidental consideration, and so the will can turn away from them. Because of the misery of his life, a man may commit suicide; because of the difficulty of learning, he may turn away from seeking truth. But in themselves, these things are the object of natural desire.

good perfectly known, cannot in any way be apprehended as non-good. The will, then, is necessitated to loving him, and cannot prefer any other object to him. In this life, however, since God is not perfectly known, he can be apprehended under the aspect of non-good, e.g., as the just judge who punishes evil. In this life, therefore, the will does not necessarily love God; the will is free with reference to God both as to exercise and as to specification.

(3) How the Sense Appetite Moves the Will

The motion of the sense appetite (passion) is sometimes so vehement that it totally impedes the use of reason. In this case there is no act of the will, for when reason does not operate, neither does the will. Under such a strong impulse of passion man is necessitated to act, not as a man, but like an animal—for such an act is not a human act.

If reason is not entirely overcome by passion, there can be no question of necessity; the will remains free. As long as the indifference of judgment remains in the reason, the will possesses dominion over its actions. This freedom of the will, however, is diminished in the degree that the judgment of reason is clouded by passion.

The sense appetite, therefore, cannot move the will of necessity. Either the will act remains free, in greater or lesser degree, or there is no human act.

(4) God's Movement of the Will

God is the only exterior mover who can, and does, directly move man's will to its act. But here we are immediately faced with a problem. Nothing can resist the divine will. Under the divine motion the human will moves infallibly to its act. How, then, can the will be free?

The problem is not solved by saying either that God does not move the will, or that the will is not free. The two truths of divine motion and human freedom are attested to by the Scriptures in many places,[8] and the authoritative voice of the Church proclaims and confirms these truth.[9] The question, then, does not concern the *facts* of divine motion and human freedom, but the *manner* in which God moves the will without prejudice to its freedom.

God is the cause of all things, and it is not the work of his providence to destroy their several natures but to conserve them. God has willed that certain effects be necessary, and these effects result from necessary proximate causes; he wills contingent effects to result from contingent causes. It would be ridiculous to say that God has created a nature and then moves it contrary to what he has determined it to be. God moves all things according to their nature.

God created the will in such a way that it is not determined to a single activity—it is free in certain areas in its action and in its choice of objects. When God moves the will, then, it moves freely, not out of necessity.[10]

God, therefore, is the cause, not only of human freedom, but also of the free act. God is the first cause of the act, the will its secondary and proximate cause. Because of the efficacy of the first mover, any effect that God determines will infallibly come about; but man determines himself as a proximate cause, so that his action remains free.

Man will *infallibly* do what God moves him to—but this is not to say that he will do it *necessarily*. He still retains the power to do the opposite, and so his performance of the act remains free. God's motion, far from destroying man's freedom, actually causes it; apart from God's causality there is no free motion, indeed, no motion whatever.

[8]"God made man from the beginning, and left him in the hand of his own counsel" (Sirach 15:14). "For it is God who of his good pleasure works in you both the will and the performance" (Phil. 2:13).

[9]Cf. Council of Trent. Sess. VI, *Decree on Justification,* Chap. 5-7 (Denz. 797-799), and Can. 4-6 (Denz. 814-816).

[10]St. Thomas, *Summa,* I, q. 83, a. 1, ad 3: "God, therefore, is the first cause, moving both natural and voluntary causes. Just as in moving natural causes he does not take away the naturalness of their acts, so by moving voluntary causes he does not take away the voluntariness of their actions, but rather he is the cause of that voluntariness. For he works in each thing according to its proper nature."

Cf. *ibid,* I-II, q. 10, a. 4, ad 1: "It would be more repugnant to the divine motion for the will to be moved necessarily, which is contrary to its nature, than for it to be moved freely, which is in accordance with its nature."

4. The Circumstances of Human Acts

A. The Nature of Circumstances

The word circumstance is derived from the Latin *circumstare*, meaning "to stand around" or "surround." A circumstance, as its name implies, is something which surrounds an act and, although outside the act, affects the act in some way. **Circumstance** is defined as *an accident of a human act already constituted in its essence.*

Circumstances are distinguished from the substance of the act.[11] The substance of the act comprises its essential elements; circumstances are accidental to the act, but modify it in some way. The substance of a human act is determined by its relation to its object. But human actions happen in the concrete, and thus involve such important factors as who performed the act, when, where, why, how.

For example, the substance of the act of theft is that it be the voluntary taking of another's property when he is reasonably unwilling that it be taken. The substance of every act of theft is the same, but each is qualified by its particular accidents. The act is differently affected according as the thief is a religious or a layman, the object stolen is cheap or valuable, the person from whom it is stolen is rich or poor, the scene of the theft is a church or a hotel lobby.

The consideration of circumstances is very important in theology, for a human act must be judged, not only in its bare substance, but as it actually happens, vested with all its circumstances.[12] Circumstances make an act to be more or less good, more or less evil, more or less meritorious or demeritorious. The manner in which circumstances affect the morality of an act will be taken up in the tract on morality.

---

[11]Although a human act, as a physical entity, is itself an accident, its essential elements are called the *substance* of the act, since they constitute its nature or essence, that is, the specific kind of thing it is.

[12]In sacramental confession, not only must the sin be confessed, but also the circumstances which gravely affect it.

B. The Number of Circumstances

Circumstances are seven in number: who, what, where, when, why, how, and by what means.

Who denotes the special condition of the *person performing the act,* e.g., that he be a priest or a layman.

What signifies the quality or the quantity of the *object,* e.g., the theft of a mink stole or a pair of shoe laces, of a dollar or a thousand dollars.

Where denotes the quality of the *place;* does the pickpocket ply his trade in a railroad station or in a church?

When denotes the quality or quantity of *time,* e.g., how long a person harbored hatred for another.

Why signifies *the intention of the person performing the act*: did a man steal in order to get drunk, or in order to give to the poor?

How signifies *the manner in which the act is done,* e.g., intensely or remissly, from passion, ignorance or contempt.

By what means denotes *the means used to accomplish the act.* Did the mother punish her child by striking him with the back of her hand, or with the skillet she wields so furiously?

The most important of the circumstances are **why** and **what.** "Why" holds the first place, because it is the end and object of the will, that by which it is moved to act. Of the other circumstances, "what" is the most important, because it denotes the quality and quantity of the object, and thus is more closely related to the substance of the act.

5. The Acts of the Will in Particular

In the preceding sections we dealt with human acts in general, i.e., according to the general conditions which are characteristic of them. But a theology which remains only on the level of the general, the universal, the abstract when dealing with human activity is about as realistic and practical as the formulas of chemistry are for the housewife concocting a stew. We must come down from the ivory tower to the particular and the concrete, to the arena of reality where human acts play their proper roles in the pursuit of man's perfection.

A. Analysis of the Complex Human Act

The complete human act is quite a complex operation. From its first inclination to an object until that object is attained we can discern a number of distinct phases in the evolution of the human act. The various acts of the will are distinguished by their relation to the end, which is the principle of human activity, and each of these acts of the will is preceded by an act of the intellect.

The voluntary act may be briefly analyzed in this way. An end is first apprehended by the intellect, which causes love and desire in the will. The intellect then judges whether the end is attainable; if it is, the will makes the intention to pursue the end. Progressing then to the means, the intellect takes counsel concerning the means which are suitable to reach the end. The will responds by giving its consent. Among the various means, the intellect decides which is best, and then the will makes its choice. All these acts are still in the order of intention, that is, on the plane of willing the end, directly, or indirectly through the means. Proceeding now to the order of execution—the plane of obtaining the desired end—the intellect commands the carrying out of the means, and the will responds by moving the other human powers to act. These powers carry out or execute the means, and when the end is attained, the will finds enjoyment in the object possessed.

So the complete human act is made up of twelve partial movements, six on the part of the intellect, six on the part of the will. The act has its beginnings in the *order of intention* and its completion in the *order of execution*. Hence the axiom: **the end is first in the order of intention, last in the order of execution.**

This succinct and very abstract analysis of the complex human act shows that the will is the source and center of human activity. Thus we may distinguish human acts from the point of view of the will into *elicited* acts and *commanded acts*. The elicited acts are those which emanate from the will itself, the commanded acts those which are produced by some other power under the movement of the will.

We will consider each of these human acts—each of these phases of the complete and perfect human act—in detail.

B. The Complex Human Act in Its Details

(1) Acts concerning the End

1. **Apprehension** is *the simple act of the intellect by which an object becomes known.* The human act necessarily has its beginning in knowledge. The will is a blind faculty and cannot tend to a suitable good until that good is presented to it by the intellect. Nothing can be willed unless it is first known. The first act of the voluntary process, therefore, is the apprehension of the end by the intellect.

2. Reacting to the knowledge of the end, the will elicits the act of **simple volition.** This is *the complacency or basic contentment of the will in the good presented by the intellect;* it is the initial inclination of the will toward the object, without reference to the means.

Only good, of course, can be the object of volition. The will is an appetite, and every appetite tends to what is good and suitable for it. Aristotle calls good "that which all things desire."[13]

But the good to which the will tends need not be a *real* good. Volition tends to the object as it is apprehended by the intellect. The will may incline to an object which is really evil, but is apprehended as good; this is called an *apparent* good, something which is objectively evil but appears to be good. The object of the will, then, is always a good, either real or apparent.

Volition is properly concerned with the end only, not the means. End and means are different classes of goods; the end is sought for itself, the means are sought only because they are useful to attain the end. Although both end and means, as good, are the object

---

[13]*Nicomachean Ethics*, Bk. I, Chap. 1.

of the will, the first act of the will aims only at the end. The elicited act of the will dealing with the means is choice.

(2) Acts concerning the Means to the End

3. Volition is concerned with the end absolutely, without any other consideration. The intellect now gives a more attentive and detailed consideration to the object, and makes a **judgment** *concerning the possibility of attainment of the end.* If the end is judged impossible, there can be no efficacious movement of the will to it; the human act stops dead at this point. If the end is judged possible of attainment, however, the will follows it with the act of intention.

4. **Intention** is an act of the will, for to tend to something belongs to the motive power of the human act, which is the will. It is defined as *the efficacious desire to attain the end through the means.* Intention is concerned not only with the ultimate end but also with intermediate ends.

Intention goes a step beyond volition. Volition is simple complacency in the end presented; intention is the desire to employ the proper means to attain the end. Although the intention of the end and the choice of the means are usually distinct acts, intention can also be extended to the means when these means are willed precisely for the sake of, and as related to the end. By one act, for example, I may will to take medicine for the sake of health.

5. **Counsel** is *the act of deliberation concerning the means.* Once the end has been intended, the intellect investigates the possible and suitable means by which this end can be achieved.

The act of counsel, although frequently necessary and highly important in human affairs, is not involved in everything we do. All important matters, of course, as a normal rule demand the inquiry of counsel in order that they may be done prudently. But things of small importance seldom need the work of counsel; in this area "snap judgments" are the usual and reasonable thing.

6. **Consent** is *the act of the will agreeing with the proposal of the means by the act of counsel.*

7. The intellect, having considered the various means which are suitable to attain the end, must now decide which of those means is the best to achieve the end intended. This is called **the last practical judgment,** for it puts an end to the deliberation of counsel. It is also called a *discriminating* judgment, because it separates the most suitable means from all the rest.

8. **Choice** is *the act by which the will elects one means in preference to others.* Choice, in conjunction with the previous act of judgment, is the act where freedom of the will is exercised. The will may choose any of the means offered, or may reject them all.

Of two means objectively equal, the will can prefer one to the other. Indeed, it can choose the lesser of two objectively unequal means. For the objectively lesser means may be considered subjectively and practically better and more useful in the concrete situation. For example, in the exercise of charity, the spiritual works of mercy are more excellent than the corporal works; but in a given situation, it is better to feed a hungry man than to instruct him.

(3) Acts concerning the Attainment of the End

9. We now move to the order of execution. The will has made its choice, which now must be carired out. This requires an act of **command,** *by which man's powers are ordered and moved to action.*

The act of command contains three elements: direction, intimation and movement. Direction is the order to execute the means. Intimation is the declaration of that order. In this respect, command differs from the practical judgment. Judgment says, declaratively, "This is to be done." Command says, imperatively, "Do this." The movement to the act comes from the will, since it is the will which moves the other powers to the exercise of their act.

Command, then, proceeds from both intellect and will. Direction and intimation are acts of the intellect, movement comes from the will. Command is essentially an act of the intellect, but presupposes an act of the will. Reason is able to move the other powers to the exercise of their acts only because reason itself is moved by the previous election of the will.

Command and the commanded acts are distinct acts, since they proceed from different powers. Nevertheless, they combine to form one moral act. They are the integral parts which make up the one human act.

The following acts are subject to command:

1) *Acts of the will.* Reason can judge that it is good to will something, and thus can follow that judgment with a command that the thing be willed. The first act of the will, volition, however, is not subject to command, since it is moved by nature or the first mover.

2) *Acts of the intellect.* The intellect, as a spiritual power, can reflect on its own acts, and so can direct those acts, just as it directs the acts of the other powers. As to exercise, any act of the intellect is subject to command. In regard to the object, however, some acts of intellect cannot be commanded, for the intellect is necessitated to assent, e.g., to first principles and demonstrated conclusions. Matters of opinion and faith, however, do not necessitate assent, and so are subject to the power of command.

3) *Acts of the sensitive appetite.* These acts, insofar as they depend upon the sensitive appetite, can be commanded, since reason can dominate imagination, from which these actions flow. But those sensitive acts which depend entirely on bodily dispositions cannot be commanded.

4) *Acts of the exterior members.* Movement of the head, hands, feet, etc., since they depend on the sensitive powers, are subject to the control of reason.

10. Use in general is the application of something to operation, e.g., the use of a bat to strike a baseball. In the human act, we distinguish active use and passive use. **Active use** is *the act of the will applying the other powers to execute the means necessary to attain the end.* For example, in the command to study, the will moves the feet to the bookshelf, the hands to take down a book and open the pages, the intellect to apply itself to the written word.

11. **Passive use** is *the application to operation of the other powers under the motion of the will.* These powers are as the instruments of the will, which is the principal cause of their movement. Passive use comprises several acts of different powers which unite with the act of the will to form one moral action.

12. **Enjoyment** (or fruition) is *rest and delight in the end possessed.* When all the means have been executed and the end is achieved, the will is satisfied. Its quest is over, and it now rests in loving possession of its object. The end is attained by the other powers, and this attainment brings joy to the will.

Perfect enjoyment comes only in possession of the last end, for only God, finally attained, can satisfy completely all human desires. A relatively last end, the culmination of a particular series, causes joy in its possession, but only imperfectly. The acquiring of a degree on graduation day brings joy, but there are many things yet to be desired and achieved.

A summary of these acts and their relationships may be found in the following chart.

Analysis of the Human Act		
	Intellect	Will
	Concerning the End	
Order of Intention	Apprehension	Volition
	Judgment of attainability	Intention
	Concerning the Means	
	Counsel	Consent
	Practical judgment	Choice
Order of Execution	Command	Active use
	Passive use°	
	Concerning the End	
		Enjoyment

*Passive use is the application to operation of all the other powers under the motion of the will, not only the intellect.

6. THE MORALITY OF HUMAN ACTS

Because they are *human,* man's acts are *moral*: "Moral acts are the same as human acts."[14] The physical essence of the human act includes freedom and voluntariness. But over and above its physical essence, the human act has also a moral essence—its goodness or its evil.

To account for this fact—recognized by public opinion, attested to by law courts and civil tribunals, certified by the centuries of human experience—we enter now the realm of moral judgment. We will discuss the general notions of morality first—its existence and nature in this section; the rule or standard of morality in **Section 7;** the sources of morality in **Section 8**—then particular aspects of morality (**Section 9**), and finally, in **Section 10,** the consequences of morality.

A. The Existence of Morality

The existence of morality is a truth that has been recognized universally and constantly by men of all times and places. Even among the most primitive barbarians a moral code has always existed. Certain actions have always been regarded as good, such as to love one's parents, to speak the truth, to keep one's promises, etc., whereas the opposite actions have always been considered evil. The universal existence of laws, courts, police and prisons likewise testifies to the fact that some of man's actions are evil, and therefore deserving of punishment.

The existence of the moral order has, of course, like so many fundamental truths, been denied. Skepticism, which denies the distinction between truth and falsehood, also denies the distinction between good and evil. Atheism, in denying the existence of God and the eternal law, does away with the supreme rule of morality. Materialism denies freedom of the will, and consequently abolishes the foundation of morality: no act—save only those concerned with happiness and the possession of man's true goal—can be morally good or bad unless it be free.

[14]St. Thomas, *Summa,* I-II, q. 1, a. 3.

The denial of so basic a truth as the existence of morality leads to absurd consequences. No law would be binding, no right inviolable, no duty obligatory; there would be no incentive for reward, no fear of punishment. Human love and justice would perish, complete chaos would reign. The denial of morality is the denial of humanity, for by definition *human* acts are morally good or morally bad.

Some have claimed that men can do no wrong, that all human actions are good. Others, like Luther, held that all the actions of men are sinful, a doctrine explicitly condemned by the Council of Trent.[15]

But morality does exist, and there is an intrinsic, essential difference between good and bad actions. The psalmist warns us, "Turn away from evil and do good" (Ps. 33:15), succinctly affirming the fact that man, by his acts, is master of his destiny.[16] And Christ himself time and again insists that his followers demonstrate their adherence to him and the Father by their concrete daily conduct.[17] "If you love me," he sums up in the discourse before his death, "keep my commandments" (John 14:15).

But what is it that makes the actions of a thing good or bad? That depends on the nature of the things. A knife is meant to cut well. If it does not cut well, its action is bad, it is a bad knife. An apple tree that produces shriveled apples is not a good tree.

Morality depends on man's nature. Man has natural inclinations to actions which are suitable to that nature and thus these actions are good; actions which are unsuitable to that nature are bad. Man's nature is *rational*: to act contrary to reason is to act contrary to nature—and this is evil. Hence direct suicide is evil, because it is an act opposed to reason, which dictates that man should follow his natural inclination to preserve his life.

[15]Sess. VI, *Decree on Justification*, Chap. 11 (Denz. 804) and Can. 7 (Denz. 817).

[16]Sacred Scripture from Genesis onward teaches the same truth over and over again in strong, explicit statements. Cf., e.g., Gen. 4:6-7, Sirach 15:14-17, 17:1, 4-7.

[17]Chapter 5 of the Gospel of St. Matthew takes this truth as its theme, but it is often repeated: Matt. 7:21; Luke 9:11 and Matt. 25:14 (parable of the talents); Lk. 12:35-47 (parable of the faithful servant); etc.

Some human actions, therefore, are intrinsically good, others by their very nature are evil.

B. The Essence of Morality

Morality is a property *inseparable* from a *human action.* It is not the same thing as freedom, for freedom belongs to the physical essence of the act and is presupposed to morality. Nor is it merely something conceived by the mind; it really exists in the human act. Reason judges morality, but does not create it.

Morality consists essentially *in a transcendental relation of the act to the rule of morals.* This means that a *human act*—in itself physically good (a beautiful spiral touchdown pass) or bad (a messy murder stabbing)—is necessarily and of its nature related to this other thing, this "rule"; so also the soul to the body, matter to form, etc.

Every act, we have seen, is specified and determined by its object; every act has an intrinsic and essential relation to its object. A physical act is constituted by its tendency to its object, the act of seeing by color, the act of willing by good, etc. So also a moral act is constituted by its relation to a *moral* object, that is, an object which falls under the rule of morals. Money, for example, is a moral object in that it belongs to some person and so gives rise to a moral right. This rule of morals, we shall see in the next section, is right reason and the eternal law.

Morality, then, let us repeat, consists in a transcendental (and therefore intrinsic and essential) relation of a human act to a moral object. But since the object is itself "moral" because of *its* essential relation to the rule of morals, this fundamental principle of human conduct is often stated: **morality consists essentially in a transcendental relation of a human act to the rule of morals.**

7. THE RULE OF MORALITY

How is the essential goodness or evil of a human act to be determined? Obviously there must be some norm or standard by which that action is measured. An architect's plan, for example, is the norm for building a house. Inasmuch as the contractor's work conforms to the architect's plan, it is good; insofar as it departs from the plan, it is bad. So a human act also must have some norm or rule by which it is measured. If it measures up to the rule, it is a good act; otherwise, it is bad.

Philosophers down through the ages to our own day hold quite divergent views as to what constitutes the rule of morality. Some teach that there is only a *subjective* rule of morality—the "moral sense" according to Thomas Reid, Herbart's "moral taste," Kant's "practical reason," motivated solely out of reverence for the law. Others hold for a single *objective* rule:

1) Hedonism (Epicurus, Helvetius): the sole criterion of morality is sensual pleasure.

2) Hobbes and Rousseau: the only rule of human conduct is the civil law.

3) Positivism (Comte, Jodl, Dewey) holds out for human custom.

4) Utilitarianism: that alone is good which is useful. This utility is variously conceived as utility for personal perfection (von Wolff), for public welfare (Comte, Mill), for the progress of humanity (Spencer).

Catholic philosophers and theologians recognize that none of these theories provides an adequate standard or rule to measure human conduct. Following St. Thomas, they teach that there is a double objective norm of morality, the first immediate and proximate, which is right reason; the second is ultimate and supreme, the eternal law. There is also a subjective rule of morality, conscience.

A. The Proximate Rule of Morality

The proximate rule of morality is *the rule which immediately regulates and measures a human act.* This proximate rule is right reason. Note that we say *right* reason, not simply reason. For man's reason is fallible and can make false judgments. Right reason is reason objectively considered, as enlightened by the eternal law and thus enabled to judge rightly of the true good to be pursued and the evil to be avoided.[18] Right reason is reason in conformity with the eternal law upon which it depends; it judges of the morality of human acts *in the universal*: that love of neighbor is good, for instance, and that murder is wrong.

A human act is good when it is directed to man's true ultimate end, for the end determines our actions. But of all the powers of the soul, it is only reason which can know the true end and the means necessary to reach it. A good act, therefore, must be in conformity with reason's correct judgment of the end. Right reason, therefore, is the arbiter of the morality of our actions, that is to say, the proximate rule of morality.

B. The Supreme Rule of Morality

The **supreme rule of morality** is *the eternal law*. Right reason cannot be the ultimate criterion of right and wrong. Human reason does not make truth, it just knows it. The measure of every truth is the divine reason, the first truth upon which all truth ultimately depends. Human reason is called right when it participates in the eternal truth of God as expressed in the eternal law.

The eternal law is "the plan of divine wisdom which ordains and directs all actions to their due end."[19] Everything in the created universe has a determined nature and performs actions which are in conformity with that nature, according to God's wisdom. Irrational creatures strive blindly to attain their own proper end, the end in conformity with their nature established by the Creator. But man, because he is rational, can direct himself. Man's end is first ordained by God through his eternal law; knowing that law, man can know his end and direct himself and his actions to it. The consequence is that the eternal law is the supreme rule or exemplar of morality, the ultimate objective standard by which human actions

[18]Right reason is endowed with the habits of synderesis (the habit of first moral principles) and moral science. In the supernatural order, reason is enlightened by faith and theology. These habits enable reason to judge moral acts in the universal. A particular judgment of an action in the concrete is made by conscience, which also requires a habit, that of prudence.

[19]St. Thomas, *Summa*, I-II, q. 93, a. 1.

are judged. Man's reason, by knowing and sharing that law, is the secondary, proximate rule of morality.

C. Conscience

Right reason and the eternal law are *objective* rules of morality. They are the exemplars according to which the goodness or badness of our actions is measured in the abstract and universal. But human actions occur as concrete and singular, and hence we must have another standard, a *subjective* one, by which particular actions are judged. This rule is conscience.

Conscience is *an act of the practical intellect which judges of the morality of an action in the concrete and singular.* It is not enough in the conduct of our lives to know, for example, that worship of God is good, and that theft is bad. We must also know that this particular action, here and now, is an act of worship, or an act of theft, and thus to be performed or avoided. The work of conscience is to apply the universal knowledge of reason to a particular action. Its vital and necessary role in the moral life will be taken up in the tract on prudence. For the present it suffices to note that, while human reason can err (culpably or excusably), the will must choose what conscience presents to it as good or be guilty of evil.

8. The Sources of Morality

What is it that makes an act to be in accord or discord with the rule of morals? Having discovered the rule or norm which measures the goodness or badness of a human act, we must now investigate the sources from which that morality of an act is immediately derived. The **sources of morality,** it is clear from the foregoing, will be those elements of a human act which make it to be in conformity or disconformity with the rule of morals. In every human act, we find three such elements: the object of the act, the circumstances which surround it, and the end for which it is performed.

The primary and essential morality of an act is derived from its object, a secondary morality from the circumstances and the end.

A. The Object

The object is that which is primarily and directly attained by the act: that to which the act, by its very nature, tends. Thus the object of justice is that which is due to another. The object is the intrinsic and essential constitutive of the kind of act this particular human action is; thus it is distinguished from the circumstances, which are accidental to the act.

The primary and essential morality of a human act, then, is derived from its object: an act is specifically good or bad in relation to its **moral** object.

But a thing is good when it has everything that belongs to its being, bad in the degree that it lacks something due to it. A blind horse has the goodness of being a horse, but suffers the evil of lacking sight. It would be incomparably worse for him, however, to be a dead horse. That is because his first perfection, his primary and essential goodness, comes from his form, the animal soul.

The same is true of actions: their essential goodness or evil comes from the form. But the form of a human action is its object. The form of any reality is its specifying principle; all acts, we have seen, are specified by their object. Just as a physical act is specified by a physical object, so a moral act is specified by a moral object. If the object is in agreement with the rule of morals, the act is essentially good; if the object is not in conformity with the rule of morals, the act directed to it is bad.

B. Circumstances

Circumstances are accidents of a human act which is already constituted in its moral essence or species,[20] that is, as the kind of moral action it is. Before circumstances enter the case, the essential morality of the act is already determined by the object. But once an act is good or bad from its object, it can be further modified by the circumstances which surround it.

[20]For the nature and number of the circumstances, cf. *supra*, 48-49.

Since particular human actions cannot be separated from the circumstances which surround them, circumstances as such give a secondary and accidental morality to these acts. Although a thing derives its primary goodness from its form, many other things contribute to its total goodness. A man is specifically a man by reason of his rational soul, but many accidents accrue to the fulness of human perfection, such as height, color, weight, health, virtue, etc. Inasmuch as a man is lacking in one or more of these he is lacking in goodness.

Since circumstances contribute to the totality of being in the action, they add to the objective and essential morality a secondary morality. Hence the following conclusions:

1) Circumstances which do not pertain to the moral order contribute nothing to the goodness or the evil of an act, e.g., to commit a robbery on Monday or on Tuesday.

2) Moral circumstances modify the morality of an act by increasing or diminishing its goodness or evil. The widow's act of almsgiving was better than that of the others, for although she contributed less, she gave all she had.[21]

There is a difference in the theft of a dollar and of a hundred dollars. The difference is not essential, for both acts are specifically the same, acts of theft. But the circumstance of quantity makes it worse to steal a greater amount than a less amount.

3) Sometimes a moral circumstance adds a new essential morality to the act. This happens when the circumstance itself has a special relation of conformity or disconformity to the rule of morals. For example, to steal a consecrated chalice adds to the sin of theft the malice of sacrilege. By its consecration, a chalice is set apart exclusively for divine worship, which gives it a new relation to the moral rule.

In such cases, the circumstance no longer remains *merely a circumstance,* but takes on the nature of object. In the example above, the theft is not merely the taking of something that belongs to another,

[21]Cf. Mark 12:41-44.

but the taking of *something sacred* that belongs to another, and thus the abuse of a sacred thing.

C. The End

The end of the person acting is one of the circumstances, but because it is the most important and has the greatest influence of any of the circumstances, it is treated separately. In order to understand its role, however, we must distinguish between the *interior* and the *exterior* act of the will. The interior act is the **elicited** act of the will, the act of willing an end. The exterior act is the **commanded** act of the will, that is, an act of one of the other powers which is moved by the will. In the act of theft, for example, the will moves the hand to reach out and take someone's purse; that movement of the hand is a commanded act of the will.

It follows from this that the end is twofold: the end of the exterior act, called the **end of the act** (*finis operis*), and the end of the interior act, called the **end of the agent** (*finis operantis*). The end of the exterior act is the objective purpose of the act, the end to which the act tends by its nature. The end of almsgiving, its object, is to relieve the needy. The end of the exterior act is not a circumstance, therefore, but is the object of that act; the end and object of the exterior act are one and the same thing.

The end of the agent, on the other hand, is the subjective purpose of the act, that is, the end which the person has in mind when he performs the act, the motive which causes the act, e.g., to give an alms in order to win the praise of others. The end of the agent is the very object of the interior act; it is only a circumstance in relation to the exterior act. Almsgiving, an exterior act good from its object (end) may be performed out of diverse motives—penance, or vainglory, or inducing another to sin—all of which are extrinsic to the act of almsgiving and do not belong to its essence. They are, then, circumstances.

The morality of a human act depends in a special way on the end. The exterior act, although it has a natural goodness or evil in its own right, derives a further morality from the direction which is given to it by the will. The exterior act and the interior act unite, after the manner of matter and form, to constitute one moral act. Since the end of the agent is the principle of the whole moral act, the morality of the interior act is extended to the exterior act. The exterior act, then, has a double morality, that which it receives from its object and that which it receives from the end of the agent. When a man steals in order to get drunk, the exterior act of theft receives from the end the secondary malice of drunkenness.

The human act, then, has three sources of its goodness or evil: object, circumstances and end. In order for the act to be good, it must be good from all three sources; for it to be bad, it need be bad from only one defect. An act which is good from its object can become evil from its circumstances or end. Almsgiving, good from its object, becomes evil if done out of a bad motive, e.g., vainglory. But an act which is evil from its object cannot become good from its end, for it is already intrinsically evil. To steal in order to perform an act of liberality remains an evil action. The end does not justify the means.

D. Moral Indifference

Are there any human actions which are morally indifferent, that is, acts which in themselves are neither good nor evil?

We can consider human acts in two ways, in the abstract and in the concrete. In the abstract an act is judged simply in relation to its object; in the concrete it must be considered as it actually happens, vested with all its circumstances.

Abstractly considered, some human acts are morally indifferent. In the abstract, an act derives its morality from the moral object alone. Some objects, however, have of themselves no moral implications, such as those of walking, talking, etc. Since these acts, in themselves, have no aspect of conformity or disconformity to the rule of morals, they are without moral good or evil, that is, they are indifferent.

In the concrete, however, no human action can be indifferent. Such an act is always surrounded by circumstances, which give it morality. If a man performs an act in proper circumstances and for a good end, that act, indifferent in itself, becomes good from the circumstances and end; if these are evil, the act becomes evil. Walking to church to hear Mass is a good act, walking to church to pick pockets is bad.

9. PARTICULAR ASPECTS OF MORALITY

A. Morality of the Interior Act

The interior act derives its morality from its object, which, we have seen, is the same as the end or purpose of the person acting. Morality belongs essentially to the interior act, for this is an elicited act of the will, the act which is formally and properly a *human* act. The exterior act in the concrete has goodness or malice insofar as it falls under the domination of the will. To walk off inadvertently with a classmate's book does not constitute an act of theft, for that act was not willed.

The interior act derives its morality from its object. But the object of the will is not only the end which it proposes (object in the strict sense), it embraces everything that is willed (*integral* object). Circumstances may thus become part of the total object of the interior act. When a man wills an act, he also wills to commit it in its concrete circumstances. To make a visit to the church is a good act. But for a women to make a visit while neglecting a sick child is not a good act, taken in its totality. The circumstance, in this case *when,* is part of the thing willed. But no one should will to do something when it should not be done, for this is not to will good. The morality of the interior act, then, *is derived from its object taken integrally.*

The interior act, in order to be good, must also be in conformity with the divine will, for God wills only that which is good. Yet in some particular act the human will may be at variance with the divine will, because we do not know all the details of divine providence. This, however, is only a *material* disagreement (on the part

of the thing willed), not *formal* (on the part of the reason for willing). We may pray for the health of a friend, but it is God's will
that this friend should die. Whatever God does, however, is in view
of the common good of the whole universe, to which all particular
goods must be referred. If, then, we will a particular good not for
itself alone but with reference to the common good known by God,
we formally conform our will to the divine will.

B. Morality of the Exterior Act

(1) Its Nature

The exterior act has an intrinsic morality of its own independent
of the will, even the divine will. In the abstract, an exterior act
(except for those that are indifferent) is good or evil of itself and
by its nature even before it is willed. This goodness or evil of the
exterior act is derived, like all morality, from the object. An act is
good or evil because it is in conformity or not in conformity with
right reason. Reason apprehends this conformity or disconformity
even before the act is willed. We are able to make the judgment
that some actions are evil by their nature (murder, theft, blasphemy) and that others are good by their nature (obedience, almsgiving, etc.)

The objective morality of the exterior act is called **material morality,** that is, the matter which the act deals with is good or bad objectively. **Formal morality** is found in the interior act, because morality essentially belongs to the elicited act of the will. Together, the
exterior and the interior act, like matter and form, constitute one
moral action.

These physically distinct acts exercise a mutual influence. The
will becomes good or bad by willing an exterior action which is in
itself good or bad. On the other hand, the exterior act has a material morality, and it becomes formal only when it is willed. The
exterior act participates in the morality of the will, because it is

executed under the motion of the will and is the effect of the interior act.

If the exterior act is of itself indifferent, its total morality is derived from the interior act, e.g., walking, an indifferent act, becomes good or evil by reason of the intention.

(2) It Influence

Does the actual performance of an act add anything to the goodness or evil of the interior act? The following considerations are answers to this complex question.

1.* The morality which the interior act derives from the exterior act adds nothing **essentially** to the interior act, because the morality of both is the same. **Accidentally,** however, the exterior act can increase the goodness or evil of the interior act:

> 1) *By multiplication.* A man decides to give up smoking as a penance, and to carry out his resolution effectively in the external order must repeat this good intention several times.

> 2) *By extension of the act.* To give up smoking for Lent means normally a longer duration for the interior act if it is carried out externally than an unrealized intention, and consequently a greater goodness.

> 3) *By intensity.* Some external actions are so pleasurable or so unpleasant that they incline the will to act more intensely or remissly. But the more intense the will is in good or evil, the better or worse it is.

2. The act exterior to the will (i.e., the commanded as distinct from the elicited act of the will) in no way changes the intrinsic formal morality of the interior act. "I say to you," Christ pointed out to the externalists among the Jews, "that anyone who so much as looks with lust at a woman has already committed adultery with her in his heart" (Matt. 5:28). The execution of the efficacious will-act by one of man's other powers is already embraced by the interior act and intended by the will: it derives its formal morality from that fact. If, given the opportunity, the will does not fulfill its intention by performing the exterior act, it is obvious that the interior act itself

is not as good or evil as it might be. On the other hand, if the will is impeded from accomplishing some act by an insurmountable obstacle, its goodness or malice is in no way diminished.

Yet the exterior act, if it has its own subjective and material morality from its object or circumstances, may add something by way of accidental reward or punishment to the interior act. He who murders in his heart is not executed by the state, although before God he may be as guilty as, or even more guilty than an actual murderer. The martyr in fact receives a crown in heaven not given to other saints, but both may possess Christian fortitude in the same degree and equally merit essential reward by its act.

C. Morality Arising from the Effect

(1) General Principles

The effects which follow from an action also have a bearing, and frequently a very important one, on the morality of human acts.

1. An effect which is intended by the agent increases the goodness or malice of the exterior act, for it is directly voluntary.

2. An effect which is foreseen but not intended increases the malice of a bad action, but does not increase the goodness of a good act. When one foresees that an evil effect will follow from his action, yet does not refrain from that act, the strong inclination of the will to evil is manifest, e.g., to steal from another knowing that it will cause extreme hardship.

But more is required for good than for evil. Since the good is desirable, reason requires that it be the object of the intention. There is no added praise in visiting a sick person merely for the sake of conversation, even though the patient is greatly cheered by the visit.

3. An effect that is not foreseen, but naturally follows from the action in most cases, increases the goodness or malice of the action, e.g., the loss of one's good name increases the malice of intoxication.

4. An effect that is not foreseen and follows only accidentally and seldom does not increase the goodness or malice of the act. In a

particular situation, however, if an evil effect could have been foreseen and thus avoided by the use of prudent judgment, the evil
effect is imputed to the act.

(2) Principle of the Double Effect

A human action often produces more than one effect. Sometimes
a single action may cause two effects, one of which is good, the
other bad. As a general rule, virtue obliges us to refrain from such
an action, but often enough, under the proper conditions, it would
be permissible and sometimes necessary to perform the act. These
conditions are four in number.

1. **The action in itself must be good, or at least morally indifferent.** It is never licit to perform an intrinsically evil action, no matter
how good the effect it produces. It would never be licit, for example, to commit perjury, even to save the life of a friend.

2. **The good effect must result immediately and directly from the
action placed, not from the evil effect.** Otherwise, it would be the
use of an evil means to achieve a good effect. The good effect,
therefore, must precede, or be equally immediate with the bad effect (not in the order of time, but in the order of causality). Thus
for a sufficiently grave reason one could sell liquor to a habitual
drunkard, foreseeing that he will get intoxicated, since the good effect (commercial gain) does not follow from the evil effect (drunkenness).

3. **Only the good effect must be intended.** To intend the evil
effect is to will evil, which is never lawful. The evil effect is merely
permitted, because inescapably connected with the good directly intended.

4. **There must be a proportionately grave reason for** placing the
act. The greater the evil, the more cogent must be the reason for
performing the act. The good effect must be greater than, or at least
equal to, the bad effect. Thus, it would be licit to kill an unjust
agressor in order to preserve one's life, but not to prevent him from
stealing goods of small value.

The principle of the double effect is the key to the solution of many moral problems. Particular applications of this principle will be found in the treatment of homicide, suicide, scandal, co-operation in evil, and other serious moral questions.

10. THE CONSEQUENCES OF MORALITY

The consequences of morality are the properties which belong to human acts as a result of their goodness or evil. In relation to the end to which they are directed, actions are right or sinful; in relation to free will they are worthy of praise or blame; in relation to just retribution, they are meritorious or demeritorious.

Good and evil are properties of all created things. This is a complete disjunction. Human actions are no exception to this rule, but insofar as they are *human*—not those of stone or bull or Gabriel—they have certain distinguishing marks, the inevitable consequences of the fact that they are not only created entities, but human.

A. Rectitude and Sin

Is there something characteristic of human acts, insofar as they are good or bad, which distinguishes them from the goodness or badness associated with natural defects or perfections, the good soaring of an eagle, the broken wing of a baby robin? Certainly so. For human action is judged good or bad by some other standard, by a rule which takes into account the specific nature of the human being as a reasonable animal.

Moral rectitude is the property of a human act as it is directed to a due end according to right reason and the eternal law. An act is called **right** (*rectus*) when it tends with due order to a good end. While the term "good" is applied to stones and eagles and persons and their acts, the term "right" properly refers to human acts alone.

Sin is the lack of this rectitude which a reasonable act should have, that is, it is the lack of due order to the end. Evil is a general term, the privation of good either in the physical subject or in its act; sin, however, is the privation of good in the human or angelic act, the act which lacks due order according to right reason to its proper end. In moral matters, however, evil and sin are synonymous, for man's only true evil is moral evil, the deprivation of this righteous order to an end; and this defect we call sin.

B. Praise and Blame

Man's human actions are good and bad, and therefore righteous or sinful—a property which clearly distinguishes them from the actions of all lower creatures. Yet not all righteous human action earns praise: the plumber who deliberately intends to mess up a repair job but instead repairs the sink perfectly despite himself is not praised, even though his is not only a good action but a righteous one, in full accord with the norms for making things. On the other hand, an expert carpenter might be defeated in his well-intended efforts to build a beautiful cabinet by bad materials or bad tools; his is a bad action, he sins against the rules of art, but this takes place in spite of his good will. In short, in that field of human operation which is making things—the province of art—neither praise nor blame is necessarily attached to human efforts.

The reason for this lies in the fact that art is a work of the intellect, whereas praise and blame are given only to those human actions where man's will is in charge. "To praise or to blame," St. Thomas points out, "means nothing else than to impute to someone the goodness or the malice of his action."[22] Only when an action lies within man's power, so that he possesses dominion over it, can it rightfully be imputed to him. This is the case, of course, with all of man's voluntary actions, for the will is the source of man's dominion.

Hence human actions are worthy of praise if they are good, deserving of blame if they are evil. In these voluntary actions evil, sin and guilt are one and the same thing.

[22]*Summa*, I-II, q. 21, a. 3.

C. Merit and Demerit

"Say to the just man that it is well, for he shall eat the fruit of his doings. Woe to the wicked unto evil: for the reward of his hands shall be given to him" (Isa. 3:10-11). In these inspired words the prophet points out an important fact of human experience. No man is a world unto himself; his human life demands the association of other men. Thus many of his acts have repercussions and influence far beyond his own private life. If he does something to another's advantage or hurt, then retribution is due to that good or evil act in justice: reward for the good, punishment for the evil. Moreover, since each individual man is a part and member of society, the good or evil done him redounds on the whole society: "who hurts the hand, hurts the man." Merit, then, is the property of a human act by which it is worthy of reward from another; demerit is the property of a human act by which it is deserving of punishment by another.

From this analysis some important conclusions follow:

1. Man can merit or demerit before individual men. By his free acts, man can disturb the balance of justice which exists between himself and other men, inasmuch as his act redounds to the good or the harm of another. The equality of justice is restored by retribution: reward for the service rendered, punishment for the harm inflicted.

2. Man can merit or demerit before the society in which he shares. As a member of one or another society, any good or harm done by an individual redounds on the whole society, be it the family, the religious community, the golf club, the city or the nation.

3. Man can merit or demerit before God. God is man's last end, to which all human actions should be ordered. Man, then, can merit reward from God by directing his actions to him, a homage to the divine good; he can incur punishment by turning away from him, not giving God the honor which is his due.

God is the governor of the whole universe. The ruler of every community is concerned primarily with the common good, and hence it pertains to him to make retribution for the good and evil done in the community. Man, therefore, can truly merit or demerit before God.

But man cannot merit from God in the rigor of strict justice, for there is no equality between God and man. Presupposing the divine ordination, however, man can merit before God either in proportionate justice (*condignly*) or on the basis of friendship (*congruously*). This point will be taken up at length in the tract on grace.

11. SUMMARY AND CONCLUSION

We can summarize this important chapter on the nature and morality of human acts in a series of moral principles. Because they will frequently be evoked or referred to in the chapters which follow, the student should make certain that he understands them, reviewing the matter already studied if necessary; moreover, they should be committed to memory as essential keys for unlocking the rich theological treasures contained in this study of man's return to God.

Here are the most important:

1. A human act is human insofar as it is voluntary.

2. The voluntary will be affected to the degree that the operations of the intellect and will are affected.

3. The object of an act determines its nature.

4. Circumstances are accidental conditions of a human act modifying its nature.

5. The several elicited acts of the will are distinguished by their relation to the end.

6. The motion of the will to universal good requires the movement of God, who moves all things according to their nature.

7. Whatever is subject to the motion of the will and the ordering of reason can be commanded by the will.

8. An action is good in the measure in which it possesses the being or perfection due to it.

9. The goodness or malice of a human act is derived from its objects, its end and its circumstances:

1) The moral object gives the human act its first and fundamental morality.

2) Moral circumstances give a secondary and accidental morality to human action.

3) The extrinsic end of the human act gives it a secondary and accidental morality.

10. The supreme rule of morality is the reason of God, i.e., the eternal law; right human reason is the proximate rule.

11. The principle of the goodness or malice of human actions is taken from the will.

12. Conscience is the subjective rule of morality, against which a man cannot legitimately act.

13. External actions may have a *material* morality derived from their object, but their formal goodness or malice arises from the will. Thus they may accidentally modify the goodness or malice of the interior will-act but never substantially change it.

14. Rectitude, praise and merit are consequences and properties of good human action; sin, guilt (blame) and demerit are consequences and properties of evil human action.

These are the chief principles concerning human acts, and they lead more or less directly to some important practical conclusions.

1. The analysis of the human act can be of very practical value in our lives, for our failures can be traced to a defect in one or another of the acts of the will. Some persons drift through life without ever accomplishing anything noteworthy because they fail in an efficacious intention of the end. They are the dreamers, the visionaries whose only achievements are the extravagant triumphs of a fanciful imagination. Others become mired in over-cautious counsel, vacillating between this means and that, too timid to make a definitive judgment. Others are full of good intentions, but lack the spark of command to move them to action.

2. Morality is the badge of humanity. To *act* for the good is the bent of all nature; to *choose* the good is the prerogative of man. Man's greatest failure is the failure of sin, the rejection of goodness. The truly successful man is the good man, for success must be measured in terms of final happiness, which is the reward of the good alone. "Before man is life and death, good and evil, that which he shall choose shall be given him" (Sirach 15:18).

3. Morality has its unshakable roots in the law of God and cannot stand on the shifting sands of public opinion or popular custom. "What will the neighbors think?" is a poor criterion for moral conduct; "everybody does it" does not make it right. It is difficult to swim against the tide, but when the goal is God the struggle is more than rewarded.

4. The soul of man is the hidden battleground of the cosmic struggle between good and evil: "our wrestling is not against flesh and blood, but against the Principalities and Powers, against the world-rulers of this darkness, against the spiritual forces of wickedness on high" (Eph. 6:12). Created in God's image, called to share in the eternal riches of the happiness of God himself, man possesses the sovereign dignity, the high destiny, the perilous privilege of realizing through his own free acts the order in the universe willed by God. Success or failure here cannot be measured by human justice, which can neither evaluate genuine virtue or true vice nor properly reward or punish it. "I have fought the good fight, I have finished the course, I have kept the faith. For the rest, there is laid up for me a crown of justice, which the Lord, the just judge, will give to me in that day; yet not to me only, but also to those who love his coming" (II Tim. 4:7-8).

5. "By thy inspiration, O Lord, anticipate our actions and further them with thy assistance. So that our every undertaking may always begin from thee and, so begun, may through thee achieve its end. Through Christ our Lord."[23]

[23]Originally one of the recessional prayers said by the priest while leaving the altar after the conclusion of Mass, this prayer is now found in the Roman Missal among the prayers of thanksgiving after Mass; in the Dominican rite, this prayer is said by the priest immediately before he descends from the altar to begin Mass.

BIBLIOGRAPHICAL NOTE

St. Thomas' remarkable and original treatise on the nature of human acts and their morality will be found in the *Summa*, I-II, Questions VI-XXI. This is presented cursorily in three pamphlets of the *TFTL* series, 26-28: *Man's Mastery*, by T. H. O'Brien, O.P.; *The Warp and Woof of Life*, by J. Fearon, O.P.; *Morality vs. Immorality*, by C. M. Lehner, O.P. *Morals Makyth Man* (New York: Macmillan, 1938) and *The Heart of Man* (New York: Longmans, 1945) by Gerald Vann, O.P., are interesting studies of the same matter from a modern practical viewpoint, and Gilson has deeply explored certain aspects of the subject in *Moral Values and the Moral Life* (St. Louis: Herder, 1931). An article by J. A. Driscoll, O.P., in the third volume of the English *Summa*, "On Human Acts," is well worth reading, and Sertillanges' brilliant exposition of the Christian conception of human action and human liberty in his *Foundations of Thomistic Philosophy* (Springfield, Ill.: Templegate, 1956) is a modern classic. *Graven Images* by Dietrich von Hildebrand and Alice Jourdain (New York: McKay, 1957) clearly shows the errors of modern "substitutes for true morality."

On Christian liberty one can profitably consult J. Mouroux, *The Meaning of Man* (New York: Sheed and Ward, 1948), Chapters 6, 7 and 8, and Maritain's *Freedom in the Modern World* (New York: Scribner, 1936). The latter's *St. Thomas and the Problem of Evil* (Milwaukee: Marquette University Press, 1942) remains one of the best available English treatments of this difficult subject. Romano Guardini's *Conscience* (London: Sheed and Ward, 1932) is outstanding in its field.

CHAPTER THREE

The Passions of Man

1. Introduction

Theology must study every activity of man which exerts an influence on his progress toward happiness. If there is wholeness in man, and a cause for wonder in the scope of his human activities, that wholeness and wonder cannot be explained by reason and free will alone. For man is a whole, not a disembodied spirit. He has a body as well as a soul; he has spiritual powers which are embodied in flesh, and when he acts he acts as an entire being. Human acts are moral by their very nature, for a human act is an act of man as man, and therefore a voluntary act. When he acts wholly, engaging both body as well as soul, does he act humanly?

Among man's actions are those which, originating from the soul's knowledge, give rise to bodily reactions, reactions which are shared

78

by man with other animals. We call these activities "passions"—not from lack of a better word, but because the term "passion" is the most apt expression of what takes place in the body once its senses have been excited by external stimuli. For "passion" means "to be acted upon," to be affected by knowledge in such a way that man suffers a bodily change, under the influence of some force outside himself. One object will give rise to love, another fear, another anger, and the result will be that we will feel physical warmth, or tremble, or experience a contraction of our facial muscles. We are acted upon by external things either pleasantly or unpleasantly, and we respond accordingly. These responses are often called emotions, too, and although passion and emotion mean essentially the same thing, the term "passion" is more meaningful, since it refers explicitly to the person affected by the change and embraces every motion and feeling of which modern psychology speaks.

St. Thomas did not expound his psychology on the passions in his tract on man, where human action was studied from a speculative point of view. The reason lies in the fact that passions, as we shall see, are *particular* activities of the sensitive appetite of man. Any study of particular human actions is eminently practical, directly connected with man's progress toward his destiny, and something, therefore, to be examined theologically—something to be judged not abstractly but concretely, with reference to the norms of morality.

Our study of the passions will begin with a discussion of their general characteristics, characteristics common to all of them. Afterwards we will inquire into the elements which constitute the individual passions. We will pattern our treatment after the outline on the page which follows.

2. The Subject and Nature of Passion

When we inquire into the subject of passion we are asking about its source. On the basis of this determination we will be able to distinguish passion from other human activities and give the precise nature of passion in a formal definition.

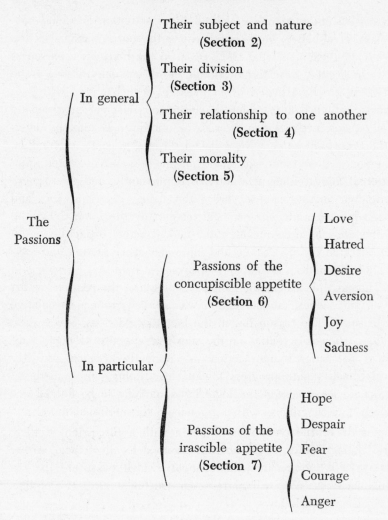

The first thing we note about passions is that, as activities, they have characteristics common to all animals: a cat will react in the presence of an enemy in the same way as man—both will bristle, showing external signs of hatred or anger or fear. Passion is not a distinctively human action, then, and certainly not characteristic of the human soul. But since the soul is the principle of a being who has a human nature—a composite of animal and spirit, body and soul— it is the accidental and remote source of all activities arising from that composite being, including its passions.

Where, then, does human passion precisely arise? Applied generally to any action in which change is involved, "passion" is derived from the Latin *pati*—"to suffer," that is, to undergo a change by reason of some extrinsic force or agent. Every passing from potency to act involves a change of some kind—from the potency to think to actual thinking is a change—but not every such change involves a bodily reaction, a response at the physical level. The human reactions of which we are now speaking, however, are characterized by just such a receptivity on the part of the human composite, usually an observable, and sometimes a violent reaction on the part of man which is physically evident. Thus, passion, which includes a physical change of this kind, is not a work of the soul's cognitive powers; cognition is a faculty which strips things of their materiality, concerned only with their underlying form and so dematerializing reality that it has no direct and necessary physical impact on the one knowing.

So passion is necessarily the work of an **appetitive faculty** (from *appetere*—to seek outside of oneself), a human power which goes out to objects as they are, in all of their materiality, regardless of the consequences at the physical level. For example, the lover of apples goes out to the object of his love as it is—its color which pleases his eye, its taste which causes his salivary glands to salivate, its smell which wrinkles his nose—a movement to something physical and material in itself which reacts physically and materially (even if sometimes imperceptibly) on the sensible subject of that movement. The mere knowledge of an apple, however, gives rise to no such reactions— as the overstuffed boy with a bushel of apples before his too big eyes can testify. In other words, cognition conquers reality, while appetition submits to reality.

The facts of introspective experience lead us to this conclusion: **passion** is *a movement of the sensitive appetite, originating from the* *knowledge of good or evil, and accompanied by some corporeal change.* The nature of passion, then, is made up of these elements:

1) **a movement of the sensitive appetite**—a motion distinguished both from acts of the will which are of a spiritual order and from other corporal motion which are *purely* bodily passions, passions which arise in the body and are terminated in the soul—hunger, for example. Passions of the sensitive appetite, on the other hand, begin in the soul and terminate in the body—for example, anger.

2) **from the knowledge of good or evil**—the appetite is a blind faculty, dependent upon knowledge apprehended by the senses, imagination, practical reason and memory. The object so apprehended is adjudged good if it is agreeable to the sensitive appetite and evil if it is disagreeable.

3) **accompaned by a physical change**—a man will flush in anger, tremble in fear, and so forth.

3. Division of the Passion

Passions are activities of man, and as such can best be understood in relation to their objects; for man's activities are characterized and specified by the objects toward which they are directed. Hence, the passions are distinct according as their objects are distinct.

The fundamental distinction between the faculties of the sensitive appetite has already been established in the first volume of this series.[1] There, the sensitive appetite was divided into two powers. The **concupiscible appetite** (from the Latin *concupiscere*, "to desire," the most dramatic activity of the concupiscible appetite) is an inclination to pursue what is suitable to man's sense nature and to avoid what is harmful (good and evil taken simply). The **irascible appetite** (from the Latin *ira*, "anger," the most impressive reaction of the irascible appetite) is also an inclination to pursue sensible good, but good

[1]Cf. *God and His Creation*, 436.

with an added note of difficulty—the pursuance of a good which is *difficult* of attainment, or the shunning of an evil which is *difficult* to avoid (good and evil as **arduous**). The reason for this distinction is quite evident: the same faculty cannot pursue both a *simple good* and a *good as difficult,* because good attracts while an evil repels, and difficulty is an evil.

Man is by nature so constituted that he is drawn to what he recognizes cognitively as good and pleasurable, and repelled by what he sees as evil and disagreeable—movements which call upon *ordinary* passions. The act of inclining toward a simple good is called **love.** Love exists whether the good object is present or absent. But when the object is absent, love gives rise to **desire,** and when the desired and loved object is present, the appetite reacts with **joy,**[2] for it finds rest in the attainment of its goal. On the other hand, the *disinclination* of the appetite to a simple evil will have its reactions. **Hatred** is the basic movement of the appetite with respect to evil, whether present or not. When faced with an actually present evil one immediately feels repugnance or **aversion,** the passion withdrawing from evil. But if the evil lays hold of the appetite so that it cannot withdraw but must remain in its presence, then one experiences the passion of **sadness.**

All of these passions or emotional reactions are movements of the concupiscible appetite. But note that because of the difference of objects—simple good and simple evil—these passions are opposed as motions. Hence, love is opposed to hate, desire to aversion, joy to sadness.

The concupiscible appetite would suffice were it not for the fact that many of the goods in man's life, as in the life of all animals, are bound up with sacrifice and difficulty repugnant to his sense nature. The animal must defend its young at the price of sensory pain; the human parent must work and sacrifice, on the sensible plane as well as on higher levels, for the good of growing children. Thus, the irascible appetite, an appetite for struggle and sacrifice, produces

[2]This movement of the sense appetite is frequently called *delight* or *pleasure.*

reactions or *emergency* passions which move toward the very things which repel the concupiscible appetite.

Confronted by a good which is difficult of attainment, the irascible appetite is moved in two ways: if it feels that it can conquer the obstacles surrounding a good, the passion of **hope** is born; but if it feels that the obstacles are completely insurmountable, then **despair** sets in. Confronted by a difficult evil, the irascible appetite has a threefold movement: **courage,** initiated by the hope that it can eventually overcome the dangers which threaten it and moves to do so; **fear,** arising when there is no hope of victory over a threatening evil, although there is still hope of escaping the threat; and **anger,** arising from the actual contact of the appetite with a difficult evil, with the result that one feels an impulse to do battle.

Like concupiscible passion, some of the emergency or irascible passions can be paired with a contrary: hope with fear, despair with courage. But unlike concupiscible passions whose contrariety consists simply in their being toward or away from contrary objects, the contrariety of the irascible passions is twofold:

1) a contrariety consisting in the members of each pair being drawn toward or repelled by *one and the same* object—thus fear causes a man to shrink away from the very object toward which he advances by courage, and hope sees the possibility of overcoming the same object that despair finds insurmountable.

2) a contrariety (similar to the contrariety of the concupiscible passions) consisting in the pairs themselves being drawn toward or repelled *by different objects*—thus both hope and despair are reactions to a difficult good and hence contrary to fear and courage which are conceived with the contrary object, difficult evil.

Anger does not have a contrary. There are two reasons for this: first, a difficult evil which is present has no contrary—when a good which was difficult is present the difficulty vanishes, and is, therefore, no longer the object of the irascible appetite; secondly, anger presupposes an evil already present, like a subpoena that has already been served, and hence no contrary motion exists whereby the evil might be eluded.

The following diagram may simplify the rather complex division of the passions:

Appetite	Objects	Passions	Reactions
Concupiscible or *ordinary* passions	Simple good	Love	Inclination to a good whether present or absent
		Desire	Inclination to an absent good
		Joy	Rest in the possession of a good
	Simple evil	Hatred	Repugnance for an evil whether present or absent
		Aversion	Retreat from a present evil
		Sadness	Restless possession of an unavoidable evil
Irascible or *emergency* passions	Difficult good	Hope	Confident impulse of overcoming obstacles
		Despair	Surrender before insurmountable obstacles
	Difficult evil	Courage	Daring in the face of evil
		Fear	Receding from the threat of evil
		Anger	Battling with a present evil

4. RELATIONSHIP OF THE PASSIONS TO ONE ANOTHER

That there is a natural order and relationship among these sensible movements and reactions we call passions is a fact discernible by

a second glance at one's own experience, even though this order
may not be immediately evident while we are actually experiencing
some emotional crisis. Hence, before we can consider the order of
each particular passion, we must bring to light their natural order
with respect to one another.

Each and every one of the irascible passions involves movement:
toward good or evil, or away from evil and difficulty. But two of
the concupiscible passions are concerned with rest rather than motion:
joy rests in possession of good; in sadness one is immobilized under
the weight of evil. Since any kind of motion precedes rest, the
irascible passions all precede joy and sadness. Nevertheless, the concupiscible passions which do involve motion precede the irascibles
because they work on the simple good, while the irascibles add the
note of difficulty to a good. Due to the fact that good always has
precedence over a related evil, love, desire, hope, despair and joy—
reactions primarily toward a good—will precede hate, passion, fear,
courage and sadness—reactions primarily toward an evil.

If, therefore, we were to list the eleven passions in the natural
order in which they usually arise, we would have the following sequence: first would come love and hate; second, desire and aversion;
third, hope and despair; fourth, fear and courage; fifth, anger; and
lastly, joy and sadness.

Joy, sadness, hope and fear, however, are called the four principal
passions: joy and sadness because in them all the other passions
reach their fulfillment and end; fear and hope, because they complete the other passions with regard to a movement of the appetite
toward something—with regard to a good, the movement begins in
love, goes forward to desire and ends in hope; with regard to an
evil, the movement begins in hatred, goes on to aversion and ends
in fear.

Love, however, because it is concerned with an absolute good
as its end, is the first of all the passions in the order of execution
and the most basic and fundamental of all movements of the sensitive appetites. It will be treated first in our discussion of the passions in particular.

5. Morality of the Passions

A. In General

Moral theology treats of passions only insofar as through their relationship to the reason and the will they penetrate the moral order. Everything that has been said thus far concerning their nature and characteristics has been only a prelude to the precise determination of their morality.

Both Scripture and Tradition bear witness to the goodness and evil of passion: the goodness of sorrow was expressed by Jesus at the death of Lazarus—" . . . he groaned in spirit and was troubled and said 'Where have you laid him?' They said to him, 'Lord, come and see.' And Jesus wept" (John 11:33-34)—and the possibility of their being evil was pointed out by St. Paul: "All they who belong to Christ have crucified their flesh with its passions and desires" (Gal. 5:24). Furthermore, St. Augustine speaks for tradition when he says that passions "are evil if our love is evil; good if our love is good."[3]

Reason is the first principle and measure of human acts, but the will is the proximate principle and measure of their goodness or evil. Hence, since a human action is one which proceeds from the deliberate will, **the passions will be morally good or evil insofar as they are voluntary.**

In themselves the passions are neither good nor evil because they are independent of reason and will, having as their source the sensitive appetite which moves because of knowledge gained through the imagination and internal senses. The sensitive appetite, however, is subordinated to reason in one way: the particular knowledge of the senses must follow the universal knowledge of reason. Moreover, both the ordinary and emergency passions are subject to the will, because when the will moves toward its object, the good, it may arouse the movement of the passions or restrain them.[4] Therefore,

---

[3]*The City of God*, Bk. XIV, Chap. 7.
[4]Cf. St. Thomas, *Summa*, I, q. 81, a. 3.

passions are voluntary and moral insofar as the will controls them under the direction of reason, which judges of their goodness or evil, their harmony or disharmony with human nature.

The question of the degrees of goodness found in the passions is a corollary of this conclusion. For a passion which is inordinate, not under the rule of reason, lessens or even destroys the goodness of an act; while any motion of the sensitive appetite which is regulated by reason adds to the goodness of an act, because it pertains to the perfection of a good moral act that the whole man act, being moved to a good object not only by the will but also by his sensitive appetite.

Without passions man would not be human. With them, when they are exercised reasonably, human life and human good are both increased and perfected.

B. The Morality of the Passions in Particular

To particularize these general notions concerning the morality of the passions and their role in human life, the following moral principles are worthy of serious consideration:

1. **Passions whch precede the consent of the will increase the intensity of the act on the part of the appetite but diminish its freedom.** As daily experience will confirm, we apprehend a sensible object much more vividly under the influence of passion, so that its attractiveness or repulsiveness (its goodness or evil for our sense nature) becomes much more apparent. In consequence, the will with greater vehemence and alacrity chooses or rejects the object so proposed.

Such an antecedent movement of the passions, however, upsets and disturbs man's reason—sometimes even to the point of destroying the voluntary entirely—as well as influencing the will. By thus impeding the tranquil deliberation of reason and the indifference of the will, passion diminishes the freedom of human action to a greater or less degree. The angry man, for example, "loses control of himself": his reason functions poorly, if at all; his will violently follows his anger and seeks to battle with the detested object; his subsequent actions are all stamped by rashness and violence; to a greater or lesser extent he is de-humanized. So, too, under the influence of passion a man may succumb to sins of the flesh he would abhor and repulse in calmer moments.

Even when no evil results from actions performed with passion as their instigator, the effect on the morality of human acts is still a considerable one. Since freedom is diminished, so also is merit, which rises entirely from free choice. To give alms is a good and meritorious act; but when one is moved more by pity to give something to a blind beggar than by reason and faith, then merit is correspondingly diminished. The same is true, of course, with respect to evil actions: antecedent passion (as in the case of the angry man) diminishes the demerit and guilt of sin by diminishing man's responsibility and freedom—his humanness.

2. **Passions which follow the will-act by way of redundance in no way affect the morality of the act.** If you deliberately choose to reject the extra drink that will tip the scales of reason, the relief and self-satisfaction that follows is a kind of reward for good, the effect of the good act. Since resultant passions of this kind do not influence the act of the will at all (although they may well be the sign of a more intense and voluntary will-act, and thus indicative of a greater goodness or evil), they neither increase nor decrease the goodness or malice of a human act.

3. **Passions which are voluntarily chosen by the will add to the moral goodness or evil of human action.** Deliberately to excite the passions in order to perform some action may be good or bad, depending on the object elected by the will, but it is always human, not merely the brute reactions of the animal side of man's nature. The just anger of Christ against the traffickers in the Temple is a case in point, as also was his sorrow at the death of Lazarus, his weeping over Jerusalem, even his agony in the garden. For in this way the total man is engaged in human action, his body as well as his soul, and the passions are powerful forces added to the will to secure the good it seeks or to overcome the evil. Moreover, a passionless man is not only an anomaly, a paradox, a freak; quite

simply he is an impossibility. Like murder, these sense movements "will out," and if man does not employ them as instruments in his pursuit of good and avoidance of evil, they will take their own revenge by anticipating his control, and thus they will lessen or obliterate his humanness.

Of themselves the movements of the sense appetites are neither good nor bad; they are simply part of man's physical equipment, necessary for his animal existence and life. But since they are subject to the imperium of reason and will, they become good or evil insofar as they are voluntary, either directly when they are commanded by the will or indirectly when the will allows them free exercise. If right reason and the human will are dominating these movements, they become morally good human actions and powerful allies in human activity; for when both of man's appetites, his sensual as well as his rational, accede to a good work, then good human action becomes easier, prompter, more intensified, more voluntary— in short, more human. Therefore it is important and even necessary to excite these sense movements in pursuing good and avoiding evil. They are, as Plato remarked, "like small flames that set fire to virtue," like soldiers assisting their lieutenant.

In sum, all of us can well afford to heed the wise counsel of Plutarch: "There is no wisdom in tearing out these affections by the root; it is neither possible nor is it necessary. What is required is to prescribe order for them."

C. Control of the Passions

To put human order, the order of reason, into our passions—that is the prescription for human living which is realized, not without difficulty or struggle, by the cardinal virtues of fortitude and temperance. But there are certain practical norms and common means which can here be suggested to assist in the right ordering of our passions.

1) *Immediately avert one's mind from any pleasurable but morally evil object as soon as it is proposed by the senses or*

imagination. Effective action on this point will be positive, not merely negative. That is, not only should we take our minds off the evil object immediately, using any legitimate distraction; more importantly, one's thoughts should be turned to good things, and particularly attentive consideration should be given to those higher motives which will dissuade us from indecent pleasures. The advice of St. Paul is very much to the point here: "Brethren, whatever things are true, whatever honorable, whatever just, whatever holy, whatever lovable, whatever of good repute, if there be any virtue, if anything worthy of praise, think upon these things" (Phil. 4:8 f.).

2) *The occasions which give rise to unhealthy passions should be sedulously avoided if possible, and immediately fled.* Experience will make us aware of the particular circumstances which customarily arouse our passions. The wrathy citizen, for example, knows that he cannot discuss politics without being easily and vehemently provoked to anger. The remedy? Keep his mouth **shut.**

3) *Above all, the passions should be deliberately ordered to higher goods.* Man must live passionately if he is to live humanly. Stoical "apathy" is all very well for statues, but a total effort to become like sticks and stones will create far more problems than it solves, and swell the waiting lines of psychiatrists. It is much more sensible because much more human to direct our passions to good than to try entirely to suppress them. Sensible love, for example, may well be ordered to Christ as he is present under the Eucharistic species; sensible sorrow can be exercised in the virtue of penance; envy can be converted into noble emulation, boldness into fortitude, and so forth.

6. THE CONCUPISCIBLE PASSIONS IN PARTICULAR

Fortified by our general knowledge of the passions, we now begin the treatment of the passions in particular. We will consider first of all those of the concupiscible appetite, and then those of the irascible appetite. Beginning with an analysis of love and ending with a discussion of anger, the main purpose of our inquiry will be to define each of the passions, give its causes and investigate its effects. Following this order, we will be rewarded with a thorough scientific grasp of each of the soul's passions.

A. Love

(1) *The Nature of Love*

Love is a passion of the concupiscible appetite because it is concerned with an unqualified good, it is not restricted to a good which is difficult of attainment. But just what is the nature of love as it is a principle of movement of the sensitive appetite? After all, love is a term used to indicate the principle of movement of any appetite: we speak of *natural love* as a movement of the natural appetite, and *rational love* as a movement of the intellectual appetite, the will. If we intend to define concupiscible love, therefore, we will have to distinguish it from these other two principles of movement.

Natural love is an inclination inherent in every being which causes the natural appetite to seek a good fitting for its nature. Thus plants bend toward the sun and heavy bodies are attracted to the center of gravity. But concupiscible love cannot be defined in terms of natural love, because the inclination of natural love takes place without any kind of apprehension or knowledge of its good object; God the Creator, the author of nature, alone apprehends this good. The sensitive appetite, however, apprehends its object by means of the internal senses and memory, as has already been pointed out. In irrational creatures this apprehension is a necessary result of being confronted with a good object; in rational creatures there is a measure of control or freedom with regard to the apprehension of this object, and as a result the sensitive appetite can be dominated by reason.

There is also a principle of movement which follows freely from man's apprehension of an object and the inclination of his will toward that object. We call this the movement of the rational appetite; its principle is rational love, the complacency or contentment of the will in a rational good which has been apprehended by the intellect, without any sensible change in the faculty. Sensitive love perceptibly differs from rational love, then, because sensitive love brings about a sensible change; for the appetite seeks a sensible good, something that can be touched and tasted and seen and so forth, and this movement toward good causes a concomitant bodily reaction.

Hence we can define the **passion of love** as *the complacency or contentment of the sensitive appetite in a good apprehended by the senses.*

Many names are given to love—dilection, charity, friendship—but the passion of love differs from all these three: dilection denotes, in addition to love, a choice, and hence cannot be in the concupiscible power; charity adds perfection to love insofar as the object loved is considered beyond compare; and friendship is like a habit rather than a passion.

A great deal of confusion surrounds the true meaning of **love of friendship** (*benevolent love*) and the **passion of love** (*concupiscible* love), for many people will love an object for a moment thinking that here is true love, and then will discard the object once passion dies. Decisions handed down by divorce courts day after day prove this fact. Therefore, a word about their differences seems to be in order.

In the first place, love's movement is twofold: toward a good which one wishes for himself or for another; and toward another *to* whom he wishes some good. The first movement is called the love of concupiscence or the love of desire, the passion of love. For example, a man may love food—for himself because it tastes good, for his children because it causes their health. The second movement is called the love of friendship, for it is directed toward another; in this way a man loves his wife, and for this reason wishes other goods for her— food, beautiful clothes, servants. Therefore, the object of benevolent love is loved *for itself,* while the object of concupiscible love is loved *for something else,* one's own pleasure or the pleasure of another.

(2) *The Causes of Love*

The first and only formal cause of love is love's object, a **good,** because the sensitive appetite is a passive faculty, unable to move without an object to bring it into act, specifying its movement. *Knowledge,* however, can also be called a cause of love, since no good can be the object of an appetite unless it has been apprehended. Experience proves that one cannot love what he does not know; a child would never love ice cream unless he first tasted it.

A final cause of love is *likeness*—the similarity between one who loves and the object of his love, a similarity which even Sacred Scripture comments on: "Every living thing loves its own kind, every man a man like himself. Every being is drawn to its own kind; with his own kind every man associates" (Sir. 13:14-15). One kind of likeness is that which exists between two things having the same quality: the sun is often referred to as a bright lamp, because both shed light. A likeness also exists between two things, one of which has an actual quality and the other a potential quality: water that is beginning to boil is said to be like boiling water.

The first kind of likeness causes love of friendship, for the fact that two men are of the same species causes one to wish good for the other as for himself. The second kind of likeness is a cause of concupiscible love—love based on the usefulness or pleasure another affords him. For he who is in potency to pleasure has a desire to experience pleasure actually, and hence will love and be like the object which gives him pleasure.

No other passion can universally cause love, because the other passions presuppose love. Hence, St. Thomas points out: "Every other passion of the soul implies either movement toward something or rest in something. But every movement toward something or rest in something arises from some kinship or aptness to that thing; and in this love consists."[5]

[5]*Summa,* I-II, q. 27, a. 4.

(3) *The Effects of Love*

Five effects of concupiscible love can be enumerated, which, because they can arise in the spiritual order and often fall under the will's control, extend to the love of the rational appetite.

1. **Union.** As an inclination or movement in the direction of the beloved, love naturally tends toward union: either a *real union,* when the beloved is present to the lover, or an *affective union,* when the appetite moves toward an apprehended object and is bound to it by affection. Thus love is the formal cause of union, but it is powerless to effect a real union.

2. **Mutual indwelling.** With regard to the sensitive appetite, mutual indwelling means simply that concupiscible love cannot be satisfied by a superficial possession of its object, but seeks to possess it perfectly by penetrating, as it were, into its very being. Thus the object loved is in the lover by being in his affections; and the lover is in the object loved insofar as the lover's contentment or complacency is rooted in the object of his love.

With regard to the rational appetite, mutual indwelling signifies that benevolent love strives to gain an intimate knowledge of everything pertaining to the beloved. The lover dwells in his beloved by reason of the fact that what is good or evil for his friends is good or evil for himself, their two wills being one. And the beloved dwells in the lover insofar as the lover wills and acts for his friend's sake as for his own. Hence, love of friendship must be a reciprocal love if it is to be true love.

3. **Ecstasy.** To experience ecstasy means to be placed outside of oneself. In the love of concupiscence, the lover is placed outside himself (carried away with love) insofar as he seeks to enjoy something outside himself. But the ecstasy which is caused by the love of concupiscence is called ecstasy in a restricted sense, since the lover seeks an exterior good *for himself,* and hence does not go out from himself absolutely.

In the love of friendship, however, a man goes out from himself absolutely, by wishing and doing good for a friend, taking care of him and providing for him for his friend's sake.

4. Zeal. Zeal is a product of love's intensity. An intense love seeks to remove everything that stands in opposition to its possession of an object. Hence, concupiscible love causes zeal which is sometimes called jealousy—for instance, a man may be jealous of his wife because the company of others may be an obstacle to his exclusive rights over her; and sometimes called envy—for example, a C student may be envious of an A student, thinking him a hindrance to his own chance of excelling.

Zeal as an effect of benevolent love, on the other hand, causes a man to repel everything that opposes his friend's good. Thus the friend of God attempts to banish every evil that is against God's honor or his will.

5. The wounds of love. Love can never harm the formal element of the passion of love, the sensitive appetite, because the object of the appetite is a good. But with regard to the material element of the passions, a bodily change, it can happen that love wounds the lover, because of an excessive change in the body. The saints often speak of the intense bodily suffering brought about by their love of God. Besides causing *the heart to melt,* love gives rise to *fervor* by which the lover burns with desire, *languor* wherein the lover is sad and desolate in the absence of the beloved, and *enjoyment* whereby the lover delights in the presence of the beloved.

Love, then, is the cause of all the lover does. The reason for this is that man acts for an end which he loves as a good. Hence, every man performs actions from some kind of love.

B. Hate

In love the appetite resonates in harmony with its object; love is consonance. Hatred is dissonance, for the appetite resonates out of harmony with the object, apprehended as repugnant and hurtful. Such an object ill befits the appetite and is, therefore, evil. And the appetite reacts against it.

Hatred may intervene at one of two stages in appetitive life. It may arise as a first passion, in reaction against what is inconsonant with one's true nature and wholesome love. It may come last of all the passions, as an effect of sadness. This latter hatred is a reaction, not against what is out of harmony with one's nature, but against what is inharmonious with traits which themselves are out of keeping with nature. Such a hatred is testimony to a corrupt nature and a degenerate character. An example would be hatred of God—the effect or daughter of the capital sin of sloth—in the man who is sad and bored with the things of God.

Love is always stronger than a corresponding hatred. But the hatred may be felt more. This is connected with the phenomenon of sensory accommodation studied in experimental psychology. Experiments show, for instance, that the surrounding temperature goes unnoticed when one's body is accommodated to it. But a variation of temperature is promptly felt, because of the change which it begins to effect in the senses. In the same way love is less noticeable than hatred because the object of love corresponds to one's present condition, whereas the object of hatred is contrary to one's present disposition and seeks to change it.

The urge to hate needs very careful rein. Hatred tends to become universalized and insatiable, so that one hates his enemy and everything connected with him and is never satisfied that an enemy has misfortune enough. In these respects hatred differs from envy, which resents only those things in which one is excelled by others, and from anger, which resents a particular inflicted evil and which is appeased once vengeance is taken or an enemy is brought low. It is hatred which causes growing youngsters to turn against all authority, causes the sinner or victim of evil habit to turn from a good end to an evil one in life, succumbing at last to malice, a sin against the Holy Spirit.

C. Desire

Desire is *the movement of the appetite in the direction of a good which is loved but absent.* This good may be an end in itself or a means to an end. If it be an end, no limit is placed upon the desire for it; if it be a means, it is desired to the extent that it implements the end. Thus a doctor sets no limit to the degree of health he desires for his patient; the healthier he can make him the better. But the doctor does set measured limits to the medicine which he desires to use as the means to health.

A further distinction needs to be made. There is a difference between the needs of nature and the desires which follow upon creative imagination. Desires connected with natural needs, such as food and drink, tend to be circumscribed in extent and limited in intensity. Desires for artificial needs invented by the human mind tend to be infinite, as with the desire for riches, a consuming passion in many men. Ths sort of desire is sometimes called *cupidity*.

D. Aversion

St. Thomas does not devote a special question to the emotion which is the contrary of desire; he points out that it does not even have its own proper name. Any name given to it is usually appropriated from another passion which bears some resemblance. Thus it is sometimes called fear, because it too is a movement away from evil; often it is known as abhorrence or loathing or hatred. In any case, it is the contrary of desire, a flight from sensible evil which is present, and **aversion** is as good a name as any. It varies in intensity from nose-wrinkling fastidiousness to headlong flight.

E. Delight

(1) Its Nature

A thing which gives spiritual delight can be possessed all at once. Eternal bliss, for instance, is the complete and perfect possession of God all at once, once and for all. This is not so with the things which satisfy the animal part of man's nature, giving rise to the passion or emotion of delight. It takes time to enjoy food, drink, sex, athletic exercise or anything else that causes bodily pleasure.

Delight or **pleasure** is *the state of quiescence in which the appetite rests satisfied in the possession of the good for which it has been striving.* From this point of view we would not call delight a passion, since passion implies motion rather than rest. But from the point of view of the changes taking place in the body during the time required to savor and enjoy the object, delight is properly called a passion.

Delight following the fulfillment of desires rooted in reason and creative imagination peculiar to man is given a special name, *joy.* Joy implies a mental life which animals do not have. This is true also of the terms used to describe the outward signs of inward joy; gaiety, cheerfulness and exultation. These descriptive terms are never applied to the emotions of brute animals.

Truly spiritual delights excel bodily delights on every important count. They are greater: men will desist from even the greatest bodily pleasures lest they be thought dishonorable; they are nobler: being rooted in a nobler part of man; they are more intimate: the sense can contact only the surface qualities of things, whereas the intellect can penetrate their very essence; they are more perfect: the mind can enoy its pleasures all at once, once and for all, but the senses can enjoy them only bit by bit; they are more sure: the delights of the senses are corruptible and soon exhausted, while spiritual pleasures are incorruptible and enduring.

Bodily delights may, however, be more strongly felt. They follow sensations, which are often more vivid than thoughts. They involve bodily alterations which are sometimes very absorbing. Most deeply felt are the pleasures which assuage sadness. The intensity of the pleasure increases with the depth of the sadness thus relieved.

One and the same object can give delight in three ways: as present, as anticipated in the future, as a past memory. Actual presence of the object causes greatest delight in the normal person, because of the physical effect actually being wrought in the body. The pleasure of anticipation is next in intensity. It is possible for a future good to be so certain that it is already present for all practical purposes, and causes pleasure very nearly the equal of actual physical presence.

Remembered pleasures are satisfying, but the bodily resonance which attends them lessens with the passage of time.

(2) *The Causes of Delight*

The sources of delight are as manifold as the activities in which a man can engage, as varied as the objects to which he can aspire. Activity and object each gives its own kind of pleasure. Sometimes, however, the object may be depressing or repulsive even though the activity regarding it be still a source of satisfaction, as in the practice of penance and mortification. One of the most pleasurable of all human activities is the act of learning, especially when the answer is found to a question which has been the cause of great wonderment.

The activities of others give delight when they express kindliness toward us, or somehow give testimony to our worth and excellence. Communion with those who share a common tie—of blood, of virtue, of learning—is a source of mutual pleasure. This is true even where the common bond is hatred of the same enemy or dislike for the same things.

(3) *The Effects of Delight*

Delight has the effect of enlarging the heart: the heart is opened like the doors and windows of a house, to let the sunshine in. The heart itself expands, the better to encompass the good which is present. Desire is increased, like the thirst for a drink which "tastes like more."

Bodily pleasures are immediately satisfying, and so absorbing that there is danger of the heart giving itself completely to them, allowing itself to be distracted from the main purpose of life, to be converted to a contrary good, or submerged in waves of passion which quench the life of reason. Pleasure must not be sought as an end in itself. It should be accepted as the corollary or by-product of wholesome activity, and as the natural concomitant of the exercise of one's faculties.

F. Sadness

(1) Its Nature

Pleasure, says St. Thomas, is rest of the soul, somewhat analogous to the peaceful rest of the body. **Sadness,** too, is rest of the soul, but it is a violent rest imposed against the resistance of nature, *a forced immobilization of the appetite in a condition repugnant to it.* Sadness is the dejection of the soul and the depression of bodily functions under the weight of present evil. Though evil from a physical point of view is nothing, since it consists in the absence or privation of good, it is apprehended by the mind after the manner of actual being, and it arouses a real reaction of the appetite.

Sadness comes when a man is deprived of his heart's desire. In fact, when there is no hope of obtaining what one seeks, the very desire itself causes sadness. If one is deprived of a good already possessed, he is more grieved than when he fails to receive something desired but not yet enjoyed.

Pleasure is the satisfaction of love and desire. Love strives for unity, and it is union with the beloved object that gives delight. Sadness is just the opposite. It arises from the deprivation of union. In a human being the greatest sadness comes from loneliness and abandonment, privation of companions and friends. Solitary confinement is a severe penance, even for the hardened criminal.

We must distinguish, however, between privacy and privation. A certain amount of separation from the world and from others is necessary, if man is to develop an interior life. There are times in a man's life when he wants to be left alone, and is the better for it. Then, too, it is possible to be surfeited when it is a question of things which should be enjoyed in moderation. Here pleasure demands a halt to union, as with excess food, drink, etc. Pain or sadness would result if such things were forced upon a man beyond their proper measure. Privation causes sadness only to the extent that one is deprived of things that perfect one's nature or present condition.

Some degree of overwhelming force is needed to impose an evil which the appetite resists. It is for this reason that one tends to fear the approach of a power superior to one's own. Only such a power can be the cause of sadness. If, however, one voluntarily submits, the greater power is the cause of delight rather than sadness.

(2) Kinds of Sadness

Sadness, in its various forms, plays an important role in a man's life. A period of mourning or sorrow makes a man more reflective, causing him to reassess his set of values. It may lead to a total change of life. Trouble can humble a man, rendering him more docile and ready to learn. God chastises those whom he loves, to teach them poverty of spirit and greater dependence upon himself. Sadness can energize a man to remedy the evils which beset him, by compelling him to devise some means of escape or by taking arms against them, as happens in contrition or sorrow for sin. Many forms of sadness could be mentioned for the benefits they bring. Hate, for example, can be changed to love through sympathy, a form of sadness.

Where sadness is too profound, and a man has no hope of escape or relief, all activity is halted. A man may even lose his mind to melancholy, becoming little more than a vegetating stump. This degree of sadness is called stupor, from the Greek word for stump.

Types of sadness may be distinguished on the basis of what one is sad about. If one is depressed by his own troubles, we call his emotion simply sadness. If one is depressed by the plight or suffering of a loved one, it is sympathy or mercy. If one is dejected by the good fortune of another, as if it were somehow an evil to himself, it is envy. If one has the feeling of being trapped by evil with no hope of escape, it is anxiety or anguish. In anxiety a man still desires to escape. Desire agitates a man from within. Anxiety, therefore, is agitated depression. St. Augustine says that no man can long desire something hopeless. When no hope of relief appears, desire dies out and a man is left in a state of retarded depression, called *accidie* or apathy, the worst possible kind of sadness. This is a condition of suspended animation or torpor in which even the will to live may be lost. In relation to the supernatural life this kind of sorrow is the capital sin of sloth.

(3) Remedies for Sadness

Sadness is the most ravaging of the emotions. Fear is second to sadness in this respect only because its object is future rather than present. No man can long endure profound sorrow. Some recourse must be sought. St. Thomas mentions many remedies, physical and psychological, which are still in use today.

Pleasure is the specific antidote to sadness, since it is its direct contrary. In the struggle between pleasure and sadness, whichever is stronger and more lasting will win out. Soothing pleasures applied in the present have a stronger effect upon the senses than do the memories of past sorrows. A cheerful environment is a big help for this reason. Self-love is more lasting than love of those who are mourned as lost. The combination, therefore, of appeal to self-love and indulgence in present joys will win out and finally expel sadness.

St. Thomas advises physical therapy: baths, drugs, rest, etc. A good cry helps, he says, because sorrow is eased when pent up troubles are given release and expression. Any expression of sadness gives some pleasure, because a man always gets pleasure from acting according to his present condition. Some persons indulge this pleasure to such an extreme that they seem happy only when they are sad.

Sympathetic friends who help to shoulder a man's troubles make his burden of sorrow seem lighter and more bearable, as when Simon the Cyrenean helped Jesus to carry his cross so that he no longer fell beneath it. The commiseration of others makes a man feel that he is loved by them, and this brings pleasure to sweeten his sorrow, as the honey sweetens the gall.

The pleasures of the mind redound to the body. It is in this way that contemplation aids in the relief even of bodily pain and sadness. With some of the Christian martyrs the joy of spiritual contemplation was able to dominate even the most cruel of tortures.

7. THE IRASCIBLE PASSIONS

A. Hope

Hope is *the passion or emotion by which one strives for a future good, difficult but possible of attainment.* Hope is related to one's power or capacity. Anything which augments a man's capabilities is a cause for hope: wealth, strength, deep conviction, know-how, previous experience, etc. We judge the future in the light of the past. Past successes form the basis of hope for the future. Where experience argues to the impossibility of a given accomplishment, it diminishes rather than augments hope.

Those who are too inexperienced or stupid to know better tend to be more hopeful than their prospects warrant. Youth is by nature more hopeful than old age, for the past is too brief to contain many disillusioning experiences, health and physical energy are boundless, and the greater part of life lies ahead. A youth is often inebriated with his power and his prospects and, like the inebriate, tends to plunge ahead with inconsiderate optimism, ready to try anything.

We are prompted to hope by our love of the good. But to love effectively requires the hope that we will find in ourselves or in others the power to obtain what we long for. In this way love and hope contribute to each other.

Hope is a confident aspiration toward what is great or difficult. When that confidence is based primarily on one's resources, it is called magnanimity. If based primarily on the help of someone else, it is called hope, although the latter term is commonly used to cover both meanings. Growth, in virtue or any difficult human attainment, demands that one aspire to something greater than what already exists. For this reason magnanimity is called by St. Thomas the crown of the virtues.

When we see that someone loves us, we look to him hopefully for the help we need. It is this hope, in turn, which gives rise to our love of him. This is why the theological virtue of hope is presupposed to the charity by which we love God. Still, the charity by which

God loves us comes before our hope. As St. John says, you love God because God has first loved you.

B. Despair

St. Thomas devotes no special question of the *Summa* to the emotion of despair. **Despair** is *the withdrawal of the appetite from effort toward the good, because the obstacles are deemed insurmountable or the good itself is thought to be too great for one's capacities.* In the man who wrings his hands helplessly in spite of having the ability to go on, this is called pusillanimity or cowardice.

To the extent that a good is difficult or delayed, says St. Thomas, it causes sadness and repels the concupiscible appetite. The irascible appetite must be brought into play if one is to advance toward the good. Hope is basic to every effort of the irascible appetite. When hope is lost and a man surrenders to despair, he is plunged into sadness from which there is no escape. This, as we have seen, is anxiety, which may deteriorate even further, into sloth.

A man may despair in one direction, though not in another. In war, for instance, a soldier may realize that he cannot win. Instead of surrendering he may fight all the more fiercely, hoping to vindicate his defeat by a glorious death. The same is true of the athlete who "goes down fighting."

C. Fear

(1) Its Nature

Fear is *the emotion or passion which causes flight from imminent harm which seems insurmountable but escapable.* Dangers in the distant future are not feared, nor are evils from which there is no hope of escape. A man does not fear something which is within his own power, no matter how evil it may be; for example, no one fears his own moral evil.

Six main kinds of fear are distinguished. *Laziness* is fear of hard work. *Embarrassment* is fear of disgrace or ridicule during the performance of an act. *Shame* is the fear of disgrace for a past deed. *Wonder* is fear of an evil or difficulty whose outcome is uncertain. *Stupefaction* is fear of an evil or difficulty which stuns the imagination. *Agony* is fear in the face of an evil which cannot be provided for.

Embarrasment causes a man to desist from his present behavior. Shame causes a man to conceal his past conduct. Wonder may prevent a man from doing anything right away, but it eventually leads to an interested study of the problem; all science and philosophy originate in wonder. When a man is overcome by stupefaction, however, he is afraid to take up the problem, because he thinks it is too much for him. Stupefaction, therefore, is a hindrance to learning. This may happen in the classroom, if the teacher or textbook makes the subject matter sound too impressive and difficult.

(2) The Causes of Fear

Fear may be aroused by anything or any person whose power exceeds our own, since such a one is able to force evil upon us despite our resistance. There is a tendency to fear anyone upon whom we are dependent or who has power over us in any way. God is feared because he has power to punish. A confidant is feared because he has power to shame us by revealing our secret life. Evil companions may be feared to the extent that they have power to entice us to sin.

Sudden events—accidents, for instance—stimulate fear. Sudden evils are the more greatly feared for the same reason that sudden changes in the temperature are felt more keenly. The sudden and sharp contrast with one's previous condition makes the change seem greater than it actually is. The longer you live with it, however, the more it tends to assume its true proportions.

Even fear itself can be feared. To the extent that one has voluntary control over his emotions, this cannot happen. But to the extent that fear is beyond one's control it can be feared. A soldier may fear that he will become frightened in battle; a sick person may fear that he will quaver if his doctor tells him that he has cancer.

Fear is intensified by a man's own weakness or by the size of the threat he faces. Anything unforeseen accentuates a man's feeling of weakness, by allowing him no time to accommodate to the situation or to plan countermeasures. Foreknowledge usually helps to alleviate fear but it can have the opposite effect, as when a person learns that he is going to be ambushed.

Not only the size of the evil and its suddenness, but its duration also will contribute to the degree of fear. An evil which promises to last twice as long as another will arouse twice the fear. Evils which are interminable or irremediable, such as the eternal loss of God or the torments of hell, give rise to the greatest fear of all.

(3) The Effects of Fear

Fear leads a man to restrict his sphere of activity, to lower his sights and moderate his ambitions; it makes a man realize his need of another's help and prompts him to take counsel. If the fear is very strong, however, it makes a man so upset that he is in no condition to listen to advice. The fearful man is himself, moreover, a poor counselor. His emotional state makes things look more terrifying than they actually are, leading to cowardly advice to those who consult him. A final beneficent effect of fear is to increase solicitude in those activities by which life's evils are avoided. This note was struck by St. Paul when he admonished Christians to work out their salvation in fear and trembling.

D. Courage

Courage is *the emotion in which one moves aggressively toward an imminent danger in the hope of conquering it.* There are modern psychiatrists who consider deep-rooted courage to be the best single criterion of a healthy, mature personality. Psychologists relate hope to a feeling of adequacy, courage to a feeling of security. Whatever contributes to hope and the sense of adequacy tends to increase one's courage and sense of security. Courage is likewise increased by anything that banishes fear or the causes of fear. A man is more courageous, therefore, if he has health, wealth, many friends to assist him (especially God), or if he has no enemies, no awareness of imminent danger.

In the exercise of courage, those who are daring by native temperament attack with full vigor. But often they meet with unenvisioned opposition, so that their attack slacks off. Those whose courage is the result of due conscious deliberation seem to work up to the attack more slowly. But frequently they find that the difficulties are less than anticipated, so that their attack intensifies. Anger is an instrument frequently employed in the work of fortitude. When anger ensues, the aggressiveness of the courageous man increases.

E. Anger

(1) The Nature of Anger

Anger is *the emotion in which one is moved to take vengeance for undue pain or evil inflicted upon him.* Anger, more than any other passion, participates in the quality of reason. It presupposes a comparison made, at least at the concrete level of sense, between the punishment which is due and the evil which is actually inflicted. This, say Aristotle and St. Thomas, is why inebriates are so often irascible and combative. Drinkers are most troublesome during the early stages of a drinking bout, when they have imbibed enough to rob them of free control of their reason but not enough to eliminate reason altogether. It is then that they are most offended by real or imagined slights. Natural instinct supplies the animal with some semblance of the rationality required for anger.

Those given to anger fall into three categories: the sharp-tempered, who are easily provoked; the dour, who remain angry for a long time; the difficult, who cannot rest until they have taken vengeance.

We have already pointed out that anger differs from hatred. **Hatred** readily tends to become universalized and to encompass the person himself. Anger is directed to the individual, toward some particular action of his by which he has offended. For this reason anger is less vicious than hatred, and less insatiable. But anger is a more heady and impetuous passion than hatred, and from this point of view it is more injurious while it lasts.

(2) The Cause of Anger

Anger always presupposes some injury or offense. All the causes of anger somehow reduce to one: belittlement. A person may feel belittled for one of three reasons—because he is despised, because his will is thwarted, or because he is treated contumeliously. Belittlement gives rise to anger because it results in sadness which is felt to be unjust.

The more exalted a man's office or position, the greater is he belittled by the same insult to his person. A rich man is insulted if you belittle his wealth, an orator if you belittle his public speaking. Those who are infirm by reason of age or physical handicap are easily hurt, and therefore easily angered.

The lower the offender's standing in relation to the one he offends, or the less he is qualified to make a criticism, the greater is the feeling of belittlement and the greater the resulting anger. But if a man, after insulting another, deliberately debases himself by a humble apology, anger is appeased; a soft word turns away wrath. The same ensues if the insulter is brought low by some misfortune or is taken in death: anger is appeased. If an angry man meanwhile becomes angry at yet another, his anger toward the first is correspondingly diminished.

(3) The Effects of Anger

Anger can amount to a veritable physical seizure, clouding a man's reason and rendering him speechless. But the overall effect of anger is most beneficial in the hands of a prudent and courageous man. We associate great achievements with the drive of the choleric man. Anger is the police force needed to keep order within the household of one's own personality, the military force needed to stave off the enemies of virtue. The body is the temple of the Holy Spirit. When temptation comes, it is like the time the money-changers came into the Temple in Jerusalem. The Christian will imitate Christ by stirring up his anger to give him the strength of soul and body needed to drive out temptation and preserve his body as a temple of the Holy Spirit and a house of prayer.

8. SUMMARY AND CONCLUSIONS

The best possible summary of the doctrine on the passions consists in the enumeration of the principles which govern this doctrine.

1. Passion is a movement of the sensitive appetite brought about by the knowledge of some good or evil and accompanied by some bodily change.

2. The passions are divided according to the differences of their objects.

3. The passions can be called morally good or evil insofar as they are voluntary.

4. Passions are ordered according to the order of their objects.

5. Love is the complacency or contentment of the sensitive appetite in a good apprehended by the senses. Hatred is the discontentment of the appetite with that which is apprehended as repugnant and harmful.

6. Delight is the repose of the appetite following upon the knowledge of its union with a sensible good. Sadness is an activity of the sensitive appetite which follows upon the knowledge of its conjunction with evil.

7. Pleasure, since it is the principle of the passions, is the rule and measure of the passions. Hence, pleasure and sorrow are morally good when they proceed from good will in conformity with right reason.

8. The perception of the object as difficult when compared with the subject's capacity is the root of differentiation of the irascible passions.

9. Hope is the movement of the irascible appetite toward a future good, difficult but possible of attainment. Despair is the withdrawal from such a good as impossible of attainment.

10. Fear is the shrinking of the irascible appetite from an imminent evil which can be avoided only with difficulty; courage advances toward the evil as something conquerable.

11. Anger is the vindictive resistance of the irascible appetite to a difficult evil which is present.

BIBLIOGRAPHICAL NOTE

St. Thomas' treatment of the material covered in this chapter will be found in the *Summa*, I-II, Questions XXII-XLVIII inclusive. Note also that the third volume of the English *Summa* contains an article by Juvenal Lalor, O.F.M., entitled "The Passions." Robert E. Brennan, O.P., has written two books on psychology which contain at least a general analysis of the passions: one, a technical work called *Thomistic Psychology* (New York: The Macmillan Co., 1941); the other, a more popular work called *The Image of His Maker* (Milwaukee: The Bruce Publishing Co., 1948). Another technical work which is worthy of perusal is *The Driving Forces of Human Nature* (New York: Grune and Stratton, 1948), by Thomas Verner Moore. Patrick O'Brien discusses the place and purpose of the emotions in harmonious living in his book *Emotions and Morals* (New York: Grune and Stratton, 1950).

Two excellent articles on the passions are Walter Farrell's "Man's Emotional Life," in *Cross and Crown*, VI (1954), 178-198, and R. Allers' "Cognitive Aspect of Emotion," in *The Thomist*, IV (1942), 589-648. *My Heart and My Flesh* by Mark Heath, O.P. (*TFTL*—29); *This Thing Called Love* by Pierre Conway, O.P. (*TFTL*—30); *Equipment for Crisis* by Joseph A. McTigue, O.P. (*TFTL*—31)—these are all readable and interesting presentations of the doctrine on the passions in popular vein.

CHAPTER FOUR

Habits and Virtues

1. Introduction

The Creator has graced man with a wonderful assortment of faculties—vegetative, sensitive and rational—to enable him to work out has salvation for himself in co-operating with God's supernatural gifts. From the womb of woman, man comes alive for a moment of time, then dies. In the interval between the coming of life and the coming of death, he must make his mark in the book of eternal life by means of distinctively human actions. What a man does in the time allotted him directly affects the destiny of his immortal soul.

To facilitate the production of man's distinctly human acts, all somehow involving the intellect and will, are added what we call habits—and especially particular kinds of habits, the *virtues* (good habits) and the *vices* (bad habits). These are intrinsic principles of operation which enable man to act well or badly with ease, readiness and pleasure. This, then, is a very important area of reality for our investigation into human action. "Turn from evil, and do good" (Ps. 33:15) is God's universal injunction to mankind; the proximate principles of human action which are good habits can ease this difficult but essential pathway to eternal life.

112

In this chapter we shall first treat of habits in general and then of good habits, or virtues. Bad habits (vices) will be treated in the next chapter. Our subjects will be developed in this order:

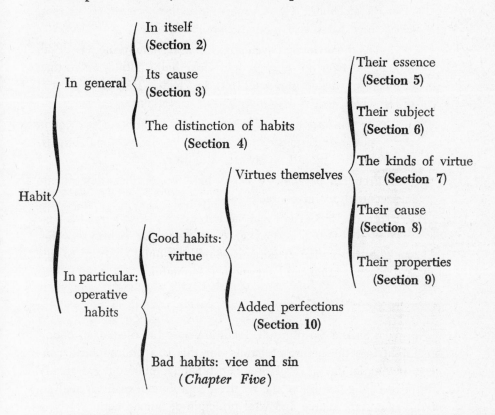

2. Habit in Itself

A. The Nature of Habit

(1) Modern Notions

The theologian's conception of habit is as foreign to the current conception of it as the modern scientist's ideas on space travel by atomic power might have been to Christopher Columbus. Men today tend to limit the notion of habit to the cursing and blasphemy of the foul-mouth in the local pool hall; or to the chain-smoker, almost unconsciously reaching for another, and then another; or to the dope addict or the alcoholic. This view of the nature of habit has its roots in one of three schools of modern psychology.

1) The **behaviorist psychologist,** basing the principle of all human behavior on reflex, would make habit nothing more than a chain—or linked series—of reflexes which function in serial order when man is confronted with a stimulus.

2) For the **response psychologist,** habit is simply a connection of physical associations, consequent upon the continual impression made by stimuli on the sense powers.

3) **Freudian psychology** likens habit to instinct, determinate and compulsory in character.

Habit so conceived makes man an automaton, led beyond his control to perform certain actions or form particular patterns of behavior. The true notion of habit is something quite contrary to this modern misconception, and far more meaningful.

(2) The Definition of Habit

Not from Sacred Scripture or Tradition does the theologian obtain an insight into the nature of habits, for this is a philosophical concept, not a datum of revelation. Fortunately, philosophy is ready with a revealing definition, the result of a profound, realistic analysis of this important source and vital principle of human actions:

A habit is *a quality difficult to uproot by which a man is well disposed or ill disposed regarding either his nature or his operations.*

To clarify this concise statement of the nature of habit we will examine in greater detail the characteristics that are here noted.

1. A habit is first and foremost a **quality.** You recall that every being in all of created reality falls into one of two classifications; it is either a **substance** or an **accident.** Every created thing either *exists in itself* (a substance: a stone, a dog, a man) or *exists in another being as in a subject of inherence* (an accident: whiteness, strength,

etc). That habit is not a substance, but rather the accidental modification of a substance, is evident.

2. There are nine different kinds of accidents; these embrace such things as height, space, color, knowledge, atomic weight, temperature, honesty, health and many more. Quality is one of these nine categories. But whereas most other accidents modify or determine the substance with respect to other things, a quality is the kind of accident which modifies or determines a substance *with regard to itself*. Such a determination of a substance can occur in various ways: 1) the shape or figure of a material thing; 2) the so-called "passion-like" qualities, such as the color of food, its flavor, its odor, its degree of heat or coldness; 3) the operative powers (faculties) of a being; and 4) the kind of modification which interests us here, **habits** —*qualities modifying and determining a substance well or badly in its being or in its operation*.

3. If a habit modifies the very nature or *substance* (entity) of a thing we call it an **entitative** habit. Entitative habits include such accidental realities as health, beauty, sanctifying grace, strength. If it modifies the *powers* of operation, we call it an **operative** habit. An **operative habit** is defined as *a quality difficult to uproot by which a man is disposed to act in a way that is easy, prompt and pleasant*. Since our primary concern in moral theology is with human behavior in relation to God, these intrinsic determinations of man's powers of acting—which so change the indifference and inertia of those powers in a permanent way as to bring facility, readiness and delight to human action—are obviously of capital importance. For good or ill, these are the proximate sources of what man does.

B. The Necessity of Operative Habits

Experience itself first informs us of the necessity of habits. Certain difficult but important tasks must be made as easy and pleasant as possible. Unless men became accustomed to speaking, reading, writing, computing, cooking, walking, studying, they would find such undertakings too burdensome, too unpleasant for frequent and intense effort.

The rational animal alone is able to cultivate habits, because he alone is determinable in the order of operation; the vital operations of plants and animals proceed from powers which are determined by nature to one object or one set pattern of operation. Rooted in human nature itself, therefore, are the conditions which make habits not only necessary but possible.

Certain conditions are necessary for the existence of habits. It is necessary: 1) that the powers be *in potentiality* to act (and so God, who is pure act, cannot have any habits); 2) that the particular powers be *undetermined* to any one particular object (hence we do not have a habit of digestion); 3) that there be *more than one way* of attaining one and the same object.

To harness his powers and put order into his actions, to act with constancy, facility and delight, man needs habit, a kind of "second nature" superimposed and perfecting human nature through its faculties. The mere ability to operate is not enough, moreover, for many of man's powers are not determined of themselves to good operation (in accord with his nature as a reasonable being) or evil operation (contrary to reason); habits are necessary in order to determine our powers to good. Hence habit strikes a middle course between the mere ability to operate and actual operation itself. Relative to the operative power, the habit is a perfecting, an act; with respect to actual operation, habit is potentiality, a capacity for this or that kind of action.

C. The Subject of Habit

In which faculties can habits be found? To answer, we need but recall that an operative habit is a disposition of a subject which is in a state of indetermination as regards operation. This indetermination to operation does not mean merely that the faculty is in potentiality with regard to act, but signifies rather a faculty's state of indifference toward many objects, or many ways of attaining a single object.

We find this essential indetermination necessary for the cultivation of an operative habit primarily in the operative powers of the soul. The intellect and will, man's chief operative powers, are the subjects of habits in the most proper sense of these terms. The will can act in diverse ways about diverse objects—for the supreme good, or for any particular good; with love or with hatred. The intellect, too, is in potency to all intelligible objects, anything that is, and can not only form concepts about them, but also judge and reason concerning them.

In a general way we may conclude that the sense faculties can also be the subjects of habits—not according as they act by natural instinct (because in this sense they are determined to one object or one manner of operating), but as they act *under the dominion of reason.* By thus sharing in reason's indetermination, these faculties can be directed to diverse objects, and ordered to them well or badly. Specifically, the sense appetites—sources of our emotions—are more susceptible of habits than the powers of sense knowledge, since they are more under the control of reason and can be directed to various objects and in various ways. Yet the internal senses can be modified by habits, as when we work under reason to better our memory or restrain the imagination. The external senses, on the other hand, cannot be directly affected by habits; by their very nature they are determined to one operation and one formal object.

Nor are there operative habits in the exterior members of the body, such as the arms or legs, or in the purely vegetative powers or motor functions—these are all determined to one object or one operation. They do not so much operate as they are operated upon, for they are instruments moving solely at the behest of the soul.

However, in a secondary sense—i.e., only in virtue of the directing influence of the rational soul—some of the bodily powers can be habituated to certain patterns of operation. Thus the hands of the machinist, the watchmaker, the surgeon and the athlete become molded to a set way of acting; their indetermination gives way to a standard-ized technique; practice has given genesis to quick, facile and even pleasing activity. Habits disposing to these questions reside *principally* in the powers of the soul, however, and only *secondarily* in the bodily powers.

3. THE CAUSES OF HABIT

A. Causes of Initial Habit Formation

There are no innate operative habits in man—that is, habits entire-ly and perfectly from nature. But there are habits which owe their existence partly to nature, and partly to some extrinsic principle. Others are caused only by some extrinsic principle.

(1) Beginnings from Nature

In the cognitive powers some habits are found *inchoatively*, by way of beginning. In the intellect inheres the habit of **understanding of first principles**: once a man grasps the meaning of whole and part, he acquires, by a partly innate habit, knowledge that the whole is greater than any of its parts; but knowledge of what is meant by whole and part cannot come except through sense experience; and hence this habit is partly from nature (from reason itself) and partly from something extrinsic to reason (sense experience). A habit may also be inchoatively natural insofar as one man, by greater acuity of his sense organs, may be more apt to understand than another; so also more sensitive sense powers as a rule dispose for better under-standing.

In the appetitive part of the soul, however, we find no innate habits, not even inchoatively. There is at most in the will an apti-tude for habits which is discoverable in the natural inclination of the appetite itself to good.

In the human body, there is a kind of beginning of habit. Some individual body types are clearly inclined to honesty, chastity or anger. Combinations of these bodily predispositions to habit are called the **temperaments;** they are each person's natural endowment. Temperament is a regular psychological pattern of reacting to stimuli and social situations; fundamentally, therefore, it is an instinctive movement, and is thus distinguished from **character,** which is the manner of reacting acquired by human choices and decisions. We cannot destroy our temperament, but we can control it and shape it into character by developing our propensities for good and disciplining the tendencies to evil by means of habits. Since the first step in self-improvement is self-knowledge, a study of one's own temperament is of considerable benefit. The chart on p. 120 may be of assistance in this self-scrutiny.

Nature itself gives us the beginnings or initial capacities for some habits, but the actual causes of habits in the operative faculties are ourselves or God.

(2) *The Work of Man*

Our own personal experience teaches us that certain habits are caused by an individual's own acts. These are called **acquired habits.** The basis for the acquisition of habits is the fact that man's powers have elements of passivity in their actions and interactions: the will can move the other powers and, when actually tending to an end, move itself with respect to means; the intellect can move itself from principles to conclusions and move the will by presenting desirable objects; etc. By such acts directed to specific objects or produced in a particular way, the indetermination of the power is overcome and its energies channeled; repetition of the same acts will make this new determination fixed and stable. While the basic potentiality of the power to act in many ways and toward a variety of objects remains, it is now determined to move easily and promptly in a certain direction, and thus brings the pleasure of accomplishment to the one acting.

Sometimes these acquired habits can be caused by one act; but far more often the acquisition of habits requires repeated acts. So, for example, by continual mortification of a desire for liquor, one cultivates the habit of sobriety, or by frequent indulgence in illicit sexual

DESCRIPTIONS	FAVORABLE INDICATIONS	UNFAVORABLE INDICATIONS	PREDOMINANT EMOTION & VICE	REQUIRED VIRTUE
Excitable (choleric): Reacts quickly and permanently to incentives. Reacts unfavorably to force; favorably to reason and to high ideals.	Great ambition; keen intellect; strong will and emotions; great powers of concentration and endurance; generous; of high ideals; tend to make capable leaders.	Strong inclinations to pride and stubbornness, very opinionated and self-confident; tends to domineer and despise others; very sensitive to humiliations.	Pride Anger Deceit Indifference *Should develop:* magnanimity.	Humility Meekness Simplicity Kindness Courage and
Optimistic (sanguine): Reacts quickly but not permanently to incentives. Needs to reflect more. Requires supervision and punishment for failures. Should learn to accept "dryness" in spiritual life.	Friendly, interesting; good mixer, willing to oblige; compassionate and able to point out another's faults; docile; candid; quickly recovers from offenses and punishment; imaginative and cheerful.	Superficial and unstable, always offering "good" reason for every change; tends to love pleasure and dread serious effort too much; over-talkative; tends to flirtation; enjoys flattery; dislikes reflection; hates loneliness, loves company; tends to depend upon "feeling" in religion.	Vanity Sensuality Envy Talkativeness Meanness *Should develop:* cheerfulness and candor.	Modesty Temperance Charity Silence Generosity Obedience.
Pessimistic (melancholic): Reacts slowly but permanently once an impression is made. Confidence must be won by kindness; must be taught to trust more in God, make more friends, cultivate more outside interests.	Inclined to reflection; prayer and meditation come quite easily. Finds peace with God. Very sympathetic and kind to others; penetrates problems, offers good advice.	Inclined to be overly serious, irresolute and dreamy; too reserved with all but close friends; fears suffering; tends to be slow, awkward, despondent; surrenders easily, then is resentful at victors; tends to be suspicious; inclined to scruples.	Sadness Fear Aversion Despondency *Should develop:* Spirit of prayer, detachment, mercy.	Joyousness Courage Charity **Hope**
Placid (phlegmatic): Reacts slowly and not permanently to impressions. Tends to be passive. Requires constant goading and surveillance.	Plodding and persevering; not easily discouraged. Demands little; has few convictions, hence, gets on with everybody.	Much inclined to ease, comfort, food and drink. Slow; unambitious; delays doing everything; unreliable; disinterested.	Dullness Sloth Sensuality Despair *Should develop:* Patience, affability, perseverance.	Temperance Zeal Abstinence Hope

pleasure one acquires the bad habit of unchastity. Once acquired, these modifications of powers incline one to perform by the habit the same acts which previously caused the habit.

(3) The Role of God

Some habits are caused, not by our own human acts, but only by God working in the soul. Such are the **supernatural** or **infused habits**, by which we are equipped to pursue a goal beyond the unaided power of human nature.[1] These new principles of operation determine man's power to know God and love him as he is in himself, and to act in other matters in a divine manner.

(4) Habit and Environment

The root of habit is an interior *active* principle, the perfection of a faculty not completely passive but already perfect as a source of self-activity. While the influence of environment on human conduct is a factor, and perhaps a large one, it can never be the immediate and sufficient cause of habit. As the principle of his own actions, man is not simply the reflection of cultural patterns but their author. Habit is his to use when he chooses, not a blind automatic response to certain social situations or the stimuli of other men.

B. Growth and Diminution

(1) Growth of Habits

When we say that habits increase, we do not mean that this increase is accomplished by way of adding more of the habit itself, as we might increase the size of a wall by additional rows of bricks. Addition supposes a plurality or multiplicity of those things which are added, and the increase of habit would then be brought about by the multiplication in the same subject of more than one habit; then we would have several habits all of the exact same species or kind, which is impossible.

---

[1]God can, of course, cause acquired habits by special intervention; those habits which we cause by laborious repeated acts he can cause in one act. He does this, in fact, when he gives someone suddenly a knowledge of the Scriptures, or imparts to an illiterate like St. Catherine of Siena the ability to read and write.

How, then, do we explain the growth or increase of habit? The growth of habit may occur: 1) *on the part of the object* of the habit itself; or 2) *on the part of the subject* in which the habit exists.

1) Habit is increased on the part of the object **extensively,** inasmuch as it now embraces new objects not before included. The habit of theology, for instance, increases as it extends to include the study of new tracts.

2) Habit is said to increase on the part of the subject **intensively,** inasmuch as one and the same habit is more surely and firmly rooted in its subject. In this way, the power in which the habit resides tends with more and more ease and readiness to its particular operation. The veteran professor and the beginning instructor are professors of the same science of mathematics, extending to an equal number of objects. But long years of study and experience give the more mature teacher a more perfect intensive possession of the habit, giving him greater ease, readiness and pleasure in the exercise of his knowledge.

To be the cause of the extensive increase of a habit the act must be one extending to an object not yet actually embraced by the habit. The man who has knowledge of all parts of a science, save one, increases that habit of science by study of the remaining part.

The intensive increase of habits is effected by the same causes which produced them in the first place, supernatural habits from God as the cause of their production and augmentation, natural habits from natural operations. Actions more intense than, or equally intense to the habit already possessed, increase that habit, or at least dispose for an increase. As St. Thomas says:

> Every such act either increases the habit or disposes to an increase thereof, if we may speak of the increase of habits as we do of the increase of an animal. For not every morsel of food actually increases the animal's size, as neither does every drop of water hollow out the stone; but the multiplication of food results at last in an increase of the body. So, repeated acts cause a habit to grow.[2]

Actions that do not equal the habit in intensity rather dispose to a lessening of the habit.

[2]*Summa,* I-II, q. 52, a. 3.

(2) *Diminution and Loss of Habits*

Supernatural habits, gratuitously caused by God, can be lost by man, not because God revokes them, but because man by sin freely rejects them.

Natural habits, as accidental forms requiring a subject in which to inhere, can be destroyed in two ways: 1) *directly*, by the acquisition of a contrary habit; 2) *indirectly*, by the destruction of the subject in which the habit inheres. All of the moral virtues and vices—good and bad habits—are capable of having contraries, because the habit may be destroyed through a judgment of reason (arising from ignorance, passion or deliberate choice) directly opposed to the inclination of the previous habit. Intellectual habits (except the habit of first principles, which has no contrary) can also be corrupted, though only directly, since the intellect is incorruptible. In this way a habit of science acquired by the intellect, such as sacred theology, can be destroyed by false principles or false reasoning processes. On the other hand, since a habit is a vital, active principle of action, it can also disappear through neglect. If the disciplined control of habit is relaxed, then an uncontrolled manner of action becomes customary: some kind of human action must take place. For example, if one never uses a foreign language which he once learned, the easy use of it quickly disappears.

C. Habit and Morality

From these observations concerning the nature and cause of habits, it is clear that they will have close relations with the morality of human action. Natural habits which have been knowingly and freely contracted through repeated acts are **voluntary**; the same is true of habits originally inadvertently acquired but subsequently approved by the consent of the will when one becomes conscious of them, or whose necessary extirpation has been neglected. On the other hand, natural habits may be **involuntary**, either because they were first acquired inadvertently and never consented to by the will, or because, once deliberately contracted, they were since efficaciously retracted through the will's firm purpose of stamping them out. Hence:

1. **Voluntary habits do not take away but ordinarily increase the voluntariness of human action.** Exceptionally a habit (drunkenness, for instance) will remove all advertence and actual deliberation from a human act, and thus will diminish the freedom of that act and its consequent goodness or evil. More frequently, however, the habit permits sufficient advertence and liberty so that the voluntariness of the act is increased, and consequently its goodness or malice also; the habitual thief is a case in point.

2. **Involuntary habits do not ordinarily take away the voluntariness of human action but always diminish it.** If the habit alone is the source of action and the act is done with complete inadvertence (offending against courtesy by vulgar speech may well be an example), it will be non-voluntary, neither good nor evil. A habit actually here and now involuntary by reason of an efficacious retraction will produce only involuntary acts, morally non-imputable; the sincerely contrite blasphemer may "slip" on occasion. But usually the case is different: involuntary habits do not force the will to action, however much they may prompt it, and thus they leave the voluntary intact; since they both disturb the reason and influence the will, however, they always diminish the voluntary. The repentant violator of chastity is not excused when habit leads him again to sin, but his very weakness makes him less guilty than one who coldly and with full deliberation commits adultery.

Since our natural habits can be good or evil, and since habits can influence our liberty to greater or lesser extent (with corresponding influence on the merit and demerit of human actions) it is evident how necessary it is to free oneself from bad habits (if any) and acquire good ones, so that we may more frequently and with greater facility perform acts of virtue.

4. THE DISTINCTION OF HABITS

Habits can be distinguished from one another in many different ways, but the radical basis for distinction of habits *as operative habits* is **according to object.** Habits which have different formal objects are specifically distinct. The reason for this is that habits are dispositions for operation, and operations are themselves distinguished according to objects. Consequently, habits too are distinguished by objects.

From this it follows that habits are likewise distinguished by reason of their subjects—that is, by reason of the faculties of operation in which they inhere—for these faculties are themselves distinguished from one another by reason of different objects. And so where we find different faculties of operation, we also will find distinct objects.

Another division of habits is that into good habits and bad habits. Habits incline man to particular actions. These actions will either be in keeping with man's rational nature (and therefore *according* to right reason), or will be contrary to man's rational human nature (and therefore *opposed* to right reason). Good habits, called **virtues**, dispose man to act in conformity with his rational nature; bad habits, called **vices**, dispose man to act contrary to his rational nature.

A final division of habits is that into **natural habits** and **supernatural habits.** Natural habits are habits which dispose to operation in accord with man's nature in terms of a natural goal, which is natural happiness. Supernatural habits are habits which dispose to operation in accord with man's supernature (grace) in terms of a supernatural goal which is supernatural happiness. St. Thomas says: "Habits are distinguished in relation to nature from the fact that one habit disposes to an act that is suitable to a lower nature, while another habit disposes to an act befitting a higher nature."[3] The "higher nature" of which St. Thomas speaks here is the participation of divine life that is man's through sanctifying grace.

5. THE ESSENCE OF VIRTUE

A. The Nominal Definition of Virtue

Having discussed the general notion of habit, we proceed to consider now a particular kind of habit: *virtue*, which is a good habit. Virtue is far more than an ostentatious show of piety, far more than purity or chastity, even though modern thinking frequently identifies

[3]*Summa*, I-II, q. 54, a. 3.

these particular qualities with virtue. The root meaning of the word should disabuse us of any such puerile notions.

The word virtue comes from the Latin word *virtus,* meaning a force or power. Related to the word for "man" (*vir*), *virtus* signifies manhood or manliness, the sum of physical and mental excellence in man. Virtue connotes, in short, something virile or manly, powers that have been brought to their ultimate limit of development or perfection. Virtue expresses this fulness of development, this realized capacity or human perfectibility of man and his operative powers.

The ultimate perfection of an operative power is, of course, found in the actual exercise or operation of that operative power. **Virtue,** however, does not properly signify the act or operation, but rather the *principle* of that operation, the good habit from which that operation flows. In this sense of the word there are frequent references to virtue both in the Old and the New Testament,[4] and it is a favorite subject of Christian thinkers in their analysis of men's journey to God.

Our analysis of virtue will be, like that of St. Thomas, in terms of the four causes: its formal cause or essence (**Section 5**); its material causes or subjects (**Section 6**); its final cause which reveals the kinds of virtue (**Section 7**); and its efficient cause (**Section 8**). The characteristics of virtue will be examined in **Section 9,** and our study will conclude by considering certain supernatural perfections closely related to virtue (**Section 10**).

B. St. Thomas' Definition

St. Thomas makes these notions more precise in his definition of virtue: **virtue** is *a good operative habit.* The genus of virtue is expressed by the word "operative habit"; the specific difference is "good," for the true perfection of virtue consists in its ordination to the good of man's nature. Virtue in its most proper sense is a morally good operative habit. Aristotle said almost the same thing in defining virtue as *that which makes its possessor good, and what he does*

[4]E.g., Sir. 24:25, Wisd. 5:13, II Pet. 1:8-9.

good as well.[5] By virtue, not only are man's actions rendered good, but man, too, is constituted morally good in his very being.

C. St. Augustine's Definition of Virtue

St. Augustine defined virtue as *a good quality of the mind by which one lives rightly, which no one can use badly, and which God accomplishes in us, without us.*[6] This definition includes the entire essential concept of virtue, listing all of its causes, and in his analysis of it St. Thomas summarizes the whole theology of virtue.

The first thing expressed in this, as in all good definitions, is the genus to which virtue belongs—in this case, the genus of **quality;** this is the remote genus of the virtues (as we have seen), and it would be even better to specify its more immediate class, its proximate genus, which is that of **habit.** The specific difference in the definition, distinguishing virtue from other qualities or habits, the bad habits or vices, is that these qualities are **good.** Thus the *formal* cause of virtue, that which constitutes the kind of thing it is, is determined.

We are told what the subject of virtue is: **the mind**—that is, the higher powers of the soul; this indicates the *material* cause, that is, the matter in which virtue exists. Also included in the definition is the end or goal of virtue (its *final* cause), which is operation: a quality . . . **by which one lives rightly.** This means that by these habits man acts in accord with reason, since some habits are always ordered to evil. Note, too, that these are habits which **no one uses badly,** which distinguishes virtue from imperfect habits, such as human faith or hope, which sometimes lend themselves to good, sometimes to evil. But virtue is the kind of principle of human acts which produces only good acts, never evil ones.

The last phrase of St. Augustine's definition—**which God accomplishes in us, without us**—indicates the *efficient* cause of the virtues,

---

[5]*Nicomachean Ethics,* Bk. II, Chap. 6.

[6]This definition is compiled from various writings of St. Augustine. Cf. *Against Julian,* Bk. 4, Chap. 3; *On Free Will,* Bk. II, Chap. 19; *Epistle 105; Commentary on the Psalms,* Ps. 118, Com. 26.

or at least of some of them. God effects the virtues, not man. Clearly, this last clause is verified only in supernatural infused virtues. For a definition of virtue applicable both to acquired and to infused virtues, these final words must be omitted.

6. THE SUBJECTS OF VIRTUE

Virtues are good operative habits. The subjects or localities where virtue inheres must be limited to the operative powers capable of such modification and determination. So the primary subjects of operative habits are the intellect, the will and the two sensitive appetites, the concupiscible appetite and the irascible appetite.

A. The Intellect

The intellect is the subject of what we call the intellectual virtues, good operative habits which determine the intellect to work well. But the intellectual virtues are not virtues in the full and perfect sense we have been speaking of up to now. We say that these intellectual virtues are virtues in a special and **restricted** sense, embracing the essence of virtue only partially. These virtues make man good, perfect, in act—but only from a particular point of view, not entirely. It is only under a certain aspect that man is made perfect by the intellectual virtues—that is, as regards a particular power of his nature —whereas the moral virtues, virtues in the absolute and unrestricted sense, render man good **absolutely,** as regards the good of his whole nature.

It is necessary to understand that these virtues which make man relatively good give the particular power in which they inhere— in this case, the intellect—an *aptitude* to operate well, a capacity which is conducive to facile and pleasant operation. But these virtues do not proximately incline the intellect to *use* this aptitude. Those virtues which give only the facility or aptitude for a good work make man good in this restricted area, and are, therefore, virtues in a restricted sense. Those virtues, on the other hand, which not only give the aptitude for good but also move man to use that aptitude are virtues absolutely, without restriction.

The skilled pharmacist, possessed of an intellectual virtue, his art of pharmacy, has a facility and capability to concoct either healing medicines or lethal potions for his clients. He has mastery over his particular domain of knowledge, but his possession of the knowledge and skill does not guarantee its good use. He need not use his virtue; even if he does use it, he need not use it rightly. But moral virtues, virtues in the absolute sense, demand to be used: a just man must perform just acts.

Virtues in the restricted sense fail to measure up to the most proper meaning of virtue. Only the moral virtues are those by which man acts rightly, and which no man can use badly.

As a consequence of this distinction, we can see that virtue is an analogical concept, whch means that it does not convey exactly the same meaning when applied to different kinds of virtues.

B. The Will

(1) The Dominance of the Will

It follows from this distinction that the subject of a habit which is a virtue absolutely can only be the will, or some power moved by the will. It is the will which moves all those other powers which in some way share in reason's guiding control. If man does anything good at all, as conducive to his true ultimate goal, it is because his will itself is good. The virtues which make man do good and do not merely give the aptitude for doing good must be either in the will itself, or in some power moved by the will.

That, from this aspect, the intellect may be the subject of virtue in its absolute sense is also possible. The intellect, when moved by a will which is well ordered to man's ultimate end, can be the subject of virtue in the absolute sense. In this way the speculative intellect becomes the subject of divine faith, and the practical intellect the subject of prudence.

(2) *The Will and the Sensitive Appetites*

Both the concupiscible and irascible appetites in man are capable of being the subjects of virtue in the absolute sense. These sensitive appetites have been endowed with a natural inclination to obey reason. Because these powers have their own proper activities, their movements may very well run counter to reason's dictates; the will must bring them under control.

The function of reason and will in controlling the passions of the sensitive appetite is considerably abetted by the help of habit. Through these determinations and under the movement of the will the sense appetites are brought to a certain habitual conformity with reason, and thus ordered to good objects and the good of the whole man.

(3) *The Will Itself*

Virtues are necessary only when an operative power has something of indetermination about it. The will does not need determination in order to will our own good, for the will of its very nature tends to this; man tends naturally, without need of any habit or virtue, to his own proper or personal good.

The will, however, is not so naturally disposed to pursue goods outside the sphere of personal good. That man be inclined to the good of his neighbor, or to some good that completely transcends or rises above the natural order of things, his power of choice needs the determinatin of virtue. Hence, man's will can become the subject of virtue in the absolute sense when directed to God or society or to neighbor, as by charity and justice and their related virtues.

7. THE KINDS OF VIRTUE

The virtues are principles of good human acts, and by acts man attains the end of human life. Theoretically, at least, man can be conceived of as having two ultimate ends: one, natural and imperfect, a natural goal which he is capable of attaining by his natural powers;

the other, supernatural and perfect, a supernatural goal which he is capable of attaining by the supernatural gifts of God. Merely human actions effected by mere human powers and habits could attain man's natural end. But man is able to attain his supernatural end, the possession of God in the beatific vision, only by means of actions which flow from supernatural or infused virtues duly proportioned to such an end.

Leaving the theoretical order, however, considering things as they concretely are, we know that man's natural end has been entirely subordinated to, and absorbed in his supernatural end. By divine revelation God has given man knowledge of a new goal of life, and he has gratuitously endowed man's powers with virtues capable of acting for that supernatural end.

In treating, therefore, of the different kinds of virtue, we shall consider: 1) the natural virtues, intellectual and moral, which are principles of purely natural acts; and 2) the supernatural theological virtues, principles of supernatural acts.[7]

A. The Natural Intellectual Virtues

There are five distinct kinds of intellectual virtues, three in the speculative intellect and two in the practical intellect. You will recall that the speculative intellect seeks knowledge simply for the sake of knowing, while the practical intellect seeks knowledge with a view to putting what it knows into practice.[8] Speculative knowledge rests in the contemplation of what is true, with no particular concern for practical sequences or the utility to which the knowledge may be put; such knowledge is sought simply as a perfection of the mind. Practical knowledge, on the other hand, has its whole reason for being in its conversion into action, that is to say, in its directing and regulating of man's operations, as in *making* things, and in *doing* things.

[7]Following St. Thomas, we shall, for pedagogical reasons, treat the supernatural (infused) moral virtues in the following section on the causes of virtue.

[8]The speculative and practical intellect are not two separate faculties, but the one intellective power ordained to different ends (cf. *God and His Creation*, 439).

(1) Virtues of the Speculative Intellect

The virtues of the speculative intellect are those which perfect the speculative intellect in the consideration of truth. There are three virtues of the speculative intellect.

1. **Understanding of first principles** is *the virtue perfecting the intellect for knowing the self-evident, or immediately evident, first principles of knowledge*:

> There are certain truths naturally known by man, immediately from the beginning, without any study or investigation: and these are the first principles, not only of the speculative order, such as that the whole is greater than any of its parts, but also of the practical order, such as evil is to be avoided and other like principles. . . . These constitute the principles of all subsequent knowledge, whether speculative or practical.[9]

2. **Science** is the virtue perfecting the intellect in *the knowledge of a particular area of reality through a consideration of its proper causes*. Science is, of course, more than physical science; it also includes the theological and philosophical sciences.

Science and understanding of first principles differ in this, that the truths attained by understanding are *immediately* evident, while the truths attained by science are *mediately* evident—i.e., by means of proof. Thus, for example, it is not immediately evident that man's soul is immortal. It is made evident by means of a proof, which gives the reasons for the truth of the judgment. There are many different individual sciences about different areas of reality, and each is a different virtue.

3. **Wisdom** is the virtue perfecting the intellect in *the knowledge of all reality through a consideration of its ultimate causes*. While the sciences view reality as cut up into sectors, each sector to be considered separately, wisdom views reality in a comprehensive, unifying whole, not in terms of causes proximate to particular phenomena, but in terms of the highest causes of all phenomena. Wisdom also judges and defends the other intellectual virtues and habits.

---

[9]St. Thomas, *De Virtutibus*, q. 1, a. 8.

(2) *Virtues of the Practical Intellect*

There are two virtues of the practical intellect: art and prudence.

1. **Art** is *the right procedure in making things.* Art works in the sphere of exterior, physical matter—building, sawing, sewing. Art, here understood as *servile* art, is to be distinguished from those liberal arts and some of the fine arts, such as playwriting, which do not involve exterior matter or transient action.

2. **Prudence** is *the right conduct of specifically human acts.* This, then, is the realm of man's moral deeds, considered as they lead toward or away from his ultimate end. The matter of the virtue of prudence lies, not in the physical world outside, but within man.

Prudence is a unique kind of virtue, for it is numbered among the moral virtues of the will as well as among the intellectual virtues. **Formally,** *as regards its essence,* knowledge, prudence is in the practical intellect as its subject, and is, therefore, an intellectual virtue; but **materially,** *as regards its content or matter,* good human actions, prudence is a moral virtue.

It is by the goodness or badness of his will, which moves all the other faculties and habits in man, that a man is good or bad. A well-regulated intellect, for instance, only renders man good in a restricted sense, as regards the particular faculty alone. Hence because the first four of the five intellectual virtues confer an aptitude for the consideration of truth—the good of the intellect—they are virtues, not absolutely, but relatively, in a restricted sense. Since, however, the use of the knowledge that a man has depends upon the movement of his will, a virtue which itself perfects the will, such as charity or justice, can oversee or control the good use of these speculative virtues. The practical conclusion is that the acts of these speculative intellectual virtues are good and meritorious when under the moving influence of a good will.

Prudence, on the contrary, disposes man to control his appetitive acts as a means to the end of human life. So it is not only, as an intellectual virtue, a virtue in the restricted sense; it is also, as a moral virtue, a virtue in the absolute sense. A prudent man not only has an aptitude to perform good moral actions, but in addition, by reason of his prudence, is powerfully inclined to perform them.

B. The Natural Moral Virtues

The moral virtues are habits by which man's appetites are well-disposed to be brought into conformity with reason, which is the norm determining the good, midway between excess and defect.

Moral virtues are necessary for man's proper moral activity because the rational and sensitive appetites in man are not entirely subject to reason. Because these faculties are properly operative in their own right, they can rise up against the control of reason. Hence, the various appetites of man must be disposed to obey reason by the discipline of the moral virtues. We speak here of the *natural* moral virtues, of acquired moral virtues, to distinguish them from the *infused* moral virtues, the supernatural counterparts of natural virtues which will be discussed later.

(1) Relationships between the Moral and Intellectual Virtues

Not every virtue is a moral virtue, but only those that reside in the will, or in the sense appetites as controlled by the will. Yet there are many in our day who deny any real difference between the moral virtues and the intellectual virtues. These trace their intellectual lineage to Socrates, for whom knowledge was supreme. He maintained that if a man had sufficient knowledge, he *could* not sin; sin was the consequence of ignorance, and man had but to cultivate the intellectual virtues and he could not fail to attain his final destiny. A grain of truth lies hidden here, for the very core of distinctively human behavior lies in reason: it is reason which points out what is good and what is evil.

But we should recall that the appetitive powers do not obey reason willy-nilly; on the contrary, they can rise against reason. St. Paul gives tongue to this universal fact of experience: "I do not understand what I do, for it is not what I wish that I do, but what I hate, that I do. . . . For I know that in me, that is, in my flesh, no good dwells, because to wish is within my power, but I do not find the strength to accomplish what is good. For I do not the good that I wish, but the evil that I do not wish" (Rom. 7:15, 17-19).

Conflicts arise in the pursuit of the reasonable good; knowledge alone fails to guarantee good conduct. The **will** can be so attached to self-love as to be disinclined to render to others what is reasonably due them, and the **sense appetites** can tend so strongly toward what is pleasurable and suffer such repugnance to what is hard and painful as to offer formidable opposition to reason:

> For a man to do a good deed, therefore, not only must his reason be well disposed by means of a habit of intellectual virtue, but his appetite also must be well disposed by means of a habit of moral virtue. And so moral differs from intellectual virtue, even as the appetite differs from reason. Hence just as the appetite, insofar as it partakes of reason, is the principle of human acts, so moral habits are to be considered virtues insofar as they are in conformity with reason.[10]

Human virtues, as habits inclining man toward the performance of good actions, must of necessity reside ultimately in one or the other of the two primary sources of human activity, the intellect or the will (or the sense appetite as moved by the will). Those habits perfecting the intellect in its consideration of truth are intellectual virtues; those perfecting the appetites in the pursuit of good are moral virtues.[11] Distinct though the intellectual and moral virtues are however, there is yet a mutual dependence among them.

1) The moral virtues may exist without the intellectual virtues of wisdom, science and art, but they cannot exist without prudence and understanding. Prudence is required in order that the good of reason may be determined for the appetitive powers; the virtue of understanding is necessary because prudence must base its judgments on the first practical principles of reason.

2) Any of the intellectual virtues, with the sole exception of prudence, may exist without the moral virtues. The reason why prudence is excepted is because the operation commanded by prudence must be directed to a good end, and it is the function,

---

[10]St. Thomas, *Summa*, I-II, q. 58, a. 2.

[11]The virtues of faith, hope and charity are not included in this division because these three, though residing in intellect and will, are supernatural virtues, and have no place in a division of strictly human virtue.

not of prudence, but of moral virtue to incline man to a good
end. Hence prudence and moral virtue are inseparable.

(2) *The Principal or Cardinal Virtues*

Some of the moral virtues are called **cardinal virtues,** from the
Latin word for "hinge," that upon which the door hangs. Cardinal
virtues, then, are those principal virtues upon which man's moral
life pivots, like the door upon its hinge. These cardinal virtues are
prudence, justice, fortitude and temperance.

That the principal or cardinal virtues are moral virtues can come
as no surprise. For the *principal* or *cardinal* virtues surely must be
virtues in the most proper sense of the world, and virtue in the absolute or perfect sense *is* moral virtue, i.e., good habits conferring both
the aptitude for a good work and the guarantee of its good use.

The number of cardinal virtues may be deduced either from a
consideration of their formal objects or from the subjects in which
they are found to reside.

1) **By reason of formal object.** In general, the formal object of
a moral virtue is simply the *good as fixed by reason;* it is the
function of moral virtue to assist man's rational and appetitive
powers in working to that end. St. Thomas thus derives the cardinal virtues from a consideration of their formal principles:

> The formal principle of [natural moral] virtue . . . is the good as
> defined by reason, a good which can be considered in two ways.
> First, inasmuch as it consists in the very act of reason, and thus we
> have one principal virtue called *prudence*. Secondly, insofar as reason
> establishes order in something else: either in operations, and then
> we have *justice*, or in the passions, and then we need two virtues.
> For it is necessary to put the order of reason into the passions in
> view of their rebelliousness to reason, an opposition occurring in two
> ways: in one way, by the passions inciting to something against reason;
> hence it is necessary that the passions be curbed: and so we have
> *temperance*; in a second way, by the passions withdrawing from that
> which reason dictates, as through fear of danger or of labor; and
> then man needs to be strengthened in that which reason dictates
> lest he turn back: and so we have *fortitude*.[12]

[12]*Ibid.*, I-II, q. 61, a. 2.

2) **By reason of subject.** There are four faculties of the soul in which the moral virtues reside, and in each of them one of the cardinal virtues: prudence in the intellect, justice in the will, temperance in the concupiscible appetite and fortitude in the irascible appetite.

Above all the virtues which regulate human action and behavior, prudence, justice, temperance and fortitude earn the right to be called cardinal virtues, because each has an object which is more important and more difficult than the objects of other virtues. Prudence is concerned with the principal act of the practical intellect, to command, rather than with counseling or judgment; justice is concerned with maintaining due responsibility for what is rightly due in such things as commercial and private bargaining and debts with another person; temperance restrains one from the more vehement pleasures of food, drink and sex; fortitude strengthens one to stand firm in the face of great danger or death itself.

The primacy of these virtues is evident. One who is able to restrain the most vehement of his carnal passions, for example, is by that fact more easily disposed for controlling his lesser passions or emotions; because he has mastered more difficult matter, he can more easily master less difficult. The individual who has the cardinal virtues possesses, at least in a rudimentary way, all the other moral virtues. The other moral virtues are related to these four principal virtues as **allied** or **annexed virtues,** since they are either concerned with secondary acts or objects, or they lack the full nature of the principal virtue to which they pertain. Thus religion, piety, reverence, obedience, gratitude are some of the virtues allied or annexed to the cardinal virtue of justice.

C. The Theological Virtues

(1) Their Existence and Nature

The theological virtues are operative habits by which we are ordered to God, our supernatural end. *Theological,* a derivation of the Greek words meaning "knowledge about God," is the proper characterization of these virtues for three reasons: 1) because both their material object and formal object or motive is God; 2) because they are infused in us by God; 3) because even their existence is known only because of God's revelation to us.

If man had ever been ordained to a merely natural goal in this life natural powers would have been sufficient to attain it. As a matter of fact, however, man's ultimate goal is a supernatural one, a goal consisting in the immediate, direct vision of the essence of God. In the face of the transcendent nature of this supernatural goal, man's natural operative equipment is hopelessly inadequate. Consequently, there must be some special supernatural apparatus given to man which will be proportioned to his supernatural goal. The fundamental supernatural principles of human action are the **theological virtues**.

Note that the object of these theological virtues is man's supernatural end, God himself; they have no direct bearing on those things that are as means to the end. That man's powers be set aright as regard the means for attaining his supernatural goal there is need for yet other supernaturally infused virtues, the supernaturally infused moral virtues, which we shall consider shortly.

The Council of Trent affirms the existence of these three theological virtues, to which Sacred Scripture bears abundant testimony: "In the very act of justification, at the moment when his sins are remitted, man receives through Jesus Christ, to whom he is joined, the infused gifts of faith, hope and charity. . . ."[13] Though the Council did not declare in so many words that faith, hope and charity are theological **virtues**, i.e., permanent habits, the universal teaching of theologians holds that faith, hope and charity are **infused theological virtues**.[14]

---

[13]Sess. VI, *Decree on Justification*, Chap. 7, "The Nature of Justification and Its Causes"; Denz. 800.

[14]The Council's use of such words as "infused" and "inhere" clearly, though not definitively, indicates that faith, hope and charity are bestowed, not as something passing, but as permanent habits. If we recall that faith, hope and charity are infused into the souls of newly baptized infants who are incapable of human actions, it becomes evident that faith, hope and charity are in them not as *acts*, but as *habits*.

The fact that there are three, and only three, theological virtues is abundantly clear from innumerable scriptural passages as well. We need only cite a well-known text from St. Paul: "So there abide faith, hope and charity, these three; but the greatest of these is charity."[15]

That there be three such virtues as faith, hope and charity, is also seen, in retrospect, to be eminently reasonable. To set his steps toward his supernatural goal, man must know this goal, and this is accomplished by **faith**. Man must move toward this supernatural end as something good and attainable, even though difficult, and this is the function of **hope**. Finally, man must attain God as good in himself, and this is brought about by **charity**.

(2) The Order among the Theological Virtues

If we were to ask which is first among the theological virtues, we would have to answer the question with a distinction. Certainly *in the order of time* none of them is first, because all of them are infused into the soul together as properties of the life-principle of supernatural existence, sanctifying grace. *In the order of nature,* faith comes first, followed by hope, then charity, for man must first know what he is to hope for, and this hope must precede love. *In the order of excellence,* charity is first among the theological virtues, since it unites man perfectly to God: it is the perfection of all the other virtues.

D. Summary

The major distinction of the virtues among themselves is indicated in summary form in the chart which follows on p. 140.

---

[15] I Cor. 13:13. For faith, cf. Mark 16:16, John 3:18, 8:24, Eph. 2:8; for hope, Ps. 117:9, Rom. 5:2, 15:13; for charity, Matt. 22:37, Rom. 5:5. This is but a sampling of the many references which could be quoted; they will be considered in greater detail in the chapters on the individual virtues.

OPERATIVE VIRTUES

Intellectual — habits perfecting the mind in knowing truth

- simply for the sake of knowledge
  - **Understanding**—perfecting the intellect for knowledge of first principles; e.g., the whole is greater than a part.
  - **Science**—perfecting the intellect in the knowledge of a particular class of reality through a consideration of its proper causes.
  - **Wisdom**—perfecting the intellect in the knowledge of all reality through a consideration of its ultimate causes.
- in order to use it
  - **Art**—perfecting right reason in making things.
  - **Prudence**—perfecting right reason in doing things.

Moral — habits perfecting the appetites in seeking *human* values

- in the practical judgment
  - **Prudence**—perfecting the intellect in commanding the kind of action best suited to reach a goal. Many auxiliary virtues co-operate to perfect prudence.
- in the appetites
  - **Justice**—perfecting the *will* to give others what is their due. (Religion, patriotism, truthfulness and respect are some allied virtues.)
  - **Temperance**—perfecting the *ordinary* appetites by moderating their pleasures according to reason. (Humanity, chastity, sobriety and modesty are some allied virtues.)
  - **Fortitude**—perfecting the *emergency* appetites by strengthening them to withstand hardships attached to reasonable, human living. (Magnanimity, patience and perseverance are some allied virtues.)

Theological — habits infused by God which dispose man's faculties supernaturally to attain God as the object of happiness.

- **Faith**—perfects the intellect to assent to revealed truth because of the authority of God who reveals it.
- **Hope**—perfects the will to strive for eternal life because of God's promise of help to attain it.
- **Charity**—perfects the will to love God with a supernatural love, in which one loves himself and others for the love of God.

8. The Causes of Virtue

A. Nature

Nature has implanted in man a foundation for virtue—namely, a natural inclination to the good of reason, and certain naturally known principles both of knowledge and action, "the nurseries of virtue," in St. Thomas' phrase. Individual men, moreover, because of bodily dispositions ("temperament") may be disposed more to the development of one virtue than of another. But these are but the beginnings of virtue. No natural virtue, intellectual or moral, is found in its full state of development as an innate endowment of nature.

And, of course, no supernatural virtue, theological or moral, is found in man from nature.

B. Human Action

Those virtues which are directed to man's natural good as determined by the rule of human reason are caused by human actions, just as any natural operative habit is. Those virtues, however, which are directed to man's supernatural good, that which is determined by the rule of divine reason transcending human reason, can be caused by God alone, since the goal is higher than the powers of nature. This is a point which demands further investigation.

C. Divine Action

That God can infuse into the powers of the soul the natural virtues attainable by repeated effort is beyond dispute. Certainly he can directly accomplish what he ordinarily produces through secondary causes; this he did do, St. Thomas holds, in the case of our first parents,[16] and the lives of the saints contain many instances of the same divine action. And he alone is the only possible cause of the theological virtues, by which we are directly ordered to our supernatural end, God as he is in himself.

[16]Cf. *Summa*, I, q. 95, a. 3.

Our present question is this: does God give us certain super-natural *moral* principles of action?

(1) Existence of the Supernatural Moral Virtues

The primary reason for asserting the existence of the infused or supernatural moral virtues is that, just as man must be disposed in the natural order not only for the end but also for the means to the end (the work of the acquired moral virtues), so also in the super-natural order man must be disposed not only for his last supernatural end but also for the supernatural means to this supernatural end. Proper determination with respect to the means is the work of the supernatural or infused moral virtues. God does not provide less perfectly and less generously for the order of grace than he does for the order of nature.

The Church has never *definitively* declared anything of the exist-ence of these virtues, but their existence is denied by no Catholic theologians and commonly affirmed by saints, doctors and theologi-ans—among the most illustrious, St. Augustine, St. Gregory and St. Thomas. The most common and more probable opinion regarding their number is that there are as many supernatural moral virtues as there are natural moral virtues.

(2) The Nature of the Supernatural Moral Virtues

The supernatural moral virtues differ **specifically** from their re-spective natural moral virtues. Although the *material objects* or con-tent of the supernatural and the natural moral virtue are the same, their *formal objects* differ. The natural moral virtue has for its formal object a good determined by reason alone, whereas the supernatural moral virtue has for its formal object a good determined by reason illumined by faith, in other words, by a supernatural standard. In-fused abstinence and acquired abstinence are both concerned with the same material object, the moderate use of food. But their norms or standards regulating this moderate use of food are quite different. The natural virtue moderates the use of food to protect the health of the body, while the supernatural virtue moderates the use of food to discipline the body and bring it into subjection in view of the goal of eternal life, so that Christians might be "fellow citizens of the saints, members of God's household" (Eph. 2:19).

The infused virtues give an *intrinsic* facility for performing certain supernatural acts, but must depend upon the *extrinsic* facility of the acquired virtues as a condition for the actual performance of these virtuous acts. A man who habitually drinks too much will receive, after a good confession, sanctifying grace and the infused virtue of sobriety; but without the acquired virtue of sobriety he will remain sober only with the greatest difficulty.

The intrinsic facility for placing a certain act consists in the inclination, rooted in the very power itself, for performing a particular operation; the extrinsic facility consists in the removal of external obstacles which impede the performance of the operation. The supernatural virtues confer this intrinsic facility for acting supernaturally, for they so elevate and strengthen man's natural operative powers as to give him not merely an inclination for, but the very *power* itself of supernatural action. But they do not confer the extrinsic facility; they do not remove the external obstacles.

The acquisition of the acquired virtues, therefore, is of tremendous importance for the Christian. The infused virtues are not intrinsically aided by the acquired virtue, but the acquired virtues do assist extrinsically by removing obstacles, such as the inordinate inclinations and desires of man's lower nature. Once these obstacles are removed, the infused virtues enable man to act easily and promptly in producing supernatural works in the various areas of human action.

9. THE PROPERTIES OF VIRTUE

A. The "Mean" of Virtue

A concept important to our study of the virtues is contained in the adage, "virtue lies in the mean," or "virtue lies in a middle course." Scripture states the same truth in other words: "Decline not to the right hand, nor to the left; turn away thy foot from evil" (Prov. 4:27).

This notion of avoidance of extremes must, however, be carefully understood: certainly virtue is far from being a continual compromise resulting in mediocrity.

The mean of virtue is not *on the part of the subject,* as though a man could not exercise virtue more than half-heartedly, could not strive with great moral energy for the perfection of goodness. The mean of virtue is *on the part of the object.* This means that virtue has for its object a middle way in its proper matter between excess and defect, precisely to the degree that right reason dictates. A man can fully enjoy drinking, but he may not enjoy it beyond the measure set by his nature as man and his vocation to heaven, right reason and divine law. Excess would be to drink too much, or to drink when, where or how drinking should not be done; defect would be not to drink in the proper circumstances and under the proper conditions as laid down by right reason. Thus, virtue consists in a "mean," conforming man's actions to a standard or measure, neither going beyond it nor falling short.

An act is good which conforms to the measure or rule of human reason or faith, morally evil if it does not. The "mean" of virtue becomes, therefore, the **mean of reason** (taking "reason" as including both the case of reason alone or as illumined by divine faith).

(1) The Mean of the Moral Virtues

All of the moral virtues observe this mean of reason. But it also happens sometimes that this *rational* mean is in addition a *real* mean—in the virtue of justice. Justice gives to another what is due him. Because justice is concerned with objective external obligations to others, the mean or standard is something wholly independent of whatever reason may determine without reference to reality. There is a right here established by objective quantity: if a man borrows ten dollars, he is obliged to pay back ten dollars. The real mean of justice consists in paying back ten dollars. To give five dollars would be an injustice; to give fifteen would go beyond justice.

The other moral virtues—prudence, fortitude and temperance—attain the mean of reason *alone,* a rational mean rather than a real mean.

There is in the virtue of sobriety no objective mean, a departure from which would also be either an excess or a defect. The *reasonable* amount one may drink differs radically with different individuals. These virtues regulate man's internal emotions or desires, which cannot be measured by the same external, quantitative rule we find in justice.

The rational mean is not something mathematical. It could not be argued, for instance, that, because eating six hamburgers makes one ill, and guilty of gluttony, and eating none at all shows lack of care for the body, therefore the reasonable norm is always to eat three. Sometimes this rational mean will be found in complete abstinence, as when a diabetic eats absolutely no sugar, or when John the Baptist abstained completely from alcoholic drink in a spirit of penance. *The rational mean is not mediocrity or compromise but the apex of perfection determined by prudence between excess and defect in a particular case.*

It is the particular task of prudence to determine the mean for the moral virtues: what is temperate or what is courageous for *this* man in *these* circumstances. Prudence will dictate for sobriety the amount of liquor a particular man can drink in the light of requirements of health, social custom, etc. Prudence will dictate for abstinence that only the prescribed amount of food be taken during Lent in order to keep the ecclesiastical law.

(2) The Mean of the Intellectual Virtues

The intellectual virtues, too, attain a real mean, for the measure of truth is objective reality itself, something external to, and independent of the consideration of the mind. An intellectual virtue is perfect when it attains things as they are. Falsehood, which is the evil of the intellect, can be had both by failing to know what is to be known and also by attributing to some object more reality than it truly has.

(3) The Mean of the Theological Virtues

Because God himself who is beyond any created measure is their object, there is no mean for the theological virtues of faith, hope and charity. It is not possible to believe too much, hope too much, love too much; their only measure is to believe, to hope, to love without measure.

Any excess or defect which might seem to be attached to the theological virtues actually comes from the circumstances or state of the subject of these virtues. One may, for instance, give himself too much to certain practices connected with contemplative prayer, which pertains to the theological virtues, if he finds it necessary to neglect the duties of his state of life—his work, his family, his health. But this excess is not really an excess *in the virtue itself,* because it does not pertain to the proper acts or proper matter of any of the theological virtues. It rather stems from the *extrinsic circumstances* or *state of the subject* in which these virtues reside.

B. Connection of the Virtues

The connection of virtues refers to *an essential dependence of one virtue upon another,* so that one cannot exist without the others in the same individual. To determine the existence of this relationship we shall have to consider each class of virtue.

(1) The Intellectual Virtues

The intellectual virtues are not necessarily connected among themselves nor with the moral virtues. One may know logic without knowing biology; a theologian may know all about charity without being a saint. Nevertheless, since all that the intellect grasps is founded on first principles, all the intellectual virtues depend on understanding.

(2) The Moral Virtues

The moral virtues in their imperfect state are not connected among themselves. A woman who by temperament might be generous to the poor might at the same time be engaged in prostitution. But in their perfect state both the acquired and the infused moral virtues are essentially connected among themselves.

The virtuous man is oriented toward morally good goals, and chooses means suitable to attain those goals; it is the work of the moral virtues to dispose and incline man toward morally good goals in life, and the work of prudence to counsel, judge and command the use of means to attain these goals. Justice, temperance and fortitude, in consequence, depend upon prudence for the realization of their perfection in human behavior. This dependence, however, is mutual, for all means are measured by the end they must attain. If prudence is to command the use of means that are truly suitable for an ultimate goal, then a man must be disposed for that goal by the right order with respect to particular goals which is set up by the moral virtues. Perfect prudence can only exist with the moral virtues. To act bravely, a prudent man must have fortitude; to act courageously, a brave man must have prudence.

The supernatural virtues, infused together simultaneously with grace and charity, are obviously linked with one another. Charity is "the bond of perfection," joining them all together in attaining an object and destiny far beyond the most perfect human capabilities, where the least defection is a total loss. Like their counterparts of the same name, they are also connected in prudence, a supernatural prudence which dictates, subject to the goals established for it, the immediate means for the proximate goals the supernatural virtues have directed and empowered human powers to realize as steps to the attainment of God.

(3) The Theological Virtues

In the state of perfect virtue, the theological virtues of faith and hope are connected in charity, for charity perfects all the virtues, directing them, informing them, as it leads them to God.

In the state of *imperfect* virtue, however, faith and hope can exist without charity. Men continue to believe in God and to hope in him even when in the state of mortal sin, when they have ceased to love him, or to direct their actions to him. But charity itself presupposes both faith and hope: we cannot love what we do not know, nor can we love what is impossible to attain. Faith may exist without hope (knowledge without desire), but hope always presupposes faith (desire for something known).

C. Equality and Inequality among the Virtues

In considering relations of equality, virtues may be compared in terms of their **objects** and in terms of their **subjects:**

1) *In terms of their objects,* the theological virtues are supreme because they have God as their object: charity is superior to faith and hope because by it man approaches nearer to God. Faith is of what is not seen, and hope is of what is not possessed, while the love of charity is of what is already possessed.

The intellectual virtues, which attain universal truth, have a more noble object than the moral virtues, which are concerned with particular goods.

Among the cardinal virtues prudence is most perfect because it resides in the reason, which is the norm of morality. Justice follows prudence, because it establishes the order of reason in man's deeds, not only regarding himself, but also regarding others. Fortitude comes third, because it strengthens man against the dangers pertaining to life and death, which are of primary concern to man. Temperance is last; it regulates the appetites in less important matters, even though matters which are necessary to preserve the individual or the species.

The infused moral virtues, since they are supernatural, are by essence superior, of course, to the acquired moral virtues.

2) *In terms of their subjects,* different men possess virtues in different degrees. Some men are better disposed than others by practice, others have a stronger natural inclination to a particular virtue, while still others have a more discerning judgment in these matters or receive a greater grace, for grace is given to each "according to the measure of the giving of Christ" (Eph. 4:9).

D. The Duration of the Virtues

The virtues are good operative habits, inhering in a soul that is immortal. We might well ask, then, if the virtues themselves will perdure into the next life with the human soul in which they reside. In the souls in heaven do there remain any of those virtues which include no imperfection, an imperfection repugnant to the state of the blessed?

The moral virtues remain in the souls of the blessed *as regards the essence of the virtue,* but not as regards its inclination to act. This merely means that there will no longer be dangers and death, and hence none of the passions concerning them for fortitude to regulate, nor desires for food or drink or sex to be controlled by temperance. Yet the appetites' conformity to right reason will remain, and this is the essence of virtue. In heaven these virtues will be applied to new operations, more fitting to the kind of life that exists there, and not to the exercises of this life.

Temperance, fortitude and other virtues concerned with the passions will be present only *radically,* however, until the resurrection of the body, as these virtues govern faculties requiring the use of the body.

The knowledge of reality attained by the intellectual virtues, which is their essential element, is itself a participation of the immortality of the intellect, and hence remains after this life. The images in the senses and the imagination (from which the intellect now gathers the raw material for its ideas) will cease to exist with the body in which they function. Truth will remain, immeasureably more meaningful, but its worldly vehicles will not be necessary.

Of the theological virtues, neither faith nor hope will exist in heaven. The obscure, unsatisfying knowledge of faith will give way to the brilliance of vision in which we possess God and are possessed by him; the blind groping of hope will give way to the unchangeable possession of God which is the happiness of heaven. Only charity will remain. Faith and hope are essentially imperfect, and in heaven they will flower in perfection into vision and possession. But charity will live on, for the perfection of love does not destroy the basic nature of love: its intensity will increase beyond measure; its object, God himself, is exactly the same. "Charity never fails."

10. ADDITIONAL AIDS FOR THE EXERCISE OF THE VIRTUES

A. The Gifts of the Holy Spirit

The life of a Christian is a journey back to God. Like every journey, this one is set apart from all others by its goal. The goal of the Christian is the vision, the possesion of God himself. It is a supernatural goal, one surpassing all the power and all the ability of created nature. And because the goal is supernatural, the means to it are also supernatural; but they must remain within the reach of man, for it is his journey, and no one else can travel the road appointed for him. The means are placed within man's reach when God elevates him to the supernatural order by grace, when he makes him a "partaker of the divine nature," infusing into him the supernatural virtues that enable human powers to perform acts that attain a divine goal and have eternal value.

With all this help, however, these acts remain more human than divine. *The way in which a man exercises a supernatural virtue is very evidently human.* It is still an act that requires thought, deliberation and the exercise of free choice on the part of man. To attain a goal so lofty and so far above us as is the vision and possession of God, we have need of a kind of activity that is more flavored with divinity. We are called to be sons of God, members of the divine household, sharers in the inheritance of Christ. And St. Paul tells us that ". . . whoever are led by the Spirit of God, they are the sons of God" (Rom. 8:14). *We are led by the Spirit of God through the gifts of the Holy Spirit.*

(1) The Existence of the Gifts

These gifts are enumerated in the Book of Isaias, where they are attributed in prophecy to Christ, of whom St. Paul speaks as the exemplar of the saints and "the firstborn among many brethren" (Rom. 8:29; Gal. 4:6):

> And the spirit of the Lord shall rest upon him: the spirit of wisdom, and of understanding, the spirit of counsel, and of fortitude, the spirit of knowledge, and of godliness (piety). And he shall be filled with the spirit of the fear of the Lord.[17]

From the very beginning of the Church, the Fathers, theologians and spiritual writers have attributed these gifts to the souls of *all* the just. Pope Leo XIII voiced this tradition when he wrote: "The just man, that is to say, he who lives the life of divine grace and acts by the fitting virtues as by means of faculties, has need of those seven gifts, which are properly attributed to the Holy Spirit."[18]

(2) *The Nature of the Gifts*

The virtues, both natural and supernatural, dispose us to obey promptly the commands of reason and reason enlightened by faith. The gifts dispose us in a higher manner to obey promptly the movement or inspiration of *the Holy Spirit,* who dwells in us through charity. And it seems, therefore, that just as our powers require habits for disposing them to be obedient to reason, so too they require habits, and not mere passing dispositions, by which we are made obedient to the Holy Spirit.

The **gifts of the Holy Spirit** may be defined, then, as *supernatural habits by which we are disposed for obeying promptly the movement or inspiration of the Holy Spirit.*

These habits are called *gifts,* not only because they are given by God, but because they dispose us to follow the impulse or suggestion of the Giver, and because they render man movable by a divine inspiration which is *a special gift* of actual grace. For this motion of the Holy Spirit is a very specialized kind of gift; otherwise it would

---

[17]Isa. 11:2-3. While the Hebrew text does not mention the gift of piety (but the Septuagint and the Vulgate do), fear is named a second time in verse 3, and in the Old Testament the terms "fear of God" and "piety" have almost the same meaning. Since the third century, tradition affirms this sevenfold number.

[18]Encyclical *Divinum Illud Munus,* May 9, 1897.

not differ from the ordinary movement of actual grace which is required even for the acts flowing from the supernatural virtues.

The gifts, then, condition man's operative powers, not for acting from their own instigation (i.e., through the ordinary channels of counsel, judgment and command) as is the case with the supernatural virtues, but for being moved from the outside, as it were, by the very movement of the Holy Spirit himself. "The wind blows where it will, and thou hearest its sound but dost not know where it comes from or where it goes. So is everyone who is born of the spirit" (John 3:8). As the sails of a ship place that ship in readiness to follow the impulse of a favorable wind, so the gifts dispose and prepare man to obey promptly the impulse of the Holy Spirit. "By means of them the soul is furnished and strengthened," writes Leo XIII, "so as to be able to obey more easily and promptly [the Holy Spirit's] voice and impulse."[19]

(3) The Necessity of the Gifts

This movement and inspiration of the Holy Spirit is necessary, not only for those who perform the more extraordinary and more excellent works of the Christian life, but also for *each* of the just, that they might persevere and grow in grace. Such is the common teaching of theologians. *The gifts are necessary that the Christian may save his soul.* Life on earth is too complex an affair for him to cope with in terms of his strictly human powers, even when elevated and strengthened by the supernatural virtues, theological and moral. "By the theological and moral virtues," says St. Thomas, "man is not so perfected in respect of his last end as not to stand in continual need of being moved by the yet higher promptings of the Holy Spirit."[20] And since, as St. Thomas points out, the need is continual and permanent, it is necessary that the gifts be in us as permanent, infused dispositions, i.e., as habits.

No man can be certain of the extent or degree of divine influence exercised in his life through the instrumentality of the gifts of the

[19]*Op. cit.*
[20]*Summa*, I-II, q. 68, a. 2, ad 2.

VIRTUES	GIFTS (Understanding)		
Faith	Understanding		to penetrate revealed truth
Charity	Widsom	divine things	
Hope	Knowledge*	created things	} to judge
Prudence	Counsel	our own actions	
Religion (Justice)	Piety		for worshipping God
Fortitude	Fortitude		to face fear of danger
Temperance	Fear†		to control desires

the intellect as enlightened by faith:

the will and sense appetites as healed by grace:

The gifts of the Holy Spirit make perfect:

*Knowledge also perfects faith, and St. Thomas treats this gift under this aspect; cf. infra, 340.
†The gift of fear also perfects hope by preserving us from presumption; cf. infra, 374 f., 696.

Holy Spirit. Their activity must always be appreciated and prayed for, and never underestimated. Our understanding of them will deepen when, later in this book, following St. Thomas, we discuss each of the gifts corresponding to a particular virtue, according to the outline on the preceding page.

B. The Beatitudes

The beatitudes, of which St. Matthew lists eight (Matt. 5:3 ff.) and St. Luke four (Luke 6:30 ff), are *actions* and not habits, the **perfect acts** of the virtues and particularly of the gifts, the most proper effects of the divine-human action which flows from these supernatural principles. The name beatitude is appropriate for these more perfect actions because they are especially conducive to man's beatitude, leading to, and meritorious of his true final beatitude or happiness: thus even in this life they bring a certain foretaste or firmly founded expectation of that happiness. We may define the **beatitudes** as: *acts that flow from the workings of the Holy Spirit in man by which man possesses happiness, beginning even in this life and perfected in the next.*

Thus the words of Leo XIII express the sentiment of the Church: "By means of these gifts [of the Holy Spirit] the soul is excited and encouraged to seek after and attain the evangelical beatitudes which, like the flowers that come forth in the springtime, are the signs and harbingers of eternal beatitude."[21] Here, then, in the program of happiness Christ announced in the Sermon on the Mount, is the perfection of human living, a level of action diametrically opposed to the ideals of the world, its means and its goals. In these great and more perfect activities is realized, by guarantee and anticipation, the aspiration for eternal life which wells from the Christian soul transformed by grace.[22]

---

[21]*Op. cit.*

[22]The full significance of the beatitudes for the Christian life is disclosed in St. Thomas' profound study of them, *Summa,* I-II, q. 69, ad 3 and 4, a reference which, though difficult, the student should consult.

C. The Fruits of the Holy Ghost

The **fruits of the Holy Ghost** are *human actions produced by the virtues and the gifts which refresh man with a certain holy and genuine delight.* The fruits are not habits or dispositions found in the soul, but rather actions which flow from habits. An action which is a fruit of the Holy Spirit is something *ultimate* and *delightful,* as the fruit of a tree or plant is the ultimate flowering of the tree and the source of pleasure for those who eat it. While these acts lack the perfection and excellence of those perfect works which are the beatitudes, they are nonetheless virtuous actions of the Christian life which are directly opposed to the works of the flesh.

In his Epistle to the Galatians, St. Paul listed the principal fruits: "The fruit of the Spirit is: charity, joy, peace, patience, kindness, goodness, faith, modesty, continency" (Gal. 5:22).[23] This is not an exhaustive but a representative listing of the accomplishments and delights of Christian virtue, covering in a general way the entire area of human action.[24]

11. SUMMARY AND CONCLUSION

The whole moral life of man, it has been well said, is theological. The achievement of the perfection which is proper to him is the progressive growth within him of the image of God unto that perfect imaging realized in the beatific vision. In the light of reason enlightened by faith, theology attempts to uncover as much as possible of the truth about our nature and its principles of action, to see that nature, its end, its well-springs of behavior as God sees them, and thereby to set forth the interior rules of human conduct arising from that nature, its supernatural destiny and its divine endowments.

[23]The Douay version, following the Vulgate, adds longanimity, meekness and chastity, bringing the number to twelve. The Greek text, however, has only the above nine.

[24]Cf. St. Thomas' analysis of the workings of the fruits of the Spirit, *Summa,* I-II, q. 70, a. 3.

God's images, we are essentially intelligences like him, beings of reason and will, captains of our fate, masters of that destiny to which we aspire. Our reason is a derivation of his eternal wisdom; enlightened by faith, informed by charity, right reason becomes the standard of judgment for all our acts insofar as it is the reflection of God's eternal law within us. And the proximate source of human action is habit—not an automatic pattern of action and reaction, but a spiritual quality which we can use when we choose to do so.

Hence the importance of good habits, of virtue, for successful human conduct in pursuit of happiness. Their function is to set up the good of right reason—that essential order of man's being and activity which consists in conformity with divine law—in those areas of human possibility and capacity which can escape the demands of his nature. In the practical intellect prudence discerns what is to be done; by participation justice places the order of reason into our actions with respect to others, fortitude into the movements of the irascible appetite, and temperance into those of the concupiscible.

Through the supernatural virtues and the gifts man's spiritual organism is brought to that higher level of perfection which enables him to live, even in this life, the life of God, and by means of this supernatural activity, culminating in the fruits and beatitudes, achieve in heaven that perfect image of the Trinity for which his nature was but the substructure.

All of this suggests certain applications of the doctrine on habits and virtues which should interest every Christian.

1. The habitual but contrite sinner may find much solace and hope in this doctrine concerning habits. Armed with sorrow and the grace of God, he is not only able to form new good habits but to destroy his deep-rooted evil habits. Every action performed by a converted sinner with his mind set on changing the past effects a real transformation in his soul. He is, with each succeeding good act, a man better equipped to persevere in his new reformed manner of life.

2. Virtues are not simply terms and divisions, but realities existing within one's very control, as much a part of man as his hands

and feet, his mind and will. St. Thomas called them good operative habits; he also spoke of them, more meaningfully, as "quasi-natural inclinations" toward the good fixed by reason. As our native operative powers are real, fully natural inclinations to particular objects, so our good habits, whether natural or supernatural, intellectual or moral, are just as real inclinations to their objects.

3. "The true Christian does not renounce the activities of this life, he does not stunt his natural faculties; but he develops and perfects them, by co-ordinating them with the supernatural. He thus ennobles what is merely natural in life and secures for it new strength in the material and temporal order, no less than in the spiritual and eternal."[25]

4. The Christian life is not one in which the natural is repressed and inhibited. On the contrary, the natural and supernatural virtues are a guarantee that human nature is acting in the way in which it was designed; they are a means leading to the full richness of human maturity.

5. "Truly in the religious crisis of our times—the gravest, perhaps, that humanity has passed through since the origin of Christianity— the reasoned and scientific exposition of the truths of faith, however efficacious it may be and is in reality, is not enough. Nor suffices the often skimpy measure of a Christian life nourished merely from conventional habits. What is necessary today is the greatness of a Christianity *lived in its fulness* with persevering constancy; what is necessary is the vigorous and valorous host of Christian men and women who, living in the midst of the world, are at every instant to fight for their faith, for the law of God, for Christ, their eyes fixed on him *as a model to imitate, as a leader to follow in their apostolic work.*"[26]

6. "Education regards man precisely as perfectible through his own activity directed by the knowledge and art of another; it sees him as capable of development through knowledge and love. The development sought in education is a development in good—a real improvement in the educable. This development is sought as something

[25]Pius XI, encyclical *On the Christian Education of Youth,* Dec. 31, 1929.
[26]Pius XII, allocution to the Sacred College, Dec. 24, 1953.

permanent and not transitory. Further, the development sought in Catholic education is complete, including physical, intellectual and moral perfection, natural and supernatural growth. Man, then, must be perfected through education in terms of his distinctively human characteristics and in terms of his divine capacities, so that the product of Catholic education will be more perfectly a man and more like unto God."[27]

7. The doctrine on virtues has ramifications for the sinner, especially for the habitual sinner, who must be warned not to overlook the cultivation of the natural or acquired moral virtues. Without them, he cannot long, and without tremendous effort, preserve the life of grace in his soul. The note of hope is found in the connection of the virtues. The sinner can have the confidence born of knowledge that the natural moral virtues among themselves, and the supernatural virtues among themselves, grow together. Hence, the sinner who is afflicted with one particular vice can be assured that his efforts to improve himself in other areas of virtue will help overcome his vicious habit as well.

[27]Thomas C. Donlan, O.P., *Theology and Education* (Dubuque: Wm. C. Brown Company, 1952), 20.

BIBLIOGRAPHICAL NOTE

The matter of this chapter is treated in the *Summa*, I-II in Questions XLIX-LIV for habits in general, and in Questions LV-LXX for virtue. For the philosophical approach to habit and virtue one may refer with profit to three works of R. E. Brennan, O.P., two of which are more technical—*General Psychology* (New York: Macmillan, 1952) and *Thomistic Psychology* (New York: Macmillan, 1941)—and one less difficult, *Image of His Maker* (Milwaukee: Bruce, 1948). Two chapters in *Moral Values and the Moral Life* (St. Louis: Herder, 1941) by E. Gilson may also prove helpful: "Virtues and Moral Character," 135-150, and "Supernatural Virtues," 215-232.

"The Gifts of the Holy Ghost" in *The Spiritual Doctrine of Sister Elizabeth of the Trinity* (Westminster, Md.: Newman Press, 1947) by M. M. Philipon presents a theologian's analysis of the writings of a Carmelite mystic concerning the gifts; this is an excellent supplement to a textbook method of presentation. *Swift Victory* by Walter Farrell, O.P., and W. D. Hughes, O.P. (New York: Sheed and Ward, 1955), and *The Holy Spirit in the Christian Life* by Ambrose Gardeil, O.P. (London: Blackfriars, 1953), are also highly recommended.

For a popular yet profitable analysis the *Theology for the Layman* series should be consulted: for habits, *In the Groove* by Paul Farrell, O.P. (*TFTL*-32); for the virtues, *The Art of Being Good* by Francis Conway, O.P. (*TFTL*-33), and *Its Own Reward* by Mannes Rogers, O.P. (*TFTL*-34); for the gifts, beatitudes and fruits of the Holy Ghost, *To Us with Love* by Walter D. Hughes, O.P. (*TFTL*-35).

The entire matter of this chapter is well presented in the essay, "The Supernatural Virtues," by T. E. Flynn in *The Teaching of the Catholic Church*, Vol. I, 622-658.

The difficult question of the connection of the virtues is treated by P. Lumbreras, O.P., in "Notes on the Connection of the Virtues" in *The Thomist*, IX (1948), 218-240, and the relation of the virtues to sanctity in "Holiness and the Cardinal Virtues" by John E. Steinmueler in *The Thomist*, XI (1950), 39-44.

CHAPTER FIVE

·

Sin

1. INTRODUCTION

In this volume we have continued to broaden and deepen our knowledge of man, the player involved in the very serious game of life. We have uncovered in very clear terms the goal or purpose of man's existence. We have seen that the goal can be attained only by actions—actions proceeding not solely from the unadorned operative powers of man, but from those powers as perfected by virtue. At least in broad outline, therefore, we have sketched what is required of man for him successfully to bring the course of his earthly life to its proper term.

This chapter, no less than its predecessors, is intended to aid man in making a success of his journey through life. But we come now to a significantly different manner of approach to the problem, to the consideration of the congenital enemy of the good life, moral evil: evil actions, evil vices.

We investigate the true nature of evil in theology that it might be the more clearly recognized and, consequently, avoided or healed.

The evil which we may call moral evil is the destroyer and ravager of happiness. Sickness, poverty, persecution, lack of friends—any physical evil whatsoever—is compatible with real happiness. Man's true happiness, his friendship with God, can stand with all evil save one, the evil of sin. Until this fact is recognized, men will continue to substitute the false, fleeting, finite goods of the world in the place of true happiness.

Our theological investigation of this greatest of human evils will follow a familiar pattern:

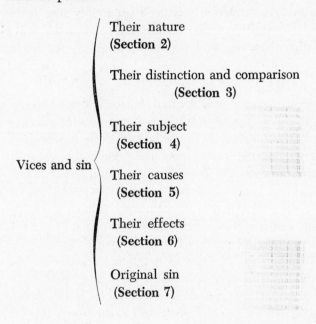

Vices and sin

Their nature
(Section 2)

Their distinction and comparison
(Section 3)

Their subject
(Section 4)

Their causes
(Section 5)

Their effects
(Section 6)

Original sin
(Section 7)

2. THE NATURE OF VICE AND SIN

By way of introduction, it should be observed that by far the greater part of this section, as well as the greater part of the entire chapter, will be taken up with the matter of sin rather than with vice. The reasons for this are not difficult to surmise. First of all, it would involve much redundancy if we were to go into great detail over the matter of bad habits or vices; a good deal of knowledge of a thing is gained from a knowledge of its contrary, and we have already at our disposal a considerable working knowledge about bad habits from our inquiry into good habits. Secondly, since habits are known only by means of their acts, it is not without reason that we busy ourselves, though not exclusively so, with bad human actions rather than the habits themselves. Finally, it is interesting to note that, while the acts that flow from the virtues have no proper or special names (we speak of a good act of temperance, a good act of justice), the acts engendered by the vices have received special names (theft, adultery, detraction), rather than simply sins against justice. For these reasons, therefore, the emphasis of our study will be placed on sin rather than vice, and we shall deal chiefly with mortal sin.

A. General Notion of Sin as an Evil

The nature of evil was treated in some detail in the previous volume. It will suffice to recall here that it denotes a lack or absence of some perfection, not a simple lack in the sense of total negation of perfection, but the lack of some perfection that ought to be present. The lack of the power of speech in a tree stump is not an evil, whereas a comparable absence of speech in a man is a very marked evil for that man. Evil, then, is not a mere negation, but a *privation* of goodness. Thus evil has been defined as *the privation of a due good.*

If this privation of good is found in some *thing* we have **physical evil**; if found in the free act of a rational creature we have **moral evil** or sin. Sin, therefore, designates the lack of perfection or goodness in some act or operation resulting from the failure of this to attain its proper term or goal. And since law is the measure according to which an act must be directed if it is to attain its end, it amounts to the same thing to speak of sin as a *deordination from an end* or as *a transgression of law.*

There are, however, three kinds of law: the laws of *physical nature,* the laws or rules of *art,* and the laws of *morality.* The birth of a mongoloid is a sin of nature, and the production of a defective bridge a sin of art. The transgression of the moral law, however, because it arises of necessity from a free will, is something worthy of blame and is imputable to the agent. As such, it merits, in technical parlance, the special and distinctive title of **fault** (*culpa*) over and above the general designation of **sin** (*peccatum*).

But because theology considers sin neither in relation to the laws of nature nor to those of art, but only in its reference to moral matters and in relation to the ultimate end which is God, the general practice has sprung up of using "sin" and "fault" in exactly the same sense, as a transgression of the moral law or a deordination from the ultimate end of man.

B. Sin, Vice, Virtue

In the very beginning of his investigation into the nature of vice and sin St. Thomas clarifies some basic concepts by comparing vice and sin to virtue.[1]

There are three things to be considered in every virtue: 1) its essence as a *good disposition* of the person; 2) the consequent *goodness* of the inclination to a good act; 3) the *good act* to which the virtue is ordained. To each of these corresponds a contrary:

1) **Vice** is contrary to virtue as a disposition, for as virtue signifies a good habit, vice signifies a bad habit.

2) Just as a good inclination follows virtue, so a bad inclination, the inclination to sin, follows vice. The **badness** (*malitia*) of vice is thus contrary to the goodness of virtue.

3) The act of virtue is opposed by **sin**. Sin is not directly contrary to virtue—for virtue is a habit while sin is an act—but to the act of virtue. Vice, therefore, is opposed directly to virtue, sin to a good act, vice's badness to virtue's goodness.

It is clear that sin has a greater evil or badness associated with it than vice, for a habit is a mean between the the operative power and its actual operation. Hence, as an operative habit is said to be more perfect—regarding either good or evil—than the operative faculty (since it *inclines* it to a certain act), so the habit is exceeded in perfection or completeness by the act which ultimately *determines* the faculty. Consequently, as all men recognize, to do evil is worse than merely to be inclined to do evil. In other words, the evil of vice comes only from the evil act to which it is ordered.

There is, however, a certain aspect under which vice may be considered as a worse evil than sin. For vice, as a habit, has a cer-

[1] *Summa,* I-II, q. 71, a. 1.

tain permanence, while the act of sin is of the moment. Likewise, vice as an operative habit is also a principle of action, a potential efficient cause of *many* sins, and, as a consequence, may be considered as being more evil than the acts which it causes. But sin, because it is the *final cause*—that which is responsible for the determination of this habit—remains, strictly speaking, worse than vice.

C. Sins of Commission and Omission

(1) In General

Up to this point we have been considering sin in terms of bad human actions. There is nothing wrong with this view of sin as long as we recognize that the picture it presents is not a total view of the possibilities of sin. St. James wrote that "he who knows how to do good, and does not do it, commits sin" (Jas. 4:17). Man can sin just as well by failing to act at all as he can by placing acts positively opposed to moral law. We must then make allowance for sins of commission and for sins of omission. The **sin of commission** is the placing of a prohibited act, and therefore is opposed to a negative precept or command; for example, theft is opposed to the negative command of the Decalogue, "Thou shalt not steal." The **sin of omission**, on the other hand, consists in the simple non-performance of an act of precept or command. He who misses Mass on a day of precept sins by the transgression of an affirmative precept.

(2) The Sin of Omission in Particular

The sin of omission, considered in its essence, does not appear to be an act, but rather a mere privation, the lack of what ought to be present. The sin of omission, however, must bear some relation to a free and deliberate act; there can be no moral culpability unless man acts voluntarily. Hence it is necessary that the sin of omission involve a positive act on the part of the sinner, *at least an interior act.* This act will precede or accompany the omission as the cause by which the sinner directly wills to omit the commanded action (I will not go to Mass) or the occasion by which he directly wills to do something other than the commanded act which will prevent him from doing what he ought to be doing (I will play golf all day Sunday). An undertaking incompatible with Mass may be one which takes place at the same time (the game of golf) or one which precedes the time of Mass (such as going on a bender on Saturday night, foreseeing the probability of not being capable of getting up for Mass on Sunday morning). In any case, somewhere along the line the sin of omission requires a free and deliberate act on the part of the sinner.

When does the sin of omission take place? It is initiated *interiorly* —and guilt is thereby contracted—as soon as man voluntarily places the cause of the omission. At that instant he intends the non-fulfillment of the command, or at least exposes himself to the real danger of its non-fulfillment. The sin is not brought to full completion, however, until the need for the fulfillment of the precept actually prevails.

As we have seen in the chapter on human acts, sin causes its essential harm in the heart of man; through evil desires and the consent thereto man's inner order is disrupted. And all this can take place before as much as a finger is raised in the external order. To man these sins of the heart are hidden, but to God, the searcher of hearts, they are an open book.

(3) *Actual Advertence and Sin*

There is a temptation ever present to man to think that if he lacks actual attention or advertence at the moment in which he places an evil action he commits no sin. This very well may be true at times, but unfortunately—and more often than not—it is only a delusion in the mind of the sinner. For some external work to be sinful it is required, and is sufficient, that it be voluntary *in some way*. Therefore, as we previously saw, it is not necessary that some sinful act be voluntary directly in itself. It is sufficient either that it be **voluntary in its cause**, as getting drunk for a certain individual leads to sins of impurity, or **voluntary indirectly** in willing some preceding omission, as when a man ought to prevent something from happening and he does not do so: a father would be responsible for the criminal actions of his son which could and should have been prevented by him.

As long as *some knowledge* of a sin's consequences is present there is sufficient advertence for contracting the guilt of sin when the cause of that sin is placed. Unless the evil action is foreseen, however, at least in a confused manner (i.e., even obscurely and indistinctly), the act would in no way be voluntary.

D. The Essential Notion of Sin

(1) Its Constitutive Elements

It is the role of theology to lead to a greater understanding of God and of all things as related to God. Some things are related to God by opposition, and among these is sin.

Sin is an evil human act. What does this mean? It means first of all that a sin is *something real*—a human act. It means further that sin is *something immoral*—an evil human act. Consequently, sin must be considered under different aspects, because it exists under different aspects.

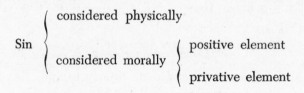

1) As a *physical entity,* sin is a human act, i.e., a real being having physical perfection like any human act.

2) *As a moral entity,* sin is a human act seen in its relation to the norm of morality, i.e., to human reason and the eternal law. Morally considered, every sin is comprised of two constitutive elements:

1) A *positive element*: the human act itself, not considered in its *physical* but in its *moral* being, i.e., as it tends to some created good which cannot be referred to the ultimate end. This element consists, then, in an **undue conversion or turning toward a creature.**

2) A *privative element* which necessarily follows from the first; the very privation or lack of rectitude or due ordination to the ulti-

mate end. This element consists in **an aversion or turning away from God.**

The privative or negative element of sin is also referred to as the **formal element;** it is this lack of due order, this absence of ordination to the ultimate end, which constitutes the voluntary act as sinful. The human act itself is referred to as the **material element** of sin. For the conversion or turning toward a created good would not be a sin, in the theological sense of the term, unless by it man were side-tracked from his true ultimate goal. In other words, the *material* of sin is the voluntary act by which man tends to something contrary to God's law; the *form* of a sin is its lack of form, the very difformity of the act, its departure from the eternal law.

(2) The Essence of Sin

Despite theological controversy on the matter, it seems clear that the essence of sin comprises both the formal and material elements of which we have been speaking. Just as we conceive of the essence of a material being as consisting in the union of a formal and material principle (for example, man as comprised of spiritual soul and material body), so too we may consider the essence of sin as resulting from the union of its formal and material elements. Sin, then, is a human action lacking its proper ordination to the true ultimate end of man;[2] it is a voluntary act including in its concept an essential disorder, a lack of conformity with right reason and divine law.

(3) The Definition of Sin

When St. Thomas comes to the matter of a definition for sin, he once again manifests his profound respect for the authority of his predecessors, in this instance that of St. Augustine.

He himself defines sin simply as *a bad human act.* This definition is fittingly fashioned: it includes the material or generic element of

---

[2]This is properly a statement of the essence of the *sin of commission;* the essence of the *sin of omission,* considered separately from the act which is its cause, consists in the privation of a fitting action as its material element, and in the privation of due order to the ultimate end as its formal element.

sin—a human act; and its formal or specific element—bad. Together the generic and specific elements of any reality give us a proper definition.

For Augustine sin is *a word, deed or desire contrary to the eternal law*.[3] This definition has the advantage of being more explicit than that of St. Thomas, although both definitions include the formal and material elements. St. Augustine explains the material element in greater detail, giving some hint of how extensive its possibilities are. When he refers the evilness of the act to its opposition with the eternal law, the supreme rule of morals, he underlines the destructiveness of sin, which not only distorts man's own nature but withstands all order, even the designs of God.

It must be observed that these definitions of St. Thomas and St. Augustine refer, in their primary and direct significance, to the *personal* and *mortal* sin of commission. Nevertheless, these very same definitions, in a secondary and indirect sense, can apply as well to:

1) the **sin of omission**, both because "affirmation and negation are referred to one same genus . . . and so *word* and *deed* denote equally what is said and what is not said, what is done and what is not done,"[4] and also because the sin of omission, in actual fact, requires some voluntary act as its cause;

2) **original sin**, if the word, deed or desire is understood as related to the will of our first parents;

3) to **venial sin**, if the badness of the act or its disagreement with the eternal law is understood not to be such as to destroy completely man's order to his ultimate end. Venial sin retards man's progress, but even in the fact of venial sin the essential ordination to the ultimate end is preserved.[5] Unless specifically mentioned, however, we shall speak in this chapter only of "perfect" sin, personal mortal sin.

---

[3]*Against Faustus the Manichean*, Bk. XXII, Chap. 27.

[4]St. Thomas, *Summa*, I-II, q. 71, a. 6, ad 1.

[5]This is another instance of the importance of an understanding of the meaning of *analogy*. We have seen that *virtue* is an analogous term, referring to moral virtue in its primary sense, to intellectual virtue in a secondary sense; so now we see that the concept of sin is an analogous concept, referring in its primary and direct sense to personal mortal sin, in secondary meanings to venial sin and sins of omission.

3. The Disinction and Comparison of Sin

What we have seen of the nature of sin is basic knowledge, but it is by no means the sum of what must be known. The Church, as a wise physician foreseeing the need for cure and subsequent prevention, commands that sins be confessed not merely in vague, general terms, but "specifically and one by one."[6] And in this same vein of thought St. Jerome wrote: ". . . if one who is ill is ashamed to make known his wound to the physician, the physician does not remedy what he does not know."[7] It is necessary, then, that the wounds which are sins be distinguished, and their true gravity or seriousness be carefully appraised.

Now vice has been exposed as being contrary to virtue, sin as contrary to virtuous acts. Both vice and sin, moreover, imply disorder, and disorder is intelligible only in terms of the order to which it is opposed—in this case, the order of virtue and good actions. Because of the contrariety between habits of virtue and vice, as well as the opposition between their respective acts, the knowledge already gained of virtue and its acts finds abundant application—the necessary changes being made—to the matter of vice and sin. Consequently, when it comes to the question of distinguishing the vices and sins among themselves, and of determining the extent or gravity of their resultant disorders, the procedure is exactly the same as that employed when the corresponding questions were asked of the virtues and virtuous acts.

A. The Distinction of Sins

(1) Their Specific Distinction

1. **Secondary divisions.** There are many accepted divisions of sins. Some of these result in a classification of sins that differ according to *kind*, that is to say, that are specifically different; others, however,

---

[6]Council of Trent, Sess. XIV, *The Doctrine on the Sacrament of Penance*, Chap. 5, "On Confession" (Denz. 899) and Can. 7 (Denz. 917).

[7]*Commentary on Ecclesiastes*, Chap. 1, v. 11.

do not result in specific distinction, but are distinguished on some other basis.

1) To this latter group belong the sins of **commission** and **omission**. Directed to the same end, and proceeding from the same motive, they do not differ specifically. So, e.g., the avaricious man in order to accumulate wealth will both steal and omit to give what he ought to give.

The division of sin into **mortal** and **venial** is another in which the distinction is not one of kind, for it is quite possible for a mortal and a venial sin to be specifically the same, as in the case of a serious and slight sin of theft. The nature of this distinction between mortal and venial sin will be treated in more detail later in this chapter.

2) To the former group of specifically distinct sins can be relegated such familiar classifications as: sins against **God, self** and **neighbor;** sins of the **flesh** and sins of the **spirit;** sins of **thought, word** and **deed;** sins of **excess** and **defect.**

Despite the abundance of classifications afforded in the preceding paragraphs, none of them pinpoints any particular sin with the precision necessary for moral theology. Even those classifications which break sin down into specifically distinct categories do not break them down to their *ultimate* species. So, to cite but one example, carnal sins are clearly distinct from those of the spirit; but it is just as clear that there exists a rather important distinction between those sins of the flesh which concern food and drink and those which are concerned with matters of sex.

2. **Primary division.** What, then, constitutes the primary or fundamental norm for determining the ultimate species or kinds of sin? In principle, the answer has been provided in an earlier chapter of this volume. For sins are human actions, defective to be sure, but none the less freely and deliberately placed by man. Consequently, as with all human acts, they denote two elements: 1) a voluntary act tending to an object; and 2) the consequent conformity or lack of conformity of that act to the standard of fitting behavior. Now sins, as bad human acts, and thereby bespeaking a lack of conformity to

the rule of good conduct, all partake of a certain sameness. In a comparable manner, all virtuous actions, denoting as they do a conformity to the rule of good conduct, also partake of a certain sameness. In order that these actions, whether virtuous or sinful, be distinguished and set apart as to their specific kinds and within their respective orders of good or evil, we must consider that to which the voluntary act tends, namely, the very object of the act itself. *It is the object, and the object alone, which provides the primal or root source for the specific distinction of sins.*

If sins are found to be distinct in kind either because they transgress this or that particular precept, or because they are opposed to this or that virtue, this is true only because, fundamentally, these sins have **objects** which are specifically different. The immediate object of the sinful act, the result it naturally produces, serves, therefore, to distinguish the various kinds of sin. The first question that must be answered in determining the kind of sin which has been committed is "What has been done?"

It is also very important in this matter of determining the different species of sins to remember that one and the same physical act, whether actually carried out or merely intended, may very well be found to pertain to two or more species of sin. "There is no reason," says St. Thomas, "why one action should not be in several, even dissimilar, moral species."[8] And this can come about, as we saw in our discussion of human acts, whenever some **circumstance** (including the *end* or *intention*) assumes a special relation either for or against the rule of reason and faith, and consequently is to be "considered as a condition of the object, and as being, as it were, a specific difference thereof."[9]

He who steals, therefore, intending to put what he has acquired to the pursuit of impure pleasures, commits one physical act but two kinds of sin, one of theft or injustice, the other of unchastity. Similarly, he who maliciously inflicts bodily harm on a cleric or upon a religious is guilty also of sacrilege, a sin against religion, because

[8]*Summa,* I-II, q. 18, a. 10, ad 3.
[9]*Ibid.,* I-II, q. 18, a. 10, ad 1; cf. also the body of the article.

he has assaulted not only this person but this person dedicated to God.

For the purposes of our investigation, therefore, it is necessary and sufficient to look first of all to the **object** or *natural result* of the act, and secondly, to the **circumstances** surrounding that act, to see whether or not any of them bring additional specification to the act.

(2) Numerical Distinction of Sins

Because we are to confess our sins not only specifically but also "one by one," it is necessary that something be said concerning the numerical distinction of sins. The question as to what kinds of sin have been committed must be followed by the question: how many?

There are two general rules to employ in discerning the number of sins committed.

1. **There are as many sins as there are complete moral objects,** i.e., objects not morally united but distinct and not coalescing into one. Sins are evil human acts, and like all human acts they denote a tendency to some special object. Consequently, sins multiply as the number of distinct moral objects multiplies.

It must be noted that this is not a question of acts that are physically distinct, for very often such separate acts have a moral unity resulting from a single intention or motive. Thus, a burglar may steal silverware, jewelry and money in the same house. This would constitute one sin of theft, because there is one moral object, of which the separate acts are incomplete parts, all belonging to the same kind of sin, namely, theft. On the other hand, a pickpocket commits as many sins of theft as he has victims, because theft against one person is an act complete in itself, having a single moral object.

Several distinct acts which are subordinated one to the other as means to the same end also form a single sin. Thus if one were first to insult another, then provoke him by actions to fight, so as finally to inflict bodily harm upon him, there would only be one sin. On the other hand, if someone were to read a pornographic magazine out of curiosity, without intending any further evil, and then, excited by what he saw, should commit a sin of impurity, he would commit two sins because the two acts were not intended as a means to one end.

But it should be noted: Although several acts, or several evil effects of one act, may constitute only a single sin, that sin is not thereby less grave than if these acts or effects constituted many distinct sins. One such sin requires more malice and, consequently, can be as grave or even more grave than several separate sins of lesser malice.

2. **There are as many sins as there are morally interrupted and repeated acts, even about the same identical object.** An act is said to be morally interrupted when it ceases to produce its effect. This may happen in three ways:

1) *When the intention is restricted, or when a contrary choice intervenes.* For example, a Catholic eating out on Friday decides sinfully to eat meat. But then looking over the menu he notices his favorite fish listed as the house special, and he changes his mind. Finally, hearing his companion extol the merits of the steak-for-two, he again changes his mind and concurs in ordering steak. He has committed two sins.

2) *When someone willingly ceases to act sinfully, without the intention of continuing.* Thus a student stealing from his roommate's wallet left on the desk hears that someone is coming down the corridor and does something else for a while. After the third party has departed, he returns to his thievery. He commits one sin, because his intention to continue stealing never ceased. On the other hand, a man looking at suggestive pictures in a magazine becomes disgusted and throws it aside. Later, he reconsiders and begins again to dwell on the same pictures. He commits two sins, because he willingly ceased acting before starting again.

3) *When the sin reaches its natural completion.* A man who drinks himself into a stupor commits a second sin if he begins to drink again after sobering up. Likewise a person who deliberately takes pleasure in impure imaginings would commit a new sin each time he began to dwell on a new distinct series of such images.

B. The Comparison of Sins

(1) Are Sins Connected?

The intention of the man who acts according to reason is different from the intention of the sinner in straying from the path of reason. For the intention of every man acting according to virtue is to follow the rule of reason; hence the intention of all virtues is directed to the same end, so that all the virtues are connected together in the right reason of things to be done, namely, in prudence.

But the intention of the sinner is not that he should deviate from the path of reason, but that rather he tend to some appetible good from which his act derives its species. Now these goods to which the sinner's intention is directed when departing from reason are of various kinds, having no mutual connection; in fact at times they are contrary one to the other. Since, therefore, vices and sins take their species from that to which they turn, it is evident that, in respect of that which completes the species of sins, they have no connection with one another. For sin does not consist in passing from the many to the one, as is the case with virtues, which are connected, but rather in forsaking the one for the many.[10]

From these words of St. Thomas it follows that the effect of sin on man is to tear him apart from deep within himself. Far from being connected one with another, sins are divisive, productive of inner strife, pitting man's powers at odds with each other. Of its very nature sin is inimical to order, for it tends to an infinitude of false goods, and these are not only unconnected but frequently incompatible. Even in this life sin foreshadows the terrifying lot that falls to the unrepentant sinner at the moment when he passes from this life to "the land of darkness and of gloom, the black, disordered land where darkness is the only light" (Job 10:21, 22).

(2) The Gravity of Sins

There are several possible rules available for determining the gravity of sins: sins opposed to the more excellent virtues are more grave than those opposed to lesser virtues; sins that result in greater

---

[10]St. Thomas, *Summa,* I-II, q. 73, a. 1.

harm are more grave than those bringing lesser harm; other things being equal, spiritual sins are more grave than sins of the flesh, because they turn a sinner away from God more, and are less affected by the influence of passion. But all of these are merely secondary rules presupposing another which is much more fundamental: **the basic gravity of sin is to be measured in terms of its moral object.**

As the object of sins tell us the *kind* of sin committed, so too it will tell us the *degree of gravity* or *seriousness* in each sin. To determine the kind of sin committed attention was directed to the positive side of sin, i.e., the tendency of the voluntary act to the specifying object. In determining the gravity of sin, we must turn to the negative element of sin, i.e., its *lack of due order* with respect to the rule of good conduct. This lack of due order results from the fact that the object of the sinful act falls short of the measure of reason and the divine law; and the degree of departure from these guiding norms determines the gravity or seriousness of that sin. *The greater the departure from reason and the divine law, the greater is the evil and the more serious is the sin.*

In the same way that a sickness or disease is more serious insofar as it strikes at a higher or more excellent part of the physical organism, so a sin is more serious if it strikes at a more noble principle. Thus, for example, a sin against the very substance of a man, such as murder, is graver than a sin which is about external things, such as theft. Of even greater gravity would be sins committed directly against God (e.g., blasphemy or unbelief).

A final element for determining the gravity of sins is to be found in the **circumstances** of sin. For the moral circumstances surrounding a sinful act may indicate either a special departure from the moral law, thereby adding a new essential morality to the act, or they may manifest at least a special willingness to do evil. In either case, the act so conditioned is made more grave by reason of the circumstance. So adultery adds the evil of injustice to fornication, and though the act is one numerically, the sinner commits two *kinds* of sins. But to steal much rather than little, though it would aggravate the sin of theft, would not add a new *kind* of malice to the action.

4. THE SUBJECT OF SIN

Man, that is, the person of man, is clearly the remote subject of human action. It is the total person who gets the credit or the blame for his free and deliberate actions, not the parts of his body nor the extrinsic instruments which he may employ in performing these acts. Every act, however, proceeds from some power or faculty of man. What, then, are the powers or faculties productive of the bad human actions called sins?

Many Protestants hold that every act of the sense appetites, even those that are involuntary, are sinful. This accounts for the severe view which many sects took, and some still take, on such things as smoking, dancing and drinking. The Church, by the way, took an official stand against these false notions as early as the Council of Trent in 1546.[11]

We have seen that vice is contrary to virtue; sin to a virtuous act. Yet both sin and acts of virtue are human acts; one is evil and the other good. Clearly, then, the human faculties are subjects of virtue insofar as their acts can be made good; they are subjects of vice insofar as their acts can be made evil. Sin can be found, therefore, proceeding from any human power whose act can be voluntary and disordered.

Just as the will, the intellect and the sense appetites can be the subject of virtue, so these faculties can be the subject of vice, and consequently of sin. But always the will, which is the principle of human action, is the principle of sin. For it is the will which is responsible for the movement of all the other powers in the exercise of their acts: we make use of the other powers only when we will.[12] Without the will, therefore, there can be no sin, and sin is found in the other powers *only in their relation to the will.* While ignorance is in the intellect, it is sinful only insofar as the will is responsible for a man's not knowing what he could and should know. The same thing is true of the sensitive appetites. Sins of intemperance such

---

[11]Council of Trent, Sess. V; Denz. 792.
[12]Cf. St. Thomas, *Summa*, I-II, q. 19, a. 1 and ad 3.

as gluttony or impurity are in the concupiscible appetite, but only insofar as the appetite so escapes the will's control as to exceed or fall short of the rule of reason or the divine law.

Thus every act of the sense appetites is not automatically sinful. The sensitive appetites are lesser well-springs of human activity, but they are not independent. It is their nature to be subject to the control of right reason and will. When they are so controlled, they are the subject of virtue; it is only when they act in opposition to this control of reason that they are the subject of sin.

5. THE CAUSES OF SIN

The problem of the causes of sin is different from that of the causes of virtue. Virtue produces a perfect human act; everything about it is positive, full of perfection and being. Sin, on the other hand—and we are speaking here primarily of mortal sin—is a bad human act; it is evil because it is defective, lacking in the direction and order that it should have. The problem of the cause of sin, then, is to find this defect which makes sin evil.

In order to discover the cause or causes of this defective order, there are three general areas to be investigated: first, we must turn within the camp of man himself and ask what part, if any, his faculties or powers play in producing this defective element of sin; secondly, what must be said of the possibility of agents extrinsic to man exercising a causal influence in the production of his sins; and, thirdly, what is to be said of sins that are the causes of other sins.

A. Internal Causes of Sin

(1) In General

We have seen repeatedly that there are two elements in every sin: *first*, there is the human act tending to an evil object; *secondly*, there is the defect, the lack of due order of this act in relation to the standard of morality. Since the defect, the lack of due order, is evil, it

cannot be the object of man's choice. The reason for this is that the
will must choose whatever it selects *under the aspect of good.* What
the will chooses, then, is only some limited, partial aspect of good
appearing in the object. But this object is inseparably bound up with
disorder. This disorder or defectiveness can be willed only indirectly. The will, therefore, *directly* produces the voluntary act of sin, intending not the evil but the apparent good; only *indirectly* does it
intend the disorder or lack of direction that is unavoidably connected
with the act. Evil, precisely as evil, cannot have a direct efficient cause,
but at best only an *accidental* efficient cause. Sin—that is, the disorder of the sinful act—is said therefore to have an **accidental or
deficient cause,** rather than a true efficient cause.

The will in choosing an evil object chooses something that has a
certain appearance of good: such is the proper act of the will; but
the thing chosen is in reality evil and disordered. Now such a choice
makes the will deficient, makes it less than it should be. The will,
then, chooses the object directly under the guise of good, and only
indirectly or accidentally its defect: the evil in sin is chosen only
indirectly as a kind of by-product inseparable from that which appears good.

Disorder, lack of due accord with reason and faith, is the essence
of sin. In the sense just described, *whatever is capable of producing
this disorder in man's acts contributes causally to the production
of sin.*

(2) In Particular

Only the will is the sufficient and completing cause of sin's being
accomplished, just as the will alone is the sufficient and completing
cause of any other human act. There are, however, other causes
which act *to dispose* the will for its choice of a sinful object; these
are the apprehensive and the remaining appetitive powers of man:

   1) The **senses,** external as well as internal, which first apprehend the sinful object; these are very remote dispositive causes.

   2) The **sense appetites,** which first incline man to the sinful
object; these, too, are remote dispositive causes.

3) The **intellect,** which does not consider the object in relation to the rule of morality, presenting thereby a partial view, a half-truth; here we have a proximate dispositive cause.

If the process were to halt here, without involving the will, there could be no sin. Sin is completed only when the will, the prime mover in distinctively human behavior, actually chooses the object presented or prepared for it by the various dispositive causes.

(3) Conclusions

Regarding the internal causes of sin we may conclude briefly as follows:

1) **Ignorance** in the intellect is a proximate dispositive cause. As to the kind and effects of ignorance, these have been sufficiently treated in previous chapters.

2) The **passions** or **emotions** of the sense appetite are remote dispositive causes. The effect of passion on human acts has also been treated above.

3) The **will** alone is the indispensable, perfecting and completing cause of sin. Especially is this so in the case of sins committed out of *malice,* i.e., those sins in which some created good or pleasure is chosen in spite of clear knowledge of the spiritual loss and offense involved. Malice is the deliberate sacrifice of spiritual goods for some gain or pleasure here and now. In most sins there is some ignorance, some weakness; but always there is malice. But those sins in which the part of ignorance and weakness are at a minimum, or even lacking altogether, represent the extreme of human perversity.

B. External Causes of Sin

When we remember that sin is a human act, it is easy to see that it can be influenced by factors extrinsic to man. The world presents the objects to his senses and sensitive appetites. God moves his will, but does he move it to sin? The devil is barred from the will but does have access to the material part of man and through this can propose things to his mind. Man, too, though incapable of directly affecting the will of his neighbor, certainly can have a hand in causing the sins of another. What kind of causality, then, is exercised by God, the devil and other men in the production of man's sins?

(1) God as the Cause of Sin

In view of the fact that mortal sin consists essentially in a disorder whereby man turns away from the order of reason and faith, and, consequently, from his last end which is God himself, it is clear that God is in no way the cause of sin. We touched upon this point when considering the question of God and his relationship to the evil found in his creation.[13] Having just finished our examination of the nature of the evil which is sin we are better able to appreciate our answer.

To argue that God causes sin is to allege that God works against himself, and this would be a contradiction, because God is supremely wise.

Moreover, the evil of sin is a privation, a lack of order that should be present. And privation, as we have seen above, does not require, indeed cannot have, a direct efficient cause, but only a deficient cause, as in the case of the erratic flight of a bird with a broken wing. The human will of itself can be a deficient cause; no further cause need be sought to explain sin. God co-operates with man in causing the act only in its physical aspect, i.e., insofar as it has a certain physical being and perfection as a voluntary act, but he is in no way responsible for the defectiveness of the act.

Nor is God obliged to prevent every evil in the world. His plan of creation allows him to draw good out of the evil which his creatures bring about. Men are allowed to abuse their liberty by choosing evil, but God offers sufficient grace to all men to choose good if they but place no obstacle to its reception. God is not, cannot be a cause of sin.

13Cf. *God and His Creation*, 352-354.

(2) The Devil as the Cause of Sin

As was mentioned earlier, no creature can act as a true efficient cause in moving man's will to sin. But that the devil is able to exercise his wiles in disposing man to sin is quite evident and well attested by Scripture.[14] His power, however, has definite limitations. We may summarize the limits of his influence as follows:

1) The devil can never be a necessary cause of sin for anyone; he cannot invade the will itself wherein alone sin is completed.

2) He is able to tempt men to sin by proposing sinful things to them and by influencing them with respect to the desirability of sinful objects.

3) Because of his angelic nature, the devil can work on the senses, especially on the imagination; he can produce any effect that is usually caused by physical movement. At most these are dispositive causes of sin.

4) There are many other causes of sin besides the devil, e.g., the world and the flesh, and these should be sought as explanations of particular sins before alleging diabolic intervention.

5) Because the devil was instrumental in causing original sin which leaves all men prone to evil, he is indirectly a partial cause of every sin.

6) The workings of the devil are limited by God, and directed to the ultimate good of those who love God. For the devil is never allowed to tempt anyone beyond his strength.

C. Man as a Cause of Sin

There are three ways in which one man is said to cause sin in another: 1) by the act of carnal generation by which original sin is transmitted to one's offspring, 2) by inducing another to sin by persuasion, suggestion, command, seduction, example, etc., which is what is meant by scandal, and 3) by co-operating in the sin of another.

---

[14]Cf. Gen. 3; Job 1:2; Eph. 6:12; Jas. 4:7; I Pet. 5:8.

Because of the special nature of original sin it will be taken up in more detail later in this chapter. Scandal, because it is directly opposed to the virtue of charity, will be treated later in this volume among the sins opposed to charity. Here, then, we will treat only of co-operation.

(1) The Nature of Co-operation

Co-operation, or participation in sin, is *help afforded to another in the execution of his sinful purpose.* Co-operation differs from scandal insofar as it presupposes the sinful intention of another, whereas scandal leads into sin one who had not yet decided on sin. Consequently, co-operation is not a cause of sin in exactly the same manner in which heretofore we have been considering causes of sin. Rather than being a cause *preceding* the ill will of another, it is a cause *concurring* in that ill will.

Now when one concurs or co-operates in the evil of another, he may contribute to the evil act either as a *subordinate agent* to the one who commits sins, providing him with the physical or moral help needful for the act of sin, or as a *co-ordinate agent* with another in the commission of the same sin, thus performing his own share in the joint act of sin. In this latter case the co-operator is always guilty, whereas there may be instances of the former co-operation when the concurrence may be guiltless.

In general, any form of co-operation in evil is morally wrong because it contributes causally to an evil effect. However, that form of co-operation is licit and permissible in which the conditions required for the application of the rule of the double effect can be fulfilled, i.e., 1) when the act of the co-operator is good in itself; 2) when he has a good intention; 3) when the evil is not the cause of the good effect; and 4) when a sufficient reason is present to justify the co-operation.

Hence, **formal co-operation,** i.e., *concurrence in the evil will of the principal agent,* is always sinful, for by it the co-operator intends the sin of another. The one co-operating is thereby guilty of a sin of the same species as that committed by the principal agent.

(2) Material Co-operation

Concerning **material co-operation**, i.e., *concurrence in the evil act of another without sharing in his evil will*, a distinction must be made.

1) *Immediate* material co-operation is the concurrence in placing an action which, according to its nature, apart from any intention of the co-operator, directly tends to produce the evil effect intended by the principal agent. This kind of co-operation is morally wrong even when done under duress. An exception sometimes could be made in certain cases when it is a question of damage done to another's property, e.g., a bystander ordered under threat of death by a gunman to assist him in carrying stolen goods from a store to a waiting automobile; in the circumstances, the owner would be *unreasonably* unwilling to permit this co-operation.

2) *Mediate* material co-operation is concurrence (which may be remote or proximate) in an action which is only a preliminary or a consequent to a sinful action. As a rule this type of co-operation is also wrong. It may be permitted, however, if the rules of the double effect may be applied—if the act performed is not intrinsically evil, for example, and if a correspondingly good reason is present.

In determining whether a sufficient reason is present, consideration must be made 1) of the *seriousness* of the sin to be committed (the more serious the sin, the more grave the justifying reason); 2) of the *proximity* of the co-operation (the more proximate the influence, the more serious the reason); and 3) of one's *obligation* to prevent the sin (if it is more probable that the sin would not be committed without one's co-operation the reason for acting is necessarily more grave).

D. One Sin as the Cause of Another

The basis for assigning one sin as the cause of others is the fact that one human act can cause another, and sins are human acts. This can happen in several different ways, according to the different kinds of causality.

One sin causes another

as an **efficient** cause

indirectly: by removing obstacles: insofar as an act removes grace or charity, or shame, or submission, or any other thing that might retard one from committing sin.

directly: by disposing man to further sin: insofar as every sin is the seed of vice, and vice is a habit inclining to sinful acts.

as a **material** cause providing the material for other sins; so, for example, gluttony and drunkenness prepare for lust, avarice provides the matter for fighting or quarrelling;

as a **final** cause one sin can become the goal for committing another; so, e.g., a man might steal in order to get drunk;

as a **formal** cause: the end determines the nature (i.e., the form) in matters of morality. So when one steals *in order to get drunk*, his sin is one of drunkenness (from the formal cause), plus the added evil or malice of theft.

Of special importance are the **seven capital sins**. These are not only acts of sin but vicious *habits* of sinning, *whose ends have special efficacy in moving men to commit other sins to attain them.* They beget other sins chiefly by acting as final causes or motives for the commission of sin, although they may also be productive of other sins as a kind of property of their special malice. Hence they have been defined as vicious acts or habits from which other vices and sins flow as from a fountain. Each of these seven sins has certain sins specially related to it and often committed because of it. These are called the "daughters" of capital vices. It should be noted, too, that these capital vices need not necessarily designate habits of mortal sin. Their pre-eminence in evil is not based on their gravity (some are only venial by nature) but rather on their influence on the commission of other sins.

CAPITAL SINS

THEIR DAUGHTERS

Pride (vainglory)—an inordinate seeking for praise and honor.

Presumption, ambition, boasting, hypocrisy, argumentativeness and disobedience.

Gluttony—an inordinate seeking of food and drink.

Mental dullness, talkativeness, coarseness, vulgarity, impurity and buffoonery.

Lust—an inordinate seeking of sexual pleasure.

Mental blindness, inconsideration, inconstancy, love of self, hatred of God, worldliness and horror of eternity.

Avarice—an inordinate seeking for riches.

Hardheartedness, anxiety for worldly things, injustice, deceit, fraud and perjury.

Sloth—an inordinate aversion for spiritual goods because of the effort required for them.

Malice, timidity, despair, bitterness, affected ignorance and curiosity about dangerous things.

Envy—sadness over another's good which is regarded as an obstacle to personal advantage.

Hatred, detraction, calumny, talebearing, joy at another's misfortune and sadness at his success.

Anger—an inordinate desire for revenge.

Quarreling, boldness, pugnacity, cursing, indignation and blasphemy.

The two most general movements of man's appetites are toward the goods he loves and away from the evils he hates. The first four of the capital sins strive to *attain* the more attractive apparent goods; the last three seek to *avoid* the more unwelcome evils. And underlying all sins is **pride**, the inordinate seeking of one's own excellence. Pride was predominant in the sin of Adam; it is present in some manner in all sins, because it makes oneself the center and goal of everything else.

6. The Effects of Sin

(1) Sin's Effects on the Good of Human Nature

By "the good of human nature" we refer to three things: a) the essential principles of man's nature, especially the soul and its powers; b) the natural inclination to virtue which is the good of reason; c) the gift of original justice. We can thus summarize the effects that sin has on these various goods:

1) Sin does not destroy or change the essential goods of nature. Sin depends upon the existence of the faculties which cause it; if it destroyed those faculties, sin would destroy itself. A sinner, howsoever depraved, remains essentially a free, rational creature with all his essential properties.

2) The inclination to virtue is diminished by each sin. Every act of sin strengthens the inclination to sin, and thus it diminishes the inclination to virtue. Acts of sin beget habits of sin which are called vices.

3) The gift of original justice was totally lost by original sin. This will be explained in detail later.

(2) The Stain of Sin

A stain results when something is soiled by contact with anything that spoils its beauty or cleanliness, as a dress or a tie is stained by spilled food. There is something akin to this in the spiritual order.

The human soul has a twofold beauty, one resulting from the light of reason, the other from the infused light of wisdom and grace. The soul is brought into contact with other things by loving them. When man loves something base, something contrary to reason and the divine law, he diminishes the twofold light which is the beauty of his soul. The loss of spiritual beauty caused by embracing something sinful is called metaphorically a stain on the soul.

This stain remains on the soul after the act of sin is finished. An ink-stain on a table cloth is not eradicated simply by setting the ink-bottle upright. Similarly, the stain on the soul is removed only when the sinner, moved by grace, repents. Then with the infusion of grace the twofold beauty is restored to his soul.

(3) The Guilt of Punishment

Well do the Scriptures tell us that "the fear of the Lord is the beginning of wisdom" (Ps. 110:10). What sinner is there who, still bearing a spark of faith and hope in his heart, does not turn to the mercy of God when he imagines that he hears addressed to him those words of Christ: "Depart from me, accursed one, into the everlasting fire which was prepared for the devil and his angels" (Matt. 25:41)? The Scriptures, Tradition and the universal preaching of the Church issue solemn warning to sinners on this matter of punishment for sin.[15] And this question of sin's punishment brings us, once again, to the matter of mortal and venial sin.

That mortal sin merits *eternal punishment* is clear from the testimony both of Scripture and of Tradition as seen in the preceding paragraph. That venial sin merits a *temporal punishment* finds similar backing from Scripture and Tradition. From Scripture we have the classic passage from St. Paul: ". . . if anyone builds upon this foundation . . . wood, hay, straw—the work of each will be made manifest . . . if his work burns he will lose his reward, but himself will be saved, yet so as through fire" (I Cor. 3:12-15). Tradition also speaks of a cleansing of the soul "after death by purgatorial or purifying punishments."[16] The fact of the distinction, therefore, rests securely on faith.

Mortal and venial sins are readily distinguished by reason of the punishment each incurs: eternal punishment for mortal sin, temporal

[15]Cf. Matt. 25:46; Mark 9:42; Isa. 66:24; Apoc. 14:11, 20-22; II Thess. 1:9; Council of Trent, Sess. VI, Can. 24 and 25 (Denz. 834-835), Sess. XIV, Can. 5 (Denz. 915); Fourth Lateran Council, Chap. 1 (Denz. 428).

[16]Second Council of Lyons, Denz. 464. Cf. also Council of Trent, Sess. VI, Chap. 11 (Denz. 804); Sess. XIV, Chap. 5 (Denz. 899).

punishment for venial sin. But the basic difference comes from the deordination found in these sins. Every sin involves a lack of due order. Mortal sin turns away from the ultimate end, the very principle of that order, and therefore it is by nature irreparable. Venial sin lacks due order to the means while preserving the order to the ultimate end; it is therefore reparable.

We must be constantly on the alert, therefore, in realizing that the term sin, when applied to mortal and venial sin, is being used in tremendously different ways. This, again, is not a division of a genus into its species, each of which shares equally in the generic perfection; rather it is a distinction of an analogous term into its parts, of which it is said principally of one, and only secondarily of the other.

Consequently, the perfect notion of sin (of which we have been treating) applies only to mortal sin. Venial sin is called sin only in an imperfect sense, and in relation to mortal sin. For it is not an act against the end or purpose of the law, since he who commits venial sin neither does what the law gravely forbids, nor fails to do what the law under serious obligation commands to be done. But he does place an act which here and now prevents his *actual* tending to God, while at the same time preserving intact the *habitual* order to that end. Venial sin, then, excludes only the actual reference of the human act to God's glory, since it does not exclude charity by which man is referred to God habitually.

As a corollary of the preceding, we may note that the fact that a particular sin is mortal or venial can be determined from a consideration of its object. For a sin will be mortal according to its genus if by it the will is directed to a thing that is in itself contrary to charity which directs man to his last end. Into this class fall, for example, all of those sins of which Scripture speaks as barring man from entrance to eternal life or the kingdom of heaven.[17] On the other hand, those actions by which a man's will is directed to a thing which denotes a certain inordinateness, but which is not contrary to the love of God and one's neighbor (e.g., an idle word, excessive curiosity, impatience)—such are called venial sins by reason of their genus.

[17]Cf. Eph. 5:5; Gal. 5:19 ff; I Cor. 6:9 ff.

Nevertheless, it must not be forgotten that since moral acts may derive their goodness and badness from the intention of the sinner or from some other circumstance, as well as from their object, it is quite possible that some sin which, by reason of its object, is generically venial may become mortal. In like manner, it can come about that a sin which is generically mortal may become venial by reason of some imperfection of the moral act, such as inadvertence.

7. ORIGINAL SIN

It is relatively easy to understand how a man may be enticed into sin by the devil or by another human being. It is easy, likewise, to understand the guilt of the sinner, for he has performed a morally evil action of his own free will. It is quite another thing to see how sin can be imputed to a person who has never performed a human act, indeed, who has not yet emerged from his mother's womb. But such is the fact. Every descendant of Adam, with the exception of Christ and his Blessed Mother, comes into the world with the stain of sin already on his soul. This is the sin of nature, which we call **original sin.**

Modern philosophy scoffs at the notion of original sin; so did the Pelagians in the time of St. Augustine. But the infallible voice of authority, the Catholic Church, has declared it to be a dogma of faith, a truth revealed by God.

Reason alone cannot prove conclusively the existence of original sin. Some thinkers, such as Newman and Pascal,[18] argue that the varied and tremendous evils which beset mankind give strong indication that "the human race is implicated in some terrible aboriginal calamity." St. Thomas gives a rational argument which leads to the probability of original sin. He points out that the defects of human nature in themselves are natural weaknesses resulting from man's composite nature. But it is reasonable to assume that God in his providence would not leave man in so unsatisfactory a condition. In view of the dignity of man's higher nature, God would have come

[18]Newman, *Apologia pro Vita Sua*, Chap. 5; Pascal, *Pensées*, Sect. vii.

to his aid, so that the body would not interfere with the work of the soul, nor the lower powers impede the intellect and will. Since, in fact, these defects do exist in human nature, it can be inferred that it is probable that they are penal, and from this one can conclude to the fact of original sin.[19]

A. The Fact of Original Sin

But where reason gives us only probability, faith gives us certainty. The existence of original sin has been defined and affirmed by the Councils of Mileve (416), Carthage (418), Orange (529), Florence (1431-1445) and Trent. In the words of the Council of Trent:

> If anyone says that the sin of Adam injured only Adam himself and not his descendants; that losing the sanctity and justice he had received from God he lost them only for himself and not for us; or that through the sin of disobedience only death and the corporal penalties were handed down to the whole human race, but not sin, which is the death of the soul, let him be anathema.[20]

But the doctrine of original sin is not an invention of the Church; it is directly revealed by Sacred Scripture. St. Paul attests to the fact: "Therefore as through one man sin entered into the world and through sin death, and thus death has passed into all men because all have sinned" (Rom. 5:12).

St. Thomas takes this text as an explicit declaration of the fact of original sin, an interpretation verified by the Second Council of Orange (Denz. 175), by the previously cited declaration of the Council of Trent, and by Pius XII in the encyclical *Humani Generis* (Denz. 3028). Since death is a penalty for sin, all men must have sinned, for all men die. Infants, however, do not incur the penalty of actual sin; therefore they must have been born in a condition of sin. This text, therefore, refers to original, not actual sin. This is a fact which the Apostle elsewhere expressly asserts: "Yet death reigned from Adam until Moses even over those who did not sin after the likenss of the transgression of Adam" (Rom. 5:14).

[19]*Con. Gent.*, IV, Chap. 52.
[20]Sess. V (June 17, 1546), *Decree on Original Sin*, n. 2; Denz. 789.

The existence of original sin is a dogma of faith, to be accepted without question. It remains for the theologian to investigate the manner in which this sin is transmitted and how it is voluntary. These are admittedly difficult questions, but their solution will shed some light on this mysterious sin of nature and show the reasonableness of the Church's teaching.

B. The Transmission of Original Sin

(1) The Sin of Adam

To understand how man has contracted sin from Adam, we must first consider his condition as he came from the hand of God.[21] Adam was created in a state of original justice, integrity and immortality.

1) **Original justice** is the theological description of this primeval condition of the parent of the human race. Basically it affirms the fact that Adam was endowed with sanctifying grace, a supernatural gift totally exceeding the order of nature, by which he was elevated to a new and infinitely more noble state of life, the participated life of God himself. Since God created man for a destiny far beyond the reach of his natural powers, to achieve that end he raised him to a new level of life by the gift of sanctifying grace.

2) **Integrity** consisted in the perfect subjection of the body to the soul and of the sense appetites to reason. This gift was not essentially supernatural; it was a perfection of man that did not raise man above the level of humanity. It was, however, a natural perfection which man, due to the inherent weakness of his nature, could not achieve unaided. Left to itself, nature could never achieve this perfection. Man's imagination and sense appetites, strongly drawn by pleasurable objects, would all too often overcome the natural dominion of reason and will. Only by diligent watchfulness and after long practice could reason keep the passions in control, and even then its dominion would not be perfect. This disharmony of man's very nature—the inclina-

21Cf. *God and His Creation*, 400-405.

tion of the lower faculties to sensible goods in conflict with the order of reason—is what is meant by *concupiscence*. To give man not only the capacity but also the facility to reach his supernatural goal, God endowed him with the gift of integrity, which banished concupiscence by establishing perfect harmony between the dual elements of man's nature.

3) **Immortality,** by which Adam was freed of the necessity of dying, was, like integrity, a preternatural gift rather than supernatural. It did not exceed the order of nature, it was a prolongation or extension of natural life. That God did actually give this gift to Adam is expressly related in the Scriptures: "Of every tree of paradise thou shalt eat: but of the tree of knowledge of good and evil thou shalt not eat. For in what day soever thou shalt eat of it, thou shalt die the death" (Gen. 2:16-17). If Adam had not sinned, he would not have had to die.

Along with immortality, Adam also enjoyed the gift of impassibility, i.e., freedom from suffering, for the ability to suffer is only an indication of, and preparation for death.

That Adam sinned by transgressing the divine command is a fact familiar to us all, related in all its essentials in the Book of Genesis (Chap. 3). As a result of his sin he lost the supernatural and preternatural gifts which God had bestowed on him. But his human nature was not corrupted, nor were his natural powers impaired. The Church has condemned the extreme opinion of Luther and Calvin that man's nature was essentially corrupted and depraved by Adam's sin, and that, as a consequence, all man's acts are evil. The "wounds of nature" of which the theologians speak are basically the natural defects of the powers of the soul in the disharmonious state of a human nature left to itself. But while Adam lost nothing of his nature as man by sin, his descendants will be born with less inclination to the good of reason (virtue) than they would have had by nature if he had not rejected God's help.[22]

---

[22]This is the very reasonable, but by no means the unanimous conclusion of many theologians. Others hold that the loss of original justice only reduced man to his natural powers, insufficient of themselves to control the conflict between his lower and higher natures without divine assistance.

(2) *The Fault of Adam*

The sin of Adam was personal and actual, a deliberate transgression of God's command; he justly deserved the consequences, the loss of his God-given preternatural and supernatural gifts. But how did we, his descendants, merit the same loss? How do we incur the guilt of his sin?

Let us start with the defects which are involved in original sin, the privation of the supernatural and preternatural gifts. This loss is the *penalty* for sin. The purpose of these gifts was to enable man to attain a supernatural end. By his first sin, Adam turned away from that supernatural end. As a result, the subjection of his reason to God, his appetites to reason, his body to his soul—all this was destroyed. Since his subjection to God was the basic reason for the other gifts which harmonized man's nature, these gifts likewise were lost. Man fell to the condition of the natural disharmony of his nature, plus his aversion from God.

But the supernatural and preternatural gifts were not given to Adam as an individual person. They were bestowed on **human nature** *in the person of* Adam. As the first man, he was constituted the spring, the head, from which (from whom) would flow *all* the things —natural, preternatural and supernatural—with which human nature would be endowed by God. The privation of the gratuitous gifts was a privation of something given to nature, human nature, not merely to the person. Consequently, the punishment of the first sin was more than personal, *it was the punishment of a nature,* that special nature created in God's image as capable of self-determination, knowledgeable and free.

This fact explains the defective nature which we have received: Adam could not generate a nature better than his own. Before sin, Adam would have generated his children in a state of original justice; after his sin, he generated a nature *despoiled* of justice.

This privation of justice has the nature of sin, for it was voluntary. It was in the power of human nature to hold on to that supernatural justice; it was in the power of human nature, of a will in that nature, voluntarily to lose it. The sin of Adam was a sin both of person and nature: *personal*, because he perpetrated it by his deliberate will; a sin of *nature*, because he lost a gift given to nature for the whole human race, committed and entrusted to his care. Hence, in all men this sin is *voluntary*, not indeed by their own will, but in the will of Adam who lost original justice for you and me and the whole of human nature. Just as actual sin results in the loss of a personal good, so original sin causes a privation of a good belonging to nature.

(3) The Transmission of Sin

This explanation is yet inadequate: it shows why man has received an infected nature; it does not explain why the loss of original justice is sinful on our part. To be sinful this act in some way must be voluntary on our part, and so far only the will of Adam has entered the picture.

To explain our voluntariness in original sin, St. Thomas has recourse to the principle of the solidarity of the human race, founded in our common nature: on the physical level (and we should never forget that we are cosmic creatures, *rational* indeed, but rational *animals*) there is a deep-rooted community, a genealogical oneness, at the very heart of humanity. Just as a political community is regarded as a single body and as one man, so the whole human race can be viewed as one man, since all have a common nature received from Adam.[23] All men, therefore, are "members of one nature." This nature is caused in individual men *by the physical act of physical generation* from Adam.

This is the foundation of St. Thomas' argument of the comparison between actual sin in the bodily members and original sin in the members of human nature. A member of the body—the hand, say—is moved to its action by the will; just so are different individuals constituted members of human nature by a similar action, the movement of generation. Through the movement of the will the hand becomes a

---

[23]If grace is built on nature, then the position of the Jews as a chosen nation is a prefiguring of St. Paul's idea of the Christian community as the mystical body of Christ, whose unity is not only natural, nor only instrumental, but the supernatural unity of "the bond of perfection," presupposing the other "principles of solidarity."

member of the personal unity of action; through the movement of generation men become members of the unity of human nature. In this way, and this way only, by physical, sexual generation, each of us is constituted a member of the human race. Any other production of a human being, escaping the physical facts of human nature and sexual generation, automatically excludes even the possibility of original sin; the first and only example is Christ.

So just as the sin of the hand is not such by its own will, but by the will of the whole man, the sin of nature is not such by the will of the individual member, but by the will of the whole. The will of the whole, in this case (for God so ordained it), is represented by Adam, in whom all men exist virtually.

Actual sin is not imputed to the hand apart from the body, but only as part of the whole man, moved to its action by the first mover, the will. In parallel, original sin is not imputed to every member of the human race physically generated as individually responsible, but as he is a part of nature and moved to the reception of his nature by the movement of generation from Adam, the first man. As a voluntary defect is transmitted from the will to the hand as part of the whole person, so a voluntary defect of nature is passed from Adam to individual men as a part of that nature. Actual sin consists in the privation of order to a due end, original sin is the privation of original justice. In the sense that we have willed it original sin is not a personal sin in us; it is a sin of nature which has been received in us. Yet, being truly a sin, it is voluntary, not by our own will, but by the will of our principle, our head, Adam. From him we receive our nature, from him we have inherited our defective nature.

(4) The Conclusion

As it came from God in the person of Adam, human nature received not only those things intrinsic to nature itself, but also the superadded and purely gratuitous supernatural gift of grace and the preternatural gifts of integrity and immortality. These gifts were in no way due to nature, but belonged to nature by reason of the divine largesse.

This gift of original justice was not the first man's personal treasure; it was entrusted to him to pass on to his descendants. As head of the whole human race he was the instrument of God in the transmission of grace to all men. But Adam sinned, and that sin was not only a personal one, it was a sin of nature. Besides his personal loss, he caused a loss in the whole of nature. Once that nature was infected by sin it was perpetuated in all mankind, for all have received their nature from Adam through carnal generation.

Original sin, because it has the true nature of sin, must be *voluntary* on our part—in some way. It is not voluntary by our own will but in the will of Adam, the physical and spiritual head of the race, of whom we are all a part by sharing his nature. In Adam we have, each of us, willed sin; through Adam we receive it.

One more question remains to be resolved. Since original sin is in the soul, which is not generated by the parent but directly created by God, how can original sin be transmitted through carnal generation? And how can a human spermatazoon, which is physical and in no sense a subject of sin, transmit a moral fault when it fertilizes the ovum?

(5) The Physical Transmission of Original Sin

Adam is the cause of human nature, not in its entirety, but in its bodily part; for all the generations of man he fulfills the physical role played by the father of each individual human family: he is the physical progenitor. Original sin could not possibly pass directly from Adam's infected soul to the souls of his descendants: nor he, nor any human father, is the efficient cause of the soul. But the body has its being by an act proper to nature, that is, by carnal generation; and the seed of man, uniting with the ovum of the woman, is the efficient cause of the body, and thus the *dispositive* cause of the soul— that is, it so disposes the body that a human soul, created by God, is called for. Since the soul is essentially related to the body, God so ordains that when the material or bodily conditions are present, he will infuse the spiritual form which is the soul. But if the body is lacking those qualities (and here the qualities are those of original justice) by which it is subject to the soul, the soul itself will lack those qualities by which it should dominate the body.

Original sin is not contained as some sort of actual reality in the seed. The spermatazoon of the male is only an instrument for the transmission of nature. But when the nature is infected, the instrument of that nature will be infected, and an infected nature will be transmitted.

C. The Nature of Original Sin

Original sin, we have seen, is truly a sin. Yet the precise nature of that sin remains to be clarified.

By original sin man is *habitually* turned away from God; it is a permanent inordinate disposition arising from the privation of harmony given by original justice. Since such a permanent disposition is a habit (both in theological and common usage), original sin must have the nature of a habit.

Yet it is not a habit in the sense that a vice is a habit. Vice is an *operative* habit, which disposes man to sinful actions. Original sin, however, is an indisposition of *nature* in relation to God; it is not ordered, except remotely, to action. It is, then, something like an entitative habit, a disposition that immediately affects the nature, rather than the nature's powers of operation. Original justice caused the habitual harmony of all the powers of the soul; original sin, the loss of original justice, leads to a contrary disposition, the state of disharmony. Like original justice, then, the subject of this sin of nature is the essence of the soul. Essentially original sin is a corrupt habit, not, certainly, infused by God, nor yet one acquired by our own acts, but innate. It is received with nature through our corrupt origin.

As in every sin, two elements are found in original sin, the formal and the material. The formal element in original sin is the privation of original justice, whose primary effect was the subjection of the mind to God, "the conversion to God," natural and supernatural, of which the Scriptures speak. The primary effect of its opposite, original sin, is the privation of this subjection, a turning away from God, an aversion to man's ultimate happiness only explicable by the loss of sanctifying grace.

The **formal** element of original sin, then, is the privation of original justice.

The **material** element of original sin is *concupiscence*—a word expressing not only the lascivious desires of man's drive for sensual pleasure, but all of his urges toward the goods which are contrary to right reason: the disorder among all the other powers of the soul. The original harmony of these powers and their powerful inclinations was the direct result of the subjection of the mind to God. Once this subjection was lost, disorder in the other powers followed as a natural consequence. The privation of original justice thus provides the material for the future sins of mankind, the essential disorder from which his personal and actual sins arise.

D. The Effects of Original Sin

The principal effect of original sin is the loss of original justice—and this, at the same time, is the very essence of the sin. For the privation of justice can be looked at from two points of view: as an aversion from God it has the nature of sin; as leaving us bereft of the power to attain supernatural happiness it is a penalty. The privation of grace affects the soul itself, but due to its loss the body and the powers of the soul are also infected with the contagion of original sin. The effects of original sin in the body and the faculties of the soul are called **the wounds of nature.**

By original sin the body was stricken with the disorder of sickness, suffering, labor and the other physical miseries of life, culminating at last in death.

The disruption of the harmony that reigned among the powers of the soul resulted in a weakness in the will in the face of evil (the wound of **malice**), great difficulty in the acquisition of truth for the intellect (the wound of **ignorance**), a weakening of the irascible power in overcoming difficulties in the struggle for the good (the wound of **weakness**), and a strong desire in the concupiscible appetite for the satisfaction of the senses (the wound of **concupiscence**).

The wounding of nature does not mean that human nature has suffered any essential corruption. Whatever belongs intrinsically to human nature has been left intact; man has been wounded in his *integral nature*. Integral nature consists in the gift of integrity, by which man's powers were united in perfect harmony. This unity has been severed by sin, like the tissues in the body are severed by a wound.

Integrity belonged to human nature, but not as naturally due to it. The natural constituents of human nature belong to it, as it were, by right; integrity belonged to it by possession of a freely endowed gift. It is quite in keeping with the language of the Councils, therefore, to say that man was wounded in his nature, that is, integral nature.

But, as St. Thomas points out, man's natural inclination to virtue is diminished by original sin.[24] In the state of fallen nature (and this would not be true to human nature in its pure state, i.e., one never elevated by grace), man is born habitually and directly opposed to God, his supernatural end, and hence indirectly averse to God, his natural end. With his will thus deprived of its order to good, man's intellect suffers the wound of ignorance (particularly the practical intellect, which judges according to one's inclination); his sensitive appetites suffer the wounds of weakness and concupiscence, for his higher powers now lack the ability to direct and control them to the good of reason.[25]

8. SUMMARY AND CONCLUSION

Sin, like all evil, is a mixture of some good with some badness. As a privation, sin requires a subject, some positive perfection, which will pay passage, as it were, for the lack of due being or perfection which comprises its formal element. Sin is a human act, a free and deliberate movement of man to an object, but to an object out of

---

[24]*Summa*, I-II, q. 85, a. 3.

[25]This is the common opinion of most Thomists; for a contrary interpretation of St. Thomas himself, see Oswin Magrath, O.P., "St. Thomas' Theory of Original Sin," *The Thomist*, XVI (1953), 161-189. Many modern theologians follow Suarez and Bellaramine in holding that the loss of original justice simply left man's powers to their natural condition of disharmony.

tune with the harmony of reason and faith. For with this tendency
to an apparent good, this conversion to the creature, there is the
concomitant aversion of turning from the rule of reason and faith,
and ultimately from the very author of these norms, God himself.

Original sin stands as a thing apart; affirming its reality, we bow
submissively to the mystery. For here we have a sin of which we are
held guilty, for which we suffer punishment, but which we have acquired without benefit of our personal act. Certainly, then, when
we speak of this fault as a sin, it is an entirely different manner
from that which is applied to actual sin.

Thus we have been introduced to the unholy triumvirate of sin:
mortal, venial and original—each in its way a disfigurement of the
divine image, a sullying of the soul's beauty, a stumbling block to
man's progress toward his perfection in God.

We may supplement what was said in the body of this chapter with
the following conclusions:

1. The danger of underestimating the evil of venial sin is a very
real one. Because venial sin does not cast out charity and the divine
life from the soul, man is not reluctant to dip, even frequently, into
its beguiling waters. But consider just a few of the dangers inherent
in the frequent repetition of deliberate venial sin:

    1) It disposes to mortal sin; for he who refuses to be sub-
ject in small matters is disposed not to be subject in greater
matters.

    2) It diminishes the fervor of charity, thereby lessening the
dispositions for the reception of actual graces.

    3) It increases disorder in the passions and causes bad habits
to form.

    4) It merits temporal punishments which must be paid in
full before entering heaven. The severity of this cleansing punishment, particularly in purgatory, should never be underestimated.

2. The modern educator and the head of the family might well
reflect on the following words of St. Augustine before seeking "new
and better" educational methods: "What is the meaning of those various threats which are used to restrain children? What the meaning of

pedagogues, masters, the birch, the strap, the cane, the schooling which Scripture says must be given a child, 'beating him on the side lest he wax stubborn,' when it is hardly possible, or not possible at all, to subdue him? Why all these punishments, save to overcome ignorance and bridle evil desires—these evils with which we come into the world? For why is it that we remember with difficulty, and without difficulty remain ignorant, are diligent with difficulty, and without difficulty are indolent? Does not this show what vitiated nature inclines and tends to by its own weight, and what succor it needs if it is to be delivered? Inactivity, sloth, laziness, negligence, are vices which shun labor, since labor, though useful, is itself a punishment."[26]

3. "O mortal man, if you remain proud in the presence of this spectacle [of the Cross], you are harder than rock, for the very stones burst. If you do not tremble even now, you are more insensible than the earth itself. If you are so busy considering your own excellence, you are more pagan than the centurion, for he said: 'Truly this was the Son of God.' If your heart remains hardened and unmoved at this sight, you are more ferocious than the mob, who, accustomed as it was to witness such sights, nevertheless beat their breast in confusion at what was transpiring. O man, if the Son of God is thus brought low, how can you be arrogant? If he is peaceful, how can you be belligerent? If he rejected honor, can you exalt it? If God despised it, how can you value it so highly? Wretched man, crush your pride, seek the last place, as your Lord sought the Cross. Be ashamed, most vile of creatures, that you have not followed Christ, crucified for you. If you are abject, why do you become haughty? If you are truly noble, why not follow him who is exalted above all other nobility? If you seek glory, what greater distinction than to follow the God of glory? If you desire knowledge, then be certain there is only one science, one philosophy: come to the lecture hall of the Cross, where you will hear the concluding lesson of the divine teacher.

"Read, I exhort you, read the book of the Cross, for there you will find all the treasures of God's wisdom and knowledge. But reflect

[26]St. Augustine, *City of God*, Bk. XXII, Chap. 22.

that he says 'hidden'; indeed, the Cross has reserved endless secrets for those who study and follow it. Study the Crucified, I urge you, for he will give you perfect triumph over self, will make you another St. Paul, crucified to the world, and the world to you."[27]

[27]Melchior Cano, O.P., *Victory over Self* (a *Cross and Crown* reprint; St. Louis: Herder, n.d.), 69-70.

BIBLIOGRAPHICAL NOTE

Sin, including original sin, finds place in Part I-II of the *Summa*, Questions LXXI-LXXXV. This matter is set forth in a popular manner in *The Knowledge of Evil* by Ferrer Cassidy, O.P. (*TFTL*-36), *The Mystery of Iniquity* by Raymond Smith, O.P. (*TFTL*-37), *Lights and Shadows* by Theophane O'Brien, O.P. (*TFTL*-39), and *Let the Punishment Fit the Crime* by Reginald Coffey, O.P. (*TFTL*-40), all of which concern actual sin; *Like Capes and Headlands* by Thomas Heath, O.P. (*TFTL*-38), treats of original sin.

For a very technical analysis one may consult "Venial Sin and Its Final Goal" by P. De Letter, S.J., in *The Thomist*, XVI (1953), 32-70, while from the viewpoint of spiritual theology Jordan Aumann, O.P., has written on "Venial Sin and Christian Perfection" in *Cross and Crown*, IX (1957), 262-270.

Eminently readable material on the condition of our first parents and the question of their fall from grace is available in *The Teaching of the Catholic Church* (New York: Macmillan, 1949), I: "The Raising of Creatures to God" and "The Fall of Creatures from God" by George D. Smith, 49-52, and an excellent article from the same work on "The Fall of Man and Original Sin" by B. V. Miller, 320-400. For an excellent work giving the up-to-date Catholic interpretation of the mysterious passages of Genesis treating of man's origin and the fall of our first parents the student should read *Beginnings* by Charles Hauret (Dubuque: The Priory Press, 1955). Detailed and rather technical treatments of the question of the transmission of original sin may be found in the following articles: "St. Thomas' Theory of Original Sin" by Oswin Magrath, O.P., in *The Thomist*, XVI (1953), 161-189, and "Heredity Guilt" by P. De Letter, S.J., in the *Irish Theological Quarterly*, XX (1953), 350-365.

A short classic that should be read by all is *Victory over Self* by Melchoir Cano, O.P. (a *Cross and Crown* reprint; St. Louis: Herder, n.d.); treating of the seven deadly sins and their remedies, this 70-page booklet is of great practical value, no matter how far one has progressed on the road to perfection.

CHAPTER SIX

Law

1. Introduction

The meaning of law, its nature and the reason for its existence are problems which have confronted the philosophers and moralists through all eras of man's long history. Even those who have tried to explain it away have realized the importance of the law in connection with human action. As we have already learned in the first chapter of this book, every man acts for an end, and not for just any kind of end, but for an ultimate end, an end called perfect beatitude, happiness, final and consummate joy. Now complete and perfect happiness consists in the knowledge of truth, or, if you prefer, the vision of truth, more commonly called the beatific vision. Law is a means for the attainment of that beatifying vision of truth. Not an end in itself, it nevertheless leads to the perfect fulfillment of natural and supernatural beatitude. For it is God's instruction for men.

Any attempt we make to discover the truth about law, its nature and effects, is dependent upon knowledge we have already gained from previous study. The first thing to be recalled is that human acts are guided both by intrinsic principles and extrinsic principles. The treatment of vice and sin concluded our exposition of the intrinsic principles of morality. Now we take one step up the ladder of knowledge concerning human acts by beginning the study of their exterior principles, namely, God and the devil.

The devil's power of inducing man to sin and of inclining him to evil has already been discussed in the first volume of this textbook series,[1] and in the preceding chapter on sin. What remains to be worked into the pattern of human acts is the way God inclines man to virtue. This he does by aiding him with grace and instructing him through law.

Grace will be covered fully in the next chaper. Let it suffice at this point to remark that, since man's final end, beatitude, is something essentially supernatural, and since he cannot raise himself up to the supernatural order by his own natural power, he must have help from God. This help we call grace.

Again, in the actual performance of human moral acts, man is directed by his reason. Man's reason, however, cannot know all of those things necessary to perform a good moral act without enlightenment. He must be instructed, especially in the supernatural order, so that he may know what goods to choose and what evils to avoid on the road to happiness. Law is God's manner of instruction, his means of lighting the way toward beatitude.

It will be helpful here to consider briefly the procedure we will follow in our study of law. Most commentators on law are just that, "commentators." They set down the definition of law and then explain the definition. No element of discovery is left to the student; the complete doctrine is presented at once. Conclusions follow principles and the important in-between steps are passed over. St. Thomas Aquinas never proceeded in this manner. In each of his inquiries, he worked out step by step, with painstaking care, the nature of a given subject, the effects flowing from the nature, and the division of the subject. Thus, in his investigation of law he began with general considerations before he treated the more particular aspects. He went

[1]Cf. *God and His Creation,* 484-486.

from discovery to discovery, analyzing each idea, so that at the end of his inquiry he had a complete logical synthesis of law. Following his example, our treatment of law will proceed according to this outline:

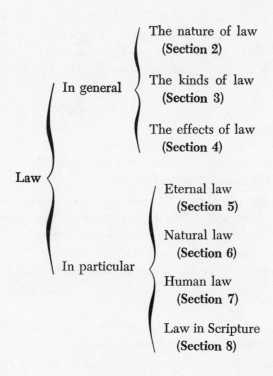

2. The Nature of Law

The very mention of the multiplicity of laws which guide us throughout life may give some cause for alarm at the outset of our inquiry. We see laws which God has given us, laws of nature, laws which are human, either civil or ecclesiastical. Admittedly, there are several species of law, but since we designate them by the same term, they must have some kind of relationship to each other. Therefore, in our study of law in general, we must look for a definition which will be valid for each kind of law. Then, when we take up the division of law in later sections of this chapter, there will be ample time to show how closely particular species of law measure up to our generic definition.

A. Description of Law

From the beginning of human history man has been living in the midst of law. From a time before the fall of Adam, down through the patriarchal era of ancient, more simple societies, through the eras of Moses, of Alexander, of Athens and Rome, and the coming of Christ and the Christianization of Europe, down all the ages and up to the present vast and intricate complexus of modern society, man has felt the presence of the law. For centuries it has guided him, instructed him, aided and restrained him. And yet, what does man really know about law? It is there, that much he knows. Whether he cherishes it as the taproot of happiness or condemns it as the threshold to tyranny, man knows that law exists. He either submits to its obligations, at least by assenting to the truth of its propositions, or he rejects its commands, chosing rather the chaos of anarchy.

(1) Historical Theories of Law

The history of the development of theories of law is the history of the evolution of ideas concerning the ultimate end, virtue and society. Zeno and the Stoics (3rd century b.c.) thought the world was governed by an impersonal reason, the Logos, an internal, blind, natural wisdom, unconscious of its own intelligence. For them, man's reason was independent of the external rule of the universe and hence morality consisted in manipulating human behaviour to fit the pattern of the reasonable decrees of nature.

Plato (427-347) and Aristotle (384-322) took one more step toward the Christian concept of law by relating it to the ultimate end, and showing the necessity of following the good of reason. And yet their final concept of law was incomplete, because they failed to co-ordinate the moral law with God and the Creator. It took St. Augustine (354-430) and later St. Thomas Aquinas (1225-1274) to give the final, clear expression of the notion of law. They recognized the relationship of law to theology, and, indeed the dependence of legal doctrine on the divine reason itself in conjunction with the divine will.

Departures from this traditional, theological idea of law have taken one of two forms. Either the role of reason has been exaggerated or it has been set aside, upstaged by the role of the will. The rational-ists elevated human reason to such a high plane that no place was given to the influence of divine reason. Along these same lines, the materialists, as well as the evolutionists and positivists, proposed theories of law which excluded God entirely. Indeed, particular ver-sions of this teaching have been set forth by Thomas Hobbes (1588-1679), John Stuart Mill (1806-1873) and John Dewey (1859-1952). For them, law comes to us only as a matter of custom. A certain ef-fective pattern of conduct is discovered, its value for society recognized in practice and thus an obligation arises to perpetuate the pattern that works, or has worked in the past. In this way law comes into being.

Even more insidious in its consequences are those theories which exclude reason entirely and play up the importance of the will. When the will is propounded as the sole source of law, sanity is scattered to the winds like bits of paper. Law becomes the will of the lawmaker; what he proposes to be done must be done. Law is placed over right. It becomes an end in itself, not a means.

American jurisprudence, under the influence of Oliver Wendell Holmes (1841-1935), stresses the importance of national economy and the sociological structure of the nation as the two main foundations of law. Law is seen as the natural consequence of public need in this or that circumstance.

(2) The Problem

Many people in trying to answer the question, "What is law?" have a tendency to describe law rather than define it. Some say that law

is authority and authority alone, whether that authority be the democratic state, the Church or a dictator. Others answer by speaking in
terms of duty and ideals. Still others attempt to define law by speaking of peace, the agreement of nations, or the friendly relationship
among men. Sacred Scripture, for example, although filled with references to law, gives no clear-cut definition, nor does Tradition. From
these and other sources we can gather descriptions of law, but no
definition.

The great differences of opinion point up the tremendous importance of the problem of definition and the difficulty of resolving that
problem. We will begin our investigation of law with, as it were, a
clean slate—that is, we will begin at the beginning and work
methodically toward a conclusion.

B. A Tentative Definition

If we are not going to take the definition of law for granted, but
rather wait until the end of our inquiry into the nature of law to
formulate a definition, we must still take the fact of law for granted.
Law exists, and all you have to do is drive through a red light or
attempt marriage without a license to prove the fact for yourself.

By taking for granted the existence of law, we can also move
forward one more step toward its definition by proposing another
basic notion to which everyone will agree. "Law is a rule and measure
of acts whereby man is induced to act or is restrained from acting."[2]
No immediate objection can rise up to challenge this tentative
definition. If we look at the facts this seems to be a rather fair
estimate of law. Certainly law is some kind of norm, a rule or measure
of human acts. The very fact that a man can be induced to act or
restrained from acting seems to prove the point. For instance, marriage is a human act. It proceeds from both the reason and the will
of the contracting parties. But if one of the contracting parties is
already married, then the law steps in and restrains him from attempt-

[2]St. Thomas, *Summa*, I-II, q. 90, a. 1.

ing a new marriage. Thus, the law acts as a norm: it measures the human act with what may be done or not done. In the example presented, it restrains the human act of marrying from being placed.

Having discovered the first key to our investigation, we can use it to unlock more doors of knowledge. The key is human acts that can be directed to do something or restained from doing something We can now ask the question, what are human acts? Or, more specifically, to what do they pertain? What is their principle, the norm according to which they are either good or bad?

An earlier chapter of this text has already given the definition of human acts and how they differ from the acts of man. There, the human reason was indicated as the measure and principle of human acts, whether these acts are good or evil.[3] There also human reason was pointed out as being the proximate principle of human activity and divine reason as the ultimate or remote principle, while, subjectively, the standard of human action is each man's conscience. In short, human reason directs human action.

Therefore, having established that law has something to do with inducing or restraining human acts, and that reason is the director of human acts, we should say a word about reason itself, for it is obvious that reason is going to play an important role in law.

Simply stated, reason is man's power of seeing the truth of things. It is the primary function of man that distinguishes him from the animals. Because of reason man can take hold of a wide variety of ideas; he can sort them and pigeonhole them, until he has put them in order, brought harmony out of chaos. Because of reason, proportions between ideas can be understood, truth and falsehood of statements can be judged, relationships between seemingly disparate objects can be seen, and even destiny itself can be comprehended. But, most important, in view of the fact that reason can distinguish and harmonize ideas, it can also draw conclusions, both in the speculative order by establishing true conclusions, and in the practical order by taking these truths and using them as a means to an end—the truth of action.

---

[3]Cf. also St. Thomas, *Summa*, I-II, q. 1, a. 1, ad 3.

C. Law: an Ordinance of Reason

(1) The Work of the Reason

What has law to do with reason? In answering this question we can draw our first conclusion concerning the nature of law. Since reason has truth for its object, and the work of the practical reason is to put into actual practice the true and best means for a given end, reason can be called the necessary directive and governing principle of human life.

In other words, the practical reason (and we are concerned here with the practical reason, because human actions actually perform some good or evil deed here and now) judges of the suitability and the proportion of certain means to a given end. But law also directs human activity, law also is a rule and measure of acts, because, as we have already learned, law either restrains or induces human activity. *Therefore, if both law and reason direct human action, then law pertains to reason,* and we can even go so far as to say that **law is an ordinance of reason.** Hence, the first element of the nature of law has been reached. Law is an ordinance of reason, or, more simply, law is a decree of reason.

(2) The Work of the Will

Ordinarily, the relationship of reason and will should present no problem in a discussion of law. We know that the will is that faculty of man which gives him the ability to move to a good that has been proposed by his reason. Just as reason has truth for its object, the will's object is a good. Alone, unaided by reason, the will would be a blind power, set off in a hundred directions simultaneously by mere caprice. And yet many seekers for the nature of law attribute the burden of law to the will. For after all, they ask, does not the making of a law involve a command, and consequently an act of the will forcing the wills of those subject to law?

We must, of course, admit that there is a voluntary aspect in every law, but we cannot admit that the will is the most important characteristic of man as a moral entity. Reason alone is the faculty which lets us judge what is right and what is wrong: reason alone can choose means to an end and, indeed, have knowledge of the end. Only reason can direct human activity. To command is a prerogative of reason, because only reason determines what should be done or what must be done. The work of the will is to move the intellect to act. We can say, then, that commanding is an act of the reason which presupposes an act of the will; an act in virtue of which reason is moved to the actual performance and completion of an act. St. Thomas puts it this way: "Reason has its power of movement from the will . . . for it is due to the fact that one wills the end, that the reason issues its commands as regards things ordained to the end."[4]

Therefore, reason gives birth to law, because reason conceives the ordering of means to an end. It creates the harmony and justice of an action, a work which the will alone would be powerless to perform since the will cannot judge what is good, but only move toward a good.

But we do not mean to imply that the will has nothing to do with the making of law. On the contrary, law is the product of the practical reason as has been pointed out before, and thus is not a work of pure thought, but thought put into action by the will. The legislator does not speculate about what ought to be, but what ought to be done. The actual doing pertains to the movement of the will.

D. Law Is for the Common Good

Thus far we have come to the conclusion that law is an ordinance of reason. And although this is the most important element to be placed in the definition, it is not the only element. Every true definition can be resolved into its four causes. With regard to law we have proposed human acts as its material cause and reason in restraining or inducing human acts as its formal cause. These two causes are called the intrinsic principles of law. Now we can inquire about the extrinsic causes or principles of law, the final cause of law, and later the efficient cause.

[4]*Summa*, I-II, q. 90, a. 1, ad 3. Cf. also *ibid.*, q. 17, a. 1.

What is the purpose of law? How can we justify it? Both of these questions ask the same thing: what is the good of law? The reason for the question is important enough because, in the final analysis, the force of any law will depend upon what it is aimed at—its end. Indeed, if there is no purpose to law, there is no necessity in forming it. A law without purpose is no law at all.

Furthermore, not only does law need an end of some kind, but that end must also be good, because if law does not presuppose a good end then it has no reason to exist. Good conduct demands that its norm be an ordinance which directs to some good end. At present, our task is to discover that end and include it as an element in our definition.

The answer is not difficult to discover. Much space has been given to the role of the practical reason in law. But the end of practical reason, that for which the practical reason chooses means, is human happiness.[5] Consequently, since law, like reason, directs human actions, it must also like reason have happiness for its end—and not just any kind of happiness either, but a happiness which will accrue to society as a whole, the perfect beatitude of the vision of God. **Law, then, is for the common good.**

We can prove this last statement in two ways. First of all, man is social by nature. He is part of a vast whole; his nature seeks perfection and completion by being part of society. The man who seeks to live apart, isolated from the rest of humanity, is a man who lives contrary to nature. Society, as such, exists as something perfect, something complete and entire. Its purpose is to assist men to final happiness. Thus man is ordained to society as an imperfect thing is ordained to the perfect, as a tiny cell is ordained to the perfect working order of the body. Consequently, the good of man is necessarily a *common* good, the universal good of society as a whole, and the laws which direct man's activity have, by necessity, the common good for their end.

Secondly, the word law is not given indiscriminately to every ordinance of reason, but only to those which are for the common good. So we distinguish law from precept, because a precept is concerned,

[5]Cf. *Summa*, I-II, q. 2, a. 7; q. 3, a. 1; and Chapter One of this book, 5-20.

not with the common good as such, but with the good of an individual or particular group of individuals. Regulations imposed by an army officer on his men, orders given by a father to his son, or even the tasks outlined by employers to employees, cannot normally be called laws. A much higher dignity attaches itself to law and also a much greater sanctity. For the law deals with a perfect society, not the imperfect societies we know as the family, army or factory set-up. The social nature of man demands that he be guided by rules which will allow him to participate fully in community life. Particular law made for a particular man alone would frustrate his natural tendency toward a common life.

This does not mean, of course, that the precepts laid down in imperfect societies should not be observed. On the contrary, they have the weight of law immediately on their establishment, if they are ultimately ordained to the common good. Therefore, the order that is established through particular regulations which are ordained to particular ends obtain the force and obligation of law when these ends are subordinated to the universal common end. Thus, for example, requirements with regard to the age and physical and moral qualities of candidates for certain governmental positions have the force of law, because the offices these men will occupy are mediately ordained to the common good. Still we must keep in mind that in this section of our study we are attempting to get an insight into the general notion of law, and thus are concerned with law as it is immediately ordered to the common good.

E. The Maker of Laws

Although we now know what law is, that is, we have two of the basis elements of a definition—*ordinance of reason and for the common good*—we must still ask about the efficient cause of law.

The question of "making laws" is a question of authority. We have already pointed out that the obligation in conscience to do an act or refrain from doing it is demanded by the common good. From this we can conclude that authority also flows from the common good, because legislation for the happiness of the community must be made by one who has authority. Authority has been well described as simply "competency in view of the common good." Those who possess the competence, then, both to understand and to realize the needs of the common good have the qualifications necessary for the making of laws.

We would be at cross-purposes here to try to determine in particular who holds legislative authority in any community. The tremendous diversity of laws would only serve to point up the many kinds of legislative authorities. In general, St. Thomas says that, since law regards the common good, then "to order anything to the common good belongs either to the whole people, or to someone who is vice-regent of the whole people."[6] From this we can conclude that the community has the right to make and enforce law, or someone who is in charge of the community has this power. The lawmakers of any particular community may be determined by examining the social and juridical structure of the community.

F. Promulgation of Law

Actually, we have come to the end of our inquiry into the nature of law. We have said what can be said about its essential definition. But still a law cannot begin to play its role in measuring the goodness or evil of human activity in relation to the common good until it has been told to the community. Just as a length of cardboard cannot be measured until a ruler is applied to it, so human action cannot be measured by law until that law has been applied to it. The law, then, begins to play its role when it is brought to the notice of the community. It must be published so that it can be known by those whom it obliges.

Publication is a condition *sine qua non* of law. This does not mean that it pertains to the essence of law, because law exists even before

[6]*Summa*, I-II, q. 90, a. 3.

promulgation by having reality in the mind of the legislator, and by being capable of directing a subject. What publication does mean is that *in order to have obligatory and directive force here and now, law must be applied to the subject.* **Promulgation**, then, is an integral part of law.

The manner of publication makes little difference as long as the law is publicly and effectively made known to the community. Not every individual must be told privately; the law is sufficently and efficaciously published when it has been made known in some customary manner, and it begins to oblige either at that time or at a time determined by the legislator.

G. The Definition of Law

The fruit of our research is the definition of law; we can now set down in full the nature of law in general, giving both its essential and integral characteristics. **Law** is nothing else than *"an ordinance of reason for the common good, made by him who has care of the community, and promulgated."*[7] In terms of the four causes, we can break up the definition in this way:

1. Material cause—human acts which are ordered by reason.

2. Formal cause—the actual ordinance of reason.

3. Efficient cause—the person or group who has care of the community.

4. Final cause—the common good; in ultimate terms, perfect beatitude.

Our summary of the doctrine on law, reached by inquiring step by step into its nature, will be the basis for the following treatment of the effects of law and the division of law. If attention and sincere consideration have been given to this present study, the understanding of subsequent doctrine should present little difficulty.

[7]St. Thomas, *Summa*, I-II, q. 90, a. 4.

3. The Kinds of Law

Since we have committed ourselves to a logical step-by-step analysis of law, we must keep ourselves on the path of truth by next investigating the kinds of law. In later sections of our study we will explain each kind of law in particular. There, the main burden of our investigation will be to discover two things: how the different kinds of law are defined; and the way in which these definitions measure up to the general definition proposed in the preceding section. At present, however, we are concerned with the broad fact that there are different species of law. Some laws have been given to us by God, some have been proposed by the Church, others come to us naturally, and still others are imposed by society. This we know, and this diversity we want to investigate.

At the outset, we must realize that the consideration of a division of law is not an arbitrary method of procedure. On the contrary, it is the next move in any logical progression. For by dividing law into its various kinds, we will ultimately bring forth with greater clarity its entire general concept.

The foundation, or basis, for our division is rather easy to determine. Our general principle states that law pertains to reason. But we can conclude immediately from this principle that, the more perfect the reason, the greater will be the dignity and extent of the law proposed. Thus, the basis for our division will be the degree of perfecton of the reason involved in making laws. In simpler terms we may state that *the basis for the division of laws is the origin of those laws.*

A. The Eternal Law

No one will argue against the fact that God has the most perfect reason. His knowledge extends to everyone and everything. He knows and understands all reality, because he knows himself intimately and he has made everything that is. And because God knows all reality with a profound knowledge, he, above all, can most perfectly order all things in the smallest detail; nothing that has been made can evade his decrees, for without him order itself would be the whimsy of chance. His reason is eternal, universal, independent and supreme, which means that the order he dictates will embody all of these notes.

Thus, the first species of law to which we can conclude will be named the **eternal law**, because it has its origin in God's eternal reason.

B. The Natural Law

Man's reason, it must be admitted, is not universal and eternal and able to order all things. The Book of Genesis, it is true, relates that "God created man to his own image: to the image of God he created him" (1:26), and we interpret these words as meaning that through creation man was endowed with an intellect and will. We cannot assume from this, however, that the intellect of man has God's power to order all things. Man's reason is a weak faculty when compared with God's.

Still, man's reason is called "reason," even though not "perfect reason." Therefore, in the very exercise of this reason, there are some things which he can naturally discover. For example, he can know what he has in common with animals and what distinguishes him from them. He can know also that all of his acts are ordained to an end. By the same token, man naturally knows that in order to attain to this end certain good acts must be performed and evil acts avoided.

In other words, the normal, functioning role of human reason can and does apprise man of the broad, elementary principles which govern human acts. Furthermore, necessity attaches itself to these principles, because they arise from the very nature of things, from the divine order established by the eternal law. We call these principles so known by men the **natural law,** for they were instilled in the nature of man when he was given life by the Creator. The second origin of law, then, is man's participation in the eternal law, his knowledge of that law as applicable to him. By discovering (not himself ordering or constructing) through unaided reason the principles, the dictates and precepts established for that nature by Almighty God, which govern his attainment of his final goal, he shares in the divine plan and governance. *This reasonable participation of the eternal law by man* is the **natural law.**

C. The Positive Law

Within the realm of reason but still dependent on the principles of natural law is another group of laws whose force is felt daily by all of us. These are the particular conclusions derived from the general principles of natural law. For example, the natural law tells us that good must be done and evil avoided. Reason takes this principle and applies it to a particular situation—for instance, that one must not disfigure another's property.

We call these ordinances **positive laws,** because they are positive determinations of the natural law. They differ, however, from the natural law on two counts. First of all, positive laws, although called supplements to the natural law, have not the necessity attached to the natural law. They are placed freely by free determination of the legislator, and require special promulgation. Secondly, those things which are prescribed or prohibited by the natural law are good or evil from their very natures, while those things which are prescribed or prohibited by positive law received their good or evil character from the very fact of prescription or prohibition.

The most important author of positive law is, of course, God. By means of the decrees revealed in the Old and New Testaments, he has set up particular **divine laws,** which man must observe in order to attain final salvation.

Man, however, also legislates in the order of positive law through the medium of **human law.** Thus, as members of a political society, our actions are governed by *civil law,* and as members of the Church we are guided by *ecclesiastical law.*

The following schema is a brief though comprehensive picture of the various kinds of law.

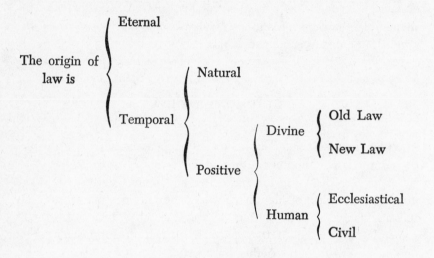

4. THE EFFECTS OF LAW

The division of law cannot help but lead to a consideration of the proper effects of law. We know from our study of its nature that law is a measure of human acts whose final cause is the common good. Our treatment of the kinds of law emphasized this fact by showing the different species, all pointing toward the common good from various angles. It is both natural and logical, therefore, to ask a pertinent question: how does law affect human moral actions so that the common good is not only attainable, but really attained? For if we agree that law is for the common good, then we must agree that it produces some effect in the life of each man, an effect ordered to making his final happiness a reality.

A. The Proper Effect of Law

A human act is good insofar as it is in accord with right reason, and evil insofar as it misses the mark of conformity with right reason.

Law, as we have already seen, pertains to reason; it is an ordinance of reason extrinsic to man which measures human acts in terms of moral goodness or evil. Thus law, like man's own reason in the internal sphere, measures the morality of human acts.

With this principle in mind, the first conclusion concerning the proper effect of law is an immediate consequence: **the whole *raison d'être* of law is to make human actions good.** In other words, the work of law is to instruct men in virtue by rectifying the actions of the whole of human life and bringing these actions into conformity with what is good.

Legislators intend laws to be obeyed; otherwise the framing of laws would be an empty gesture. If the legislator frames true laws, those which are directed to the common good, then the proper effect of law will be perfectly realized in his subjects. It will make them good *absolutely,* without qualification.

On the other hand, legislators who make laws which are useful only to their society or a small group of subjects cannot expect the perfect realization of the proper effect of law in their subjects. Not every law makes men good without qualification. The man who obeys the civil law will be a good citizen, although he will not necessarily be a good man in every respect. The reason for this is that the root of moral goodness is internal, whereas law is always an extrinsic principle of action.

B. Other Effects of Law

If we inquire further into the nature of law, other effects will be discovered. These other effects, although not dependent on the nature of law itself, are, nevertheless, dependent on the nature of the human acts which law directs. It is important to recall at this point, then, that human acts differ according to their objects. Thus, if an action is placed whose object is in conformity with right reason, then that action is a *good action.* On the other hand, when an action is posited whose object is something contrary to right reason, the action is *evil.* Again, sometimes an action is placed whose object does not directly pertain to reason; for example, closing a door or taking a walk. We call these human acts *indifferent* acts.

When we speak of human acts and the way they derive their moral character from their object, however, we are speaking in abstract terms. So acts which are indifferent when considered abstractly lose their indifference when performed here and now: there is a motive, good or bad, behind every human action.

When we apply the law to these different kinds of human action, we notice immediately that its directive force changes in character with each kind of human action.

1) When the action to be placed has a good and virtuous object, then the law directs this act by a *command*. Thus the fourth commandment tells us, "honor thy father and mother," because obedience and piety toward our parents is an act of virtue. Laws of this kind are often called **affirmative laws**, because they affirm the generic goodness of an object.

2) When the action to be performed has an evil object, the law steps in and *forbids* the placing of that action. For example, the civil law forbids driving through a red light, because the object of that action will disrupt traffic, and hence the public order. Laws of this kind are sometimes called **negative laws**, because they deny the generic goodness of certain objects.

3) When the action has an indifferent object as its goal, the law merely *permits* the action to be placed. So a sign posted near a river may read, "swim at your own risk." This means that swimming in these dangerous waters is neither condoned nor forbidden, but merely permitted, because the object is neither good nor evil, but depends on the prowess of the individual.

4) Having considered the *directive power* of the first three acts of law, we can add here another effect of law which pertains chiefly to positive laws. This is the *coactive power* of law, i.e., its power of punishing those who transgress the precepts of law. Although punishment is not in itself a true act of law, it is one means of insuring obedience to the law. For oftentimes the only reason (not, to be sure, the perfect one) for placing an

action or omitting an action is the fear of a penalty attached to the law.

It should be noted that law is said to punish, but not to reward. This does not mean that law does not or cannot provide rewards. It indicates, rather, that there is nothing distinctive about bestowing rewards, which law may do in common with many other agencies. However, only competent authority may inflict punishment, and this is distinctive of law.

A summary of what we have learned in this section can be drawn up schematically in this way.

The effect of law in
- those subject to law is **virtue.**
- the acts of law itself is
  - to command
  - to forbid
  - to permit — a **directive power.**
  - to punish—a **coactive power.**

With this consideration of law's effects we can conclude our treatment of law in general. Now we can begin our investigation into the particular aspects of the various species of law.

5. THE ETERNAL LAW

The main burden of our investigation is over. What remains to be completed is the treatment of the different species of law. This object will be accomplished in the next four sections. The primary concern of such an inquiry will be to define each kind of law, and then compare this definition to our generic concept of the nature of law. Then we will be able to judge in which species law is most perfectly realized.

A. The Existence and Nature of the Eternal Law

The existence of the eternal law is deduced from the fact that the world is ruled by divine providence.[8] Providence is the idea or plan existing in the divine reason of the order of creatures to their end. God creates for a definite purpose and then sets in motion every created thing. The detailed plan of providence rests upon eternal, universal principles. These universal principles, existing eternally in God for the direction of all actions and movements to their proper end, comprise what we call the eternal law.

Divine reason stands in relation to the movement of all things to their end as the plan of civic order in the mind of the legislator stands in relation to the governance of his subjects. Providence makes particular, detailed blueprints for the direction of every creature. Divine governance executes these blueprints at the appointed times and in the designated manner.

Our use of the phrase "eternal law" is perfectly accurate. This law is eternal because it exists in the mind of God. This plan is truly a law. It is a command directing the movement of creatures to their end; hence it is an act of the intellect conjoined with the will. It is an act of God who is Supreme Ruler of the universe. It applies to the entire universe, and directs it to the supreme common good who is God himself.

All of the essential notions of law seem to be verified in the foregoing. What remains to be considered is the way the eternal law is made known. Every law is promulgated by the word of the lawgiver, and the eternal law is promulgated in the divine Word, in whom are expressed "all things that are in the Father's knowledge, whether they refer to the divine essence, or the Persons, or the work of God."[9] It is the Word who is the perfect expression, the promulgation, of the eternal law. This role is appropriated to him because the Word proceeds from the Father in the way all ideas, including laws, proceed from reason.

[8]Cf. *God and His Creation*, 219 ff.
[9]St. Thomas, *Summa*, I-II, q. 93, a. 1, ad 2.

Gathering together the elements of the preceding analysis, we define **eternal law** as *the plan of divine wisdom directing all actions and movements to the supreme good of the universe, promulgated in the divine Word.*

This, then, is the perfect, unique and supreme law. It is identical with God, it is the essence of God, but our limited minds must conceive of it as something distinct, for the total reality of divinity is too vast to be grasped at once. Everything else will deserve the name "law" in proportion to its resemblance to the eternal law.

B. Man's Knowledge of the Eternal Law

The supreme law of the universe is supremely important to those who are subject to it. It is not enough for men to know *that* the eternal law exists: they must know *what* it is and something of its details if they are to be under its direction in a characteristically human fashion.

The disheartening reality which we must all face, however, is the knowledge that we cannot know all of its details, because we cannot know God in his essence. What we do see of the eternal law is a mere reflection. But at least that is something. The very fact that we can know truth in some measure, at least the truth of common principles, is proof that we can participate in the eternal law.

So even those to whom the words "eternal law" are meaningless have a *material* knowledge of it as the underlying cause of the natural law and of any truth whatsoever that they might know.

C. The Primacy of the Eternal Law

The eternal law is the supreme law. The theological proof of this fact can be set forth in the following manner. Whenever we observe a hierarchy of governors, there is always one who is recognized as supreme governor and who frames the plan of civil governance. Those who also govern in their own right, but who are subordinate to the supreme governor, must accept this plan and make their own laws in accord with it. In the same way, the eternal law is the plan of government in the Supreme Governor, God. Therefore, all other laws which are made by those who are subordinate to God—and there is no doubt that every human governor is inferior to him—must be derived from the eternal law, in direct proportion to their participation in his right reason. For this reason St. Augustine says, "there is nothing just or legitimate in temporal law that men have not taken for themselves from the eternal law."[10]

Ultimately, then, the eternal law is the basis for all obligations. It is the foundation for the essential order of reality in the universe, for the natural inclination of all things to their proper ends, and, as will be shown, of the natural law in man.

D. The Extent of the Eternal Law

The eternal law governs all the fixed and necessary things of the universe by ordaining their natures to their objects. It governs all contingent creatures by giving them power and instinct, and impressing within them the directive principles of their natures which account not only for their accomplishments but also for their defects. Thus the eternal law is verified in all creatures, which are passively governed by this participation of God's governance, known as the "laws of nature."

Man is governed under the eternal law in such a way that he truly governs himself and also governs others. To understand this, it is necessary to recall that man shares with lower creatures certain natural powers and inclinations which are subject to the eternal law through the "law of nature." Over and above this, he is subject to the eternal law by the very fact that he has knowledge of it. It must be noted, however, that this twofold subjection to the eternal law, viz., through natural inclinations and through knowledge, works imperfectly in evil men. The vicious habits of wicked men weaken their natural inclination to virtue, and their natural knowledge of good. For this reason the actions of evil men are imperfectly subject to the eternal

[10]St. Augustine, *Concerning Free Will*, Bk. I, Chap. 6.

law. Indeed, the wicked are really less perfectly human. But although the wicked are not perfectly subject to the eternal law in their free actions, their subjection to involuntary sufferings is increased, because the eternal law includes the punishment of those who act against it.

Good men, on the other hand, are perfectly subject to the eternal law in their free actions, and under its provision they freely attain the rewards appointed by the eternal law for those who love God.

6. The Natural Law

A. The Existence and Nature of the Natural Law

The existence of the natural law is affirmed by St. Paul: "When the Gentiles who have no law do by nature what the Law prescribes, these having no law are a law unto themselves. They show the work of the Law written in their hearts" (Rom. 2:14 f.)

Experience proves the operation of what men call the "law of nature" or "physical laws," which are observable throughout the order of the universe. Man, however, is subject to the eternal law in a special, fixed way conformable to his nature as a rational, moral being.

By a natural, spontaneous and quasi-instinctive judgment, man's reason directs him to do some things and restrains him from doing others. These basic dictates, everywhere and always generally the same, are compelling evidence for the existence of a natural law in man. It is man's distinctive share in divine wisdom. Therefore, it is clear that *man's rational participation in the eternal law* is the **natural law.**

This definition of natural law includes all of the elements pertaining to the definition of law in general, because:

    1) there is an ordinance of reason—rational participation is accomplished only intellectually;

    2) made by him who has charge of the community—namely, God, the author of nature;

3) for the common good—the moral well being of the whole community; and,

4) promulgated—by being impressed in the intellect of every man, and in the same way to all.

B. The Precepts of the Natural Law

Like all law, the natural law belongs to the practical order; it is not a principle of knowledge only, but of action. In the order of knowledge, the very first thing known is *being*, the notion of which is included in whatever anyone knows. Consequently, the first indemonstrable principle of knowledge is based on the difference between being and non-being: *the same thing cannot be and not be at the same time and under the same aspect.*

Similarly, in the order of action, the basic notion is *good*, for the good is what all men desire, and *every act is performed to attain some object which appears good to the agent.* Consequently, the first precept of the natural law is: **Good is to be done and pursued, and evil is to be avoided.** All other precepts are based on this, so that whatever the practical reason naturally apprehends as man's good belongs to the natural law as something to be done, and whatever it naturally apprehends as evil as something to be shunned.

In view of this, the other precepts of the natural law will follow the order of man's natural inclinations. Now we discern a threefold level of "nature" in man, and this underlies a threefold division of the precepts of natural law.

1) Man has an inclination to good in accordance with the nature he shares with all substances. But every substance seeks its own preservation according to its nature. Hence, self-preservation and the avoidance of death and injury pertain to the natural law.

2) Man shares inclinations which are proper to his animal nature. Thus, self-reproduction and care of offspring pertain to the law of nature.

3) Man possesses distinctively rational inclinations. Thus the desire to know the truth, even about God, and the desire to live peaceably in society are human inclinations. Hence the avoidance of ignorance, the treatment of others as he would be treated by them, and the worship of God—all belong to the natural law.

Now all these basic precepts, and the many more that can be added, have a unity because they are all applications of the most basic law; do good and avoid evil. In other words, *act humanly*, i.e., **live virtuously.**

C. The Universality of Natural Law

In maintaining that the natural law follows natural inclinations a serious difficulty arises, for different men are inclined to different things; some desire pleasure, others honor, and so forth.

This difficulty can be solved by recalling that there is a difference between speculative and practical knowledge. Speculative knowledge is concerned with necessary and unchanging truths. The sum of the angles in a triangle *always* equals two right angles; it cannot be otherwise. In speculative knowledge, principles *and* conclusions are universally true. Practical knowledge, on the other hand, is concerned with changing contingencies; it directs human actions.

In both speculative and practical matters, the most general principles are the same for all and are equally known by all. But when we descend to the particular conclusions of speculative principles, although the truth is the same for all, it is not equally known by all. For example, everyone recognizes that a mathematical whole equals the sum of its parts, but not everyone knows enough geometry to recognize the application that the angles of the triangle equal two right angles.

Now in the particular conclusions of practical reason, not only is the same conclusion *not* true for everyone, but even when the truth is the same, it is not equally known to everyone. For example, it is universally true that good is to be done and evil avoided. From this it follows that goods entrusted to another should be returned to their

owner. This conclusion is right in the majority of cases, but it admits
of particular exceptions: a revolver, for example, should not be
returned to a man who wants it for the avowed purpose of killing
his wife. And the more complicated the situation, the greater possibility that the principle will not apply in a concrete case.

D. Primary and Secondary Precepts

Authors usually cite two distinct kinds of precepts of the natural
law. This distinction is of considerable practical importance.

1) *Primary* precepts of the natural law are those which promote the principal ends of nature either by imposing acts which
attain them or by forbidding acts which obstruct them. For instance, since bodily health is a primary goal of nature, the excesses both of gluttony or starvation are prohibited by a primary
precept of the natural law: they obstruct a principal goal of
nature.

2) *Secondary* precepts of the natural law either promote the
subordinate goals of nature or facilitate the attainment of its
principal goals. Thus gluttony or starvation would contravene a
secondary precept if it interfered with a man's capacity to work
properly, which is a subordinate goal of nature.

E. Knowledge of the Natural Law

What has been written about the universality of the natural law
might appear highly unrealistic, to put it mildly, to an experienced
policeman, social worker or foreign missionary. To all that has been
said they might well reply. "The theologians just haven't met the
people I deal with." Experience demands that any realistic theory
of natural law account for the very obvious departures so frequently
observed.

Two things must be recalled as a basis for offering a solution to
the problem of knowledge of the natural law. First, the distinction
between the primary and secondary precepts, the former of which

are more basic to nature and are universally known to all. Secondly, the natural law is in man as a kind of habitual knowledge, and man is not constantly adverting to everything he knows habitually—he adverts to it actually only when he wishes to.

To admit that a man would not have habitual knowledge of the primary precepts of the natural law would be to admit the existence of a living contradiction: an irrational man. It would be a complete perversion of his nature for a human being to say, "Evil, be thou my good." Such a reversal is as destructive to humanity as ground glass is to the digestive tract. The same is true of the laws of self-preservation, self-reproduction and of living humanly in their most fundamental forms. All men have habitual knowledge of these laws, else they cease to be human.

But a man can have *habitual* knowledge of something and still not advert to it *actually* in a particular situation. Consequently, rage, lust, fear or some other passion may affect a man so strongly that he cannot apply the general precept of the natural law to a particular situation. It is only in this way that man can be ignorant of the primary precepts of the natural law.

Men can be ignorant, even habitually, of the secondary precepts of the natural law. These are either deduced or inferred from the primary precepts, and each step in the application increases the possibility of error. Evil environment, vicious customs and corrupt habits are causes of this ignorance.

F. The Law of Nations (*Ius Gentium*)

Midway between the natural law and the positive law stands a special kind of law known as "the law of nations" or *ius gentium*. While it has its roots in nature, it is not immediately apparent as is the natural law. While it depends upon human reason, it is not the product of legislative processes.

The law of nations is common to all men. It is the result of a determination of the natural law made by human reason in the light of certain contingent facts without the intervention of authority. The most common example is the law establishing the necessity of private property.

The natural law requires that man's social life, which demands the use of material possessions, be orderly, industrious and peaceful. But experience teaches that *de facto* men are not orderly, industrious and peaceful in using commonly owned goods. Hence, the possession of private property is required for man's social life in his present state.[11]

In this argument, reason juxtaposes a principle of natural law and a universal, contingent fact. The result is the inference of a quasi-positive law which is morally universal in application.

The *ius gentium* was historically compounded of the tribal law of foreigners (hence: *gentes*) and the Roman Law, but in the evolution of jurisprudence it came to represent what all nations agreed to be right.[12] So while it is not the same as "international law"—which is properly a kind of positive law—the *ius gentium* is indispensable in formulating international laws.

7. HUMAN POSITIVE LAW

The natural law provides man primarily with the fundamental, unchangeable and indemonstrable principles of human behavior, which guide him toward his distinctly human happiness. Yet the natural law provides only more general guides, and man lives from day to day in the midst of concrete circumstances which are subject to innumerable modifications. Therefore, between the general principles of natural law and the more particular situations of everyday life there must be some bridge in the form of specific directives. These directives are made by positive laws.

The **positive law** is not like the natural law, which wells up from within man; it is *posited*, that is, laid or imposed upon its subject by a

[11]Cf. the excellent re-statement of this argument for the natural right of private property by Leo XIII, in his great social encyclical, *Rerum Novarum.*

[12]For an excellent historical conspectus and a doctrinal summary, cf. J. M. de Aguilar, "The Law of Nations and the Salamanca School of Theology," *The Thomist,* IX (1946), 186-221.

specific decree of an extrinsic authority. But all positive law has this in common: it is something passed for human welfare. It is diversified both in terms of exactly what kind of welfare it envisages, and in terms of the authority which makes the law. Hence the positive law is divided thus:

$$
\text{Positive Law}
\begin{cases}
\text{Human}
\begin{cases}
\text{Civil} \\
\text{Ecclesiastical}
\end{cases} \\
\text{Divine}
\begin{cases}
\text{Old Testament} \\
\text{New Testament}
\end{cases}
\end{cases}
$$

In this section we will consider human positive law and reserve the discussion of divine positive law to the next section.

A. The Existence and Nature of Human Law

Human law is either ecclesiastical or civil, depending upon which of the only two perfect societies in the world issues the law. While our general considerations will apply to both kinds of law—the particularities of these laws are more properly the field of jurisprudence than of theology—most of the examples and applications will be taken from the more familiar area of civil legislation.

The reason for the existence of human law is simple: necessity. Natural law does not provide directions that are specific enough to afford adequate guidance through the complexities of life, something more particular is needed, and that something is the human law.

A dreamer may object that, since laws are naturally designed to make men good, the purpose could be better achieved by exhortations than by the force of law. But a realist like St. Isidore will reply: "Laws are made so that by fear thereof human audacity might be curbed, that innocence might be safeguarded among the good and that among the wicked themselves the tendency of harming others might be held in check."[13]

Every human law must be in accord with man's rational nature, and the first rule of the practical reason is the natural law. Hence, from what has been said thus far, we can define **human law** as *the ordination of human reason by which society* (i.e., the state or Church, and its members) *is directed immediately to temporal happiness and aided mediately to perfect beatitude by him who has care of the community, and promulgated.*

There is no problem in comparing this definition with our general definition of law. But it should be noted that there are two ways in which human laws can be derived from the natural law: *first,* as a conclusion from a principle (e.g., that one should not sell opium except as medicine may be derived from the principle that one should not harm any man); *secondly,* as a precise determination of a general principle (e.g., the natural law establishes that evil-doers should be punished, and human law determines exact punishements for specific kinds of evil deeds).

B. The Conditions for Human Law

The nature of human law as a particular determination of the principles of the eternal and the natural laws for the welfare of mankind demands that certain conditions be fulfilled in it.

Because it depends ultimately on the eternal law, human law must **foster religion.** Hence, those human laws which tend to abrogate God's rights to be worshipped cannot have the force of true law.

Because it must harmonize with the natural law, human law must be **helpful to discipline.** This means, then, that the laws must be *just,* because human discipline depends primarily on the order of reason. Human law must also be *possible of observance* by its subjects. This is a difficult and important consideration for the lawgiver, who must take into account the personal capacities of his subjects (their moral strength, level of education, their habits and tendencies, their age, and so forth) and, further, take cognizance of their social capacities

[13]*Etymologies,* Bk. V, Chap. 20.

(their economic development, history, customs). Now all this merely means that the human law is not an abstraction, that is, the best *possible* law; rather, it is a concrete directive which attains perfection by effectively moving its subjects to the end envisaged, that is, it is the best law possible *in these circumstances.*

Finally, human law must **promote the common good.** If it fails to do this, an essential condition of all law is lacking, and the measure is no law **at all.**

C. The Force of Human Law

(1) *The Human Law and the Common Good*

It is essential that the human law be directed to the common good, for it is not framed solely for an individual case, nor is it enacted on a temporary basis. Since, however, law promotes the common good, then by its very nature it will not provide a solution for every individual matter perfectly, nor will it tend to change.

Yet human law will fail not only in respect of a minority of individual cases; it will also fail to suppress every vice. Thus, the law does not strive to suppress every vice from which the virtuous abstain; it represses only the more grievous vices, from which it is possible for the majority to abstain. Especially does the human law prohibit the vices against justice, because society perishes when injustice flourishes.

The principle of the temporal common good determines not only that human law does not suppress all vices, but also that the law need not prescribe every act of virtue. Absolutely speaking, the human law may enjoin acts of any virtue. In practice, however, the law prescribes only those acts of virtue that are ordainable to the common good either directly or indirectly.[14] Thus the human law commands the payment of just debts, but it does not enjoin the duty of almsgiving.

---

[14]"Human law is ordained to the civil community which is social. But social life is carried on through external acts by which men deal with each other. This kind of social communication is a matter of justice, which properly directs the human community. Consequently, human law makes no precepts except about acts of justice, and if it commands acts of other virtues, this is only insofar as they assume the nature of justice." St. Thomas, *Summa,* I-II, q. 100, a. 2.

(2) *Human Law and Morality*

From the fact that human law is ordained to the common good, we have deduced three conclusions regarding the force of human law:

1) Law cannot extend to every particular case.
2) Law cannot repress every vice.
3) Law cannot effectively promote every act of virtue.

Now this indicates clearly that morality demands far more of man than conformity to human law. Yet the law should not be despised on this account as a defective instrument. It is a good instrument *for its purpose,* which is to attain the temporal common good. The temporal common good is not an ultimate goal for man, but a morally necessary condition for working out his pursuit of a higher goal. Human law establishes and preserves the general climate of virtue which is man's natural moral climate.

Although it is clear that human law does not make man perfectly virtuous, that is, so that he acts virtuously *from a virtuous motive,* the problem of the relationship between legality and morality is not settled so easily. We must ask further if man has a moral obligation to comply with human law: is there an obligation in conscience before God to obey man-made laws, so that he who breaks them is guilty of sin?

To answer this important question, it is necessary to recall the distinction between a just law and an unjust law. In the case of an unjust law—which is an abuse of law rather than a law—there can be no moral obligation to obey *arising from the nature of law,* for the nature of law does not exist in unjust laws.

Now if the unjust law contravenes a higher law, it is immoral to obey it, for ". . . we ought to obey God rather than men" (Acts 5:29). But if the object of the unjust law is not something evil of itself, there can sometimes be an obligation to obey in order to avoid scandal or disturbance of the public order, for which a man should be willing to yield his right.

On the other hand, just human laws have the power to bind in conscience. This is abundantly true of those laws which partake

of the force of natural law because they are proximately derived
therefrom. But it is also true of the particular determinations of
natural law which rest on the authority of human rulers.

This moral obligation which arises from the human law presupposes that all conditions for a just law be present: 1) that the law
be for the common good; 2) that the law be enacted by a competent
authority; 3) that the law be equitable in assigning burdens proportionately among the citizens.

It is clear, then, that human law can impose a moral obligation to
perform even heroic acts, e.g., to risk one's life for the defense of the
nation. It is equally clear that laws which make disproportionate
demands upon some do not *of themselves* beget any moral obligation,
although the avoidance of scandal or disturbance may demand their
observance in view of the common good.

(3) Penal Laws

Is it possible to have a law which begets no moral obligation to
observe it? This is a celebrated question in theology, and one which
has been disputed among various authors since the 16th century,
although its roots go back much farther.[15] The problem concerns
what are called "penal laws," which are distinguished by some theologians from precepts which oblige in conscience, and considered to
be legal ordinances whose transgression of itself does not beget any
sin whatever. All theologians agree, however, that they do impose
the moral obligation of submitting to a penalty either assigned by
the legislator or to be assigned by a judge.

Civil legislators do not, as a rule, concern themselves with internal acts, nor do they ordinarily state that they do not intend to
oblige their subjects in conscience. By what standard, then, may

[15]If need should arise for a discussion of the problem of penal law, which is
very abstruse, it is suggested that the teacher present a digest of the conflicting
views set forth in: Riley, Noonan, Herron, "Panel Discussion—The Problem of
Penal Law," *Proceedings of The Catholic Theological Society of America*, X
(1955), 259-284. Cf. E. T. Dunn, S.J., "In Defense of the Penal Law," *Theological
Studies*, XVIII (1957), 41-59. The author supplies references to views other
than his own.

this or that civil law be designated as merely penal? The only practical guide will be the customs of the people and the conclusions of prudent men.

But it may be stated as a general rule, derived from the nature of law itself, that any law which is judged to be merely penal must deal with matters of minor moment which have only a remote connection with the common good. Thus, for example, laws governing the parking of automobiles which impose a fine for overtime, excise taxes and customs duties, hunting and fishing regulations, etc., are generally thought to be only penal laws.

(4) Final Problems

The principle of the common good must be invoked again to answer two final problems on the force of human law. First, may a subject ever act outside the letter of the law with good conscience? Secondly, what degree of guilt attaches to the transgression of various laws?

Law is for the common good, and sometimes the literal fulfillment of the law defeats its own end. Laws which guarantee the inviolability of a man's home, for instance, will be defeated if a passerby could not break in to extinguish a blaze. Precisely as an ordinance for the common good, laws will sometimes fail in particular instances. Whenever it is possible, recourse should be had to authority before acting outside the letter of the law, but when emergency prevents this, then necessity brings its own dispensation to act for the common good, even outside the letter of the law.

The degree of moral guilt arising from transgressing a human law is fixed generally in terms of the common good:

1) When the thing commanded or forbidden by the law is something grave and closely related to the common good, then it is mortally sinful to break the law, e.g., draft-dodging in war time.

2) When breaking the law involves a grave infraction of justice or charity, then the infraction is mortally sinful, e.g., selling liquor to intoxicated persons.

(5) Recapitulation

Legality and morality are not co-existive. More is required to be a good man, and especially to be a good Christian, than is needed to be a good citizen or a good subject. Just human law, however, does provide a reliable guide to a virtuous life *within the limits of the goal it seeks and the authority it enjoys*. No one can be a good man or a good Christian by condemning human law.

D. The Changeableness of Human Law

Many factors such as scientific and economic advance provide reasonable grounds for changes in human laws, but it is clear that changes must not be made without careful consideration. The permanence of law—a kind of legal inertia—creates a climate of custom which affords precious security to human social life.

Change may also be wrought in human law by dispensations. **Dispensation** is *a relaxation of the obligation of a law granted by competent authority in a particular case in which the law would otherwise oblige.* Sometimes a particular law, although generally conducive to the common good, wreaks harm on a particular individual or in a special case, either by preventing some greater good or by causing some evil. In such cases, the proper authority may dispense his subjects from observing the law. Thus the civil government may waive some requirement for obtaining citizenship, and the local Ordinary may dispense from the law of abstinence on a national holiday which falls on a Friday.

E. Civil and Ecclesiastical Law

It is possible to divide human law into several kinds (national, city, international, etc.), but that is more properly the work of jurisprudence and of political philosophy. For our purposes it will suffice to mention the division into civil and ecclesiastical law. A comparison of the two under several headings will serve to illustrate both their likenesses and their differences.

1. Both are ordinances of human reason. Civil law directly derives from the natural law. Church law does not ignore the natural law, but rests upon the higher authority of Christ: "Whatever you bind on earth shall be bound also in heaven; and whatever you loose on earth shall be loosed also in heaven" (Matt. 18:18).

2. Both suffer the defects inherent in human law. Thus, Church law, unlike the divine positive law, does not of itself extend to internal motives and intentions. Like civil law, it regulates man's *external* conduct.

3. Civil law is directed to the *temporal* common good, which is an end in the order of nature. Church law is directed to the spiritual common good, which is supernatural. Church law directs man's *external* acts to this goal.

4. Civil law is enacted and promulgated by civil authority; Church law is enacted and promulgated by ecclesiastical authority which, ultimately, rests on the authority of Christ, the invisible Head of his Church.

8. Divine Positive Law

In the context of history, there are two great facts that explain the failure of natural and human law and that also call for a higher type of guidance. These facts are man's elevation to the supernatural order, i.e., his vocation to a life of divine grace, and man's fall through original sin.

We now turn to a consideration of that supernatural, divine law which is the indispensable guide for man who has been called, and re-called, to seek his happiness in God.

A. Existence and Nature of the Divine Law

God, who is the Supreme Lawgiver, legislates from all eternity in the eternal law. In time he legislates through the laws of nature impressed upon the irrational creation and through the natural law written in the hearts of men. Beyond these legislative functions which are intimately bound up with divine as well as created being, God emerges as a framer of positive laws in the affairs of men. For the particular determination of human action, when the question of the supernatural order is raised, needs supplementation from other than created sources.

We have only to turn to the Old and New Testament to convince ourselves of the existence of such laws, for they are communicated through revelation. Considering this fact, we may define the **divine positive law** as *an ordination of divine reason, which by the free and positive will of God was immediately brought forth and promulgated for directing men to their supernatural end.* Once more all the elements which pertain to the generic concept of law are fully present, and with a truly unassailable perfection. Our study will begin with the revelation of the Old Law and conclude with the New Law.

B. The Law of the Old Testament

(1) Its Perfection and Imperfection

We have seen that law is measured as good or bad in terms of its relationship to reason. The conformity of the Old Law with that higher divine reason which governs not only the natural order but the supernatural order as well will thus be the criterion of its goodness. To recognize agreement (or disagreement) at this level, however, man's unaided natural reason is entirely inadequate. Yet reason elevated and enlightened by faith can see the correspondence of the Old Law with divine reason, and hence concludes to the essential goodness of this divine positive law.

The Old Law repressed sinful concupiscence, which is contrary to reason: "You shall not covet your neighbor's house. You shall not covet your neighbor's wife . . . nor anything else that belongs to him" (Exod. 20:17). Moreover, the Old Law forbade every kind of sin, and any sin is contrary to reason. Thus it is clear that the Old Law was a good law because it was in conformity with the order of things, natural and supernatural, established by divine reason.

To say something is good, however, is not to say it is perfect. Law is a means to happiness, and the Old Law was directed to the perfect happiness of the vision of God. But the Old Law of itself could not bring men to that vision; it could only render some assistance by withholding them from sin, which obstructs beatitude. Only divine grace can effectively bring men to God, for ". . . . . the gift of God is life everlasting in Christ Jesus our Lord" (Rom. 6:23). We may conclude from this fact that the Old Law was good, but it was not perfect; it *disposed* men for salvation, but did not cause it *effectively*.

(2) *The Purpose of the Old Law*

God's Law in the Old Testament disposed men for salvation precisely by preparing men for receiving Christ. The Old Law *bore witness* to Christ: "For if you believed Moses you would believe me also, for he wrote of me. But if you do not believe his writings, how will you believe my words?" (John 5:46 f.). The Law also *disposed men* for the coming of Christ—"our tutor unto Christ," in St. Paul's words (Gal. 3:24)—by withdrawing them from idolatry and by surrounding them with the true worship of God.

This Law was given exclusively to the Jews: "He has not done thus for any other nation; his ordinance he has not made known to them" (Ps. 147:20). And why were the Jews so favored? Because Christ was to be born of them. And why was Christ to be born of the Jews and not of some other race? "For love of your fathers he chose their descendants . . ." (Exod. 4:37). And why did God so love the Jews that he chose them for the unique distinction of being the forebears of Christ? This is a question of divine choice to which God has not revealed the answer.

C. The New Law of the Gospel

Christ came to bring the good news of salvation to all men, and his coming marked the introduction of the New Law. Yet this New Law was not a repudiation of all that had gone before. Christ himself expressed the perfect attitude toward the Old Law: "Do not think that I have come to destroy the Law or the Prophets. I have not come to destroy, but to fulfill" (Matt. 5:17). The New Law, then, must be regarded as the *fulfillment*, the *perfecting* of the Old. It is from that point of view that we will consider the New Law of the Gospel under this threefold division:

The New Law
- Considered in itself
- In comparison with the Old Law
- In terms of its contents

(1) The New Law in Itself

The New Law marks the final stage in God's plan for man's salvation; nothing further will be added. Consequently, the New Law must really effect man's salvation; it must actually accomplish what the Old Law promised and foreshadowed. Salvation, however, consists in union with God, and this is accomplished by grace, which is given to the followers of Jesus Christ. Now in view of these truths, the term "law" as applied to the Gospel has a twofold meaning:

First and principally, the New Law is the grace of the Holy Spirit given to those who believe in Christ. "For the law of the Spirit of the life in Christ Jesus has delivered me from the law of sin and of death" (Rom. 8:2). Grace itself is ". . . the law of faith" (Rom. 3:27), written in the hearts of Christians, truly an ordinance of divine reason leading men to the supreme common good, God himself.

Secondly, the New Law consists in certain precepts which dispose men to receive the grace of the Holy Spirit and to use it well in the Christian life. So the New Law contained in the gospels and epistles manifests the truths about Christ which men must believe, and through which belief they receive the grace of the Holy Spirit. Moreover, the New Law contains precepts which withdraw men from worldiness to prepare them for ". . . the Spirit of truth whom the world cannot receive, because it neither sees him nor knows him" (John 14:17). Finally, the written New Law exhorts men to a life of virtue in keeping with the grace of Christ.

Thus the New Law is principally the grace of the Holy Spirit written by God himself in the hearts of men by the presence of the Holy Spirit; and secondarily, it is a law written in the New Testament to guide men in the Christian life.

The written letter of the New Law, however, has power to justify men only when it exists in conjunction with the interior grace of the Holy Spirit.

(2) The New Law and the Old

In view of Christ's express intention to fulfill the Old Law and not destroy it, the Old and New Laws cannot be distinguished by opposition. Both the Old and the New Law have the same end, which is to *make man obedient to God.* The God of both Testaments is the same. *Consequently, the Old and the New Law are not specifically different, for both have the same object.*

Yet, neither are they identical, else the coming of Christ would have been in vain. *They do not differ in kind, but rather in the degree of perfection.* The Old Law was like a tutor of children; the New Law is a law of the spiritually mature. The New Law is the law of perfection because it is the law of charity, and charity is the bond of perfection.

But precisely how is the New Law a fulfillment, a perfection of the Old? This was accomplished in two ways:

1) Regarding the end of the Law which was to justify men: the New Law accomplishes through the Passion of Christ what the Old Law foreshadowed in ceremonies and promised in words.

2) With respect to the perfecting of the precepts: Christ fulfilled the precepts of the Old Law both by his deeds and by his teaching. By his deeds because he was born under the

Old Law, and he chose to be circumcised and to observe the other precepts which were obligatory at that time; and by his teaching in three ways: 1) by explaining the true meaning of law, and thus he fulfilled the law by showing that even the internal acts of sin fall under the prohibition (cf. Matt. 5:21 ff., 27 ff.); 2) by indicating how the statutes of the Old Law could be more surely observed; and 3) by adding thereto certain counsels of perfection.

(3) The Contents of the New Law

As we have already seen, the principal content of the New Law is the grace of the Holy Spirit. But in addition, the New Law contains precepts which regulate man's acts. Some of these acts are prescribed because they lead to grace, like the sacramental acts of baptism and the Eucharist. Other acts are commanded because they flow from divine grace through love, e.g., Christians are commanded to profess their faith (Matt. 10:32). Still other acts are forbidden because they are opposed to divine grace, e.g., Christians are forbidden to deny their faith (*ibid.*).

But beyond these acts which are indispensable to the manifestation or preservation of divine grace in the soul, the Christian is left free to decide what he should do and what he should avoid. The New Law is called "the perfect law of liberty" (Jas. 1:25), because it leaves men free to choose their way along the paths of virtue, whereas the Old Law made many minute regulations and left little choice. Under the influence of the grace of the Holy Spirit, man is endowed with a kind of supernatural instinct that makes him do freely the things that are becoming to grace and shun whatever is opposed to it.

The external acts explicitly regulated in the New Law are of three kinds: 1) the sacraments, which cause grace; 2) certain good acts which necessarily manifest grace, like professing the faith, assisting the needy; and 3) certain evil acts which are opposed to grace, like murder, adultery.

These, then, are the general outlines of the teaching of the law of the Gospel as St. Thomas envisages them.

(4) The Evangelical Counsels

In keeping with its nature as "the perfect law of liberty," the New Testament offers certain counsels (or, if you prefer, recommendations) to Christians. This marks a sharp difference from the Old Law in which we find no counsels, but only commandments. Counsels, which are left to the option of those to whom they are offered, are different from commandments, which impose obligations upon those subject to the law. The commandments of the New Law impose obligations in matters that are indispensable for attaining eternal happiness; the counsels offer advice in matters that make the attaining of this goal more certain and more expeditious.

Man must work out his salvation along the straight and narrow path of virtue which lies between the things of this world on the one hand, and spiritual goods on the other. Should anyone give himself up to worldly things so as to make them the rule and reason for all he does, and to place his whole happiness in them, then he must necessarily abandon spiritual goods. This fatal disorder is prevented by keeping the commandments, which prevents any sinful use of the things of this world. It is not necessary, therefore, to renounce the things of this world in order to secure the joys of the next.

But a renunciation of the things of this world provides a more certain and expeditious way to secure the things of heaven, and the evangelical counsels are offered by our Lord in the New Law for this purpose.

Now all the goods of this world may be classified generally under the three headings of material wealth, carnal pleasure and honor. The evangelical counsels of poverty, chastity and obedience offer a way of dealing with these goods which will enable the Christian to employ them better for the purposes of eternal salvation.

But there are two ways to observe these counsels: either absolutely, so as to make a complete pattern of life as is done by vows in the religious life; or in limited particular respects, as is done by Christians who are not members of religious communities.

For example, a diocesan priest professes the counsel of perpetual chastity; Christians may freely give alms, or the married may practice continence temporarily, or a man may refuse to follow his desire to sue a debtor. All of these are acceptances of the counsels in particular ways which do not make them a complete way of life. The counsels are a declaration of complete dependence upon God, and a distinctive note of perfection in the New Law.

9. SUMMARY AND CONCLUSION

With law touching upon every phase of human experience, practically limitless applications of this doctrine are possible. The following are chosen with a view to promoting discussion along lines of more general interest.

1. "Whatever happens, whatever change or transformation may take place, the purpose of all social life remains the same, ever sacred, ever obligatory: the development of the personal values of man, who is made in the image of God; whatever legislator or authority he may obey, every member of the human family remains bound to secure his immutable ends. He has therefore always the inalienable right—a right which no opposition can destroy and which all, friends and enemies alike, are bound to acknowledge—a right to a constitution and an administration of justice inspired by the conviction and understanding that it is their essential duty to serve the common good."[16]

2. "If one has not been brought up under right laws, it is difficult to obtain from one's youth a right training in virtue; for it is not pleasant for most people, especially when they are young, to live temperately and hardily. . . . This is why some men hold that lawgivers ought to exhort and guide men to virtue, on the assumption that those who have been well trained in habits will

---

[16]Pius XII, radio broadcast, "Con sempre nuova freschezza," *Acta Apostolicae Sedis*, XXXV (1943), 13.

attend to such influences; and that punishments and penalties should
be imposed on those who disobey and are of inferior nature, while
the incurably bad should be completely expelled.[17] For the good
man and he who lives under a sense of honor will be obedient to
reason; and the baser kind, who grasp at pleasure, will be held in
check by pain like beasts of burden."[18]

3. "When in the Course of human events, it becomes necessary
for one people to dissolve the political bands which have connected
them with another, and to assume among the powers of the earth,
the separate and equal station to which the Laws of Nature and of
Nature's God entitle them, a decent respect to the opinions of mankind requires that they should declare the causes which impel them
to the separation.

"We hold these truths to be self-evident, that all men are created
equal, that they are endowed by their Creator with certain unalien-
able Rights, that among these are Life, Liberty and the pursuit of
Happiness. That to secure these rights, Governments are instituted
among Men, deriving their just powers from the consent of the
governed."[19]

4. "Such is the rush of present-day life that it severs from the
divine foundation of revelation, not only morality, but also theoretical and practical rights. We are referring especially to what is
termed the natural law, written by the Creator's hand on the tablet
of the heart (Rom. 2:14) and which reason, not blinded by passion
or sin, can easily read. It is in the light of the commands of this
natural law that all positive law, whosoever be the lawgiver, can
be gauged in its moral content, and hence, in the authority it wields
over conscience. Human laws in flagrant contradiction with the
natural law are vitiated with a taint which no force, no power can
amend."[20]

[17]Cf. Plato's arguments on these points in (respectively) the *Laws* (a work of
his maturity) and *Protagoras* (virtue is knowledge and can be taught).

[18]Aristotle, *Nicomachean Ethics*, Bk. X, Chap. 9.

[19]The Declaration of Independence.

[20]Pope Pius XI, encyclical *Mit brennender Sorge* (On the Catholic Church in
Germany), March 14, 1937.

5. "It is international law that must make secure and defend the life of that peace; but an international law which recognizes its foundations in that natural law written by God in the very conscience of every man, and from it derives ultimately its binding force. The alernative is the law of the stronger; and then the defences of peace will collapse under the first attack launched by those for whom might makes right."[21]

6. "The fundamental theory of liberty upon which all governments in this union repose excludes any general power of the State to standardize its children by forcing them to accept instruction from public teachers only. The child is not the mere creature of the State; those who nurture him and direct his destiny have the right, coupled with the high duty, to recognize and prepare him for additional duties."[22]

[21]Pope Pius XII, *Discourse to Members of the U. S. Senate Military Affairs Committee*, November 2, 1945.

[22]Oregon School Case: U. S. Supreme Court Decision, June 1, 1925.

BIBLIOGRAPHICAL NOTE

The matter of this chapter is covered in Questions XC-CVIII of the First Section of the Second Part of the English *Summa* (Volume I). Of those questions, XCIX-CV are lengthy considerations of the precepts of the Old Law in great detail; a brief summary of these is available in popular style in *Of Shadow and Substance* (*TFTL-44*), by Richard M. Heath, O.P. Three valuable aids in understanding the text of the *Summa* are *Preface to Happiness* (New York: Benziger Bros., 1950), by E. F. Smith, O.P., and L. A. Ryan, O.P., 212-222; an excellent short article by Walter Farrell, O.P., in *The Great Books—A Christian Appraisal* (New York: Devin-Adair, 1949), Harold C. Gardiner, S.J., ed., I, 44-49; and a brief though scholarly introduction by Vincent McNabb, O.P., entitled *St. Thomas and Law* (London: Blackfriars, 1955), which will be found among the Aquinas Papers.

Those interested in more profound inquiries may consult *The Metaphysical Foundations of Thomistic Jurisprudence* (Washington: Catholic University Press, 1939), by K. Kreilkamp, and "A Question About Law," in *Essays in Thomism* (New York: Sheed & Ward, 1942), by M. J. Adler.

The doctrine on law is explained in more popular style by Edward P. Farrell, O.P., in *An Obliging Teacher* (*TFTL-41*), John Fearon, O.P., in *The Path of Reason* (*TFTL-42*), and Robert A. Morris, O.P., in *Guardian of the Public Good* (*TFTL-43*). Eminently readable and brief, with some excellent contemporary examples, is *Order and Law* (Westminster: Newman Press, 1954), by Aegidius Doolan, O.P.

A great deal has been written about the vast subject of natural law. A rather complete study which is readily available is *The Natural Law* (St. Louis: Herder, 1949), by H. A. Rommen. The translator has added copious notes to this work which enhance its utility. Jacques Maritain also makes some profound, though clear, statements about natural law in his book *The Rights of Man and Natural Law* (New York: Charles Scribner's Sons, 1943).

CHAPTER SEVEN

Divine Grace

1. INTRODUCTION

"The principal element in the New Law is the grace of the Holy Spirit which is bestowed upon us inwardly."[1] This idea is the bridge which leads us from considering God as an instructor by his law to the study of God who enables us to share the divine life through his grace.

Consonant with St. Thomas' viewpoint, the aspect of this tract remains theocentric. It is God himself, and *not* his grace, who is the extrinsic principle of man's acts, for divine grace works within man, suffusing the very depths of his being. God made man to be receptive of his grace, and man receives it gracefully, for grace becomes a "second nature" to man.

Man is the image of God. This is the theological definition of man, the key to his relationship with God. By a creative act of love he establishes man as an intellectual substance whose powers of reason and will bestow an aptitude for the knowledge and love of God himself, and thus make that nature imitative and expressive, not only of the divine nature, but even of the Trinity. Human achievement

[1]*Summa*, I-II, q. 106, a. 2.

251

will thus radically consist in the progressive perfecting of this "image of creation" through man's own acts of intellect and will.

But God's tremendous love gives even more to man than a nature expressive of divinity. His journey to God will consist in the progressively more perfect realization, through his own supernaturalized acts of intellect and will, of the higher image which sanctifying grace produces, unto its consummation in glory. And it will be accomplished, indeed, by man's acts, but through the special assistance of God—itself a grace, an actual grace or transitory divine movement of the supernatural order.

The importance of this study of God's supernatural help can, therefore, hardly be overestimated.

It will be treated in this order:

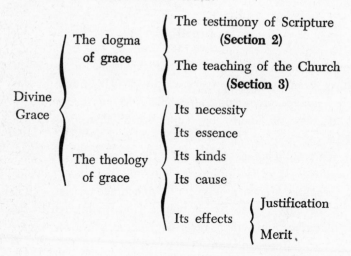

Divine Grace

The dogma of grace
- The testimony of Scripture (Section 2)
- The teaching of the Church (Section 3)

The theology of grace
- Its necessity
- Its essence
- Its kinds
- Its cause
- Its effects
  - Justification
  - Merit

THE DOGMA OF GRACE

2. The Testimony of the Word of God

Our English word *grace* derives from a long line of antecedents, even the earliest of which had religious meanings. It is thought to derive ultimately from the Sanskrit *gír*, "a hymn of praise,'" which is related to *gurtah*, "praised."

The Greek word for grace, *charis,* derives from a root meaning refulgence, light or splendor. From this, various meanings developed in classical writings: 1) physical loveliness—similar to our English "gracious" and "graceful"—(this meaning has no theological counterpart); 2) such "grace" usually evokes the reciprocally "good graces" of others, and hence there is a second meaning, *favor* or *benevolence;* 3) benevolence, in turn, often impels the giving of *gifts*: grace is a gift in this third meaning; 4) and the receiving of a gift calls for the gratitude, the *giving of thanks,* which is the fourth meaning in the Greek.

The Latin word for grace is *gratia.* It is used in the same senses as the Greek *charis* explained above. The Latin *gratia* also connotes the condoning of faults and the granting of dispensations, as well as the motive for an action.

It is from this ancient background, mostly classical, that our English word *grace* comes through the Old French. Its meaning in the theological context becomes clear from scriptural usage.

But while both the Old and the New Testaments employ words signifying *grace,* there is a profound difference in the meaning of the terms in the two Testaments:

> It is indeed true that in those of the just who lived before Christ the Holy Spirit resided by grace, as we read in the Scriptures concerning the prophets, Zachary, John the Baptist, Simeon and Anna; so that on Pentecost the Holy Spirit did not communicate himself in such a way "as then for the first time to begin to dwell in the saints, but by pouring himself forth more abundantly; crowning, not beginning his gifts; not commencing a new work, but giving more abundantly" (St. Leo the Great: *Homily III, On Pentecost*). But if they also were numbered among the children of God, they were in a state like that of servants, for "as long as the heir is a child, he differs in no way from a slave, though he is master of all; but he is under guardians and stewards until the time set by his father" (Gal. 4:1 f.).
>
> Moreover, not only was their justice derived from the merits of Christ who was to come, but the communication of the Holy Spirit after Christ was much more abundant, just as the price surpasses the earnest and the reality excels the image. Wherefore St. John declares: "As yet the Spirit had not been given, since Jesus had not yet been glorified" (7:39). So soon, therefore, as Christ, "ascending on high," entered into possession of the glory of his kingdom which he had won with so much labor, he munificently opened out the treasures

of the Holy Spirit: "he gave gifts to men" (Eph. 4:8). For "that giving or sending forth of the Holy Spirit after Christ's glorification was to be such as had never been before; not that there had been none before, but it had not been of the same kind" (St. Augustine, *On The Trinity*, Bk. IV, Chap. 20).[2]

A. The Old Testament

The Septuagint employs the Greek *charis* in its various senses to translate several different Hebrew words.[3] Thus, as Pope Leo XIII pointed out in the citation quoted above, while divine grace was a reality in the times of the Old Testament, the doctrine on grace was imperfect and only a foreshadowing of that to come through the revelation of Christ. In fact, there is very little in the way of clear and explicit explanation of grace in the Old Testament, because the necessity and supernatural nature of internal grace had not been revealed at that period. But the Old Testament does speak of the mercy, faithfulness, kindness and love of God—all of which pertain to the divine benevolence, which is "uncreated grace."

There is an emphasis upon the external blessing of God (e.g., on the deliverance of his people from suffering and tyranny) and upon the gratuitous graces by which the prophets were illumined. Yet we find a significant insistence upon the mercy of God in remitting sins: "Who is a God like to thee, who takest away iniquity, and passest by sin of the remnant of thy inheritance? He will send his fury in no more, because he delighteth in mercy" (Mic. 7:18). This and similar passages refer implicitly to the grace which causes the justification of sinners.

Moreover, the doctrine of grace is implied and foreshadowed in God's familiar friendship with Adam, with the patriarchs and the prophets, and in their faith and obedience. They walked with God, made agreements with him, and were beloved by God (cf. Sir. 44-45).

---

[2]Pope Leo XIII, encyclical *Divinum Illud Munus,* "On the Holy Spirit."

[3]1) *beauty,* "Charm is deceptive and beauty fleeting . . ." (Prov. 31:30); 2) *favor,* "Noe found favor with the Lord" (Gen. 6:8); 3) *a gift or benefit,* "Jacob answered, 'They are the children that God has graciously given your servant,' " (*ibid.,* 33:5); 4) *the giving of thanks,* "A fool has no friends, nor thanks for his generosity" (Sir. 20:15).

Abraham was God's "friend" (Isa. 41:8). To the prophets were promised the gifts of renewed hearts and spirits (cf. Ezech. 11:19; Zach. 12:10).

B. The New Testament

The Greek *charis,* "grace," is widely used in the New Testament, but in varying degrees of frequency. Although it is not found in the Gospel according to St. Matthew, it occurs eight times in St. Luke, and four in St. John's Prologue; in the Acts it is found seventeen times; it is employed twelve times by St. Peter in his First Epistle; St. Paul uses the word over one hundred times throughout his writings. Moreover, in New Testament usage *charis* acquires a new meaning besides the four found in the Old Testament, for it properly signifies something freely and gratuitously bestowed *by God*: "Even so, then, at the present time there is a remnant left, selected out of grace. And if out of grace, then not in virtue of works; otherwise grace is no longer grace" (Rom. 11:5 f.).

The synoptic gospels teach that the kingdom of heaven is not a temporal government, nor one consisting only in external observances; rather it is chiefly, although not exclusively, an internal reign in the hearts of men. It is something revealed to little ones, and only they can enter it. And conversion to this kingdom is the result of a divine call and of divine assistance. This is clear from the call of the apostles, of Mary Magdalen, of Zacheus and of others. Peter was able to confess his faith in Christ only because the Father revealed it to him.[4] Christ's teaching contradicted the doctrine of the Jewish teachers who exaggerated the role of free will in salvation so much that they minimized man's dependence on the grace of God.

St. John declares that Christians receive grace from Christ's fulness of grace, for he came that they might have life, and that they might have it more abundantly (John 10:10). Indeed, no one can come to Christ to share in this divine life unless he be drawn by the grace of the Father (John 6:44).

[4]Cf. Matt. 16:17 ff.

St. Peter speaks of divine grace with great incisiveness. He describes the life of habitual grace: "For indeed his divine power has granted us all things pertaining to life and piety through the knowledge of him who has called us by his own glory and power—through which he has granted us the very great and precious promises, so that through them *you may become partakers of the divine nature*, having escaped from the corruption of that lust which is in the world" (II Pet. 1:3 f.). He also describes the effects of actual grace: "But the God of all grace, who has called us unto his eternal glory in Christ Jesus, will himself, after we have suffered a little while, *perfect, strengthen and establish us*" (I Pet. 5:10).

St. Paul dwells on grace at considerable length and in many places.[5] He affirms the opposition between the Old Law and grace (Rom. 6:14). He uses the failure of the Jews to observe the Law and the pagans' inability to avoid sin as proofs of the necessity of grace (Rom. 2:3; 7:8). He states the need for grace to believe (Phil 1:29); the fact that his own calling came through grace (Gal. 1:15 ff.); that the fruit of his apostolate is the result of grace (I Cor. 15:10 f.).

It is St. Paul who puts the great question: "For who singles thee out? Of what hast thou that thou hast not received? And if thou hast received it, why dost thou boast as if thou hadst not received it?" (I Cor. 3:7). And it is from him that we learn the answer: "So then there is question not of him who wills nor of him who runs, but of God showing mercy" (Rom. 9:16); "for it is God who of his good pleasure works in you both the will and the performance" (Phil 2:13).

3. THE TEACHING OF THE CHURCH

Over the course of centuries since the time of Christ, many errors have arisen on the subject of divine grace. The Church has refuted these errors both by the writings of her great teachers and by official

[5]To gain some insight into the teaching of St. Paul on grace, the student should read: Rom. 3:21-26, 5, 6, 8; Eph. 2:4-8; Tit. 2:11-14, 3:4-7.

pronouncements of the *magisterium*.[6] The four principal errors are those of Pelagianism, Semi-Pelagianism, Protestantism, Baianism and Jansenism (these latter two being treated together).

Definitive and authoritative refutations of these successive errors have enabled the Church to put the great revealed mystery of grace in clearer and brighter light. As Christ's teacher she has affirmed the absolute transcendence of this gift of God over the entire created order, and the potentialities and exigences of all creation; she has restated the absolute gratuity of this greatest of God's gifts. At the same time, however, the essential goodness of human nature as it comes from the hand of God has been insisted upon, and the sovereign freedom of man's will has been strenuously defended against pessimistic excesses. Between the exaltation of human nature which renders grace superfluous (Pelagianism) and the degrading of human powers that reduced man without grace to a monster of evil (Jansenism) appears the true role this gift of God is to play in the lives of men.

It is the duty of speculative theology to analyse this role for us.

THE THEOLOGY OF GRACE

The determination of what has been revealed to us by Almighty God about grace in Sacred Scripture and Tradition, of what the Church proposes for us to believe with respect to this revelation—this is only the first of the theologian's tasks, the preoccupation of that branch of his science which is known as "positive" theology. Once the facts have been ascertained, however, the Church entrusts her theologians with the more profound office of investigating these facts to determine their nature, correlating them and comparing them with other truths, both natural and supernatural, and organizing the knowledge so obtained, not in an artificial system or extrinsic frame of reference, but rather into an organic "vision in depth."

[6]Explicit references to the Church's teaching will constantly be made in the course of this study.

With St. Thomas as our guide, our present endeavor will be to obtain just such a total and integral view of the revealed mystery of divine grace. Logically we should begin this inquiry, like all scientific inquires, with the question, "Does this thing exist?" But since faith assures us of the answer, we probe a little deeper, seeking to ascertain the reasons for its existence, *why* it is, what role it is designed to play. Hence the opening section—the necessity of grace, our need for grace (**Section 4**).

With this foundation we can then analyse the nature of grace (**Section 5**), the divisions or various kinds of grace (**Section 6**), the causes of grace (**Section 7**), and conclude our study by discussing the workings of grace, i.e., its effect, justification (**Section 8**) and merit (**Section 9**). This well ordered and logical procedure should help greatly to keep our thinking straight as we plunge deeply into a profound and eminently practical subject.

4. THE NECESSITY OF GRACE

Grace exists. Why? Why does God so freely, so lovingly give man this special divine assistance? St. Paul's insistence on the weakness of man and on the impotence of the sinner gives one answer: grace is necessary as a remedy, a medicine, to heal man of the wounds of sin. But his equal and contrasting insistence on man's call to sanctification, to the perfection of God himself, illustrates another aspect: grace is necessary for man to achieve his high destiny, his supernatural happiness. On the one hand, then, man's weakness, his miseries; on the other, his high calling, his supernatural possibilities. Only careful analysis will clearly delineate the function of God's special help in our lives.

To answer our question as accurately as it demands, we must recall certain truths from our previous studies. First of all, all creatures are dependent on God, not only for their creation and for their conservation in being, their continuing in existence, but for their every action, their every operation and motion and movement. Divine assistance, then, divine movement is absolutely necessary if the creature (angel or aardvark) is to *do* anything, to inaugurate an action and carry it through to a successful conclusion.[7] But it is not this general movement of creatures by God (called "premotion" with respect to its inauguration and "concursus" with respect to its execution) of which we are now inquiring. Our question concerns a *special* divine assistance, over and above this divine help necessary for any created movement whatsoever.

Secondly, we have seen the necessity of distinguishing between the natural and the supernatural orders; the first is proper and connatural to the created order considered in its own natures and ends; the second is proper and connatural to God alone, although God has chosen to raise men and angels to this infinitely higher plane. Obviously the needs and necessities of one order may be quite diverse from those of the other.

Lastly, the historical facts of man's existence must be taken fully into account. These lead theologians to distinguish three "states" in which man has been found:

1) *The state of original justice.* God created Adam in such a fulness of sanctifying grace that not only was his a divine life and destiny but also a perfect integration and harmonizing of all his faculties, his reason perfectly subject to God, his lower appetites and body perfectly subject to reason.

2) *The state of fallen nature.* Stripped of grace and preternatural gifts, human nature is left "on its own": subject to sorrow and death, ignorance in the intellect, malice in the will, and faced with the rebellion of the lower powers. Moreover, since this is a sinful condition, it becomes now more difficult for "fallen man" to do good and avoid evil than had he never been elevated to the supernatural order.

3) *The state of restored nature.* Through Christ man dies to sin and lives once again through God's grace the divine life, to share the blessedness of God. But the wounds of sin are not

---

[7] Cf. *God and His Creation*, 84 ff. (God as First Mover of all things), 202 ff. (efficacy of the divine will), and 475 ff. (divine governance).

entirely healed in this state, nor does man enjoy the other preter-natural gifts God showered on Adam.[8]

With this background we can begin to answer this vital question concerning our need for grace, treating the following points:

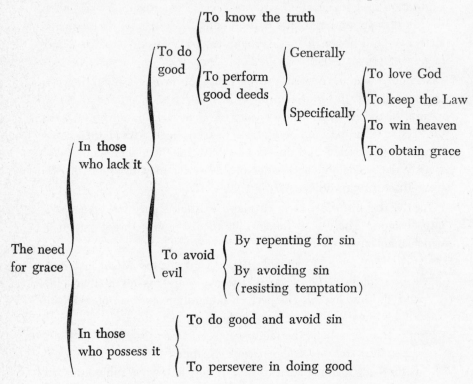

A. Grace and the Knowledge of Truth

Man's intellectual knowledge manifests his distinction from lower creatures. It is his hallmark, his sign of distinction. Since divine grace

[8]For greater precision, some theologians further distinguish two other "states," never historically realized, the "state of pure nature" (man without any special gift) and the "state of integral nature" (human nature plus special, non-super-natural divine help to render it integrated and harmoniously controlled by reason). These further precisions and rather subtle distinctions need not enter our considerations for the moment, but it should be noted that in St. Thomas' vocabulary the "state of integral nature" is not that here described but rather the state of original justice (Adam) insofar as it conferred perfect rectitude with regard to the operations of nature.

is viewed as God's assistance to man, it is logical to inquire first into the role of grace in man's most distinctive function: Is man able to know truth without the aid of divine grace?

Bearing in mind the distinctions noted in the preliminary remarks of this section, we can reach the following conclusions:

1) For knowing any truth, whether natural or supernatural, God's movement of the intellect is necessary. For every movement must be reduced to the First Mover, and the reduction of the intellect from potentiality to act is a movement and subject to this universal law of dependence.

2) For knowing *natural* truths, man does not need the help of *supernatural* grace. The light of natural intelligence suffices for knowing natural truths. "If anyone says that the one and true God, our Creator and Lord, cannot be certainly known with the natural light of human reason by means of things that have been made, let him be condemned."[9]

3) Divine grace is necessary for knowing supernatural truth. The natural light of reason suffices for natural truths, but it cannot attain the truths above the level of nature. For supernatural truths, a supernatural light is needed, and this light comes as a divine gift, and is supernatural grace. Hence, *if* man is to know truths beyond his natural capacities, he must have a principle of knowledge commensurate with such truths, and this principle is a light of faith, or revelation, or prophecy, etc., which is gratuitously bestowed upon him by God—that is to say, a supernatural grace. Thus it was that our Lord said after Peter had confessed Christ, "Blessed art thou, Simon Bar-Jona, for flesh and blood has not revealed this to thee, but my father in heaven" (Matt. 16:17).[10]

4) Sometimes, by a special grace, God instructs someone miraculously in matters which they could know naturally, as he did in the case of St. Catherine of Siena and certain other saints.

[9]Vatican Council, Sess. III, *Constitution on Catholic Faith,* Chap. 2. "Concerning Revelation," Can. 1; Denz. 1806.

[10]"If anyone says that by the power of nature he can think anything good which pertains to the salvation of eternal life as he should, or choose or consent to salvation, i.e., to the preaching of the Gospel, without the illumination and inspiration of the Holy Spirit, who grants delight to all in consenting to and believing in the truth, such a one is deceived by an heretical spirit, not understanding the voice of God saying in the Gospel, 'Without me you can do nothing' (John 15:5); and the saying of the Apostle, 'Not that we are sufficient of ourselves to think anything, as from ourselves, but our sufficiency is from God' (II Cor. 3:5)." Second Council of Orange, 529, Can. 7; Denz. 180.

Every man, then, depends on God, first, for his intellectual faculties, and, secondly, for the premotion which actualizes them in knowledge. Over and above this, the faithful are indebted to God for a supernatural light whereby they are able to know things above the limits of nature, and it is this grace which is needed for knowing supernatural truth.

B. Grace and Good Deeds

Knowledge is the principle of truly human action. If man needs grace for certain kinds of knowledge, must he have it also for the performance of certain good actions?

Here we must recall the various "states" in which man has historically existed, and the difference between the natural and the supernatural orders. Then the question, "Is supernatural grace necessary for good acts?" can be answered under four headings:

1) Man needs movement from the First Mover to do any good, whether natural or supernatural. This is clear from the first conclusion of the preceding section: just as man does not exist of himself, so neither can he act of himself. This is universally true of any state in which man exists or could exist.

2) Before the fall, man was able to desire and to perform naturally good works without supernatural grace. Nature itself, under the ordinary movement of God, could do all naturally good works, for these were commensurate with natural powers.

3) In the state of fallen nature, man can do naturally good deeds that are proportioned to his wounded powers.[11] Original sin did not destroy nature, and therefore even a sinful man can perform objectively good works—conduct business, till the soil, build homes, etc. Sin, however, so wounds nature that it cannot any longer do every possible natural good without failing in some respect; to will and perform the totality of good works propor-

---

[11]This is a teaching of faith. Cf. Council of Trent, Sess. VI, *Decree on Justification* (1547), Can. 5: "If anyone shall say that after the sin of Adam, man's free will was lost or destroyed, or that it is something merely nominal, indeed a title without reality, and moreover, a fiction introduced into the Church by Satan, let him be condemned"; Denz. 815. Cf. *ibid.*, Chap. 5, "The Necessity for Adults to Prepare Themselves for Justification"; Denz. 797.

tioned to human nature, man needs the medicinal remedy of grace.

4) If man is to desire or accomplish any supernatural good, then grace is necessary for him in whatever state he may be. The reason is that there must be a proportion between the principle and the action it produces. But a natural principle is in no way proportioned to supernatural acts, and hence some special divine assistance is necessary to elevate man to the supernatural level, and to move him in the supernatural order.

Thus our Lord tells us: "As the branch cannot bear fruit of itself unless it remain on the vine, so neither can you unless you abide in me. I am the the vine, you are the branches. He who abides in me, and I in him, he bears much fruit; for without me you can do nothing" (John 15:4 f.). This is explicitly taught by the Church in the Sixteenth Council of Carthage[12] and the Second Council of Orange.[13]

It is evident from these conclusions that, before the fall, man was dependent upon grace for one reason, viz., to wish and to do supernatural good. Now, after the fall, we depend on grace for two reasons: first, to be healed, at least partially, of the wounds of sin; secondly, to will and to do works of supernatural virtue. And, in either state, in every supernatural act man needs the premotion of actual grace.

Sin, then, makes us more dependent upon God. But God's grace heals nature first, so that the natural and supernatural orders are not distinguished by opposition, as materialists allege, but rather by addition. *Grace perfects nature; it does not destroy it.*

The distinctions and principles of the two foregoing sections can now be applied to more specific problems relating to our need for grace.

(1) Grace and the Love of God

Chief among all morally good deeds is to love God above all else. We are concerned here with that natural love whereby every creature seeks its own proper good because of the common good of the entire

[12]Can. 3-8; Denz. 103-108.
[13]Cf. *supra,* note 10.

universe. "God draws all things to love of himself," as Pseudo-Denis says.[14] Among irrational creatures, this "love" is the natural tendency toward the orderly working of the universe; it is the inclination to follow the "law of nature." In man, it is this and something more: he has, from his higher powers of reason and will, not a blind but a *rational* inclination to prefer God as the greatest good above all others, because God is the Creator—the principle of everything man is and of all that he has. This natural love, of course, is of an entirely different and lower order than the supernatural friendship of divine charity.

Before the fall, human nature was perfectly ordered, and it was connatural for man to refer all love for creatures to God, and to subordinate himself to God. Because of this perfect order in human nature itself, man naturally loved his Creator more than himself and more than any creature. For this natural love no grace was needed, but only the physical premotion of God in the natural order.

After the fall, however, human nature was wounded and its powers disorganized. Man tends now to seek his personal interests without reference to the common good, to the love of God. To restore man's passions to the dominion of reason and man himself to the dominion of God, a healing grace is necessary. This is not merely a convenience, it is a *necessity*: human nature is wounded, and the patient cannot cure himself.

(2) Grace and the Natural Law

Before the fall, man could have kept all the precepts of the natural law without any special help of grace, for the natural law prescribes only what corresponds with the inclinations of nature in its undamaged state. This conclusion is also clear from the fact of original sin: had man not been able to keep the law, he could never have sinned by transgressing it.

By the same token, nature wounded by sin is not able to keep all the precepts even of the natural law, because the totality of com-

[14]*On the Divine Names,* Chap. IV, nn. 1, 11.

mandments is beyond the strength of wounded nature. After sin, man needs healing grace to be restored even to the fulness of his natural moral abilities.

But over and above the simple *fact* of keeping the commandments, there is a question of the reason *why,* and the *manner* in which they are observed. To keep the commandments because of friendship for God and in a manner befitting divine charity is what we are called upon to do: "If you love me, keep my commandments" (John 14:15). To make obedience the expression of love, to obey out of friendship, is the work of charity, and this requires grace, whether before the fall or after. Here again it is a matter, not of convenience, but of simple necessity, as the Church teaches: "If anyone shall say that divine grace is given through Jesus Christ only that man might live justly and merit eternal life with greater ease, as if he were able to do both by his free will without grace, but with difficulty and hardship, let him be condemned."[15]

And even after man is made a friend of God through grace, he still needs the actual movement of God's grace in all his acts of friendship.

(3) Grace and Eternal Life

The crowning reward of divine friendship is the beatific vision wherein we see God, not "through a mirror in an obscure manner," but "face to face" (I Cor. 13:12). The attainment of this reward is farther beyond nature's powers than the act of seeing is beyond the power of the ear, and for the same reason—a lack of proportion between the power and the goal. "The gift of God is life everlasting" (Rom. 6:23). It is impossible for man to merit eternal life without divine grace.[16] As St. Augustine says, "It is certain that eternal life is the reward of good works, but the very works for which it is conferred on us are the results of God's grace."[17]

[15]Council of Trent, *loc cit.* Can. 2; Denz. 812.

[16]This is defined by the Church in the Second Council of Orange and in the Council of Trent, *loc. cit.*, Can. 1-2; Denz. 811-812.

[17]*On Grace and Free Will,* Chap. 8.

(4) Preparing for Grace

The consummation of friendship with God which is eternal life depends upon his grace. What of its beginnings? How is this friendship begun? Can man prepare himself for grace by his natural powers? The Pelagians and Semi-Pelagians answered in the affirmative. They hold that man could, so to speak, pull himself up to divine life by his bootstraps.

Our Lord gives a negative answer to the question. "No one can come to me unless the Father who sent me draw him" (John 6:44). From this it is clear that the preparation for grace itself must begin with grace, and does not come from purely natural effort and good will. But if grace is necessary to prepare for grace, then it seems that the contradiction of an infinite series of preparations is being suggested.

Such, however, is not the case, for there are two distinct kinds of preparation to be considered:

1) *Preparation for eternal life,* which consists in being made a friend of God through **habitual grace** which effects a lasting change in the recipient. No previous habitual grace is required as a preparation for this, so that no infinite series of habitual preparatory graces is here involved.

2) *Preparation for receiving habitual grace,* which is effected by the transitory divine movement of **actual grace.**

To prepare oneself for grace is freely to turn oneself to God, and this turning is accomplished by an actual free movement of the will by God. "Convert us, O Lord, to thee, and we shall be converted" (Lam. 5:21). In this action of turning oneself to God man does what he is capable of doing, but with the special assistance of God. Hence, what is impossible to man by himself becomes possible to him through the movement of actual grace.[18]

---

[18]The necessity for grace in order to prepare for grace is defined by the Second Council of Orange, Can. 3; Denz. 176. "If anyone shall say that without the preceding inspiration of the Holy Spirit and without his assistance, man can believe, hope, love or repent in the way that he should so that the grace of justification may be given him, let him be condemned" (Council of Trent, *loc. cit.,* Can. 3; Denz. 813).

C. Grace and the Avoidance of Sin

As we have seen, the man without grace is confronted by formidable obstacles in striving to do good. We now view the condition of man without grace from another aspect, in his efforts to overcome evil. There are two problems: first, does man need grace to repent of his sins; secondly, does man need grace to resist temptation?

(1) Grace and Repentance

What can the sinner do to repent of his sin? This is a question of such universal relevance that no one can afford to ignore it. We say that the soul is dead through mortal sin. By every human standard, death is an irremediable evil. Is the same true of the death of mortal sin, so that despair is the only refuge of sinners?

Sin is an evil act by which one turns from God to creatures. To repent of sin is not simply to interrupt the act of sin, for when the act of sin ceases, the guilt remains; repentance restores to man that which he lost through sin. In every mortal sin, however, man suffers a triple damage:

1) The stain of sin, which is the loss of the soul's beauty; this is a spiritual disfigurement.

2) A disordering of human nature resulting from the turning of the will away from God.

3) The debt of eternal punishment.

Repentance, if it is to be effective, must repair this threefold damage.

St. Paul clearly teaches that repentance is a work of grace. After describing the slavery of sin he says:

> But when the goodness and kindness of God our Savior appeared, then not by reason of good works that we did ourselves, but according to his mercy, he saved us through the bath of regeneration and renewal by the Holy Spirit; whom he has abundantly poured out upon us through Jesus Christ our Savior, in order that, justified by his grace, we may be heirs in the hope of life everlasting.[19]

This is also defined by the Church as a matter of faith.[20]

[19]Titus 3:4 ff.

[20]Second Council of Orange, Can. 4 (Denz. 177); cf. Can. 14 (Denz. 187), 15 (Denz. 188) and 19 (Denz. 192); Council of Trent, *loc. cit.*, Can. 1 (Denz. 811) and 3 (Denz. 813).

How precisely does grace restore the repentant man to his sinless state by removing the threefold loss of sin?

1) The splendor of the soul is a reflection of the light of divine grace. "O Lord, let the light of your countenance shine upon us" (Ps. 4:7). This beauty is restored by the gift of habitual grace.

2) The disorder of the will in turning from God is removed by an actual grace which redirects the will to God.

3) The debt of eternal punishment is removed by the mercy of God, against whom the offense is committed.

All this being true, what role does free will play in the matter of repentance? St. Paul calls upon his converts, "Awake, sleeper, and arise from among the dead, and Christ will enlighten thee" (Eph. 5:14). We must not think of grace as coercion. The Spirit moves things "strongly but sweetly." Hence the free will, whose free movement is made a reality by the movement of actual grace, turns to God, and God grants to the repenting sinner the light of his justifying grace.

Here we have some insight into Christ's words, "Without me you can do nothing" (John 15:5). What saves the sinner from despair, then, is not his own resources, but solely the mercy of Christ.[21]

(2) Grace and Temptation

The man who is without grace needs grace to recover from sin by repentance. Does he also need grace to resist temptation?

In order to answer this problem adequately we must recall the distinctions previously made regarding the states in which man can exist. With these distinctions in mind, the question of the need of grace in resisting temptation may be answered according to these conclusions:

---

[21]If the sinner of himself cannot help himself, what can he do for those for whom he has been the occasion of sin? This question drives home the dreadful responsibilities contracted by those who have given scandal (the leading of others into sin). Human efforts to repair scandal often come to naught. Some who will agree to share a sin will not agree to abandon it; others are beyond reach. In these cases frequently the only recourse the giver of scandal has is that of prayer, for by prayer man can ask God to pour forth his grace upon the other and repair the harm of sin which the one who has done the damage cannot undo.

1) In the state of original justice, man is able to avoid all sins against the *natural* law. Nature's powers, when they are unimpaired by sin, are able to keep the natural law perfectly without any special supernatural help from God; the divine conservation and motion at the natural level would suffice for this.

However, if integral human nature is viewed as elevated to the supernatural state, so that man would be obliged to keep supernatural precepts, like those of faith, hope, charity and of the other supernatural virtues, then supernatural grace would be necessary for him to avoid sin. Not in any state is nature capable of living the supernatural life.

2) In the state of restored nature, a man healed by habitual grace is able to avoid all mortal sins. The healing effects of habitual grace apply directly and principally to the mind, i.e., to the intellect and will, although perfect order among the passions is not restored. Sin, in order to be mortal, must be a perfectly human act, proceeding from an act of the deliberate will—that is to say, sin must be an act of the mind. Hence since man's mind is healed by grace, he is able, with the help of actual grace, to resist all mortal sins. This is expressly taught by the Church: "If anyone shall say that the commandments of God are impossible to observe even for a man who is justified and living under grace, let him be condemned."[22]

3) In the state of restored nature a man healed by habitual grace is able to avoid each single venial sin, but not all of them, except by a special divine privilege.

The redeemed man must be able to avoid each venial sin or it would cease to be sin, for no one is responsible for the unavoidable. Still the wounds of sin remain in the passions of those redeemed by grace. St. Paul says, "I myself with my mind serve the law of God, but with my flesh the law of sin" (Rom. 7:25). Because of this residual disorder, a man occupied in regulating one passion may easily lose control of another. Thus a man struggling against anger over the unpredictable movements of the driver in the car just ahead might fail in the courtesy due to his wife if she asked a question at the wrong moment. The Christian, faced with the multiplicity of temptations to venial sin, is like a man under attack by too many mosquitoes; he is capable of killing or warding off each of them, but when too many come at once, some are bound to sting him. In moral mat-

[22]Council of Trent, *loc. cit.*, Can. 18; Denz. 828.

ters, unlike arithmetic, the totality is something more than the sum of the parts.

The possibility of absolute sinlessness on the part of the redeemed, except by a special privilege, has been authoritatively denied by the Church. "If anyone shall say that man once justified can sin no more, nor lose grace, and that therefore he who falls and sins was never truly justified; on the contrary, that he can avoid all sin, even those that are venial, for his whole life, except by a special privilege of God, such as the Church holds regarding the Blessed Virgin, let him be condemned."[23]

4) In the state of fallen nature, one who has not been healed by habitual grace, i.e., one who perseveres in sin, can avoid each mortal sin for a time, but he cannot long remain without sinning anew.

St. Gregory says that "a sin not soon removed by repentance drags man down to another sin by its very weight."[24] While the sinner is under no necessity to remain constantly at the business of sinning—his every act is not a sin[25]—the man who destroys his rectitude by turning away from God leaves himself open to the assaults of temptation which his disordered faculties cannot long resist.

St. Thomas explains the plight of the unrepentant sinner in this way: "For when a man does not have his heart so fixed on God that he would not be willing to be separated from him either to have any good or to avoid any evil, many things come upon him, and to obtain them or to avoid them (as the case may be) man turns from God by breaking his commandments, and thus he sins mortally."[26]

From these conclusions we can see that grace is the only bulwark against temptation. Yet if man falls, it is himself who fails, the failure and fault are his alone. For Christ promises, "My grace is sufficient for thee" (II Cor. 12:9).

---

[23]Council of Trent, loc. cit., Can. 23 (Denz. 833); cf. also Sixteenth Council of Carthage, Can. 6, 7 and 8 (Denz. 106-108); condemnation of certain propositions of Michael Molinos, Denz. 1275-77, 1282-83.

[24]Homily XI on Ezechiel; cf. St. Thomas, Summa, I-II, q. 109, a. 8.

[25]This is the authoritative teaching of the Church. "If anyone shall say that all works done before justification, in whatsoever manner they were performed, are truly sins or worthy of God's hatred, or that insofar as anyone strives to dispose himself for grace, he only sins the more gravely, let him be condemned." Council of Trent, loc. cit., Can. 7; Denz. 817.

[26]Summa, I-II, q. 109, a. 8.

D. Grace and Spiritual Progress

Up to this point, our study has centered upon those who lack divine grace, with the exception of some conclusions regarding the avoidance of venial sin in those who live the life of grace. We now turn to an investigation of spiritual progress in those who live the life of habitual grace. This topic will be developed more fully later, but now two fundamental questions must be answered in terms of man's *need* for grace once he possesses it. The first regards our need for actual grace; the second, our need for grace to persevere.

(1) Man's Need for Actual Grace

Human acts require two things: first, the possession of a faculty (e.g., the intellect) and then its use. The faculty itself is something permanent, it pertains to the order of *being;* its use is transient, it pertains to the order of *action.*

There is a parallel in the spiritual life. Man needs first a permanent, habitual gift by which his wounded nature is healed, and, having been healed, is elevated to the state of friendship with God. In this state of restored nature man is capable of manifesting his divine friendship by supernatural acts which have meritorious value in God's sight. This *habitual grace* is a sharing in the divine nature; it is to the soul in the supernatural order what the soul is to the body in the natural order, for just as the soul is the principle of life for the body, so also is grace the principle of supernatural life for the soul; it is permanent of its very nature.

Over and above this principle of life, man needs the motion of God whereby he acts in accord with the supernatural life of grace. This transient divine motion is called *actual grace.* "For it is God who of his good pleasure works in you both the will and the performance" (Phil. 2:13).

Now this divine motion is required for two reasons in a man already justified through habitual grace:

1) Every movement of every creature depends ultimately on motion from the First Mover. Grace is not exempt from this

universal law of dependence, because grace perfects nature and does not destroy it. As in the order of nature, so also in the supernatural order God's assistance is always necessary.

2) In addition, there is a more special need for actual grace. The healing effected in wounded human nature by habitual grace is not complete. Man's lower appetites retain some of the disorder and rebelliousness of sin: man's nature is a volatile composite of spirit and flesh, with conflict between the two an inevitability save through a harmony imposed by special gifts, like the preternatural gifts of the state of original justice that were lost by sin; to overcome this reluctance of the flesh, the rebellion of man's lower nature, special divine assistance is necessary. Then, too, the intellect remains partially under the cloud of ignorance begotten of sin, so that man fails to weigh all circumstances according to objective spiritual values, and he does not attain to perfect self-knowledge. Hence, he needs the motion of actual grace to guide and guard him.

The effect of habitual grace, then, in no sense makes man independent of God; rather it makes him even more dependent on God, who must preserve and activate habitual grace by his actual graces. The Church herself assures us of this important fact: *"Concerning the assistance of God. It is of divine gift when we both think aright and restrain our steps from falsity and injustice; for as often as we do good, God works in us and with us, in order that we may act."*[27]

(2) Man's Needs for the Grace of Perseverance

Arriving somewhere is one thing; remaining there may well be quite another, as any party-crasher is apt to learn and as a soldier well knows who has wrested a contested hill from a determined enemy.

[27]Second Council of Orange, Can. 9; Denz. 182. Cf. Council of Trent, *loc. cit.*, Chap. XVII, "Concerning the Fruit of Justification": ". . . for since Jesus Christ himself as the 'head into the members' (Eph. 4:15), and as the 'vine into the branches' (John 15:5), continually infuses his strength into those justified; a strength which always precedes their good works, and which accompanies and follows them, and without which they could in no wise be pleasing and meritorious before God, etc. . . ."; Denz. 809.

Once man obtains a share in the divine friendship through God's mercy in bestowing habitual grace upon him, he needs actual grace for every good act, and to avoid each temptation. The "grace of perseverance," however, is simply a continuation in God's friendship until death, and such constancy requires that actual graces be supplied continuously to preserve man in habitual grace. This sustained giving of the actual graces necessary to bring man to the end of life as a friend of God is itself a special gift which is the result of predestination.[28] Hence the definitive statement of the Church: "If anyone shall say either that one already justified can persevere in the justice he has received without the special help of God, or that with such help he cannot persevere, let him be condemned."[29]

A very practical conclusion: this grace of final perseverance should be sought continually in prayer. St. Paul instructs us to "'. . . work out your salvation with fear and trembling" (Phil. 2:12), and St. Thomas observes that "grace is given to many to whom perseverance in grace is not given."[30]

5. The Essence of Grace

That a special divine assistance of the supernatural order does exist is a certainty, taught by divine revelation, authoritatively proposed by Christ's Church; and we have seen why this special gift is necessary for man immersed in the misery of sin and yet dedicated to the successful pursuit of a supernal vocation. In theology as in the lesser sciences, working from effect to cause is recognized scientific procedure. From what grace does for us, then, it seems logical to attempt to determine (so far as man can obtain a theological understanding of the mysteries of faith) what grace is. With the teachings of Scripture, of the Church, of the Fathers and of St. Thomas to direct our

[28]Cf. *Summa*, I, q. 23; *God and His Creation*, 227 ff.
[29]Council of Trent, *loc. cit.*, Can. 22 (Denz. 832); cf. Denz. 826.
[30]*Summa*, I-II, q. 109, a. 10.

investigation, we should be able to obtain a deeper knowledge of God's gift of grace.

But before we proceed, one point requires clarification. Grace exists, to be sure. But is it a reality distinct from God, something belonging to the creature so graced? Or is it only God's favor, without any reality in the creature enjoying divine benevolence? That it is truly a distinct entity is implicit in all that has been said before, of course. But now it is necessary explicitly to establish that fact, before attempting to determine what grace is.

A. The Reality of Grace

(1) The Revealed Truth

Grace is something real, a positive entity, intrinsic to man, distinct both from God and from man, his soul and his powers; it is not just the extrinsic favor of God (Calvin), nor the imputation of Christ's justice to us (Luther), nor good works without any intrinsic supernatural principle (de Bay):

> The sole formal cause [of justification] is "the justice of God, not the justice whereby he himself is just, but whereby he makes us just," namely, the justice given by him whereby we are renewed in the spirit of our mind; nor are we only regarded as just—we are indeed just and are truly said to be so. Each one receives his own justice within himself, according to the measure which the Holy Spirit allots to everyone as he will, and according to the individual disposition and co-operation of each.[31]

The Church teaches, therefore, that grace is: 1) a **real entity** (the justice given by God whereby we are not only regarded as just but

---

[31]Council of Trent, *loc. cit.*, Chap. 7, "The Nature and the Causes of the Justification of a Sinner" (Denz. 799). Cf. *ibid.*, Canon 11 (Denz. 821): "If anyone shall say that men are justified either by the sole imputation of the justice of Christ, or by the sole remission of sins, excluding grace and charity which is poured forth in their hearts by the Holy Spirit and remains there, or even that the grace by which we are justified is only God's favor, let him be condemned." The Council of Vienne, 1311-12, had chosen as more probable and more in harmony with Church doctrine the opinion which held that grace and the virtues were infused in the soul as habits, but the Council did not define it as a matter of faith; cf. Denz. 483.

are truly just); 2) **supernatural** (by it men share in the very justice of God); 3) **intrinsic** (each receives this justice in himself); and 4) a **created entity** distinct both from God (not the justice whereby he is just, but distinct from him as effect from cause—the Holy Spirit) and from the soul and its powers (it is a supernatural renewal of the spirit of our mind).

This pronouncement only makes explicit what was clearly the intent of God's revelation. The words and figures of speech employed in Sacred Scripture describe grace as just such an interior supernatural reality: it is "our life," a "seed," an "earnest," a "seal," an "anointing," a "regeneration."[32] Through his prophet, Ezechiel (36:25-27), God had promised:

> I will pour upon you clean water, and you shall be cleansed from all your filthiness, and I will cleanse you from all your idols. And I will give you a new heart, and put a new spirit within you: and I will take away the stony heart out of your flesh, and will give you a heart of flesh. And I will put my spirit in the midst of you: and I will cause you to walk in my commandments, and to keep my judgments, and do them.

And Christ taught the woman at the well of this promised gift of supernatural life: "He who drinks of the water that I will give him shall never thirst; but the water that I will give him shall become a fountain of water, springing up unto life everlasting" (John 4:14). The Apostle states the same truth less metaphorically: "The charity of God is poured forth in our hearts by the Holy Spirit who has been given to us" (Rom. 5:6), and urges his disciple, Timothy: "Do not neglect the grace that is in thee" (I Tim. 4:14).

The supernaturality of grace, its reality as a created entity interiorly changing man—such are the truths revealed in these and many similar passages of Sacred Scripture, and they were so interpreted in this very realistic sense by the Father.[33] Why, then, the Protestant difficulty?

[32]Cf. Rom. 6:4; I John 3:9; II Cor. 1:22, 5:5; Ephes. 1:13-14; John 1:13; I Pet. 1:23.

[33]Cf. *infra,* footnote 36.

(2) *The Explanation of Theology*

As we have seen, the word "grace" can have several meanings: *actively* it means the love one has for another; *passively*, a gift which is given out of such a love; and *effectively*, the gratitude of the beneficiary for the gift. In which of these senses—and here lies the Protestant dilemma—is grace now used?

The theologian, working from the data of faith, does not hesitate. He argues thus:

> "Grace" in this context is that by which man becomes pleasing to God and acceptable to him, i.e., the object of God's special love in the supernatural order.
>
> **But:** divine love is not determined and caused by the goodness which is in things themselves but is, on the contrary, the cause of that goodness.
>
> **Therefore:** the man who is pleasing to God in this way and loved by him cannot but possess in himself some reality caused by God.

The first statement of this "argument" (the **major**) is simply the affirmation in different words of the wonder about which only God could tell us: that despite man's sinfulness and unworthiness God loves him with a special and most intimate love. This is not that general love in virtue of which "he loves all things that are" (Wisd. 11:24), giving them their natural being; this is that special love for men which makes them like unto God, cleansed of sin, sons and heirs.

But God's love (a point unknown or deliberately ignored by the heretics) does not work like ours. Human love seeks the good, the lovableness it lacks, in some pre-existing thing. Divine love, on the contrary, seeks no good from any creature: God *is* love, subsisting goodness. Thus, as the second statement points out (the **minor**), God's love is the cause of the good which he loves in those whom he loves, this good being a communication of his own subsisting goodness.[34]

---

[34]Cf. *Summa*, I, q. 20, a. 2; *God and His Creation*, 208 ff.

Sometimes, to be sure, "grace" may signify God's eternal love itself; but normally, and as used here, it means a supernatural gift interior to man which God freely gives us.

(3) Conclusion

The conclusion we have reached as to the existence of grace as a supernatural entity is valid, it is evident, not only for the habitual gift infused into the souls of the just which we call **sanctifying grace,** but also for the transitory divine movement known as **actual grace.** In this section, however, we will concentrate on the investigation of the nature of sanctifying grace. Since it is *supernatural,* since it is a distinct *entity,* there will be two points of inquiry: 1) how is grace supernatural (its formal and specific aspect)? 2) what kind of being is it?

B. The Formal Aspect of Grace

(1) Preliminary Notions

In what precise sense is grace *supernatural?* We know already that the supernatural in its fullest meaning (which is here in question) so exceeds the entire order of created natures (really existing or only possible), so transcends the powers and exigencies of each and every creature, that it can neither be a natural thing, nor come from the principles of nature, nor in any way be demanded by nature: of its very being it infinitely surpasses all of nature and therefore all that may be conceived as owed to nature.[35] The *supernatural,* then, is **that which is connatural to the Godhead alone and proper only to God as he is in himself**—not as conceived by us nor with respect to those perfections he has in common with his creatures, but precisely

---

[35]Theologians distinguish the *intrinsically* supernatural, which is such in virtue of the interior principles of its being (the Godhead, for example; sanctifying grace, etc.), from beings intrinsically natural and only *extrinsically* supernatural because ordained to an end above nature (eating, ordained by charity to man's supernatural goal) or produced in a manner entirely beyond nature (miracles). The first sense, which is the most proper sense of the word, is used here.

as he transcends the entire order of created natures: *subsistent being, pure act—the divine nature and all that follows from the Godhead under its most formal aspect.*

Is grace—a created entity, a reality distinct from God—thus *connatural* to God? Certainly not, obviously not, in the sense that it would be substantially identical with God; it is patently absurd, a contradiction in terms, that anything created should, in virtue of intrinsic, substantial principles, be that which God is by essence: subsistent being and pure act. Nevertheless God does communicate what is exclusively and properly his to his rational creatures; grace is truly and intrinsically supernatural. This can only come about if what is communicated is not fully and adequately what God is, but rather only partially, incompletely, inadequately so—a sharing of what is God's, not an identity; a lesser realization, an imitation, not a duplication. *Grace is a partaking, a participation* (= "taking part of") *of what is connaturally and properly God's.*

But every participation involves two elements, the precise thing which is shared; and the manner, degree or extent of partaking of that shared thing. What of God's do we share by grace? And in what way is this participation realized by grace?

(2) *Grace: a Participation of the Divine Nature*

All creatures participate in the divine perfections—existence, or life, or intellectuality, these are common to God and his creatures, but the infinite perfection they possess in God cannot be communicated to any creature. Yet grace is a *supernatural* participation, a sharing of something exclusively God's. And thus if the infinite mode of these common perfections cannot be shared, then there must exist divine perfections which not only in their manner of existing in God (infinitely) but of their very nature are proper to God alone: such a participation would be intrinsically supernatural (of something connatural to the Godhead alone as proper only to him), even though the partaking would be realized in an inadequate, limited and finite manner. Which of these exclusively divine perfections does grace share in?

The answer can only come from revelation; before a reality so intimately divine, human reason is as blind as a stone. And in his love and mercy God does tell us: *grace is a participation of that very nature which is God's alone,* and thus a communication of that intimately divine life shared only by the Father and by the Son and by the Holy Spirit.

To teach this revealed fact, St. Paul did not hesitate to adopt the pantheistic expression of a pagan poet. "In [God] we live and move and have our being," he instructs the Athenians, "as indeed some of your own poets have said, 'For we are also his offspring'" (Acts 17:28). St. John phrases the same truth no less realistically: "Behold what manner of love the Father has bestowed upon us, that we should be called children of God; and such we are. . . . Beloved, now we are the children of God, and it has not yet appeared what we shall be. We know that, when he appears, we shall be like to him, for we shall see him just as he is" (I John 3:1-2). But we can only be sons of God and like to him, "born of God" (John 1:13) and "reborn, not from corruptible seed but incorruptible" (I Pet. 1:23), if we share the very nature of the Father. This is the fact which moves St. Peter to state bluntly that we have become "partakers of the divine nature" (II Pet. 1:4), and St. Paul to call grace a new life (Rom. 6:4), a renovation of our souls (Ephes. 4:23), and even a second creation (Gal. 4:15; Ephes. 2:10).

A sharing of God's own nature and life—that, God has revealed to us, is exactly what sanctifying grace is. So clear is the testimony that this divine marvel, beyond man's wildest imaginings, farther from his gaze and guess than the unknown limits of outer space, is nonetheless unhesitatingly and constantly affirmed by the Fathers in the name of the Church.[36] St. Thomas but echoes this received tradition when he writes: "The only begotten Son of God, wishing to make us

---

[36]So universal and continual is their teaching on this point as to constitute an infallible witness of the revealed truth; the multiplicity and variety of their assertions preclude any citations here. For specific (although incomplete) references, cf. M. J. Rouët de Journel, S.J., *Enchiridion Patristicum,* 14 ed. (Barcelona: Editorial Herder, 1946), "Index Theologicus," p. 773, nn. 356-361, especially n. 358.

partakers of his own divinity, took upon himself our human nature, that having become man he might make men gods."[37]

And so against the pretensions of proud humanism, against the despair and pessimism of Luther and Calvin, and now against the encroaching tide of modern secularism the Church affirms the shining truth of grace, of the higher, Godlike nature which destines man for God's own perfection and the riches of the happiness proper to God. Every day in the Roman Mass the priest recites the beautiful prayer expressing this truth:

> O God, who in creating human nature didst marvellously ennoble it, and hast still more marvelously renewed it, grant that by the mystery of this water and wine we may be made partakers of his Godhead, who vouchsafed to become partaker of our humanity, Jesus Christ, thy Son, our Lord.[38]

(3) Grace: a Formal and Physical Participation

From what has been said above it will be easy to answer our second question concerning grace as a participation, namely, in what

[37]Lesson for the Office commissioned by the Church for the feast of Corpus Christi (cf. P. Mandonnet, O.P., *Opuscula Omnia*, V [Paris: Lethielleux, 1927], 465). This is a more or less direct borrowing from the Fathers, several of whom employed the same phrases: St. Athanasius (*On the Incarnation of the Word and against the Arians*, 8), St. John Chrysostom (*Homilies on St. Matthew*, 2:2), St. Augustine (*Letter 140* [to Honoratus], Chap. 3, n. 9), St. John Damascene (*On the True Faith*, Bk. IV, Chap. 8).

It is worthy of note that St. Thomas devotes not a single article in the *Summa* to this aspect of grace, although he explicitly calls it a "participation of the divine nature" (I-II, q. 110, a. 3 and a. 4) in his treatment of the essence of grace, and it serves as the key of that treatment and can be directly and immediately deduced from it. This would be an inexplicable omission if history did not teach us that this truth was so much a part of received tradition in his time as to serve as an unassailable *principle*, not a conclusion to be discovered or defended, as we now must do in the face of the Nominalists' doubts and difficulties and Protestant denials. For the rest, this revealed fact is so constant and recurring a teaching of his as almost to be a theme: II *Sent.*, d. 26, q. 1, a. 3 and ad 2, a. 4 ad 2 and ad 3; IV *Sent.*, d. 5, q. 1, a. 3, q1a. 1; *De Ver.*, q. 27, a. 1, ad 6, a. 2 and ad 7, a. 3, a. 6; *Con. Gent.*, III, chap. 147 and chap. 151; *Summa*, I, q. 13, a. 9 and ad 1, a. 10; I-II, q. 112, a. 1, q. 113, a. 9, q. 114, a. 4; II-II, q. 24, a. 7; III, q. 2, a. 10, ad 1, q. 3, a. 4, ad 3, q. 62, a. 1 and a. 2; *De Car.*, a. 2, ad 15; etc.

[38]Prayer at the Offertory of the Mass. The Church has never found need to issue a solemn declaration defining this truth, no doubt because it is so clearly taught by her ordinary *magisterium*.

manner does grace share in the divine nature? There are various kinds or degrees of participation, summarized in this outline:

$$
\left\{
\begin{array}{l}
\text{formal} \left\{
\begin{array}{l}
\text{moral} \\
\text{physical} \left\{
\begin{array}{l}
\text{univocal} \\
\text{analogical}
\end{array}
\right. \\
\end{array}
\right. \\
\text{virtual}
\end{array}
\right.
$$

If the participating subject and the thing participated share intrinsically and formally in one common form, then the participation is *formal;* thus goodness is a form common to God and creatures, participated in *formally* by the creature. Such a form may be of the moral order, like dignity or sanctity or justness, and then the participation, although formal, will be *moral.* Or it may be of the order of beings and entities, of the physical order, and then the formal participation will be *physical,* as dog and cat properly and physically partake of the same common form, animality. On the other hand, if no common form is shared, then the participation is called *virtual,* either because the one participating has a power to produce an effect proper to the thing participated or because that which is formally contained in the one participating is found in the participated thing only causally and eminently (in this way every created nature may be called a *virtual* participation of the divine).

In the light of these distinctions we can immediately conclude that grace is not only a virtual participation but **formal,** since it is a true and real sharing of that unique form which is the divine nature, physically and formally imitating that radical principle of properly divine operations. It is a **physical** participation also, not merely moral, for by it we share not only God's sanctity, dignity, etc., but their basic root, i.e., the physical entity which is the divine nature. This participation is not univocal, of course, as if the divine nature were absolutely the same in God and in us, like animality in the cat and the dog; it is an **analogical** participation, in the sense that by grace we are in the accidental and created order what God is in the substantial and uncreated order.

Grace, then, is *a formal and physical but analogical participation of the very nature of God.*

C. Grace as an Entity

We have seen what grace is precisely under the aspect of its supernaturality; now we must determine what kind of *being* it is, what place it holds in the hierarchy of created realities. Undoubtedly this is a profound and therefore difficult inquiry, but the scientific formulation which is its end offers a necessary and very practical clarification of the nature of grace.

With our previously acquired knowledge of what grace is, we can, with the guidance of St. Thomas, reach the following conclusions:

1. **Grace is an accident.** All of created reality is divided into two great clases, that of *substance* (things which exist of themselves and in their own right: a man, the tree outside the window) and that of *accident* (realities which modify substances and exist only in dependence on them: the wisdom of a man, the beauty of the tree). It is clear that grace must belong to the accidental order of things: it inheres in the soul, something contrary to the very nature of substance but quite proper for accidents. Moreover, since grace is intrinsically supernatural, if it were a substance, then what is proper and connatural only to God would belong to it by nature, not by participation; these things would then be common both to God and to this created being, and hence no longer supernatural.

Grace, then, is an accident, but what kind of accident is it? Only further specification will produce an accurate knowledge of its nature.

2. **Grace is a quality.** All of revelation points to the fact that sanctifying grace is a permanent form within us,[39] disposing us in our being itself for divine life and divine activity—not temporarily, or now and

---

[39]The same scriptural arguments are valid here as those used to show the interiority of grace, *supra*, 274-275. Moreover, the statements of the Council of Trent so clearly imply this (cf. Denz. 796, 798, 799, 800, 803, 809, 813, 821, 834, 894) that many theologians hold that the permanence of grace as a distinct interior form is a matter of faith, its denial heretical. It is not defined, however, that grace is a quality or habit in the philosophical sense, although this is a theologically certain conclusion.

again, but habitually: a renovation, a regeneration, a re-creation. It is the life-principle of an utterly new kind of life, the supernatural life which is natural for no creature; and thus we declared grace to be a formal and physical participation of the very essence of God (subsistent being and pure act) precisely as that essence is the root and principle of divine operations.

Aristotle described **quality** as that kind of accidental reality "by reason of which a being is said to be such or such" (a man wise or a tree beautiful), a notion preserved by the technical definition given by philosophy: *a modification or determination of a substance in itself*. It seems clear that this is exactly the sort of thing sanctifying grace is, a perfecting disposition of a created substance in itself.

St. Thomas reaches the same conclusion by a compelling and revealing argument:

> It is not fitting that God should provide less for those whom he so loves that they can possess supernatural good than for the creatures whom his love orders to the possession of natural good. For natural creatures, however, he has so provided that he not only moves them to natural acts but also gives them definite forms and powers to serve as principles of action, in order that creatures of themselves might be inclined to these acts. In this way the movements whereby they are moved by God become easy and connatural, according to the assertion of the Book of Wisdom, "She governs all things well" (8:1).
>
> So much the more, then, does he infuse certain forms or supernatural qualities in those whom he moves to the attainment of eternal supernatural good. In virtue of these qualities they are moved by him agreeably and promptly to possessing eternal good.
>
> And so the gift of grace is a certain quality.[40]

3. **Grace is a habit.** It is but a short step from the conclusion that grace is a quantity to the fact that grace is that species of quality which philosophers and theologians call *habit*. For habit is that type of quality which disposes its subject well or ill in itself, and is difficult to change. Certainly grace disposes us well, since it does so for eternal life. Not so obvious, perhaps, is the fact that grace is difficult to change. Yet we have established the fact that it is something permanent, we have styled it a "second nature," we speak of it as a

[40]*Summa*, I-II, q. 110, a. 2.

state of existence,[41] with all the stability and firmness that the term implies. Actually it is not easy for one living in grace to commit the mortal sin which destroys the divine life of his soul.[42] Inhering in the mind, strengthening all our spiritual faculties, grace is never simply lost, it does not fade or melt away, it does not slip from our grasp. No, only by the deliberate act, the free choice of the created in place of the divine, does man enter the state of spiritual death which is sin. Man does not "fall" into sin as into a hole, he jumps in.

4. **Grace is an entitative habit.** If grace is a good habit, is it not identical with virtue? Not with acquired virtues, since it is supernatural; not with the infused moral virtues, whose primary concern is the human, not the divine; not with faith or hope, which may still remain even when grace ceases to exist. The only virtue with which grace might be identified is charity.

Yet both Sacred Scripture[43] and the Church[44] speak of them separately, as of distinct realities. Following this hint, the theologian concludes with certainty that grace and charity are two different things.

Sanctifying grace is primarily and *per se* a participation of the divine nature, existing in us after the manner of a nature; charity, on the other hand, is an immediate principle of operation. But for all of created reality there is necessarily a real distinction between a nature and its powers.[45] Since grace perfects nature and does not pervert or destroy it, this same difference between nature and power will be maintained at the higher level of supernatural life.

Since grace is a habit but not a virtue (a good operative habit), then it must be an *entitative* habit, one which modifies and disposes the entity itself rather than its powers. Just as beauty disposes the whole

[41]"Justification is a passing from the state in which man is born a son of the first Adam, to the state of grace and 'adoption of sons of God' (Rom. 8:15) through the second Adam, Jesus Christ our Savior"; Council of Trent, *loc. cit.*, Chap. 4, "Description of the Justification of the Impious and the Manner of Justification in the State of Grace" (Denz. 796).

[42]Cf. St. Thomas, *De Veritate*, q. 27, a. 1, ad 9.

[43]Cf. II Cor. 13:13; I Tim. 1:14.

[44]Cf. Council of Vienne (Denz. 483), Council of Trent, *loc. cit.*, Chap. 7 (Denz. 799) and Can. 11 (Denz. 821).

[45]St. Thomas, *Summa*, I, q. 54, a. 3, q. 77, a. 1.

material substance of the tree, so grace is the kind of accidental reality which modifies and perfects the soul itself in its essence, becoming the divine form of that soul and its supernatural beauty. Thus also this communication of the divine nature is constituted the single, common substratum of the various supernatural faculties which physically and necessarily emanate from it[46] (as in the natural order man's powers flow from the soul's essence as properties of it), and through these powers it is also the common substructure of man's divine operations. In very truth, sanctifying grace, even though it is not a substance, is a **supernature**, divinizing man in the root and principle of his being and his activity.

D. Theological Perspectives

The scientific analysis of grace just completed provides us with a meaningful and profound theological definition: **sanctifying** or **habitual grace** is *a supernatural entitative habit by which intellectual creatures participate physically, formally, but analogically, in the divine nature as it is in itself.*

A wonder so divine as grace can never be fully understood by man, for that would be to understand God himself. But a brief consideration now of the effects it works within us may aid us to a deeper appreciation of this singular mark of divine predilection.[47]

1. By grace we share in God's own nature, in that essence which is subsistent being and that nature which is pure act. Moreover, directly but secondarily we also share in the essential attributes of God (immediately, through the virtues and gifts which flow from grace) and in the divine fecundity and inexpressible circulation of divinity which is the Trinity (mediately—by means of virtues and gifts—through the divine actions of which we are capable).

---

[46]For this reason St. Thomas very often calls habitual or sanctifying grace "the grace of the virtues and the gifts."

[47]For a fuller development of these important points see M. J. Scheeben, *Nature and Grace* (trans. by Cyril Vollert, S.J.; St. Louis and London: B. Herder Book Co., 1954), Chapter IX, "Qualities and Effects of Supernature," and Chapter X, "Powers and Acts of Supernature."

2. Thus the image of the Trinity which is our birthright as intellectual creatures is immeasurably perfected by grace. The imperfect and remote analogy of nature with the divine Persons issues through this "image of re-creation" in a faithful reflection and perfect resemblance of that transcendent, mysterious process by which the one divine nature is possessed by the Trinity of divine Persons.[48] For by the powers which grace brings we can know God's essense *as it is in itself*, and thus form an internal "word" of God and a love expressive and imitative of the Spirit.

3. By grace we share the divine sonship of Christ. What the Word of God is by his divine nature, the Son of God, we are by grace, for we truly are his offspring, possessing by participation the identical divine nature which is Christ's. The fact of our divine adoption as sons is insisted on by St. Paul;[49] the stupendous reality of the fact is made real by grace: we are his sons because he begets us in his image and in a similarity of nature.

We are of the very family of God, loved by God with that selfsame love with which he regards his natural Son, not servants of the household only but his friends (John 15:14-15). And if we are sons, we are also heirs (Gal. 4:7): by grace ours is the divine inheritance of the personal goods of God, ours a right to the infinite riches, the infinite happiness which belong to God alone.

4. Grace enables us to live the life of God himself. We share in God's own nature, and that nature is the root principle of divine knowledge and divine love and divine beatitude, for us as for him. By this new nature even our natural powers of action are transformed, re-created, divinized, so that even the most meager and inconsequential of man's actions is of divine value, intrinsically greater than the noblest natural effort of the world's greatest genius.

---

[48]The perfection of this supernatural imaging of the Trinity is realized by supernatural acts, and thus more perfectly in the beatific knowledge and love of God; but since everything exists virtually in its principles, this image of grace will be found in all those who possess the supernatural virtues and gifts. Cf. *God and His Creation*, 458 ff.

[49]Cf. Rom. 8:14-17, 30; Ephes. 1:5; Gal. 4:5.

5. "If any one love me, he will keep my word, and my Father will love him, and we will come to him and make our abode with him" (John 14:23). God is everywhere as the source and conserver of all beings, the cause of their every movement. But in those in the state of grace he dwells as in a temple, our friend and our guest: Father, Son and Holy Spirit are really and physically present in a new and singular way, precisely as objects of our participated divine knowledge and love, of our possession and enjoyment. When we share in the divine knowledge from which the Son proceeds as Word, he is sent into our hearts as the Word of the Father; by our love of God by charity, which is like his love from which the Spirit proceeds as fruit and term, the Holy Spirit is given to us; and the Father is present also, known and loved as principle of Son and of Spirit.[50]

6. For those who are in the state of sin, original or personal, sanctifying grace provides a remission of sin and a spiritual renovation of the interior man, for grace makes men holy with the holiness of God. This supernature shares in the divine holiness by imparting to our nature an excellence, purity and stability in goodness such as belong only to the Godhead, and consequently brings about a removal from the evil which is sin which is as great as the change from nothingness to infinity.

6. THE DIVISIONS OF GRACE

A great deal has been written about the kinds of grace, and how they are divided. Much of this writing is both highly technical and controversial, and practically all of it is beyond the scope of a text such as this. For our purposes it will suffice to give the general divisions of grace, both essential and accidental, and to offer a brief explanation of St. Thomas' teaching on the harmony of freedom and the impulse of actual grace.

[50]Cf. Pope Leo XIII, *Divinum Illud Munus* (encyclical on the Holy Spirit) and Pope Pius XII, *Mystici Corporis*.

A. The Various Kinds of Grace

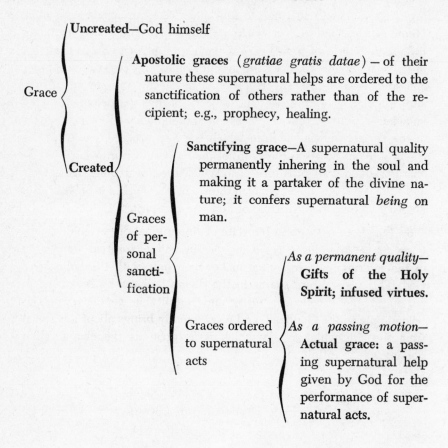

Uncreated—God himself

Apostolic graces (*gratiae gratis datae*) — of their nature these supernatural helps are ordered to the sanctification of others rather than of the recipient; e.g., prophecy, healing.

Sanctifying grace—A supernatural quality permanently inhering in the soul and making it a partaker of the divine nature; it confers supernatural *being* on man.

As a permanent quality— **Gifts of the Holy Spirit; infused virtues.**

As a passing motion— **Actual grace: a passing supernatural help given by God for the performance of supernatural acts.**

Grace — Created — Graces of personal sanctification — Graces ordered to supernatural acts

(1) Graces of the Apostolate

Apostolic graces are provided to prepare some men to bring other men to God. Accidentally, they may aid in the recipient's sanctification, but that is not their primary function. Since only God can draw a man to himself by an internal movement of the will, the apostolic graces work externally by teaching and persuading.

The enumeration of these graces (representative rather than exhaustive) is given by St. Paul (I Cor. 12:8-10). St. Thomas explains them as means for proclaiming the teaching of Christ, and for persuading others to accept that teaching. Teaching and persuasion require three things: first, a knowledge of the doctrine; secondly, an ability to confirm the doctrine; and thirdly, an ability to propose the doctrine clearly and persuasively. Hence, the apostolic graces are divided in this way:

1) To insure adequate konwledge of divine doctrine, there are three graces: **faith, knowledge** and **wisdom.**

2) To enable the apostle to confirm his doctrine he should be equipped to do things that only God can do, and thus there are the graces of **healing** and **miracles;** and he should be able to disclose things that only God can know, and for this there are the graces of **prophecy** and the **discernment of spirits.**

3) Finally, the apostle should be able to communicate his message clearly, and for this there are the graces of the **gift of tongues** and of the **interpretation of speech.**[51]

(2) Graces of Personal Sanctification

Graces of personal sanctification (*gratia gratum faciens*) are ordered to the sanctification of the recipient, although accidentally (e.g., through good example) they might help others. These are the principal graces, for through them man is effectively brought to God and not merely disposed for God, as he is through the apostolic graces.

As we have seen, **sanctifying grace** is an accidental but permanent modification of the soul, in virtue of which man really and truly, although analogously, shares in the very nature of God and the divine life. But like the soul, this grace is not immediately operative, although it is the radical source and principle of divine operations. From this "second nature" flow the powers of divine life in man, the supernatural modifications of his natural powers which constitute the proximate principles of his participated divine life: the **theological virtues** (faith, hope and charity), the **infused moral virtues** (prudence, justice, fortitude, temperance), and the **gifts of the Holy Spirit.** Beyond these permanent supernatural qualities, man needs God's special

[51]*Summa,* I-II, q. 111, a. 4. Cf. III *Con. Gent.,* Chap. 154, for an interesting and detailed account of these special graces.

activating assistance to bring his supernatural potentialities into actual operations and sustain these acts at the level of divine activity: **actual grace.**

The special divine movement which is actual grace gives rise to an accidental division of grace (where grace differs from grace not by essence but only under some secondary aspect) of great practical importance.

B. Accidental Divisions of Grace

Of the various ways in which actual graces can accidentally be distinguished from one another, the following two most directly affect us in the practical order.

(1) Operating and Co-operating Grace

Depending on its effect on the will, actual grace is divided into *operating* and *co-operating* grace. The initial grace of repentance, for example, is an "operating grace," under the influence of which the will is moved by grace rather than moving itself. Once the will is aroused, however, the grace becomes "co-operating" as soon as the will begins to move itself with the assistance of grace. In other words, the selfsame grace is called "operating" when it moves the will to act, "co-operating" when it divinely assists the will so moved in the fulfillment of its action.

(2) Sufficient and Efficacious Grace

Actual grace is also divided accidentally into *sufficient* and *efficacious* grace. This distinction is based on the role of proximity of actual grace in the production of supernatural acts. We will discuss this division in the section which follows.

C. Human Freedom under Grace

Any effort to solve the problem of man's freedom under the impulse of actual grace must be prefaced by the realization that no ultimate solution is possible in this life. A supernatural mystery is here involved, and the human mind cannot comprehend the workings of God: divine motion is identified with the divine essence, which is infinite, and therefore cannot be comprehended by any creature. This fact, however, should not prevent men from striving to understand what God has revealed to the best of their ability. It is reasonable to seek an explanation which is free of intrinsic contradiction and capable of refuting objections, even though in so profound a matter such an accomplishment assumes commanding proportions.

Underlying this problem, there are two truths of faith which must be held without deviation or compromise. The first truth is that God is the first and universal cause of all things; God's knowledge is universal and infallible and not caused in any way by creatures. The second truth of faith is that man is free, even in his supernatural acts. About these two truths there is no problem.

The problem arises precisely in attempting to harmonize these two truths of faith, and it may be expressed in two questions:

1) How can God move the will in such a way that it remains truly free?

2) How does God know the free movements of the human will?

(1) Principles of the Solution

Four truths must underlie any adequate solution of this problem:

1) Every being in potency must be moved to act by a being already in act.

2) God's knowledge is not caused by creatures; rather it is the cause of creatures.

3) Man's will cannot be determined by anything created, because it is free or undetermined regarding everything except the beatific vision.

4) The motion of God's grace extends not only to the substance of a thing or to its act, but also to every mode and circumstance that affects them.

(2) Solution of St. Thomas

It is the teaching of St. Thomas that actual grace is of two kinds:

1) **Sufficient grace** is a passing supernatural motion from God which brings the will to a perfect preparation *in the order of potentiality* and makes the will adequately proportioned for the performance of a salutary act.

2) **Efficacious grace** is a passing supernatural motion from God which applies the prepared will to *act*, so that man performs an act meritorious of salvation.

Thus for St. Thomas, grace is *intrinsically* efficacious. It does not become efficacious because the will accepts it; nor is it efficacious because it is given in congenial and opportune circumstances, which then have a role in determining what man will do. Rather, efficacious grace is efficacious *because God makes it so.* By means of *physical* premotion (as opposed to *moral* persuasion) grace not only reduces the will to act, it causes the mode of freedom in the act and sustains the will in its act.

(3) Objections and Resolutions

Historically and practically, certain objections come to mind against this explanation of St. Thomas. Their solution will throw further light on the subject.

1. *Sufficient grace is made superfluous; what is sufficient grace sufficient for?* It is a principle verified in philosophy that a being in the state of potency must be *prepared* for act; it progresses from remote to proximate potency. Sufficient grace pertains *to the order of potency*, and in that order it suffices to prepare the will for efficacious grace. Sufficient grace is certainly not of itself sufficient for salvation, because it cannot produce any acts by itself. But it must be remembered that efficacious grace could not be effective unless sufficient grace were sufficient in its own proper order.

2. *Physical premotion destroys freedom by determining the will to its act.* This is an anthropomorphic concept. Physical premotion, far from destroying, rather *causes* the freedom of the act, for the divine

motion causes not only the act but the very mode of the act, its freedom. The very manner in which this act occurs—*freely*—must come from God.

St. Thomas offers this explanation:

> Free will is the cause of its own movement, because man moves himself to act of his free will. Nonetheless, it does not necessarily pertain to liberty that what is free should be the first cause of itself, just as it is not required for one thing to be the cause of another that it be the first cause.
>
> Now God is the first cause moving both natural and voluntary causes. And just as by moving natural causes he does not prevent their acts from being natural, so in moving voluntary causes he does not prevent their actions from being free, but rather causes this [freedom] in them; for he works in each one according to its own proper nature.[52]

3. *The Council of Trent teaches that the will can reject grace.*[53] *Therefore, grace is not intrinsically efficacious, but extrinsically, through the consent of the recipient.* That the will remains *able* to resist efficacious grace is true; but *actual* resistance to efficacious grace is never offered, otherwise the grace would not be efficacious.

A celebrated distinction is employed here to show exactly how the will remains truly free when premoved to a determined act by efficacious grace. When the movement of grace and the act so determined are considered together (*in sensu composito*), then the will cannot fail to perform that act. When the grace and the determined act are considered separately (*in sensu diviso*), then the will can fail to perform the act.

When man combines his ability to sit with the act of sitting (*in sensu composito*) then he cannot stand, although at the same time he retains the power to do so (*in sensu diviso*).

4. *Sufficient grace is useless, for it cannot produce an act without efficacious grace.* We have shown that sufficient grace is *indispensable* in its proper domain, which is the order of potency. Sufficient grace makes man responsible for his failure, for God does not deny efficacious grace to those who receive sufficient grace except because of some fault which precedes the withholding of efficacious grace (at

---

[52]*Summa*, I, q. 83, a. 1, ad 3.
[53]*Loc. cit.*, Sess. VI, Can. 4; Denz. 814.

least in the order of nature, if not of time). Whoever are saved are saved by God's mercy, and whoever are lost are lost through their sin.[54]

7. The Causes of Grace

Under this general heading we shall consider not only the elements which enter into the production of grace but also man's role in preparing for grace and his ability to recognize whether he possesses grace or not.

A. The Cause of Grace

(1) The Principal Cause of Grace

By sanctifying grace a man becomes the adopted son of God; he shares in the divine nature by a participated likeness; he is raised to a supernatural life that is beyond the needs and powers of all created nature. It is evident, then, that this marvellous gift can come only from God. The greater cannot come from the less; what is proper to God alone, *his* nature, *his* life, can only be shared by his giving and his gift. If man is to become like to God, only God can effect this as the principal efficient cause.

This is taught by the Psalmist: "For a sun and a shield is the Lord God; grace and glory be bestows" (83:12). And the Church proposes the same teaching as a matter of faith.[55]

(2) The Subject of Grace

Although God is its principal efficient cause, properly speaking, we cannot maintain that grace is created. Creation eliminates any pre-existing subject, and grace always exists in some subject, i.e., either in a man or in an angel. Grace is an accident, like whiteness; its existence is entirely in its subject, it has no independent existence.

---

[54]A resumé of one of the most celebrated controversies about actual grace is had in: Aelred Whitacre, O.P., "The *Congregatio de Auxiliis*," *Dublin Review*, 376 (1930), 71-87.

[55]Council of Trent, *loc. cit.*, Chap. 7; Denz. 799.

Whence, then, does it come? Grace is said to be brought forth by God from what is known as an "obediential potency," of a kind found only in rational creatures. Human nature is in that higher stratum of intellectual beings where only God and his angels are companions. As such it is in potency to supernatural perfections which can be realized by no natural agent but only by God, whom it "obeys" in order to receive from him whatever he chooses to give. This receptivity for divine action, a certain absence of opposition to supernatural fulfillment—this is a purely passive aptitude, to be sure, in no way ordained to operation nor demanding completion. Thus in the natural order a piece of marble (unlike a bowl of soup, for example) possesses an obediential potency of becoming a statue, should a Michelangelo so shape it; but it has no need to become a figure of Moses, it retains all its natural being and perfection even though this potency is never realized.

But passive though it is, obediential potency is very real. None of the lower orders of being—dog or flower or stone—possesses any such aptitude for supernatural perfecting through God's gracious action; on the contrary, by nature theirs is a non-receptiveness, a repugnance to such elevation. Men and angels, being intellectual, do have this capacity, however, and God brings forth from it the wonders which are his graces. It is for this reason that theologians hold that man, precisely as he is a natural image of God (i.e., endowed with intellect and will) is capax Dei, capable of being, of knowing and loving God as he is in himself, not by natural powers but by supernatural elevation.

(3) The Instrumental Causes of Grace

God himself is the principal, physical, efficient cause of grace. Between himself as principal cause of grace and man as the recipient, God has established certain instrumental causes of grace. These are the sacred humanity of Christ and his sacraments of the New Law, which are the physical instruments by which God communicates to men through Christ a share in the divine life.[56]

---

[56]A detailed explanation of this instrumental causality may be found in Christ, and His Sacraments, 151-155, 303-312. For Mary's role in the distribution of grace, cf. ibid., 276-278.

Two things must be noted here. First, God does not limit his causality of grace to the sacraments; he remains the principal efficient cause and may confer grace by means other than the sacraments. God does not become a prisoner of his own institutions, even—as in the case of the sacraments—when he makes them the ordinary means of conferring grace. What these extraordinary means of salvation may be has not been revealed to us, but the reality of their existence is deduced from the general doctrine that God wills that all men be saved.[57] Secondy, even when one man possesses grace, he is not thereby capable of communicating it to others. For grace never becomes natural to man; he has it only by participation. Similarly, an adopted son is not able to adopt others into the family which accepts him.

B. Man's Preparation for Grace

(1) *The Need for Preparation*

A transformation as complete as that effected by habitual grace requires some disposition in the recipient for this participation of the divine nature. Habitual grace is an accidental form which transforms the soul, and a form so perfect and permanent requires, according to the ordinary dispositions of divine providence, that its subject be disposed to receive it, just as wood must be dried before it can be enkindled.

The *initial* disposition for the reception of sanctifying grace by those who have the use of reason is produced through the movements of actual grace. This is completed by a *perfect* disposition which is concomitant with the infusion of sanctifying grace itself. In the case of infants, however, through the merits of Christ the entire preparation is concomitant with the infusion of sanctifying grace. Infants are not subject to the movement of actual grace because it affects the intellect and the will, the use of which they do not yet enjoy. In this

---

[57]Cf. *De Veritate*, q. 14, a. 11, ad 1. Helpful in this question is: Francis S. Shea: "The Principles of Extra-Sacramental Justification," *Proceedings C.T.S.A.*, X (1955), 125-149.

instance grace perfects nature, but it is an exception which does not eliminate the need for nature.

When a man is moved by actual grace he is not reduced to the state of God's puppet; there must also be a free movement of his will.[58] But this movement of the will under the impetus of actual grace does not presuppose a prior motion of grace as its own preparation; otherwise there would be an endless series of preparations.

(2) God and Man

There are two elements, then, in the preparation of man for habitual grace: the impetus of actual grace whereby God is the primary mover, and the action of the free will which is the secondary cause of the preparation. If, however, we were to consider the efforts of the free will independently of the impulse of actual grace, then no such purely natural effort could possibly attain sanctifying grace. Grace infinitely exceeds all the needs and powers of nature.

Divine grace is bestowed through God's love; it cannot be seized by any human effort. If, however, man's efforts to prepare himself for grace are inspired and sustained by actual grace, then such preparation will infallibly obtain sanctifying grace. Originating with actual grace, man's preparation becomes proportioned to the effect of disposing him for supernatural life. Thus Christ says, "Everyone who has listened to the Father, and has learned, comes to me" (John 6:45). It is in this sense—and only in this sense—that one can understand the famous axiom: "God does not deny grace to him who does what lies within his power to attain it."

Preparation for grace as well as the bestowing of grace is God's work in the order of efficient causality; preparation for grace, under the impetus of grace, is man's work in the order of physical dispositive causality. These are correlatives, not alternatives. It is perfectly true

---

[58]This is defined as a matter of faith by the Council of Trent, *loc. cit.*, Can. 9 (Denz. 819): "If anyone shall say that a sinner is justified by faith alone, so that this is taken to mean that nothing else is required whereby he co-operates to obtain the grace of justification, and that it is unnecessary that he be prepared and disposed by the action of his own will, let him be condemned."

to say that we must pray *because* everything depends upon God, and we must work *because* everything depends upon ourselves.

(3) The Possession of Grace

Since not only grace but the preparation for grace is God's work, do all men, regardless of their dispositions and their efforts at preparation, share equally in the divine nature?

Obviously, from one point of view, sanctifying grace, insofar as it confers a participation of the *same* divine nature and marks the beginning of possession by creatures of the *same* God, is the same for all.

Yet it is equally obvious that not all men share equally in the possession of grace. Why this difference? Radically, of course, this is explained by God's willingness to admit different men to different degrees of intimacy in his friendship: "To each one of us grace was given according to the measure of Christ's bestowal" (Eph. 4:7). He alone provides the initiative. But since you yourself must respond to this invitation—or any other man for that matter—the reason for the differences of the sharing in this grace come down to the generosity with which each man prepares himself, under the influence of God's movement, to receive so great a gift. And this diversity of possession of grace produces a harmony and variety in the beauty and perfection of Christ's Church: a column-sitter like St. Simeon Stylites may possess greater initial grace than a king like St. Louis of France.

C. Man's Knowledge of Possessing Grace

If grace results in such a complete transformation and is so intimately present, it would seem reasonable that a man would be acutely aware of either its presence or its absence. Nothing is more important than to lead the life of grace; nothing more tragic than not to. Can one be sure of being in the state of grace?

Clearly, a man can be certain of having grace if God reveals this fact to him, as when he said to St. Paul, "My grace is sufficient for thee" (II Cor. 12:9). But apart from such special revelation, no man can have absolute certainty of being in the state of grace. To have such knowledge would require a reading of the divine mind, and "who has known the mind of the Lord, or who has been his counsellor?" (Rom. 11:34).

Yet if anyone is to make wholehearted efforts in the spiritual life, he must have some assurance of grace. No one will walk very far amidst difficulties toward what he fears may be a mirage.

The attitude of the Christian toward his personal possession of divine grace must be based upon two realities: first, upon an unshakable faith in the mercy of God, the merits of Christ and the efficacy of prayer and the sacraments; secondly, upon a realistic appraisal of human weakness, that frailty which prompted St. Paul to warn us to ".... work out your salvation with fear and trembling" (Phil. 2:12). But bearing these factors always in mind, it is possible to have a *conjectural* knowledge of being in the state of grace. Such a knowledge will be based upon signs of the workings of grace in one's life.

These signs of the presence of grace are both negative and positive. *Negatively,* it is a sign of grace if one's conscience is free of any awareness of mortal sin. This may be a weak indication for those who are tepid and neglectful in their spiritual duties, but it comes close to moral certitude in the devout. Mortal sin is never an accident, it is a catastrophe; and a devout person is not likely to forget such a serious deliberate fall. This sign is greatly strengthened when it is accompanied by persevering sorrow for past offences, a true contrition which involves a firm resolve not to offend God again, and implies a willingness to endure temporal suffering rather than to sin grievously. *Positively,* the presence of grace is discerned in its fruits: to find joy in divine things such as the sacraments, prayer and hearing the word of God; to fulfill the divine will by keeping the commandments, and especially by performing the works of charity toward one's neighbors.

Conscious of the presence of these signs in himself, a man can be at peace in the realization that he enjoys the divine favor and is truly a friend and an adopted son of God.[59]

[59]For a brief and clear treatment of this entire question, cf. P. De Letter, S.J., "Am I in the State of Grace?", *Cross and Crown*, XI (1959), 140 ff.

8. THE FIRST EFFECT OF GRACE: JUSTIFICATION

Having seen our need for God's special assistance, what it is, how it is obtained, it remains now only to consider what it does, what we can do through and by means of this divine gift. Two chief effects are caused by grace: the first is justification, whereby a man is made holy and pleasing to God; the second is merit, which is the right to eternal reward earned by the justified man through his supernatural acts. Justification is prerequisite for merit, and hence it is treated first. Respecting this result produced by grace three things must be considered:

Justification
- Its nature
- Its elements
- Its excellence

A. The Nature of Justification

Properly speaking, justice implies the giving to each one what is his due; it means the establishment, conservation or restoration of due order between individuals and among groups. Of its nature justice implies a relationship to others; "self-contained" justice—justice toward oneself—is a metaphorical idea. Yet nonetheless there is a basis in reality for this metaphorical usage: whenever there are parts of a single totality that must be set in a harmonious order among themselves, "justice" may be established among them, the proper relationship of part to part and part to whole.

In the present context, "justification" is thus used metaphorically to designate that effect of sanctifying grace whereby a man is removed from sin by having his reason made obedient to God (part to whole) and his lower powers subject to his reason (part to part). Justification, in everyday terms, consists in making a sinner into a saint. Spiritually, it is the restoration of the prodigal to an honored place in the home and among the children of his heavenly Father: it is the raising of the spiritually dead to supernatural life.

Father apart than heaven and earth are the Catholic and Protestant views of justification. For Luther and his followers, man is a sinner and remains such all his life. Without effecting any internal change in the sinner, God can *impute* to him the justice of Christ; and this God does, provided only that the sinner firmly trusts that God thus "justifies" him. Such justification is entirely extrinsic to the sinner; it does not remove his sins, it does not change him at all, it simply cloaks sin with the merits of Jesus Christ, as the dirty city streets are covered by snow. As long as the sinner firmly trusts that God does so impute Christ's merits to him, he remains justified in God's sight, even if he should sin again. In such a view justification is a *juridical* entity rather than a *spiritual* reality; the former is comparable to a court declaration that a man is innocent (and this may have nothing to do with his abiding internal guilt); the latter is a true internal renovation by which the sinner is truly changed from within from an enemy into a friend of God.

The full import of the divergence in these views will become clear as we explore the Catholic teaching in greater detail.

B. The Elements of Justification

To understand the true meaning of justification, it is important to keep in mind that so radical a change requires a movement of man from the state of sin or injustice to the state of grace or justice. The sinner is turned away from God in his pursuit of some created good, which he seeks in some way that is opposed to the divine order; in every sin there is an element of disorder, a disorganization of man's forces going astray in pursuit of some satisfaction that is beyond the limits established by the sweet yoke of divine love. To repair this, a contrary motion must be set up, an entirely new center of gravity established, a complete re-orientation, not of this or that desire, but of one's total being. So also must the man who walks south turn his back on the north. To accomplish this unrepentant and total re-dedication to God an infusion of divine grace is required.

This is why the Church expressly teaches: "If anyone shall say that men are justified either by the imputation of the merits of Christ alone, or by the remission of sins alone, to the exclusion of grace and charity which is poured forth in their hearts by the Holy Spirit and inheres in them, or also that the grace by which we are justified is only the favor of God, let him be condemned."[60]

A city is not rebuilt simply by ceasing to bomb it; neither is a man justified simply by ceasing to sin. A positive movement back to God is required, and man himself cannot make such a movement; it must come from the same God who was offended by sin. God must make a special act of love for the sinner, and that act of love results in an infusion of grace whereby an enemy is changed into a friend.

In keeping with man's nature and the nature of justification, the following elements are essential, although they are usually implicit and not clearly distinct in the consciousness of the sinner who returns to God:

1) The infusion of sanctifying grace.

2) Following upon this (subsequent in nature not in time), a movement of man's free will toward God, for God moves each creature according to its nature, and man is endowed with free will.[61]

3) An act of faith is required for justification in adults. "Having been justified therefore by faith, let us have peace with God through our Lord Jesus Christ, through whom we also have access by faith unto that grace in which we stand, and exult in the hope of the glory of the sons of God" (Rom. 5:1 f.). Psychologically, no one can desire what he does not know. Hence, the

---

[60]Council of Trent, *loc. cit.,* Can. 11; Denz. 821.

[61]"If anyone shall say that the free will of man aroused and moved by God does not co-operate with God awakening and calling him by an assent whereby he prepares and disposes himself for obtaining the grace of justification; or that man cannot resist grace if he wishes, but that he does nothing at all and is entirely passive like something lifeless, let him be condemned." Council of Trent, *loc. cit.,* Can. 4 (Denz. 814). Cf. *ibid.,* Can. 9, quoted *supra,* note 58.

It follows that adults must have an intention in receiving the sacraments of baptism or penance whereby they are justified; or at least a desire for these sacraments if they cannot be had in danger of death. Infants, who contract original sin through carnal generation, are justified by Christ through the spiritual regeneration of baptism.

mind must first assent to the truths of God before the will can turn to God.[62]

4) An act of detestation for sin is required in justification. "Cast away from you all your transgressions by which you have transgressed, and make to yourselves a new heart and a new spirit" (Ezech. 18:31). It is impossible for a man to turn to God while he clings to his sins.[63]

5) Finally, justification requires the forgiveness of sin by God. Only thus is peace restored between man and God. In this forgiveness the movement of justification is terminated.

These five elements essential to justification take place *simultaneously*, in an instant. An agent of limited power must labor to prepare his materials before he can work with them, as the metal must be softened in the forge before it can be shaped by the ironworker. This is not true of the omnipotent God, who disposes his creatures perfectly in the instant when he wishes to justify them.

How, then, can we understand those painful conversions of some sinners which take years? Ultimately, such delays are reducible to the divine will, which may leave a man to overcome many obstacles before returning to God's grace, possibly to teach us something of the chasm which separates the sinner from God. Whatever precedes the infusion of grace is a remote preparation; sometimes it is lengthy, sometimes instantaneous. But justification proper occurs in the instant when one begins to be the friend of God.

C. The Excellence of Justification

The justification of sinners is so clearly a sign of God's personal interest in each of his children, and so obviously contrary to the sinners' deserts, that we may reasonably inquire if this be God's greatest work. There are many aspects to such a question, and an answer

---

[62]This need for faith is expressly taught by the Church: Council of Trent, *loc. cit.*, Chap. 8; Denz. 801. Cf. Heb. 11:6, Rom. 4:5.

[63]This too is explicitly the teaching of the Church. Cf. Council of Trent, *loc. cit.*, Chap. 6 (Denz. 798), Sess. XIV, *On Penance*, Chap. 4 (Denz. 897).

must be sought in comparisons rather than in a simple affirmation or negation.

There is a sense in which creation is a greater work than justification, because creation begins with nothingness, whereas justification is the re-creation of a sinner in divine love. Yet this excellence of creation is offset by the fact that creation terminates in a good of the natural order, whereas justification brings man to a sharing in the divine nature, which is an eternal good. "The good of grace of one man," St. Thomas does not hesitate to say, "is greater than the good of nature of the entire universe."[64]

In the supernatural order, the glorification of the just confers a greater grace upon them than justification bestows upon sinners; the grace of the heavenly homeland is more precious than the grace of the wayfarer. Yet we must remember that the just man is *worthy* of glory, whereas the sinner has absolutely no claim upon divine forgiveness. In terms of those who receive it, then, justification is a greater gift than glorification.

Sometimes justification is said to be miraculous, as in the case of the conversion of a sinner under unusual circumstances. In the sense that justification is uniquely a divine work, there is about it an element of the miraculous. Yet sinners who are justified have a capacity, an obediential potency for divine grace, and hence justification, marvel that it is, is not ordinarily miraculous, since it takes place according to the customary workings of supernatural providence. Conversions may be called miraculous, however, if they occur in a manner beyond the ordinary rules of the spiritual life. The slow, gradual maturing that characterizes spiritual growth is sometimes dispensed with, as it was in the case of St. Paul. However, any kind of miracle is a rarity, and it would be unforgiveably presumptuous to expect miraculous conversion as the way of salvation.

9. THE SECOND EFFECT OF GRACE: MERIT

It is proper to speak of man meriting either reward or punishment. Theologically, however, **merit** is *that property of a human act where-*

[64]*Summa*, I-II, q. 113, a. 9, ad 1.

by it is worthy of a supernatural reward. Our consideration of merit will follow this order:

$$\text{Merit} \begin{cases} \text{Its nature} \\ \text{Its foundation} \\ \text{Its conditions} \\ \text{Its objects} \end{cases}$$

A. The Nature of Merit

That an adopted child should have a share in his foster-father's affection is more readily to be expected than that he should enjoy rights over the father's possessions. When the father is God the Creator and the adopted child a mere creature, the prospect of the creature having real rights is amazing. But how else can one understand the words of St. Paul? "The Spirit himself gives testimony to our spirit that we are sons of God. But if we are sons, we are heirs also; heirs indeed of God and joint heirs with Christ . . ." (Rom. 8:17).

All merit is based on an exchange: someone does something for another, and receives a reward in exchange. Sometimes this exchange is based on justice; sometimes on suitability or fittingness. Thus, there are various kinds of merit.

Merit
- Condign—when the merit rests upon justice.
  - According to strict justice—when the one rewarded is entirely independent.
  - According to proportionate justice—when the one rewarded has received the principle of merit from the rewarder.
- Congruous—when the merit is based upon the mercy and friendship of the rewarder, or upon the suitableness of the request of him who receives the reward.

The essential problem here, first stated in the Old Testament, was thus formulated by St. Paul: "Who has first given to [the Lord] that recompense should be made him?" (Rom. 11:35). By the fact that man is a creature, all that he is and all that he has and all that he does is already God's. How can a creature do anything for God or give anything to him? This already poses a problem in relation to the goods of the natural order; much greater indeed is the problem in the wholly gratuituous order of grace. How can a right to a reward be based upon a gift to which man has absolutely no claim? How can the transcendent God be made a debtor to his creature?

B. The Foundations of Merit

The answer to these questions lies in the divine decree whereby God binds himself to grant merit. He directs that man's actions under grace shall be worthy of a reward; when the reward is granted, God is—so to speak—being just to himself in fulfilling his own decision to reward the meritorious deeds of men. God seeks no profit from man's acts; rather he seeks his glory, the manifestation of his own goodness. Underlying the justice whereby he rewards our good deeds is his mercy by which he binds himself to make these deeds worthy of a reward.

Every creature obtains what God ordains for it: the sun shines; grass grows; animals eat, grow and reproduce, etc. Men also obtain their divinely appointed goal of eternal reward, but they attain it by their free acts, and hence their actions are meritorious. This is not true of creatures which are not free.

God's intention to reward man's acts is revealed throughout the Scriptures.[65] The same truth is taught by the Church as a matter of divine faith: ". . . And eternal life should therefore be set before those who persevere in good works to the end (cf. Matt. 10:22), and who hope in God. And it should be proposed to them as the grace mercifully promised to the sons of God through Jesus Christ, and 'as the reward' which, according to the promise of God himself, must

[65]Cf. Matt. 5:12, 25:34 ff.; Mark 9-40; II Cor. 5:10; II Tim. 4:8.

certainly be given to them for their good works and merits. . . ."[66] And
the Church underlines this teaching by insisting that these merits are
not a mere fiction:

> If anyone shall say that the good works of a justified man are so
> much the gifts of God that they are not also the good merits of the
> justified man himself; or that, by the good works which are performed
> by him through the grace of God and the merit of Jesus Christ (whose
> living member he is), the just man does not merit an increase of grace,
> everlasting life, and (if he shall die in the state of grace), the posses-
> sion of that same everlasting life, and even an increase of glory, let
> him be condemned.[67]

But in what sense of the term can man be said to *merit* a reward
from God? Regarding condign merit, which is based on justice, man
cannot merit anything from God *according to strict justice*. For strict
justice obtains only between equal and independent parties, and
man is neither equal to, nor independent of God. The only condign
merit that is possible for man is that which is based upon justice *in a
proportionate sense*: on the supposition that God has ordained that
good works shall be meritorious, and that he first gives man "the principle of merit," i.e., grace, then there is established a proportional
equality between God and what there is of God in man and his
works.[68] It is in this sense that there is true merit based upon justice
between God and man: God freely makes a divine gift a divine debt.

Certain physical feats are beyond man's power. For example, his
voice cannot carry over a distance of several miles. Yet his voice can
be picked up, amplified and broadcast by electrical energy so that
he may be heard at great distances. By virtue of a power extrinsic
to it, the human voice becomes capable of communication that exceeds

---

[66]Council of Trent, *loc. cit.*, Chap. 16, "On the Merit of Good Works"; Denz.
809. Cf. Denz. 429, 834.

[67]*Ibid.*, Can. 32; Denz. 842.

[68]". . . so much is attributed to good works in the Scriptures that Christ
promises even to whoever gives a drink of cold water to one of his least followers, that he shall not be without his reward (Matt. 10:42), and the Apostle
declares: 'For our present light affliction, which is for the moment, prepares for
us an eternal weight of glory that is beyond all measure' (II Cor. 4:17). Nonetheless, the Christian should not either confide in himself or glory in himself
rather than in the Lord, whose goodness toward all men is so great that he
ordains the very things which are his gifts to be their merits. . . ." *Ibid.*, Chap. 16;
Denz. 810.

its power. Similarly, man's acts cannot of themselves have any efficacy at the level of divine life. But they can be elevated and enriched by grace so that they become proportionately commensurate to supernatural goals and rewards. The price for this is the Blood of Christ, paid for fully and for all by the Savior's death; it is the just claim of Christ to a divine reward, and this reward he shares with men through sanctifying grace. "It is now no longer I that live, but Christ lives in me" (Gal. 2:20). The divine life he won for us he gives us through sanctifying grace; this life is the foundation of merit.

C. The Conditions for Merit

Several conditions must be fulfilled for an act to be meritorious:

1. **A positive act is required for merit; omitting to act is not meritorious.** An internal act by which one abstains from some external deed is, of course, a positive act and therefore can be meritorious. Of a righteous man it is said: "He could have sinned but did not; could have done evil, but would not" (Sir. 31:10).

2. **A meritorious act must be voluntary and free.** Just as a man cannot be held accountable for things beyond his control, so neither is he rewarded for acts that are not truly his own.

3. **A meritorious act must be morally good.** Sinful acts are opposed to God's glory, which is enhanced by meritorious acts. (Cf. Matt. 6:1 ff.)

4. **A meritorious act must be supernatural in origin, i.e., it must proceed from grace.** The greater cannot come from the less.[69]

5. **A meritorious act must be directed to God as to its end.** Such an act must be related to the love of God; otherwise there would be no reason to expect a reward from him. "Therefore, whether you eat or drink, or do anything else, do all for the glory of God" (I Cor. 10:31).

6. **Merit is limited to acts of this present life.** Eternal life is the final goal of all merit; once it is possessed (i.e., heaven) or assured (i.e., in purgatory) it can no longer be earned. "For all of us must be made

---

[69]Cf. Council of Trent, *loc. cit.*, Chap. 16, quoted *supra*, note 68.

manifest before the tribunal of Christ, so that each one may receive what he has won through the body, according to his works, whether good or evil" (II Cor. 5:10).

7. **Merit can be gained only by those in the state of grace.** "I am the vine, you are the branches. He who abides in me, and I in him, he bears much fruit; for without me you can do nothing" (John 15:5). "If anyone shall say that divine grace is given through Jesus Christ merely to facilitate man's living justly and meriting eternal life, as if he could do both, although barely and with difficulty, by his free will without grace, let him be condemned."[70]

All the foregoing conditions presuppose that the foundation for all merit has been established by divine decree as already explained.

D. The Objects of Merit

It remains to be seen what things may be merited, and under which kind of merit various goods fall. We must recall here that nothing supernatural can be merited condignly according to strict justice, because the equality needed for such justice cannot exist between man and God. Practically, all condign merit rests upon a proportionate justice. Besides this, there is only congruous merit. The following are the various objects of these two kinds of merit:

1. **The good deeds of a man in the state of sanctifying grace merit eternal life** *condignly.* "I have fought the good fight, I have finished the course, I have kept the faith. For the rest, there is laid up for me a crown of justice, which the Lord, the just Judge, will give to in that day, yet not to me only, but also to those who love his coming" (II Tim. 4:7-8). The gift of grace establishes a proportion between man's acts and the reward of eternal life, which is thus a true reward in justice.

2. **No one can merit his initial actual grace in any way.** Just as no one can reproduce himself, so neither can he begin to generate his own supernatural life.

[70]Council of Trent, *loc. cit.*, Can. 2; Denz. 812. Cf. Denz. 1012; 1015; 1017 f.

3. **No one can merit his initial sanctifying grace** *condignly*. The very principle of merit does not itself fall under merit, for this would be a vicious circle.

4. **A man who has received the initial actual grace may, in a wide sense of the term, merit** *congruously* **to receive the initial sanctifying grace.** Properly speaking, the foundation for congruous merit is friendship with God, which is established only through sanctifying grace; it is fitting, or congruous, that God should heed the requests of his friends. In a wider sense, however, it is also fitting that God, entirely on a basis of mercy rather than friendship, should add gift to gift, mercifully granting sanctifying grace to the sinner whom he has previously moved by an actual grace.

5. **No man can merit** *condignly* **an initial grace for someone else.** No one merits the beginning of the life of grace for himself, nor can anyone do this for his neighbor. To merit condignly for others is reserved to Christ, "the author of salvation" (Heb. 2:10). "Neither is there salvation in any other. For there is no other name under heaven given to men by which we must be saved" (Acts 4:12).

6. **A man in the state of grace can merit grace for others** *congruously*. Such a man is God's friend, and it is fitting that God should hear his request. St. Stephen prayed for those who stoned him; one of these was Saul who became St. Paul (Acts 7:54-60).

7. **A man in the state of grace cannot merit now the the recovery of grace after some future fall.** Mortal sin destroys every basis of merit in the sinner. "But if the just man turn himself away from his justice, and do iniquity . . . all his justices which he has done shall not be remembered" (Ezech. 18:24). ". . . we may be said to be justified freely, in the sense that nothing that precedes justification, neither faith nor words, merits the grace of justification. . . ."[71] The restoration of sinners to grace is entirely the work of divine mercy.

8. **A man in grace can merit both** *congruously* **and** *condignly* **an increase of grace and charity.** Grace is a share in divine life, and all

---

[71] *Ibid.*, Chap. 8; Denz. 801. On the revival of previously gained merit in one who is re-converted to God after mortal sin, cf. *Christ, and His Sacraments*, 449; see also Denz. 807.

that pertains to this life falls under merit. Now life is not only a goal, it includes means, among which are growth and increase in grace. This is taught both in the Scriptures and by the authoritative declarations of the Church.[72]

9. **Man cannot merit** *condignly* **to persevere in grace until death.** To claim perseverance as due in justice would be to insist upon impeccability as man's due in this life. Perseverance is the continuance in grace until death, and it implies freedom from serious sin. This can only come as a special gift of God; it cannot be earned as a payment, it can only be sought in prayer as a favor. This is expressly taught as a matter of faith by the Church.[73]

10. **Temporal things can be merited only insofar as they are truly necessary or useful for eternal life.** The just merit that measure of temporal prosperity or adversity that is conducive to their eternal welfare.

10. SUMMARY AND CONCLUSION

Methods of self-improvement always find a ready market. Courses in charm, good grooming, health, correct speech, dancing and dieting are available in endless variety. Best-sellers teach how to win friends and influence people, how to acquire the power of positive thinking, how to stop worrying and start living, and a host of other techniques for success and betterment. Religion itself is advertised as an element in success—"How to use God in enriching your life." The gospel of success has many evangelists, and many devoted adherents.

All of this, theologically, is a recrudescence of Pelagianism; all of it poisons the atmosphere in which the Christian must live; some of it, surely, he must breathe in. Living amid the militant secularism and the pervasive naturalism of the age, he finds more opposition than support in his attempt to attain the supernatural destiny to which

---

[72]Cf. Matt. 25:26-29; cf. Council of Trent, *loc. cit.*, Can. 32, quoted *supra*, 307.

[73]On this important matter, all should read: Council of Trent, *loc. cit.*, Chap. 13, "The Gift of Perseverance"; Denz. 806.

he is called, and the successful use of God's grace upon which he is dependent for the attainment of his divine vocation. Sanctifying grace, inhering in the very essence of the soul, effecting at the very root of man's being a profound change, makes of him, in short, a different *kind* of being.

There is a subtle temptation for the Christian to anaesthetize himself with the thought that, after all, he's only human; it is part of his calling rather to goad himself with the conviction that grace has made him divine. "I admonish thee to stir up the grace of God which is in thee" (II Tim. 1:6).

Grace is a principle of life; it is not given simply to be preserved, but to be increased and diffused. The man of the parable who buried his talent was condemned, not for having lost something, but for having failed to use it profitably (Matt. 25:14 ff.).

Before all else, the Christian must labor constantly to be aware that he is ". . . the stranger in this world, the citizen of the city of God, predestinated by grace, elected by grace, by grace a stranger below, and by grace a citizen above."[74] Unless he nourishes that conviction by frequent reflection, he cannot fulfill his destiny to collaborate in the work of his own sanctification begun through grace, and by that collaboration to advance the restoration of all things in Christ and achieve that perfection of the divine image of the Trinity in the soul which is his manifest destiny.

An awareness of grace, a devout reflection on its meaning, an effort to penetrate its implications, will call forth the efforts necessary to comply with its demands and to fulfill its promise. And that means to live in the world *as a Christian*: to love the world not for itself, but for Christ; to serve the world not for worldly gain, but to gain it for Christ; to remind the world that all its pursuit of happiness cannot be won by human effort, for true happiness is something divine that can be had only through the grace of Christ.

[74]St. Augustine, *The City of God*, Bk. XV, Chap. 1.

BIBLIOGRAPHICAL NOTE

St. Thomas Aquinas' treatment of grace can be found in the *Summa*, Part I-II, Questions CIX to CXIV. The most authoritative and complete modern work on this subject is *Grace* by Reginald Garrigou-Lagrange, O.P. (St. Louis: Herder, 1952); the same author also applies this doctrine to the spiritual life in *Christian Perfection and Contemplation* (St. Louis: Herder, 1937) 80-113. *Nature and Grace* (St. Louis: Herder, 1954) by M. J. Scheeben is a thorough and revealing study, and there are many valuable references in his great work, *The Mysteries of Christianity* (St. Louis: Herder, 1946). A book emphasizing the effect of sanctifying grace on the interior life of the soul is *Our Life of Grace* by F. Cuttaz (Chicago: Fides, 1958); a survey of grace in somewhat more popular vein is *The Theology of Grace* by Jean Daujat in the series, "Twentieth Century Encyclopedia of Catholicism" (New York: Hawthorn Books, 1959).

Two valuable articles by E. Towers will be found in *The Teaching of the Catholic Church* (New York: Macmillan, 1949) I, 549-621, dealing at length with both sanctifying and actual grace. Walter Farrell, O.P., is the author of the article, "Divine Grace," in the Benziger English *Summa*, III, 3277-3288. Many applications to the spiritual life of the doctrine on grace are found in *The Mystical Evolution in the Development and Vitality of the Church* by John. G. Arintero, O.P. (St. Louis: Herder, 1950), 41-285; the author quotes freely from the mystics and other spiritual authors on the matter of grace. *Cross and Crown* has published two articles on grace with emphasis on the spiritual value of the doctrine: "The Gift of God" by F. L. B. Cunningham, O.P., VIII (1956), and "Grace, the Life of the Soul" by Aegidius Doolan, O.P., VI (1954), 88-97.

CHAPTER EIGHT

Faith: Beginnings of Eternal Life

1. Introduction

With this chapter a transition takes place from what is usually called *general* moral theology to that termed *special* moral theology. All that has preceded this point has looked to the moral life of man and his relations with God with the eye of an artist penning a rough, over-all sketch of his subject. The general lines of man and morality have thus been marked out and investigated in some detail—his ultimate goal; human action and its norms; the good habits which serve as means to his destiny; the tragic deformity of sin; God's assistance through law and grace. Man's moral life, however, is a tapestry woven, not out of the insubstantial yarn of universal and abstract principles and truths, but out of the stuff of concrete and particular actions. It is necessary, then, for the full perfection of moral theology, that its general analysis of the question

314

of man and morality be followed by a detailed consideration of the particular kinds of actions—and thus of the virtues which are their source—that men must exercise in the concrete living of the Christian life.

To live a Christian life, however, does not mean putting an end to variety in one's way or manner of living. Despite their common identifying stamp of "Christian," the faithful are free to choose certain states of life that will provide their particular pathway to eternity. Consequently, the moral theologian must consider the actions and virtues which pertain commonly to all conditions and walks of life, and also those which pertain in a special manner only to certain men. It will be the task of the remainder of this volume to treat in particular concerning these actions, virtues and states.

In the concrete scheme of the economy of salvation, the perfection of man consists in conformity to Christ. "For those whom [God] has foreknown," wrote St. Paul, "he has also predestined to become conformed to the image of his Son, that he should be the firstborn among many brethren" (Rom. 8:29). Grace gives to the soul, in a marvelous and mysterious manner, a likeness to Christ—nay, makes men "partakers of the divine nature" itself. And just as grace conforms the soul to Christ, it is supernatural virtue which conforms man's powers to Christ. The question of the moral perfection of man may be reduced, therefore, to the matter of the supernatural virtues. There must exist virtues setting man in proper alignment with his supernatural goal, and virtues, as well, setting him aright in regard to the means proportionate to, and necessary for attaining that transcendent destiny. To satisfy the first requirement, there are the three **theological virtues;** to satisfy the second, the four infused **cardinal virtues** and their entourage of subsidiary virtues. And since man must be oriented properly to his goal before he can set out to attain it, it is first necessary to consider the theological virtues, and among them, in the first place, the virtue which establishes man's initial contact with the author of the supernatural, the virtue of faith.

The treatment of this virtue will follow the order laid down in this outline:

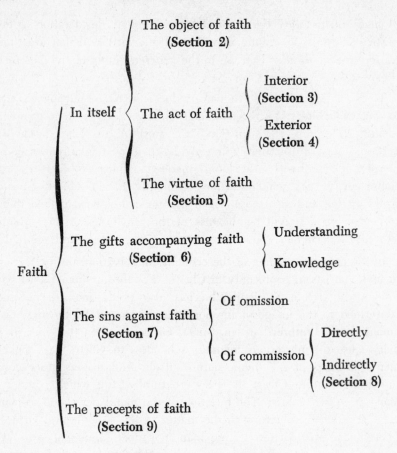

Faith
- In itself
  - The object of faith (Section 2)
  - The act of faith
    - Interior (Section 3)
    - Exterior (Section 4)
  - The virtue of faith (Section 5)
- The gifts accompanying faith (Section 6)
  - Understanding
  - Knowledge
- The sins against faith (Section 7)
  - Of omission
  - Of commission
    - Directly
    - Indirectly (Section 8)
- The precepts of faith (Section 9)

2. THE OBJECT OF FAITH

A. The Notion of Faith

The Catholic Church has a unique and widespread reputation for incredible narrowness, stubbornness and intolerance. From the vociferous and belligerent Blanshards to the quiet and friendly non-Catholic neighbor next door, this is generally singled out as an outstanding mark of the Catholic Church. Yet, ironically enough, it may be just this apparently hide-bound "intolerance" that may one day bring these very same persons into "the harbor of truth and the unity of faith."

The reason for the "unco-operative" attitude of the Catholic Church is to be found in the revealed truths concerning the virtue of faith. This Catholic "attitude" is best expressed by St. Paul:

> If we or an angel from heaven should preach a gospel to you other than that which we have preached to you, let him be anathema! As we have said before, so now I say again: If anyone preach a gospel to you other than that which you have received, let him be anathema. . . ! For I give you to understand, brethren, that the gospel which was preached by me is not of man. For I did not receive it from man, nor was I taught it; but I received it by a revelation of Jesus Christ.[1]

(1) The Revelation of Christ

This revelation of Christ is nothing but the sum of the truths he wished his followers to believe: it is a unity, a whole whose diverse parts are formally connected and integrally related—the one gospel of our Lord and Savior Jesus Christ. Hence it follows that the faith by which men actually place belief in this Gospel must likewise be **one.** Whether the word "faith" is used to designate the *body of truths* which are the object of belief, or whether it is used to signify the *act* or the *habit* which places the believer in contact with these truths, it is characterized by the attribute of oneness or unity. "One Lord, one faith, one Baptism; one God and Father of all" (Eph. 4:5-6).

The reason for this determined attitude on the part of the Catholic Church to preserve the unity of faith is to be found precisely in the nature of the revelation made to it by God. "God, who at sundry times and in divers manners spoke in times past to the fathers by the prophets, last of all in these days has spoken to us by his Son" (Heb. 1:1-2). *God has spoken to man*—and he has spoken "things hidden from the foundation of the world" (Matt. 13:35).

How false is the claim that the faith of the Catholic is a sin against the freedom and liberty of man! By his faith, goes up the cry, the Catholic degrades himself—becomes less human—enslaves himself to the totalitarian regime of the Church of Rome. True, the Catholic

---

[1] Gal. 1:8-9, 11-12.

makes a surrender. But, paradoxically, this surrender frees him to walk familiarly into the hidden life of God. Faith removes the barriers of the natural order which shield, from the world and man, the inner life of the Godhead. Certainly it is true that "since the creation of the world his invisible attributes are clearly seen—his everlasting power also and divinity"; yet these things are grasped by man only as "being understood through the things that are made" (Rom. 1:20). God—his existence and something of his nature—can be known by reason alone, but only in terms of the finite and limited things of nature which he has brought forth from nothing. This approach to God is not direct. It must begin from the world of nature; it must proceed from an analysis of the artist's handiwork to a knowledge of the artist himself. Such knowledge is certainly imperfect and limited, it is to a large extent negative, and it is always forced to proceed from effect to cause.

(2) The Mysteries of God

This is not at all true of the knowledge that comes by means of faith in God's revelation. The barriers of nature crumble before the power of a simple act of faith, revealing a completely new and transcendent aspect of the author of nature. Faith reveals not only many naturally attainable truths; far more importantly, a vast new order of truth rising completely above the natural capacities of the human mind appears before the believer. By faith the veil is drawn back to disclose what theologians call **the supernatural order of life and truth** in God. Faith brings into the focus of man's intelligence "the unfathomable riches of Christ . . . , the mystery which has been hidden from eternity in God" (Eph. 3:9).

St. Paul, truly the master of this subject of divine faith, attests to the marvels thus revealed:

> But we speak the wisdom of God, mysterious, hidden, which God foreordained before the world unto our glory, a wisdom which none of the rulers of this world has known; for had they known it, they would never have crucified the Lord of glory. But, as it is written, "Eye has not seen nor ear heard, nor has it entered into the heart of man, what things God has prepared for those who love him."[2]

[2] I Cor. 2:7-9.

Faith, in short, opens our minds to gaze on the ineffable supernatural mysteries of God.

(3) The Definition of Faith

This, then, is that singular gift of God for which St. Paul gives the profound and meaningful definition: **faith** is *"the substance of things to be hoped for, the evidence of things that are not seen"* (Heb. 11:1). It is faith which implants in man the first beginings ("the substance") of his eternal happiness ("of things to be hoped for"), and makes him absolutely certain of the hidden mysteries and glories of God ("the evidence of things that are not seen").

A far more technical description of faith is to be found in the formal definition of the Vatican Council, in the Church's infallible assertion that:

> Faith is a supernatural virtue whereby under the inspiration and assistance of grace we believe those things revealed by God to be true, not because the intrinsic truth of these things has been perceived by the natural light of reason, but because of the authority of God himself revealing, who can neither deceive nor be deceived.[3]

Any discussion of the Catholic notion of faith reduces itself, in effect, to nothing more than a commentary or explanation of what is contained in these two classic definitions. In order to understand their content more fully, it will be necessary to consider separately the **object**, the **act** and the **virtue** of faith.

It is the first point which directly concerns us in this section, for in moral matters the object absolutely determines the kind of act and habit which is involved. Moreover, all of us are more familiar with *what* we believe and *why* we believe than we are with our process of believing, or the supernatural gift which makes this act possible. From common, everyday experience we recognize that belief is nothing more than the acceptance of another's testimony concerning some particular matter which is unknown to the believer himself. As with every act man performs, this acceptance must be reasonable. But one does not reasonably accept the testimony of another unless he judges that his informant is truly *in possession of*

---

[3]Sess. III, *Constitution on the Catholic Faith*, Chap. 3, "Concerning Faith"; Denz. 1789.

the facts (knows what he is talking about), and, even more, that he *is willing to communicate his knowledge without deception* (straight from the shoulder). To consider these two points is to inquire into the matter of the object of faith. And all faith, whether natural or supernatural, is found to have a twofold object, namely a **material object** (the things to be believed) and a **formal object** (the reason or motive for believing). We shall discuss the latter and more important first.

B. The Formal Object of Faith

The formal object of faith is the reason or motive that moves man to assent to the material object. The material object answers the question, "*What* is believed?" But the formal object provides the answer for *why* man believes. Man assents to all the truths contained in God's supernatural revelation "because of the authority of God himself who reveals them, who can neither deceive nor be deceived."[4] The reason, and the only reason, for man's acceptance of supernatural truth is the authority of God himself. If God speaks to man, there can be no doubt as to the truth of his message. His knowledge is infinite; his veracity beyond question. And since God *has* spoken, the case is closed.

To anticipate, once again, the ever recurring objection—yes, it is true that the Catholic believes only what his Church proposes for his belief. Ecclesiastical authority, however, while determining the form in which the articles of faith will be proposed, does not *reveal* the truths which are to be believed. God alone reveals; the Church simply points out—and infallibly so—precisely what has been revealed by God.[5]

[4]Vatican Council, *loc. cit.;* Denz. 1789.

[5]The question of the Church's role as infallible custodian and teacher of God's supernatural revelation, as well as the matter of that revelation itself—its existence and nature—properly pertain to the defensive part of the wisdom which is theology, i.e., to Christian apologetics. A detailed treatment of this subject is beyond the scope of this chapter. The reader may consult any apologetics text for a greater exposition of this important doctrine, e.g., *Evidence for Our Faith* (Notre Dame, Ind.: University of Notre Dame Press, 1952), by John H. Cavanaugh, C.S.C.

"Therefore we too give thanks to God without ceasing, because when you heard and received from us the word of God, you welcomed it not as the word of men, but as it truly is, the word of God, who works in you who have believed" (I Thess. 2:13).

C. The Material Object of Faith

The material object of faith is the truth, or body of truths, accepted by the believer. In the case of the supernatural act of faith, the material object is **the content of God's supernatural revelation.** How is this to be discerned? The infallible authority of the Church has declared that it is to be found "in the written books and in the unwritten traditions received by the apostles from the mouth of Christ, or delivered to us by the hands of these same apostles under the inspiration of the Holy Spirit."[6]

It is the plan of God that his message be communicated to individual men, not by the inner promptings of the Holy Spirit as many Protestants hold, but "through the hands of the apostles." Divine revelation is, therefore, a *public* matter. God has determined from all eternity that his "good news," the Gospel, would be broadcast to the world through the tangible medium of his visible Church whose Head is Jesus Christ. "All power in heaven and earth has been given to me. Go, therefore, and make disciples of all nations . . . , teaching them to observe all that I have commanded you" (Matt. 28:18-19). It follows, then, that when the Church speaks, Christ speaks; and when Christ speaks, the Father speaks: "The word that you have heard is not mine, but the Father's who sent me" (John 14:24); "my teaching is not my own, but his who sent me" (*ibid.* 7:16). To guarantee that his message will be public and open to all men—not the plaything of individual vagaries or personal feelings, not the football of miscreants and malcontents, not the private province or production of an elite—Christ established an infallible witness and objective proponent of his truth.

[6]Vatican Council, *loc. cit.*, Chap. 2, "Concerning Revelation"; Denz. 1787.

It is the function of his Church, not to tell man that the things God has revealed are true, but merely to point out what truths actually were revealed. And this function of the Church has been defined quite clearly when the Vatican Council expressed the material object of faith in the following formula:

> All those things are to be believed, on divine and Catholic faith, which are contained in the written and unwritten word of God, and which are proposed by the Church as divinely revealed, whether that is accomplished through her solemn pronouncement, or through her ordinary and universal teaching power.[7]

In short, the Church is in no sense the cause of divine faith, but she is the necessary transmitter, custodian and interpreter of the faith of Christ—indispensable as she is infallible, the instrument of God without which (*conditio sine qua non*) faith for any of us would be impossible.

Among all that a man believes by "divine and Catholic faith," is there not one truth which stands out as the keystone? This brings up the question of the *primary* and the *secondary* material objects of faith and its answer will further increase our understanding of this theological virtue.[8] The **primary object** is that which is immediately, directly and of itself attained by any act, habit or power, and that by reason of, and by means of which other things are attained; color is the primary object of sight, for example, and through color, by reason of it, we see other visible things. Those things attained by reason of the primary object are called the **secondary object**.

(1) The Primary Object

God himself, the first and primary eternally true being, is the principal object of divine faith. The divine essence as it is in itself—not as known through its effects—certainly exists as the first of all truths, and it is the Godhead *in itself*, in its supernatural being, which is the prmiary object of our faith; this truth, then, transcends all our

---

[7]*Loc. cit.*, Chap. 3, "Concerning Faith"; Denz. 1792.

[8]Modern theologians reserve the term "material object" for the secondary material object alone, calling the primary material object the "formal object *quod*" and the motive the "formal object *quo*." We have preferred to use the traditional terminology, which is that of St. Thomas, as being both more accurate and less confusing.

natural powers of knowledge. All other truths which are revealed by God are the object of belief because of their connection with this first truth, and they are assented to by reason of that first truth. "From this point of view," writes St. Thomas, "the object of faith is in some way the First Truth, insofar as nothing falls under faith at all except in relation to God; so also the object of the art of medicine is health, since nothing is considered by it except by reason of its relation to health."[9]

(2) The Secondary Object

The total content of faith is *all* that God has revealed and *only* what he has revealed—no more, no less. Among revealed truths we will find some secondary truths which are **directly** and of themselves connected with God, such as the divinity of Christ, the sacraments, the Church, etc. Others, however, will have only an **indirect** relationship with God, no necessary connection with doctrine or morals (the scriptural account of the Jewish captivity, for example); but no matter how unimportant they may seem to be, these truths have also been vouchsafed for by God himself and are thereby contained in the public deposit of faith.

Moreover, there are still other truths which are not expressly stated in the sources of revelation but equivalently enunciated in some other revealed truth. These **implicit** truths are the object of divine faith when they are contained in an **explicit** truth as parts of a whole, for knowledge of some totality is also at least implicit knowledge of its constituent parts. It is explicitly revealed that the apostles received the Holy Spirit on Pentecost; implicit in this truth is the fact that St. John received the Spirit. Implicit truths of this kind are part of the deposit of faith because, equivalently and so far as meaning is concerned, they have been stated by God himself.[10]

[9]*Summa*, II-II, q. 1, a. 1.

[10]Private revelations as well as public revelations are guaranteed by the same authority, God himself; but for the former this is true only *for those to whom such revelations are given*. Hence even when they are "approved" by the Church, like those of Lourdes and Fatima, no one is obliged to believe these private revelations; such an approval means only that they contain nothing opposed to faith and morals, that there is sufficient evidence for accepting them *on human faith* without superstition. It would not be right, then, to treat such "approved" revelations with contempt.

(3) *The Evolution of the Material Object*

In the divine plan, public revelation closed with the death of the last apostle, and so no new truth will be publicly given by God unto the end of time. Yet it seems evident that some evolution of faith, some growth in the content of belief, has occurred during the centuries of the Church's existence: the dogmas of the Immaculate Conception, the infallibility of the pope, the Assumption, for example, were all defined within the last hundred years or so.

This is not a case, however, of adding new truths to old; all of these, all revealed truth, was proposed from the beginning by the Church and at least implicitly believed by every Catholic in every century. What has occurred is a subjective development on the part of the faithful, a clearer and deeper understanding of divine truth. For the Church as a whole, this evolution of the material object of faith takes place in three ways:

1) The clearer and more accurate expression of truths (before stated in popular language and somewhat vaguely) by the invention of precise, scientific formulas and terms—e.g., "hypostatic union," "transubstantiation."

2) The explicit affirmation of an implicit truth contained in a more general truth. Thus the doctrine of the necessity of grace for the beginnings of faith was developed from the more general doctrine that grace is necessary for every salutary work.

3) The speculative and express proposal of a truth taught and believed from the beginning in practice. From the beginning, for example, the Church never repeated baptism, confirmation or holy orders; this practice contained the doctrine that these sacraments imprint an indelible character on the soul.

Progress in knowledge of the objects of belief will take place for the individual Catholic in two ways: 1) through study of the teachings of the Church (one objective of your theology course); and 2) through the special inspirations of the Spirit working through his gifts. By one way or another—and preferably by both—the individual Catholic can fulfill his obligation to grow in the knowledge of God and his Christ unto the fulness of Christian maturity.

(4) The Characteristics of the Material Object

We can summarize this whole consideration of *what* is believed by divine faith by pointing out two facts: 1) its object must be **true** (could God deceive us? or would we believe these astonishing things if he had not deigned to reveal them?); 2) its object is necessarily **obscure**—something "unseen" because supernatural or intimately connected with the supernatural, and therefore not coercing the intellect's assent. At one and the same time, consequently, faith is most certain and disturbingly, provocatively unsatisfied.

3. THE INTERIOR ACT OF FAITH

From what we have seen of its object, we can conclude that the act of faith establishes contact between two minds, the divine and the human: God communicates divine truth, and man receives it on the word of God. This very special commitment on man's part to a higher order of things, to the plane of divine truth and life, merits our close scrutiny, so necessary is it for us, so revealing of our relations with God. It takes place within us, first of all, but in certain circumstances it is necessarily exteriorized, for the personal gift of faith is still a public affair, with important repercussions in the social order. So we will consider both the interior and exterior act of faith.

A. The Nature of the Interior Act of Faith

St. Augustine states that to believe is "to consider with assent."[11] The believer, then, is a mind *investigating* truth, not having full and complete evidence of it. And yet, although he considers inevident truths, there is still a firmness in the adherence of his intellect: he **considers**, to be sure, but *with assent*.

---

[11]*Concerning the Predestination of the Saints,* Chap. 2, n. 5.

(1) Analysis of the Act of Faith

Of its very nature the intellect always looks for evidence for its conclusions. Since in supernatural faith this proof is unavailable because the truths themselves are obscure, the intellect must be led to assent in some other way.

It is the will that moves the intellect to give its assent where direct proof is wanting. Belief—the act of faith—is an operation elicited by the intellect, but imperated, or commanded, by the will. The things we believe are not evident to the human intellect—for instance, that Our Lady could be a virgin, even in giving birth to Jesus. We admit this proposition revealed by God because the will decides it is good to give credence to God who told us this truth, and so the will moves the intellect to admit this proposition as true. Clearly we can see that *no one believes unless he wills freely to believe.* We can present the faith to our non-Catholic neighbors, but, since the truths of faith are not evident, they will believe only if they will to believe.

The will is free, but since it is engaged with a supernatural object its own activity is not enough, it must also be moved by God's grace.

St. Thomas includes all these elements in his definition of the act of faith. **Faith** is *"the act of the intellect assenting to divine truth under the dominion of the will as moved by God's grace."*[12]

From this analysis it is evident that faith, a supernatural act about a supernatural object, immeasurably transcends mere erudition about religious matters or persuasion about rational truths, as rationalists hold. It is far more than the Protestant's concept of a confidence, a reliance on God's mercy; it is *knowledge* of mystery, imperfect and obscure but a real glimpse of eternity. The views of Luther, Calvin and their modern disciples are confined to the affective, subjective order, while faith for a Catholic is a firm judgment based on God's word. And yet faith in this realistic Catholic sense is much more than a soberly intellectual conviction, though it always begins with that. A loving faith, energized by charity, overflows into good works,

[12]*Summa,* II-II, q. 2, a. 9. Cf. *De Veritate,* q. 14, a. 1.

the keeping of God's law: "So faith too, unless it has works, is dead in itself" (Jas. 2:17).

(2) *The Judgment of Credibility*

The act of faith is an assent of the intellect commanded by the will. But there is an operation of the intellect prior even to this command of the will. Since the will cannot demand the assent of the intellect before the intellect has previously judged that such an assent should be given, before the act of faith takes place an act of the intellect is necessary. This we call a **judgment of credibility:** that the truths of faith are not only believable, but must—*if we are to act reasonably*—**be believed.** Thus there are three stages in this complex act:

1) A judgment of credibility by the intellect, by which we judge that these truths must be believed.

2) A free act of the will by which we *will* to believe, commanding the intellect to assent to these truths.

3) The essential act of faith itself in the intellect, by which we actually assent to this truth, affirming that it is true.

(3) *The Motives of Credibility*

The judgment of credibility requires two allies: the **preambles of faith** and the **motives of credibility.** The preambles of faith are propositions which must be accepted by reason antecedently to the act of faith, preparing the way for it: such truths as the existence of God, his infallible knowledge and veracity, etc.

The motives of credibility are those arguments for the fact of revelation which lead us to the very brink of the act of faith. They are signs by which the existence of revelation is proved, because they cannot be explained on any natural basis. They are not, however, a cause of the act of faith; if they were, they would be indistinguishable from the formal object or motive of faith, the authority of God revealing. But by showing that it is reasonable to believe they dispose us remotely for the act of faith; since we must act reasonably, this is to say, in effect, that we *must* believe. The *motive of faith*, on the other hand, moves us proximately, in the very act of faith.

The *external* motives of credibility are the working of miracles and the fulfillment of prophecies, and the sanctity, unity and spiritual fecundity of the Church, showing the Church as a divine institution, the guardian of revelation. The life of the Church precisely as a motive of credibility is seen, not as supernatural and divine (for this view of the Church is believed by faith), but as a natural phenomenon in the light of history.

The *internal* motives of credibility are such things as the sanctity of Christ and the sublimity of his doctrine, objective facts naturally inexplicable. They do not prove the existence of divine revelation with strict certitude, but frequently they have a greater personal impact on the inquiring non-Catholic.

Purely interior motives for believing, such as one's own personal religious experience and the soul's instinct to faith, are too subjective to be certain and evident proofs of revelation. Furthermore, they tend to reduce the faith and its causes to the level of natural emotional inclinations, though these may, of course, be steppingstones to the faith.[13]

B. The Necessity of Faith

Since "without faith it is impossible to please God" (Heb. 11:6) and to come into the fellowship of his children, it follows that justification comes to no one who does not possess faith, and that no one shall attain to eternal life except "he who has persevered to the end" (Matt. 10:22) in it.[14]

It is only by a humble act of belief—his own, or the Church's— that man can possibly know of the supernatural end for which he has been destined, and it is only by being aware of its existence that he can take any steps toward his goal. Application of this fundamental principle, however, gives rise to many practical problems

[13]For a profound analysis of these psychological motives see Newman's *Grammar of Assent*.
[14]Vatican Council, *loc. cit.;* Denz. 1793.

concerning the matter of the necessity of faith. Their solution necessitates an important distinction.

Something can be termed necessary for salvation either by a *necessity of means or* by a *necessity of precept.* A necessary means of salvation is some absolute condition without which that end cannot possibly be attained. Hence, if such a means is wanting—whether due to one's fault or not—the end simply cannot be achieved. So, without eyes one cannot see; without grace no one can be saved. A necessity of *precept* arises when something is obligatory for salvation by the special command of legitimate authority, which imposes it as a condition for attaining salvation, but not in such an absolute manner that salvation could not be attained in some other way. By the law of the Church, attendance at Sunday Mass is necessary for all Catholic adults, but not so absolutely necessary that no one can be saved without its fulfillment.

Consequently, no excuse makes any difference whatsoever when it is a question of a necessity of means; on the contrary, inculpable ignorance or moral impossibility excuses from things necessary from precept alone. There are some things necessary, however, both by a necessity of means and a necessity of precept, and faith is among these.

(1) The Necessity of Means

1. **Habitual faith is necessary for all men by necessity of means, so that without it no one can be saved.** St. Paul stated simply and without any limitation that "without faith it is impossible to please God" (Heb. 11:6). This doctrine is itself a matter of faith: in the case of baptized infants and others lacking the use of reason, the habit of faith suffices for justification and salvation.

2. **The act of faith is required by necessity of means for all adults.** "He who believes and is baptized shall be saved" (Mark 16:15). Those who have attained the use of reason are obliged to tend to God *by their own personal actions.* Since no one can possibly advance to his supernatural goal unless he knows about it through faith, an actual and explicit act is absolutely necessary.

The inevitable question arises at this point as to the fate of those sincerely ignorant of God's supernatural revelation, whether they lived before, during or after the time of Christ. Little profit is to be gained by searching any farther for a solution than in the inspired words of St. Peter: "Now I really understand that God is not a respecter of persons, but in every nation he who fears him and does what is right is acceptable to him" (Acts 10:34-35). St. Thomas sets an example for us in this regard, when he stated simply that "if they shall do that which is in their power to perform, the Lord shall provide for them according to his mercy."[15] As for the manner in which this might be accomplished, this was Thomas' mind:

> If one brought up in ignorance of the Gospel were to follow the lead of natural reason in seeking after the good and avoiding evil, it most certainly must be held that God would either reveal those things necessary for salvation through an internal inspiration, or he would direct to him some preacher of the faith, as he sent Peter to Cornelius (cf. Acts 10:1 ff.).[16]

3. **With at least implicit faith one must believe all those things revealed by God and proposed by the Church for belief.** That faith should extend to all whatsoever God has revealed follows from the formal motive of faith itself. For God is truth, both in knowing and in revealing; hence, when he speaks he is to be believed.

But for God to demand an explicit belief in each and every truth that he has revealed and that the Church has proposed would be to place an impossible obligation on the vast majority of mankind. And certainly God does not command the impossible. Nevertheless, at least some of his revelation must be believed explicitly, as we shall see when discussing the precept of faith.

4. **With explicit faith one must at least believe in God's existence as man's supernatural last end and in the fact that he is the rewarder of good and the punisher of evil.** The major theological source of this teaching is the authority of St. Paul: "For he who comes to God must believe that God exists and is a rewarder to those who seek him" (Heb. 11:6). But a consideration of the nature of faith itself

---

[15]*Commentary on the Epistle to the Romans*, Chap. 10, lect. 3.
[16]*De Veritate*, q. 14, a. 11, ad 1.

leads to the same conclusion: for no one can freely and deliberately approach a goal that is unknown to him, and the supernatural goal of man's life is known *only by faith*; moreover, for man to make the move to approach to God as the goal of his existence a motive is required, and this motive is the supernatural reward of heaven.

St. Alphonsus and St. Thomas were of the opinion that, in addition to the two truths just mentioned, explicit belief must also be extended to the mysteries of the Incarnation and the Trinity. Though their conclusion is a subject of controversy among theologians, their position has the strong scriptural support of St. Peter and St. Paul: "For there is no other name under heaven given to men by which we must be saved" (Acts 4:12) and "there is one God, and one mediator between God and man, himself man, Christ Jesus" (I Tim. 2:5). St. Thomas reasons that man must believe the Incarnation explicitly, because in this mystery is provided *the only way by which men are to be saved*. And since the Incarnation is the mystery in which the Son of God was conceived in the womb of the Virgin Mary through the powers of the Holy Spirit, there is no way of believing in the Incarnation without at the same time including belief in the Trinity. So authoritative is this view that, in administering baptism to a dying unbeliever, the Church requires that the person should be questioned, if time allows, about his belief in all four truths. If he professes belief in only the first two, he can be baptized, but only conditionally.

(2) *The Necessity of Precept*

The necessity of rendering internal assent to the revealed word of God follows necessarily, and quite naturally, from the relationship existing between God and man. For if God speaks to man, refusal to accept his message surely amounts to an insult directed either to his truthfulness, or to his wisdom, or to the divine majesty itself. But besides this intrinsic necessity, God himself *commands* belief, that no man may err in so vital a matter: "he who does not believe shall be condemned" (Mark 16:16). And thus St. John remarks: "This is his commandment, that we should believe in the name of his Son Jesus Christ . . ." (I John 3:23).

The extent of this precept will vary widely according to the degree of one's instruction in the things of faith and, even more especially, according to one's particular vocation in life. Consequently, those charged with the care of souls, such as bishops and pastors, and even parents, instructors of religion, etc., are held to a more perfect knowledge of the faith than the simple faithful.

In general, however, *all men* are obliged to render internal assent to the principal truths of the Christian faith. This obligation is generally considered to be satisfied by belief—in substance at least—in the following points of doctrine: the Apostle's Creed, the Ten Commandments, the Lord's Prayer, the sacraments necessary for salvation, and any other sacraments which one is about to receive.

The inner assent of faith should be forthcoming on the part of the believer immediately upon his being made aware that some truth has actually been revealed by God. For faith, wrote St. Paul, "depends on hearing" (Rom. 10:17). How often must the act of faith recur in one's life? The Church has condemned the statement that one's initial act of faith is sufficient.[17] Hence the act of faith should be repeated frequently during life and, most probably, at the time of one's death as well, for at this moment especially, one is required to believe in the mercy of God and the reward he holds out for those who love him.

4. The External Profession of Faith

The basis for the obligation of external confession of faith is quite unmistakable:

> . . . everyone who acknowledges me before men, I also will acknowledge him before my Father in heaven. But whosoever disowns me before men, I in turn will disown him before my Father in heaven (Matt. 10:32-33).

The external act of faith is, therefore, the full burgeoning of the inner conviction of the mind. Thus body and soul unite in testifying to the word of God. In this manner, too, the faithful manifest before

---

[17]Decree of the Holy Office, March 4, 1679, 17th condemnation; Denz. 1167.

men tangible evidence of their membership in the visible Church of Christ. Just such a distinctly social confession of faith is the Church's own liturgy. Pope Pius XII said:

> The worship she offers to God, all good and great, is a continuous profession of Catholic faith and a continuous exercise of hope and charity. . . . In the sacred liturgy we profess the Catholic faith explicitly and openly, not only by the celebration of the mysteries and by offering the Holy Sacrifice and administering the sacraments, but also by saying or singing the Credo or Symbol of the Faith . . . and likewise by the reading of Holy Scripture, written under the inspiration of the Holy Ghost. The entire liturgy, therefore, has the Catholic faith for its content, inasmuch as it bears public witness to the faith of the Church.[18]

The command to acknowledge the faith externally involves a negative and a positive element:

1. **Negatively,** one is never permitted outwardly to deny the faith, for there is never a time when it is licit to deny God and the truth of God. One can sin in this way either by a *direct* and *explicit* verbal repudiation of the true faith, thus joining the inner renunciation of the mind with external expression; or, *indirectly* and *implicitly*, if without the intention of denying the faith interiorly, one places an external action which has all the earmarks of a denial of faith, e.g., partaking of "communion" at a Protestant service.

Though such direct and indirect denial is never permissible, circumstances could arise when *to conceal* one's faith would become not only permissible but even obligatory, provided always that sufficient reason warranted it, and that it did not entail any direct or indirect denial. Thus a priest or even a lay Catholic in time of persecution would be under no obligation to go about publicly proclaiming his faith; and similarly, a convert, for a sufficiently serious cause, could keep his conversion secret for a time.

2. **Positively,** one is obliged to make external profession of his faith: 1) whenever silence would do great injury to the honor of God or fail to win great honor for him; and 2) whenever silence would result in spiritual harm to one's neighbor. Injury to God's honor

[18]Encyclical *Mediator Dei,* Nov. 20, 1947.

would be found in the denial of the faith in the presence of the public authority, or even before a private individual if such a one were motivated by a hatred for religion. As for one's neighbor, one would be obliged to profess the true faith before him if silence would be certain to drive him further from the faith or even seriously impede his approach to it.

The practical guiding norm in all questions relating to the external profession of the faith, and a norm never to be lost sight of, is found in the following words:

> . . . the end of faith, as of all the virtues, ought to be referred to the end of charity, which consists in the love of God and neighbor; and, consequently, whenever the honor of God or the advantage of neighbor demands, a man should not be content merely to be united by faith to God's truth, but ought to confess his faith outwardly.[19]

5. The Virtue of Faith

A. Its Existence and Nature

Faith is more than a transitory act proceeding now and then under the intermittent influence of God's actual grace. The Scriptures speak of faith rather as a permanent disposition or quality that is requisite for salvation. St. Paul writes in this vein; "We, however, are not of those who draw back into destruction, but of those who have faith to the saving of the soul" (Heb. 10:39); "he who is just lives by faith" (Gal. 3:1; Rom. 1:17).

At the moment of his justification, when he is ingrafted into Christ, the sinner receives, along with sanctifying grace, "all these things infused simultaneously: faith, hope and charity."[20]

In this sense, then, faith was defined by the Vatican Council as "a supernatural virtue whereby we believe," and by St. Thomas

---

[19]St. Thomas, *Summa*, II-II, q. 3, a. 2, ad 1.

[20]Council of Trent, *loc. cit.*, Chap. 7, "The Nature of Justification and Its Causes"; Denz. 800. Before justification, faith exists, it seems, only as an *act* performed under the influence of an actual grace. Its presence as a *habit* would seem to be when it accompanies the first appearance of sanctifying grace in the soul.

as "a habit of the mind by means of which eternal life is begun in us, making the intellect assent to things that are not evident."[21]

The virtue of faith is absolutely necessary in order that the intellect may attain to the heights of God's supernatural message. As the eye can establish visual contact with the colored objects surrounding it only by means of physical light, so the intellect—the eye of the mind —is able to contact the supernatural revelation of God only through the instrumentality of some "light" proportionate to the nature of that revelation. And this "light" is precisely the divinely infused, theological virtue of faith.

B. Formed and Unformed Faith

Despite the astonishing perfection faith bestows upon the intellect, it still does not rise out of the category of an intellectual virtue. In spite of its supernatural dignity, therefore, it remains marked by a pronounced limitation of perfection. The intellectual virtues, it should be recalled, confer only a partial perfection on man; of their nature they seek, not the good of the whole man, but the good of the intellect alone. Hence the good scholar or the good artist is not thereby *the good man*.

Faith, of itself, cannot transcend its properly intellectual nature; it opens the door on supernatural truth, but nothing more. For this knowledge to be raised up outside the strictly intellectual sphere and directed to the good—and therefore to the ultimate goal—of the whole man, something other than faith must do the directing. And it is in exactly this manner that faith is directed by charity. It is charity which orders the acts of all the virtues to the true ultimate goal of man. Faith, then, loses its imperfection, becoming transformed from a dead to a living faith, from faith *unformed* to *formed* faith, only when the will orders it to the goal of the whole man, under the influence of charity.

Formed or **living faith** is so called because it is informed or animated by charity; thus it is oriented to man's supreme end, friendship with

[21]*Summa*, II-II, q. 4, a. 1.

God. **Unformed** or **dead faith,** on the contrary, is simply faith without its soul, cut off from charity. It remains a true virtue, however, because it does perfect the intellect in regard to its proper object, God himself and all revealed truth. But because of a bad will, turned from God by mortal sin, it is an imperfect virtue, lacking proper orientation to the ultimate goal.

C. The Subject of Faith

The discussion of the subject of the act of faith, while bearing primarily on the faculty (*proximate* subject) which properly elicits the act, includes also the question of the persons capable of placing this act (*remote* subject).

(1) The Faculty of Faith

The proximate subject of the act of faith is man's speculative intellect. This simple fact, taught by the Church for centuries, is in direct contradiction to the Protestant notion of faith as a kind of *confidence in God.* "If anyone should say that the faith that justifies is nothing other than a confidence in the divine mercy which does away with sin because of Christ, or that it is this confidence alone by which we are justified, let him be anathema."[22] Faith, far from being an act of the emotions or of the will, is of the intellectual order, even though its assent is caused by the will.

(2) The Possessors of Faith

The remote subject of the act of faith—those persons capable of making the act—fall into two classes. First, there are all living men, with the exception of all formal unbelievers; these unbelievers, as long as their obstinacy continues, block the movement of grace essential for the act of faith. Secondly, the souls in purgatory, since they have not yet attained the beatific vision, possess faith. The angels

[22]Council of Trent, Sess. VI, *Decree on Justification,* Can. 12; Denz. 822.

and blessed in heaven are incapable of this act because for them the obscurity of faith has given place to vision. The damned, both angels and human souls, have no contact with the supernatural; they are completely cut off from the gifts of God. Though the devils are said to "believe, and tremble" (Jas. 2:19), their belief is neither supernatural nor free; it is a mere natural faith forced on them by the very sharpness of their natural intellectual equipment.

D. The Cause of Faith

Anything and everything which has to do with the progress of man toward his supernatural goal must of necessity have its origin in God. "No one," Christ said pointedly to the Jews, "can come to me unless the Father who sent me draw him" (John 6:44) and, with even more explicit reference to faith, "no one knows the Son except the Father; nor does anyone know the Father except the Son, and him to whom the Son chooses to reveal him" (Matt. 11:27). From all that has been said to this point, it is clear that faith, whether its *act* or the *virtue*, can have no other cause but God himself.

Faith increases along with the growth of sanctifying grace. As faith is infused along with this grace, so it parallels it in growth. It follows, then, that God is the cause of the increase of faith as he is the cause of the increase in grace. By actions performed in the state of grace, man merely *merits* an increase of grace and faith; it is God who gives the increase. Though one's frequent and fervent acts of faith may produce a certain facility for eliciting similar acts in the future, this facility is not from a supernatural, but a natural habit.

The loss of faith can only be accomplished through a mortal sin of disbelief. One does not lose faith by sloughing off one truth at a time. It is possessed whole and entire, or it is lost totally; when any of faith is lost, all is lost. The reason for this is that when one denies even one truth, he necessarily rejects, in favor of his own judgment, the infallible revelation of God and the infallible teaching of the Church, destroying thereby the very foundation of his faith.

E. The Effects of Faith

Faith brings to man the only full and true picture of reality. In it God stands out as the rewarder of good and as the punisher of evil. For really to know God means to know him not only as the cause (for those who love him) of the eternal joy of heaven, but also as the one who, in passing judgment on sinners, consigns them to an eternity of punishment in hell. To believe in such a being and yet not fear him would certainly be to act unreasonably. This kind of fear, a direct effect or by-product of unformed faith, is called by theologians **servile fear.**

Faith also presents God as the only infinite good, the most desirable object to which man could aspire, the beneficent Father who lavishes unsurpassing love on his adopted children. When man is effectively and affectively united and subjected to God by means of grace and a faith animated by charity, servile fear gives place to **filial fear.** To the degree one grows in the love of God, to just such an extent his fear of eternal punishment gives place to the reverential fear of the child, who stands in horror of being separated from the tender love and care of his parents. Servile fear centers attention more and more on oneself; filial fear, on the contrary, directs one more and more to focus attention on God.

In addition to engendering salutary fear of God, faith is responsible for another effect, called by St. Thomas "The purification of the heart." By raising the mind to supernatural truth, faith directly frees man from the defilement of error, while at the same time it provides a basis for moral purity. Even unformed faith guarantees intellectual purity, but when charity impregnates faith this purfication is brought to its perfection by ridding the will of evil.

6. THE GIFTS ACCOMPANYING FAITH

When a man enters new and strange surroundings, he becomes painfully aware that the ready and easy familiarity which marked his former life in his native locale has left him. How many college freshmen away at school for the first time can attest to this fact! In its own unique way, faith catapults man into the world of the supernatural. "You are now no longer strangers and foreigners, but you are citizens with the saints and members of God's household" (Eph. 2:19). Man can hardly be blamed for not feeling completely at home in such an atmosphere.

It is the function of the gifts of understanding and knowledge to provide an air of connaturality for the mind of man in this world of supernatural truth. These gifts supply the flexibility and familiarity not furnished by faith itself, and make man more at home in this new and transcendent domain which is God's own world.

A. The Gift of Understanding

The **gift of understanding** may be defined as *a quality infused into the mind enabling it, under the impulse of the Holy Spirit, to penetrate the mysteries accepted by faith by means of a simple, intuitive perception.* The intellect thus equipped and under the influence of the Holy Spirit operates on a supernatural plane. Under the aegis of this gift, the human mind is enabled to live among the truths of faith with a ready and easy familiarity; a new perspective is achieved that gives deep insight into the things of God. Thus this gift enables some to penetrate the meaning of the Scriptures, others to discern the divine plan in souls; to some it gives a particular knowledge of Christ, of the mystery of Mary, or an understanding of the redemption, of providence, of the Real Presence.

Understanding is not a gift reserved for the select few who are far advanced on the way to sanctity. On the contrary, it is destined for all—its only requirement is the presence of sanctifying grace. Without this gift, the ordinary Christian is doomed to failure in living his life according to the divine plan, for his every action must embody divine truth, and be enlivened with the divine life. Without the gift of understanding, such an accomplishment is impossible.

Though all who are established in grace possess this gift, not all possess it to the same degree. In its lowest state, it will provide for a somewhat elementary penetration of the truths of faith sufficient to enable man to satisfy his obligations and to resist the ordinary difficulties that might arise. Those who live the life of the counsels will have a higher degree, perceiving more profoundly the content of supernatural truth. Finally, the highest degree of this gift will be found in the saints, those chosen souls who have so generously responded to God's graces and who are living the mystical life of grace, experiencing, through the inspiration of the Holy Spirit, an intimate knowledge of the presence of divinity.

B. The Gift of Knowledge

The **gift of knowledge** may be defined as *a quality infused into the mind enabling it, under the impulse of the Holy Spirit, to judge of created and human things in the light of the world of faith.* This gift makes an adjustment on man's view of the world. An unbeliever sees the world only as it appears to be; the Christian sees it as it is. God, as it were, shares his own view of creation with man by means of faith and the gift of knowledge. In effect, a twofold movement may be distinguished in the mind under the impulse of this gift: first, it judges on the true worth of creatures, realizing that they have come from God, and are to be used for his glory; secondly, in beholding the things of creation, it looks upon them as the footprints of God, bringing man always to a vital awareness of the nearness of God to his creation.

These two gifts, then, have as their function to further perfect the virtue of faith: the former accomplishes this by surpassing the simple adherence to revealed truth by means of the *intuitive perception* of their meaning; the latter *judges* all of creation in terms of the truths of faith.

7. SINS OPPOSED TO FAITH

Faith, as the "substance of things to be hoped for," constitutes the substructure of the spiritual life, "the foundation and root of all justification." Those sins, therefore, which would destroy or even endanger this precious gift assume an extremely grave malice. Further-more, as an added aggravating feature the loss of faith throws wide open the door leading to sins of every kind and description. As long as the sinner preserves his faith, he retains within himself the foundation of hope, the small spark capable of rekindling the flame of saving desire.

The sins against faith can be classified as either **sins of omission** or as **sins of commission.** To sin in the first manner, by omission, amounts simply to a deliberate failure to place an act that falls under the precept of faith. Thus, for example, one who failed to make an act of faith at the time of his death would sin by omitting an interior act that is obligatory. So, too, the Catholic father who would fail to speak up for the faith in the presence of his children when it was attacked by a non-Catholic neighbor would certainly be neglecting his obligation to profess the faith. In the light of the previous discussions concerning the necessity of the act of faith, the question of the sins against faith by omission offers no particular difficulty; a failure to place any of these necessary acts, either internal or external, amounts to a sin against faith.

Attention will be directed at this juncture exclusively to sins opposed to faith *by some contrary act,* i.e., to **sins of commission.** The outline on the next page provides a listing of the sins to be considered (including, for the sake of completeness, the sins of omission). In this section we will consider only the direct sins against the internal act of faith, that is, sins of unbelief; indirect sins against the internal act of faith and the sin of blasphemy will be matter for later treatment **(Section 8).**

A. Direct Sins against Faith in General

Unbelief is the contrary of faith. The man who has never had the word of God's revelation preached to him through no fault of his own, however, cannot be blamed for his state which is contrary to faith. This state of unbelief is what theologians call **negative unbelief,** and it is in no way sinful.

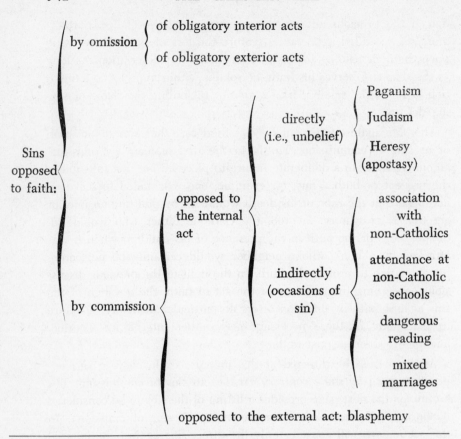

Sins opposed to faith:

by omission
- of obligatory interior acts
- of obligatory exterior acts

by commission
- opposed to the internal act
  - directly (i.e., unbelief)
    - Paganism
    - Judaism
    - Heresy (apostasy)
  - indirectly (occasions of sin)
    - association with non-Catholics
    - attendance at non-Catholic schools
    - dangerous reading
    - mixed marriages
- opposed to the external act: blasphemy

To be a sin, unbelief must involve a deliberate rejection of faith. This **positive unbelief** is *any act by which someone deliberately refuses to assent to a truth sufficiently proposed to him as revealed by God.* Such unbelief necessarily involves both contempt on the part of the will and obstinacy on the side of the intellect. Briefly, it may be said to consist in *any deliberate and obstinate refusal to believe.*

This refusal to believe may be found in a variety of subjects: 1) in one who has **never** possessed the Christian faith—the pagan; 2) in one who formerly possessed it, but **only in its pre-figures and prophecies**—the Jew; and 3) in one who formerly possessed it **in its full reality,** i.e, as culminating in **explicit** faith in Christ—the heretic.

Pagans and Jews do not reject faith in Christ after having accepted it; only the heretic does this. By no means, however, is everyone classified in ordinary speech as "a pagan," "Jew" or "heretic" guilty of the sin of unbelief. As designating sins against faith, these designations are to be taken *in their strict formal sense,* in the technical meaning given them by theology. Even though, *in a material sense,* these words signify some deficiency of belief in some of the truths commanded by precept, it would certainly be unrealistic, irrational and uncharitable to maintain today that every Jew, Protestant or pagan is involved in a serious sin of unbelief.[23] Those in the above categories are demnominated sinners only *when their rejection of the faith results from a deliberate and pertinacious will.* Hence, in our country, the greater number of Jews and Protestants unquestionably are to be ranked as *material* rather than *formal* unbelievers. They have been brought up in their unbelief from infancy, and have never sincerely doubted even momentarily the truth of their own faith.[24]

Were one of these material "unbelievers" seriously to question his religious position, seriously to doubt the truth of his religion (or lack of it), he would be obligated to investigate the facts. And if the facts of God's revelation and the claims of Christ's Church were honestly presented to him, then he would be obliged to the assent of faith, for God will give to sincere seekers the grace of conversion on his personal commitment to him. Knowledge, of course, is not enough, and pride and prejudice may well impede acceptance; but the seeker who is literally or figuratively on his knees may well receive the gift of eternal life. But the case is entirely different for the Catholic, for he possesses the true faith. Any truly voluntary *doubt* against the faith is gravely sinful; a genuine doubt is the

[23]These terms as technical theological expressions arose in the ages of faith, when the Christianity of Europe was so thorough and complete as to provide little subjective excuse for sins of unbelief. The Jew or pagan in "the lands across the seas" would be considered as non-believing (without faith—*negative* unbelief), not as unfaithful (*against* faith).

[24]It is under this aspect that the famous axiom *outside of the Church there is no salvation* must be understood: anyone who lives and dies outside the Church *by his own fault* will definitely be damned. Cf., against the radical and untraditional position of the Feeneyites, the letter of the Holy Office to Archbishop Cushing (*The Church Teaches* [St. Louis: Herder, 1952], 279).

equivalent of holding that faith is uncertain. But when the ordinary Catholic says that he entertained "doubts" about this or that mystery of faith, seldom, if ever, does this mean that he considered it actually as uncertain. This expression usually means that he experienced difficulty in grasping *how* it might be so. A thousand difficulties, Cardinal Newman pointed out, do not constitute a single doubt. Faith guarantees a doctrine's **truth**—*not its understanding*.

For pagan or Jew or disbelieving Catholic, in some imporant respect, the various types of formal unbelief are alike, for each completely destroys faith by rejecting its formal motive—the authority of God revealing. The heretic, however, offers (at least objectively) the greatest insult to God: he has turned his back on the truth after having once possessed it in its fulness. Certain aspects of this sin of heresy warrant further consideration.

B.　Heresy: The Particular Sin of Unbelief

Formal heresy is *the voluntary and obstinate denial by a baptized person of one or more truths revealed by God and proposed by the Church for belief.* The heretic deliberately denies the truth *despite his knowledge* that the Church proposes it as divinely revealed. This act is mortally sinful of its very nature; it does not admit any lightness of matter. For such an act involves the formal contempt of the truthfulness and authority of God himself.[25]

Apostasy is the name reserved for *the complete and total repudiation of the Christian faith on the part of a baptized person.* The apostate denies in its entirety what the heretic rejects in part. The net result in each case, it is to be remembered, is the same: complete destruction of the virtue of faith. Apostasy is not a sin specifically distinct from heresy; they differ in degree, not in kind. The Church attempts to open men's eyes to the devastating nature of these two

[25]Schism, which is the refusal to submit to the Vicar of Christ or to communicate with the members of the Church subject to him, attacks the unity of Christ's Mystical Body; as such it is directly opposed to charity (cf. Chapter Ten). Only too frequently, unfortunately, the formal schismatic is also a formal heretic, particularly since the definition of papal infallibility.

sins by providing severe ecclesiastical penalties for those who commit them *publicly*. The principal penalties are an excommunication specially reserved to the Holy See and denial of Church burial.

It should be remembered that both these sins are contrary to the *interior* act of faith; one is guilty of formal heresy or apostasy, therefore, even if he does not manifest his unbelief externally.

It is for this reason—the internal denial of faith—that the Church so vigorously opposes such religious societies as the Masons. In our country the individual Mason is, perhaps, seldom aware that he is committing himself to a religion in joining such a "benevolent fraternal society," one whose avowed public aims are so laudatory, so humanitarian, so unselfish, so liberal. Unfortunately, the Masons and their allied societies are, in secret, not only dedicated to the eradication of the Church—the political histories of too many nations of Europe and South America can supply documentation on this point—but proponents of a natural religion (less delicately, of sheer paganism), as their ceremonies of initiation to the various degrees testify.[26] Whatever the social or financial advantages of membership in such organizations, the Catholic will clearly recognize that it constitutes formal apostasy for one convinced of its tenets—a *complete* denial of his faith.[27] So serious and proximiate is this danger, and so subtle its temptation, that the Church excommunicates anyone who would even join the Masons or a similar secret anti-Catholic religious society (Can. 2335).

C. "Toleration" of Non-Catholics by Catholics

We come now to a very practical question: what should be the attitude of Catholics toward other religions? If the Catholic Church is indeed the true Church and her doctrines indeed revealed by God, then all religions which hold doctrines contrary to hers are to that extent false religions, even though their adherents be in good faith.

[26]For an objective but very revealing analysis see W. J. Whalen, *Christianity and American Freemasonry* (Milwaukee: Bruce, 1958).

[27]So true is this that many Protestant sects (the Missouri Synod of the Lutheran Church is an example) "read out of the Church" those who subscribe to a Masonic society.

In the modern world, where society is no longer solely Catholic nor Christian peoples inclined to admit that the Catholic Church is the one, true religion, the Catholic is faced with a paradox: if he gives his allegiance to the Catholic faith, on what basis can he maintain an attitude of toleration regarding other Christian and non-Christian religions? Is it not intrinsically immoral to permit other faiths to function? Obviously this question has great relevance in the United States where non-Catholics harbor considerable fear that Catholics will abbreviate the rights of non-Catholics if they come into political or social power.

Of the objective truth of the Catholic faith as the sole witness to divine revelation there can be no doubt. Nor can there be any doubt that, objectively speaking, all men are obliged to seek out and give their free adherence to this Catholic faith.

But on the practical level, are Christian states and Christian individuals permitted to tolerate the pesence and activity of objectively false religions? Pope Pius XII answered this question clearly:

> The question is raised whether . . . toleration is permissible, and whether, consequently, positive repression is not always a duty. . . .
> Could God, although it would be possible and easy for him to repress error and moral deviation, in some cases choose the "non impedire" without contradicting his infinite perfection? Could it be that *in certain circumstances* he would not give man any mandate, would not impose any duty, and would not even communicate the right to impede or to repress what is erroneous and false? A look at things as they are gives an affirmative answer. Reality shows that error and sin are in the world in great measure. God reprobates them, but he permits them to exist. Hence the affirmation: "religious and moral error must always be impeded, when it is possible, because toleration of them is in itself absolutely immoral," is not valid *absolutely and unconditionally.* . . .
> The duty of repressing moral and religious error cannot therefore be an ultimate norm of action. It must be subordinate to *higher and more general* norms, which *in some circumstances* permit, and even perhaps seem to indicate as the better policy, toleration of error to promote *a greater good.*
> Thus the two principles are clarified to which recourse must be had for the answer to the serious question concerning the attitude which the jurist, the statesman and the sovereign Catholic state is to adopt in consideration of the community of nations in regard to a formula of religious and moral toleration as described above. First,

that which does not correspond to truth or to the norm of morality objectively has no right to exist, to be spread or to be activated. Secondly, failure to impede this with civil laws and coercive measures can nevertheless be justified in the interests of a higher and more general good.

The Catholic statesman . . . will permit himself to be guided by weighing the dangerous consequences that stem from toleration against those from which the community of nations will be spared, if the formula of toleration be accepted.[28]

Toleration of moral and doctrinal error may, then, be permitted as God permits evil in the world, if the advantages—such as the good accruing to the community of nations—outweigh the evil effects.

8. OTHER SINS AGAINST FAITH

Sins opposed to faith destroy the very foundations of salvation. "Without faith it is impossible to please God," says St. Paul (Heb. 11:6). Those who are blessed with the faith have a serious obligation to preserve it. This means that they must not reject the faith, and also that they must not expose themselves imprudently to the danger of rejecting it. There are certain persons, places or things which can constitute a serious occasion for committing a direct sin of unbelief. Needlessly to expose oneself to such occasions is an indirect sin against faith. While there are many such dangerous occasions, four of them are deserving of special mention: joining with non-Catholics in religious affairs; attendance at non-Catholic schools; dangerous reading matter; and mixed marriages. Besides these indirect sins against the internal act, we will also consider the sin of blasphemy, directly opposed to faith's external act, the confession of faith.

A. Religious Co-operation with Non-Catholics

In any society where a variety of religious beliefs is professed, Catholics and non-Catholics associate frequently in business, social and political life. Such association will occasionally extend into the area of religion.

[28]Address to Italian jurists, Dec. 6, 1953.

There is a definite Catholic policy governing co-operating with non-Catholics in religious activities. This position is frequently misunderstood by non-Catholics; sometimes it is neglected by Catholics; occasionally it is criticized by both. For a number of reasons, this entire area of religious co-operation offers fertile ground for suspicion, hostility and other offences against charity and civic peace. An understanding of the principles upon which Catholic practice is based is indispensable for personal guidance in the face of complex and frequently embarassing situations; it is also essential for fulfilling the injunction of St. Peter to "be ready always with an answer to everyone who asks for a reason for the hope that is in you" (I Pet. 3:15).

All Catholic practice in associating with non-Catholics in religious activities is governed by the principle that **the Catholic Church, and she alone, has received from God the fulness of teaching and the perfection of worship whereby men must be saved.** Every norm for conduct in these matters is but a logical application of that principle.

(1) The Nature and Kinds of Religious Co-operation

Co-operation in religious activities is any kind of sharing in non-Catholic religious exercises or worship. It includes attendance at church services, offering prayers together, uniting in the reception of sacraments, building and maintaining places of worship, publishing and selling devotional literature, singing in choirs, contributing to religious causes, and many other similar activities.

The various forms of co-operation are classified as follows:

$$
\text{Co-operation in religious activities:}
\begin{cases}
\text{public} \begin{cases} \text{active} \\ \text{passive} \end{cases} \\
\\
\text{private} \begin{cases} \text{active} \\ \text{passive} \end{cases}
\end{cases}
$$

Public co-operation exists when the non-Catholics are engaged as an organized religious group in specifically religious exercises; e.g., divine service in a non-Catholic church. When the non-Catholics are performing some religious act simply as private persons, the co-operation is **private;** e.g., saying grace before meals in a private home. *Active* co-operatoin is present when the Catholic contributes positive acts of his own to non-Catholic religious practices—singing hymns in non-Catholic services or reciting non-Catholic prayers, for example. *Passive* co-operation exists when the Catholic is simply present without contributing any positive acts to the non-Catholic worship, as in the case of attending the funeral of a friend in a non-Catholic church.

(2) General Norms Governing Co-operation

1. Active co-operation in non-Catholic religious practices is forbidden by divine positive law. St. Paul forbade his converts to partake of the religious banquets which often accompanied the worship of their pagan neighbors.[29] And Christ warns: "Whoever disowns me before men, I in turn will disown him before my Father in heaven" (Matt. 10:33). To join in any false or unauthorized worship implies a denial of faith, and this is condemned by the Savior himself.

2. Passive co-operation in non-Catholic religious exercises is forbidden only when the circumstances create the danger of scandal or of the loss of one's faith. Divine law does not forbid mere bodily presence at such rites.

3. The general norms governing public co-operation are expressed in the canons of the Church:

1) "It is unlawful for the faithful to assist actively at, or to take part in the religious services of non-Catholics."

2) "A passive or merely material presence at funerals and weddings and similar solemnities of non-Catholics may be tolerated for the sake of civil duty or honor, because of a grave

---

[29] I Cor. 10:20 f. Cf. Fernand Prat, S.J., *The Theology of St. Paul* (Westminster: Newman, 1952), I, 117 f.

reason (to be approved by the Bishop in a doubtful case), pro-vided there is no danger of scandal or of loss of faith."[30]

3) "One who spontaneously and with full knowledge helps in any way in the propagation of heresy, or who co-operates in divine worship with heretics contrary to the provision of Canon 1258, is suspected of heresy."[31]

4. Private co-operation, either active or passive, is lawful only when *all* of these conditions are fulfilled:

1) there must be no proximate danger either of scandal or of loss of one's faith;

2) any remote dangers must be justified by the principle of double effect; and

3) there must be a sufficient reason for the co-operation.

(3) Practical Applications

While the Church issues general directives such as have been seen above, every contingency is not covered by a specific law or decision. Hence, there is great need for prudent judgment in particular cases. Theologians and canonists have written extensively on these problems, and their opinions are safe norms.[32] The following are some of their conclusions covering the more common instances of co-operation in non-Catholic religious activities.

1. Catholics may not act as sponsors at a non-Catholic baptism. Sponsors actively co-operate by asking for baptism in the name of the infant, and this is to seek a sacrament from an unauthorized minister. Passive co-operation at baptism is licit only when the conditions explained above are fulfilled.

2. In cases of extreme necessity (such as danger of death) when a Catholic priest is unavailable, a Catholic may seek the sacraments

---

[30]Can. 1258.

[31]Can. 2316.

[32]For an excellent and extensive summary, cf. J. R. Bancroft, *Communication in Religious Worship with Non-Catholics* (Washington: Catholic University Press, 1943). A brief summary excellent for classroom use is Francis J. Connell, C.SS.R., *Co-operation of Catholics in Non-Catholic Religious Activities* (Washington: The American Ecclesiastical Review, 1956).

of penance and extreme unction (and, according to some theologians, viaticum) from a validly ordained non-Catholic priest, provided that proximate danger of scandal and of loss of faith are removed.

3. A Catholic nurse may, at the request of a non-Catholic patient, inform a minister that a member of his church desires a visit. A Catholic hotel-owner may post notices of non-Catholic services in his lobby. A Catholic publisher may accept similar notices for his paper. These are merely information services which do not imply any promotion of the worship involved.

4. On the contrary, the Catholic nurse may not urge the services of non-Catholic religious officials upon her patients, nor may Catholics promote advertisements which urge people "to attend the Church of your choice." These activities actively promote worship which Catholics hold to be false, or contribute to the false principle of indifferentism that "one church is as good as another."

5. Generally, Catholics may not be official witnesses, bridesmaids or best men at non-Catholic weddings, for this is active participation in their worship. The same holds true for Catholics acting as pall-bearers at non-Catholic funerals. In certain dioceses some of these functions are considered not to pertain to the religious ceremony itself, and permission to fulfill them can be obtained.

6. Catholics may not sing or play instruments at non-Catholic services. This is always active participation.

7. When Catholics are lawfully engaged in public passive co-operation at non-Catholic services, they may do whatever courtesy and propriety demand. E.g., they may stand and sit with the congregation, and men may wear their hats during Orthodox Jewish ceremonies. Catholics, however, should not kneel during non-Catholic services (this is commonly considered by non-Catholics to be active assistance), except in those schismatic churches where the Blessed Sacrament is present.

8. Catholics taking oaths in the civil courts may use whatever Bible is presented as in general usage for all citizens.

9. While traveling, Catholics are not obliged to attend Mass on Sunday if the precept can be fulfilled only by attending Mass offered

by a non-Catholic priest. Such attendance is active co-operation in an unauthorized act of worship.

10. Near relatives, especially parents, brothers and sisters, could rarely have reason sufficient to justify their presence at a non-Catholic marriage ceremony for a Catholic member of their family. To attend such a ceremony would seem to approve the breaking of solemn laws of the Church, and would almost certainly give rise to grave scandal.

11. Catholics may not attend anti-Catholic funerals, such as those of apostates who chose to be cremated as a final gesture of contempt for the Church, or those wherein speeches against the faith are to be delivered. If grave obligations exist in these circumstances, they may be discharged by a visit to the wake.

12. Catholics may pray together privately with non-Catholics. It is understood that whatever prayers are used do not contain any false doctrines.

This is but a sampling of more commonly encountered cases involving religious co-operation. In understanding these norms and in applying others, it is important to be mindful of the great difference between charity and tolerance toward people of other beliefs, on the one hand, and compromise in religious truth on the other. Catholics are obliged to show charity toward all, and they are also obliged to be true and loyal to the faith which they have received as a most precious gift from God. In all matters we must be courteous and respectful toward the legitimate rights of our fellow citizens. But whenever the truths of salvation taught by Christ's Church are at stake, we cannot purchase the approval of men by being disloyal to the faith of God.

B. Attendance at Non-Catholic Schools

The Catholic attitude toward schooling is simply a corollary flowing from the Catholic evaluation of faith. Faith is so integral and indispensable an element in the Christian life as to pervade all of life's activities. The school is among the most influential factors in the experience of the young. If the truths of faith are excluded from its curriculum, and if the values and the influence of the faith are not operative in the school, the Christian education of the child must necessarily suffer.

The Church has a divine command from Christ to "teach all nations" (Matt. 28:19). Supernaturally she is the mother of men—whom she generates, nurtures and educates in the divine life of grace through her sacraments and her teaching. To obey this command of Christ and to fulfill this role of supernatural motherhood, the Church operates and directs her own schools, and watches over the spiritual welfare of those of her children who must attend (a growing problem in our day) other schools.

The school is an agency of education subsidiary and complementary to the family, the Church and the state. It operates on authority delegated chiefly by the parents, and its duty is the parental duty of preparing the child for his role as a member of the Mystical Body of Christ and as a citizen of the state. The school must respect the rights of all whose authority it shares.

The primary interest of the Church is in the spiritual welfare of her children. This concern is clearly expressed in the Canon Law regulating the education of the young:

> The education of all Catholics from their childhood must be such that not only shall they be taught nothing contrary to the Catholic faith and good morals, but religious and moral formation shall hold the most important place.
>
> Not only parents (as provided in Canon 1113), but also all those who take their place have the right and the most serious obligation of providing for the Christian education of the young.
>
> In every elementary school, religious formation must be imparted to the children in a manner suited to their age.
>
> Youths who attend higher schools are to receive a fuller religious training, and the Ordinaries shall see that this is given by priests conspicuous for their zeal and learning.[33]

These laws clearly provide for the positive elements in the religious education of the young in the schools. But just as the healthy child requires not only good nourishment but also protection from disease,

[33]Cf. Can. 1372-73.

so too Christian education demands that the child be safeguarded from influences that would weaken or destroy his faith. The law of the Church also provides safeguards against these dangers:

> Young Catholics shall not attend non-Catholic, undenominational or mixed schools (i.e., those which are open also to non-Catholics). It is up to the Ordinary alone to decide, in keeping with the instructions of the Holy See, under what circumstances and with what safeguards to prevent loss of faith it may be tolerated that Catholic children attend such schools.[34]

The important thing to note is that the principal concern of the Church is with the spiritual health of her children. It is clear from divine revelation that faith, together with sanctifying grace, is God's greatest gift to man. Voluntarily to take on oneself an avoidable risk of casting aside this great treasure for their children, as parents who send them to non-Catholic schools do, implies not only ingratitude toward the giver, but also a willingness to risk the loss of salvation for those they have brought into the world.

No one can deny that attendance at any non-Catholic school involves some degree of danger to faith. At best, such schools must create a neutral atmosphere in matters of faith. A teaching that is ignored can easily be regarded as irrelevant; such an atmosphere is the incubator of indifferentism: "He who is not with me is against me; and he who does not gather with me scatters" (Luke 11:23). At worst, non-Catholic schools disparage or attack the faith, and strive to extirpate it from the minds and hearts of their pupils.

In certain circumstances, Ordinaries may allow Catholics to attend non-Catholic schools provided adequate provision is made for their religious instruction and if they are not exposed to direct attacks against their faith. Hence the importance of "release time" periods for grammar school and high school students, and Newman Clubs and allied organizations at the college level. But no permission can ever be obtained to attend a school which is positively anti-Catholic; the natural and divine laws are as inflexible against spiritual self-destruction as they are against suicide.

---

[34]Cf. Can. 1374. For a detailed study of this entire problem, cf. C. H. Boffa, *Canonical Provisions for Catholic Schools* (Washington: Catholic University Press, 1939), 77-126.

C. Dangerous Reading

Education is not confined to schools. Reading is a potent influence in shaping attitudes and in acquiring convictions. Many books deal directly with matters of faith, and many more are concerned with them either indirectly or by implication.

It is precisely because of the influence of reading upon the religious faith of her children that the Church is concerned with the judgment of books. The encouragement and support of literature and art has been part of the Catholic tradition from earliest times; this is only the effect of the Church's general concern for the enrichment of the human mind as an adjunct of her principal mission of salvation. But the protection of the faith against the effects of harmful reading requires more formal organization, just as the state passes practically no laws to promote good eating habits and very many laws against the sale of tainted or unwholesome food.

The primary norm in regulating man's choice of reading is to be found in the natural law. The natural law is antecedent to, and independent of all man-made laws, whatever their origin. Consequently, even if no positive law had ever been passed to regulate reading, no one would be free from all restrictions to read whatever attracted his curiosity without regard for the consequences to faith and morals.

The natural moral law obliges all men to avoid any grave danger to faith or morals. There are many books which constitute just such a danger. For that reason, the reading of such books is forbidden to all by natural law. Thus there are many books not specifically prohibited by any particular law which would be forbidden for everyone, because they are generally a grave danger to faith and morals. In addition, there are many books which would be forbidden by natural law to particular individuals. (e.g., to the young or to the uninstructed) because of their special susceptibility to the harmful influence of certain books.

These general norms of the natural law are made explicit and are augmented by the Church, first, by the general laws which govern the prohibition of books; and, secondly, by the list of specific titles expressly condemned and placed on the Index of Forbidden Books. The following categories summarize the more commonly applicable regulations of the general laws which forbid the publication, reading, possession, sale or translation of:

1. Books which designedly defend, propagate or persuade people to accept heresy or schism.

2. Books which undertake to destroy the truths which are fundamental to religion, e.g., the existence of God, the spirituality of the soul, the freedom of the will, the possibility of divine revelation or of miracles, etc.

3. Books which assiduously attack either natural religion, or the Catholic faith, or good morals. This does not include books which may make some slurring remark or which may include some brief objectionable passage; rather it refers to books which set forth many arguments or which devote the equivalent of a chapter to such purposes.

4. Books written by non-Catholics which professedly treat of religion, unless it is clear that they contain nothing of consequence contrary to the Catholic faith.

5. Books which attack any article of Catholic faith, which assiduously defend any error condemned by the Holy See; which deride divine worship; which strive to destroy ecclesiastical discipline; or which attack, repudiate or demean the concept of the hierarchy, of the clerical state or of the religious life.

6. Books which teach or propagate superstition and similar perversions of true religion.

7. Books which defend as moral the practices of duelling, suicide or divorce.

8. Books which present Masonry and similar secret sects, not as pernicious, but as useful to the Church and civil society.

9. Books relating new miracles, prophesies, visions, etc., or promoting devotional novelties, when they are published in despite of canonical regulations.

10. Books which publicize spurious indulgences, or those proscribed or revoked by the Holy See.

11. Any images of our Lord, the Blessed Virgin, or the angels and saints which are not in keeping with the spirit and decrees of the Church.

12. Editions and translations of the Sacred Scriptures which are published by non-Catholics.

13. Books which professedly discuss, describe or teach impure and obscene topics.

The foregoing summary of the general classes of prohibited books is also to be applied to daily papers, periodicals and other publications, unless it is made clear that only books are meant.[35]

---

[35]Cf. Can. 1384.

In addition to these general categories of prohibited books, there is also a list of specifically condemned titles. This is the **Index of Forbidden Books.** The majority of titles on the Index comprises theological and philosophical studies considered to be particularly harmful to faith or morals. A much smaller number is prohibited because of obscenity. All books contained in the Index belong to some category of the general laws on the prohibition of books, but not every forbidden book—nor even the major portion of them—is listed by title in the Index.[36]

It should be noted that permission to read books forbidden by general law or specifically on the Index may be obtained from the local Ordinary, generally through the diocesan chancery. A sufficient reason must be offered for sustaining the dangers involved—serious research, scientific studies, etc. Merely securing the necessary permission, however, does not confer any guarantee against these risks, and individual readers must be guided by prudence in these matters.

D. Motion Pictures, Television and Radio

The general attitude toward books is applicable to the more recent types of communication, when due allowance is made for the differences among the arts concerned. The motion picture—and, more recently, the radio and television—have multiplied the means of communication, of entertainment and of influence. It is clear that these newer scientific developments and the arts which use them create many problems in the moral sphere.[37] The Christian must use prudence to insure that these media do not jeopardize his faith

[36]The Index, and translations thereof, are published by The Vatican Polyglot Press for about $3.00. Copies may be obtained from the larger Catholic bookstores or borrowed from Catholic libraries. For explanation of the Index, cf. R. A. Burke, *What Is The Index?* (Milwaukee: Bruce, 1952); an eminently practical booklet is, P. M. J. Clancy, O.P., *The College Student and Forbidden Books* (Chicago: Cathedral Book Club, 1948). For further discussion see "The Problem of Prohibited Books and the American Catholic Intellectual," *Proceedings of the Society of Catholic College Teachers of Sacred Doctrine*, VI (1960) 83-96.

[37]Two of the late popes have written encyclicals on these arts. Both should be read. Cf. Pope Pius XI, encyclical *Vigilanti Cura* (On Decent Motion Pictures), June 29, 1936; Pope Pius XII, encyclical *Miranda Prorsus* (On Motion Pictures, Radio and Television), September 8, 1957.

or morals. He must be docile to his superiors and willing to accept the counsel of wise judges in choosing what he will watch and hear. He must be as quick to commend and support what is good as he is to condemn what is harmful. And if he be favored with talent and training, he should at least consider the possibility of dedicating his efforts to improving these arts which can be so helpful to learning and culture, and to an indispensable relaxation characterized by Christian joy.

E. Mixed Marriages

No other association between humans is so intimate, so constant and so prolonged as marriage. When the partners are divided upon religious convictions, an essential avenue of communication about indispensable matters is either obstructed or closed. An area of communication becomes an area of compromise; what could be a common source of healing is made an additional irritant. Mixed marriages create very special dangers to the Catholic's faith; that is why the Church is unalterably opposed to them.[38]

The concern of the Church about the loss of all religious spirit consequent upon mixed marriage is shared by many non-Catholic religious leaders. The loss of faith among Catholics in *valid* mixed marriages has been shown in recent sociological studies. Whereas only 5% of non-Catholic partners are converted during their marriage, over 40% of the Catholic spouses cease to practice their religion; around 40% of all children born in such marriages are either unbaptized, or baptized as Protestants, or simply baptized without recieving any instruction in the faith. The results of *invalid* mixed marriages are, naturally enough, even more appalling.[39]

[38]This subject has been treated at length in: T. C. Donlan, O.P., *et al.*, *Toward Marriage In Christ* (Dubuque: The Priory Press, 1957), 22, 58 ff., 62, 120 f. An excellent, imaginative and brief presentation of the problem in practical terms, based on a true life experience, is available in an inexpensive pamphlet, *I Love You, But* . . . (Union City: The Sign Magazine, 1952).

[39]John L. Thomas, S.J., "Mixed Marriages and the Future," in *Sanctity and Success in Marriage* (Washington: 1956, Family Life Bureau).

F. Blasphemy

The sins against the internal act of faith are many, and most of them are by nature very grave. We have still to consider, however, one area of human failure with respect to the obligations of faith: that of acting against its external act. Any assertion, either vocal or written, that some truth of the faith is false, or that some erroneous doctrine is true, is certainly a sin against the obligation to profess the faith outwardly. Such sins, however, are not formally distinct from the inner denial of faith that takes place in the mind, being merely its full flowering in the external order.

There does exist a sin, however, that of its very nature is contrary to the external profession of faith, and that is blasphemy. For **blasphemy,** in its strictest meaning, is *the utterance of contemptuous speech against God.* Here is a sin necessarily involving outward manifestation; it is a *public* act of its very nature. It is an out-and-out affront to God's honor, accomplished by the contemptuous denial to God of something that is his, or the attribution to him of something that does not belong to him. In this wise, blasphemy offends against faith since it attempts to disfigure the concept of God that faith presents. Since the object of this scorn is the infinite majesty of God, blasphemy admits of no lightness of matter; it is of its nature mortally sinful. Only inadvertence or lack of awareness of one's action can lessen its gravity.

9. THE PRECEPTS OF FAITH

To someone without faith, a command to believe would be quite meaningless. How, then, can there be any meaningful positive precept of faith? The answer is that faith in God's existence must first be accepted before a man can be subject to any precepts to believe the other articles of faith. "He who comes to God must believe that God exists" (Heb. 11:6). This beginning of faith comes as a gift, and once it is accepted, it becomes the foundation whereon rest all the

other precepts we have previously considered to believe the truths
of divine revelation.

10. SUMMARY AND CONCLUSION

It is extremely difficult fully to appreciate the importance of faith.
The majority of Catholics—we so-called "born Catholics"—have been
rubbing elbows with mystery so long that its aura of transcendent
excellence usually loses some of its brilliance. Faith becomes something taken for granted, and its nature as a completely gratuitous gift
of God is too often forgotten or overlooked. Against these tendencies
the faithful must wage relentless war.

Man has absolutely no claim or right to faith. It is pure gift on
the part of God; its supernatural character is proof of this. And faith,
first, last and always, is of the supernatural order. For by faith alone
is man enabled to share in the living knowledge of Christ, to
participate in his own personal contact with his Father. To share in
this supernatural revelation of God is not something simply difficult
for man to accomplish, it is absolutely impossible without God's help.
With St. Paul, the believer must say, "by the grace of God I am
what I am" (I Cor. 15:10).

The act of faith, proceeding from a divinely implanted supernatural virtue and under the divinely instigated movement of actual
grace, enables man to accept the only all-inclusive view of reality
as it truly is. Men are brought into a universe that consists in much
more than appears to earthly eyes, or that can be discerned by
reason's natural capacities. A whole supernatural order of life and
truth completes the picture of things as they really exist. And the
only truly healthy mind is that which embraces both the natural and
supernatural aspects of this real order. This can only be done through
the supernatural virtue of faith: a gift supernatural in origin, in
purpose, in manner of operation.

When God thus enables the mind of man to assent to his word,
then, and only then, does man begin to contact eternity. The "Credo"
of the believer is the beginning of his salvation, truly eternal life

begun. Thus is given meaning to the words of the Preface for the Mass of the dead: "For to those who believe in thee, Lord, life is only changed, not taken away; and in exchange for the dissolution of this earthly dwelling place they receive an eternal home in heaven."

The world today could profit much from a sincere, humble and prayerful consideration of this first of the theological virtues. And the following points might serve well as springboards to further thought concerning the world today and the faith of Christianity:

1. "The source and root of all the evils which affect individuals, people and nations with a kind of poison, and which confuse the minds of many is this: ignorance of the truth—and not only ignorance, but at times a contempt for, and a deliberate turning away from it. This is the source of all manner of errors which, like contagious diseases, pass deep into minds and into the very blood stream of human society and turn everything upside down, with serious damage to all individuals and to the whole human race."[40]

2. "Moreover, there are those who, though they do not deliberately attack the truth, yet by neglect and extreme carelessness work against it—as if God has not given us a mind to search for and arrive at the truth. This depraved manner of acting leads by an easy path to the ridiculous opinion that there is no difference between the true and the false, and so all religions are equally true.

"To use the words . . . of our predecessor, 'this kind of reasoning was aimed at the destruction of all religions, and particularly of the Catholic, which, since it alone is true, cannot without serious injustice be placed on a level with the others.'

"Moreover, to reckon that there is no difference between contraries and opposites has surely this ruinous result, that there is no readiness to accept any religion either in theory or in practice."[41]

3. "In the giddiness of material progress; in the victories of human ingenuity over the secrets of nature and over the forces of the elements of the earth, the seas and the sky; in the anxious competition to surpass the summits reached by others; in the arenas of daring research, in the

[40]John XXIII, encyclical *Ad Petri Cathedram*, June 29, 1959.
[41]*Ibid.*

conquests and in the pride of science, of industry, of laboratories, of factories; in the greed for money and for pleasure, in the tense effort toward a supreme power more feared than contended for, more envied than equalled; in the turmoil of all this modern life, where can the naturally Christian soul of man find peace? Perhaps in finding contentment in itself? Perhaps in boasting to be king of the universe, enveloped by the fog of illusion which confuses matter with the spirit, the human with the divine, the momentary with the eternal?

"No! Intoxicating dreams do not calm the storm in the soul and a conscience put into turmoil by the impetus of mind which stands above matter and, aware of its unrejectable immortal destiny, steps over toward the infinite and toward immense desires. Approach those souls and question them. They will answer you in the language of a child, not of a man.

"They did not have a mother who would speak of the Father in heaven when they were children; they grew up between walls without a cross, in homes where religion was not mentioned, in fields far away from altar and from steeple; they read books from which the names of God and Christ were absent; they heard priests and monks and nuns vituperated; they went from the countryside, from the city, from their homes—went to the factory, to the shop, to the halls of knowledge, to every art and work, without entering a church, without knowing the parish priest, without a good thought put in their hearts."[42]

BIBLIOGRAPHICAL NOTE

The subject matter of this chapter is paralleled in St. Thomas' *Summa*, II-II, Questions I-XVI. The Benziger edition of the English *Summa*, III, 3289-3305, contains an excellent article by James R. Gillis, O.P., that covers the same matter in a style at once popular, exact and to the point. Martin D'Arcy, S.J., has written two valuable works on

[42]Pius XII, address to the leaders of Catholic Action, May 3, 1951.

this subject, *The Nature of Belief* (London: Sheed and Ward, 1934) and *Belief and Reason* (London: Burnes, Oates and Washbourne, 1946).

Francis J. Connell, C.SS.R., has an article emphasizing the need for greater awareness and understanding of the faith on the part of the ordinary Catholic, so that he might be able to speak about it intelligently with non-Catholics: "The Need of a Knowledge of the Faith," in the *American Ecclesiastical Review*, CXXVI (1952), 195-203. For a look at faith as conceived by St. Paul, plus some worthwhile references to Protestant theology, consult Fernand Prat, S.J., *The Theology of St. Paul* (Westminster, Md.: The Newman Bookshop, 1927), II, 233-253, 450-455. "Act of Faith," by H. F. Davis in *Theology Digest*, I (1953), 119-122, also considers the Protestant view of faith and compares it with the Catholic position. On the technical side, but of value for those interested in the mechanics of the act of faith, the following may be consulted: "St. Thomas and the Act of Faith," by B. Duroux, in *Theology Digest*, IV (1956), 87-91, and "Function of Natural Reason in Eliciting the Act of Faith," by P. Parente, in the same periodical, I (1953), 157-160. A not too difficult article portraying the role of apologetics in regard to faith is "Faith and Apologetics," by P. DeLetter, S.J., which appears in the *Irish Ecclesiastical Review*, LXXXII (1954), 310-321. Faith in relation to man's spiritual life is the subject of "Life of Faith," by Bishop G. A. Beck in *Blackfriars*, XXXVII (1956), 148-164, an excellent article wherein faith is related to many very practical points of current interest. On the spiritual repercussions of faith two good articles are "Spirituality for All: Divine Activity," by J. J. McDonald, O.P., in *Cross and Crown*, IX (1957), 92-108, and "Grandeur of Faith," by H. M. Christmann, O. P., in the same periodical, IV (1952), 344-355.

For help in solving the many practical cases that arise concerning one's obligations toward the faith the following are quite valuable: "Co-operation of Catholics in Non-Catholic Activities," by F. J. Connell, C.SS.R., in the *American Ecclesiastical Review*, CXXXIV (1956), 98-108, 190-200, 240-250; "Obligation of Professing the Faith," by the same author in the same periodical, CXXVIII (1953), 81-89, and CXXIX (1953), 28-37.

CHAPTER NINE

Hope: The Assurance of God

1. INTRODUCTION

The Christian concept of hope is necessarily a theological concept, for the nature of hope and its precise dimensions are known only by divine revelation: ". . . the eyes of your mind being enlightened, so that you may know what is the hope of his calling, what the riches of the glory of his inheritance in the saints, and what the exceeding greatness of his power towards us who believe" (Eph. 1:18-19).

But just as grace presupposes nature, so revelation presupposes human life and human activity. Revelation is *for* man: what God tells us, even when bearing the stamp of divine mystery, is revealed in terms of what man already knows and understands. Hence divine faith is likened to the seed of human faith already planted in man's nature; divine charity is likened to the perfecting of man's natural emotion of love; supernatural hope is spoken of by God as something like the feeling of hope that ebbs and flows in man's daily life.

Hope, then, is first of all a passion residing in the sense appetite, an emotion bridging the gap between desire for some good and the joy of its attainment. Hope looks to the future, to some good not yet possessed, for man does not waste his hope on some good he already has. Hope, too, is concerned only with a good which demands a stalwart courage, a good difficult of attainment: these emotional energies will not be squandered on something lying easily within his grasp. One the other hand, hope's gaze does not long contemplate the impossible; it would be a useless expenditure to hope for some good impossible of attainment.

This, then, is human hope: a movement of the sense appetite toward 1) an *unpossessed* good, 2) waiting somewhere in the *future,* 3) *difficult* of attainment, and yet 4) *capable* of being attained. Equipped with these basic natural notions, we shall search out the characteristics of *supernatural* hope, as they have been revealed by God, according to the following outline:

The theological virtue of hope

{

Its existence and definition
(Section 2)

Its object and necessity
(Section 3)

Its subject of inherence
(Section 4)

The gift of fear
(Section 5)

Sins against hope
(Section 6)

The precept of hope
(Section 7)

2. THE EXISTENCE AND NATURE OF HOPE

A. The Existence of Hope

The existence of supernatural hope, precisely because it is supernatural, can be known only by divine revelation. Its roots, in fact, are planted far back in the revelation of the Old Testament. The unique vocation of Israel made it the perfect proving ground for supernatural hope, which was explicitly inaugurated with God's promise to Abraham: "I will make a great nation of you. I will bless you, and make your name great, so that you shall be a blessing" (Gen. 12:2). Thereafter the true nature of hope was revealed little by little, the history of Israel being a record of the advance from one hope to another in a journey toward the precise object of all Old Testament hope, the promise of a new kingdom and a Messias, ". . . whose empire shall be multiplied, and there shall be no end of peace: he shall sit upon the throne of David, and upon his kingdom . . ." (Isa. 9:7).

Then Jesus appeared as the Savior, and the hope of the Old Testament was realized in the establishment of the kingdom of God on earth: "The kingdom of God has come upon you" (Matt. 12:28). This kingdom was a spiritual one, not the material power many Jews had been expecting; as such it offered a new and even greater object of hope, *the hope of eternal life*, of a kingdom of the elect, who shall rise to glory at Christ's second coming. And this kingdom is both gift of God and reward for individual merit: "If thou wilt be perfect, go, sell what thou hast, and give to the poor, and thou shalt have a treasure in heaven" (Matt. 19:21).

It is this fuller, more perfect concept of supernatural hope which is the object of the Church's pronouncement. Thus the Council of Trent declared: "faith, unless hope and charity be added to it, neither unites one perfectly with Christ, nor makes him a living member of his body."[1] And the same ecumenical synod condemned anyone who says that "the just ought not, for their good works performed in God, to expect and hope for eternal reward from God, through his mercy and the merit of Jesus Christ."[2] Hence the Church proposes for belief both the existence of supernatural hope and its dependence on the mercy and aid of God.

[1]Sess. VI, *Decree on Justification*, Chap. 7, "The Nature of Justification and Its Causes"; Denz. 800.

[2]*Ibid.*, Can. 26; Denz. 836.

B. The Nature of Hope

In the light of what we know about human hope we can interpret the facts of revelation so as to formulate a theological definition of divine hope. **Supernatural hope** is *a divinely infused virtue by which, with certain confidence, we expect, by divine assistance, eternal happiness and the means of attaining it.*

This definition describes the nature of the theological virtue of hope, containing all of its important elements:

1) a genus, by which hope is distinguished from the mere human passion of hope and all natural virtues—**a virtue divinely infused;**

2) its proper act, which distinguishes hope from other divinely infused virtues—**to expect;**

3) an essential property—**with certain confidence;**

4) its material object, that which hope obtains—**eternal happiness and the means to attain it;**

5) the formal object, the motive or reason for our hope—**by divine assistance.**

3. THE OBJECT AND NECESSITY OF HOPE

To obtain a deeper appreciation of this great theological virtue, we must examine more closely some of the cardinal features of hope—its dual object, eternal happiness and divine aid, its relationship with the other theological virtues, its necessity. But although we shall consider separately the material and the formal object of hope, it should be emphasized that in reality they are inseparable: if we strive to possess eternal happiness without reliance on divine assistance, we destroy hope; if we depend on divine assistance to will anything other than eternal happiness and its means, our efforts are equally destructive.

Any faculty, any habit, any virtue, any operation possesesss such a dual object; they are, as it were, its matter and form, its body and soul, its genus and species. *What* faith attains, for example—i.e., its material object—is all that God has revealed. The aspect or formality *by which* faith attains what it attains—the formal object—is the authority of God revealing. Knowledge of both of these gives us an insight into the nature of faith, and for a similar knowledge of hope we now ask: what are its objects, and what do they tell us about this virtue?

A. The Material Object

All hope, even the human passion of that name, urges man toward good. But the good man hopes for by supernatural hope is an infinite goodness, a goodness consonant with his supernatural destiny: this good is eternal life, which consists in the enjoyment of God himself. This is the kingdom of God realized in its perfect state, the vision of the divine essence, of God the supreme good. This is the primary object of hope.

But in the very movement of hope toward its primary object, man's supernatural destiny, there is included everything which helps man toward its attainment, every necessary means to reach this end—remission of sin, increase of sanctifying and actual grace, particular virtues, material goods, the fulfillment of the duties attached to one's state of life.[3]

B. The Formal Object

One of the Church's formulas for an act of hope begins in this way: "O my God, relying on thy infinite goodness and promises. . . ." This is an explicit expression of the means by which eternal happiness will be attained, the promise of God; and, implicitly, it includes other divine attributes which underlie this means. The problem to be solved, then, is the determination of that precise attribute in God which is the proper basis (formal object) on which hope depends for the attainment of its goal.

---

[3]Jesus Christ himself pointed this out: "But seek first the kingdom of God and his justice, and all these things shall be given you besides." (Matt. 6:33). Cf. Rom. 5:2; Titus 1:2; Heb. 6:18; I John 3:2.

In the first place, the material object of hope is the kingdom of God, which transcends our own unaided power. We must rely, therefore, on the almighty power of God—his omnipotence—aiding us here and now in order that a good of such surpassing difficulty may become possible for us. *The formal object or motive for hoping is, it seems clear, the omnipotence of God actually assisting us.* Why does the Christian confidently expect eternal happiness and the graces necessary for his realization of it? Because he trusts that God, almighty in power, is actually going to help him, is actually helping him here and now.

This is implied in Scripture: "You have hoped in the Lord for evermore, and in the Lord God mighty forever" (Isa. 26:4); "and God is able to make all grace abound in you, so that always having ample means, you may abound in every good work" (II Cor. 9:8). It is also equivalently affirmed by the Church: ". . . let no one promise himself anything as certain . . . although all ought to place and repose a very firm hope in God's help."[4]

And yet the omnipotence of God would not help us attain the object of our hope unless God were kindly disposed toward us by his mercy: "But I . . . trust in the kindness of God forever and ever" (Ps. 51:10). Furthermore, the certainty that God will aid us by his power depends on God's faithfulness to his promises: "Let us hold fast the confession of our hope without wavering, for he who has given the promise is faithful" (Heb. 10:23).

Nevertheless, the *proximate* motive or formal object of hope is the assisting omnipotence of God, the means whereby hope obtains what is hoped for, although this necessarily presupposes God's mercy and God's fidelity to his promises.[5] Note that the motive of our hope is not the mere omnipotence of God; the knowledge that God *could* aid us by his power is not enough. It is his actual exercise of that power on our behalf which is our assurance that our hope is not vain.

Since the power of God is the principal efficient cause of our salvation, we hope primarily in him. God, however, also uses creatures as a foundation for each man's hope for salvation—the merits of Christ's

---

[4]Council of Trent, *loc. cit.*, Chap. 13, "The Gift of Perseverance"; Denz. 806. Cf. also Gen. 15:1; Ps. 17:3; Ps. 118.

[5]Cf. St. Thomas, *De Virtutibus,* q. 4, a. 1.

humanity; the prayers and sacrifices of the saints and martyrs, especially of the Blessed Virgin; grace and the prayers of our friends and relatives; the sacraments; and, not least of all, our own merits in this life. This does not mean that we hope in other men as though they were the primary causes of our journey toward eternal happiness; rather, we hope in them as in secondary or instrumental causes in dependence on divine omnipotence, subordinate causes through whom we are helped in obtaining certain goods ordained to happiness.

C. Hope in Company with Faith and Charity

Hope, then, is a supernatural virtue, both because of its dual object —the omnipotence of God helping us and the goodness of God to be shared by us—and because it is caused by a supernatural principle, grace. Thus, since the act of hope is a supernatural means to a supernatural end, it must itself be supernatural.

Hope, like faith and charity, is a theological virtue because it adheres to God as its object. But there is a difference in the way hope adheres to God which makes it distinctive. Charity adheres to God for his own sake; faith adheres to him as he is the font of the knowledge of truth; but hope adheres to him as he is the *source of perfect goodness*—that is, through hope, we are confident of divine aid for attainment of eternal life. Without faith there would be no object of hope, for faith's knowledge provides an object: faith is "the substance of things to be hoped for" (Heb. 11:1). Charity has an even closer relationship with hope—first of all because, as we shall see, hope, like charity, is a virtue of the will; and secondly, because both are a kind of love.

Hope's love is what we might call a **love of need,** and this distinguishes it from the higher love of charity. Many Protestants deny or minimize the supernaturality of hope, because according to them it is essentially inordinate and imperfect, its love selfish and mercenary: we desire God as a good for ourselves, and we love him for the sake of an attached reward.

In answer to this objection, we must state that the love of hope, although imperfect, is still supernatural. It is imperfect only when compared with the love of charity, which is the complete form of love. Hence, it does not *exclude* the higher motive of charity, but merely *abstracts* from it.

Simply because we love God as *our* good is not to deny that he is *in himself* supremely good and supremely lovable for his own sake. Hope does not act for a reward alone, as though having no thought for any higher motive of operation. A spiritual reward, however, can be a powerful incentive in this life, and is certainly paramount in God's plan for man, satisfying a desire he himself implanted deep within human nature. After all, a necessary condition of all our willing and loving is that everything we will or love be good *for us;* otherwise, we would never will or love it.

Our love, then, is selfish only in the sense that we refer God to ourselves as the source of perfection is referred to the mere capacity for perfection. We are potency; God is act. We desire to have our potency actualized by perfect act. This love is certainly not a disordered love; God himself willed that his Son become incarnate for man's sake, which does not mean that God thereby became subordinate to man, but rather manifested God's own superiority, for his perfection alone could remedy man's imperfection. God is man's highest good. We do not desire him as a means for our own end and reward, but rather as the object and end **which** is attained. In other words, man is merely the end **for which** the object of hope is obtained. God is desired by man, therefore, not as a means is desired for an end, but as the perfect is desired for the perfectible.

Consequenly, hope's love leads to charity, a journey from imperfection to perfection, from limited contemplation to an unlimited joyful contemplation, and from personal exclusiveness to an inclusive, all-embracing identifying union with both God and neighbor. Without charity hope would be a dead virtue. Although hope can exist in the soul devoid of charity, it is perfect hope and a perfect virtue only when enlivened by charity. Where charity has been driven out, as in the soul in the grip of mortal sin, hope is called *unformed hope,* because its ultimate perfection—its "form"—is lacking. Hope without charity is not fully orientated to man's last end.

D. The Necessity of Hope

Hope can be considered as a habit or as an act. The habit of hope, the inclination toward eternal happiness, is absolutely necessary as a means of salvation for all men, children as well as adults. This necessity flows from the very nature of salvation itself, since the flowering of charity which is eternal life is unattainable unless it be hoped for: "For faith, unless hope and charity be added to it, neither unites one perfectly with Christ, nor makes him a living member of his body."[6]

The act of hope, the very expectation of the supernatural goal, is absolutely necessary for adults having the use of reason, since these must deliberately tend toward and confidently expect supernatural salvation. Indeed, the act of hope is commanded both of sinners and those in the state of grace alike. This means, in general, that the act of hope is morally necessary for the just, since hope naturally follows upon faith, which is ncessary for all: "Trust in him at all times, O my people! Pour out your hearts before him; God is our refuge!" (Ps. 61:9).[7]

4. THE SUBJECT OF HOPE

Hope is the personal and proper possession of man the wayfarer, who trudges the road of life toward God, whom he neither sees nor possesses but, nevertheless, desires as his good. Hence it is an act of man's appetitive power; and, since God is a divine good, not a sensible one, the act of hope by which man desires God belongs to his higher appetitive power, the will, rather than to his lower

---

[6]Council of Trent, *loc. cit.*, Chap. 7, "The Nature of Justification and Its Causes"; Denz. 800.

[7]Cf. also Wisd. 2:22; I Cor. 9:24 f.; Heb. 3:6, 13:14.

appetite. The will, then, is the proximate subject of inherence for the theological virtue of hope.

Since the wayfarer sets as his goal a good which is future and difficult of attainment but still possible, man alone can possess this virtue. The blessed in heaven no longer hope because eternal life is present for them, not future. Even Christ did not experience hope, for in this life he always possessed the beatific vision. On the other hand, Our Lady had infused hope while she lived on earth, since the beatific vision was not yet hers.

Hope remains, too, in the souls in purgatory, because their happiness is still future, still arduous and difficult of attainment, something to be earned through suffering. The fact that those in purgatory are certain of eternal life is of no consequence, for certitude is actually part of theological hope. The damned in hell have no hope, because eternal happiness is no longer possible for them.

Hope is infused in the soul of the warfarer at the same time as sanctifying grace, faith and charity. It is not necessarily lost, however, when charity is lost, i.e., with the commission of any mortal sin. Hope is destroyed in two ways: 1) *directly*, by the sins contrary to hope, despair and presumption; 2) *indirectly*, when faith, the foundation of hope, is lost through a sin of infidelity.

The act of hope gives its possessor absolute certainty of salvation, because from faith we have certitude that the omnipotence of God cannot fail: so we are infallibly sure that God's power can, and will, assist us in attaining salvation and the means of salvation.

But there is still a measure of uncertainty in hope, which is due to man's fragile and inconstant humanity. It is the risk of unfulfillment. Although God does not and cannot fail us, yet our own free will can fail by placing an obstacle to God's power—sin. *On the part of the motive of hope*, this is to say, hope is absolutely certain, for God's power cannot fail us. But *on the part of the subject of hope* there is no such certainty: our own free will can place sin as an obstacle to our attaining heaven. From this point of view, then, hope's certitude is conditional: we are certain that we will obtain eternal life by God's power *if* we use the means of salvation given to us and persevere to the end. If the condition is not fulfilled, hope will not attain its goal. But it is important to remember that the possibility of failure comes, not from hope itself, but from the debility of man the wayfarer.

5. THE GIFT OF FEAR

The spiritual heights to which supernatural hope can soar cannot be understood without reference to the gift of fear which implements the work of hope.[7a] Supernatural fear, which exists in the will, is analogous to the emotion of fear in the sense appetite. Like the passion of fear it causes man to flee from an imminent evil, which, though vincible, can be overcome only with difficulty. This fear flows both from love and from hope, since man fears that he will lose, or never obtain the object of his love and hope. These two then, fear and hope, mutually assist each other to preserve man from either presumption or despair.

But whom—or what—do we fear? We do not fear God, for he is the supreme good. What we must fear, then, is some evil which either comes from God (such as punishment for sin) or destroys our union with him (such as sin itself).

There are three kinds of fear we can have toward God: 1) by **servile fear** we fear God as the avenger of sin, the just inflicter of penalties; 2) by **filial fear** we fear sin as sin—that is, as an offense vile to God in himself; 3) between servile and filial fear stands a third type of fear called **initial fear,** a kind of beginning or imperfect state of filial fear, by which we renounce sin—partly because of punishment for it, and partly because sin is detestable to God in himself.

All these three kinds of fear are supernatural in character, and hence all are pleasing to God. Opposed to them is mundane or **worldly fear,** by which we fear an evil proceeding from some creature more than we fear God, an evil which makes us willing to offend God by sin.

[7a]The gift of fear also perfects temperance; cf. *infra,* 696.

Filial fear alone is properly the gift of the Holy Ghost. It differs specifically from servile fear in that it avoids sin, not because of the punishment, but because of the nature of sin itself, the offense against our heavenly Father.

6. SINS AGAINST HOPE

Every virtue stands in the middle, on the high ridge between excess and defect, carefully balancing man and his actions so that he will not be precipitated into either abyss.

Hope, too, is a mean, a medium, which keeps a sharp eye on the limitations of fallen human nature, for man can sin by defect if he despairs of attaining eternal life, and he can sin by excess if he presumes to attain it by his own power.[8] And so to complete our discussion of hope, we will treat of the sins opposed to it.

A. Despair

Despair is a sin opposed to hope by defect. **Despair is *an act by which one turns away from eternal happiness, rejecting all expectation of obtaining it.***

What a paradox it is to desire something, but spurn it as impossible of possession! Yet this is the torment of the despairing man. He forms a judgment that eternal life is *not possible* for him, either because it appears *excessively difficult* or because it is not really *future*, as if God were not to give him the necessary help. Just as hope in the will presupposes the intellect's judgment that eternal happiness is possible, so despair in the will presupposes a previous judgment that eternal happiness cannot be attained, though this intellectual affirmation leading to despair is not the act of despair itself.

True despair is never a light sin; it is always mortal (supposing both sufficient advertence and deliberation) and especially injurious

[8]The "mean" of the theological virtues necessary for salvation must be properly understood; cf. *supra*, 145-146.

to God—because he who despairs contemns the divine omnipotence and rejects hope. Given even the smallest quantity in the object, it will be a mortal sin—mortal *ex toto genere suo*.

Despair is a more serious sin than the sins opposed to the moral virtues, for its object as a theological virtue is God, not some created good. Infidelity and hatred of God are, however, more serious than despair, because they are opposed to the truth and goodness of God in himself, while despair is against God insofar as we share his goodness by our trust in the promised assistance of his power. Despair is, however, especially dangerous, because without hope men cannot rise from vice and evil. And, in fact, the first step in conquering any habit of sin, especially the sins of the flesh, is to be convinced that this sin *can* be overcome.

B. Presumption

The word "presumption" indicates any immoderate or excessive hope. But not every form of presumption, theologically speaking, is opposed to the virtue of hope.

In one form, presumption causes a man to tend toward a good possible to him but which, in fact, exceeds his own power. This presumption is opposed to hope only in a roundabout way, inasmuch as a man would mistakenly presume to obtain by his own powers something possible only to divine power—like the sanguine father who hopes to build his new home in six weeks, when six months would be a highly optimistic prospect.

A second kind of presumption is more relevant to our discussion. It is that presumption which tends toward some good as though possible by divine power and mercy which is actually not possible at all—as when one hopes that God, by his power, will grant pardon for sin without true repentance on the part of the sinner. This is what we mean when we refer to presumption as a sin of excess opposed to hope: the expectation of salvation through God's grace without our co-operation; or, on the contrary, the expectation of salvation through our own efforts without God's assistance.

We can, therefore, define this second kind of presumption as *the rash and inordinate expectation of attaining beatitude by means not ordained by God.*

By presumption, a man may sin either directly or indirectly against hope. That presumption which is *directly* against hope is immediately opposed to the very motive of hope, the power of God aiding us. It destroys hope in one of two ways: either by excessive reliance on one's own power to obtain eternal happiness, or by relying on the power of God to give us something which is impossible to give, as to supply forgiveness of sin without repentance.

The presumption which is *indirectly* against hope does not actually oppose the formal motive of hope nor destroy hope, but looks to the material object of hope in a rash and inordinate way—as, for example, by hoping for supernatural goods outside the scope of divine providence, or by hoping for goods never promised by God, or by using the certainty and infallibility of the motive of hope to sin more freely.

Both sins against hope are mortal. But a sin directly against hope does not admit of light matter, while an indirect sin against hope does.[9]

7. THE PRECEPT OF HOPE

The natural and divine law imposes under mortal sin a precept of hope, namely, that we confidently hope for the supernatural happiness promised us: "For in hope we were saved" (Rom. 8:24).[10] This precept is both negative and positive. The negative precept forbids the rejection of hope through despair or presumption; the affirmative precept commands us to elicit an act of hope on certain occasions, particularly: 1) at the dawn of reason when eternal life is sufficiently proposed to us as our goal toward which we should tend; 2) at the

---

[9]Because it destroys the very nature of hope, its formal object, presumption directly against hope is mortal *ex toto genere suo*. Presumption which is indirectly against hope is mortal *ex genere suo*—that is, it admits of lightness of matter.

[10]Cf. also Heb. 3:6; I John 3:3.

point of death, when we are but one step away from the attainment of eternal life; and 3) frequently during life, especially in temptations against hope, or when hope is lost through sins contrary to it, or when other virtues and precepts oblige to at least an implicit act of hope, as when we receive the sacraments.

8. SUMMARY AND CONCLUSION

Hope is God's special gift, a help given to us to move steadily and confidently toward our supreme good, which is future, possible and difficult of attainment: eternal happiness and the means to attain it. So that we might not grow weak when faced by the adversities of the world, God has rooted deep at the core of this virtue a most certain foundation, his own infallible power helping us.

Hope depends on faith, for we must believe that eternal life lies ahead of us and that divine power will assist us on our way toward it. Hope also depends on charity, its very life and spirit, for charity draws us to the goods to be expected.

There is no place in the Christian life for the melancholy or despair with which the search for worldly happiness confronts man, continually destined to heartbreak and disappointment. The world was not created to absorb the energies of the human soul, nor its love. It is a way-station through which we pass, pausing only momentarily. Our attention must always be fixed on the future, for there we will find a happiness altogether worthy of us.

Christian hope combats the cynicism of modern life. The Christian soul is never oppressed by the tedium of daily living, because it knows that God's power, manifested in the workings of divine providence, can overcome all obstacles. Thus one of the effects of supernatural hope is surrender to divine providence. In this sense the Christian is independent of the difficulties of life. His resting place is not here, but far up ahead—ahead in eternity.

The theology of hope gives rise to many practical conclusions, applicable to the daily life of every Christian.

1. "Trust in God means the abandonment of oneself—with all the force of a will sustained by grace and love, in spite of all the doubts suggested by appearances to the contrary—to the wisdom and the infinite love of God. It means believing that nothing in the world escapes his providence, whether in the universal or in the particular order; that nothing great or small happens which is not foreseen, wished or permitted, always directed by providence to its exalted ends."[11]

2. "Where will the soul of man, which is naturally Christian, ever find peace? Will it be in mere self-complacency? Will it be in its vaunted mastery of a universe cloaked in the fog of illusion which confounds matter with spirit, the human with the divine, things that pass with things that endure? No, these delirious dreams will never set at rest the tumult of the soul and the conscience of man, restless under the impulse of a mind which soars above matter, and which goes on, conscious of an immortal and unchangeable destiny, toward the infinite, toward aspirations which have no bounds."[12]

3. "His ascension into heaven recalls to mind that day on which our poor lowly nature was, in the Person of Christ, raised above all the host of heaven, above the ranks of all the angels, above the sublimity of all the powers, to the throne of God the Father.

"In this order of divine events we are so rooted that, when that which claimed our reverence was withdrawn from men's sight, God's grace became yet more marvelous, and faith did not fail, and hope did not falter, and love did not grow cold. For this is the power of worthy souls, this is the glory of those who truly believe: to believe, without faltering, what is unseen by the eyes of the body, and there fasten their desires where sight cannot follow."[13]

[11]Pius XII, radio broadcast, June 29, 1941, "Divine Providence in Human Affairs."

[12]Pius XII, address to the workers of Italian Catholic Action, Sept. 4, 1940.

[13]St. Leo the Great, *Sermon 74* (second of the Ascension).

BIBLIOGRAPHICAL NOTE

The doctrine of this chapter is treated in the *Summa*, II-II, Questions XVII-XXII. A useful reference is the article on hope in the *Catholic Encyclopedia*, VII, 465-467. Several good articles in *Cross and Crown* treat various aspects of the doctrine on hope: "Hope, the Forgotten Virtue," by J. McSorley, C.S.P., II (1950), 255-265; "Hope the Self-Seeker," by P. Lumbreras, O.P., III (1951), 174-189. "Divine Activity," by J. J. McDonald, O.P., IX (1957), 92-108; and "Hope in a Nuclear Age," by Mary J. McCormick, X (1958), 67-74.

CHAPTER TEN

Charity: Divine Friendship

1. INTRODUCTION

"Aloneness," remarked the poet Auden, "is the condition of man." The statement is profoundly true. For the heart of man is a hunger as illimitable as it is insatiable, and never can man find in the parcels of the present the wholeness and fulfillment of that lonely hunter, his heart. This out-reaching of being toward the reality which lies about and beyond him characterizes his nature and his activities and his destiny. Made for God by God, where else will he find his fill? "Our hearts are restless, O God, until we find our rest in thee."

But the fact is that God does respond, freely and gratuitously, to man's aloneness and emptiness: God loves man. All of creation is a mark of divine love, a love of which "the earth is full" (Ps. 32:5, 118:64); "you love all things that are and loathe nothing that you have made . . . and how could a thing remain, unless you willed it, or be preserved, had it not been called forth by you?" (Wisd. 11:24-25). But the love of God for man is something entirely different, entirely special, causing Job to meditate: "What is man, that you make much of him, or pay him any heed? You observe him with each new day, and try him at every moment!" (Job. 7:17-18). The God of love had placed Adam in a garden especially planted for him, given him a helper, destined them, our first parents, to bodily immortality and eternal happiness, and after their sin gave them hope of again attaining his love.

This divine love forged a covenant between Yahweh and Israel, and despite the unfaithfulness of his people God showered them with favors and blessings, never withdrawing his love for them: "With an everlasting love have I loved you" (Jer. 31:3). In their turn the Israelites were to love him: this was the foundation and the summary of the whole Law and the prophets.[1] Again and again Moses repeats this theme: "Hear, O Israel, the Lord our God is one Lord. Thou shalt love the Lord thy God with thy whole heart and thy whole soul, and with thy whole strength . . ." (Deut. 10:12).[2]

Man gives expression to this love for God in a precise observance of the Law. Throughout the Old Testament the expressions "to fear God," "to love God," "to keep his commandments," "to walk in his ways" are interchangeable. Only too often, however, this observance of God's law was shadowed by servile fear, or degenerated into merely external observances. Against this, and a self-righteous exclusivism, the prophets emphasized the gratuity of divine love, and the necessity of an inner movement of the spirit, rather than the merely external keeping of the precepts of the Law. But only with the coming of Christ would there be fully revealed the necessity of mans' love of God, and its significance.

Israel was also commanded: "Thou shalt love thy neighbor as thyself" (Lev. 19:18). But the universality of man's love for man was yet to be revealed. Just as its cause, Yahweh's preferential love, was confined to the Jewish people, so love of neighbor meant love of one's fellow Hebrew.

The New Law, the law of grace, proclaims these good tidings: God's special love, his favors and his blessings are no longer reserved for

[1]See Matt. 22:7; Mark 12:30; Luke 10:27.
[2]See also Deut. 11:1, 13:22, 30:16.

Israel. The preaching and parables of Christ make clear that the status of a son of Abraham is not sufficient title to the love of God. "For I have come to call sinners," he declared, "not the just" (Matt. 9:13). This absolutely free quality of God's love is emphasized in the parables of the lost sheep (Luke 15:3-7), the prodigal son (Luke 15:11-32), the workers hired at the eleventh hour (Matt. 20:1-16). Not justice, not the rights of the just man, not even the prerogatives of the chosen people move God to his love of esteem and choice. His gift is an entirely free act, and it is given to all men, regardless of race or condition, color or position.

The emphasis placed in Christ's preaching upon the love that God bestows on sinners brilliantly illuminates the truth that divine love is productive. God loves men, and in loving them gives life, and that more abundantly. God does not love men because they are good: they are good because he loves them.

And the response of men should be as free, as generous, as whole-hearted as God's predilection and benevolence for them. The whole life of Jesus is an act of loving God above all else. In word and example, he teaches that man must set the love of God before all things. He reaffirms that the whole Law and the prophets is summed up in the two greatest commandments: the love of God and of neighbor (Matt. 22:37; Mark 12:30; Luke 10:27). The will of his Father was his guide in all things, even to the death of the Cross: "Yet not my will but thine be done" (Luke 22:42).

This primary love of God is to be directed to himself as well, "for I and the Father are one." The overriding supremacy that this love of God must have can be no more strongly emphasized than in the warning: "If anyone comes to me and does not hate his father and mother, and wife and children, and brothers and sisters, yes, and even his own life, he cannot be my disciple" (Luke 14:26-27).

No longer in this newly revealed universality of divine love can the love of one's fellow man be restricted to those united by ties of kinship or nationality. The charity of man for man is to be an imitation of God's love for man, and is to be marked by the same gratuity. In the sermon on the mount, Jesus sets forth this new commandment:

> You have heard that it was said, "Thou shalt love thy neighbor, and shalt hate thy enemy." But I say to you, love your enemies, do good to those who persecute and calumniate you, so that you may be the children of your Father in heaven. . . . For if you love those who love you, what reward shall you have? Do not even the publicans do that? And if you salute your brethren only, what are you doing more than others? Do not even the Gentiles do that?
>
> You therefore are to be perfect, even as your heavenly Father is perfect.[3]

The restless, hungry, lonely heart of man will find its solace, its satiety, its communion in the love of God. So we are assured by God himself in his inspired word, by his Word of inspiration. But what is this love on our part for him who, in all truth, is love itself? What is its nature, its characteristics, its causes and effects? The deeper significance of this reciprocal love of God and man which embraces all men will be the object of our present inquiry. We will put our questions in the sequence outlined on the opposite page.

2. THE NATURE OF CHARITY

There is only one possible way of attempting to discover what the reciprocal love of God and man is: since it is a result of divine benevolence, a gratuitous gift which surpasses all that man might reasonably desire or long for, a relationship so special that only the vaguest and most uncertain of clues can be obtained from our ordinary sources of information (the world which lies about us), only God himself can delineate the meaning of this love, the existence of which he so abundantly testifies to. Our inquiry into the nature of divine love, then, must first of all begin with a searching of his revelation if it is to obtain the meaning of so astounding a fact. First of all we must see what God has told us about this special love; only then can we examine it under the aspect of habit, and proceed according to the order of reason to discuss its subject, its object (**Section** 3) and its act (**Section 4**).

---

[3]Matt. 5:43-48; cf. Luke 6:27-38.

The nature of charity
(Section 2)

The object of charity and the
order of its objects
(Section 3)

Charity in itself

The acts of charity
(Section 4)

To love: hatred of God

Sloth

To joy

Envy

Charity

The vices op-
posed
(Section 5)

To peace: discord

To beneficence: scandal

The precepts of charity
(Section 6)

The corresponding gift of wisdom
(Section 7)

A. Charity as Friendship

(1) The Word of God

Almost from the first page of the Bible we are informed that the reciprocal love of God and man is a love of friendship. The fact is most clearly stated, as we might expect, in the New Testament:

> This is my commandment, that you love one another as I have loved you. Greater love than this no one has, that one lay down his life for his friends. You are my friends if you do the things I command you. No longer do I call you servants, because the servant does not know what his master does. But I have called you friends, because all things that I have heard from my Father I have made known to you. You have not chosen me, but I have chosen you, and have appointed you that you should go forth and bear fruit and that your fruit should remain; that whatever you ask the Father in my name he may give you. These things I command you, that you may love one another.[4]

But he who in the beginning walked in the garden of man in the cool of the day (Gen. 3:8) never scrupled to reveal that his love (and man's response) was a love of friendship. To Abraham, father of the chosen people, this friendship was given: "They must remember how Abraham was tempted, and being proved by many tribulations was made the friend of God" (Judith 8:22); Moses also: "And the Lord spoke to Moses face to face, as a man is wont to speak to his friend" (Ex. 33:11). Not only the leaders were so privileged, however; God's love for Israel and for each individual was like that of a mother for her children,[5] as intimate as a bridal or marital relationship (the theme of the Canticle of Canticles),[6] strong as the love of a father for his child.[7] This love of friendship is perhaps most movingly expressed in the prophet Osee:

> Because Israel was a child, and I loved him: and I called my son out of Egypt.
> And I was like a foster father to Ephraim, I carried them in my arms: and they knew not that I healed them.

[4]John 15:12-17.
[5]Cf. Isa. 49:14-15.
[6]Cf. Isa. 54:6-7, 62:4-5; Jer. 2:2, 3:1, 12; Osee 1—3.
[7]Cf. Ex. 4:22; Deut. 1:31, 8:5; Jer. 3:19-20; Mal. 1:6; Osee 4:14.

> I will draw them with the cords of Adam, with the bands of love: and I will be to them as one that taketh off the yoke on their jaws: and I put his meat to him that he might eat.[8]

But this reciprocal love between God and man was as yet only partially understood. The full significance of divine friendship is revealed by Jesus Christ, and so new and complete a thing is this that the writers of the New Testament find it necessary to "invent" a new word to describe it: they adopted the Greek word **agape**, which we translate as *charity*, to describe a divine love of esteem and choice (root meaning of the term) which transforms man to his innermost being, making him a lover of God on the most intimate level, that is to say, God's friend.

Thus with St. Paul we can perceive the truth of this new and marvelous fact: for us, God is "the God of charity" (II Cor. 13:11), a friend whose free, spontaneous and completely gratuitous love is made evident by the supreme sacrifice of his Son upon the Cross:

> For why did Christ, at the set time, die for the wicked when as yet we were weak? For scarcely in behalf of a just man does one die; yet perhaps one might bring himself to die for a good man. But God commends his charity towards us, because when as yet we were sinners, Christ died for us.[9]

Among all the virtues, he insists in his beautiful hymn to love (I Cor., Chap. 13), man's love of friendship for God is pre-eminent. Thus also the second great precept of charity is of the first importance: "Owe no man anything except to love one another; for he who loves his neighbor has fulfilled the Law" (Rom. 13:8); and again, "be you, therefore, imitators of God, as very dear children, and walk in love, as Christ also loved us. . ." (Eph. 5:1-1).

With St. John, the scriptural witness to the doctrine of charity is complete in every sense of the word. He sums up and puts in order all that the Old Law and the synoptic gospels had said of divine friendship. So dominant is the theme of charity that no brief selection of texts can do justice to it. No other sacred author so thoroughly presents the doctrine of charity: of God's love for us, of the love we

---

[8]Osee 11:1-4.
[9]Rom. 5:6-8.

must have for God, of the love of neighbor for the love of God. The theme is perhaps best seen in a single passage from the first epistle:

> Beloved, let us love one another, for love is from God. And everyone who loves is born of God, and knows God. He who does not love does not know God; for God is love.[10]

With St. Thomas, then, we may gather from God's own words that the kind of love which we designate by the word "charity" is that highest and most intimate type of love called "friendship." More fully to understand this, we must analyze the notion expressed by this relationship.

(2) The Notion of Friendship

Charity is friendship with God and all the children of God.[11] But what is friendship? This is the question we must now answer through an analysis of the notion of love.

We can distinguish a twofold love in the heart of man. There is the **love of concupiscence** by which man's love and desire goes out to some good that is seen as benefiting himself; thus a man loves food, clothing, football, dances. It is a love that is turned inward, that seeks good things for the satisfaction of the one desiring them; it is a self-centered love, even though not always selfish in the bad sense of the term. Indeed, even the most exalted affection has something of the love of concupiscence mixed with it: one who is drawn to a saintly person so that he may grow in virtue, or to a wise man that he may grow in wisdom, is moved by this sort of love.

A deeper, truer affection is the **love of benevolence.** Here the object is not the profit and satisfaction of the one loving, but the good

[10]I John 4:7-8.

[11]The mind of the Church in connection with this idea may be seen from the language used by the Council of Trent in its decree on justification: "By the voluntary acceptance of grace and of the gifts . . . the unjust man becomes just, an enemy is made a friend. . . . The meritorious cause [of this justification is] God's well-beloved Son, our Lord Jesus Christ who, *when we were enemies* (cf. Rom. 5:10) *by reason of his very great love, by which he has loved us* (Eph. 24), by his most holy passion on the wood of the Cross merited justification for us, and made satisfaction to God the Father for us. . . ." Sess. VI, Chap. 7; Denz. 799.

of the beloved: the love of husband for wife, parents for children, David for Jonathan. It is a movement of the soul that cannot go out to material things but only to *persons,* to those capable of enjoying spiritual goods. It is a disinterested love, for the beloved is sought for what he is, not for what he can do. This is the first characteristic of friendship.

If to this benevolence or well-wishing there is added **the return of love**—a *mutual* seeking of the other's good—the love is truly one of friendship. In human affection, as the products of Hollywood and the "Dear Abby" and "Dear Dorthy Dix" letters witness, it is possible to love without being loved in return. For true friendship, however, there must be mutual love.

A third note is found in friendship: **communication.** This is a oneness of friends, a sharing. It is not merely the exchange of confidences, but a certain identification with a friend. *A friend is another self.* The attachment and union that arises among comrades in arms, among citizens united in defence of their country by bullet or ballot, between husband and wife, between parent and child—all are examples of this highest form of human love. This communication is an active one, a community of action: living together, working together, playing together, praying together.

In summary, then, three notes mark friendship: **benevolence,** or disinterested well-wishing; **reciprocity,** or a mutual loving and being loved; and **communication.**

(3) Charity of Friendship

1. Charity is **benevolent,** it is not self-seeking; rather, it is directed toward the good of one's friend. By charity man loves God and all that is of God for the sake of God. Charity seeks to give glory to God and to promote his honor. It is different from the love of concupiscence by which man seeks to gain pleasure or profit for himself. St. Paul exemplified the benevolence of true charity when he said: "For I am ready not only to be bound but even to die at Jerusalem for the name of the Lord Jesus" (Acts 21:13). God's

love for man is perfectly benevolent, for the whole purpose of creation is to share the supreme good of eternal happiness with those whom God loves. "I have loved you with an everlasting love" (Jer. 31:3).

2. Charity, like all true friendship, must be **mutual.** It cannot be onesided. By charity man returns the love which God has already shown for him: "I love them that love me" (Prov. 8:17). Christ promises his willingness to love us. "He who loves me will be loved by my father, and I will love him and manifest myself to him" (John 14:21).

3. Friendship demands that the friends have **something in common,** something shared as the basis of the friendship. Yet what common ground of friendship is there between man and God? The God who is man's friend in charity is not the God whom man knows from his effects in nature, nor yet the God known by the reasoning of philosophers. Rather this is God as he is in himself and as he reveals himself to man. It is God as he is known by supernatural faith, who is beyond the farthest reach of all unaided natural powers. A common ground for friendship with God on this supernatural plane can only come from God himself. And it does come from him—through the gift of divine grace which makes men "partakers of the divine nature" (II Pet. 1:4). "In this is the love, not that we have loved God, but that he has first loved us, and sent his Son a propitiation for our sins" (I John 4:10). By grace we become the adopted sons of God, we share in the divine nature. This, then, is what we have in common with God as the basis for the divine friendship of charity. "God is trustworthy, by him you have been called into fellowship with his Son, Jesus Christ our Lord" (I Cor. 1:9).

The profoundest mystery in divine friendship is this communication between God and man. The Scriptures express the fact, for we are likened to associates and fellow citizens of God (Eph. 2:19; I Cor. 1:9; I John 1:3), to his brethren (John 22:7), to his spouse (Eph. 5:23; Apoc. 19:7, 21:3). The most frequent and most powerful expression of this sharing of the divine nature is the comparison of children to their father. St. John exhorts us "Behold what manner of love the Father has bestowed upon us, that we should be called the children of God; and such we are" (I John 3:1-2).[12]

The communication essential to friendship comes immediately from the active sharing of divine life, enjoying even now his happiness with him, working together with him and his friends for the spread of his kingdom among men, a new dimension and dynamism for human activity. This active communication will culminate in the eternal enjoyment of God together with God and his friends in the beatific vision. Its more distant foundation is sanctifying grace, which makes us of one race, one family with God in his glory. This is most powerfully expressed in the Scriptures by the comparison of father and child, for here are summed up the sharing of nature, the reverence (and inequality) that flow from such a relation, the balance of love and justice, the actual living of a life together, the necessity of love for other children of God, and the reason for it.[13]

It is from this sharing of the very life of God that there flow all the implications of friendship revealed in the Scriptures and emphasized by the Fathers:

1) The gratuity of God's love for man, and its consequent, that man's love for his fellows must reflect that gratuity, even to loving his enemy, for the friend of one's friend is a friend.

2) The pre-eminence of this love above all others. Founded as it is upon a sharing of the inner nature and happiness of God, all other loves can be no more than a reflection of this one.

3) Though man is placed on the path of perfection by the friendship of God, the fulness of friendship and communication is realized only in heaven.

B. Charity as a Virtue

(1) Its Nature

Charity lifts man beyond the limits of his human nature and enables him to be at home with God and with the things of God. It is

---

[12]See also Matt. 5:44; John 1:12; Rom. 8:16.
[13]Cf. Cardinal Cajetan, *Commentary on the Summa*, II-II, q. 23, a. 1.

difficult to comprehend the greatness of this privilege. St. Thomas states it simply: ". . . charity is the life of the soul as the soul is the life of the body."[14] This gives an insight into the meaning of the phrase, "mortal sin is the death of the soul." Of its nature, charity is a permanent and lasting friendship. It cannot be lost by accident as can our mortal life; it can only be cast away by a kind of deliberate spiritual suicide.

The friendship of charity, then, is permanent or habitual. St. Paul tells us that ". . . the charity of God is poured forth in our hearts by the Holy Spirit who has been given to us" (Rom. 5:5). It is an effect of the Holy Spirit, and the effect is twofold. Charity gives us a share in the divine nature, makes us children of God and adopted sons of the divine household. It also gives us the ability to live at this divine level, to perform actions that are of eternal value in the sight of God. These actions must not be like the halting steps of an infant; they must be the sure steps of an adult who is at home on the way to the mansions of the heavenly Father. Charity attains God; it unites us to God. St. Augustine says that charity is a virtue which, when our affections are properly ordered, unites us to God, for by it we love him.[15]

Man's acts of love which mark his friendship with God call for some created principle in his soul. It is the role of virtue to make man good in himself, and to render his natural faculties inclined to prompt and joyous action, but natural virtues look to the good of reason, to the right ordering of man's actions to his natural end. Some such similar source of supernatural action is needed as well in the souls of men "whose citizenship is in heaven" (Phil. 3:20). It is not sufficient for charity that a man should desire the happiness enjoyed by the blessed in heaven; even the wicked desire that. True heavenly ciitzenship is exercised by him who seeks the central good above all, who loves God above all things, who lives in order that God's goodness may be known and loved by all men. As the earthly patriot takes

---

[14]*Summa*, II-II, q. 23, a. 2, ad 2.

[15]*On the Morals of the Catholic Church and the Morals of the Manichees*, Bk. I, Chap. 11.

arms against any threat to his nation, so the man of charity repels any threat to the good in himself or in others.

Human friendship is not a virtue in itself. It rather follows on virtue, for our love goes out to a friend because of his goodness. The divine friendship of charity, however, is a virtue, since it joins us to God. Its object—God in himself as he is supremely happy and the author of happiness—makes charity the greatest of all the virtues.

The note of *friendship with God* gives a unity to the virtue of charity. Earthly friendship may stem from a vast diversity of ends: utility, pleasure or, in friendship at its best, goodness. In charity the end is *one*: the divine goodness itself, loved for itself, and by reason of which all other things are loved. Again, the sharing, the common-ness, the *communication* in earthly friendships may arise from a hundred ties of blood, of nationality, even of common commercial interest. In charity the bond of union is forged from the sharing in the very life of God and in divine beatitude. Men are friends of God because by his grace they share in his nature, his life, his activity, his happiness.

All of this is summed up in the definition commonly given by theologians: **charity** is *a divinely infused theological virtue by which we love God for himself, and ourselves and our neighbors for the love of God.*

(2) Its Excellence

It is widely held among Protestants that faith is the most excellent virtue, and that man is saved by faith alone. Charity is conceived as the handmaid or instrument of faith, so that one who truly believes will live according to his faith. Everyday experience shows clearly that this theory does not work in human affairs. The very existence of hell argues against it, for hell is reserved for those who knew better and failed to do better.

As a principle of good human actions, virtue consists in attaining the rule or measure of human acts. Charity is a virtue because it unites us to God, who is the supreme rule of human actions. It is a distinct virtue, attaining a proper object which is different from that of all other virtues. The object of charity is God himself, precisely as he is infinitely good and lovable for his own sake. "So there abide faith, hope and charity, these three: but the greatest of these is charity" (I Cor. 13:13).

There are not several kinds of charity, but one only. Howsoever different the people we love in charity—friends, relatives, parents, enemies—all are loved for one reason, because of the goodness of God; and a share in the same divine happiness is desired for them all. God himself is the principal object of charity; all others are included for the love of God.

Charity is the most excellent of all virtues because it attains God himself as its proper object. The moral virtues are concerned with human actions as means to the end, as steps in life's journey. The theological virtues are concerned with the goal of the journey, and this is God. Faith attains God inasmuch as he is truthful in his revelations. Hope attains God precisely as he is good for us, and it relies upon him to bring us to the supreme good of eternal happiness. Charity attains God himself in his infinite goodness without any limitation and independently of our personal advantage. Indeed, ". . . the greatest of these is charity."

(3) Its Necessity

Mortal sin destroys charity. Does it also destroy the other virtues a man may have? To answer this important practical question, it is necessary to recall the doctrine on virtue in general and the distinction of virtues previously explained (Chapter Four). This is essentially a moral question, a problem concerning man's direction to his true final goal. From this aspect, it is clear that the intellectual virtues such as wisdom, science and art can exist and increase without charity, because these virtues do not directly perfect the will by which man chooses to seek or to reject his final happiness. A man's sins need not interfere with his science.

But what of the moral virtues of temperance, justice and the like? Can they exist without charity? If we speak of the *infused* moral virtues which God gives us as part of the supernatural organism, they cannot exist apart from charity. Their whole purpose is to lead man to his true final end which is God. Once the order to that end is destroyed and the soul no longer lives in charity, then the infused moral virtues cease to exist. "And if I distribute all my goods to feed the poor, and if I deliver my body to be burned, yet do not have charity, it profits me nothing" (I Cor. 13:3).

If we consider the *acquired* moral virtues, which are the products of repeated acts of justice, temperance and the like, the case is different. These natural virtues can exist in man without charity, because they dispose man well in regard to some good in the natural order. Acquired temperance, for instance, disposes man to behave reasonably in the enjoyment of pleasures. Now such reasonable enjoyment is a legitimate goal in itself, but it should be further dedicated supernaturally to God by charity. If charity is absent and reasonable enjoyment is sought for itself without this supernatural relation to God, the essential natural goodness of such enjoyment still remains. Consequently, acquired virtues can remain in a man who has rejected the divine friendship.

In fact, our faith confirms what our experience teaches us: that people are not wholly corrupted by a mortal sin. The goods of nature remain in the seriously sinful man, but the disorder of his supernatural life creates many difficulties in the practice of the natural virtues. Man is not composed of air-tight compartments. There is vital interaction between the principles of nature and of grace.

Finally, there are certain patterns of living that masquerade as virtues. Some misers, for example, practice great self-denial because of their vicious and disordered love of acquiring money. These counterfeit virtues effectively destroy charity by turning man away from God.

(4) Charity, the Form of All Virtue

It is the common teaching of theologians that charity is the "form" of all other true virtues. As the soul, the form of the body, gives it life, so charity vivifies and inspires the virtues by directing them to the final goal which is God himself. This does not mean that charity replaces the other virtues, but that it elevates them to a higher supernatural end which of themselves they could not attain. Justice, for example, seeks to give to another what is due him, and every virtuous payment of a debt will always be the work of justice. But charity will direct the works of justice and of the other virtues to the love of God. Because it thus "conceives" the acts of these virtues in the love of God, it merits to be called the "mother" of all virtues.

We have seen a number of different senses in which scholastic terminology uses this word "form." Here it is to be taken in the sense of *directing end,* rather than of a constitutive principle. Thus the *purpose* for which a satellite is to be launched determines its overall design, its instruments, even the actions of its launchers to the final countdown: it is its "form."

Hence charity does not stand to the other virtues as the soul stands to the body, as an intrinsic and constitutive principle; sanctifying grace fulfills that role. But it shapes and directs the actions of the other virtues to their end, which is God.

So vital is this function of charity that without it no other true virtue is possible. Quite simply, a virtue which is not ordered to the end of charity is not a virtue at all. The financial prudence of the miser, the calculated temperance of the hypocritical office seeker, the daring of the bank-robber are directed to false goals. Even the particular virtues, whose ends are goods of a limited nature, find perfection only insofar as they are shaped and molded by charity to the ultimate end of man. By its pre-eminence and by this commanding role, charity gives order and direction to all the acts of all the virtues of man. The equitable actions of the just, the reasonable restraint of the temperate, the deliberate daring of the courageous take on a new integrity and dimension when elevated and guided by the love of God.

For supernatural living, then—the life to which God calls us as his children and heirs—charity is absolutely essential.

C. The Subject of Charity

Love is so often identified with feelings that many people think that loving God is simply a manner of feeling kindly toward him.

It is fortunate indeed that charity does not reside in our feelings, for they are so fickle and subject to change that a friendship with God based upon feelings would be as unstable and changeable as a weather-vane. But, as we have seen,[16] our feelings are closely dependent upon the senses, while God is a spiritual good that cannot be grasped by the senses. The object of charity is the *divine goodness*, let us insist, a good which can only be grasped by the intellect and desired by an intellectual appetite. Charity, it is clear, must reside in the will. Sometimes charity overflows into our feelings, to be sure, to bring a special joy or delight to those who love God. But this is something accidental. Charity is not a matter of how we feel, but of what we *are* and what we *do*. "You are my friends if you do the things I command you" (John 15:14).

D. The Cause of Charity

"The charity of God is poured forth in our hearts by the Holy Spirit," says St. Paul (Rom. 5:5). Thus do we learn that charity is infused into our souls by God. Charity is a divine friendship, which is founded upon participation of God's own life and of his everlasting happiness. This divine life and this everlasting happiness are something wholly supernatural, entirely surpassing all our natural powers. Consequently, their source must be none other than God himself. Charity is necessarily an infused virtue, as the Church teaches.[17]

An important conclusion follows from this fact: *the measure of charity is not the natural capacity of the recipient, but rather the generosity of the divine giver.* Those whom nature favors with a splendid physique or a keen mind and those whom fortune grants educational opportunities or wealth are not thereby necessarily those whom God loves more as his friends. No creature can cause charity, but only God. And ". . . to each one of us was given according to the measure of Christ's bestowal" (Eph. 4:7).

[16]Cf. *supra*, Chap. Three, 79-82.

[17]Second Council of Orange, Can. 25, *On the Charity Whereby We Love God* (Denz. 198); cf. Council of Trent, Sess. VI, *Decree on Justification*, Chap. 7, "The Nature of Justification and Its Causes" (Denz. 799).

(1) Growth in God's Love

Can man love God more and more each day? From the notion of charity as friendship, we would expect that it can increase. We know that friendship differs in degree with different people, and with the same people at different times. That charity can increase is clear from the Scriptures: "Rather are we to practice the truth in love, and so grow up in all things in him who is the head, Christ" (Eph. 4:15); "he who is just, let him be just still; and he who is holy, let him be hallowed still" (Apoc. 22:11). The same truth is stated by St. Augustine, who tells us that charity merits increase so that by increase it may merit perfection.[18] It is reflected in the prayer for the 13th Sunday after Pentecost: "Grant us, O Lord, an increase of faith, hope and charity," and forms part of the official teaching of the Church.[19] For we are all wayfarers, journeying homeward to God, and the increases of charity are the steps along the way.

The possibility of an increase in charity raises the problem of how that increase may occur. Divine friendship is not a quantitative thing, to which we can add part after part. Charity cannot grow by the addition of other kinds of charity, as a man might grow by adding new weight. Nor does it increase extensively, by extending its field of operations. Intellectual habits may grow in this way: a student of grammar increases his habit when he masters usages which he did not know previously. But the least degree of charity extends to every object which we are bound to love. To hate one of his children is to destroy our love for our heavenly Father.

Rather, charity increases by *intensification*, by being shared more and more, to a greater and greater degree, by those who are the friends of God. To say that the charity of one is greater than that of another is to say that one person's acts of charity are more fervent, more intense—that the life of one is more perfectly subject to the divine friendship than the life of another.

---

[18]*Letter 186;* cf. *Commentary on the Gospel according to St. John,* Treatise LXXIV, n. 2.

[19]Council of Vienne (1311-12), condemnation of the error of the Beghards and Beguines (Denz. 471); Council of Trent, *loc. cit.,* Chap. 10, "On the Increase of Justification" (Denz. 803) and Can. 24 (Denz. 834).

Just as God is the author of charity by pouring forth the divine friendship into the hearts of men, so God is the principal cause of the increase of charity. "Now he who provides the sower with seed will both give you bread to eat and will multiply your seed, and will increase the growth of the fruits of your justice" (II Cor. 9:10). Yet this is not to deny man himself a real part of the increase of charity. Man's good actions truly merit for him an increase of the divine friendship, as the Church clearly teaches.[20] Man's good actions concur in the increase of charity by preparing him for, and making him worthy to receive a greater intensification of the divine friendship.

(2) Acts Which Increase Charity

We must further ask: does *each* act of charity cause the habit to increase? Let us recall that charity grows by intensification, as a man grows more human as the rule of reason more perfectly penetrates and controls all—even the most animal—of his faculties. The polished speech of an orator is more human than the lisping of a child precisely because reason controls the oratory more perfectly. As in the acts of other virtues, there are different degrees of perfection in the acts of charity.

The degree of man's love for God is measured by his most intense, his greatest act of charity. To increase the degree of his charity, then, he must dispose himself by an act more intense than the level which he has already attained. Thus by a more fervent reception of Holy Communion, by an act of greater sacrifice for another, or by a great effort of self-denial to avoid offending God, man would dispose himself for a more intense life of friendship with God, and he would thereby merit that God should raise him to a more intimate friendship. But what of those acts of charity that fall short of the degree one already possesses? Do these so-called "remiss acts" have any effect on the increase of charity?

If someone had attained a degree of charity that could be represented by the number 9, clearly an act of charity having a fervor represented by 3 would not increase the habit here and now. Yet

[20]Council of Trent, *loc. cit.*, Can. 24 and 32; Denz. 834, 842.

this "remiss act" is truly an exercise of charity, and, as such, merits eternal life. Moreover, *every act of charity also merits an increase in charity*. The answer, says St. Thomas, is that the reward of eternal life is bestowed at the proper time, that is, at the instant when eternal glory begins. At that moment every good deed, even those that could have been better, will receive a suitable reward. "And whoever gives to one of these little ones but a cup of cold water to drink because he is a disciple . . . he shall not lose his reward" (Matt. 10:42). This is also the case with the increase of charity that each and every act, even less intense acts, merits; it is not conferred at the moment, but at the proper time—at a future time when we strive for an increase of charity.

From this doctrine we learn the practical importance of striving for more fervent acts of charity. These merit an *immediate* increase of the divine friendship, and thus lead to a constant progress in union with God. Growth in divine friendship is a matter of quality rather than of quantity. A single fervent act of the Blessed Virgin would be preferred by God to the tepid acts of countless Christians; the conversion of a sinner like St. Paul or St. Mary Magdalen to a high degree of sanctity will please God more than the conversion of many sinners to a life of tepidity.

Thus for the friend of God who places no obstacle to divine grace, the possibility of an indefinite growth in God's love opens up. He shares more perfectly in the limitless love of God which is the Holy Spirit himself; he is urged on to greater heights by the infinite power of God; his soul expands and grows under the impulse of a growing charity; his heart learns new hungers from the very love it feeds upon.

(3) Love without Limit

Charity is friendship with God. One limit of charity would be reached if God were loved *as much as he is lovable*. But God is infinitely lovable because he is infinitely good. Consequently, the limit or perfection of charity can be attained only by God himself, and it is found only in the intimate life of the Blessed Trinity.

Another perfection of charity is found when a man loves God *as much as he can.* Absolutely speaking, that would mean always loving God actually, without any distraction whatever. This degree of charity is possible to man only in heaven, where he will be free of all concerns, of every necessity and every desire except that of loving God.

In this life, there are some who earnestly try to give their time to God and to the things of God as much as they can, and who occupy themselves only with what is absolutely necessary for this earthly life. This is the perfection of charity possible to men on this earth, but not all who are friends of God love him so perfectly. More commonly, those who have charity give their whole heart to God habitually, which means that they do not think or desire anything contrary to God. This is common to all who are God's friends; in its lowest degree, it represents the minimum of charity required for salvation.

There is a manner of speaking to describe the different stages of growth in charity by a comparison with man's dvelopment in the natural order. It is found in the writings of many of the Fathers of the Church and is used here by St. Thomas. It sets up a threefold distinction among the degrees of charity according to the different pursuits to which man is brought by the increase of charity:

1) **The charity of beginners** who are in the *purgative way* is principally concerned with avoiding sin and with resisting the appetites which move man in opposition to charity.

2) **The charity of the proficient** who are in the *illuminative way* is chiefly occupied with strengthening charity by more intense acts. Proficients feel the onslaught of sin less, and tend to perfection with greater security. Yet, like the builders of Jerusalem, they work with one hand and carry a sword in the other (II Esdras 4:17).

3) **The charity of the perfect** who are in the *unitive way* aims chiefly at union with and enjoyment of God. This degree is exemplified by St. Paul who desired ". . . to depart and to be with Christ" (Phil. 1:23).

It must be noted that these degrees are very general classifications. They are distinguished by the principal occupation of each, without excluding other divine concerns which will occupy souls in the various degrees.

(4) The Lessening of Charity

It is clear that acts of charity can be of different degrees of fervor. But what of the habit of charity? Can it also *decrease* in intensity? The answer is found by considering the possibilities for decrease. Divine friendship cannot decrease by eliminating some of its objects; that would be to substitute hatred for love and thus to destroy the virtue, for the least degree of charity must reach to all those whom we are bound to love. Neither can the degree of charity be lessened *directly* by the venial sins of the man who has charity. The sick man who ardently desires health will sometimes break his diet without ceasing to want to be healthy. But charity is the love of God and of others precisely because they are God's; charity, then, is essentially directed to the end or goal of man's life. Just as an inordinate desire for, or use of the means does not directly decrease the love for the goal, so neither does venial sin dirctly decrease man's union with God who is his goal. Neither does venial sin merit the decrease or loss of charity, for a just God will not inflict the gravest punishment for any but the gravest fault.

Indirectly, however, man can dispose himself for a decrease in the fervor of his habit of charity. By ceasing to perform acts of charity the ardor of charity is cooled. By sinning venially, man makes it impossible to act out of charity at the same time. We cannot combine an act of rash judgment with an act of charity of offering ourselves to God at Mass. So just as acts of charity, even remiss ones, dispose the soul at least remotely for the intensification of the habit of charity, the lack of acts of charity—venial sin—disposes the soul for a lessening of the intensity of charity—that is, a lessening of the influence of divine friendship in all our thoughts, words and actions.

Moreover, venial sin disposes for mortal sin. Venial sin is the occasion for God to withhold his special actual graces; it cools the fervor of charity and makes us comfortable in evil; it nourishes our disorderly affections.

(5) The Loss of Charity

Charity is never lost by accident any more than it is picked up by chance. We acquire charity by freely co-operating with God's grace; to lose it we must freely give it up, throw it away.

Charity consists in man's loving God above all things and subjecting himself entirely to him by referring all that he is and all that he has to God. Charity inclines man to love God in such a way as to desire to please God in all things. That means that man must unite his will to that of his divine friend by keeping God's commandments. Whatever is contrary to the commandments is contrary to God's will and, consequently, contrary to charity. Mortal sin, however, is nothing other than a bad human act by which man chooses something contrary to God with full knowledge and consent. Such a choice destroys the divine friendship. Mortal sin is completely opposed to charity. The man who faces east must necessarily turn his back on the west. The mortal sinner must as a result exclude God from his rightful place as the principal love of his life.

God infuses and preserves charity in the soul as the sun infuses and preserves light in the air about us. When we close a shutter against the light of the sun, we plunge a room into darkness. So, too, when we give our hearts to some creature, to some pleasure, we close our souls to the light of God's grace and plunge them into spiritual death. "For the wages of sin is death, but the gift of God is life everlasting in Christ Jesus our Lord" (Rom. 6:23).

This does not mean that we cannot love anyone or anything besides God. It does mean that there must be an order in our love, and that God must come first by being preferred to all others. St. Augustine says, "Too little does he love thee who loves aught besides thee that he loves not for thee, O Love who ever burn and are never quenched."[21]

[21]*Confessions*, Bk. X, Chap. 29.

3. THE OBJECT OF CHARITY

A. The Formal Object of Charity

Charity is the unifying force of all the virtuous acts of the Christian. This power of union comes from charity's nature as divine friendship, and from the fact that its formal object is *one*. In all moral matters, the specific nature of an action (or a habit) is determined by the formal object to which the action is directed. Just as the eye grasps the whole world of material things because of light and color, so the virtuous man loves all that he loves *by reason of his love of God*.

The primacy of the love of God is seen in all the texts we have examined from the Old and New Law. Revealed as well is its formal nature as *object*: "And this commandment we have from him, that he who loves God should love his brother also. . . . In this we know that we love the children of God, when we love God and do his commandments" (I John 4:21; 5:2).

We may distinguish a double note in man's friendship with God. God is loved first of all as *object*, for he is all good, and as *formal* object, for other things are loved because they pertain to him, or are ordered to him. We love our neighbor, for instance, because he is a child of God.

With the principle in mind that God is loved for himself, and all other things for the love of God, the many diverse objects of man's affections fall into place.

B. The Material Object of Charity

Charity is a divine friendship between man and God. Like every true and perfect friendship, it extends beyond the person of the friend to all who are his, to all who are related to him. "And this commandment we have from him, that he who loves God should love his brother also" (I John 4:21). This does not indicate a division in charity;

it does not mean that there is one kind of charity for God, another for ourselves, still another for our neighbor. God is loved in himself for himself; all others are loved for the sake of God, that is, because they are, or can be, his friends. Every act of charity is specified, is made to be what it is, because it is directed to God as to its object. Thus there is only one charity which extends to many objects in terms of their relationship to God.

The divine friendship is based upon a sharing in eternal happiness, upon a participation of the divine nature begun in this life and made perfect in heaven. God is the principal cause and the object of this eternal joy, we ourselves and our neighbors share in it directly, and it will be shared indirectly by a kind of overflow by our bodies. The principal objects of charity, then, are 1) God; 2) ourselves; 3) our neighbors; 4) our bodies.

(1) The Love of Self

The love of ourselves in God is the measure of our love for others. We are commanded to love our neighbors *as we love ourselves* (cf. Matt. 19:19). By the friendship of charity we are united to another; but we are already identical with ourselves in a more perfect union. Hence the usual notion of friendship does not apply to this love a man has for himself, which is *above* friendship; this love is the form and root of friendship, for our friendship with others consists in doing unto them as we do unto ourselves. "Friendly relations with one's neighbors, and the works by which friendships are defined," Aristotle observed some time ago, "take their origin from a man's relations with himself."[22]

But when we consider charity as that special friendship with God which animates all our actions, then we do love ourselves with a divine love of friendship—precisely as something belonging to God. In charity, then, we love ourselves as the friends of God, and we love our neighbors both as God's friends and our own.

[22]*Nicomachean Ethics,* Bk. IX, Chap. 4.

(2) The Love of Neighbor

Who is our neighbor? The term "neighbor" properly refers to an intellectual creature who is capable of sharing eternal happiness with us. It includes, therefore, all men and all angels, except only those who, having persevered in mortal sin by their own free choice, have been condemned to hell for their unrepented offenses. Yet the love of charity extends even to the damned—not that we can possibly have friendship for them, but we do love what is good in them and wish this good to remain for the glory of God. Similarly, this divine friendship also excludes animals, because they are not able to share in eternal happiness. Indirectly, however, animals may be the objects of charity insofar as we want them to manifest God's honor, as did St. Francis of Assisi, or insofar as we desire men to have them and to use them well.

The term "neighbor" includes our fellowmen, even those who are sinners and our enemies. To love sinners does not mean to desire what they want nor to rejoice in what brings them joy, for they desire the pleasures of sin and rejoice in them. We love the sinner in terms of his capacity for loving God, we desire him to become a friend of God. This means that we must hate the sin by which he separates himself from the love of God. Every truly Christian love of sinners must include a hatred for his sin.

Our Lord has commanded: ". . . love your enemies, do good to those who hate you, and pray for those who persecute and caluminate you, so that you may be children of your Father in heaven" (Matt. 5:44). Enemies are those who hate, offend or injure us, and also those whom we think do these things. An enemy either is evil or is regarded as such. Now we are not required to love anyone precisely as he is our enemy, for this would be a perverse love of another's wickedness. Rather, we are commanded to love our enemies precisely because they are, or can become, God's children through charity.

Charity must be expressed in action. Therefore, enemies may not be excluded from the common signs of friendship which we show to all men. It would be contrary to charity to exclude an enemy from the prayers we offer for all men generally. We must always be prepared to assist an enemy who is in extreme necessity, although we are not bound to show him special favors or signs of friendship outside of the special case of necessity. Freely to seek out one's enemy and to offer him special signs of friendship when he has no extreme need for them is a sign of the perfection of charity whereby we wish to overcome evil by good.

(3) Love of Our Bodies

Our bodies are legitimate objects of charity. St. Paul urges us to "... present ourselves to God as those who have come to life from the dead and your members as weapons of justice for God ..." (Rom. 6:13). The true Christian love of the body is marked by a desire to use its members in the divine service. This is in direct opposition to the worldly worship of the body. The rule of charity to our bodies was expressed by Christ: "He who finds his life will lose it, and he who loses his life for my sake will find it" (Matt. 10:39).

C. The Order of Charity

Charity tends to God as to the principle of eternal happiness. The friendship of charity is based upon a sharing in that happiness, and so all those who are included in charity must stand in some definite relationship to the principle of charity who is God. There is, consequently, an order according to which charity is to be exercised.

Every human being is limited in the exercise of charity. Frequently a Christian must make choices among those who stand in need of his charitable assistance, because he cannot help all. Occasionally these choices are difficult, as in the rare case of the man who must choose between rescuing his mother or his child from a burning building, or who must choose to save either the life of a dear friend or the life of a worthless brother.

There is a fundamental distinction which will help greatly to make clear the problems faced in the choices that must be made.

Objectively (on the part of the one loved)—
when a greater good is willed to one
rather than to another.

One is loved
more than
another

Appreciatively—when one is preferred to another because he is
known to be better.

Subjectively (on
the part of the
one who loves)

Intensively—when one is loved
with greater feeling and stronger
affection than another.

The order of charity is to be judged according to the order
of *appreciative* love, which proceeds from a judgment of reason.
It does not depend upon a sentiment of affection based upon
our closeness to someone, as in the case with *intensive* love—God
commands us, not to feel love, but to have love. The order of appreciative love, which generally includes the order of objective love,
is based upon the union of the one loved with God; the order of
intensive love is based upon the union of the one loved with ourselves.

In the light of these distinctions and principles, the following conclusions may be made:

1. We are bound to love God more, both *objectively* and *appreci-*
   atively, than ourselves or our neighbor. The reason is that God
   is infinitely better than any creature. Hence we must prefer
   him to everyone else; we must prefer to suffer any evil, even
   the greatest, rather than offend him in the smallest matter.

2. *Objectively,* our love for ourselves and for our neighbors should
   be equal, for we must desire for them a share in the same eternal
   happiness we hope to have ourselves. *Appreciatively,* we should
   prefer ourselves above our neighbors, in the sense that we may not
   do ourselves the slightest spiritual harm even to secure their greatest good. E.g., charity forbids anyone to commit a venial sin—even

an excusing lie—in order to do his neighbor any good, no matter how great. *Intensively*, men necessarily love themselves more than their neighbors.

3. The goods men possess are those of the soul, or of the body, or of external possessions. This is the order of *appreciative* love with respect to these various goods (the order of preference):

    1) One's own spiritual good.
    2) One's neighbor's spiritual good.
    3) One's own physical well-being.
    4) One's neighbor's physical well-being.
    5) One's personal possessions.
    6) One's neighbor's possessions.

4. Neighbors who are closer to God than ourselves, e.g., Our Lady and the saints, must be loved more than ourselves *objectively*, i.e., we must desire for them a higher degree of glory in proportion to their greater union with God.

5. Neighbors who are better must be loved more *appreciatively* than those who are close to us. E.g., we must will a greater good to an honest acquaintance than to a dishonest brother.

6. Those who are closer to us may be loved more *intensively* than others who may be better than they are. E.g., a mother has a more intense love for a wayward son than for an upright nephew. Intensively, our love for our parents is greater than our love for God, humanly speaking, because they are closer to us. If this love proceeds from charity, then God himself will be more loved intensively, for his love will be the reason for our love of our parents. In every case, however, we must prefer the will of God to the wishes of our parents.

7. In matters pertaining to natural origins and survival, relatives must be loved more *appreciatively* than friends and associates. A man is obliged to assist his parents, children, wife, brothers and sisters before he cares for his friends, although all of them may be suffering equal need.

8. In matters pertaining to the temporal common good, our native land and our fellow citizens are to be loved more *appreciatively*

than others. The same principle of preference, both in temporalities and spiritualities, is applicable to those who are ". . . of the household of the faith" (Gal. 6:10).

4. THE ACTS OF CHARITY

The divine friendship of charity is a virtue that embraces God, ourselves and our neighbors. What are the acts by which this virtue is extended or applied to those whom we must love? What effects does charity produce? The outline facing this page shows the various acts and effects of charity.

A. Love

The proper and distinctive act of charity is, not to be loved, but rather to love someone else. Friends are praised for loving, but if they are loved and refuse to love in return, they are blamed. The same truth is clear from the example of mothers, whose great love, unselfish and unseeking, seeks to love rather than to be loved. This love is not simply an act of good will, but adds to that an affection for the beloved.

What of our love for God? Can we love him in himself or only because of his gifts? If we love the divine gifts and not the divine giver, then we do not have charity but an acquisitive, concupiscible love.[23] But from the things it knows the soul learns to love what it knows not: God's gifts dispose us to advance in his love. The favors he bestows, the rewards we hope to receive from him, even the punishments we hope to avoid through him, all can and should lead us to love God himself. The Church, in fact, condemns the teaching that it is sinful to live a good life because of the hope of an eternal reward.[24]

We gain our knowledge of God through other things, but after he is known in himself we can put these helps aside as the cripple

---

[23]Cf. supra, Chap. Three, 92-94.
[24]Council of Trent, loc. cit., Can. 31; Denz. 841.

Principal: **Love**—affectionately willing good to others.

Acts and effects of charity

Secondary

Internal

Joy—delighting spiritually in divine friendship for God and others.

Peace—a union of hearts among many and a unity of desire in each.

Mercy—a heartfelt compassion for the misery of another which impels us to relieve him if we can.

External

Beneficence—manifesting benevolence by doing good to others.

Almsgiving—bestowing gifts out of compassion for the needy and out of the love of God.

Fraternal correction—prudent and merciful admonition of a sinner for his spiritual good in an effort to assist him in correcting himself.

when he is cured casts away his crutches. "We no longer believe because of what thou hast said, for we have heard for ourselves and we know that this is in truth the Savior of the world" (John 4:42). So, too, our love must reach beyond the gifts to the giver himself.

No human heart can enclose the infinite goodness of God. Yet there are ways for man to fulfill the command to love God with his *whole* heart, for a man can love all that pertains to God, and he can do this with all his might by referring all he is and all he has to the love of God. The measure of the love of God, says St. Bernard, is to love him without measure.

It is sometimes thought that the difficulty of a deed is the measure of its excellence. It is more difficult to love an enemy than a friend; hence, it will be said, it is more meritorious. But is this really the case? Goodness, not difficulty, is the measure of merit. It is more meritorious to love God than to love one's neighbor, simply because the object of the act is better in itself. The Blessed Virgin in caring for her son would merit more than all the martyrs in their torments, because she had a higher degree of charity. On the other hand, she merited more on Calvary than in those acts that were easier.

There are two kinds of difficulty: *objective*—which arises from the greatness of the deed; and *subjective*—which arises from the weakness of the doer. Now an objective difficulty in an act of charity increases merit, because it requires a high degree of charity to do great deeds of love. On the other hand, a subjective difficulty indicates a defect of charity and indicates a lessening of merit.

Another example of this principle is found in the love of enemies. In itself, it is better to love one's friends who are better and closer than one's enemies. This is evident from the opposite, that it is worse to hate one's friends than one's enemies. Yet there is a sense in which the more difficult deed of loving one's enemies is a better and more meritorious act. Only a pure motive of charity, i.e., the love of God, will lead us to love our enemies, because they are not lovable in themselves. Other things being equal, to love an enemy requires a stronger charity that will extend to an object so remote as an enemy.

Not every difficulty is a sign of merit, but only such difficulty as is a sign of a better act, one proceeding from greater love.

B. Joy

It is possible to crowd a lifetime with pleasure without ever tasting real joy. Spiritual joy is an effect of charity. It can be possessed only by the friends of God, it never comes to one who lives in opposition to the will of God. "For the kingdom of God does not consist in food and drink, but in justice and peace and joy in the Holy Spirit" (Rom. 14:16). It was of such spiritual joy that Christ spoke when he said, "These things I have spoken to you that my joy may be in you, and that your joy may be made full" (John 15:11).

Spiritual joy is a rejoicing over God's own goodness and over our sharing in that goodness through divine grace. Just as the sensible passion of delight follows upon the possession of a sensible good desired and loved, so supernatural joy arises in the will of those who share in the blessedness of God through charity. Spiritual joy can coexist with sorrow over our past sins or the sins of others. Indeed, such sorrow is itself a result of true charity. But this in no way diminishes the reality of the joy that comes from the possession of the divine friend. One of the best signs that a soul is in grace is that it delights in the things of God and sorrows over the recollection or the possibility of being separated from him by sin.

C. Peace

All men desire peace in the sense that they wish to be unmolested in the pursuit of happiness. Yet all do not mean the same thing by peace, any more than they mean the same thing by happiness. Among groups and nations, "peace" implies a unity, a common agreement to "live and let live." Properly speaking, such a state is called *concord*. Concord is usually confined to some limited aspect of life. There can be military concord without political agreement; there can be domestic concord without real love.

Peace includes concord (which is an amicable relationship with others) and adds something more. Peace extends to a unity of desire within the individual; it includes the notion of harmony within the individual and of the individual in relation to God. True peace is found only in good men who seek what is good. Evil can never put man at rest: "there is no peace to the wicked" (Isa. 48:22).

True peace flows from both justice and charity. "And the work of justice shall be peace" (Isa. 32:17), because justice removes the obstacles to peace. But most properly, peace is the fruit of charity, which unites men's desires, and men themselves, in the orderly unity of divine friendship. Since charity establishes the proper order of all our relationships, internal and external, in ordering all things to God, it produces a peace of soul surpassing all understanding. "Much peace have they that love thy law" (Ps. 118:165). "Peace," says St. Augustine, "is the tranquillity of order."[25] Peace is not a virtue, but the fruit of virtue.

All acts of charity, we have seen, are meritorious, but a special place and a special reward are set aside for those who, from charity, strive actively to bring about peace. Peacemaking is listed among the beatitudes (cf. Matt. 5:9), and the beatitudes are the most perfect acts of perfect virtues. Here we see the friendship of charity come full circle. The reward merited by the peacemakers echoes the formal sharing of the divine nature that makes charity possible: "Blessed are the peacemakers, *for they shall be called the children of God.*"

D. Mercy

If there were no suffering, there could be no mercy. The proper matter for mercy is the sufferings of others which we seek to share and somehow make our own out of charity. Mercy is evoked by any affliction, but more by those for which the sufferer is not

[25]*City of God*, Bk. XIX, Chap. 13.

responsible, and most especially by those which a man strove diligently to avoid.

Charity is a unitive force; it makes us rejoice over the good of our neighbor and makes us sorrow over the evil that befalls him because we consider his fortunes in a manner our own.

Mercy is charity's response to the suffering of others. This third effect of charity is defined as *the heartfelt compassion for the misery of another which impels us to relieve him if we can.* Mercy in this sense is not merely the emotion of sympathy, the pang in the sensible appetite that follows on the suffering of another. It is an act, and a habit, of the will. It is called into play by any affliction, but especially by those for which the sufferer is not responsible. It will be particularly marked in the case of those evils which the sufferer has tried to avoid. The destitution of one who has lived an honorable life, the dereliction by ungrateful children of loving parents, the innocent overwhelmed by war or natural catastrophe—all are particularly evocative of mercy.

Mercy is not the fruit of charity in the same way as peace and joy. It is a **virtue** in its own right, for it has the function of *moderating the passions.* It has its own special object: *relief of the evil that another suffers.* It has a special relation to charity in that it comes under its command, and therefore shares the character of that supreme virtue.

Mercy cannot be the greatest of *human* virtues, for those which unite man directly to God surpass it. Yet it is the greatest of the virtues exercised towards man's neighbor, for it has something of the godlike attribute of power. Only the seeing can lead the blind, and he who aids his neighbor must, exactly in the measure in which his aid is effective, be stronger and better than the unfortunate. The merciful man, even when faced with the irremediable suffering of another, continues to practice the virtue by carrying out St. Paul's counsel: "Rejoice with those who rejoice; weep with those who weep" (Rom. 12:15).

To be merciful, a man must be willing to suffer with another. While no sorrow can intrude upon the inexpressible joy of the divine life, God's mercy is infinitely more perfect than man's, for he makes our sorrows his by conquering them and healing them by his limitless power. Nothing escapes God's providence: ". . . the very hairs of your head are all numbered" (Matt. 10:30). Every work of God is a work of mercy; even his works of justice are founded upon mercy.

E. Beneficence

Beneficence simply means doing good to someone, and the result of charity is that a man does good to his friend. In this general sense, then, beneficence is an act of charity. But very often, the good that is done to someone is something special, and the result of another virtue that is more properly concerned with the good deed. Some acts of beneficence flow immediately from mercy, justice or patriotism, and only remotely from charity as commanding the acts of these other virtues.

It should be obvious that beneficence is a matter of moral obliga-tion, that one *must* do good. The will of man, granted the physical ability, does what it wants. The will informed by the love of charity has the obligation of willing good to others and, as a consequence, the same obligation of *doing* good for them.

"Therefore, while we have time," says St. Paul, "let us do good to all men, but especially to those who are of the household of the faith" (Gal. 6:10). Thus we learn that beneficence must be regulated according to the circumstances of place, time and person, as indicated by the order of charity. It is not possible to do good actually to everyone. Therefore, the acts of charity must be measured according to the principles that regulate the order of charity.

F. Almsgiving

Almsgiving is an act rooted in charity and exercised through the virtue of mercy. Its object is to relieve the needy by giving them gifts for the love of God. Almsgiving is essential to Christian living. "He who has the goods of this world and sees his brother in need and closes his heart to him, how does the love of God abide in him?" (I John 3:17).

There are many different kinds of almsdeeds corresponding to the different needs of men. There are *seven corporal works of mercy*, intended to relieve physical needs: to feed the hungry; to give drink to the thirsty; to clothe the naked; to harbor the harborless; to visit the sick; to ransom the captive; to bury the dead. And there are *seven spiritual works* to relieve spiritual needs: to instruct the ignorant; to counsel the doubtful; to comfort the sorrowful; to reprove the sinner; to forgive injuries; to bear with those who trouble and annoy us; to pray for all, both living and dead. This traditional listing is not exhaustive, of course; many more works of mercy will occur to the charitable soul as needs differ and circumstances change.

There are two circumstances that determine the obligation of almsgiving: the need of the recipient, and the ability of the giver. We are speaking here strictly about *obligation;* as a work of special generosity more may be done as a matter of *counsel.*

The need of the recipient of alms may be judged according to the three kinds of necessity:

1) **Extreme necessity** exists whenever there is moral certitude of the imminence of eternal damnation, death or some equivalent evil which cannot be avoided without help. Evils considered equivalent to death are: loss of reason, health or liberty, and conditions which would be brought on by such ills as a grave psychological shock, malnutrition or imprisonment for life.

2) **Grave necessity** exists either when the aforementioned evils may probably occur and cannot be avoided without serious difficulty; or when the certainly imminent evils are not extreme, but grave (e.g., unjust imprisonment for a time, serious disgrace, serious illness, loss of considerable money that would make living difficult).

3) **Common necessity** exists whenever anyone encounters some special difficulty in sustaining his life or his dignity. Sinners ordinarily are considered to be in common spiritual need; beg-

gars are considered to be in common temporal need, unless graver need is evident.

The second circumstance that determines the obligation of almsgiving is the ability of the giver in terms of his possessions. A man's possessions may be evaluated in three ways:

1) *Necessities of life* are required to sustain the lives of their owner and his dependents, such as food, clothing, etc.

2) *Necessities of state* are those goods, over and above what is required for life itself, which are needed to maintain a man and his dependents in a manner in keeping with their station and position in life. An estimation of these goods must take into account reasonable provisions for future expenses such as education, retirement income, etc.

3) *Superfluities of state* are those goods which exceed what is required to provide properly for one's state in life. Some have maintained that the richest men never have anything beyond what their state demands. This false view, which would comfort the miserly rich and rob the poor of the help the rich should give, has been condemned.[26]

The chart on the opposite page deals only with what is of strict obligation in charity; it will serve to indicate the various degrees of the Christian obligation to give alms.

But no chart, table or fixed percentage can assign the obligation of the individual Christian to give alms. The obligations of justice can be fixed precisely, but not those of charity. The objective order of charity may serve as a first approximation for a norm, but even this is subject to many variables. The greater need of a stranger here and now may outweigh the lesser indigence of a distant cousin.

The complexities of our society and culture are reflected even in the merciful act of almsgiving. Organization is increasingly necessary for the effective handling of funds given to relieve distress. The heartstrings—and pursestrings—of the well-endowed and merciful man are tugged at by many worthy appeals: that of a bishop for

[26]Decree of the Holy Office, March 4, 1679, 12th error; Denz. 1162.

When our neighbor's need is . . .	and the source of alms are goods . . .	then the obligation to give is . . .
Extreme	Necessary to life	None—unless the needy are public personages.
	Necessary to state	Grave—neighbor's life is preferable to our dignity.
	Superfluous to state	Grave.
Grave	Necessary to life	None.
	Necessary to state	Grave—without grave hardship to self.
	Superfluous to state	Grave.
Common	Necessary to life	None.
	Necessary to state	None.
	Superfluous to state	1) Grave—to give *something* to *someone*. (A neighbor's decency is preferable to our superfluity.) 2) None—to relieve *every* necessity, or to give to one in particular. 3) None—to seek out the poor, except when there might be extreme necessity, or when it is a duty.

the charities of his diocese, the United Fund for humanitarian purposes, church carnivals, funds for the relief of certain ills—and a host of others.

What is the duty of the virtuous man in this regard? No one, not even the wealthiest, is obliged to contribute to all. Here the rule given by St. Thomas that discretion must be used in the giving of alms enters in.[27] He observes that considerations of personal relationship, sanctity and utility (both for the person helped and the common good) must all enter into the decision. The objective order of charity, especially with regard to "those of the household of the faith" must be considered. A weighing of the need of the eventual recipients and even the personal note of intensive love, of preference for one form of relief over another, can serve to determine a contribution to organized charity.

The obligation to assist others out of liberality, beneficence, magnificence or legal justice can be binding even when our neighbor does not suffer any necessity whatever. The obligation in charity of giving alms does not exhaust the larger question of the proper use of superfluous goods. St. Basil expresses the truly Christian attitude when he says: "If you acknowledge your possessions as coming from God, is he unjust because he apportions them unequally? Why are you rich when another is poor, unless it be that you may have the merit of a good stewardship, and he the reward of patience? It is the bread of the hungry that you withhold, the naked man's cloak that you have stored away, the shoe of the barefoot that you have left to rot, the money of the needy that you have buried underground; and so you have injured as many as you might help."[28]

Christian almsgiving should be: 1) *prudent*—assisting the truly poor (Thess. 3:10); 2) *gracious*—without embarassing them (II Cor. 9:7); 3) *generous*—to aid many (Tob. 4:9); 4) *prompt*—lest the poor despair (Prov. 3:28); 5) *unostentatious*—only for the love of God (Matt. 6:1-4); 6) *just*—neglecting no duty (Sir. 4:1, 8; Luke 19:8-9); 7) *well ordered*—considering all circumstances (Matt. 5-23); 8) *universal* (cf. Luke 6:31-35).

---

[27]*Summa*, II-II, q. 32, a. 4.
[28]*Homily on St. Luke*, 12:18.

G. Fraternal Correction

Almsgiving is a kind of beneficence that cares for our neighbor's needs. **Fraternal correction** is a kind of beneficence—a spiritual almsgiving—that looks after our neighbor's spiritual welfare. It may be defined: *an act of mercy whereby we strive to care for our neighbor's spiritual need by prudently admonishing him in an effort to prevent him from sinning or to lead him to repentance.*

Christ insists that we have an obligation to offer fraternal correction, and he tells us explicitly how it is to be done:

> But if thy brother sins against thee, go and show him his fault, between thee and him alone. If he listen to thee, thou hast won thy brother. But if he does not listen to thee, take with thee one or two more so that on the word of two or three witnesses every word may be confirmed.[29]

This act of charity must be exercised with great prudence, lest it be done from a motive of pride and lest the sinner be made even worse by being corrected.

It is easily seen that superiors—bishops, public officials, parents, teachers, confessors, etc.—have a special and grave obligation to correct those who are subject to them, which often extends to the correction of relatively minor faults. They can commit serious sins by neglecting this duty. Even equals, who have no official authority, have an obligation to correct their fellows, but the obligation of equals occurs far less frequently than that of superiors. When the following five conditions are present simultaneously, a Christian has the obligation to correct an erring neighbor in a spirit of charity.

1) *Serious matter*—i.e., a grave sin which was certainly committed. Private individuals need not correct others for venial sins, nor are they to pry into the hidden sins of others. (Cf. Prov. 24:14.)

2) *Real necessity*—there is no need to correct one who is going to correct himself.

3) *Usefulness*—there must be reasonable hope that the correction will be heeded. If one is certain that the correction will

---

[29]Matt. 18:15-17.

do no harm (e.g., will not provoke blasphemy, etc.) while it may do good, he is bound to make it. If there is serious doubt about its utility, correction need not be made, except in cases where one's neighbor might die in serious sin or fall into worse sins if not corrected.

4) *Possibility*—the risks we must take in correcting others must be proportioned to our neighbor's need. No one may refuse to correct another simply because of fear of offense or anger.

5) *Opportunity*—the correction should be made graciously and charitably, without needless embarrassment and publicity. Sometimes we must await a suitable opportunity.

Every true Christian would warn his neighbor against robbers or disease that would ruin his fortune or his health; should he do less to protect him from the destruction of his soul?

5. THE VICES OPPOSED TO CHARITY

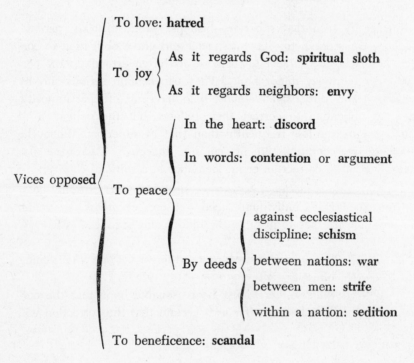

Vices opposed

To love: **hatred**

To joy
- As it regards God: **spiritual sloth**
- As it regards neighbors: **envy**

To peace
- In the heart: **discord**
- In words: **contention** or **argument**
- By deeds
  - against ecclesiastical discipline: **schism**
  - between nations: **war**
  - between men: **strife**
  - within a nation: **sedition**

To beneficence: **scandal**

Since charity is love, the love of God and man, the sins and vices which are its enemies will be those that strike first of all at love itself, and then those that attack the effects of charity in the soul. Following St. Thomas' method, we will consider the various sins and vices against charity as they are opposed to its acts and habits.

Some of these vices can be understood sufficiently in terms of their definitions, others will require further explanation.

A. Hatred

Hatred is *an act* (and a habit) *by which a man regards someone or something, seen as harmful or repugnant to him, with malevolence.* It is the contradictory of love, and basically is of two kinds:

1) **Enmity,** by which a man *wishes evil* to someone who displeases him. There is no question here of mere indifference, or of a simple not-wishing-well. Enmity in its extreme form is a positive desire for the death, damnation and destruction of the other person. It is directly opposed to the *benevolent* friendship of charity, and is always sinful.

2) **Detestation,** by which one *opposes* something or someone regarded as harmful or displeasing to himself. It is the contrary of *concupiscible* love, and is sinful if it is directed against a person, but not necessarily so if it is directed against a quality of a person. One may virtuously detest vice or sin in a sinner. One may even feel repugnance at physical habits or social lapses of someone without sin. In the latter case, however, there is an obvious danger of being disposed to hatred.

(1) Hatred of God

God cannot be hated *in himself,* for he is all goodness. To hate him would be, not vicious, but insane. Nor can even the most depraved sinner hate God for those gifts which have no evil in themselves: life, health, reason and the like. The man who curses his life—or takes it—is railing, not against the gift of God, but against some evil in it that he regards as unbearable.

The sinner can hate God for those of his *effects* which are contrary to an evil will: just punishment, the laws against sin and so on. This hatred, which embraces both enmity and detestation, is **the greatest possible sin**, for it is contrary to the highest object of charity itself, which is the highest virtue.[30]

Hatred of God is placed by the theologian as a special sin against the Holy Spirit. It is not a capital sin, but rather the culmination of other sins. It is the last plunge into the abyss, the final dissolution of a soul corrupted and shattered by other vices.

(2) Other Hatreds

Hatred of sin is not sinful, but rather an act of charity, whether it be of our own sin or of our neighbor's. Hatred of our neighbor himself is gravely sinful. As charity is a uniting force, welding and binding into one all the virtues of the one who loves, so its contrary, hatred, destroys the unity and integrity of the personality. Other sins may work a greater harm to one's neighbor—theft, murder and the like—but none indicates or causes a greater disintegration in the soul of the sinner himself. Spiritually speaking, hatred is an ulcer, for the sinner consumes himself in the corrosive forces of his own disordered soul.

B. Sloth and Envy

(1) Spiritual Boredom

Ordinarily, man delights in the presence of his divine friend. But the friendship of charity imposes many obligations, as we have already seen. It is possible for someone to regard these obligations as burdens rather than as privileges; he becomes saddened and oppressed and weary until, finally, he neglects to do good. *This peculiar sadness which leads to a neglect of the spiritual duties that flow from sharing in God's friendship is called* sloth.

Sloth produces a kind of spiritual paralysis that leads to a neglect of our duties. When it is directed against our sharing in the divine

[30]Cf. St. Thomas, *Summa*, I-II, q. 73, a. 4.

goodness it is a special mortal sin. Sloth is also a capital vice which leads a man to commit many other sins, called its "daughters":[31]

Daughters of Sloth

- withdrawing men from what oppresses
  - by flight
    - from the goal—*despair*
    - from the means
      - which are the counsels—*timidity*
      - which are the commandments—*apathy*
  - by resistance
    - to men—*spite*
    - to spiritual goods—*malice*
- plunging men into evil distractions
  - *uneasiness of mind*
  - *curiosity*
  - *verbosity*
  - *restlessness*
  - *instability*

(2) Envy

Sloth is a sadness occasioned by the divine goodness. Envy is *a sadness over our neighbor's good which is regarded as evil, inasmuch as it lessens our own excellence.* Because envy is opposed to charity—one is saddened by that very good of another which would make a charitable man rejoice—it is a mortal sin. Some

[31]For a brief, practical analysis of this vice and for concrete remedies against it, cf. Melchior Cano, O.P., "Victory over Self," *Cross and Crown*, VIII (1956), 149-153. This also treats of some of the other vices opposed to charity.

imperfection of the act, or lightness of matter, can, however, make it venial only. Envy is a *capital* vice because it incites man to sin, either to avoid sorrow or to satisfy its demands.

The moral conflict aroused by envy has three stages, each marked by a special sin begotten as a "daughter" by this vice:

1) It begins by striving to ruin another's reputation, either secretly (*whispering*) or openly (*detraction*).

2) It increases with efforts to defame others. If these are successful, there is *joy at another's misfortune;* if unsuccessful, *sorrow at another's prosperity* results.

3) It ends in *hatred*—hatred of neighbor first of all, and then, since our neighbor's good is from God, envy is also the mother of hatred of God.

C. Sins Opposed to Peace

Hatred and sloth destroy the integration of the soul that charity produces, and *interior peace* is lost in their wake. There are other sins, special ones, which are more directly contrary to the *union among men* which is the result of charity. Their special nature—and special danger —demands that we consider them. First is **discord** in the hearts of men; next **contention** in words; then the deeds: **schism, war, strife** and **sedition.** Their very names are a catalogue of disaster.

(1) Discord

The vice of **discord** is one that strikes at the end of charity itself, for it is defined as *dissension with regard to the good of God or our neighbor.* We are bound by charity to assist and to foster that good. The best intentioned among men may differ, and even warmly, as to *how* God's good or our neighbor's is to be fostered, while in full agreement that it must be done; but discord does not arise concerning means, it involves the end itself, the good we should will.

The adage has it that it takes two to make a quarrel, but in the differences that arise from the vice of discord one of the two parties may be acting virtuously, while evil festers in the heart of the other. More often, perhaps, charity is deficient in both.

Discord springs from pride and vainglory, for the discordant parties seek to have their own way, come what may. True concord is reached, not by the submission of the will of one to that of the other, but by the acceptance by both of the will of God.

(2) Contention

If discord finds expression in vocal argument, it is called **contention**. As a sin, contention is the *impugning of truth*—or even the defence of truth, if it be done in an inordinate way. Like discord, it arises most generally from pride and vainglory. It may appear surprising to find contention listed among the sins against charity, rather than against truthfulness. But its malice lies, not in the uttering of falsehoods, but in the direct attack on a neighbor's spiritual good, his opportunity to know the truth, or on him as a person for defending it.

Verbal argument, even somewhat heated argument, is not in itself contentious. The public speaker from pulpit or platform who is exposing the truths of faith may choose to employ a vigorous style. He is not contending against truth, but arguing against error. The same thing is true of an attorney arguing his case in court. He may not use falsehood, nor attack that which is manifestly just, but he may present the points that favor his cause with all the legal and rhetorical skill at his command. So, too, in other polemical matters, or in the campaign of a political candidate. St. Thomas, a most able disputant himself, notes: "If the attack on falsity with a due measure of acrimony be called contention, then contention is laudable."[32]

The operative phrase in this statement of St. Thomas is "due measure." Even the defender of right and truth may not use sarcasm and personal invective to make his point.

D. Sinful Deeds Opposed to Peace

(1) Schism

Schism is contrary to the bond of charity which unites the faithful in the Church of Christ. It is *the refusal of a baptized Christian to be subject to the Supreme Pontiff, or to have communion with the mem-*

[32]*Summa*, II-II, q. 38, a. 1.

bers of the Church subject to the Roman Pontiff.[33] Schismatics incur an excommunication specially reserved to the Holy See.[34]

Whereas heresy is opposed to the unity of faith, schism is opposed to the unity of charity that should exist in the Church. By "unity" here is meant the unity of discipline, of government under one visible head. There is a destruction of the unifying bond of charity in the schismatic's withdrawal, for that bond not only links man to man in the Church, but links them all to the common father, the Vicar of Christ.

Grave enough in itself, schism prepares the way for even graver sins. It is less grave in itself than heresy (although both are mortally sinful), for heresy destroys the virtue of faith, which has God himself as its object, while schism wars against an *effect* of charity. History has shown, and the sad experience of schismatic groups of our own day bears witness, that heresy does grow out of schism.[34a]

The schismatic who does not fall into heresy retains **unformed faith.** The bishops and priests in schism retain the *sacramental power* as well. Bishops are truly consecrated, the priests they ordain are truly priests, and their Mass continues the sacrifice of Calvary. This sacramental power remains, for in administering the sacraments man acts only as the instrument of God. By reason of his withdrawal from the source and fount of authority, however, the schismatic loses the *power of jurisdiction.* He can have no authority over the faithful, and knowingly to approach a schismatic to receive the sacraments is gravely sinful.[35]

(2) Warfare

Warfare is *an armed conflict between nations.*[36] It can be waged defensively to repel aggression or offensively to secure redress for

---

[33]Cf. Can. 1325.

[34]Cf. Can. 2314.

[34a]The important distinction between *formal* and *material* sins (see the chapter on faith, 343) should be recalled and applied here.

[35]In the case of extreme necessity it would be permitted to ask for the sacraments.

[36]Following the great Spanish theologian, Francisco Vitoria, O.P., many modern theologians treat war as a sin against justice. In truth they have good reason for this classification, since nations nowadays are not united by the common bond of Christian friendship as they were (at least theoretically) during the ages of faith. War today is more directly a sin against concord and the order of justice than against peace and the order of charity.

injuries. The Manicheans and the followers of Wycliff maintained that war was always evil. This position is taken by several Protestant sects today, notably the Quakers. Luther taught that it was evil to resist the scourge of God by warring against the Turks. These and similar views of extreme pacifism have been condemned by the Church.[37] The Christian position is that warfare can be lawful under certain circumstances.

Three conditions are traditionally laid down for a just war:

1. **It must be declared and waged by public authority.** Because of the economic expenditures and complexity of organization required, this is a matter of course today. The fundamental reason, however, lies deeper. The cannon of the French armies of Louis XIV bore graven on their muzzles: *Ultima ratio regum,* "The last argument of kings." In differences between sovereign nations, there is no higher political authority to whom appeal may be made for decision. When diplomatic negotiation has failed, the nation, through its supreme authority, may take to arms to defend its rights.

2. **It must be waged for a just cause.** There must be a wrong to be righted, or a punishment to be inflicted on those against whom war is waged. "Preventive" war as such is unjustifiable.

3. **The one waging war must have a good intention.** A war, rightly begun and for a just cause, may be rendered unjust by a bad intention on the part of the ones waging it. Political or economic gain, revenge, vindictiveness, are motives which can vitiate a good intention.

From this it should be clear that war is not intrinsically evil. Its final end is the restoration of the peace of charity. We speak of a "just" rather than a "charitable" war because, as we have seen above, peace among men requires that justice be established.

Other considerations enter in. In the past, armed conflict was confined to actual participants. In the age of the atomic and hydrogen bomb, of bacterial and chemical warfare, the whole population of a nation is exposed to death and injury. It is an established principle

---

[37]E.g., Leo X, bull *Exsurge Domine,* June 15, 1520, against certain errors of Martin Luther (Denz. 774); Pius IX, "Syllabus" of Modern Errors, Dec. 8, 1864 (Denz. 1762).

of moral action (and of civil law as well) that only that force may be used against an aggressor which is necessary to repel him. The position of many today who speak of "total war" and regard all citizens of a nation as combatants because they contribute by labor or taxes to the support of the armies is morally indefensible. The destructive effect of modern warfare, it can be argued, of its very nature will go beyond that needed or permitted by justice.

It was noted in explaining the first condition that the fundamental right of a nation to wage war is based on the fact that the ultimate defense of its rights cannot be achieved in any other way. In a modern world where ties of communication and economic interdependence have made the human community more closely united, the need for an international political organization is implicit. Such an organization would exercise the functions among nations that the supreme political power does within the individual nation: judicial powers, executive powers, including police powers, even legislative powers. Only such an organization with effective means at its disposal can rid the world ultimately of war. It would be a material disposition to the reign of the peace of charity among nations.[38]

(3) Strife

The violation of peace known technically as **strife** was discussed by older theologians as a sort of private war in which one took matters of defense of rights into his own hands. The range wars of our own Wild West are an example of strife. It is defined as *a physical encounter in which one individual tries to kill or injure another.*

Strife presupposes an unjust attack by one party, together with the intent to harm the other. It is a sin opposed to charity, for it

[38]The complex problems posed by the threat of atomic warfare are both grave and urgent. The flavor of contemporary papal teaching on these subjects may be learned in the following writings of Pope Pius XII: Christmas Message, 1943 (*Catholic Mind*, 42 [February, 1944], 65-76; Christmas Message, 1948 (*ibid.*, 47 [March, 1949], 179-87); Easter Message, 1954 (*ibid.*, 52 [July, 1954], 438-40); Christmas Message, 1955 (*The Pope Speaks*, 2 [Winter, 1955], 301-14); Christmas Message, 1956 (*ibid.*, 3 [Spring, 1957], 331-46).

destroys peace, and to justice as well. Its gravity will depend upon the harm intended and accomplished.[39]

(4) Sedition

The sin of *strife between factions of the same state* is called **sedition.** It shares the malice of strife among persons and also of war, because it is contention between parties who are prepared to take to arms. It goes beyond strife in gravity, for it is directly contrary to the common good.

The full flaring of such strife is **civil war,** but even the plotting of such strife is sedition, and the guilt of the violation of charity falls most heavily on those who foment seditious activity.

Just as war may sometimes be undertaken to restore the balance of justice and the peace of charity, so civil war and revolution may sometimes be virtuous. A people who try to overthrow a tyrannical regime by force are acting for the common good. For their action to be truly virtuous, the injustice of the regime must be manifest, and no peaceful remedy available. In addition, the evils that follow from the rebellion may not be greater than those suffered under the tyrant.[40]

E. The Vice Opposed to Beneficence: Scandal

(1) Its Nature

The word **scandal,** in its origins, means a stumbling block. Theologically speaking, it is a stumbling block in our neighbor's progress toward God. It is defined *as a word or deed which is evil (or which seems to be evil) that occasions the spiritual ruin of another.* It

[39]The form of strife in which combatants meet by pre-arrangement and with deadly weapons is called *duelling.* Both parties gravely violate charity, and the Church has levelled the punishment of excommunication on all who participate in any way in duels. Cf. Canons 2351, 1240, § 4.

The discussion of the morality of prize-fighting or, more generally, of boxing belongs rather to justice or prudence than to charity.

[40]Some who argue against the impossibility of a just war among nations today use this principle. Effectively speaking, they say, any war is a civil war, by reason of the interdependence of nations. And the destruction caused by modern weapons is worse than any imaginable evil.

should be noted that not only evil deeds or words are scandalous, but even those, indifferent in themselves, which have the appearance of evil. The word or deed does not necessarily cause the spiritual downfall of another. It may sometimes be merely the occasion of it.

Scandal, then, is not shock or surprise, nor is it a word or deed that causes shock, surprise or raised eyebrows. *It involves leading another into sin.*

(2) The Kinds of Scandal

The various kinds of scandal are indicated in outline on the facing page.

(3) The Malice of Scandal

The following conclusions summarize the doctrine on scandal:

1) *Passive* scandal is always a sin—either mortal or venial—on the part of the one who is scandalized, because passive scandal is nothing other than the sin he commits. E.g., a man hears a calumny which leads him to commit the sin of rash judgment; the rash judgment is the passive scandal.

2) It is always sinful to give *active* scandal (Matt. 18:6). This is true even if the scandalous action only appears to be sinful. E.g., a Catholic lawyer pleads a divorce action without troubling to reveal that he has the bishop's permission, although he reflects that his silence will give rise to rash judgment among his associates.

3) Both active and passive scandal can exist independently of the other. Scandal can be given without being taken; it can also be taken without being given (pharisaic scandal, or scandal of the weak).

4) *Diabolical* scandal is always mortally sinful. *Simply direct* and *indirect* scandal may be either mortal or venial sins, depending on the intention, the nature of the action, the degree of contempt for another's spiritual welfare, and the resulting passive scandal.

5) There is an obligation to repair damage done by active scandal. For indirect scandal, the implicit reparation of contrary good example

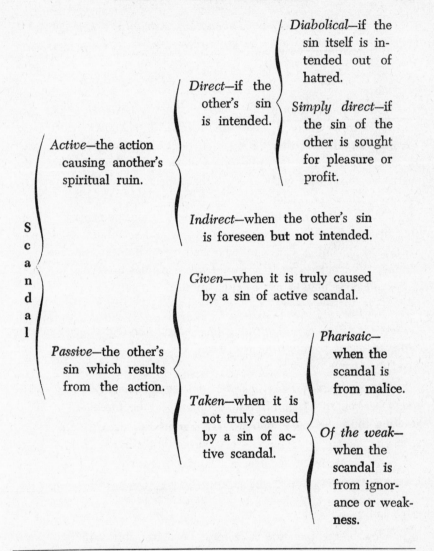

Scandal

Active—the action causing another's spiritual ruin.

Direct—if the other's sin is intended.

Diabolical—if the sin itself is intended out of hatred.

Simply direct—if the sin of the other is sought for pleasure or profit.

Indirect—when the other's sin is foreseen but not intended.

Passive—the other's sin which results from the action.

Given—when it is truly caused by a sin of active scandal.

Taken—when it is not truly caused by a sin of active scandal.

Pharisaic—when the scandal is from malice.

Of the weak—when the scandal is from ignorance or weakness.

ordinarily suffices. For direct scandal, explicit reparation is required: one who scandalizes another by evil advice must correct it; one who publishes bad books must try to stop their circulation, etc. Public scandal must be repaired publicly under the guidance of the bishop or other competent authority.

(4) The Avoidance of Scandal

The following rules govern the avoidance of scandal:

1. *Every truly evil deed which could give scandal must be avoided.*

2. *Every deed having the appearance of evil which could give scandal is to be avoided, unless there is an urgent and grave reason for performing it.* If there is no such reason, then every effort must be made to remove the appearance of evil, e.g., by explaining the matter to those who will see it. If the appearance of evil cannot be removed, then the action may not be performed. A private citizen could shoot a fleeing robber, for example, without pausing to explain that he was a robber, even though this would scandalize those who witnessed it; but a Catholic who had permission to eat meat on Friday could not do so if it would be a scandal to others to whom he would be unable to make explanation.

3. *No one may omit what is necessary for salvation* (e.g., to profess his faith), *or for fulfilling the natural law* (e.g., not to lie), *in order to avoid scandalizing the weak, for no one may do evil that good may come.*

4. *No good deed need ever be omitted to avoid pharisaic scandal.* Occasionally an indifferent action could be foregone to avoid exciting the malice of others.

6. The Precepts of Charity

In view of the fact that love must be a free gift, and that there is no commandment about love in the Decalogue, it seems that there is no true precept commanding an act of charity. Yet in answer to the question about which is the greatest commandment Christ stated: "Thou shalt love the Lord thy God with thy whole heart, and with thy whole soul, and with thy whole mind . . . and . . . thou shalt love thy neighbor as thyself" (Matt. 22:37-39). The teaching of the Church reaffirms the same point: there is an obligation to make acts of charity.[41]

The freedom of the act of charity is not destroyed by the commandment, however; obligation is against the will only of those who are turned away from what is prescribed, as we see in the case of those who obey from fear alone. But the precept of love can only be fulfilled freely, and hence is not contrary to true liberty. The precept of charity is not contained in the Decalogue explicitly, but rather is included in all the commandments, because they are directed to the love of God and of neighbor.

The precept of charity includes both the love of God and of our neighbor. "And this commandment we have from him, that he who loves God should love his brother also" (I John 4:21). Indeed, the two precepts of the love of God and neighbor include all the rest, for "on these two commandments depend the whole Law and the prophets" (Matt. 22:40).

The precept to love God "with your whole heart" means that we must have the highest love for God *appreciatively*, and that nothing can be loved more than God, contrary to God, or equally with God. God must be preferred to any other object of love, even though *intensively* we may love others more than God during this life.

The command to love God entirely cannot be fulfilled perfectly in this life, but it indicates to us the perfection of love that is the lot of the blessed in heaven. "God therefore does not command impossibilities; but in his command he admonishes you both to do what you can for yourself, and to ask his aid in what you cannot do," St. Augustine reminds us.[42]

When we are told to love our neighbor *as ourselves*, it means that our neighbor is to be loved *in the same way* as ourselves, not equally. Objectively, we wish the same eternal happiness for others that we desire for ourselves, and we love our neighbor as we love

---

[41]This was made clear by the condemnation of the opposite opinion, first by Alexander VII in a Decree of Sept. 24, 1665 (Denz. 1101), and later by the Holy Office, March 4, 1679 (Denz. 1156-57).

[42]*On Nature and Grace*, Chap. 50.

ourselves for the love of God, and not for whatever we can gain from him. But charity forbids us to prefer our neighbor's salvation to our own so that we would sin for his sake. In this way, we must always love ourselves more than anyone else, for the precept of charity in the gospel indicates that the order of charity itself is a matter of precept.

7. THE GIFT OF WISDOM

A. The Gift Itself

All love is a unitive force; it begets a similarity between those who love. The divine friendship of charity is no exception. Charity unites men to God and stamps them with a resemblance to their divine friend. Now the most noble and distinctive part of man is his reason, whereby he is able to know and judge all things and where he guides his life. If man is to be able to judge things by divine standards, his mind must be raised up beyond its natural limits. In those who are God's friends by charity this is accomplished by the gift of wisdom. "For there is naught God loves, be it not one who dwells with Wisdom" (Wisd. 7:28).

The **gift of wisdom** is *a divinely infused habit that makes the mind docile to the movement of the Holy Spirit in the contemplation of divine things, and in the judgment of all things, both human and divine, according to divine standards.* The nature and necessity of these gifts of the Holy Ghost has already been explained. Here we shall examine some of the workings of this particular gift.

The gift of wisdom is in the intellect, for it enables man to make judgments, and these are intellectual acts. The gift is far superior to the acquired intellectual virtue called wisdom, both because it deals with supernatural things which no natural virtue can attain, and because it operates almost effortlessly, like a kind of divine instinct, whereas the acquired wisdom must proceed by the more or less halting steps of reason in its judgments.

The gift of wisdom differs from infused faith, although both perfect the intellect. Faith makes us *assent* to divine truths; wisdom goes further and enables us to *judge* in the light of the truths accepted on faith. An example will help to make this clear. We sometimes give assent to historical facts concerning World War II; yet we are not able to judge these facts properly, because we remain ignorant of their causes. So, too, it is one thing to accept on faith the fact of Adam's sin, and quite another to judge wisely that God permitted this sin in his providence for the sake of a greater good which was the Incarnation.

From this gift, we acquire a reverent familiarity with divine standards, we adopt a divine viewpoint in our judgments, we glow in the experience of being "at home" with God. Wisdom springs from charity; it can be found only in the souls of God's friends. "Because into a soul that plots evil wisdom enters not, nor dwells she in a body under debt of sin" (Wisd. 1:4).

St. Thomas ascribes the seventh beatitude, "Blessed are the peacemakers, for they shall be called the children of God," to those who have this supernatural gift. It is the function of wisdom to put things in order, and to judge them well. Now peace is called the "tranquillity of order," and all those who have charity know this peace within their own hearts—their lives are well-ordered, and they are able to contribute to the right order of the lives of others. To set things in proper order is the task of the wisdom which flows from charity. Peacemakers, then, are blessed because they possess this gift of the Holy Spirit.

And fittingly are they called "the children of God," for God's only begotten natural Son is wisdom incarnate. By participating through charity in the gift of wisdom, man attains by adoption to the sonship of God, and becomes a co-heir with Christ.

B. The Vice Opposed to Wisdom

The opposite of wisdom is called either *folly* or *stupidity*. The wise man has an acute and penetrating sense to judge things aright; the foolish or stupid man has a sense that is blunted and dulled so that he judges poorly. We are not here concerned with the dullness that is due to some natural defect, but rather to that lack of judgment about divine things that comes from being immersed in the things of this world to the exclusion of God.

The wisdom of this world is generally folly by divine standards; and the wisdom of the friends of God is often the object of worldly ridicule. Divine and worldly wisdom are opposed as good and evil; if one grows, the other must decrease. The folly that leads a man to plunge into the pleasures of this life until he forgets God is surely a sin. It is more exact to say that this folly is the result of sin, for no one would directly choose those things that make them foolish about the things of God.

Folly is a subtle poison. It begins with an unrestrained admiration of the things of this world and leads to excessive desire for them. Soon it makes man forgetful of his moral obligations in his effort to enjoy the pleasures of life. At some time he comes to the state where he calls the worst enemies of his soul "his friends"—his very food has become poison. Most frequently, unrestrained lust forges the chains of this folly that bind a man to evil pleasure and blind him to any divine consideration that would make him repent and change. But this folly has a limit even in this life, and that limit is reached when "the fool says in his heart, 'There is no God'" (Ps. 13:1). After that point, there is no progress, not even downward. Instead, life becomes a dizzying and boring circle, around which a man marks time, awaiting the moment of supreme folly when he throws away his soul for all eternity.

8. SUMMARY AND CONCLUSION

Life is characterized by change, variety and complexity. That is a lesson brought home to every man sooner or later with the passage of the years. The past comes to resemble a half-forgotten play, acted out by strangers. The future is clouded over by uncertainty and hedged about by innumerable contingencies. The palpable present is peopled by unpredictably changing circumstances that make it elusive of man's control. In the midst of the myriad needs, rights and duties that arise daily, man sometimes resembles a juggler who tries to keep too many Indian-clubs, plates and hats in the air all at once. A careful investigation of moral principles, even when it has progressed only thus far, must deepen the realization of life's complexity.

Understandably, men search for some unifying principle whereby the multiple elements of living may be put in order and managed well. This should be something like the architectural principle whereby countless stones are raised into a towering pyramid, so that they both converge into and flow from its apex. It must be some principle within man, for he himself is the focal point of all the divergent experiences and elements which make up his life. It must be a principle capable of encompassing the subhuman and the supernatural, for these varied elements enter into man's life. Finally, this unifying principle must govern and explain not only the relations between the elements of each life and the individual; it must govern and explain the relation of each individual to the totality of reality of which he is a part.

Only love can meet all the demands for such a principle, for love is the proper principle of union and of unity, as has been shown. It is clear that the love which is the unifying force of life cannot be simply a love of concupiscence which seeks pleasure or utility, for such love must draw everything to man's level, and thus, in a sense, debase the higher goods in his life. This must rather be a love of friendship which expands the heart in the service of another who is regarded as the self. Yet not even a humanly perfect love can make man a friend of God; such a love must be divine, and it must be initiated by God. Only a divine love can suffice to harmonize all that man has and all that he is with God who calls us to himself. "No longer do I call you servants . . . I have called you friends" (John 15:15).

This divine love is charity. In existence and nature it "surpasses knowledge." Here we enter upon the mysterious ways of God, for no man ever dreamed of being a friend of God until God revealed

his love to us. But once the reality of charity is revealed, its importance becomes evident. "Man is the perfection of the universe; the
spirit is the perfection of man; love, that of the spirit; and charity, that
of love. Wherefore the love of God is the end, the perfection and the
excellence of the universe."[43]

These are some of the implications of this teaching:

1. There are many paradoxes in love. The fact that man is the
subject of specifically distinct kinds of love which are not necessarily
harmonized guarantees that he will experience some conflict. Christ
promised this: "He who loves father or mother more than me is not
worthy of me; and he who loves son or daughter more than me
is not worthy of me. And he who does not take up his cross and
follow me is not worthy of me. He who finds his life will lose it,
and he who loses his life for my sake will find it" (Matt. 10:37 ff.).

2. While it is true that our neighbor is the "secondary" object of
charity, it would be spiritually fatal to construe "secondary" here
as meaning optional or merely accidental. "Secondary" here bespeaks
an order between two indispensable objects of love, God and neighbor. The charity which unifies life is itself unified. "If anyone says,
'I love God,' and hates his brother, he is a liar. For how can he
who does not love his brother, whom he sees, love God, whom he
does not see? And this commandment we have from him, that he
who loves God should love his brother also" (I John 4:20 f.).

3. "All the faithful, without exception, are members of the Mystical
Body of Christ. It follows that the law of nature, and still more
pressing, the law of Christ, imposes upon them the obligation of giving
a good example by a truly Christian life: 'For we are the fragrance
of Christ for God, alike as regards those who are saved and those
who are lost' (II Cor. 2:15). Today, all are more and more concerned
in their prayer and sacrifice not only about their own private needs,
but also about the great intentions of the reign of God in the world
according to the spirit of the Our Father, which Jesus Christ himself
has taught us."[44]

[43]St. Francis de Sales, *Treatise on the Love of God*, Bk. X, Chap. 1.
[44]Pope Pius XII, address to the World Congress of the Lay Apostolate, Oct.
14, 1951.

4. Christian charity is not a sentiment or a feeling; rather it is a convinced and unalterable dedication that must find expression in deeds. Particularly needed for our day is the specialized and organized expression of charity which is Catholic Action.[45]

5. Christ assures us that giving a cup of cold water will not go unrewarded (Matt. 10:42). This is certainly not because of the value of the drink, nor even simply because it is given to another, but rather because in being given to our neighbor the cup is given to Christ. In what way is Christ present in our neighbor? What of the promised reward if the cup be given to an enemy of Christ?

6. "Can we say that everyone is called to the apostolate in the strict sense of the word? God has not given to everyone either the possibility or the aptitude. One can hardly ask a wife and mother, who has to look after the Christian upbringing of her children and has to work at home besides to help her husband feed their little ones, to do apostolic work of this kind. The vocation to be an apostle is, therefore, not addressed to all alike.

"It is certainly not easy to draw an exact line of demarcation showing precisely where the true apostolate of the laity begins. Should it include, for example, the education given by the mother of a family, or by the men and women teachers engaged with holy zeal in the practice of their profession? Or the conduct of a reputable and openly Catholic doctor whose conscience never wavers when there is a question of the natural and divine law and who fights with all his might in defense of the Christian dignity of married persons and the sacred rights of their offspring? Should it include even the action of the Catholic statesman who sponsors a generous housing policy in favor of the less fortunate?

"Many would be inclined to answer in the negative, seeing in all these examples merely the accomplishment, very laudable in itself but obligatory, of the duties of one's state. We recognize, however, the powerful and irreplaceable value, for the good of souls,

---

[45]For a detailed explanation of charity as the foundation of this apostolate, cf. Pope Pius XII, "Magna Charta of Catholic Action," Sept. 4, 1940, translated in: Stephen Anderl, *Religious and Catholic Action* (La Crosse: St. Rose Convent, 1947), 127-43.

of this ordinary performance of the duties of one's state by so many millions of conscientious and exemplary faithful.

"The apostolate of the laity, in its proper sense, is without doubt to a large extent organized in Catholic Action and in other forms of apostolic activity approved by the Church; but, apart from these, there can be and actually are, lay apostles, those men and women who see all the good to be done and the possibilities and means of doing it; and they do it with only one desire: the winning of souls to truth and grace."[46]

7. "In the misery of man's earthly sojourn there remains always the consoling fact that he can grow in divine love; that he can climb higher; that his likeness to the divine model can ever become more pronounced; that the soul's relationship with the divine friend can ever grow in tenderness and intimacy and rapture. The significance of our condition as wayfarers consists in the opportunity it provides to advance, through our personal efforts sustained by grace, in the virtue of charity and the unfolding of the divine friendship."[47]

[46]Pope Pius XII, address to the World Congress of The Lay Apostolate, Oct. 14, 1951.

[47]Jerome Wilms, O.P., *Divine Friendship* (Dubuque: The Priory Press, 1958), 130.

BIBLIOGRAPHICAL NOTE

St. Thomas treats of charity in the *Summa,* II-II, QQ. XXIII-XLVI. An excellent article which considers the application of charity to contemporary social problems is "Social Charity" by Most Rev. Aloysius J. Muench, D.D., which is in Vol. III of the English translation of the *Summa,* 3326-36. A group of French theologians and experts in other fields have published a worthwhile symposium, *Love of Our Neighbour* (London: Blackfriars, 1955). Generally less technical and wider in scope is a series of articles in a special issue on "Love of God," *The Life of the Spirit,* VIII (1953), nn. 86-7.

The Perfection of Man by Charity by Reginald Buckler, O.P. (St. Louis: Herder, 1954), *The Mind and Heart of Love* by M. C. D'Arcy, S.J. (London: Faber and Faber, 1954), and *The Love of God* by Aelred Graham, O.S.B. (New York: Longmans, 1940) are three practical and outstanding works of more than passing interest. Two books by Reginald Garrigou-Lagrange, O.P., are also of great value: *The Love of God and the Cross of Jesus* (St. Louis: Herder, 1951) and *Our Savior and His Love for Us* (St. Louis: Herder, 1951). An excellent small work and highly recommended is *Divine Friendship* by Jerome Wilms, O.P. (Dubuque: The Priory Press, 1958).

Among the many articles on the doctrine of charity and its applications the following may be noted: G. J. Budde, "Christian Charity, Now and Always," *American Ecclesiastical Review,* LXXXV (1931), 561-579; P. De Letter, S.J., "Hope and Charity in St. Thomas," *The Thomist,* XIII (1950), 204-248, 325-352; Dominic Hughes, O.P., "Dynamics of Christian Perfection," *The Thomist,* XV (1952), 247-288; Reginald Masterson, O.P., "Charity, the Bond of Perfection," *Cross and Crown,* IX (1957), 214-230.

CHAPTER ELEVEN

Prudence

1. INTRODUCTION

Having studied those virtues which have God for their object, theology now turns its attention to the virtues which help man to attain God. In treating, therefore, of "the movement of the rational creature toward God," theology begins its most practical consideration at this juncture. The four cardinal virtues, prudence, justice, fortitude and temperance, are the principal *means* that a man must employ to attain that *end*—Almighty God—toward which he is orientated by the theological virtues.

The first of the cardinal virtues, prudence, is widely misunderstood and thereby, it would seem, widely abused. Young people often look upon this virtue with timidity, either because they fear its dictates will set unwanted restraints upon their freedom of action, or because youth, proverbially, shies away from the patient counsel that is an essential ingredient of prudent activity. The misfortune of such an attitude—an egregious error in right moral living—lies in the simple fact that prudence is the most important of all the cardinal virtues because it is the director of them all.

To facilitate our study of this key virtue of human living, we will follow this plan:

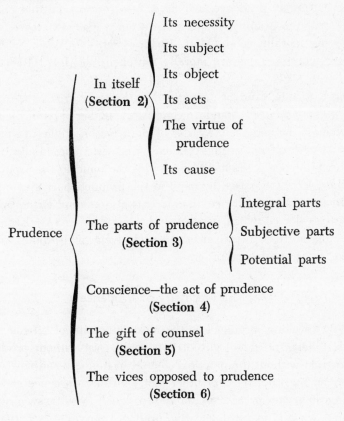

Prudence
- In itself (**Section 2**)
  - Its necessity
  - Its subject
  - Its object
  - Its acts
  - The virtue of prudence
  - Its cause
- The parts of prudence (**Section 3**)
  - Integral parts
  - Subjective parts
  - Potential parts
- Conscience—the act of prudence (**Section 4**)
- The gift of counsel (**Section 5**)
- The vices opposed to prudence (**Section 6**)

2. PRUDENCE IN ITSELF

Generally speaking, the word prudence is understood to imply a correct knowledge with regard to moral action. To ask if something is prudent is to question whether or not a particular action is morally acceptable. Notice that the accent is upon action, for prudence is normally applied either to a person who is thought to act properly, or to the actions of such a person. Rightfully do we speak of a prudent person and of a prudent action.

Somewhat more exactly prudence is described as a practical knowledge that directs moral action. Yet this description is not a definition of the virtue of prudence, which is our concern in this chapter. Holy Writ, for example, applies the term equally to those whose actions are morally good (Matt. 10:16; I Pet. 4:7; Wisd. 8:7), and to those whose actions are morally reprehensible (Luke 16:8; Rom. 8:6-7).

Philosophically, **prudence** is defined as *the order of right reason applied to doing things.* It stands in contrast to another habit of the mind, art, which is defined as "the order of right reason applied to making things." In thus contrasting prudence and art,[1] the implication is obvious. Prudence is the habit which aids the mind in the production of *human acts.* Art assists the mind in the production or manufacture of *things:* artifacts. Prudence, therefore, is also a *moral* virtue because it regulates deeds, which pertain to the moral order. Art is only an intellectual virtue; it is concerned exclusively with things, which pertain to the ontological order.

A. The Necessity of Prudence

Simply speaking, prudence is the most important of all the moral virtues. Indeed, no moral virtue (if it could exist without prudence) can function without the practical counsel in the here-and-now which is supplied by prudence. For other moral virtues are concerned with ordering man toward a certain end or goal, with answering the question: what is to be done? But prudence strives to see that the means to achieve these various goals are properly ordered, thus answering the question: how is this to be done here-and-now? Consequently, prudence is the most valuable, the most indispensable of all moral virtues, for it overshadows them all, directs them all, claims a hearing in every human act of supernatural value.[2]

[1] Cf. St. Thomas, *Summa,* I-II, q. 57, a. 3 and a. 4.

[2] This is not to deny that charity is (as we saw in the last chapter) the form of all the virtues. Charity is called the "form" of the theological and moral virtues because it directs them perfectly to the ultimate end of man. Prudence is also the "form" of the other moral virtues because it directs them, according to right reason, to the proper means for attaining the ultimate end.

B. The Subject of Prudence

Human actions never occur in the abstract. A human action is always a singular, concrete occurrence. Precisely for this reason, it may seem strange that prudence should be subjected in the intellect. For, as the student of logic will recall, what properly pertains to the intellect of man is abstract, universalized ideas. How, then, explain that prudence is subjected in the intellect and yet deals with singular things?

The apparent difficulty here is readily solved by appealing to an important distinction. **Formally,** prudence is an intellectual virtue, that is, a virtue given to facilitate an intellectual activity; but **materially,** prudence is a moral virtue, because the matter with which it deals is moral action—a material, then, of singular, concrete realities. Consequently, prudence is said to pertain to, or to be subjected in the **practical intellect.** The speculative intellect of man is concerned with those things which are to be known—with knowledge, whether or not this knowledge is to be turned to any practical use. Once the mind directs its knowledge to action, then the practical intellect is the proper subject of this knowledge. Since the virtue of prudence is concerned exclusively with the application of universal truths to particular affairs, it is said to be a virtue which is seated in the practical intellect.

C. The Object of Prudence

Prudence is not primarily concerned with the knowledge of universal truths, but with the application of these truths to particular situations. The universal truths themselves are understood by other intellectual habits—by wisdom, science and understanding, by synderesis and moral science. The knowledge supplied by these habits is utilized by prudence in particular situations. Speculative knowledge concerning the end of temperance, for example, will inform an individual that three martinis are too many for him before supper; prudence will command him, here-and-now, to stop at two. Speculative knowledge concerning the end of charity will instruct the individual never to speak unkindly of another; prudence will command him, as he walks to class with another student, to refrain from unkind remarks about the professor.

It follows, therefore, that the object of prudence is the singular, concrete moral action of a man. This moral action may be concerned with any one, or several, of the theological or moral virtues. Regardless of the virtue concerned, the moral action of that virtue is the *material*—the **object** of prudence. Thus, the precise material object of the virtue of prudence is the right ordering of man's moral actions, which are acts of any of the intellectual, moral or theological virtues.

Concerning the object of prudence, however, two factors should be distinguished:

1) In dealing with human actions, the formality with which prudence is primarily concerned is this: certain actions are now to be commanded because they are suitable or even necessary means to a good end; or, certain actions are to be avoided as unsuitable.

2) The motive or purpose for every prudent judgment is the **practical truth** of these actions, that is, that these actions *truly* conform to the moral law, or that they *truly* are acceptable means to a justifiable end. In other words, the **motive** (*formal* object) of prudence is that the performance of these actions amounts to truth in practice. This does not deny that the actions are also seen as desirable. While prudence primarily regards human actions under the aspect of truth, secondarily it regards them under the aspect of good. This emphasizes the twofold character of the virtue as partly intellectual, partly moral.

The function of prudence with regard to the works of the other virtues is to establish, in concrete situations, the mean of virtue.[3] Prudence does not decide for the other virtues the proper end of each. Rather it is the proper work of prudence to dispose the necessary means for the attainment of the end of each virtue—but, again, in the particular situation. Thus prudence will dictate how,

[3]Cf. Chapter Four, 143-146.

when, where, how much, by whom and the other circumstances that always occur in the concrete. In directing the case of the present moment as to its circumstances, prudence is ordering the means to the end. And by so ordering these means, it is seeking to avoid the two extremes which are violations of virtue: excess (too much, too many, too often, etc.) and defect (not enough, too seldom, too few, etc.).

But to repeat, there is no question here of prudence establishing speculative truths; it *applies* such truths to the workaday actions of the individual. This is accomplished by a practical syllogism, whose **major premise** is a universal truth, whose **minor premise** is a particular fact of the here-and-now; and whose **conclusion,** consequently, is a *command* of prudence. For example:

It is an injustice to deprive the worker of his just wages. (A speculative truth, expressive of the end to be attained by the virtue of justice.)

But: *To pay this engineer two dollars an hour is to deprive a worker of his just wages.* (A practical truth, calculated by prudence which has considered all necessary factors or circumstances: hours worked; engineer's ability, education and contribution to the product; salary needed for working wage, etc.)

Therefore: *It is an injustice to pay this engineer two dollars an hour.* (This conclusion, drawn by prudence, is the act of *command,* which, however, can be expressed—as in this case—by way of intimation or declaration, as we shall see in the next section.)

In such reasonings prudence manifests its superiority over the other virtues. Other virtues are concerned with ends, to be sure, while prudence is concerned only with means; yet it is nonetheless true that, in practice, the production of a virtuous act manifests the superiority of prudence. For in the singular instance, in the production of *this* act, prudence does establish the end to be attained. *This* might be an act of justice or liberality or religion or piety or of any moral virtue; but in the concrete situation *this* would be a mean between excess and defect, the practical end to be accomplished, and it is prudence which determines and commands it. Absolutely considered, therefore, prudence is a virtue that is concerned with means; but it is nonetheless concerned with ends to be attained in the here-

and-now situation. Thus, it is in very truth the most important (if not the highest) of all moral virtues.

D. The Acts of Prudence

(1) In Themselves

The Young Christian Workers, a movement of Catholic Action founded in our time by the Belgian, Canon Cardijn, approach the social situations which they seek to influence with the formula: "See, judge, act." The true genius of this successful formula lies in the fact that it is simply a popular restatement of the three acts of prudence, technically known as counsel (or deliberation), judgment and command. The prudent man is one who employs these three steps in every moral action. The three acts, however, while accomplished successively, are inseparable companions. All three must concur when the prudent man exercises his virtue of prudence. It is entirely true that often his use of one or more of these acts is so rapid—because so truly habitual—that it is difficult for him to distinguish one from another. Nevertheless, prudence is exercised only when all three acts, counsel, judgment and command, are brought into play.

1. **Counsel** is *an act of inquiry by which the mind seeks the knowledge that will form the basis for a judgment.* Since prudence presupposes an end already established (in the abstract), this act of counsel will be concerned with means. When faced with the burden of making a judgment concerning some contingent singular—always the case where prudence is concerned—it is usually necessary for the mind to take counsel, to make inquiry. For singular things are uncertain and doubtful, by reason of their complexity and the variability of circumstances. Unlike universal truths, singulars are continually subject to change, and consequently the act of counsel or deliberation is a necessary preamble to the action of the prudent man.

2. **Judgment,** as the second act of prudence, is an activity of the spectulative intellect. Its function is normative, directive; for *it does nothing more than to establish, as a proposition, that the means which*

deliberation has discovered are good and should be adhered to, or evil and to be avoided. (The act of conscience, studied later in this chapter, is allied to the second act of prudence, insofar as judgment perfects the act of conscience. Conscience, however, is not always under the good influence of prudence; hence, conscience and judgment are not fully synonymous.)

3. **Command,** because it alone is actually concerned with the action to be performed (the preceding acts have only a speculative interest in this action) is the most important act of prudence. It is entirely possible for a man to make adequate deliberation regarding some particular situation, and to formulate a right judgment relative to the proper mode of action, and still fail to be prudent. If there is no act of command, then there is no act of prudence. The act of command is the crux of prudence. But, on the other hand, command without the preceding acts does not constitute an act of prudence. Command that flows from caprice instead of counsel, or from prejudice instead of sound judgment, is not prudence.

The act of command is an act of the practical reason, the intellect directing by way of intimation or declaration. Yet behind this intimation or declaration is presupposed an act of the will. For the reason is set into motion, so to speak, by an anterior act of the will: the will willing to reason. But it is not precisely this anterior act with which we are concerned in dealing with command. Given the act of the will, the reason gives orders, either indicatively: **this is what you must do;** or imperatively: **do this!** But because what is more formal, more essential, in this act is the *order* involved—that is, the declaration which necessarily determines what is to be done—it must follow that command is an act of the practical reason.

(2) The Acts of Prudence Exemplified

These acts are perhaps best explained through an extended example. Imagine yourself in the middle of a currently popular novel. To your surprise you find that the novel contains some suggestive passages. It is not difficult for you to see that the author is not a pornographer; he intends no filth for filth's sake. But in the development of his characters, the plot requires that he place them in shoddy situations, picturesquely detailed. Your immediate problem is the question: may I continue reading this novel (or this passage of the novel) without violating the virtue of chastity? Or should I lay the book aside altogether?

Prudence is here summoned to handle a concrete case touching upon the virtue of chastity. Entering the scene, prudence must first take counsel or deliberate. That is to say, it must consider the circumstances of the present situation, and it must examine the means available to keep chastity intact. This deliberation discloses several factors: you are easily tempted by written accounts that seem not to bother many other people; in the past you know of no single instance where, in reading such passages, you have not been guilty of at least doubtfully sinful entertainment of evil thoughts; and it is clear, you must admit, that the present passage is the kind of sequence which has caused you trouble before. Moreover, past experience also reminds you that the only valid means to avoid sinful thoughts in this circumstance is to discontinue reading the book. No, not even to omit suggestive passages as you come to them is sufficient; for you have tried this in the past, but found that it was necessary to read some of them or lose the train of the fiction; and on that doubtful excuse you have continued to the point, woefully, of mortal sin.

The second act of prudence, capitalizing upon this investigation of counsel, must now assert itself. This is the act of judgment. Prudence now judges on the basis of its prior investigation. And the judgment is quite unequivocal: I should lay this book aside; I should discontinue reading it altogether. This is my prudent judgment.

Pause momentarily, though, and notice that you have not yet completed an act of prudence. We have seen that the most important of prudence's acts is the third, the act of command. After all, there are many people who arrive at the judgment that a certain book should not be read, or reading it should be discontinued. It is because they fail to follow this judgment that they fail to act prudently.

Consequently, the third act, following upon judgment, is the simple command: *put down the book;* as an act of the virtue of chastity, *set it aside.* Notice that the true act of command will be characterized by promptness. It will be immediate. Do it now!

E. The Virtue of Prudence

Earlier we inspected a general definition of prudence which pointed up the general character of the virtue as the approach of right reason to moral matters. While there are many qualities that may be denominated by the term "prudence," the word most properly applies to the moral virtue, which is the subject of this chapter.

Most scientifically, therefore, **prudence** is defined as: *the divinely infused virtue by which, given due counsel and judgment, practical reason commands in the concrete a true manner of acting as a means to man's supernatural ultimate end.* The elements of this definition are explained as follows:

1) **virtue:** prudence is a good moral habit which cannot be employed in the performance of evil actions, but is of utility only in the production of good acts. As a habit, prudence is a power by which one produces acts easily, with delight and promptly—a habitual power, therefore, that may rightfully be called a "second nature," since, when truly possessed, this power becomes a part of a man, and is difficult to take from him.

2) **divinely infused:** actually, this distinguishes the infused from the acquired moral virtue. Supernatural prudence differs from natural prudence causally in that the former is given to the soul by God with sanctifying grace, while the latter is acquired by dint of repeated acts, over a long period of time, and often with notable difficulty.

3) **given due counsel and judgment, practical reason commands** is a phrase expressing the three integral acts required for a truly complete act of prudence.

4) **practical reason,** as already noted, is the subject of this virtue, while most other intellectual habits are seated in the speculative intellect.

5) **in the concrete** is an essential element of the definition, because the virtue of prudence has for its material object *moral* actions that are contingent, particular and singular.

6) **the true manner of acting** expresses the formal object of prudence, viz., particular truth in moral matters.

7) **as a means to man's supernatural ultimate end:** the material object of the virtue—and this must be clearly understood—is never the ultimate end of man, but only those human actions which take man toward that end.

Besides telling us what prudence is, the definition also tells us what it is not. Hence, the following points are noteworthy:

1) Prudence is not a theological virtue, for these have God for their object and direct us toward God as toward our ultimate end, while prudence is concerned with the means toward that end.

2) Prudence is not simply an intellectual habit, such as wisdom, science, etc., because these are not found in the practical reason, but are speculative habits. In the foregoing definition, prudence is clearly seen to differ from art which also directs a man's activity, but in regard to *making*, not in regard to *doing*. Moreover, art and the other intellectual virtues can be used badly, for evil purposes, without the habit itself being frustrated. Prudence, on the contrary, can never be used badly because it is a moral virtue.

3) Prudence differs from all the other moral virtues, for none of these is in the reason as a subject, but are in the appetitive powers of man. And it is well to insist that reason is the subject of prudence, for this virtue is assigned the *knowledgeable* direction of one's life in and through the other moral and theological virtues.

4) To speak of the three integral acts of prudence in the definition, finally, is to set prudence apart from all of its allied virtues (i.e., subjective and potential parts) which deal with one or another of these acts, but never with all three.

F. The Cause of Prudence

"So with old age is wisdom, and with length of days understanding" (Job 12:12). When the sacred poet characterizes wisdom as a property of those advanced in age, it is clear that he is speaking of prudence as an acquired virtue, or at least of the perfection of the use one can make of the infused virtue. To appreciate the biblical statement, however, one needs a clear knowledge of the origins of this virtue.

Already we have differentiated between a natural or acquired moral virtue, and a supernatural or infused moral virtue.[4] Here, certain accessory truths connected with the causes of prudence ought to be emphasized.

In the first place, while it is true that every soul in possession of sanctifying grace, even the newly baptized infant, has the supernatural virtue of prudence, it does not follow thereby that every person in the state of grace will act prudently. For all of the supernatural virtues require a natural, acquired counterpart to facilitate—indeed, even to make possible—the ordinary use of the infused virtue. Thus, the inebriate who is newly restored to grace through the sacrament of penance has the supernatural virtue of temperance in his soul; but this will not permit him easily to practice sobriety in the future unless he has the natural virtue of temperance. Similarly with prudence: no Christian will be capable of utilizing his divinely infused virtue of prudence with ease and assurance until, through repeated acts and over a long period of time, he gradually trains his faculties in the pattern of prudence.

Therefore, it is necessary to distinguish between the cause of the natural virtue and the cause of the supernatural virtue. Acquired prudence is caused by repeated acts, conscientiously produced, with difficulty, over an extended period of time. Supernatural prudence, on the other hand, is rightly called *infused* because it is produced in the soul exclusively through the power of God, who bestows this gift as a normal complement of sanctifying grace.

Keeping these truths in mind, we can establish the following conclusions:

1) Natural prudence is not a virtue that will be characteristic of young people; they have simply not had time to acquire it.

2) Supernatural prudence will be found in young and old when they are in the state of grace.

3) An adult in the state of grace who has acquired an adequate degree of natural prudence will possess supernatural prudence both as a habit and as an act.

---

[4] Cf. *supra*, Chap. Four, 142-143.

4) Young people, as well as adults who have acquired no natural prudence to speak of, will possess, when in the state of grace, supernatural prudence as a habit. Further, they will possess supernatural prudence as an act in regard to those things which are indispensable for eternal salvation.

5) The reason why one not in the state of grace has no supernatural prudence is that he is no longer directed toward a supernatural goal. By mortal sin, he has voluntarily surrendered his direction toward a supernatural end. With this surrender, all of the moral virtues are lost, since these are concerned with the supernatural actions that bring a man toward that end.

3. The Parts of Prudence

Earlier, we saw that a cardinal virtue has three kinds of parts.[5] From the point of view of the conditions necessary for a perfect act of the virtue, it can be divided into **integral parts**; the various species of a cardinal virtue, which contain its whole nature and power, are called its **subjective** parts; its **potential** parts are those other virtues that are similar to it, but which lack a total conformity to the cardinal virtue.

A. Integral Parts of Prudence

The conditions necessary for the perfection of the act of prudence, called the integral parts of prudence, are eight in number. The key act of prudence is the rational command to perform a definite concrete action. Yet preceding command there must be two auxiliary acts, namely, counsel and judgment. Five conditions or integral parts must be simultaneous with the act of counsel; three are necessary for the perfection of the practical judgment. For counsel, one must have: 1) memory, 2) understanding, 3) docility, 4) shrewdness and 5) reasoning. Judgment requires: 6) providence, 7) circumspection and 8) caution. These integral parts may be readily explained.

[5]Cf. *supra,* Chap. Four, 137.

(1) Concerning Counsel

For the knowledge needed in the act of counsel the prudent man must *remember* his past experiences, for only through memory of the past can he find the necessary aid to discern the moral implications of the problem facing him now. Further, he must have an *intellectual grasp* of the principles of morality and of the peculiar situation to which he must now apply them. Since human life involves an infinite variety, it would be impossible for any one man to gain all this knowledge on his own; consequently, the prudent can must be *docile* to the advice of others more prudent than he. *Shrewd* he must be, too, to estimate rightly how the means available to him can be used to solve his moral problem. Finally, that his counsel be complete, he must use the *deductive reasoning* process, so that from this acquired information new conclusions and judgments may enlighten his mind about the moral problem at hand.

(2) Concerning Judgment

In the formation of the practical judgment which immediately precedes command, three acts are necessary. The prudent man must be *provident*: he must look ahead to his ultimate end, in order to see how the action he contemplates is ordained to it. Further, he must be *circumspect,* viewing all the circumstances that may morally affect the action which he intends to command. This is so because a moral act does not exist in a vacuum, but in a definite place, at a determinate time, and so forth. (We saw earlier that the seven circumstances can, often enough, render an action morally good or morally evil.)[6] Finally, the prudent man must be *cautious,* that is, prepared to deal with those unforeseen difficulties which might spoil the action that his practical reason will command.

(3) Practical Value

Before dealing with the other parts of prudence it would be well to note here that sometimes little or no explicit attention has to be given to these integral parts. When, in fact, prudence becomes

[6]Cf. *supra*, Chap. Two, 62-65.

habitual with a man, these actions become almost second nature. In certain clear-cut moral cases, moreover, as in the avoidance of an obvious violation of law, much deliberation is not needed. In important decisions of the moral life, however—for example, in the choice of a vocation, or in the dilemma often presented by proximate occasions of sin—one must be careful that each of these acts is considered and is present; otherwise a man's prudent decision will be less than perfect.

B. The Subjective Parts of Prudence

The subjective parts of prudence are the various species contained within the genus of the virtue. Prudence, as has been seen, is concerned about the ordering of means to end, and therefore there are as many kinds of prudence as there are ends to which means can be ordained. In general, we can distinguish the following species:

1) **Personal prudence** regulates the ordering of human acts to the ultimate end of the individual.

2) **Domestic prudence** deals with the direction of family activity to the accomplishment of the purpose of family life.

3) **Political prudence** handles the co-ordinated activity of citizens to achieve the proper end of the state.

C. The Potential Parts of Prudence

The potential parts of a cardinal virtue are distinct yet annexed virtues which produce acts secondary and preparatory to the principal act of the cardinal virtue. Consequently, while resembling the cardinal virtue, the potential parts lack its power. Prudence has three potential parts: *eubulia, synesis* and *gnome.*[7]

1. **Eubulia** (the aptitude, capacity, talent for good counsel). This is the virtue whereby the prudent man judges well about the means to

[7]Because these Greek words are difficult to render into English or Latin, theologians have traditionally retained the original Greek. We will use this terminology and provide the English equivalents taken from *A Lexicon of St. Thomas Aquinas,* edited by Deferrari, Barry and McGuiness (Washington: Catholic University of America Press, 1948).

attain an intended end. Some may say that it seems unnecessary to have a special virtue productive of the act of counsel, since counsel is an act of prudence. But St. Thomas explains that "it belongs to prudence to take good counsel by commanding it, to *eubulia* by eliciting it."[8] In other words, the act of good counsel comes directly from the virtue of *eubulia*, which is moved to produce this act by the superior virtue of prudence.

2. **Synesis** (the virtue of common sense in practical affairs) is the virtue by which a man makes a good judgment about events, according to the common rules of life, that is, according to the natural and positive law.

3. **Gnome** (the ability to judge rightly about the extraordinary things of life) is a virtue which enables a man to judge what his conduct ought to be according to a higher law. To the prudent man, it is evident that in extraordinary situations the common rules do not apply. In such circumstances the virtue of *gnome* comes into play. It is *gnome*, for example, which inspires the prudent judgment that continued health, or the works of charity, demands that one omit attendance at Sunday Mass.

4. CONSCIENCE

A. The Definition

Popular parlance will speak of conscience in a manner at variance with theological usage. Ordinarily, we refer to conscience as a kind of habit or faculty within man. In popular piety, conscience is "the voice of God," an inner voice designed by the Creator to admonish, warn or urge the individual in matters of right and wrong. Less happily, it is sometimes considered a disturbing faculty whose mission is to ruffle man's composure when he is tempted to transgress the bounds of good morals. Moreover, we refer to the examination of

[8]*Summa*, II-II, q. 51, a. 2, ad 1.

conscience as the inspection of a permanent power within man that records his good and evil deeds (principally his evil ones).

In reality, the inner voice of conscience is nothing more than a man's practical intellect reasoning that certain actions are good or bad, and this in conformity with the natural law impressed upon it by the Creator. When "conscience" forbids excesses in the matter of food and drink or the unjustified taking of another's property, "conscience" happens to be nothing more than the practical intellect at work. And when one "examines his conscience," this inner power to which he somewhat vaguely refers is nothing more than memory recalling the good and evil committed in past life.

Theologically, as already noted, conscience is to be understood as the second act of the virtue of prudence,[9] the act of practical judgment. Conscience, therefore, is defined as: *the proximate practical judgment concerning the uprightness of human action, considered in the concrete.* It should be well understood, therefore, that conscience is an *act*, not a habit or a power or faculty; and an act concerned with the particularity of moral actions.

B. Division of Conscience

Theologians commonly distinguish between (1) true and erroneous conscience; and (2) certain and doubting conscience.

(1) True and Erroneous Conscience

1. **Definitions.** A *true conscience* is one which correctly deduces a course of action from true moral principles. An *erroneous conscience* is one which incorrectly deduces a course of action from false principles *which are thought to be true.* Erroneous conscience may be vincibly or invincibly false, depending on the nature of the ignorance

---

[9]Strictly speaking, the act which we call conscience is not identical with the second act of prudence (judgment). One can lose prudence, and still have acts of conscience. Conscience is said to be the second act of the virtue in the sense that this natural act of the practical intellect is perfected by the good habit or virtue of prudence.

which is the source of falsity. In addition, an erroneous conscience may be scruplous, lax, perplexed or pharisaical:

1) A *scrupulous conscience* is one which, for little or no reason, judges an action to be morally evil when in fact it is not.

2) A *lax conscience*, by contrast, is one which formulates judgments on insufficient grounds which make that which is seriously sinful to be venially sinful, or that which is sinful not to be sinful.

3) A *perplexed conscience* is conscience-in-dilemma, for it judges (wrongly, of course) that sin will be committed whether one performs or omits a given act.

4) A *pharisaic conscience*, like the lax conscience, is one which minimizes serious sin; but unlike the lax conscience, it magnifies matters which are not at all, or only slightly sinful.

2. **Rules for true and erroneous conscience.** In practice, the formulation of a right and certain conscience can be a most complicated matter. When this is so, a parish priest, confessor or spiritual director should be consulted. Normally, however, the following rules will be the basis for every moral evaluation of conscience:

1) *The formulation of a right, unerring conscience obliges everyone.* Conscience is the subjective norm of moral conduct for every individual. Because every individual is obliged to bring his life into conformity with the moral law, it follows that he must be assiduous in establishing the subjective, proximate standard—right conscience—without which it is impossible to conform to the law.

2) *A* **true** *conscience, or one that is* **invincibly** *in error, must be followed when it commands or forbids a given action.* In regard to invincibly erroneous conscience, one must follow its dictates for the simple reason that to fail to do so would be to violate the proximate norm of morality. The case is exemplified by the person who stands before the theatre marquee believing the advertised motion picture to be a near occasion of sin, when in fact it is unobjectionable for general patronage. The misinformed movie-goer is obliged *not* to enter the theatre, since

one must follow an invincibly erring conscience. The war-time soldier of an unjustly aggressive nation is bound to defend his comrades by killing an assailant, if subjectively his conscience tells him that the conflict is morally justified.

3) *A vincibly erroneous conscience must not be followed, but neither must one act contrary to such a conscience.* As stated in the first rule, one is obliged to act only with a right conscience. Hence, no action may be taken until a vincibly erroneous conscience has been corrected. That one may not act with such a conscience follows from the fact that no one may expose himself to the danger of doing evil. If, however, all good efforts fail to produce a correct conscience, one must follow the surer, safer course—and this for the same reason, namely, lest one needlessly expose oneself to the danger of sinning.

(2) Certain and Doubting Conscience

1. **Definitions.** A *certain conscience* is one which judges, with no fear of being in error, that a given course of action is lawful or unlawful. A *doubtful conscience* is either one which sees equal reasons, or no reasons, for affirming either of two contrary courses of action, or one whose judgment is not free of fear of error (for good, insufficient or bad reasons).

The moral doubt of which we are here speaking is twofold, inasmuch as the mind may doubt either the existence of a law (and this is *a doubt of law*) or the existence of some particular fact (this is *a doubt of fact*). Moral doubt, in addition, may be positive or negative: it is *positive* when based on serious reasons, *negative* when based on reasons that are light.

2. **Rules for certain and doubtful conscience.**

1) *Only a certain conscience may be followed.* But it must be remembered, on the other hand, that "in human acts on which judgments are passed and evidence required, it is impossible to have demonstrative certitude, because they are about things contingent and variable. Hence, *the certitude of probability*

suffices—the conviction which attains truth in the greater number of cases, even though it should fail in the minority."[10] The only certainty that one may reasonably demand of conscience is moral certainty: that which is derived from the majority of cases, under normal conditions and circumstances.

2) *In the state of positive doubt, one may not act.* No one, as already stated, may place himself in the near occasion of sin. When perplexed by a conscience in the state of positive doubt, one must refrain from acting or he must attempt to dispel the doubt. In the latter course, when sufficient diligence has failed, one may have recourse to one of the indirect or reflex principles. These are:

a) *An uncertain or doubtful law does not oblige.* This principle refers to an *objective* doubt of law, that is, when the meaning or intention of a law is commonly doubted by prudent men. It does not refer to subjective doubt, as is often found in those who have little or no acquaintance with the principles of interpreting law. If a law stated that "liquor could be served only on church-going days," Catholics, Protestants and Jews would all have a legitimate objective doubt about the law's meaning.

b) *In subjective doubt, one must presume the law to be certain.* To act otherwise, once more, would be to incur the serious danger of committing evil.

c) *In matters of commutative justice, possession is nine-tenths of the law.* If I have a Bulova wrist watch, you are going to have to prove that it was originally yours and illegitimately taken from you against your reasonable will.

3) In regard to the sacraments, and other actions which have an immediate and necessary connection with eternal salvation, *the safer course must always be followed.* Moreover, when a question involves the clear rights of a third party, the safer course must likewise be pursued.

---

[10]St. Thomas, *Summa*, II-II, q. 70, a. 2.

5. THE GIFT OF COUNSEL

Because it is concerned with activities to be performed here-and-now, the gift of counsel is allied to the virtue of prudence, and is designed to help and perfect it. Its particular purpose is akin to the purpose of the act of counsel. Both are concerned with means to an end; both are intended to provide the mind with adequate instruction and awareness concerning what has to be done for the sake of an end to be attained. Prudence derives this knowledge through the research of reason, functioning through the integral parts of the virtue. But by the gift of counsel, God the Holy Spirit infuses into the mind a perception and an appreciation of those avenues of human conduct which a man ought here-and-now to follow. Hence, what prudence does in an ordinary manner (especially through its act of counsel), the gift of counsel does in a higher manner, that is, through a loving union and connaturality with God.

Yet the Holy Spirit moves the soul according to human custom. Grace does not destroy, but presupposes and perfects nature. God pours his counsel into the soul not suddenly, but with normal discourse and inquiry. That is to say, the gift of counsel does not obviate deliberation. Rather, it builds upon this human factor. The gift, therefore, should not be visualized as a lightning bolt of sudden inspiration hurled by God, but rather as a divinely patient and sure direction leading our steps in the processes of discourse and inquiry. Yet because all of these processes are followed under the inspiration of the Holy Spirit, the gift of counsel can do what prudence can never accomplish: it can remove all uncertainty and doubt concerning things which one must do.

And this, precisely, is why the gift of counsel is a necessity in human life. "The deliberations of mortals are timid, and unsure are our plans" (Wisd. 9:14). There are very many singular, contingent things in human life which can easily escape our attention. Even in a man's spiritual life, complexity is an ever challenging hazard. To overcome this obstacle, the generosity of God gives us the gift of counsel. By it, God, who comprehends all complexity with a single sweeping gaze of his eternal vision, aids prudence's deliberation so that "man is directed as though counseled by God."[11]

The gift of counsel belongs to all who are in the state of grace. But it admits of degrees of perfection. All sanctified souls possess counsel with regard to those things that are necessary for eternal salvation, namely, the keeping of the precepts. A further degree of this gift will incline one to follow the evangelical counsels of Christ. The highest degree of counsel will inspire one perfectly to fulfill these evangelical counsels. The gift of counsel, moreover, is possessed by those in heaven. There, however, it could hardly be concerned with things to be done toward an eternal life already possessed; but it is functional in the blessed, since it is the source whereby God communicates temporal truths to the saints. By it, the minds of the saints are moved to acts of praising God, and of praying for wayfarers who seek and need their intercession.

6. THE SINS AGAINST PRUDENCE

Like other moral virtues, prudence can be violated by excess or by defect. Prudence, therefore, strikes a happy mean between two extremes. One sins against prudence by exceeding (so to speak) the mean of this virtue, or by falling short of it.

A. Sins by Defect

Deficient prudence—prudence by defect—is known, generally, as *imprudence*. The term, however, includes many specific kinds of shortcomings. In fact, there are four species of imprudence, each of which is opposed to, or is in violation of one of the three acts of the virtue.

(1) Precipitation

Precipitation (precipitancy; haste) is *a sin of indeliberation*. It is opposed to the act of counsel, and amounts to an unwise and

[11]St. Thomas, *Summa*, II-II, q. 53, a. 1, ad 1.

excessive haste in acting. Failure to take sufficient counsel concerning an action to be performed will usually lead to disaster of greater or less moment. The young couple entering marriage with no thought of the sacrifices and trials which will soon challenge them are imprudent by precipitation.

(2) Inconsideration

The sin of **inconsideration** (thoughtlessness) is opposed to the act of judgment. It entails *a rashness with regard to judgment*, insofar as factors and possibilities that should be seriously, deliberately considered in a prudent judgment are, in fact, neglected, if not held in downright contempt. Sins of lust or impurity are frequently the result of inconsideration. Either through habit, or owing to the vehemence of passion, or even because of wilful contempt, the judgment that this occasion of sin is here-and-now to be avoided will often never be made.

(3) Inconstancy

Inconstancy amounts to *a reflection of the prudent judgment that has been made*. Hence, inconstancy is opposed to the act of command, inasmuch as the act of command is impeded by inconstancy. The collegian who promises attendance at daily Mass during Lent is guilty of inconstancy when he abandons this good intention on Ash Wednesday morning.

(4) Negligence

Negligence is also a sin against the act of command, for it *is directly opposed to solicitude, a necessary quality of command*. Solicitude failing, the command of prudence is not carried out. Negligence, then, is a failure to actualize the command in an external action. The sins of omission, discussed in a previous chapter,[12] are, generally speaking, instances of imprudence. One who fails to perform the necessary daily mortifications and prayerful exercises which he has judged and commanded for himself as indispensable means to a life of purity sins by grievous negligence.

[12]Cf. *supra*, Chap. Five, 164-166.

B. Sins by Excess

One cannot, strictly speaking, sin by excess against prudence, for there is no such thing as too much prudence. Yet there are moral actions that parade under the guise of prudence, and have an unfortunate resemblance to it. This prudence by excess (to speak improperly) is known as **false prudence.** The vice of false prudence manifests itself either because it is concerned with means (whether good or evil) that are ordered toward an evil end; or with a distinctively evil means directed toward an end (whether good or evil); or with a failure of due moral solicitude. The "daughters" of false prudence (vices opposed to prudence "by excess") are the following.

(1) Carnal Prudence

Carnal prudence (prudence of the flesh) is the vice castigated by St. Paul when he writes: "For the wisdom of the flesh is hostile to God, for it is not subject to the law of God, nor can it be. And they who are carnal cannot please God" (Rom. 8:7-8). Carnal prudence is deceptively similar to the virtue of prudence; indeed, misunderstanding the motives of another, one can readily attribute to him the virtue of prudence when, in fact, his actions proceed from the "wisdom of the flesh." Carnal prudence is always concerned with an *evil* end to be attained; but it is termed a kind of prudence because it wisely selects the means necessary to attain this evil goal. The seductor, all too often, can cleverly arrange circumstances to accommodate his lust. One might be tempted to praise him for the ingenuity of his plans, while (of course) despising his crime.

(2) Craftiness

Craftiness (astuteness) is concerned with *the use of evil means for the attainment of an end that may be good in itself.* Christ's parable of the unjust steward (Luke 16:1) exemplifies the vice of craftiness: "And the master [of the household] commended the unjust steward, in that he had acted prudently." Again, while not condoning the evil perpetrated by the steward, the master in Christ's parable can admire him for seeking a good end: security for his future. The implied conclusion is that his astuteness in employing evil means might well be imitated by the faithful in their use of good means.

(3) Excessive Solicitude

Excessive solicitude (worldly care; worry; anxiety), like negligence, is opposed to solicitude, but for a different reason. Where negligence takes insufficient care to execute the commands of prudence, excessive solicitude goes beyond the limits set by right reason. In fact, it is *an inordinate concern for materialities*. Materialism is an obvious example of this vice at work in modern society. Birth control is another, inasmuch as it expresses an over-anxiety for bodily health, or social status, or the family budget.

7. SUMMARY AND CONCLUSION

The urgency of the virtue of prudence cannot be overstated. Because it is the virtue which directs the activities of all the other virtues in the concrete performance of human actions, there can be no true moral virtue when one lacks the virtue of prudence. Moreover, the perfection of the other virtues in the actions they perform will (under normal circumstances) be in direct proportion to the perfection of prudence possessed by one striving to act virtuously.

1. "If moral science is hesitant and imprecise in the abstract, this is even more true when we come down to apply it in detail to concrete instances—those covered neither by art nor by precedent. For the factors at work in human deeds are indefinitely variable. Accordingly, decisions must be left to each person's prudence."[13]

2. "It is well known what great efforts and pains lovers of money will patiently subject themselves to, and from what great pleasures they will abstain, in their desire to increase their wealth or in their

[13] St. Thomas, *Commentary on the Nicomachean Ethics,* Bk. II, lect. 2.

fear of diminishing it; with what great shrewdness they pursue gain, and how prudently they avoid losses; how they are usually afraid to take the property of others, and sometimes even disregard loss to themselves in order not to lose more in its quest and litigation.

"Because these traits are well known, it is right for us to be exhorted to love wisdom to the extent that we most eagerly seek it as our treasure, acquire more and more of it, suffer many trials, restrain desires, ponder the future, so that we may preserve innocence and beneficence.

"Whenever we act in this way we are in possession of true virtues, because our objective is true, that is, is in harmony with our nature in reference to salvation and true happiness."[14]

BIBLIOGRAPHICAL NOTE

St. Thomas treats the doctrine on prudence in the *Summa,* II-II, Questions XLVII to LVI. Few books have been written on this subject in English; so it might be well for the student to consult the works listed in the general bibliography where he will find at least a short summary of Thomistic teaching on prudence.

There are, however, several articles on prudence which can be found in various periodicals: "Prudence and Morality," by J. R. Connery, S.J., in *Theological Studies,* XIII (1952), 564-582; "Prudence, a Necessary Virtue," by A. Muntsch in *Review for Religious,* VIII (1949), 82-85; "The Intellectual Virtue of Prudence," by W. A. Gebhard in *The Thomist,* VIII (1945), 413-456; "The Virtue of Prudence," by F. J. Connell, C.SS.R., in *Journal of Religious Instruction,* XI (1940), 322-327; and "The Virtue of Prudence" by J. W. O'Brien in *Journal of Religious Instruction,* IX (1939), 420-424.

[14]St. Augustine, *Against Julian,* Bk. IV, Chap. 3.

CHAPTER TWELVE

Justice

1. INTRODUCTION

The state of world affairs today between nations, society and the individual, private citizens and their neighbors, is a state fashioned in terms of justice. Wherever we turn in the sphere of human activity problems arise concerning what is just: human rights, unjust aggression, strikes, racial integration, capital punishment—these are a mere sampling of the myriad controversial issues which can be answered only by a correct notion of the nature of justice.

Whenever justice is analyzed, such a wide variety of meanings is set forth that it would be impossible for the ordinary man to interpret them intelligently. Nevertheless, there is one simple idea of justice to which everyone can unhesitatingly adhere without fear of misunderstanding, the idea that everyone is to be given his due. This is a traditional notion of justice which reaches far back into antiquity, even to the remote era of the wandering Ulysses, for in the fourteenth book of the *Odyssey* these words appear: "The gods respect those who do what is right and just."

Hence justice, the second of the cardinal virtues and the first of the moral virtues, concerns our relations with some other. It is not just a matter of doing these others favors or being friendly with them, but of giving them their exact due. The aim of this virtue is to establish a relationship of perfect equality between ourselves and others.

We must remember, however, that the legalistic attitude of justice is insufficient in the life and activity of the Christian. To be successful our just actions must go beyond a minimum obligation: they must be caught up in the wider vision of charity. Then alone can justice be a human ideal and its study capable of providing insights into our duties toward God, the state, our parents and neighbors.

The very fact that justice rules human actions and gives to *others* their due shows it to hold a place of pre-eminence over fortitude and temperance. By regulating the passions, they make man virtuous with regard to himself alone, and not with regard to his neighbors. Thus the treatment of justice logically precedes that of fortitude and temperance.

In this chapter we shall treat the virtue of justice in general, the subjective parts (or species) of justice, together with their opposing vices, and its integral parts. Treatment of the potential parts of the virtue will be reserved to the chapters on religion and on the social virtues.

On the following page is outlined the material we will consider.

2. JUSTICE IN ITSELF

A. Right

The fundamental notion presented in the introduction to this chapter is by no means the ultimate analysis of the virtue of justice. Rather, it is a preliminary step to a closer scrutiny of this virtue, a common idea in the mind of mankind of what justice should be. If "to give each man his due" were all that could be said of justice, its

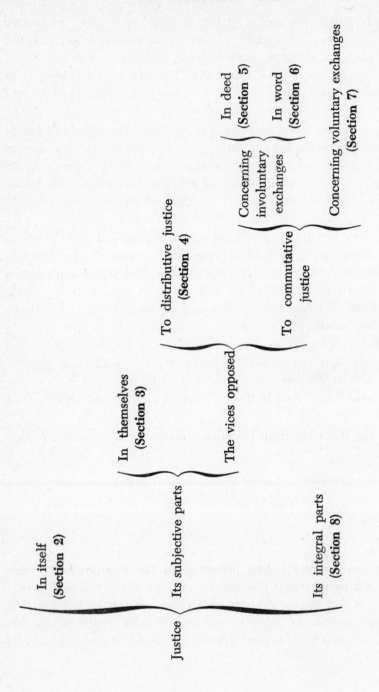

Justice

- In itself
  (Section 2)
- Its subjective parts
  - In themselves
    (Section 3)
  - The vices opposed
    - To distributive justice
      (Section 4)
    - To commutative justice
      - Concerning involuntary exchanges
        - In deed
          (Section 5)
        - In word
          (Section 6)
      - Concerning voluntary exchanges
        (Section 7)
- Its integral parts
  (Section 8)

concept would be so simple as to preclude further study. But justice implies too much, embracing as it does every relation that members of a society have toward one another, to warrant summary treatment. Hence, in order to draw a complete picture of justice, we will have to inquire by a logical progression into its every aspect.

The first hurdle we must overcome is an understanding of the object of justice—that which determines or specifies the act of justice, that is, an object which ultimately causes this man in these circumstances to give another his due.

There is a characteristic of man, basic to all of his human activities, which makes him want to dominate and absorb every object of his desire. He reaches out with his hands to grasp food, he fills his eyes with nature's beauty, he has dominion over the birds of the air and the beasts of the field—a dominion granted by God himself in his command to Adam: ". . . fill the earth, and subdue it, and rule over the fishes of the sea, and the fowls of the air, and all living creatures that move upon the earth" (Gen. 1:28). And through knowledge, by his penetration of the very essences of things, he makes everything he knows a part of himself. Thus he is related to other things in a manner which causes them to be drawn in some way to himself.

But when man is faced with another creature of equal powers of absorption and domination, an entirely new relation springs up. The impact which results when man meets man creates, necessarily, a re-evaluation of man's power of subduing what he desires. For he recognizes that his neighbor has and exercises the same kind of control as he over objects of desire. And this recognition is a realization that here is an object which can neither be absorbed nor penetrated. Rather, instead of drawing his neighbor to himself, he must go out to him: a movement which can be understood in terms of respect for his neighbor's *rights*. In other words, he must see to it that his neighbor's free actions remain as inviolate as his own: he must give him his due.

Due or right, then, is *presupposed* to justice. "Since," St. Thomas says, "the act of justice consists in giving to each that which is his own, the act by which a thing becomes one's own properly precedes the act of justice."[1] Hence, the *object of justice, that which specifies it, is right.* Having drawn this conclusion, we must inquire into the existence and nature of rights, their origin and their division. This is a necessary step, both for the sake of clarifying the whole concept of justice and because the obligation to do justice would not exist unless first the idea of the due, the right, entered in. We give fair warning, however, that the ideas which will be expressed in the next few pages need close study if they are to be comprehended.

(1) The Existence and Nature of Rights

To prove the existence of rights, little more need be done than to give an example, for common human experience attests to their existence. Thus, although the worker who is out of a job does not get paid, once he begins work again, something due to him comes into being—his wage: by the very fact that he does something, whether it be bricklaying, digging, accounting, teaching or practicing medicine, something is now due him. The actual rendering of what is owed we call justice; the fact that this action of payment is truly due him is his right.

An investigation of the nature of right is initiated at this point, for the commonalty of mankind understands right to pertain to the sphere of doing or acting—the practical order; it is something in human acts. Thus when a man says, "I have a right to a home," he means that he alone is permitted to enter that home, to live in it and to destroy or sell it. Right, then, has to do with action—this man's action or someone else's. The question remains: is my right objectively my freedom to act (or omit an action) or my security that you will not interfere by your action or omission with my will?

The seed of an answer has already been planted: right pertains to the sphere of performing acts. Through his acts man tends toward an end. Human acts, however, are of two kinds: one kind consists in the use of exterior goods (for example, to drink coffee); and the other does not use exterior goods (for example, to move the hand, to sing). Therefore, the means by which man inclines toward his end

[1] II *Con. Gent.,* Chap. 28.

are primarily his acts and secondarily exterior things, which are either necessary or useful insofar as they are implicated in human activity.

Man, however, is a social being. He depends on his fellow men in both a negative and positive way: negatively, insofar as others can impede him from performing necessary activities for his end; and positively, insofar as he needs the acts of others and their collaboration to attain an end. Hence man works for his end not only by his own actions but also by the actions of other members of society. Wherever, therefore, human life is united in a society, each man is bound to perform and to omit many actions, so that all can, in a fitting way, succeed to their proper end.

The proper term of right, then, as we use it when speaking of the social milieu—the object to which it tends of its nature—**is the actions and omissions of another person.** If we were to say that the object of right is some "thing," then that "thing" would signify the action or omission of another person. Material things are objects of right only mediately, insofar as they are objects of some human activity which is the immediate object. Hence rights cannot exist unless there are at least two men. Right essentially consists in a relation to the acts of another, because even to speak of actions or omissions implies that there is another person besides the subject of a right. A right, then, is a relation whose subject is one person and whose object is the act or omission of another person; the subject has a relation to the act or omission of the other person as to something owed him.

Bearing in mind that right pertains to the order of acting, we can clarify the meaning of right even more. For it is evident, from all that has been said about human action in other chapters, that the sphere of acting has for its principle the end. From this it follows that the relation of what is due, a right, is a relation caused by the fact that man is ordered to an ultimate end—happiness. But God in his wisdom orders man to the attainment of his end through certain necessary means. We have already noted that external objects of human activity are one kind of necessary means. But a relationship to such objects cannot pertain to right, because they are restricted to one's own action; they are never referred to others.

But also included as necessary means for the possession of ultimate happiness are the actions and omissions of other men, and hence they are directed toward this same end. For example, my relationship to my end causes another relationship by which I am ordered to certain acts and omissions of my neighbor as things owed to me, to help me secure my happiness.

Reason tells us this: for how easy it is to lead another person into sin by one of our actions and endanger his right to natural happiness! Our knowledge of this basic fact is the same as the knowledge of our moral obligation to act according to what is right for our neighbor.

All men are equally ordered to their perfection. No man is for the sake of another man, because this would indicate inequality. But in the plan of God men are equal to one another from the fact that they are related to one another as *owed* to one another, that is, by their actions or omissions, as necessary means for the end. Hence there is a moral necessity of conserving this equality through their own human activities. Right is caused by this equality in the order of final causality, for this equality is the goal of right: right exists so that men can be equal, each one having the necessities for attaining his own end. We must take notice, however, that this is a *proportional* equality—that is, one proportioned to the needs and the means of the individual: a richer man does not need as much a guarantee of some of his rights to property as the state should furnish for a less wealthy individual; a poorer man, conversely, may not need much protection from robbers.

We can now formulate the complete definition of right. **Right** *is a relation between one person and the action or omission of another, by which the person is related to this action or omission as to something owed to him, caused by his ultimate goal and for the purpose of establishing an equality.* Thus, because of the final goal, eternal happiness, an employee, by an act of his employer, must receive the wage owed to him so that he can have the ability to pursue happiness on an equal footing with other men.

The concept of right we have been considering up to now is an **objective** one, for it considers right as it is the object of justice.

There is, however, a more personal idea of right, right as it belongs to you or to me here and now. In other words, right can be thought of in a **subjective** way, and in this sense can be defined as *the moral faculty or capability of performing or omitting an action.* By "moral faculty or power" we mean that one man has preference in the use and disposition of a certain object. Thus a man has an inviolate and legitimate right to life and private property. Indeed, even if the use of private property were curtailed by a superior force, the moral claim would still exist.

When one says, therefore, "I have the moral faculty of performing this action," he is really saying, "It is permissible for me to do this because this action or object is related to me as something owed to me"—which is only to say that none of the others—other men, other persons—have any right to dispose of my action or my disposal of this object. In other words, *my* **right** means that you cannot by your actions or omissions interfere with my actions or failure to act, and *yours* is the right to be accorded the same treatment from me.

(2) *The Origin of Right*

Since human rights are the foundation of the social order, a certain importance must be attached to the discovery of their source. Where do rights come from? There are two possible answers to this question: rights are either created by man or given by God.

The sixteenth century gave birth to political and moral theories which attempt to remove God, as Creator and ultimate end, from human life. These theories, which can be linked together under the title of "Positivism," recognized the law of animal nature, the law of might makes right, as the sole rule of human conduct. Hence, men are not united by nature, but are strangers and even enemies to one another. Because, however, men do live together, order can be achieved only by transferring individual rights to the community. According to these theories, then, rights originate from collective human authority. No man has rights because he is a man; rather, he gets rights from the state. We all know the consequences of these theories—totalitarianism in its most base forms: fascism, nazism, communism.

Hence, we must say that God is the *ultimate* source of human rights. Our existence and everything about us depends on God who created us. Law, morality and society have been founded on God and his eternal law. Nothing can move from beneath his authority, and so rights also come from him.

But man must be considered the *proximate* source of human rights. The dignity of the human personality demands certain rights, for man has an ultimate goal which it is his right to obtain, and a right to the necessary means for its attainment. Hence man does not serve the state: the state serves man; and if certain obligations are imposed upon him by the state, he must be given the freedom to carry them out.

Consequently, animals cannot have rights, because they have no ultimate goal in God. They have no dignity as personalities and for this reason can be used legitimately (but not mistreated) by man.

So far we have been considering natural rights, the inalienable rights which belong to our God-given nature. But besides these basic and essential rights there are others which arise from positive law, whether divine ("right" to the sacraments) or human ("right" to vote). We will return to this point shortly.

(3) Kinds of Right

Law may also be called "right." The English language does not preserve this usage, but other languages both ancient and modern do. For example, the law of the Church is called in Latin, *jus canonicum;* in French, it is *droit canon.* Both *jus* and *droit* signify right. The law gives rise to rights and guarantees them.

Different kinds of law give rise to different kinds of rights. Important in this respect is the distinction between natural law and positive law.

The natural law gives rise to **natural rights**, that is, rights which are based on the very nature of man. Our Declaration of Independence considers life, liberty and the pursuit of happiness to be natural rights. This means that they exist quite independently of human law and even of any special positive promulgation by God. They are reflected in the nature of man and can be known by the exercise of human reason.

Positive law gives rise to *positive rights*. The right to a free education in a public school belongs to children in America by reason of our positive laws. While natural rights often are inalienable and unchangeable, positive rights can, of course, be changed by a change in the positive law.

There is a third kind of right which stands midway between natural and positive rights. This is the right which is founded upon the "Law of Nations," or *jus gentium*. Such a right is derived as a conclusion from the natural law, by reason of some universal contingent fact. The right *to acquire* private property is a natural right, that is, the natural law ordains, in general, that material things are for man, and man can acquire dominion over them. But the actual *distribution* of private property—that this man should own some particular property, and that man should own another—is a right of the Law of Nations. This is based on the natural right of man over material creation, together with the universal fact of social disorder and difficulty which would (and does) arise from completely common ownership.

The correlative of right is **obligation.** An obligation is the moral *necessity* of performing or omitting an action. A right in one man implies a corresponding obligation in another—the obligation to respect that right.

In human affairs, obligations come before rights. Indeed, we have rights in order to enable us to fulfill our obligations as men. In an absolute sense, however, rights come first, for God has rights absolutely, and no strict obligations.

B. The Virtue of Justice

(1) Its Nature

Having seen what the specifying object of the cardinal virtue of justice is, we can more easily grasp the classical definition: **justice is** *the constant and perpetual will to render to everyone what is his due.*

It is obvious that we are using "justice" in this context in a sense entirely different from that frequently employed by the Scriptures to signify holiness, the complexus of all the virtues ("Blessed are they who hunger and thirst for justice. . . ." Matt. 5:6), or any good work ("Unless your justice exceeds that of the Scribes and Pharisees. . . ." Matt. 5:20), or justification ("Grace is from many offenses unto justification." Rom. 5:17). To illustrate this more clearly, we will scrutinize the definition in detail.

1) The words "constant and perpetual" in this definition indicate that justice is a habit. This means that it is a firmly established quality in the will, possessing a certain stability which renders it difficult to remove.

2) Justice is in the will. As a habit, it inheres in the will itself. The subject of prudence is the intellect; fortitude and temperance are in the sense appetites. Only justice affects the will directly. It is not, therefore, an intellectual habit, but a moral one, since the will's business is doing, not knowing. It avails little for a man to know what is just, if he does not *will* the just thing.

3) In the last part of the definition, it is stated that justice always involves another person. It looks to another: it is a *social* virtue. A man cannot, strictly speaking, be said to be just or unjust to himself. This is a virtue which always involves someone else. Since the family society is so close-knit—husband and wife form a unity—strict justice cannot find a place among members of the same family. No, the "other" must be entirely apart from the just man, "opposed," in a sense, in all his inalienable rights and his inviolable personality.

Looking at this definition from another angle, we can see that it outlines the various objects of the habit of justice. The matter with which it deals is the external operations of man—not his thoughts or his passions—and exterior things insofar as they are connected with these external actions. But the primary material object of justice, that which it chiefly, directly and for its own sake intends and procures in deeds and with things, is *the just,* the equality owed to another. In other words, it is the perfect equality which is owed and which should be absolved between the debt of one man and the demands of the rights of another man; by this equality our actions are proportioned to the right which is owed to the other. Hence the immediate and proximate motive of justice, its **formal object** *on account of which* it renders what is owed and establishes this equality, is the special virtuousness of this very equality, which is found in the fact that that which is *his* is given to this other. Because it is good, a debt and just, we will to render what is owed to another and thereby establish (or preserve) equality between him and ourselves.

Two things should be emphasized about the conclusions of this analysis. First of all, it shows that justice necessarily has reference *to another*, to another principle of activity like ourselves, to another person distinct by reason of his intellect and his own will. Not only, then, is it impossible to be just or unjust to oneself; moreover, we cannot act unjustly to a person who consents to our action: *one can neither act unjustly without willing it, nor suffer unjustly if one consents to it.* Thus if there are venial sins of injustice (which is a grave sin in itself) then the lightness of matter arises from the fact that the injured party cannot reasonably consider himself a victim of strict injustice.

Since justice is concerned with our neighbor, it follows, in the second place, that its field will be that of external human operations, of our communications with other men: they are the means and the occasion for the necessary adjustments with our neighbor. Justice, in short, makes man qualified to apply external realities (operations, material good, words) to other men and to set up relations and communication with them. And the basic activity of all, that from which all just acts flow, is the exact and virtuous discernment and determination of "mine" and "thine," of that which is due to you and that which is due to me. To settle a department store charge account, for example, I must pay for the articles purchased; but that payment presupposes my previous judgment that this sweater is now *mine*, and consequently my ten dollars is no longer mine but *yours*.

The final consequence of all this is that justice is not only a habit but a *good* habit, a moral virtue which makes its possessor good and his actions good also. For justice **regulates**—that is to say, puts the rule (*regula*) of reason into—human operations, and thereby renders man's operations good. Hence Cicero remarked that good men are so called chiefly because of their justice, from which it follows that "the luster of virtue appears above all in justice."[2]

(2) The Kinds of Justice

It is an ancient tradition of moral science to see justice as a *general* virtue, one which has its finger in every pot, so to speak; we find this reflected not only in the Greek and Roman moralists but in the use Sacred Scripture makes of the word and the idea. It was St. Thomas, however, who gave precise meaning to this rather vague concept:

> Justice . . . directs man in his relations with other men. But this may occur in two ways: first, as regards his relations with individuals; secondly, with respect to his relations with others in common, insofar as a man who serves the community serves all those included in that community. Accordingly, in its proper meaning justice can be directed to the other in both senses.
>
> It is evident, however, that all who are included in a community stand in relation to that community as parts to a whole. But the part as such is something of the whole, and thus whatever is the good of the part can be referred to the good of the whole. From this it follows that the good of every virtue—whether it directs man in relation to himself or in relation to other individual persons—is referable to the common good, to which justice is ordered. And according to this the acts of all the virtues can belong to justice, insofar as it ordains man to the common good.
>
> It is in this sense that justice is called a general virtue. And since it is proper to law to direct to the common good, hence it is that justice, "general" in the aforesaid manner, is called *legal justice*—because, namely, through it man is in harmony with the law directing the acts of all the virtues to the common good.[3]

The implications of this determination of the nature of **general** or **legal justice** are quite remarkable. It is a special virtue, with its own

[2]*Concerning Duties*, Bk. I, Chap. 7.
[3]*Summa*, II-II, q. 58, a. 6.

special and distinct object: the common good; it is a particular *kind* of virtue, not a generic virtue which is subdivided into various species. Neveretheless, it is still a general virtue, inasmuch as it directs the acts of the other virtues—all the virtues—to its own end, moving them by way of command. Just as charity (a distinct special virtue) directs the acts of all virtues to the divine good and is thus "general," so legal justice is quite properly styled **general** because it directs all virtuous acts to the common good. Hence it is a virtue principally and architectonically of the sovereign, secondarily and administratively in the citizens of the state.

But, obviously, besides this virtue ordained to other men considered in their social and sociological relationships as they constitute a whole (community or state), there is need for a virtue relative to other persons considered in their singularity and individuality. This virtue is **particular justice**, whose object is particular social goods. It regulates man's external actions and his use of external things with reference to other individual persons, for it is by these actions and things that man communicates with his fellow and establishes relations with him.

(3) The Mean of Justice

Every moral virtue consists in a mean between extremes, a medium between an excess and a defect. In the other virtues this medium is determined by the rule of reason, and the medium is not necessarily the same for every individual nor in every circumstance. In the matter of temperance, for example, one man may find that it is reasonable for him to eat three hamburgers, another may find that one is reasonable for him, and a third may discover that the only reasonable thing to do is to pass up hamburgers altogether.

In this respect, justice differs from the other virtues. The medium of justice is determined, not by reason (which only discovers it), but *by objective reality*—by the objective rights which are due to others. If I owe a man five dollars, it is five dollars which justice requires that I return—not two, and not ten. The medium of justice is **mathematical** in every case. In the case of commutative justice, it is even *arithmetical*. In the case of distributive justice it is *geometrical* or proportional; that is, each must be given what is his due *in proportion* to his merits or demerits.

(4) The Excellence of Justice

The common good of society is greater than the particular good of any individual member, for it more perfectly reflects the perfection of the goodness of God: it is, in Aristotle's phrase, "more divine." General justice, then, will clearly be the foremost of all the moral virtues; it embraces in its comprehension even the lofty virtue of religion, not that it surpasses it in excellence, but in the sense that religion is the highest part of legal justice.

Even particular justice has a special eminence among the moral virtues. First of all, its subject is the rational appetite, vastly superior to the sensitive appetites which are the subject of the other moral virtues; for the will will extend the empire of justice into all powers of the soul. Secondly, it seeks the good of our neighbors, and it is more noble to achieve and defend the good of the other than solely to have reference to one's own private good. Particular justice to be sure, does secure our own good—the good of the virtuous person who is well disposed toward another—but in so doing it redounds to the good of that other, and is a sign of greater human activity and greater efficacy.

C. Injustice

For the foregoing analysis of justice it is evident that its contrary, injustice, will be a very serious matter. Whether the injustice be opposed to general justice or to particular justice, it is a distinct sin and a distinct vice with its own special malice. It is obvious that a man who violates legal justice lacks respect for the common good; it is obvious how dangerous such an attitude will be for good moral conduct, for human living, for it is a kind of selfishness which can lead a man to commit every sin imaginable. Violations of particular justice are also dangerous sins of selfishness, destroying the necessary relations and communications which must exist among men.

But the malice of injustice is even greater than these reflections suggest. For it is a direct contradiction of that charity which gives life to the soul. Whereas charity efficaciously moves us to will and perform the good of our brethren, injustice deprives our neighbor of his most elemental goods. Infallibly it inflicts injury on the other, our brother in Christ. Hence by its nature injustice is a mortal sin. So true is this, so serious this sin, that lightness of matter here means only that what is done is not considered to be altogether contrary to the will of the one who suffers; to take an apple, for example, is only venially unjust because it is probable that our neighbor is not hurt or displeased by our action.

The special and grave malice of injustice is only found, of course, in those who do what is unjust intentionally. Material injustice may be committed through ignorance or out of passion, but unless it is directly willed no formal sin of injustice can be imputed to one so acting. Hence the important conclusion: no man can do an injustice except willingly; no man can suffer an injustice except unwillingly.

D. The Act of Justice: Judgment

Judgment belongs properly to a judge—one who determines what is right and just. But in its wider meaning it includes the decisions made in every speculative and practical matter. With regard to practical matters we do not ordinarily consider the act of judgment in itself, because the judgment of a virtuous man about his performance of an act of virtue has value only in the light of that virtue. For example, the judgment of a temperate man is important only in virtue of his act of temperance and is not studied for its own sake.

But since justice is a social virtue, embracing those who judge, places of judgment and so forth, it is surrounded by a dignity which is filled with significance in the social order. Furthermore, the very nature of justice demands that the act of justice be treated in itself. So we must consider the nature of judgment and its conditions, and finally arrive at a definition of judgment if we want to show its particular importance.

(1) The Nature of Judgment

The first thing we note about judgment is that it has an objective value all its own. For the just man must make judgments according to universal principles that have already been laid down, principles over which he has no control. For example, the just man cannot judge divorce to be legal when the eternal law forbids it. Thus, although judgments may mirror the particular dispositions of the subject, they have, over and above any personal and private considerations, a considerable effect in his relations with other men.

Furthermore, a just judgment is perfect even before it has been carried out, because the act of judging attains the medium between excess and defect immediately. It is a true external activity modifying relations to others. For instance, a judgment deciding the ownership of property is more important than the handing over of that property to its rightful owner, because before the judgment the owner has only a tentative relationship to his property, while after the judgment the relation became certain.

Judgment, then, must be the principal act of justice, that from which all others proceed, for other acts of justice imply an explicit judgment or one which is taken for granted. We are speaking here, it should be noticed and remembered, with respect to *general* (legal) justice, although our remarks will be analogously applicable to *particular* justice as well.

Of itself, of course, judgment is an act of the intellect, and in practical matters of the practical reason. But right judgment implies an aptness on the part of the one judging for judging rightly. In this way judgment proceeds from the virtue of justice in matters which concern that virtue.

(2) Conditions of Judgment

In order to make our definition of judgment explicit, we must inquire into the conditions necessary for a just judgment.

1. **It must proceed from an inclination of justice.** If this were not a necessary condition, many judgments would be made contrary to the inclination of justice and hence would violate the law. In the ordinary course of life no man—and especially those in authority—can avoid making many judgments. But he should take care that such judgments be just. In order that they be so, they must be made from the right motive: from a desire for justice, not from envy or anger or simple dislike.

2. **It must be expressed by prudent reason.** This means that a man's reason must be certain and his motive solid when he makes a judgment. Anyone who judges without recourse to prudent reason judges either on mere suspicion or lack of trust (**rash judgment**). Judgments made from mere suspicion are unjust and, therefore, sinful. The gravity of the sin will vary according to the gravity of the injustice involved. To doubt a person's virtue or intentions from light motives may not be very serious; to judge him certainly malicious, with little evidence for the fact, would be worse; actually to condemn him on suspicion would be unjust in the extreme.

Suspicion has three principal sources: 1) it can occur from simple dislike of a person—we are more apt to think evil of our enemies than of our friends; 2) it can arise from the existence of vice in the one who judges—a good man tends to think good of others, a bad man imputes his own malice to everyone; 3) finally, the tendency to suspicion can arise from experience—old people are notoriously suspicious because they have seen a great deal of the malice of men. It is worthy of note that many sins which people refer to as "sins against charity" are really sins against justice. Rash judgments and imprudent suspicions are sins of this kind.

It is obvious that the safer and more prudent course for a virtuous man is to avoid suspicion and hasty judgment. When we are in doubt, it is always better to give the facts a happy interpretation. In acting in this manner we may occasionally, or even often, make wrong judgments, but we will not commit the sin of injustice: "it is better to err frequently through thinking well of a wicked man than to err less frequently by having an evil opinion of a good man, because in the latter case an injury is inflicted, but not in the former."[4]

3. It must be made by one who is in the position of authority in any society. Authority is necessary for human society if justice is to be preserved. He who is unqualified to pronounce judgment but does so anyway is said to be a usurper of judgment. God, of course, is the supreme authority, but he is not the only judge; he has so constituted men that they are competent to judge in certain areas. Thus, a true judge on the human level in the area of general justice must be one who has legislative authority: he alone can determine the welfare of the community prudently; he alone can frame laws which govern social activity; he alone can apply in concrete cases the universal principles of law. Other men participate in the judgment of authority insofar as they adhere to it and carry out its sentence.

(3) The Definition of Judgment

From what has been said, then, we can define the **act of judgment** as *an act resulting from an inclination of justice, and expressed by prudent reason as it is embodied in one with competent authority over a society.*

As a corollary to this conclusion we may add that it is necessary to judge according to the written law. Otherwise judgment would fall short of natural right (a thing which is just because of its very nature) and positive right (a thing which is just because of an agreement between men), for laws are written to manifest both of these rights.

3. THE KINDS OF JUSTICE

Having seen what justice is in itself—its object, nature, opposed vices and its act—we now begin an inquiry into the *parts* of justice. As we saw with respect to prudence, a cardinal virtue may be divided into **subjective parts** (the different species or kinds of the principal virtue), into **integral parts** (the acts or conditions necessary for the

[4]St. Thomas, *Summa*, II-II, q. 60, a. 4, ad 1.

perfect functioning of the virtue, comparable to those integral parts
—arms and legs, for example—without which the body cannot properly
function), and into **potential parts,** virtues which are akin to the
principal virtue by reason of their formal object although lacking its
full power. In this chapter we will consider the subjective and integral
parts of justice; its potential parts will be studied in the two following
chapters. In this section our subject is the various kinds or species of
justice.

We have already seen that general or legal justice is a special
virtue, distinct from all other virtues by reason of its object, the
common good. But particular justice, which is directed to the private
individual, demands further specification; for as part of the community the individual is related to other parts, other individuals, and
yet there is quite another relation existing between the whole,
the community, and himself as part. So there are two distinct kinds
of particular justice: one which governs the proportionate distribution of common goods to the private individual, **distributive
justice;** and one concerned with the mutual dealings between two
persons, **commutative justice.** Both will have the same matter—the
use of certain externals, of persons, things or services. But distributive
justice will direct the external operations dealing with these materials
from the point of view of *distribution,* and its medium or mean will
be a proportional one. Commutative justice, however, directs *exchanges* (*commutatio* in Latin; hence the name for the virtue),
voluntary or involuntary, between two persons; its medium is an exact
arithmetical equality.

We must now examine these three virtues of justice in detail,
adding a more specific treatment of the act of commutative justice
which is restitution.

A. General Justice

(1) *Its Nature*

From the notions previously acquired about this kind of justice,
it is fairly simple to reach a definition. **Legal justice** is *a virtue which
directs human acts owed to the common good to that end.* It is a

distinct virtue which inclines men to give to the community as such that which is owed to it. Directly and of its nature, therefore, general justice is concerned with the common good, which is like its proper end and its object, and its formal object is the special virtuousness of procuring that same common good. The good here in question, we have noted, is greater than the private good of any individual, superior, more eminent, nobler; it is not simply the aggregate of particular individual human goods, mathematically added up, but **the common temporal happiness of the entire society,** a perfect sufficiency of human life duly subordinated to eternal beatitude. It consists *essentially* in those virtues which are exercised for perfect human living, whether contemplative or active; *integrally* in the other sciences and arts of mankind; *by way of consequence* in a common friendship and peace which flow naturally from virtuous living; and *instrumentally* in a certain abundance of those exterior goods whose use is necessary for a well-organized society.

It is natural for man to live in society, for without the assistance and co-operation of other men the individual would find it most difficult (if not absolutely impossible) to secure his temporal happiness and, in consequence, his final destiny. This being so, it is necessary for him to direct his acts to the common good. Hence every man, whether superior or subject, has need of the virtue of legal justice. Principally, of course, this virtue will be found in those who govern the society, the rulers, to whom it belongs to establish laws and prescribe the means to procure the common good and the best administration of the state, to the end that each member of the society will rule himself as the common good and the perfection of the state demand. In subjects this virtue exists secondarily, for they bring into actual execution the means set up by the ruler when they accommodate themselves to the same end by fulfilling his laws. As Aristotle points out, the object of legal justice is not that which is equal but that which is conformable to law, not equality but conformity to just laws.

(2) The Obligations of Legal Justice on the Part of Rulers

While general justice is a virtue that must be cultivated by all the citizens, it is above all the characteristic virtue of those who govern.

For them it will be a firm and constant will to secure, by practical measures, the common good which this virtue inspires them to love. Generally these measures will take the form of laws for the good of the whole, laws in conformity with the natural law and with the constitutional laws of their community. Hence they deeply offend against justice if they legislate or govern in view of private ends, of party interests or of those of some political caste; this is but a more subtle modern form of tyranny and despotism. Similarly, they must, *in view of the common good,* distribute the duties and burdens which are necessary for public administration (taxes, offices, public responsibilities, etc.) equably—not arithmetically but proportionally, taking due account of each individual's social conditions, professional and legal status, and the advantages he derives from society.

It is the right and duty of the ruler, further, to safeguard the inviolable rights of the individual and to facilitate his development as a human being. To this end the state possesses the just power and the obligation to establish and enforce codes of public morals, to set up censorship of books, movies, radio and TV programs, etc., and effectively punish violators of its laws. There is a definite limit to public authority, however, namely, the rights of the Church, the family, the individual human person. Pope Pius made this point explicit in a radio broadcast on June 1, 1941:

> The care of such a common good does not supply so extensive a power over the members of the community that, in virtue of it, the public authority can interfere with the evolution of individual activity . . . , decide on the beginning or the ending of human life, determine at will the manner of man's physical, spiritual, religious and moral movements in opposition to the personal duties or rights of man, and to this end abolish his natural rights to material goods or deprive them of efficacy.

A major area of responsibility for rulers is that of international relations. Undoubtedly the solidarity of mankind and modern means of contact and communication establish the fact of an international community—not yet effectively organized at the constitutional level. It is a plan mapped out by God himself, the late pontiff declared, that "all peoples—in peace and not in war, in collaboration and not in isolation, in justice and not in national selfishness—are meant to make up a great human family bent on the advancement of common interest, through mutual aid and a fair distribution of this world's goods which are a treasure entrusted to men by God."[5]

But at the same time individual nations have their own proper rights and duties, as well as those in common with other states. Only justice can guarantee the equable protection of the respective rights of each nation and balance them against the rightful demands of international common good. Agreements, treaties, international conventions—unquestionably abused in the past to secure the interests of a few "power nations," and thus irrational, immoral and unjust— are the practical means at the present day of obtaining international harmony and the common good of nations.

If all else fails, the common good of the individual state must be defended with arms; declaration of war in defense of one's country is the duty of the ruler, who must judge the situation according to the canons of justice and charity. In these circumstances, war (by definition a just war) is an act of virtue, of the virtue of legal justice, but it must be waged justly as well as entered upon for reasons of justice. Past failures in this area have been regrettably frequent; only too often nations, for lack of an effective *international* authority, arrogate to themselves the power of decision of matters that could only be justly arbitrated by some superior tribunal. The unhappy result has been the increasingly more tragic wars of modern times, many, if not most of which are inaugurated unjustly and immorally.

(3) The Obligations of Legal Justice on the Part of Citizens

General justice is said to reside only secondarily in the individual members of the community, but this should not be misinterpreted to mean that it is somehow superfluous and second-rate; indeed it is most necessary for every man, an indispensable virtue on the natural and supernatural level, and its excellence for the citizen is of as high an order as it is for the ruler. Generally speaking, legal justice enables the citizen to fulfill the laws of the community virtuously and to

[5]Christmas Message, 1949.

collaborate with his fellows for the common good and for the development of the social order, as well as to discern when laws, duties and services are unjust.

In one sense, of course, every violation of every virtue is at least indirectly a sin against legal justice, although it is not formally so unless committed out of contempt for the common good; a general corruption of morals, nonetheless (a condition toward which we seem to be speeding in the United States), is a form of national suicide, a fact history abundantly attests. But there are certain actions which so immediately affect the common good that, even when "legal," they violate justice. A prime example is the widespread and casual divorces of our era, which destroy family life and thus attack the state as its very root, a social evil causing increasing alarm for all who are concerned about the common good, regardless of their religious differences. Still more direct are the attacks of those who seriously disparage the government and promote dissension; these are sins of sedition, dangerously close to treason and gravely harmful of the common good, and their prime perpetrators in our day are the Communists.

Among the many obligations of citizens there are three that need to be looked at more closely, since they are primary and fundamental: voting, military service and the payment of taxes.

1. **Voting.** In a democratic society whose citizens elect their own governors, there exists a real necessity of selecting proper representatives to fill the respective offices. It is a duty of the citizenry in general, then, to fill these offices justly, according to the demands of the common good and the well-being of the society, and to vote justly on such laws and issues as are submitted directly to them for approval or rejection. To vote properly is thus a virtuous act of legal justice; it is not only a privilege but a right and a duty. Consider these authoritative words of the late pontiff:

> It is a right and a duty to draw the attention of the faithful to the extraordinary importance of elections and the moral responsibility which rests on everyone who has the right to vote. Beyond any doubt, the Church intends to remain outside and above political parties, but how can she remain indifferent to the composition of a parliament, when the constitution gives it power to pass laws which so directly

affect the highest religious interests and even the condition of the life of the Church herself? Then there are also other arduous questions, above all the problems and economic struggles which closely touch the well-being of the people. Insofar as they are of a temporal order (though in reality they also affect the moral order) churchmen leave to others the care of pondering and treating technically with them for the common welfare of the nation.

From all this it follows that it is a strict duty for all who have the right, men or women, to take part in the elections. Whoever abstains, especially out of cowardice, commits a grave sin, a mortal fault.

Everyone has to vote according to the dictates of his own conscience. Now, it is evident that the voice of this conscience imposes upon every sincere Catholic the duty of giving his or her vote to those candidates, or those lists of candidates, who really offer sufficient assurances for safeguarding the rights of God and the souls of men, for the real good of individuals, families and society, according to the law of God and moral Christian doctrine.[6]

2. **Military service.** In most countries today the national defense, under the guidance of military leaders, is the job of the citizens; the days of mercenaries are long past. This, then, is another area for the workings of legal justice, since the defense of the commonweal obviously devolves upon the members of a particular society. Military service is a kind of tax which is paid by personal service on the part of the citizen.

When a just law requires military service, the citizens are bound in justice to give such service. It would be a violation of legal justice to seek exemption from service by illegal means. To mutilate oneself, to lie, to bribe examiners and officials in order to avoid service, are all sinful actions. Desertion is such a sin, and the deserter is bound in conscience to return to service. (Though he might be excused if the penalty exacted were extreme; no one would be obliged to give himself up if he would thereby face a death sentence.) Those who are not drafted into service but volunteer for a stated period are further bound by commutative justice to fulfill the agreement.

3. **Taxes.** Taxes are absolutely necessary if society is to operate efficiently. Every citizen should be willing to bear his fair proportion

[6]Pope Pius XII, address to the delegates of the International Conference on Emigration, Oct. 17, 1951.

of the burdens of government. Our Lord himself clearly taught this: he himself paid taxes (Matt. 17:23-26); he pointed out our obligation to "render to Caesar the things that are Caesar's" (Matt. 22:21), in reply to a question directly relating to the coin of tribute. The Apostle wrote to the Romans: "Wherefore you must needs be subject, not only because of the wrath, but also for conscience' sake. For this is also why you pay tribute, for they are the ministers of God, serving unto this very end. Render to all men whatever is their due; tribute to whom tribute is due; taxes to whom taxes are due; fear to whom fear is due; honor to whom honor is due" (Rom. 13:5-7). It is noteworthy that St. Paul makes the payment of taxes a matter of justice.

It is necessary that the responsible parties observe justice in the imposition of taxes. Taxes must be imposed by competent public authority, for a good reason and in due proportion, observing the dictates of legal and distributive justice. Experience teaches us that many persons dispute the justice of certain taxes today. There are those, for example, who consider the federal income tax unjust because at certain points in the graduated scale it appears almost confiscatory. It should be emphasized, however, that the individual citizen has no right to judge a law unjust (thereby absolving himself from obedience) on his own authority, for a light motive or on mere opinion. It is fanciful to suppose that an ordinary citizen would possess the high degree of specialized knowledge in theology and in economics to be able to judge such a matter competently. A certainly and evidently unjust law would not bind. Cases of doubt, however, should be resolved practically in favor of the community.

Taxes, then, in themselves bind in conscience. It is the common opinion of theologians that **direct taxes** always give rise to such an obligation.

In this connection it may be contended that many tax laws are merely penal—that is, that they bind, not under pain of sin, but only under pain of punishment. It is possible to make a case for this point of view. The usual norms of judgment should, however, be scrupulously applied. What is the intention of the lawmaker? The lawmaker is presumed to intend to bind the citizens in conscience in cases which immediately contribute to the common good and are crucially necessary to public order. It must be conceded that at least *some* tax laws are of this kind. Another norm is to be found in the kind of penalty attached to the violation of the law in question. If a law is enforced by light sanctions—light fines and short jail sentences, imposed without a jury trial—then it is possible that it is a merely penal law. But where the penalty is severe—a heavy fine or a long term of imprisonment, for example—the presumption is that the law is intended to bind in conscience.

In cases where taxes are imposed after a *declaration* on the part of the citizen, the obligation in legal justice does not rest primarily on the declaration; this would seem to be merely penal law. Caution should be exercised, however, in applying this norm to concrete circumstances. A lie is always a lie, and a sin in its own right. Furthermore, many tax forms require a declaration *under oath*. This would seem to be an indication that the legislator intends to bind in conscience even to the declaration. A violation of an oath would, in addition, be a sin of perjury which is of itself serious.

(4) Particular Sins against General Justice

It is quite clear that an **unjust war** seriously injures the common good of another nation; because of the many physical and moral evils it causes and occasions, this would be a most grave sin. The unjust waging of war falls in the same category. Indiscriminate bombing (negating the difference between military and nonmilitary objectives), "total war" (which obliterates the distinction between combatant and noncombatant), and "ABC warfare" (atomic-bacteriological-chemical) are horrendous modern means that could scarcely, if ever, be morally justified, however just and good the end. Unfortunately there are many less spectacularly evil means whose common use makes modern war difficult to justify morally and theologically.[7]

[7]For a more detailed examination of the problems of war from the ethical point of view, cf. Austin Fagothey, S.J., *Right and Reason* (St. Louis: C. V. Mosby Company, 1959), 555-578.

Genocide is another terrible sin against legal justice. It is explicitly defined in Article II of the Genocide Convention of the United Nations as follows:

> Genocide means any of the following acts committed with intent to destroy, in whole or in part, a national, ethnical, racial or religious group as such:
>
> a) killing members of the group; b) causing serious bodily or mental harm to members of the group; c) deliberately inflicting on a group conditions of life calculated to bring about its physical destruction in whole or in part; d) imposing measures intended to prevent births within the group; e) forcibly transferring children of the group to another group.

Although such practices have been engaged in from time to time since the dawn of history, only in modern times have they been so systematically and scientifically and brutally employed. Nazi Germany was guilty of this very grave sin, and behind the Iron Curtain Soviet Russia even today perpetrates these actions which annihilate the common good and are one of the grossest examples of man's inhumanity to man.

A third most serious sin against legal justice is of more immediate concern, **compulsory segregation.** As the Declaration of Independence states, all men are created equal—that is, created with the same nature and the same fundamental rights by God, redeemed by his Son, equally bound by his laws and made for the same destiny: equal, then, in human dignity and human rights. Men are unequal, of course, in talent and achievement, in culture and personal characteristics. But to discriminate against a group solely on the accidental fact of race or color, regardless of personal qualities and achievements, is to deny the truth that God has created all men with equal rights and equal dignity.

Enforced segregation, then, is unreasonable and unjust, and a grave violation of general justice. This is so for two reasons:

1) In itself and by its very nature it imposes a stigma of inferiority upon the segregated people.

2) In practice it has led and does lead to oppressive conditions and the denial of basic human rights.

Between the excess of rashness and the defect of inaction, prudence must find a way to establish racial justice in our country. The problems are many and ancient, the attitudes and prejudices are deep rooted and complex, the situation vital and urgent. But for justice's sake, and for the love of God (for compulsory segregation seriously offends against love of our neighbor), we and our nation must face this challenge and meet it.[8]

(5) Conclusion

The remarks we have made concerning the nature of general justice and its obligations will be proportionally applicable to those less perfect societies within the state which are lesser communities and have a less exalted and analogous common good—municipalities, states, clubs, labor unions, etc. Due proportion being guarded, they will also be applicable to that other perfect human society, the divine-human society of the Church of the Word Incarnate; this fact will be made more clearly and in greater detail when we speak of the Mystical Body of Christ in the third volume of this series.

B. Distributive Justice

Distributive justice is *that virtue by which society (or its head) distributes goods and burdens among its members, according to the merit, dignity and need of each.* Even more than legal justice, then, this is the special virtue of the ruler, of those who govern. For while the efforts of every man, ruler and subject, are useful and necessary in fostering the common good, the establishment of a just and equitable distribution among the several members of society is particularly the work of a prudent and just governor. Necessarily he must consider many men in his distributive actions, since he must institute comparison among their relative merits or necessities, even if he only confers an honor or an onus on one person.

[8] All students should read the statement of the American hierarchy, Nov. 13, 1958, on the subject; cf. *The Catholic Mind,* LVII (1959), 82-87.

Distributive justice regulates the relationship between the state and the individual citizen. It is equally important to recognize that society has duties toward its citizens, that the citizens too have rights. Neither is this difficult to concede. Difficulty may arise, however, in recognizing the unique determination of the medium of the virtue which applies to distributive justice. The mean, as we have explained, is proportional. An excessively naive view of justice would be tempted to judge the mean of this virtue in terms more appropriate to commutative justice. We are very much in love with the idea of equality, but equality, too literally interpreted, could actually work injustice. It would be wrong, for example, to ask a poor man to pay the same amount of taxes as a rich man. The state must distribute rights and duties, rewards and burdens, according to the varying needs and deserts of its citizens. This cannot be done with perfect arithmetical equality.

Directly and principally distributive justice has to do with the distribution of goods, for of its nature it regards others rather than demands things for itself. But what are these goods? In general, they are the good social conditions of the community: the security of order, the guarantee of individual rights, the establishment of decent economic conditions, and so forth. These goods of the community the ruler must grant to every man, but according to his ranking in the society, so that each may achieve in his own sphere that development of virtuous human living which is the prelude to eternal happiness.

There are secondary goods of the community also—the various public offices, its rewards, assistance and subsidies, and the honors the society bestows for public merit. Whether ordered to the common weal, such as offices and public functions, or to the personal betterment of the citizen, such as benefices and honors, these particular goods must equally be distributed with justice. Functions granted to certain citizens for the administration of public affairs and the procuring of the common good must be entrusted only to those whose honesty, competence and qualifications guarantee successful (or at least virtuous) fulfillment of duties; this is admirably taken care of in our country by the civil service. Honors, favors and rewards should be granted only to those who have merited them from society.

The principal burdens handled by civil society are those of taxation and military service, which we have already considered. We need only emphasize that these, too, must be distributed justly, i.e., not with arithmetical equality, but in proportion to the situation and abilities of the individual. Moreover, whereas general justice looks at these levies on the community's members from the point of view of the common good, distributive justice is duty bound to consider them with respect to the good of the individual.

C. Commutative Justice

Commutative justice is *the virtue whereby a man renders to each one, by a constant and perpetual will, what is his exact due in the exchanges that can take place between two persons.* It is evident that this virtue resides in the private individual and regards the relations of private person to private person, part to part; it is not the immediate concern of the ruler (although he will supervise such transactions among men to see that justice is preserved for the good of the community), nor does it directly affect the common good (although it will have obvious repercussions in the social order). Commutative justice has the same remote material as distributive justice, as St. Thomas points out:

> Justice is about certain external operations, viz., distribution and exchange. These consist in the use of certain externals, whether things, persons or services: of things as when one man takes from or restores to another that which is his; of persons, as when a man does an injury to another's very person, e.g., by striking or insulting him, or again by showing respect for him; and of services, as when a man justly exacts a work of another or does a work for him.[9]

But the two virtues have entirely different points of views, for the one is concerned with distribution while the other restricts its control to the transactions which take place between individuals, whether they be voluntary or involuntary. Commutative justice, moreover, has

[9]*Summa*, II-II, q. 61, a. 3.

an arithmetical medium. What the individual owns is his. Everyone must be willing that he have it, and that if it be taken from him it be restored. An ancient adage has it that *res clamat domino,* a thing cries out for its owner.

We will have much more to say about commutative justice when we discuss in particular the justice and injustice of various exchanges and transactions. For the present, however, we must consider the proper and specific act of commutative justice which is restitution.

(1) The Nature of Restitution

Commutative justice demands a perfect parity between men in the untroubled enjoyment of their rights. Injustice upsets natural balance in two ways: first, there is an objective inequity to be repaired; second, there is the guilt of injustice. The first requires restitution; the second is taken care of by punishment. We are not at all surprised when a judge not only requires a thief to make good what he has stolen but imposes a penalty as well.

When a person has been deprived of his rights either through some kind of injury or some unjust violation, the disturbed balance of justice must be restored by proper and timely action. What belongs to a man does not cease to be his simply because it is actually removed from his possession. It still belongs to him and must be restored by the person who inflicts the injury. Indeed, the precise thing which has been taken away must be restored.

The work of restoration falls to the act of restitution—an obligation which is grave if the injury was grave and light if the injury was light. In its wide sense we can define restitution as the return of anything received, whether through loan or deposit or theft. But, strictly speaking, **restitution** is *the act by which a return of property is made to him who has been deprived of it, or by which an unjust damage is made good.* It is the proper and distinctive act of commutative justice.

It is obvious that the obligation of restitution requires that what was unjustly taken be restored, for justice is necessary for salvation and he who refuses to make restitution when he is able to do so violates justice: "Behold, the wages of the laborers who reaped your fields, which have been kept back by you unjustly, cry out; and their cry has entered into the ears of the Lord of Hosts" (Jas. 5:4). Should restitution of the thing taken prove impossible, however, something equivalent may be substituted. But it should be remembered that this is licit only when restitution of the actual article is impossible.

(2) The Sources of Restitution

A consideration of the sources of restitution follows upon the two possible reasons why man is bound to restore the property of another: he either possesses another's property or he has damaged another's property.

1. **Unjust possession.** Anyone who is in possession of goods owned by another is obligated to return them eventually to the legitimate owner. But many times a person may possess another's goods and think them his own: we call this kind of a person *a possessor in good faith*. For example, a thief steals a bicycle from one boy and sells it to another. The buyer is a possessor in good faith. The true owner, however, recognizes the bicycle and proves his ownership. In this case the buyer must return the bicycle to its owner and try to get his money back from the thief. But if the buyer discovers the true owner before a claim is put in, he can return the bicycle to the thief and ask for his money, because returning the stolen article does no further damage to the owner. Furthermore, if the possessor in good faith loses or destroys the bicycle in some way before the owner claims it, he has no obligation to the owner.

On the other hand, a *possessor in bad faith* is the same as a thief: he possesses another's property unjustly and he knows it. Hence he is bound to return this property to its rightful owner, or its equivalent, even if the goods have been destroyed inadvertently. Furthermore, he must make good every loss which the owner has suffered due to the thief's unjust possession—for example, if a farmer loses his crop for want of a plough which has been stolen, the unjust possessor must restore not only the plough but also the ordinary profit on the farmer's crop.

It strictly follows, then, that a receiver of stolen goods has the obligation of restitution. This obligation would hold even after the goods have passed from his possession. Anyone who seriously cooperates in a violation of commutative justice is bound in the same way. The single exception to this rule is the case of a person who accepts custody without accepting responsibility, and who, without fault of his own, loses possession of the entrusted goods. In such a case he is excused from restitution because the possession of the goods was without any intention of injustice and without any benefit to himself.

2. **Unjust damage.** Unjust damage may be defined as *a voluntary and injurious act by which one man causes his neighbor to suffer some loss, either of property or of good name.* In both cases the balance of justice is disturbed: in the first case an unjust person is enriched at the expense of his neighbor; in the second case the wrongdoer, although not enriched in terms of property, still voluntarily damages his neighbor, which is the same thing as stealing from him. As Shakespeare wrote:

> Who steals my purse steals trash; 'tis something, nothing;
> t' was mine, t' is his, and has been slave to thousands;
> But he that filches from me my good name
> Robs me of that which not enriches him
> And makes me poor indeed.[10]

The moral law demands that restitution for damage be made only when damage results from a sinful will to cause harm. Inadvertent or accidental damage is not unjust because it is not deliberate, and hence there is no moral obligation of restitution, unless the civil law, which can legislate against negligence and carelessness, passes judgment that restoration must be made. But even before

---

[10]*Othello*, Act III, Sc. 3.

the civil law steps in, charity dictates that we pay in some way for inadvertent injuries.

(3) The Circumstances of Restitution

Restitution is to be made as soon as it is morally possible to the person who has been deprived of his rights. It does not help the balance of justice to restore property to a third party, unless the rightful owner is impossible to find. Thus if a thief who has stolen a ring from a passerby cannot discover the identity of the possessor, then he is permitted to sell the ring and make restitution by giving the proceeds to the poor; in any case, he cannot keep it himself.

There are many ways to make restitution, ways which can be used either openly or secretly: the item or money can be sent through the mail without further explanation; a gift can be bestowed, as long as the one who has been damaged does not return a gift of equal value; free labor can be given. Restitution to the city or state, however, should be made according to the statutes of law, if such laws are provided. Otherwise one can buy government bonds, savings bonds or postage stamps, and destroy them.

(4) Causes Excusing from Restitution

Occasionally, restitution to the owner may be legitimately deferred or even permanently excused. One can delay restitution if for physical or moral reasons restitution is impossible for a time. For example, the wrongdoer may be gravely ill, or he may be poverty stricken, or he may be in college and restitution would force him to give up his studies.

Furthermore, it may happen that restoration of a man's property would be actually harmful to him. If I have stolen a gun which the owner wants in order to shoot himself, I am not obliged to immediate restitution. I may defer this action until a more suitable time.

Restitution is deferred permanently when the owner voluntarily condones a debt by excusing the wrongdoer from restitution, or when compensation is made. For example: you owe a friend $100 and your friend owes you a suit valued at $100. It is easy to see that the two debts can be mutually destroyed by the agreement of both parties.

D. Conclusion

The essentials of the three different kinds of justice have now been considered in sufficient detail to warrant passing on to another task. Legal justice, distributive justice and commutative justice are the great virtues which regulate man's relations with his fellow man on the basic natural level of right and obligation, although they are far from embracing all his just activities, as we shall see when we consider the potential parts of this cardinal virtue.

Today there is a great deal of discussion about "social justice." It does not seem, however, that this is a special virtue nor a special species of particular justice. All justice is defined by some reference to society; in this sense, all justice is "social." The various affairs which are governed by so-called "social justice" are easily reducible to the species of justice which we have examined. Does an employer fail to pay a living wage? He is violating commutative justice by failing to give the worker what is his by right. He is probably violating distributive justice, because the society of employers and workers is a kind of community of which the employer functions as director. He may be violating legal justice as well, if his substandard wage is contrary to positive statutes. The traditional threefold division of justice appears to be adequate to meet every situation.

Our next consideration, then, will be of the vices opposed to distributive and commutative justice (we have already discussed some of the sins against legal justice). Since the latter virtue involves both involuntary and voluntary transactions between two men (involuntary when someone uses another man's possession, person or service against his will, voluntary if he transfers his possessions freely to another man), these vices will be of two general kinds. Specifically, however, they may be outlined as follows:

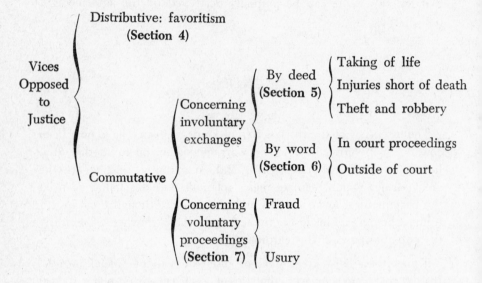

4. THE VICE OPPOSED TO DISTRIBUTIVE JUSTICE

The vice opposed to distributive justice is called *acceptance of persons* or **favoritism.** The norm of distributive justice demands that the good things of society be distributed according to a certain proportion, based upon need and merit. Favoritism occurs whenever other motives irrelevant to this norm are used in the distributions of society's benefits and burdens.

Favoritism is a serious evil in society. It is the cause of corruption in government and has, in various periods of history, disfigured the beauty of the Church itself. It is wrong for a man in power to appoint his relatives to office solely because they are his relatives. Everyone admires loyalty; but misguided loyalty in politicians can be disastrously injurious to the common good. The ability to turn out the vote does not necessarily qualify a man to hold public office. It certainly does not *entitle* him to hold office.

Favoritism is a vice which exists in those responsible for the direction of society, and vicious indeed in its consequences for society itself, for the ones guilty of it, and for the recipients of its tainted favors.

5. Sinful Deeds Opposed to Commutative Justice

The relations between individual men which are controlled by the virtue of commutative justice have as their elemental basis the fact that the human person is endowed by his Creator with a special dignity (he is the image of God) and characteristic rights. Among the most fundamental of these natural rights—which strictly demand from other men and the society of man the constant and perpetual will (the virtues of justice) to conserve and foster them—are the right to life and the right to property. To attack these basic rights is seriously to offend against justice, for the individual is reasonably (and understandably) unwilling that this exchange should take place. Here we will consider three such vicious kinds of attack: those which involve the taking of life; those which, falling short of so final an offense, involve serious bodily injury; and those which violate man's right to property.

A. The Taking of Life

One of the Ten Commandments is "Thou shalt not kill." The right to life is fundamental: it is, indeed, the basis and the condition of every other natural right. The right to life, however, is not absolute. This commandment, simple as it sounds, needs to be understood.

Not many present-day Americans worship dogs. But a great many of them are hopelessly sentimental. It has become an axiom of journalistic practice that the place for an animal story is on the first page; it has "human interest." The tale of a starving puppy will evoke as many tears as the tale of a starving child; sympathy is widespread for monkeys who are sent to outer space; scientists who experiment with animals are looked upon with jaundiced eye.

Sentimentality toward animals is unsound both philosophically and theologically. Reason tells us that the inferior is for the superior;

revelation declares that plants and animals exist for man's use and under his dominion.[11]

In the context of a tract on justice, it is only just to point out that only the intelligent creature is the subject of rights. A right is essentially a dominion of free reason over an object or action. Without intelligence and will, rights do not and cannot exist. Plants and animals have no rights: they exist for man, they are his to use, they fulfill their noblest purpose when they serve him.

Cruelty to animals may be sinful, but it is not a sin against justice, not a violation of rights. Man is meant to act reasonably. When he abuses rather than uses lower creatures, he acts against reason. This is, of course, immoral. He cannot become brutal, give free vent to every passion, go to excess in any activity, and still maintain virtue.

(1) The Penalty of Death

The prohibition against the taking of life, then, is against the taking of human life. It is not, however, an absolute prohibition. It is a prohibition against the *unjust* taking of human life. The commandment intends to forbid **murder,** an act which has many different forms we will have to examine.

There are times when society can exact the supreme penalty of a man, the penalty of death. Society is ruled by the exigencies of the common good, and the individual is related to the common good as a part to the whole. Often enough the part must be sacrificed to the well-being of the whole. We do not hesitate to amputate a limb if this is necessary to save the life of the whole body. Neither should we hesitate to amputate a dangerous member of society.

Opponents of capital punishment forget that the purpose of penalties is not uniquely the reformation of the criminal. Penalties often are and should be **medicinal** as far as the culprit is concerned. If we can turn a bad man into a good one, a criminal into a useful citizen, this is good and desirable. But our concern for the erring should not blind us to the needs of orderly social life. Penalties are often medicinal in the sense of *preventative*: they prevent further crime—

---

[11]Cf. Gen. 1:29, 11:3.

not only on the part of the person being punished, but on the part of other individuals. The death penalty was attached to the federal law against kidnapping, not because it was thought that kidnappers could not be reclaimed or were not worth reclaiming, but in order to discourage this particular type of crime. It seems to have effectively done so.

Let us not forget, also, that penalties are needed which are not only medicinal but **vindictive;** vindictive, not in the sense of issuing from cruelty, but in the sense of restoring the balance of justice destroyed by crime.

The execution of criminals is the province of public authority. No matter how vicious a criminal is, it is never licit for private citizens to take the law into their own hands. The reason is that the execution of criminals is for the protection of the common good. It belongs, therefore, to those who have official care of the community. Furthermore, the experience of history has shown that mob "justice" is an extremely dangerous thing. Private individuals, and groups of private individuals, all too easily forget the common good and begin thinking of their personal advantage. A crusade against public criminals can easily turn into a vendetta against private enemies. Individuals are too easily ruled by passion, too quickly given to judgment with flimsy evidence, too prompt to act on impulse. Society would become chaotic if the power to execute the criminal were to pass into private hands.

These remarks suffice to preface our study of various forms of taking life which work against commutative justice.

(2) Suicide

Suicide may be defined as *an action or omission which of its nature will cause one's own death*. It may be *direct*, if death itself is intended as an end or a means, whether explicitly or implicitly. Such an action, which so grievously violates the stewardship God has given to man, is of its nature gravely sinful, admitting (obviously) of no lightness of matter; for it is harmful not only to the individual who thus takes authority into his own hands but to society itself, and injurious to divine rights as well. It is forbidden by natural law (the law of self-

preservation and the community's right to its members) and by
divine law:

> Learn then that I, I alone, am God,
> and there is no God besides me.
> It is I who bring both death and life,
> I who inflict wounds and heal them,
> and from my hand there is no rescue.[12]

Moreover, the Church inflicts grave penalties on those who attempt
suicide[13] and deprives deliberate suicides of Christian burial and the
liturgical prayers for the dead (Can. 1240, §3).

Even *indirectly* to take one's own life is unlawful unless there is a
just and proportionate cause. The principle of double effect must be
applied in all cases. The just and proportionate causes that could
justify taking one's life indirectly are three:

1) **Public welfare.** Priests, doctors, policemen may expose
themselves to death for the sake of their duties; a soldier may
give his life to bomb an enemy installation.

2) **Spiritual welfare,** including the advance of science and
culture. Missionaries may go among cannibals or behind the Iron
Curtain; explorers may seek to discover new routes or new
regions; a man in shipwreck may give up his life preserver
to another; a woman may leap from a window to preserve her
virtue (but only if there is some real hope that her life could
be spared—without such hope, it would be direct suicide).

3) **Physical welfare** that results from escaping a greater danger
to life or a worse form of death. A condemned man could risk
life in order to escape certain death; a man trapped in a burning
building could risk life to escape burning, but he could not
hurl himself to certain death from a very high building, for this
would be direct suicide. (A certain *danger* of death is not the
same thing as certain death itself.)

(3) Murder

1. **Direct killing.** The death penalty is a punishment for wrong
doing. No authority, private or public, can morally take the life
of an innocent person. This means that **abortion** and **euthanasia** are

[12]Deut. 32:39; cf. Sap. 16:13; Rom. 14:7-8.
[13]Can. 985, §5, 2350, §3.

never licit: they are, quite simply and literally, **murder.** (We are speaking here of direct abortion and the direct killing of the aged and incurably ill; later we shall speak of the morality of indirect killing.) An aged person may well be a burden on his family and upon society; life for others might well be more pleasant without him. But he is not a criminal. He has done nothing to deserve a penalty which society reserves for its worst malefactors. The relationship of the individual to society as part to whole is not so literal as to do away with the dignity of the human person nor to eliminate natural human rights. An unborn child may be unwanted, he may be a difficult burden, he may even endanger the life of the mother. He is, nonetheless, a human being, possessing an immortal soul and an inalienable right to life. He is not even capable of sin, which alone would earn for him the penalty of death.

2. **Unjust aggression.** Rights have to be defended. The very existence of rights implies the existence of coaction—that is, the ability to defend one's rights with force. Because man is a social animal, and in order to preserve order in society and avoid the abuse of excesses, we reserve the exercise of violence in the protection of rights to public authority. Occasionally, however, recourse to public authority is impossible. In such a case the right to defend one's life and property, even by violent means, reverts to the individual.

A man may defend himself against an unjust aggressor even to the point of taking a human life. Precautions are necessary, however, lest the action lose its aura of justice. The defense must be against an aggressor—that is, someone who is *actually*, here and now, *unjustly* attacking me. I cannot shoot a man who has expressed the intention of killing me, I cannot track down a malefactor after the deed has been done and vindicate my rights. He must be in the act of aggression. **Due proportion** must also be used in the application of force. It is wrong to kill an aggressor who could be stopped with a blow. It is wrong to shoot him in the head when a shot in the leg would incapacitate him. It would be out of proportion to defend my watermelon patch against children with the use of a shotgun.

In all of these cases, and many others, it is important that the proper intention guide one's actions. A man can virtuously intend the preservation of justice. He can intend this, and act on this intention, even if the preservation of justice results in harm to another. It is justice he intends, not the harm. He is, and can be, willing that the harm occur. But this is secondary to the principal intention which motivates his action.

3. **Indirect killing.** In the last case, we have another example of the principle of the double effect. This same principle determines the morality of numerous other cases of *indirect killing*, such as indirect abortion, the indirect taking of one's own life, and similar cases. Abortion would be licit if it results from some legitimate medical procedure necessary to preserve the health of the mother—a necessity, incidentally, which is not supposed to arise from the mere fact of pregnancy. Here we have an example of an evil effect, not intended, but permitted for the sake of the good which is intended.

The accidental taking of life is not morally imputable. We are responsible only for our free voluntary actions; things which occur outside our intention are not sinful. It is possible, of course, to be responsible *in cause* for what is an apparent accident. A deliberately negligent driver is held responsible for the death he causes, and rightly so: careless driving, breaking traffic laws controlling public safety, driving too fast, are all violations, and often serious ones, of legal justice and one's obligations to himself, even when no accident occurs; injury to another or another's property violates commutative justice as well, and obliges one to restitution.

B. Injuries Short of Death

The greatest bodily injury that can be inflicted upon man is death. Short of death, there are lesser injustices, all of which may be reduced to duelling, mutilation, physical assault and incarceration. Each of these will be considered separately.

(1) Duelling

Duelling, a personal conflict between two individuals using deadly weapons, is forbidden by the natural law and by the Church. So serious a violation of justice is it, and yet so possible (one has only to recall Aaron Burr and Alexander Hamilton, or their modern equivalents), that the Church punishes duelling with the penalty of excommunication (Can. 2351) and with deprivation of Christian burial (Can. 1240).

The intrinsic immorality and gravity of duelling stems from two facts: it exposes a human being, without sufficient reason, to the danger of death and to the danger of unjustly taking a human life. It cannot be defended as legitimate self-defense, for there is no actual aggression. If genuine rights are in the balance, recourse can more reasonably be had to law or to arbitration. Duels are usually entered into in order to repair damaged honor. This is a childish and unreasonable undertaking. Neither reputation nor honor can really be protected or restored by recourse to arms.

(2) Mutilation

1. Its nature. Mutilation is *the removal of a member from the body, or an operation whereby the use of a member or an organic function is suppressed.*[14] Mutilation poses many moral problems, and some of them are very difficult to solve. To this area belong a host of questions: medical experimentation on humans; anaesthesia; lobotomy; organic transplantation; cosmic and plastic surgery; the various medical and surgical techniques which result in the suppression or destruction of the generative functions; the medical and surgical rectification of sexual anomalies; and many similar matters.

Obviously, many of these problems are of a highly technical nature and are the proper province of medical and theological specialists. Any detailed exploration of these cases would be outside the province of a general text.[15] Here we will present simply a treatment of the fundamental principles governing mutilation, in order to assist in the formation of correct views on matters that may attract general interest.

[14]Blood transfusions and skin-grafts are not mutilations in the strict sense. They do not destroy anything necessary for bodily integrity, and nature quickly repairs the temporary loss sustained.

[15]A selection of more technical references will be found in the bibliography at the end of the chapter for the benefit of those who have occasion for further study.

2. Principles of solution. Basic to the understanding and solution of the complex problems of mutilation is what theologians call *the principle of totality*. St. Thomas expresses the principle thus:

> Since any member is a part of the whole human body, it exists for the sake of the whole body, just as an imperfect thing exists for what is perfect. Hence a member of the body is to be disposed of according to the needs of the whole body. Now a member of the human body is indeed useful of itself for the good of the whole body; yet it can happen accidentally that it might be hurtful, as when a diseased member infects the entire body. Therefore, if a member is healthy and functioning according to its natural disposition, it cannot be removed without harm to the entire body. . . . If, however, a member is diseased, and therefore a source of infection to the whole body, then it is lawful, with the consent of its possessor, to remove the harmful member for the health of the whole body. For each one is charged with the care of his own health.[16]

The full meaning of this principle, it seems clear, can be understood only in the light of the general teaching of St. Thomas on the substantial unity of the human person.[17] Physical life and health depend upon the subjection of the body to the soul; sickness, suffering and death are due to some lack of this subjection. Hence man instinctively shrinks from illness and death, which are threats to his very being or his well-being. This natural aversion serves to emphasize the psychosomatic unity of the human person.

As a consequence of the substantial unity of body and soul, of the human person, St. Thomas' teaching on mutilation must be correctly interpreted as pointed to the good of the *person* and not simply of his body.

This same doctrine is propounded in recent papal teaching. Pope Pius XI states:

> Christian doctrine establishes, and the light of human reason makes it entirely clear, that private individuals have no other power over the members of their bodies than that which pertains to their natural ends; and they are not free to destroy or mutilate their members, or in any other way render themselves unfit for their natural functions, except when no other provision can be made for the good of the whole body.[18]

[16]*Summa*, II-II, q. 65, a. 1.
[17]Cf. *Summa*, I, q. 74.
[18]Encyclical *Casti Connubii* (On Christian Marriage), Dec. 31, 1930.

The same basic truth is expressed and expanded by Pius XII:

> As far as the patient is concerned, he is not absolute master of himself, of his body or of his soul; he cannot, therefore, freely dispose of himself as he pleases. Even the motive for which he acts is not for him the only sufficient determining factor in the case. The patient is bound by the immanent purposes fixed by nature. He possesses the right to use, limited by natural finality, the faculties and powers of his human nature. Because he is the user (and not the proprietor), he does not possess unlimited power to allow acts of destruction, of mutilation against his anatomy or its functions. But in virtue of the principle of totality, of his right to employ the services of the organism as a whole, he can allow the destruction or mutilation of individual parts, when and to the extent that it is necessary for the good of his being as a whole. He may do so to assure the existence of his being or to avoid—and, naturally, to repair—grave and lasting damage which could otherwise be neither avoided or repaired. . . . The principle of totality itself affirms only this: where the relationship of a whole to its part obtains, and in the exact measure it obtains, the part is subordinated to the whole, and the whole can dispose of the part in its own interest.[19]

This principle of totality, by itself alone or in conjunction with the principle of the double effect, is applicable to many and most of the problems which arise concerning human ailments.

3. **Application of principles.** Among the many problems that arise on this score—difficult and complex as they are, and not easily amenable to just solutions—some few admit of so clear an application of moral principles as to serve as a guide and an example in more difficult cases. Hence the following conclusions.

1. Any medical or surgical treatments which cause mutilation (excluding the mutilation of the generative faculties and danger to the unborn child of a pregnant woman) may be morally justified by the principle of totality when they offer solid hope of genuine benefit to the patient which could not be attained by simpler means that are reasonably available. This principle governs the vast majority of surgical and medical procedures—as appendectomy, tonsillectomy, lobotomy, antibiotic and hormone therapy which may have harmful

---

[19]Address to the First International Congress on the Histopathology of the Nervous System, Sept. 13, 1952. Cf. *Irish Ecclesiastical Record,* LXXXI (1954), 222-230; *The Catholic Mind,* LI (1953), 305-13, for the complete text in English.

side effects, X-ray or cobalt irradiation which may impair or destroy organs and functions, plastic surgery, etc.

2. Medical or surgical treatments which create danger to the unborn child of a pregnant woman may not be justified by the principle of totality. It is clear that the fetus is not a part of her own body subordinated to the health of the mother. A pregnant woman may not be treated as if she were not pregnant. Dangers to the fetus must be solved by the principle of double effect.

3. Surgical and medical techniques which involve *direct* sterilization of the subject cannot be justified by the principle of totality. The reason for this is that the generative function as such is not subordinated to the individual; it is related more directly to the common good than other human parts, and in consequence man has less direct dominion over his generative faculties. "Direct sterilization— that is, the sterilization which aims, either as a means or as an end in itself, to render childbearing impossible—is a grave violation of the moral law, and therefore unlawful."[20]

Surgical and medical techniques resulting in *indirect* sterilization, however, may be justified by the principle of totality. Indirect sterilization is any technique which, while attaining an independent and legitimate object, inevitably results in sterilization as a by-product which is neither desired or intended. Thus, for example, Pope Pius XII affirmed the liceity of castration to relieve complications arising from carcinoma of the prostate.[21]

It is imperative in every application of the principle of totality to cases of mutilation that all necessary conditions be verified. These are enumerated as three by Pope Pius XII:

1) The continued presence or function of an organ must cause serious damage to the organism or constitute a threat to it.

2) This harm cannot be avoided or notably reduced except by a mutilation which offers real hope of relief.

[20]Pope Pius XII, address to the Italian Catholic Union of Midwives, Oct. 29, 1951.

[21]Pope Pius XII, address to the Congress of the Union of Italian Urologists. It is to be noted in this case that the organ which is removed or rendered inoperative is *not* diseased, but that its preservation or functioning involves a serious danger to the whole body, either directly or indirectly.

3) There must be reasonable expectation that the mutilation and its consequences will be offset by the good resulting from the removal of danger, relief of pain and other beneficial effects.[22]

4. Medical experimentation. Medical experimentation (in the form of unproved remedies applied in extreme cases for the benefit of the subject) can be judged by the principle of totality alone, or in conjunction with the principle of the double effect. Special moral problems arise, however, when the experimentation is tried for the benefit of others, and not because of the needs of the subject himself.

To begin with, man does not have perfect dominion over himself; he is a steward rather than a proprietor. Hence the consent of the subject alone cannot provide moral grounds for unrestricted experimentation. It is obvious that experimentation conducted by violence (as in the Nazi abattoirs) or by restraint (as may happen in prisons or so-called charity wards) is wholly indefensible on moral grounds.

Yet it does seem that experimentation on willing subjects for the benefit of others may be morally permissible when ordinary laboratory research, dissection and experimentation on animals proves impossible, inadequate or impracticable.[23] Such experimentation must be governed by the laws of justice and charity. It cannot directly inflict grave injury or death, and every reasonable precaution must be taken to avoid even indirect causing of grave injury or death.[24]

5. Organic transplantation. A final question of mutilation concerns the transplanting or grafting of parts taken from another human being. There is no real moral problem in autografts (those in which one part of the subject's body is used to aid another part of his body), as in skin grafts from the leg to repair burns on the face. This is covered by the principal of totality. Neither is there any moral problem in the transplanting of skin and organs from cadavers or legitimately am-

[22]*Ibid.*

[23]Cf. *supra*, the statement of Pope Pius XII, 515.

[24]A clear discussion of this entire problem is available in Gerald Kelly, S.J., *Medico-Moral Problems* (St. Louis: The Catholic Hospital Association, 1958), 261 ff. This book is highly recommended for a fuller study of the matter treated in this present section.

putated members, provided the consent of all parties concerned is obtained. The problem centers on "donor" transplants, wherein one party submits to an operation which is not for his own good.

There is a considerable interest in, and widespread discussion of the problem of organic transplants among theologians. The matter is far from settled. It should be noted, however, that a forceful argument against the practice is contained in the words of Pope Pius XI quoted above.[25] Many reputable theologians who are proponents of the liceity of transplantation base their arguments chiefly on the law of charity, which envisages the beneficiary of the transplant as "another self." It has yet to be shown, however, that this view can be harmonized with the papal teaching already mentioned.[26]

6. **The moral necessity of mutilation.** It is within a man's rights to allow mutilation, but it is by no means his obligation in every case. So sacred is the integrity of the human body that it may be preserved even at the cost of life itself. The man with the gangrenous leg may permit its amputation; he may also refuse to allow the operation. It is a principle of morality that one must take all the ordinary means to preserve his life. As to extraordinary means, he is free,[27] and any major surgical operation is reasonably considered, by doctors as well as theologians, as an extraordinary means. Confusion may easily arise here as to the meaning of "ordinary." It does not mean "ordinary or normal surgical procedure"—it may well be ordinary surgical procedure to amputate a gangrenous limb. "Ordinary" and "extraordinary" in this context indicate whatever can or cannot be done without a great deal of trouble, pain and danger. A human judgment is to be made, not a technical, scientific, medical one.

7. **Punitive mutilation.** Public authority can, upon sufficient provocation, take away life itself. Certainly, then, it can inflict lesser penalties. Mutilation as a punishment can be licit, but it must be imposed for a real crime, and one for which it is an apt remedy.

[25]Cf. *supra*, 514.

[26]For a discussion of the question and a bibliography of sources, cf. Gerald Kelly, S.J., *op. cit.*, 246 ff.; John P. Kenny, O.P., *Principles of Medical Ethics* (Westminster: The Newman Press, 1952), 108 ff.

[27]For a detailed discussion, cf. Gerald Kelly, S.J., *op. cit.*, 128 ff.

The Church's stand against sterilization of the poor or feeble-minded is well known. The reasonableness of this stand is crystal-clear. Mutilation is a punishment; it cannot be inflicted upon those who have committed no crime. Whatever benefits to society may be imagined to come from such action, it remains a flagrant violation of justice.

So even sterilization could be used as a punishment for a real crime—if it were truly a vindictive remedy, justly inflicted, for sins against society. But the opposition to its use as such is most reasonable and hence it is strenuously protested against by the Church: it is an inept punishment: it causes no pain, it does not prevent further crime. It even makes sexual crime easier. It follows from this that sterilization of the innocent (of mental patients, for example) is a violation of human rights that has neither medical nor political justification, and no moral theological ground on which it might justifiably stand.

(3) Physical Assaults

Punishment by beating is by definition a lesser thing than mutilation. Presumably it causes no permanent harm to the bodily organs, but only temporary pain, and so is licit even to private authority—the operative word here is "authority." Private persons cannot inflict punishment except under special circumstances. The state may order a thief to be given ten lashes; parents may spank their children. But authority is necessary to inflict any punishment at all. I cannot spank my neighbor's child without that neighbor's consent. Sometimes, of course, the consent is implicitly given.

Certain court decisions in recent years have upheld the right of school teachers to inflict corporal punishment upon pupils on the grounds that they stand *in loco parentis*, in the place of the parents—and surely, if teachers are delegated with parental authority to assume educational responsibilities, they have the parental rights of discipining the child, besides whatever rights might privately accrue to them in virtue of the virtue of revenge. It is presumed, of course, that such punishment is inflicted by authority and that it is moderate. No parent could chastise his child to the point where corporal punishment becomes mutilation. The purpose of the punishment must be the preservation of justice, the inflicting of a just penalty. Beating subordinates is not licit when it is motivated by passion or cruelty.

According to the teaching of many modern theologians, boxing or prize-fighting (and especially professional boxing) falls into the category of these sins against justice. "The manly art of self-defense" is a euphemistic phrase for a practice essentially brutal and brutalizing. Boxing is not self-defense: of all forms of sport in which man is pitted against man, boxing alone has as its prime and direct object the physical injury of the contestants. Profesional football, hockey and even basketball may be rougher sports, involving more wholesale body contact; but their immediate purpose is not the injury of an opponent (if an individual player should intend injury, or deliberately employ means, however legitimate, from which injury would quite likely follow, then clearly he would be morally unjust). But medical experience shows that boxing necessarily produces severe body damage: hematuria occurs in 65-89% of boxers after a bout; 60% of boxers develop neurologic and psychic changes in the brief span of five years—two instances from limited surveys which support the medical opinion that boxing is always potentially dangerous to life and health, and often actually so.[28]

Boxing is not a manly art. It is opposed to virtue, and thus to the good of man and to true manliness. Three reasons support this conclusion:

1) Of its very nature boxing tends to result in serious and unjustifiable injury to its participants.

2) These very effects are directly intended by the prizefighter, at least implicitly.

3) Prizefighting of its very nature appeals primarily to the brutish instincts of both participants and spectators, and therefore constitutes a deordination of man's rational nature.

[28]Cf. Eugene G. Laforet, "Boxing: Medical and Moral Aspects," *Linacre Quarterly*, XXV (1958), 56-67. It is significant that scholastic boxing has been disapproved by the Joint Committee on Health Problems in Education of the National Educational Association and by the American Medical Association; cf. the editorial "Safeguards in Boxing," *Journal of the American Medical Association*, CXLII (1950), 1298.

(3) Incarceration

Mutilation injures bodily integrity, beating interferes with bodily well-being, and imprisonment restricts liberty of action. Imprisonment affords no special difficulties. It, too, can be a legitimate means of punishment, provided that it is applied by proper authority and in due proportion.

Justice demands that every man's rights be respected, but by disorderly actions men can lose the exercise of certain rights. Punishment for crime is justly inflicted out of consideration for the good of the society of which the individual is a part, and may legitimately take the form of depriving offenders of their liberty.

Unless imprisonment for some length of time is inflicted by public authority and with due regard for justice, it is morally unjust.

C. Theft and Robbery

As sins against commutative justice, theft and robbery despoil the individual of his right, of something that is his. In this instance it is some tangible and material thing that is unjustly taken from him, and before we can analyze the injustice done, we will first have to establish man's right to own property.

(1) The Right of Private Property

1. **Its meaning.** Man has a right to life, he has a right to bodily integrity, and he has a right to property. Scripture attests that lesser creation was intended by God for man's use and that it is subject to his dominion. The Church has always been the defender of the right of private property.[29] The social encyclicals of Pope Leo XIII are classic documents on this subject.

Americans are little inclined to socialism at this time. During the depression of the 1930's some of our citizens suffered temptations. But there is little doubt that private property, free enterprise, individualism—all are part of our national tradition. But in contemporary society we hear a great deal of complaints about the "welfare state." Many people think that the government is begin-

---

[29]Cf. Pope Leo XIII, encyclical *Rerum Novarum,* May 15, 1891.

ning to encroach upon the right of private property and to destroy our precious private initiative. Whatever be the truth of this charge, we still remain the least socialistic of modern societies. It is possible even that we exaggerate the absoluteness and the sacredness of private ownership.

All nature belongs, of course, to God. He made it. It is his. He has given over to man the right to *use* the created universe. God, however, remains the owner. The created universe belongs to man— man with a capital "M"—to the human race. Does this mean that property should be held in common? How do we justify the actual division of property?

It is clear that, since the natural law intends lesser creatures for man's benefit, it at least *allows* the division of the world into privately owned property. The actual division is seen to be necessary when human reason looks closely at the nature of man and the needs of society.

2. Its necessity. That individual men should have property which is, properly speaking, their own is seen to be necessary for three reason:

1) Because otherwise (human nature being what we know it is) men would not take sufficient care of their common possessions. What belongs to everyone belongs to no one, and usually no one takes care of it. It would be only natural to human weakness for each individual to leave the care of the common possessions to someone else. The incentive for solicitude would be gone.

2) Because an orderly society demands that articles be earmarked for private use. Nothing but confusion could arise from common ownership.

3) Because private ownership is the best way to preserve peace. Common ownership would give rise to quarrels and disputes over the use of property. Private property inclines individuals to be content with their own share of this world's goods.

3. The nature of private ownership. The right to private ownership includes the right to provide for the future. A father is the natural head of his family and has responsibility for its members. It is in accord with the natural law for him to set aside something for a rainy day, to provide for his children's education, to think of the time when he will no longer be with them. The passing on of private property from father to son, by natural succession or by testament, is likewise a corollary of the doctrine of private ownership.

When all this is said, certain reservations have to be made. The private ownership of property is quite in accord with the natural law. But it is not something absolute. Ultimately all things belong to God; less remotely, but importantly, all material things belong to the human race. It is possible for common right to take precedence over private. Thus, in cases of extreme necessity, property becomes common once more. A starving man has a **right** to food. If there is no other way of obtaining it, he may literally take it from another man's table. In so doing he is not stealing, he is merely claiming what is rightfully his.

Christian theologians commonly hold that the superfluous property of the extremely wealthy is not a completely private affair:

> A man's superfluous income is not left entirely to his own discretion. We speak of that portion of his income which he does not need in order to live as becomes his station. On the contrary, the grave obligations of charity, beneficence and liberality which rest upon the wealthy are constantly insisted upon in telling words by Holy Scripture and the Fathers of the Church.
>
> However, the investment of superfluous income in securing favorable opportunities for employment, provided the labor employed produces results which are really useful, is to be considered, according to the teaching of the Angelic Doctor,[30] an act of real liberality particularly appropriate to the needs of our time.[31]

A man has a right to private property; he has a right not merely to sustenance and security, but to sufficient goods to maintain himself in his station in life. But whatever he possesses over and above this carries obligations. He has obligations to society, and to the poor. His excess wealth belongs more to the poor than it does to him.

---

[30]*Summa*, II-II, q. 134.
[31]Pope Pius XI, encyclical *Quadragesimo Anno*, May 15, 1931.

Finally we must recognize that an assertion of the right of private ownership does not alter the primacy of the common good. Society has rights as well as individuals; governments have rights. There are clear cases in which the common good must take precedence over private advantage. Every civilized nation recognizes the right of eminent domain. When property becomes necessary to the welfare of the community it ceases to be a merely private affair. Our insistence on the rights of individuals should not lead us to become anarchists. Governments are for the sake of governing. There may be such a thing as too much government, but this does not mean that any government at all is an excess.

This twofold aspect of property, individual and social, was emphasized by Pope Pius XI:

> First, let it be made clear beyond all doubt that neither Leo XIII, nor those theologians who have taught under the guidance and direction of the Church, have ever denied or called in question the twofold aspect of ownership, which is individual or social accordingly as it regards individuals or concerns the common good. Their unanimous contention has always been that the right to own private property has been given to man by nature or rather by the Creator himself, not only in order that individuals may be able to provide for their own needs and those of their families, but also that by means of it the goods which the Creator has destined for the human race may truly serve this purpose. Now these ends cannot be secured unless some definite and stable order is maintained.[32]

4. The definition of private property. Taking all these factors into consideration, we can define the **ownership of property** as *the perpetual and restrictive power or right, retained by just limits and flowing from the natural law, to dispose of something as one's own.* This definition can be explained in the following manner:

1) **Perpetual and restrictive power or right** signifies a complete and exclusive ownership, independent of the state, of other societies and of other individuals.

2) **Restrained by just limits** means that the ownership of property is a limited right, not an absolute one. Thus, *extreme necessity* places all property into common hands; the law of *eminent domain* allows the state to take over private property

[32]*Loc. cit.*

when the common good demands such a move, although compensation must be made; and the law of *charity* requires that the wealthy give their superfluous riches to the poor.

3) **Flowing from the natural law.** The right to own private property flows directly from principles of the natural law. Hence all men have a right to use the goods of this world. Pope Pius XII forcibly re-stated this social teaching of the Church:

> The native right to the use of material goods, intimately linked as it is with the dignity and other rights of the human person, provides man with a secure material basis of the highest import on which to rise to the fulfillment, with reasonable liberty, of his moral duties. The safeguarding of this right will ensure the personal dignity of man and will facilitate for him the attention to and fulfillment of that sum of stable duties and decisions for which he is directly responsible to his Creator.[33]

Since the fall of Adam, private property has most especially become a moral necessity. Once man lost the state of innocence, his inclination to sins of selfishness demanded that property rights be respected for the preservation of peace in the social order.

4) **To dispose of something as one's own** means that the individual can alienate, sell, give, exchange, use, enjoy or destroy this thing (whether corporeal like land or a house, or incorporeal like honors, benefices, etc.) on his own authority, exclusive of any other individual's interference. This he must do, of course, reasonably, morally, justly.

(2) Sins Contrary to Private Ownership

Specific sins against the right of private property are theft and robbery. Each consists in depriving someone of what is rightfully his. The thief does it by fraud and deceit; the robber accomplishes it in the open, by violence. Theft is malicious because it is opposed to justice; it takes on an added malice because it is insidious. Robbery is sinful because it violates justice; its special malice comes from the violence it employs. Both of these sins upset the balance of nature, which must be restored by the act of restitution.

[33]Pope Pius XII, radio broadcast, June 1, 1941.

Theft may be defined, then, as *the unjust taking of another's property, the owner being reasonably unwilling, with the intention of keeping it.* Theft by stealth is called *simple* theft; if violence is used it is *robbery.* This is a vice directly contrary to commutative justice, but it offends against society as well. In consequence, to determine the gravity of the sin from the standpoint of the amount taken there is a double standard: *relative* (based on the harm done to the individual) and *absolute* (based on the harm done to society).

1) Generally speaking, the relative sum for a grave sin of theft is the sum sufficient for a day's support for a man and his family.

2) The absolute sum for grave matter is more difficult to determine; by definition it will be a sum so large that society would suffer seriously if it could be stolen without serious sin even from the wealthy or from rich corporations. It has been reasonably suggested that a sum equivalent to the weekly wage of the better paid unskilled laborer would constitute absolute grave matter; this would be about $75 today.

Small thefts may coalesce—i.e., be grouped together to constitute grave matter—if the thief keeps the money until he accumulates a large sum, or if he intends ultimately to take a large sum by these means, or if they are so closely united that they constitute one moral act. When a person steals only at intervals, however, it would take a larger sum to constitute mortal sin than if he did it in one act, and the same is true of thefts of small amounts from different people; one and a half times as much is a reasonable estimate for the larger amount.

In certain highly restricted circumstances a man may recover what is owed him by helping himself secretly to what is his. This practice, called *occult compensation,* is generally forbidden; but if no other way is possible, the debt is certain, and there is no danger to himself or his family, then it might be permissible. But occult compensation is never permitted to employees who have freely contracted for a certain wage; even though the amount is actually below the living wage, they can never justly help themselves to what they think they deserve.

6. Sinful Words Opposed to Commutative Justice

Having discussed the vices opposed to commutative justice by unjust deeds, we must now take up another set of vices which disrupt the balance of justice among equals: injurious words. Injurious or sinful words are spoken in two areas of social relationships: 1) in court of law; and 2) privately. We shall speak first of injustices which are committed in judicial proceedings. To accomplish this task we shall have to inquire about injustice in words among judges, plaintiffs, defendants, witnesses and lawyers.

A. Injustice in Judicial Proceedings

(1) Justice and Injustice in Judges

The first requisite for a just judge is that he possess jurisdiction. He is a public person and has a public power which cannot be assumed by an individual on his own initiative. Not only must a judge be legitimately appointed or elected to office, but he must possess jurisdiction over *this* defendant; that is, he must possess authority over the person on whom judgment is passed. For example, a secular judge does not have jurisdiction in ecclesiastical cases.

Since a trial is a matter of public interest it is regulated by law. A judge is bound by evidence. As an individual he may, indeed, possess a great deal of knowledge about this case, but he may not justly use this knowledge. His judgment must be based upon the evidence presented in court according to the laws which regulate trial procedure. This is the reason why people with preconceived notions are excused from jury duty, and why jurors (who really function as judges) are protected from newspaper publicity and comment on cases which they are trying

Judges (and jurors) must be impartial. They must guard against the sin of favoritism. That is, they must not allow themselves to judge from personal prejudices, likes or dislikes, or knowledge privately obtained. This would be to do violence to the judicial system and to introduce practices which, though conceivably beneficial in a particular instance, could only lead to abuse if they were to become widespread.

(2) Justice and Injustice of Plaintiffs

The office of prosecutor is likewise a public charge. Private individuals have no general obligation to act as accusors, nor should they do so except under certain conditions. The conditions are two: 1) the crime should be one that involves the public good; 2) it should be susceptible of proof. Hence faults that are strictly private concern God alone and should not be denounced to those in authority unless their divulgence will benefit the common welfare. Furthermore, those who make charges must be capable of giving evidence for the facts they have set forth.

Catholic tradition requires that a serious accusation be reduced to writing. This is because, in a serious matter, no one should be condemned on merely spoken words, which are often vague and liable to ambiguity and misinterpretation. It is reasonable, too, that the defendant know the exact nature of the crime of which he is charged, in order to be able to prepare a defense. He also has a right to know his accuser, as well as the nature of the crime with which he is charged.

No man is obliged to accuse himself of a crime, even if he be guilty, nor can force be used to make him confess. The law is principally concerned with external actions, and hence if insufficient evidence is at hand by which to convict the accused, there is simply no basis for judgment. No one need testify against himself, and every man is innocent until proved guilty. This is the nature of law.

False accusation is patently sinful, and seriously so. It is a sin against the defendant, whose rights are violated, and it is a sin injurious to society itself. Even the accusation of a true criminal must be truthful in order to be just. Lies cannot be told in order to convict even a certainly guilty defendant: the end does not justify the means.

(3) Justice and Injustice of Defendants

The defendant in a trial is being judged according to the law. He may, therefore, use every defense which the law allows, but he may not use unjust means of defense. A lie is immoral, and a lie may not be told even in self-defense, nor may the defendant rely on perjured testimony (lying under oath). He may refuse to answer questions when the answers are self-incriminating—the law allows this—but he may not tell a direct falsehood.

Advantage might well be gained by besmirching the character of the prosecution's witnesses. This would be an unjust means, and illicit. Every legitimate means of defense may be employed, including appeal; but not even the end of self-defense justifies immoral means.

A justly condemned man, though he may exhaust all legal means of defense and appeal, is not allowed to defend himself violently. The situation is otherwise with one who is unjustly condemned. Having exhausted the means provided by public authority, he may now defend his rights on his own.

(4) Justice and Injustice of Witnesses

Witness, too, must observe the rules of law and of justice. The function of witness may be distasteful, but it can be an obligation. Charity may demand that one give testimony in order to avoid damage to another person or to society. Strict commutative justice may demand it when it is a part of one's official duty. An arresting officer, for example, is not exempt from being a witness. Legal justice requires testimony from one who receives an official subpoena.

There are times when testimony can be refused. A priest must certainly refuse to give testimony regarding information he has received in sacramental confession. Certain classes of professional people, such as lawyers and doctors, are repositories of natural secrets.[34] Such secrets need not be revealed provided they were

[34]Professional secrets are technically "implicit entrusted secrets." Cf. the excellent article by Robert E. Regan, O.S.A., "Problems of Professional Secrecy," *Proceedings of The Catholic Theological Society of America*, X (1955), 152 ff. This article is highly recommended as a concise and clear solution of problems of great practical interest.

learned in an official capacity and there is no danger of injury to innocent third parties. It is interesting that lawyers are willing to grant generous exemption from testimony to themselves on this ground, but are reluctant to grant it to others, to clergymen and doctors, for example. Often such matters are regulated by positive law, but it is difficult to see how the natural law would regard a lawyer as more privileged in this respect than a doctor.

The most serious sin which a witness may commit is to give false testimony. This is immoral on three separate counts: 1) It involves perjury, a mortal sin which does not admit of light matter, because testimony is always given under oath; 2) it is a violation of justice— a mortal sin which does admit of light matter; 3) it is a lie, a sin which is generically venial.

(5) Justice and Injustice in Lawyers

Perhaps the most important question which can be asked about lawyers is whether they can justly assume the advocacy of an unjust cause. To answer it we must distinguish between civil and criminal trials.

No lawyer can justly defend an unjust cause in a civil case. The reason is that by so doing he would be offering co-operation in injustice. This is perhaps a hard saying, but a true one: it is the only principle of action which can save the integrity of the legal profession. To accept a fraudulent damage suit against a street-car company would be to co-operate with robbery; to accept a divorce case would be to co-operate with the destruction of family society.[35] These actions cannot be justified by appealing to the liberality of law. Civil suits are simply not in the same category with criminal suits in this respect. Nor can they be condoned on the plea that "someone else will take the case." One sin does not justify another.

Criminal cases are in another category altogether. A lawyer may offer to defend a man even when he knows him to be certainly

---

[35]There are certain circumstances when it would be permissible for a lawyer to handle divorce cases, even those of Catholics. Cf. Donlan, *et al., Toward Marriage in Christ* (Dubuque: The Priory Press, 1957), 56.

guilty. The reason is that positive law presumes every man innocent until he is proved guilty. Guilt must be proved. In such a case no harm is offered to any third party. In the larger sense the common good is served rather than injured, because it is the common good which demands the presumption of innocence.

B. Verbal Injustice outside Judicial Proceedings

Injurious words spoken outside of judicial processes can be committed on all sorts of occasions, public or private. We distinguish the principal sins in this area of injustice according to the diverse injuries intended by the sinful speaker. Some words deprive an individual of the benefits connected with virtue by unjustly imputing guilt to him for some evil. Thus, tribute to the existence of virtue paid to an individual by his neighbor under the names of honor, fame and friendship is repudiated through contumely, defamation and vicious whispering; and the tribute to virtue paid by one's conscience to oneself under the title of self-respect can be lost through the derisive speech of another. We shall treat each of these sins in more detail.

(1) Contumely

Contumely is more easily recognized by the names "reviling" or "insult." In general, to insult someone is to deprive him of the honor and respect that should be paid him by his neighbor. Reviling can be exercised by deed—for example, blows or contemptuous gestures —but it is more properly effected by word. As St. Augustine says: "Compared with words all other signs are very few, for words have obtained the chief place among men for the purpose of giving expression to whatever the mind conceives."[36] Hence deeds are a source of contumely only insofar as they have the significance and force of words.

There are two characteristics of an insult worthy of particular notice: an insult is always given in the presence of a victim; and it

---

[36]*On Christian Doctrine*, Bk. II, Chap. 3.

is an expression of complete contempt, which seems to show that reviling often springs from anger, insofar as they both have revenge for their end. **Contumely** is therefore defined as *the unjust dishonoring of a person who is present.*

Besides reviling a person for any guilt or punishment which he has incurred, man has devised other ways of heaping insult upon his neighbor: he *taunts* him because of some bodily defect such as blindness; and he *upbraids* him for being inferior to himself—for example, by reminding him spitefully that he has had to be loaned money or has needed help with his studies.

Contumely can be mortally sinful—indeed, as serious a sin as theft or robbery, for a man has a right to his honor no less than to his possessions. Thus if the intention of the reviler is to bring dishonor upon his neighbor, he must pay for the damage done with the same coin by which it was inflicted—speech. But if, on the other hand, he meant merely to correct his neighbor for some fault, he does not commit sin formally but only materially and accidentally, although, at times, correction through insult may be venially sinful. Hence the lesson we can learn from contumely is always to use the power of speech with moderation.

(2) Detraction

Detraction is often given the more colorful name "backbiting," because it consists in injuring a person's reputation behind his back, its purpose being to undermine his title to fame. Modern authors distinguish two types of backbiting: simple detraction and calumny. These two species of sin are defined in terms of truth and falsehood. Simple detraction ruins a person's reputation by telling the truth about him, by revealing his sins. Calumny accomplishes the same purpose by means of lies. St. Thomas gathered both types under a single sin, on the grounds that the purpose or effect of both is the same: the unjust depriving of a person's good name. **Detraction** may be formally defined as *the unjust blackening through words of the reputation of one who is absent.*

The unjust defamation which both simple detraction and calumny attain is a mortal sin in itself, since, as St. Thomas says, "it is a serious thing to take away the good esteem of another, because among man's personal possessions nothing is more precious than his good name; if he lacks it, he is hindered from doing many things well."[37] It may be necessary, however, to utter words which defame: the common good or the good of an individual may demand such utterances, and would justify the telling of facts whose disclosure in other circumstances would be sinful.

In practice we can decide the gravity of defamation by considering:

1) *the person who speaks,* who, if he is an important man or one noted for his prudence, will cause more harm than a vacillating, talkative person;

2) *the persons who listen*—if they are many and influential, grave injury more easily follows than if they were few and unimportant;

3) *the person injured*—if he is worthy of high dignity and has a good name, then he will suffer greater harm than a worthless character (thus, for example, it would be a greater sin to defame a bishop than to defame a notorious gangster);

4) the *motive* which causes the revelation of fault—no motive justifies calumny, although simple detraction can have reasons which excuse from the sin, as has been noted.

Backbiting, like all sins of injustice, demands restitution. With regard to simple detraction this can be accomplished by using every lawful means to excuse the sins one has unjustly revealed. With regard to calumny, restitution must be made in a public way.

(3) Whispering

Tale-bearing or whispering is a particularly vicious sin against justice. We can define **tale-bearing** as *unfavorable speech made in secret to another person for the purpose of destroying one of the noblest relationships necessary to human life, a virtuous friendship.* The main sin of tale-bearing seems to be connected with the breaking up of a friendship completely, for the whisperer's purpose is to turn friends into enemies.

[37] *Summa,* II-II, q. 73, a. 2.

Whispering is, from its nature, a mortal sin—more serious than detraction and even than calumny, for friendship is a greater and nobler human good than fame or honor. But it admits of light matter, because often the injury is slight, so that friends are not turned into enemies.

(4) Derision

Like the other sins of speech against commutative justice, **derision** or mockery discredits another: it is defined as *attributing some defect or evil to another in a joking manner in order to embarrass him.* Derision, unlike the serious tone of other forms of verbal injustice, is spoken in fun and has as its chief goal to make another's defects an object of laughter. The result of derision is to cause the victim of this injustice to suffer shame.

The gravity attached to mockery depends upon the degree of contempt intended by the derider. When he makes light of a serious matter, he commits a mortal sin, for he exhibits grave contempt for his victim, acting as if he were entirely worthless. When he treats a light evil in a light way, no contempt is exhibited, although serious embarrassment may ensue. If the one who suffers derision does not take the slight too seriously, only a venial sin is committed. Furthermore, the gravity of derision can be judged by the person to whom it is directed. To mock God is the worst form of derision; to mock one's parents is next in gravity; and to mock holy persons is especially grave because their virtues deserve honor, and derision prevents men from imitating their holiness.

(5) Cursing

Besides imputing the evil of guilt through contumely, detraction, whispering and derision, sinful speech can also employ the evil of punishment. There are the verbal injuries which we commonly class under the single name "cursing." When a man curses his neighbor, for example, he wishes that some kind of evil will befall him. Since all men have claim to our love and respect, such a wish is unjust, for it means we desire evil as evil to befall another. In this formal sense, **cursing** is the *dishonoring by which one begs evil as evil for* *another person.* Cursing is, then, clearly distinguished from blasphemy, obscenity and mere vulgarity.

Cursing can be expressed in two ways:

1) *imperatively*, when one is vested with the authority to determine that punishment is to be inflicted on a person—as when God condemns sinners to eternal or temporal punishment, judges sentence criminals, the Church pronounces anathemas upon those who resist her authority;

2) *as a desire*, when one has neither the power nor the authority to command punishment, but expresses a wish that some misfortune befall a person.

The gravity of cursing depends again upon the intention of the one who curses: if the intended evil is ordered to some good, no sin is involved. Thus, with regard to imperative cursing, the punishment inflicted upon a criminal may be evil for him, but morally it is ordered to the good of justice. With regard to curses expressed in the form of a desire, one may wish that a murderer be hanged, not because of the suffering involved, but for the protection of the community.

By its nature, unjust cursing, which intends the evil of another precisely as it is evil, is a mortal sin, both because, as St. Paul points out, neither "the evil-tongued nor the greedy will possess the kingdom of God" (I Cor. 6:11), and because such cursing manifests hatred. It will be a correspondingly graver sin by comparison with the ones who are cursed and the love and honor we owe them, and in proportion to the gravity of the evil desired for the other. Cursing does, however, admit of light matter. Often, too, one curses either because his temper has been suddenly aroused or from habit, without really wishing evil to anyone.

7. Contractual Exchanges and Their Opposed Vices

Man's social nature is manifest in every exercise of the virtue of justice, and it is precisely as a social being that he suffers from injustice. The socio-political climate and economic structure of any given era will create and modify occasions for justice and injustice, but the basic truth remains constant: these things profoundly affect man at the very roots of his being.

The whole area of rights and duties wherein justice and injustice flourish has expanded both in scope and complexity with the emergence of our technical civilization. For an understanding of the more basic problems involved, some knowledge of the various titles to property and of the nature of contracts is prerequisite.

A. Ownership and Its Titles

(1) Private Ownership

Ownership, we have seen, is the exclusive right to control and dispose of property at will. Man's right of ownership over the material things of this world is a corollary that flows immediately from his natural right to life, for life cannot be sustained without property. Unlike economics (which is the systematic study of the production and distribution of wealth in view of the economic welfare of the community), moral theology is vitally concerned with moral problems connected with ownership.

This concern is aptly expressed by Pius XII:

> The Church aspires to bring it about that private ownership should become, in accordance with the plans of divine wisdom and with the laws of nature, an element in the social system, a necessary incentive to human enterprise, and a stimulus to labor. All this is for the benefit of the temporal and spiritual ends of life, and consequently for the benefit of the freedom and dignity of man created in the image of God, who in the beginning granted to man dominion over created things for his service.[38]

It is clear from this teaching that ownership is a moral right, and it is a moral right that is fundamental to human dignity. Human personality is the highest value of the temporal order. The state and all other institutions, the entire social and economic structure, are ordained to provide man with the means of fulfilling "the altogether personal obligation of maintaining and bringing to greater perfection his own material and spiritual life."[39] Ownership is indispensable for

[38]Address on the reconstruction of the world on a true Christian foundation, September 1, 1944.

[39]Pius XII, address on the fiftieth anniversary of Rerum Novarum, June 1, 1941.

fulfilling this obligation. It is also necessary for family life, for "only private ownership can provide the head of a family with the healthy freedom he requires to carry out the duties allotted to him by the Creator for the physical, spiritual and religious well-being of his family."[40]

(2) Titles to Ownership

It is clear that the Christian view sees ownership as a moral and a human entity that is the safeguard of human dignity. As a consequence, Christians have an obligation to strive for the diffusion of the opportunities of ownership to all. But how may title to ownership be acquired?

By virtue of his human nature, man has the right to ownership. Now this is something abstract, and it must be concretized in the actual possession of some particular piece of property. This is accomplished by a **title**, which is some historical fact that reduces the abstract right of ownership to the concrete right to control and dispose of this piece of property as the owner wills. These titles are seven in number:

1) *Occupancy*—taking possession of something that has no owner to make it one's own.

2) *Labor*—creating new values by working on raw materials.

3) *Gift*—gratuitous donation of ownership to another.

4) *Trade*—any exchange or purchase.

5) *Inheritance*—possession through legacy.

6) *Accession*—appreciation in value of one's property.

7) *Prescription*—gaining of another's property through lapse of time.

B. Contracts

(1) Their Nature

Most of these titles are reducible to the general heading of **contract**, which is *the consent of two or more persons to the same agreement.* In general, contracts are of three types:

[40]*Ibid.*

1. **Gratuitous contracts** confer a benefit on one or some of the parties only, as in a gift.

2. **Onerous contracts** impose obligations on all parties, as in a lease.

3. **Aleatory contracts** (from the Latin *alea*, meaning hazard or chance) concern fortuitous and future events, as in an insurance policy.

Any contract may be either *explicit* or *implicit*, depending upon whether it is made formally in words or writing or simply contained virtually in the acceptance of some office, such as that of a physician. Every contract requires two things: first, an act of the intellect understanding and proposing the agreement; secondly, an act of the will consenting to the contract.

(2) The Kinds of Contracts

Sufficient for our purposes in general will be a schematic presentation of the various kinds of exchanges that can arise between individuals on a contractual basis and bind in commutative justice. They are listed on the opposite page.

Contracts are intimately bound up with the whole matter of private property. Not every contract is about property, and not all property is acquired by contract, but every deliberate transfer of property involves a mutual agreement of offer and acceptance, and this is a contract. Most relevant to our purposes are two types of contract: the first is buying and selling, which involves the exchange of property for money under the title of trade; the second is the labor contract. Buying and selling presents the moral problem of the just price; the labor contracts involve the just wage. Each will be considered separately.

C. Buying and Selling

(1) The Conditions of Justice

The contract of purchase and sale is founded on the natural law, which binds the parties by virtue of their consent to its terms. Positive law may, however, add certain conditions for the sake of the common good, as when it demands that titles to real estate be re-

Contracts

Gratuitous

Unilateral

Promise: a contract whereby a person freely and spontaneously obliges himself to give something to another or omit something.

Gift: the generous offer of part of one's possessions to another who accepts it.

Last will and testament: the final and complete disposal of goods made by a man to be effective at his death.

Bilateral

Loans for use: the gratuitous loan of a thing to be used for a definite purpose and for a specified time.

Deposit of goods: a contract in which some moveable good is placed in the custody of a person on condition that it be returned when the depositor demands it.

Agency: a contract whereby one party undertakes to conduct some action or business.

Loans for consumption: a contract by which the ownership of some good consumed in its first use is given to another, who is obliged to restore its equivalent in kind at some future date.

Onerous

Buying and selling: an onerous contract by which some commodity is given for a price and a price paid for the commodity.

Renting: a contract by which one person (the renter) allows another (the tenant) the use or fruits of real property in return for a specified price.

Labor contract: one by which one party (the employee) promises another (the employer) certain services or work in return for a specified wage.

Aleatory

Insurance: a contract by which one person (the insurer) in return for a fixed sum undertakes to pay compensation for any damage which another (the insured) may suffer by involuntary chance.

Betting: a contract in which two or more persons disputing the truth of some event tender a sum to be given to the person who was right.

Gambling: a contract in which a reward is given to the winner of a contest undertaken as a pastime.

Lottery: a contract whereby on payment of a certain sum the right is acquired of obtaining some prize, if the person is lucky.

corded or that purchase and sale of stock by officials in their own company be made public.

The seller must *own* whatever he sells; he must *disclose* its substantial defects (i.e., those which make an object notably useless for the primary and manifest purpose of the buyer); he must *deliver* the purchased article or its duplicate in the same condition as at the time of the sale; he must *charge* a just price. If asked, he must either reveal accidental defects or declare that the object is being sold "as is."

The buyer must accept what he has purchased and he must pay the just price for it within the time determined by the contract or by custom.

(2) The Just Price

The just price presents an economic problem inasmuch as it is a price, and a moral problem inasmuch as it is just. The consideration of a just price is limited to ordinary goods exchanged in daily commerce. The sale of rare articles or the conduct of private transactions must abide by the just price, but they cannot establish a standard of values for scaling prices; ordinary business in stable commodities alone can do that.

The **just price** of an article is *its value expressed in money*. It is based on the intrinsic value of the article and the consequent loss of profitable investment which the seller endures because of his sale. *Money* is legal tender accepted as the medium of exchange. *Value* is the article's capacity to satisfy human wants. The just price, then, is the true monetary value of an article; it is the sum that can purchase other goods which have equal capacity to satisfy human wants.

Buying and selling are acts of commutative justice, based on the principle of equality which determines that the buyer receive the equal of what he pays and that the seller receive the equal of what he gives. This notion of equality does not exclude the notion of profit because the seller has a right to a reward for his industry and ingenuity within the limits of justice.

The just price cannot be an inflexibly fixed sum because human wants are subject to too many variations. Neither can the just price be the product of individual whims, for this would simply establish the immoral practice of selling a man his own necessity, as when a starving man would be charged whatever he is willing to pay for food; in this situation the purchasing power of money would decrease in inverse ratio to the increase of a purchaser's needs. The consequence is that the just price must be based on the value of goods to men generally, and not to some particular individual in certain circumstances.

The just price reflects the value-judgment of the public expressed in the open market under conditions of competition. The public estimate of the capacity of goods to satisfy human wants is translated into monetary values. This determines the *natural* price of goods, and it is the just price where competition prevails.

The just price can be the natural price; it can also be an *artificial* price determined by government action. This is known as the **legal price**, which is established by law for goods which could easily be manipulated contrary to the common good. Examples of the legal just price are found in public utility rates and transportation charges.

In the comparatively uncommon sale of rare objects like masterpieces of art, the just price is more elastic, being determined within the relatively small group of those who deal in such things. In auction sales like the stock exchange, the highest bid determines the just price.

Finally, the just price is flexible, ranging between the highest just price and the lowest in response to changes in the value-judgments of the buying and selling public. To trade within these limits is just; to buy or sell outside them is an injustice demanding restitution because it is a violation of commutative justice.

D. The Labor Contract

(1) Its Nature

The **labor contract** is *an agreement whereby one man hires out his labor to another for a wage.* Employment is not the same as investment in a company. The employee receives the security of a fixed income in the form of salary. The employer receives the profit from his investment. The employer takes the risk of loss. The employee shares neither profits nor losses.

The wage contract is an equitable agreement. The employer may not take all the profits and then inflict losses upon the workers in adverse periods. The payment of a just wage is his primary obligation; if he cannot pay it, he has ordinarily no moral right to engage in business. The worker receives a steady income from his labor. It is his labor that he sells, and when he has been justly paid for it, he has no claim upon profit as he has no liability for losses.

The establishment of a *minimum* just wage poses many formidable problems, many of which are moral. It is beyond our scope to attempt a solution in terms of dollars and cents; we wish simply to indicate certain principles and factors which must enter into a moral judgment of these problems.

(2) The Just Wage

The object of the labor contract is the exchange of the result of the laborer's work for a just wage. This entire matter is of crucial importance in our highly industrialized civilization in which it has ever-increasing importance in terms of the common good. It is also fertile ground for moral discussion. Although the principles involved are clear and certain, many conclusions remain tentative and in the category of informed opinion; certitude is difficult to establish when many variable contingencies must be considered. Here we make no claim to solving these complex problems; rather, we will present a summary of the basic principles involved, together with an indication of some of the more common trends of theological thought on the subject.

To begin with, a man's labor is not just one among the many commodities offered on the market. The determination of the just wage is not the same as the determination of the just price. Labor is essentially something human: it is the ordinary means for sustaining human life, it involves the dignity of the human person, and thus it cannot drop below that point where subhuman conditions would prevail. It is here that the just wage becomes much more a moral than an economic problem.

The labor contract is a reasonable means for getting work done rationally under competent direction; it brings both employer and employee proportionate benefits for their respective contributions to their mutual endeavor. The object of the contract is to exchange the fruit of the laborer's work for a just wage. The laborer sells his part in the product to the employer. How is this part to be valued in money? The answer to that question determines the just wage.

The fact that the product results in part from the fruit of human labor gives it a certain intrinsic and relatively constant value that is quite independent of the price it commands in the market. The reason for this is that the product must bring to the worker a wage that is sufficient for him to attain the purpose of human labor, which is a decent standard of living according to a just appraisal of his socioeconomic status.

It is important to note that the worker contracts only for the value of his labor's contribution to the product; thus he has no direct claim upon the whole value of the product such as he would enjoy through partnership with the employer. The limitation of the worker's *strict rights* is clearly taught by Pius XII:

> It would be just as untrue to assert that every particular business is of its nature a society, with its personnel relationships determined by the norms of distributive justice to the point where all without distinction—owners or not of the means of production—would be entitled to their share in the property, or at the very least in the profits of the enterprise. . . . The owner of the means of production, whoever he may be—individual owner, workers' association or corporation—must always within the limits of public economic law retain control of his economic decisions.[41]

Thus it is clear that in commutative justice the worker has a strict right only to a just wage. In *equity*, however, he has a title to a share in surplus profits, but his primary and strictest right is to the steady income of a just wage, free from the risks of partnership.

The minimum just wage must rest upon the most stable basis possible to preserve the worker from the hardship of fluctuating

[41]Address to Catholic employers, May 7, 1949.

income, insofar as the economy will allow. The **minimum just wage** is *the amount that any regularly employed unskilled worker should be paid for his labor.* To establish a workable general norm, skilled workers whose services command higher salaries, and exceptional employees like part-time workers, the handicapped and children, must be excluded. All these workers must be paid justly, but their specialized circumstances will not allow their wages to establish a norm for all. Their just wages will be determined by proportionate increase or decrease from the norm established as minimal for the unskilled worker.

The just wage must be measured according to the needs of life itself, for men work so they might make a living for themselves and their dependents. That is the universal purpose of those who work. The minimum just wage, then, must supply the essentials of human life.

In *Rerum Novarum* Leo XIII taught that the minimum just wage must enable the worker to lead a decent life proportionate to his social status. This teaching was clarified by Pius XI in *Quadragesimo Anno* to mean a **family living wage,** which should be determined in relation to three interdependent factors: first, the value of labor; secondly, the financial condition of industry; and thirdly, the needs of society.

Such a wage must be adequate to provide the worker and his family with a decent, modest home; sufficient decent food and clothing; reasonable rest and relaxation; ordinary recreation; and some surplus for emergencies and modest insurance coverage. But these items must be measured by realistic standards that do not confuse luxuries with necessities, at the same time making due allowances for the increases made in the standard of living.

While theologians agree that a family wage is due to the worker in justice, they dispute the precise kind of justice that governs the contract. All agree that an *individual* wage is due in commutative justice, and that any violation of the minimum just wage begets the obligation of restitution. Some claim that the family wage is due by the same kind of title, while others make the family wage an obligation of distributive justice, the violation of which would not require restitution. Protagonists of both views claim papal authority for their position, but no indisputable text can be cited by either side. Regarding employers' obligations, then, it is best to say for the present that the individual minimum wage is due in commutative justice, and the family wage in distributive justice.[42]

(3) The Right to Work

Man has a *right* to live and he must also have a *duty* to work, because men generally must live by their work. The duty to work is the foundation for man's **right to work**. Man's work must be the means of improving himself precisely as human. Thus man has no right to work which destroys his health or his life, which retards his development because it fails to challenge his capacities, which exposes him to grave spiritual and moral dangers, or which harms his social nature or the society of which he is a part.

This right to work is variously limited in the interest of the worker and his fellows, and in the interest of society generally. These limitations are sometimes established by nature, for all do not have the talents necessary for every kind of work. Professional groups often limit access to their profession; the same thing is true of certain unions. Employers restrict the right to work for their companies. The government sometimes bars certain people from some employments by law or directive.

A common form of restriction upon the right to work is enforced by the closed shop, or the union shop policies which require **membership** in a certain labor union as a necessary condition of employment. Within recent years, this form of restriction has been opposed by the proponents of what are called "right-to-work laws."[43]

[42]This entire matter is concisely treated in Jeremiah Newman, "The Just Wage," *Theology Digest,* V (1957), 120-26. A critique of this article by Edward Duff, S.J., is summarized in the same issue, 127 f.

[43]An excellent theological appraisal of the controversy over so-called "right-to-work laws" is given by John C. Cronin, S.S., and Francis W. Carney, "The Morality of Right-to-Work Laws," *Proceedings of the Catholic Theological Society of America,* XII (1957), 193-215. A divergent view is presented by John E. Cogan, S.J., *Voluntary Unionism for Free Americans* (Washington: National Right To Work Committee, 1957).

(4) Profit-Sharing

The workers' right to a share in profits cannot be based upon commutative justice, because such sharing is not part of the customary labor contract. There is a case in equity for such sharing, however, and many moralists and economists claim that profit-sharing has many advantages for all concerned. It does appear to be a practical way to effect the greater distribution of wealth and the more wide-spread ownership so constantly called for by the popes. But it is important in discussing this problem not to go beyond the limits imposed by the nature of the work contract, and to make the error of resting the case for profit-sharing upon commutative justice. The case should rest upon equity—which pertains to the area of moral obligation rather than of legal debt.[44]

(5) Labor Practices

What is the moral status of such practices as the union shop and the closed shop? In principle, these practices cannot be considered as immoral. Indeed, the worker must exercise his own right to work in such a way as to foster his fellow-workers' rights. Now collective bargaining is the only practicable means the worker has to protect his basic rights in the labor market. As a social being he has a duty and a right to associate with his fellows, particularly in view of the common good. If the union, *both in avowed intent and in actual administration,* is devoted to fostering the workers' perfection by just collective means which individuals alone could not attain— so that without the collective activities of the union he would be deprived of the opportunity to achieve his perfection through work—then the worker is obliged to support the union. The worker remains free, of course, to work in other circumstances of his own choosing. Then, too, it savors of injustice for some to accept the benefits secured through good unionism while they absolve themselves of the obligations inherent in union membership and union activities.

---

[44]There is a vast amount of literature on this subject, and it can best be consulted through periodical indices. One highly significant experiment in profit-sharing was inaugurated by Mr. Albert Coburn of Beaumont, Texas. The operation of the plan is described by Pacificus Kennedy, O.F.M., "Profit-sharing Prophet," *Friar,* V (1956), 47-51.

A formidable moral problem confronts the members of unions which, either by intent or by actual administration, show that they are in effect opposed to the perfection of the worker or to the common good of society. In such cases the worker would be wrong to co-operate actively, and he would have the duty to strive within the limits of his capacities to improve or to supplant the union.

The universality of the right to work indicates a parallel obligation resting upon society generally to provide adequate opportunities for employment. In times of prosperity this poses no great problem, but in times of financial depression the problem becomes extremely acute. Under these circumstances labor and business organizations have obligations to co-operate for the equitable relief of hardship, and if private enterprise will not or cannot safeguard the workers' rights, then the state has the obligation to do so. The problems of the unemployed and the unemployable must be the constant object of concerted efforts, and must be handled in a manner similar to that indicated for general unemployment in depressions.

(6) The Strike

Organized labor's ultimate weapon to secure its demands is the *strike, an organized stoppage of work. Direct* strikes involve workers who labor under the same grievances; *sympathetic* or secondary strikes are called by workers who have no grievances of their own in order to support other workers who have; *general* strikes are work stoppages throughout an entire country to secure political ends.

Direct strikes are justifiable by the principle of the double effect. Workers have a natural right to organize in order to secure justice by limiting those profits which employers seek to gain unjustly through curtailing just wages or maintaining poor working conditions. When a just grievance is the cause, there is proportionate reason for a strike called by a legitimate union as a last resort which will use just and peaceful means of persuasion.

Secondary or sympathetic strikes are justified only when directed against unjust employers. It is immoral to make the innocent suffer for the crimes of others. General strikes amount to political revolutions and must be judged by principles relating to political action.

A lockout is a stoppage of work by the employer. It is his ultimate weapon against injustice on the part of workers. Like the strike, it must be judged by the principle of the double effect. Sympathetic lockouts, which shut down all factories in a given locality in order to break a strike in one of them, are immoral, because the suffering caused among the many is not proportioned to whatever gains may be secured for the few.

A boycott is an organized effort to suppress trading with a particular company. This tactic is to be judged in the same way as a strike. Secondary boycotts are directed against firms dealing with the boycotted company in order to insure the effectiveness of the action. A company whose own policies are above reproach should not be made to suffer for the injustices of others in business. The secondary boycott must be judged in the same way as sympathetic or secondary strikes.

E. The Sins against Justice in Voluntary Exchanges

(1) Fraud

The various acts by which justice is violated in buying and selling are grouped together under fraud. This includes every violation of the just price, concealment of substantial defects in merchandise, the substitution of inferior goods, the delivery of damaged goods, unreasonable delay in payment, etc. **Fraud,** then, is *commutative injustice perpetrated by violating the contract of buying and selling.* As an act of injustice, fraud is of its nature a mortal sin, but it admits venial violations when smaller sums are involved.

(2) Usury

Usury etymologically signifies the price of a thing's use. In a technical context it means *the price charged for the use of something borrowed, or profit realized from a loan on the unique title of the loan itself.*

The principle upon which usury is judged to be in violation of justice is that it is not moral to sell the same thing twice. Two types of goods may be involved in a loan: goods whose use involves their consumption, and goods whose use is distinct from themselves. In the first case, if one charges for the use of a consumptive good there is no second title at all; the thing is not distinct from its use. It would not be right to sell a bottle of wine and then charge a person for drinking it. In the second case, there is a charge made for something which does not belong to the lender: the use of the thing is transmitted by the fact of the loan. Money is an excellent example of a consumptive good. It disappears when it is used.

Thus is summarized the ancient argument against usury. For St. Thomas, usury was not *excessive* interest, it was any interest whatever that was taken on the sole title of the loan itself.

Today, the trend is to consider money differently than as a means of exchange. With the proliferation of opportunities for ready investment through capitalism, money is coming to be regarded in some quarters as a good which fructifies. Money invested, they say, begets more money. For such thinkers, usury is a crime against the positive law which forbids excessive interest, rather than against the natural law which prohibits charging for the use of a consumptive good.

In the last analysis, the underlying theories of money do not affect the practical moral judgments of interest-taking. The more recent theory holds for an **intrinsic** title to interest; the ancient concept allows interest to be taken for reasons **extrinsic** to the contract or loan. A lender may justly charge for the expenses of the loan (*damnum emergens*), or for the inability to make advantageous purchases while his money is on loan (*lucrum cessans*), and for the risk he takes of losing the principal (*periculum sortis*). These titles are surely valid today, and no competent moralist would deny the liceity of accepting a just price for a loan in view of them.

It is safe to say that in today's society there usually exist such extrinsic titles to moderate interest. In practice, borrowing and lending contracts are strictly regulated by civil law. It is to be presumed that the law is just, unless the contrary is manifestly evident. There still exist, however, individuals who operate as "loan sharks," charging exhorbitant interest which cannot be justified by any known moral principle.

8. THE QUASI-INTEGRAL PARTS OF JUSTICE

The integral parts of any virtue are those acts which must concur as necessary conditions for the perfect exercise of the virtue. These integral parts are spoken of by analogy with comparable things in the physical order, as the roof, walls and foundation are integral to a house. When predicated of virtues, these acts are called "quasi-integral" parts.

If justice is regarded as a special virtue whereby each one gives what is due to his neighbor, then there are two special acts which must be present in the perfect act of justice. The first of these acts is to do the good that one's neighbor deserves; the second is to avoid the evil that is harmful to him.

Justice *establishes* an equality among men regarding things and actions; this it does by positive acts of doing good, whereby each one renders to others what is their due. Justice also *preserves* the equality it establishes; this it accomplishes by avoiding evil which is harmful to others. Avoiding evil does not consist in not acting at all; rather it is a positive act of the will resisting evil to preserve the balance of justice.

Thus, there are two acts which concur in the perfect act of justice: doing the obligatory good, and resisting the undue evil. These are the quasi-integral parts of justice, which cannot exist apart from them.

9. SUMMARY AND CONCLUSION

This chapter has been concerned with the general principles of justice and the more common ways in which justice is violated. It is not an exhaustive treatment. It is rather a statement of principles and norms.

The assimilation of the material will be best achieved in its application to problems and cases presented by the teacher. It will promptly emerge that moral judgments are not easily made and that moral theology is a complicated business. The mind grasps principles with comparative ease; it applies them with much travail. Unfortunately for our desire for comfort, and for the natural appetite of the mind for clarity and certainty, moral cases involve not only principles but contingent facts as well. There is a great deal of room for error in determining facts and relating them to principles.

This should be no occasion for discouragement. Moral science requires experience, and ease will increase as experience is acquired. It should never be forgotten that the possession of a virtue itself imparts a certain ease in judging the matter of the virtue. Nobody can recognize justice more quickly or easily than a just man.

Our treatment of justice reaches its most significant statement in the social doctrine of the Church. Some of the more striking pronouncements of modern pontiffs will serve as conclusions to this chapter.

1. "The social question is undoubtedly an economic question, but even more than that it is a question which concerns the ordered regulation of human society. And, in its deepest sense, it is a moral and therefore a religious question. As such it may be summed up thus: Have men—from the individual to the people, and right through to the community of peoples—the moral strength to create such public conditions that in the life of society there will not be any individuals nor any peoples who are merely objects (that is to say, deprived of all rights and exposed to exploitation by others), but all instead will be subjects—that is, having a legitimate share in the formation of the social order, and able, according to their art or profession, to live happily and tranquilly with sufficient means of support, protected efficiently against the violence of an egoistic economy, in freedom defined by the general welfare, and with full human dignity, each respecting his neighbor as he respects himself?"[45]

2. "We have said that the state must not absorb the individual or the family; both should be allowed free and untrammelled

[45]Pope Pius XII, address to the youth of Italian Catholic Action, Sept. 12, 1948.

action as far as is consistent with the common good and the interests of others. Nevertheless, rulers should anxiously safeguard the community and all its parts: the community, because the conservation of the community is so emphatically the business of the supreme power that the safety of the commonwealth is not only the first law, but is a government's whole reason of existence; and the parts, because both philosophy and the Gospel agree in laying down that the object of the administration of the state should be not the advantage of the ruler, but the benefit of those over whom he rules. The gift of authority is from God, and is, as it were, a participation of the highest of all sovereignties; and it should be exercised as the power of God is exercised—with a fatherly solicitude which not only guides the whole but reaches to details as well.

"Whenever the general interest of any particular class suffers, or is threatened with evils which can in no other way be met, the public authority must step in to meet them. Now among the interests of the public, as of private individuals, are these: that peace and good order should be maintained; that family life should be carried on in accordance with God's laws and those of nature; that religion should be reverenced and obeyed; that a high standard of morality should prevail in public and private life; that the sanctity of justice should be respected, and that no one should injure another with impunity; that the members of the commonwealth should grow up to man's estate strong and robust, and capable, if need be, of guarding and defending their country.

"If by a strike, or other combination of workmen, there should be imminent danger of disturbance to the public peace; or if circumstances were such that among the laboring population the ties of family life were relaxed; if religion were found to suffer through the workmen not having time and opportunity to practice it; if in workshops and factories there were danger to morals through the mixing of the sexes or from an occasion of evil; or if employers laid burdens upon the workmen which were unjust, or degraded them with conditions that were repugnant to their dignity as human beings; finally, if health were endangered by excessive labor, or by work unsuited to sex or age—in these cases there can be no question that, within certain limits, it would be right to call in the help and authority of the law. The limits must be determined by the nature of the occasion which calls for the law's interference— the principle being this, that the law must not undertake more, nor go further, than is required for the remedy of the evil or removal of the danger."[46]

3. "He who would have the star of peace to shine permanently over society must do all in his power to restore to the human person the dignity which God conferred upon him from the beginning. He must resist the excessive herding together of human beings, as though they were a soulless mass. He must set his face against their disintegration in economic, social, political, intellectual and moral life, against lack of solid principles and firm convictions, against their excessive reliance upon instinct and emotion, and also against their fickleness of mood. He must favor, by all legitimate means and in every sphere of life, social forms which render possible and guarantee full personal responsibility in regard to things both temporal and spiritual."[47]

4. For a just and true peace—not merely concord, and far more realistic and perfect than cold war "co-existence"—Pope Pius XII in his Christmas message of 1939 pointed out the principles that must be recognized to establish internal order and international harmony. This "five-point peace program" embraces the following principles:

1) The right of life and independence for all nations, whether they be large or small, strong or weak. 2) The liberation of the nations from the heavy burden caused by the race for armaments, and from the danger that material force, instead of protecting rights, will lead to their violation. 3) Creation or reconstitution of international institutions, eliminating mistakes of the past, calculated to guarantee the fulfillment of peace terms, and with the power to revise and correct them where necessary. 4) Provision for meeting the real needs and just demands of nations and peoples as well as ethnical minorities.

[46]Pope Leo XIII, encyclical *Rerum Novarum* (The Condition of Labor), May 15, 1891.
[47]Pope Pius XII, Christmas message, 1942.

5) The penetration of leaders and peoples with the spirit of intimate, acute responsibility, springing from the observance of the divine law, moral justice and universal love.

5. "A charity which deprives the workingman of the salary to which he has a strict title in justice is not charity at all, but only its empty name and hollow semblance. The wage-earner is not to receive as alms what is his due in justice. And let no one attempt with trifling charitable donations to exempt himself from the great duties imposed by justice. Both justice and charity often dictate obligations touching on the very same subject matter, but under different aspects; and the very dignity of the workingman makes him justly and acutely sensitive to the duties of others in his regard."[48]

6. "How completely deceived are those inconsiderate reformers who, zealous only for commutative justice, proudly disdain the help of charity! Clearly charity cannot take the place of justice unfairly withheld. But, even though a state of things be pictured in which every man receives at last all that is his due, a wide field will nevertheless remain open for charity. For justice alone, even though most faithfully observed, can remove indeed the cause of social strife, but can never bring about a union of hearts and minds. Yet this union, binding men together, is the main principle of stability in all institutions, no matter how perfect they may seem, which aim at establishing social peace and promoting mutual aid. In its absence, as repeated experience proves, the wisest regulations come to nothing. Then only will it be possible to unite all in harmonious striving for the common good, when all sections of society have the intimate conviction that they are members of a single family and children of the same heavenly Father, and further, that they are 'one body in Christ and everyone members one of another,' so that 'if one member suffer anything, all members suffer with it' (Rom. 12:5).

"Then the rich and others in power will change their former negligence of their poorer brethren into solicitous and effective regard, will listen with kindly feeling to their just complaints, and will readily forgive them the faults and mistakes they possibly make. Working-

---

[48]Pope Pius XI, encyclical *Divini Redemptoris* (On Atheistic Communism), March 19, 1937.

men too will lay aside all feelings of hatred or envy, which the instigators of social strife arouse so skillfully. Not only will they cease to feel weary of the position assigned them by divine providence in human society; they will become proud of it, well aware that every man by doing his duty is working usefully and honorably for the common good, and is following in the footsteps of him, who, being in the form of God, chose to become a carpenter among men, and to be known as the Son of a carpenter."[49]

BIBLIOGRAPHICAL NOTE

St. Thomas' consideration of the virtue of justice in itself and its subjective and integral parts is taken up in the *Summa*, II-II, Questions LVII-LXXIX. There is an abundance of material written in English on this subject, of which we can give only a cross-section. Josef Pieper makes a rather penetrating study of the deeper implications of the human phenomenon of justice in his work entitled *Justice* (New York: Pantheon, 1955). Papal teaching is very important for the cogency of the Church's application of moral principles to modern social problems. Valuable in this respect will be: *The Pope's New Order* by Philip Hughes (New York: The Macmillan Co., 1944); *The Church Speaks to the Modern World: The Social Teachings of Leo XIII* by Etienne Gilson (Garden City, N. Y.: Doubleday and Company, 1954); *Forty Years After: Pius XI and the Social Order* by Raymond J. Miller, C.SS.R. (St. Paul: Radio Replies Press, 1947); *Papal Thought on the State* by Gerard F. Yates, S.J. (New York: Appleton-Century-Crofts, 1958); and an article in the periodical *The Pope Speaks*, V (1959), 209-213, entitled "The Church and Social Progress," by Pope Pius XII. A rather technical study of St. Thomas' concept of general justice can be found in Jeremiah Newman's *Foundations of Justice* (Cork University Press, 1954).

[49] Pope Pius XI, encyclical *Quadragesimo Anno* (Reconstructing the Social Order), May 15, 1931.

Other aspects of justice can be examined at length in *Distributive Justice* (New York: The Macmillan Co., 1922) and *The Church and Labor* (New York: The Macmillan Co., 1920), two works of almost classical stature by John A. Ryan; *Social Justice* by W. F. Drummond, S.J. (Milwaukee: The Bruce Publishing Co., 1955); and *Catholic Social Principles* by John J. Cronin, S.S. (Milwaukee: Bruce, 1950).

Among the many books expressing the viewpoint of Catholic theology on medical problems, three are particularly recommended: Charles J. McFadden, O.S.A., *Medical Ethics* (3rd ed.; Philadelphia: Davis, 1953), the most extensive text on the subject in English; Gerald Kelly, S.J., *Medico-Moral Problems* (St. Louis: The Catholic Hospital Association, 1958), a concise reference work which covers the entire range of relevant problems, valuable for itself and as a guide to the literature in the field; John P. Kenny, O.P., *Principles of Medical Ethics* (Westminster: Newman, 1952), a brief text which is clearly written and offers excellent material for a one-semester course in medical ethics. Periodical literature on medical ethics is very extensive. An excellent bibliography is given by John J. Lynch, S.J., "A Topical Index to Moral Problems of Medicine," *Linacre Quarterly*, August, 1954.

Other articles of interest in the vast field of justice are the following: "An Approach to the Problem of Restitution," by H. Renard, S.J., in *Modern Schoolman*, XXXVI (1959), 77-89; "Distribution of Wealth," by J. M. Paul in *Social Order*, VIII (1958), 207-212; J. V. Schall's "Totality of Justice: from Justice to Friendship" in *The Thomist*, XX (1957), 1-26; "Justice and Charity," by J. Lacroix in *Theology Digest*, II (1954), 182-185; "The Scope of Distributive Justice," by D. O'Donoghue in *Irish Theological Quarterly*, XXI (1954), 291-308; "Malice and Gravity of Injustice," by Sister Therese in *Irish Ecclesiastical Record*, LXXXVII (1957), 47-50; "Morality and Racial Segregation," by Archbishop J. F. Rummel in *The Catholic Mind*, LIV (1956), 296-300; "Morality of Mutilation: towards a Revision of the Treatise," by G. Kelly, S.J., in *Theological Studies*, XVII (1956), 322-344; "No Place for Rain: Is Our Society Subsisting without Either the Vice of Injustice or the Virtue of Justice?" by Walter Farrell, O.P., in *The Thomist*, XII (1949), 397-424; and "Theology of Social Action" by J. Newman in *Irish Theological Quarterly*, XXII (1955), 31-48.

On the problems of modern warfare, three articles in *Theology Digest* should be consulted: Pelayo Zamayón, "Morality of War Today and in the Future," *Theology Digest*, V (1957), 2-5; John C. Ford, S.J., "The Hydrogen Bombing of Cities," *ibid.*, 6-8; John R. Connery, S.J., "Morality of Nuclear Armament," *ibid*, 9-12. An unusually provocative article, one well worth reading by everyone, is Victor White, O.P., "The Morality of War," *Life of the Spirit*, IV (1949), 97-104.

A concise and excellent treatment of the fundamental problems of penology, invaluable in its field, is the survey by Illtud Evans, O.P., *et al.*, "The Purpose of Punishment," *Blackfriars*, XXXVIII (1957), 195 ff.

Required reading in the field of Church-state relationships in education is the exceptional article, "A Case of Distributive Justice," by William Gorman in the pamphlet *Religion and the Schools* (New York: The Fund for the Republic, 1959).

CHAPTER THIRTEEN

Religion

1. INTRODUCTION

The virtue of religion is a *potential part* of the virtue of justice.
A potential part of a virtue is so called by comparison with the soul
and its potential parts. Each potential part (the intellect, for example)
accounts for some of the soul's activities; no one part represents all
that the soul is able to do. Or, to put it another way, the human soul
is able—is in potency by reason of the intellect—to apprehend, to
judge and to reason, activities which are a part, but only a part,
of what the soul is able to do. The intellect is therefore a potential
part of the soul.

Similarly the virtue of religion accounts for a part of the activity of
the virtue of justice. It represents one specific area of the activity of
which justice is capable. As a virtue annexed to justice two things
regarding religion should be observed: 1) religion has something in
common with justice—both virtues are concerned with a debt to be
paid to another; 2) religion lacks some power, some perfection
which justice has. Justice, involving a relationship between one
man and another, is able to pay its debt in perfect equality.
Religion, based upon a relationship between man and God, is
powerless to pay God as much as is owed to him.

But while these facts sufficiently underline the kind of duties and the nature of the obligations which religion implies, they tell us nothing of the excellence of the virtue. For religion is the most eminent of all the virtues, including justice, which are concerned with human action as their object. Our relations with God in the supernatural order, to be sure, are founded in faith, burgeon in hope, flower and fructify in divine friendship. But still we are creatures, only the more dependent on God for the love which elevates us to his truth, his power, his very life. And as grace presupposes and perfects nature, as fraternal charity presupposes and perfects the necessary basic relationship with our fellowman which is procured by justice, so the theological virtues presuppose the judicious rectification of our relations with God and our reactions to our different duties, in order to bring to proper supernatural perfection the homage and service of which religion is the source. This intimate alliance with faith, hope and charity perhaps best suggests the pre-eminence of this virtue which has to do with our creaturely relations with our Creator, our Lord, our Savior, our Alpha and Omega.

The virtue of religion will be considered according to this outline:

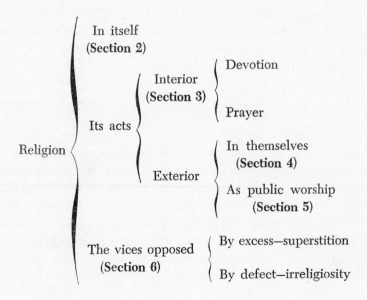

Religion
- In itself (Section 2)
- Its acts
  - Interior (Section 3)
    - Devotion
    - Prayer
  - Exterior
    - In themselves (Section 4)
    - As public worship (Section 5)
- The vices opposed (Section 6)
  - By excess—superstition
  - By defect—irreligiosity

2. RELIGION IN ITSELF

A. Its Meaning

The word "religion" is probably derived from the Latin word which signifies *a binding together*. Man is bound in a variety of ways to a multitude of persons and things, but the binding together which is all-important for him is his relationship with the being who is the First Cause of *everything* man is, and the *ultimate* reason for which man exists.

This relationship between man and God is of its nature one in which man subjects himself to God and strives by whatever means are his to render to God the worship, the acknowledgment of dependence, the gratitude which are God's strict right. As First Cause God is the author of every perfection which man has; as Ultimate End he is the reason for every perfection of which man is capable. Religion, then, based upon completeness of dependence, is concerned with a completeness of subjection and of worship.

The greatest of the Christian virtues, charity, is a friendship between God and man. It establishes, therefore, mysterious gift of God that it is, some kind of equality between God and man. It is an equality only of proportion, it is true, *but it is truly an equality*. Such equality has no place in the virtue of religion. Religion is the virtue of the servant, the virtue of subordination.

B. The Nature of Religion

Because religion is concerned with man's subordination to God, it is a virtue essential to man's perfection. Man's perfection demands independence of things less than he is, but it equally demands subordination to what is greater than he. Man is made independent of lesser things by the activities of the virtues of fortitude and temperance to be explored in following chapters. By these two virtues man is freed: 1) from the infinity of inordinate fears that beset his life; 2) from the tendency to enslave himself to the pleasures that appeal to the senses.

If a man does not dominate these fears and these pleasures they will dominate and enslave him. Man's perfection *demands* independence of these things.

But to what advantage would man hold himself aloof from a slavish subordination to that which is less than he is, if at the same time he refuses subordination to his superior? If man cuts himself off from the source of his perfection, whence would that perfection come? St. Thomas points out:

> By the very fact that we revere and honor God our mind is subjected to him. In this its perfection lies, since a thing is perfected by being subjected to its superior. The body, e.g., is perfected by being quickened by the soul and the air by being illuminated by the sun.[1]

Religion, then, is a most special virtue, and its activity is essential to man's perfection. Since the theological virtues have God himself under several aspects for their objects, religion is not a theological virtue. The **material object** of religion is those actions of man which he performs in recognition of God's supreme dominion over all his creatures: *the worship of God*. Because it deals with human actions it is a moral virtue. Because it directs human actions to the worship of God it is the highest of the moral virtues, having among them all the highest object.

What is the aspect or motive in virtue of which man offers his actions to God—the **formal object** of religion? By reason of his supernal excellence God has a strict right in justice to the testimony his subject, man, can give to that excellence and to the witness man can bear. By his acts of worship, then, man seeks to pay this debt, to establish an equality, so far as he can, between himself and God. Obviously this can only be an imperfect and relative equality, one established only in consideration of man's limited ability and God's free acceptance of this service in lieu of the full recognition that is his objective due. But it is the special rightfulness of this relative equality, its goodness and justice, which moves man, immediately and proximately, to render due worship to the transcendent God.

Hence we may define **religion** as *the moral virtue which inclines man to manifest to God the worship that is his right as the First Cause of all things*.

[1] *Summa*, II-II, q. 81, a. 7.

C. The Excellence of Religion

Religion has a special relationship with the other moral virtues: it occupies a central position between the other moral virtues to which it is superior, and the theological virtues to which it is inferior. For this reason it plays a unifying or commanding role in the activities of the other moral virtues. In a manner similar to the way in which the acts of *all* the virtues are incomplete and imperfect unless they are unified in charity and commanded by charity, so the acts of the moral virtues are incomplete and imperfect unless they are unified in religion and commanded by religion in the service of God and in recognition of his supreme dominion over all creatures.

To religion, in this role of unifying and commanding the activities of all the moral virtues, St. Thomas gives the special name **sanctity** (*holiness*). There is a sense in which the activities of all the moral virtues are implicit in, and required for the practice of the virtue of religion. Hence **moral sanctity** or perfection (the Christian perfection inherent in the practice of the moral virtues) is *formally* in the virtue of religion, just as the **totality** of Christian perfection is *formally* in the virtue of charity.

Sanctity implies two things:

1) *Purity*—i.e., freedom from contact with baser things: "Purity is necessary," says St. Thomas, "in order that the mind may be applied to God, since the human mind is soiled by contact with lower things, just as all things depreciate when admixed with baser things—silver, for example, when mixed with lead."[2] Without this freedom, this "purity," the mind of man becomes so preoccupied and fascinated—as by the legendary hypnosis of the basilisk—that it cannot be applied to God; sense images, sense movements simply overpower it. Hence the advice of St. Paul: "Strive for peace with all men, and for that holiness without which no man will see God" (Heb. 12:14).

2) *Firmness*—i.e., the stability of union with the superior. Fully to be dedicated to God, to the service that will give all of oneself

[2]*Summa*, II-II, q. 81, a. 8.

and one's activity, necessarily indicates an unrepentant commitment, an immobility where deviation is catastrophe. Again the Apostle gives us the worthy and just explanation: "I am sure that neither death, nor life, nor angels, nor principalities, nor things present, nor things to come, nor powers, nor height, nor depth, nor any other creature, will be able to separate us from the love of God, which is in Christ Jesus our Lord" (Rom. 8:38-39).

Both of these are the work of the virtue of religion. Religion presupposes that man is reasonably withdrawn from inferior things and firmly unites him to God as his first beginning and last end.

3. The Interior Acts of Religion

God's right to man's reasonable service is universal, i.e., it includes everything that man is and everything man makes use of in attaining his final goal. Consequently everything that man is or that he makes use of should be represented in some way in his worship of God. A complete listing of the acts of religion shows that this is, in fact, the case.

Man offers to God the two highest faculties of his soul, the will and intellect, by the acts of **devotion** and **prayer.** He offers his body by **adoration.** External things are given to God by **sacrifices, oblations, first fruits, tithes** and **vows,** which are promises to offer something to God; these external things belong in some sense to man. But he also makes use in his worship of God of things which are God's. These are either the **sacraments**—material things which God has chosen to be the signs and causes of his grace—or **God's name.** The importance of the sacraments in man's sanctification and the space their study requires demands that they be reserved for consideration to the last volume of this work, and because they are not alone acts of worship of God but also relics of Christ's passion and death—the perfect sacrifice of thanksgiving, praise, petition and propitiation—their treatment there is most fitting. The name of God is used by man in the

worship of God in three ways: in the taking of an **oath;** in **adjuring**
or inducing another to speak truthfully; or in right actions for the purpose of prayer or **praise** of God.

To clarify these points the following outline may be proposed:

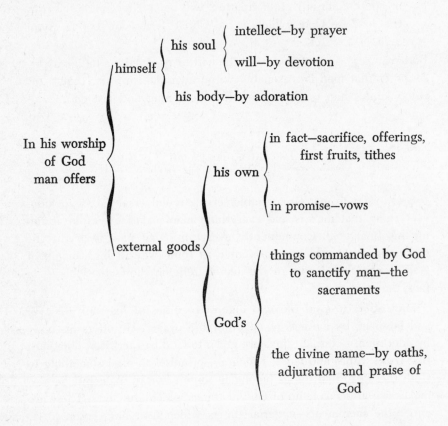

In his worship
of God
man offers

himself
 his soul
  intellect—by prayer
  will—by devotion
 his body—by adoration

external goods
 his own
  in fact—sacrifice, offerings,
   first fruits, tithes
  in promise—vows
 God's
  things commanded by God
   to sanctify man—the
   sacraments
  the divine name—by oaths,
   adjuration and praise of
   God

We shall first of all discuss the interior acts of the virtue of
religion, reserving for the following section (**Section 4**) the detailed
examination of its external acts. So we now take up the two great
human acts which are man's virtuous acknowledgment of the creative
transcendence, the sovereign authority and the overwhelming love
of God.

A. The Act of Devotion

(1) Devotion in Itself

The first and principal act of religion is **devotion**—a weak and much maligned word which badly seeks to render in English the virile Latin *devovere*, "to submit oneself absolutely, with all the power and energy of one's rational will." St. Thomas defines devotion as *a promptness of the will in those things that concern the worship of God*, "the will to give oneself readily to things concerning the worship of God."[3] By this promptness St. Thomas understands an eager and utter dedication of the will itself to the worship of God. The will is the source of all human movement (human acts as opposed to acts of man). This is true whether the actions be actions of the will itself or actions of other powers that are moved by the will. Consequently, if the will itself is eagerly and without reservation dedicated to God's service, it follows that the whole man is so dedicated. This is the importance of devotion in man's life and the reason why it is the first and principal act of religion. Without devotion there can be no true act of religion—a fact we recognize, even when our words drain the reality of much of its vitality and force, in speaking of a "devout" prayer, a "devout" sign of the cross or a "devout" sacrifice.

The will of man must first be dedicated, truly and wholly consecrated to God's service; then, as mover of all man's activities, it stamps its character, its type of movement, on all man's efforts to worship God. In this respect a parallel between charity and religion suggests itself:

Habit	Principal Act	Secondary Act	Object
charity	love	almsgiving	union with God
religion	devotion	adoration	subjection to God

[3] *Summa*, II-II, q. 82, a. 1.

Every secondary act of the virtue of charity must be moved and characterized by charity's principal act, which is love: almsgiving which is not moved and molded by love is not almsgiving at all. Just so, neither is any act of religion a true act of worship of God unless it is moved and shaped by the eager and utter dedication of the will to God which is devotion.

(2) The Cause of Devotion

Since the principal concern of a theological text on the virtues must be with the infused virtues, our interest is in the acts of the supernatural virtue of religion, even though all of the demands, duties and obligations of man's worship of God are based on the natural relationship which obtains between creature and Creator. With respect, then, to the principal act of supernatural religion, the chief cause of devotion must be God himself. Only God can be the principal cause of a supernatural habit such as religion, or, by the gift of actual grace, of the acts which proceed from that habit. Such a virtue and its activity are as much a gift of God and as far above man's natural powers as is sanctifying grace itself. God is, then, the extrinsic cause of devotion.

But the cause of devotion within man is meditation or contemplation. This contemplation is principally a consideration of two things: the goodness and loving-kindness of God, and man's own shortcomings and dependence upon God. A profound awareness of both truths is necessary for devotion. God is our Creator; and supernatural insight informs us of a more intimate and loving relationship: he is our Father. He has, therefore, a strict right to complete service on the part of his creature, of his son. On the other hand, consider man's own shortcomings—not exclusively nor even principally one's own sins, the acts of rebellion and disobedience and ingratitude, but rather the more basic condition of man as creature, his need to lean upon God as the source of whatever perfection is possible to him, and so removed from God that he is infinitely our creditor with regard to our gratuitous sharing in the intimacy of his own life, the inexpressible communication of divinity which is the Trinity of divine Persons.

Well may we exclaim with St. Paul, "What hast thou that thou hast not received. And if thou hast received it, why dost thou boast as if thou hadst not received it?" (I Cor. 4:7).

Meditation or contemplation is the necessary intrinsic cause of devotion; in fact there can be no devotion without it. Whether it be the first halting attempts of the beginner at meditation, or the lofty infused contemplation which is beyond man's power to acquire, or any stage of progress between them, awareness of God's infinite goodness and man's own inadequacy is essential to devotion. A thing must be known to be willed, for the object of the will is the good proposed by the mind. Since God is lovable above all things, it is the consideration of the Godhead itself which is most powerful in inciting to love and consequently to devotion. Yet because of the weakness of man's intellect, he is led to knowledge and love of the divine through knowledge and love of sensible objects, "through knowing God through visible things he is caught up to love of things invisible" (Preface of the feast of Christmas): "Since the creation of the world his invisible attributes are clearly seen—his everlasting power also and divinity—being understood through the things that are made" (Rom. 1:20). This is why meditation on what pertains to the humanity of Christ is so powerful in exciting devotion.[4]

(3) The Effects of Devotion

The direct and principal effect of devotion is joy, because devotion is chiefly caused by a consideration—immediate or through the humanity of the Son of God—of God's goodness. Direct considera-

[4]This is not only the recommendation of a speculative theologian and practical mystic like St. Thomas (*Summa*, II-II, q. 82, a. 4, ad 2), it is also the advice of that practical Carmelite theologian, the speculative Spanish mystic, St. Theresa of Avila: "I can clearly see—and since that time have always seen—that it is God's will, if we are to please him and he is to grant us great favors, that this should be done through his most sacred humanity, in which, his majesty said, he is well pleased. Very, very many times have I learned this by experience—the Lord has told it to me. I have seen clearly that it is by this door that we must enter if we wish his sovereign majesty to show us great secrets. Even if you reach the summit of contemplation, therefore, you must seek no other way: that way alone is safe. It is through this Lord of ours that all blessings come. He will show us the way, we must look at his life—that is our best pattern" (*The Life of the Holy Mother Theresa of Jesus*, Chap. 22).

tion of man's defects causes sorrow—a sorrow that is according to God: "the sorrow . . . that produces repentance that surely tends to salvation, whereas the sorrow that is according to the world produces death" (II Cor. 7:10). Indirectly, however, an awareness of God's goodness causes sorrow, for man is not perfectly united to God in this life; and in the same way a knowledge of man's defects causes joy, for it arouses hope of God's help. And thus the psalmist sings: "athirst is my soul for God, for the living God. When shall I go and behold the face of God? My tears are my food day and night" (Ps. 41:3-4). The eager and complete surrender of his will to God produces in man this strange mixture of joy and sorrow. Yet man's life, even in this present state, ought to be more and more filled with joy as his surrender to God becomes more and more perfect; if it is not, the sign should be interpreted as a lack of holiness (sanctity), of an attachment to baser things or a lack of firm dedication to the divine service.

The joy of devotion is called by St. Thomas "a spiritual joy of the mind."[5] Is there any connection between this joy and a feeling of devotion, what is called *sensible* devotion? To answer this question— by no means an unimportant one—we must observe, first of all, that devotion itself is an act of the will; in itself, then, devotion has nothing to do with passion or feeling, and the senses of themselves know nothing of the object of devotion. On the other hand, experience shows that feelings and sensible devotion have much to do with man's worship of God.

The answer to this practical paradox lies in the unit of the human being. Although man has many diverse principles of activity to correspond to the diverse principles of his nature—matter and spirit—he is, nonetheless, *one thing substantially*. If the will is set in motion toward an object proper to it, a corresponding movement of the feelings or passions is to be expected, because man is one thing. If the sense appetite moves toward an object proper to the senses a corresponding movement of the will (always allowing for its freedom) is to be expected. Thus when the will, incited by a consideration of

[5] *Summa*, II-II, q. 82, a. 4.

God's goodness and man's shortcomings, surrenders itself eagerly and completely to God, and when the spiritual joy which is the effect of such an offering floods the soul, it is not to be wondered at that sensible feelings like love, desire, pleasure and hope take vehement possession of the soul. It is difficult to see how a normal human being in a normal condition can continue to surrender his will eagerly and completely without arousing such feelings. Devotion itself would seem in such a case to be halfhearted and remiss.

God himself teaches us in the Incarnation the importance of the visible and the sensible; Christ instituted the visible Church and the seven sacraments to teach the same truth; the Church in her liturgy, in her insistence on ceremony and rite, and in her multiplicity of "devotions" to aid devotion pays tribute to the truth that man needs objects he can see and hear and touch in his spiritual worship of God. The spiritual act of devotion and the spiritual joy it causes will overflow normally into the feelings of the senses. And feelings, if they are not sought for their own sake, will influence devotion itself.

B. Prayer

(1) Its Essence and Object

The second interior act of religion is prayer. It is described by St. John Damascene as "the lifting up of the mind to God,"[6] and in this general sense would include any such movement of the intellect and will to God, arising not only from the virtue of religion but from the theological virtues, from penance or humility or from similar virtues; so meditation and contemplation are frequently called "mental prayer." More properly, however, prayer is restricted to the raising up of the mind to God which flows from religion, such acts as praising and blessing God, thanksgiving and petition. In the most proper sense of the word, only this last act of petition is prayer, and it is defined as *the pious petition of suitable gifts from God.*[7] This

[6]*On the True Faith*, Bk. III, Chap. 24.
[7]St. John Damascene, *loc. cit.*

points up the fact that prayer is an explicit manifestation of our desires to another, in order to obtain something from him **by way of a favor;** it is a request for **fitting** gifts, things that we may properly ask from God and he may in all propriety give us; and it is made to **God alone,** who alone can of himself fulfill these desires.

Hence prayer is concerned with getting things done, and getting them done in an orderly and reasonable manner. So it is an act of the **practical reason,** of man's intellect (presupposing an act of the will) ordering and ordaining things in the practical order. By his practical reason man is the cause of things in two ways: 1) *by commanding* those things that are inferior to him—his bodily members and other men who are subject to him; 2) *by requesting* something of those not subject to him—equals or superiors. In either case— by command of those things within his power or request with regard to things outside his power—man is a true *cause* through his practical reason of what is accomplished, a perfect cause in the first instance, a disposing cause which induces to the effect in the second.

By prayer, i.e., by humbly imploring God for the things he needs that are not within his power, man **worships** God. He admits his dependence upon God as the First Cause of all that man is and the Ultimate End who alone can perfect him. Man subjects his practical reason to God in the admission that he is not commanding but beseeching. Hence just as the act of devotion offers the will itself to God, so the act of prayer offers to God man's noblest faculty, his intellect. In the Christian who prays fervently for the things that he needs, this intention to worship God is usually implicit rather than explicit; but prayer as an act of worship is the most important aspect of man's beseeching God. Of its very nature it demands subjection of the reason to God.

From this analysis of prayer it is clear that two things are required of a being who prays:

    1) *intelligence*—since prayer is a way of arranging to get things done according to a proper and fitting order;

    2) *need*—since prayer is essentially a petition, a beseeching for what we cannot produce or effect by ourselves alone.

These two requirements make prayer man's proper activity. He alone in material creation is intelligent; his need is measured by the tremendous destiny that is completely above his nature but his only true goal.

Since prayer is worship of God, it is offered to God alone as to the one who fulfills man's needs. But it is fittingly directed to God through Our Lady, the angels or the saints, that our prayers may be effective through their prayers and merits; thus many of the Church's prayers implore the intercession "of Christ our Lord," "through our Lord Jesus Christ, who livest and reignest with thee in the unity of the Holy Spirit, world without end"—"for there is one God, and one mediator between God and man, himself man, Jesus Christ" (I Tim. 2:5).[8] In fulfilling what man asks in prayer God does not change the decrees of his divine providence: prayer does not alter the divine will. Rather his providence has eternally decreed that many things will be accomplished through secondary causes, including human acts, and high among these acts and causes is prayer. "We pray, not that we may change the divine disposition, but that we may petition that which God has ordained to be fulfilled by our prayers."[9]

(2) The Conditions of Prayer

The question, "*Why* should man pray?" is sufficiently answered in the preceding section on prayer: it is an act of worship of God. In prayer man offers and subjects to God his noblest faculty, the reason, in an activity which is most proper to his nature. But in this section the following points need to be considered: 1) *what* man should pray for; 2) *whom* man should pray for; 3) *when* he should pray.

1. **The things to pray for.** A simple rule which determines what man may ask of God in prayer is this: *it is reasonable to pray for anything that it is reasonable to desire.*[10] Since first things should be desired first, the same rule can be used to determine the order in which man should seek good things from God. Man is not obliged

---

[8]Since Christ is God, prayers may also be directed to him: "If you ask me anything in my name I will do it" (John 14:14).

[9]St. Thomas, *Summa*, II-II, q. 83, a. 2.

[10]Cf. St. Augustine, *Letter 130* (to Proba), Chap. 12.

in prayer to ask only in a general way for what God knows to be good for him; he may petition God for definite things for which he feels a need. As a reasonable being with the obligation of directing his own life intelligently, he must obtain the things necessary for his perfection and well being. Some of these things are not within his power to command, and for these he prays and petitions in particular.

Some things are so completely good for man that they cannot possibly have an evil result: the eternal vision of God in heaven and the means by which man merits it are in this category. Almost everything else, however good it may be in itself, however desirable, can bring an evil result to this particular man or at this particular time. Consequently all else should be sought in prayer under the condition that it be in God's provident plan for the individual's good. What a man may reasonably desire and seek of God in prayer will differ for different men, in different states of life and at different social levels.

The most perfect of all prayers is that composed by Christ himself at the earnest entreaty of his disciples.[11] "If we pray meetly and justly," St. Augustine remarks, "we can say nothing else but what is contained in this prayer of our Lord."[12] St. Thomas comments on this fact as follows:

> Since prayer is like an interpretation of our desires before God, it is only right to ask for something in our prayers when it is right to desire it. But in the Lord's Prayer not only do we ask for all that we may rightly desire, but also in that very order in which we should desire them, so that this prayer not only teaches us to ask but also directs our affections.
>
> It is clear, however, that the first object of desire is the end, and then whatever is ordained to the end. Now our end is God, toward whom our affections tend in two ways: first, by our willing the glory of God; second, by willing to enjoy his glory. The first belongs to the love whereby we love God in himself, and the second to the love whereby we love ourselves in God. And thus the first petition is stated: *hallowed be thy name;* and the second: *thy kingdom come*, by which we ask that we may come into the glory of his kingdom.

[11]Cf. Matt. 6:9-13; Luke 11:1-4.
[12]*Loc. cit.*

To this same end a thing directs us in two ways: in one way, by its very nature; in another way, accidentally. The good which is useful for an end directs us to that end of its very nature, and this in a double manner. First of all, directly and principally, according to the merit by which we merit happiness by obeying God, and in this respect we ask: *thy will be done on earth as it is in heaven.* Secondly, in an instrumental way, assisting us to merit, as it were; and in this respect we say: *give us this day our daily bread.* This may be understood either of the sacramental bread, whose daily use is profitable for man and in which also all the other sacraments are understood, or of the bread of the body, connoting our entire bodily sustenance. For the Eucharist is the chief sacrament, and bread is the chief food. . . .

We are directed to happiness accidentally by the removal of obstacles. But there are three things which exclude us from happiness. First of all sin, which directly excludes one from the kingdom; to this refer the words: *forgive us our trespasses.* Secondly, there is temptation, which hinders us from observing the divine will; and to this refer the words: *and lead us not into temptation*—not that we thereby ask not to be tempted, but not to be overcome by temptation, which is "to be led into" temptation. Thirdly, there is present punishment, which impedes a sufficiency of life; and with respect to this we say: *deliver us from evil.*[13]

Expressive as it is of the divine friendship of charity—of our love for God, for self, for neighbor (do we not plead in the plural?)—the Lord's Prayer has been traditionally recognized in the Church as a perfect preparation for Communion, and thus finds its place in the liturgy of the Mass. Indeed, Christ most abundantly fulfilled his disciple's request to teach us to pray.

2. **The persons to pray for.** By reason of the bond of charity man ought to desire good things not only for himself but for others, and consequently he should pray for others, not only for the just but also for sinners. The Christian is bound to love even his enemies— love of one's enemies is a special mark of those who follow Christ, as we have seen;[14] he is therefore bound to pray for his enemies. But he is not obligated to pray for a particular enemy unless that enemy is in some special extreme need, just as he is not bound to love his enemy by a particular motion of love. A man is obliged, however, not to exclude his enemy from his prayers for all men. An example of

[13]*Summa,* II-II, q. 83, a. 9.
[14]Cf. Matt. 5:43-48.

sinfulness in this regard would be to make a mental exception of an enemy while saying the words of the Canon of the Mass: "Be mindful, O Lord, . . . of all here present."

3. **The time of prayer.** Since prayer is so proper an activity of man there is a sense in which prayer should be continual: "Pray without ceasing" (I Thess. 5:17).[15] Man prays for what he desires, and what he desires he desires in charity or love of God. Everything a man in the state of grace does he should do at least virtually from the desire of charity. So in the sense that charity, the cause of prayer, is continual, prayer is continual.

But prayer itself is subject to frequent interruptions by other activities. The Christian who lives by charity will live a life of continual prayer by making sure that his prayer is interrupted by other activities, and not that his other activities are occasionally interrupted by prayer. The grace of final perseverance, the most precious of all God's gifts, should be the object of frequent prayer, since it is entirely a gift of God and cannot be merited or caused in any way by man himself. The obligation to pray at a particular time can bind under pain of mortal sin if the result of refusing to seek God's grace would be to commit mortal sin.

(3) The Kinds of Prayer

By reason of the manner in which it is performed, prayer is divided into mental prayer and vocal prayer, private prayer and public prayer.

1. **Mental prayer** is accomplished by interior acts alone; it is either meditation (a loving *discursive* consideration of religious truths) or contemplation (a loving *intuitive* consideration and admiration of religious truths). **Vocal prayer,** however, originates in the mind but is expressed externally through signs, usually by means of words vocally produced.

2. **Private prayer** is that offered by the Christian in his own name, whether mentally or vocally, by himself alone or in common. **Public prayer** is that which is offered in the name and by the authority of

---

[15]Cf. Luke 18:1 ff.

the Church in the form prescribed by the Church. It may be said in common or by a single individual, but it is always vocal and fulfills three conditions: 1) it is offered by a person deputized by the Church; 2) the prayers used are those instituted by the Church; 3) it is performed in the name of the Church. On the whole, prayers said in common, whether private or public, are better and more efficacious, as expressive of the unity of charity: "For where two or three are gathered together for my sake, there am I in the midst of them" (Matt. 18:20). Vocal prayers also have a special usefulness, since they may arouse interior devotion, they express the whole man and not only his mind, and they are a natural release for the spiritual joy of the soul; but it is frequently useful, sometimes indispensable and always laudable to pray to our Father in secret.[16]

(4) The Necessity of Prayer

Prayer is a necessary means of salvation for adults, not because of its nature (although the necessary worship of God is impossible without a loving movement of the soul toward him, which is prayer in the wide sense), but according to the ordinary laws of providence. For God does not customarily grant the actual graces necessary for salvation—and especially the gift of final perseverance—except to those who pray. Moreover, he has himself commanded us to pray: "Be assiduous in prayer," admonishes the Apostle (Col. 4:2);[17] and besides this divine precept the natural law itself (presupposing the ordinations of divine providence previously spoken of) imposes a like command.

Thus there is a serious obligation to pray frequently during life (several times a year, it would seem), and theologians commonly hold that the precept binds at the outset of man's moral life and when in danger of death. The precept likewise obliges, but for incidental reasons, when prayer is necessary to fulfill other precepts (e.g., Sunday Mass), in moments of grave temptation and in times of serious disaster, especially if it should be public.

[16]Cf. Matt. 6:6.
[17]Cf. Luke 18:1; Eph. 6:17-18; I Thess. 5:17.

(5) The Effects of Prayer

Because prayer is conversation with God, and by reason of charity conversation with a close and intimate friend, it brings refreshment and delight to the soul if it proceeds (as every act of religion should) from devotion. Another effect of prayer, one which it has in common with every act of virtue performed in the state of sanctifying grace, is **merit**. Because prayer is meritorious it is also **satisfactory**, i.e., it merits or causes the remission of venial sin and of the punishment due to sin. But the effect of prayer which is proper to prayer, which only prayer produces, is to obtain from God the things man needs which are not within the power of man to command. This effect of prayer is called **impetration**—obtaining something by beseeching a superior. And it is in virtue of this effect that that which is essential to prayer, the worship of God, is produced.

Under certain conditions prayer, *even the prayer of one in mortal sin,* infallibly obtains what is sought of God. This is not by reason of the meritorious power of prayer; it is based solely on the infinite mercy of God and on his promise: "Ask, and it shall be given you; seek, and you shall find; knock, and it shall be opened to you. For everyone who asks, receives, and he who seeks, finds; and to him who knocks, it shall be opened" (Matt. 7:7-8).

The conditions under which prayer obtains the favor a man seeks are:

1) *That it be pious,* i.e., an act of worship, based on humility, flowing from charity, faith and hope. In the case of the sinner these acts (except, perhaps, for faith and hope) would proceed not from the infused habits but from actual graces.

2) *That what is sought be something necessary or useful for salvation.* This, of course, may include even material benefits.

3) *That what is sought is for oneself.* Prayer which obtains the favor of God presupposes the subjection of the will by devotion. The will of another may not be subjected to God.

4) *That it be persevering.*[18]

---

[18]Cf. Matt. 15:22-28; Luke 11:5-8.

4. The Exterior Acts of Religion

The worship rendered by the Church to God must be, in its entirety, interior as well as exterior. It is exterior because the nature of man as a composite body and soul requires it to be so. Likewise, because divine providence has disposed that "while we recognize God visibly, we may be drawn by him to love of things unseen."[19] Every impulse of the human heart, besides, expresses itself naturally through the senses; and the worship of God, being the concern not merely of individuals but of the whole community of mankind, must therefore be social as well. This obviously it cannot be unless religious activity is also organized and manifested outwardly. Exterior worship, finally, reveals and emphasizes the unity of the Mystical Body, feeds new fuel to its holy zeal, fortifies its energy, intensifies its action day by day.[20]

The chief element of divine worship, the chief acts of religion, must be interior. God cannot be worthily honored unless the mind and the heart of man turn to him in quest of perfect life. But man's external actions are signs of internal reverence, and through them the whole man comes into play, with all his God-given faculties. So now we come to consider these exterior acts, which may be divided as follows:

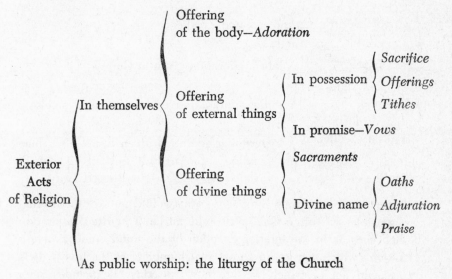

Exterior Acts of Religion

In themselves

Offering of the body—*Adoration*

Offering of external things
- In possession
  - *Sacrifice*
  - *Offerings*
  - *Tithes*
- In promise—*Vows*

Offering of divine things
- *Sacraments*
- Divine name
  - *Oaths*
  - *Adjuration*
  - *Praise*

As public worship: the liturgy of the Church

[19]Preface of the Nativity.
[20]Pope Pius XII, encyclical *Mediator Dei*, Nov. 20, 1947.

We will treat the exterior acts of religion in themselves in this section, and these acts as the public worship of the Church in **Section 5.**

A. Adoration

In testimony of another's excellence and superiority, man is accustomed to manifest his submission to such superiority by certain signs. Thus a baseball crowd will rise to its feet when the President enters the ball park; the enthusiastic crowd in St. Peter's will fill the basilica with applause as the Pope is carried down the middle aisle. Obviously it is the internal act of reverence which is important here—standing on one's feet during the seventh inning stretch does not count as an act of reverence of the President; but, as with sacrifice, such is man's composite nature that he seeks to express this interior sentiment by perceptible signs.

If reverence is due to men, it is obvious that adoration pre-eminently is owed to God, for his excellence and superiority are uncreated and supreme. But since there are varying degrees of excellence and superiority we may distinguish different grades of adoration:

Civil—based on natural, created excellence

Religious (based on supernatural excellence)

latria: adoration given to God

dulia: adoration given to saints and angels

hyperdulia: adoration given because of some unique supernatural but created excellence, as, e.g., to Our Blessed Lady

Since we are creatures composed of a twofold nature, intellectual and sensible, we offer God a twofold **latria:** a *spiritual* adoration (which consists in the interior devotion of the mind); and a *bodily* adoration (which consists in an external humbling of the body). It is this second act of which we are now speaking. It includes such things as genuflections, inclinations of the head, joining of the hands in prayer, standing at the reading of the Gospel, kneeling at the consecration of the Mass, etc. **Adoration** in this sense may be defined as *an external manifestation of reverence for, and submission to God made by a suitable act or gesture.*

Exterior adoration which does not flow from the devotion of the will is not an act of religion but a mere external appearance of one; it is one of the hypocrisies for which Christ condemned the pharisees.[21] Adoration has for its purpose either the arousing of devotion, since man is naturally led from the material to the spiritual, or the expression of the total dedication of the will to God which is essential to religion.

These physical acts and gestures of religion are external signs of an interior reverence. They are performed not as if they added anything to God, but to aid man in arousing the internal spirit of submission and worship which is the essence of religion. To attempt to do away with such physical signs is to deny the reality of the physical side of human nature, and to increase the difficulty of discharging the debts of religion.

Some acts of adoration are performed privately, as when a man kneels to say his prayers, but many special acts of adoration are confined to churches which are specially designated for religious ceremonies as an aid in the spirit of devotion.

B. Sacrifice

(1) In General

The central and most important of all the external acts of religion is sacrifice, the act by which external things belonging to man are offered exclusively to God in worship. Certain other actions and other possessions of man may be offered to creatures as signs of reverence, but not sacrifice—it is offered to God alone.

Sacrifice is defined as *an offering which a priest makes to God by changing or destroying some object in order to manifest God's domin-*

[21]Cf. Matt. 23:27-28.

ion and our subjection. Special emphasis must be given to the various elements of this definition to grasp this unique religious reality.

1) Since man is a dependent being, naturally subject to a higher power, he must give explicit recognition of his inferiority and God's supremacy. But he must pay homage to God *in his own human way.* Now it is natural to man to convey his sentiments by perceptible signs. So to express the submission of his being to God (and this is the spirit and heart of true sacrifice), he will externalize his homage through signs. Basically, then, sacrifice, is an *offering,* a giving up or surrender of self. This interior sacrifice is symbolized when man offers God one of the inferior creatures placed at his disposal. For man is God's steward, and hence given dominion over the things of this world; to give up such a sensible object to God appropriately represents his self-giving.

2) But as his spiritual sacrifice is entire and complete, the symbolic action must express this perfect submission. Hence the sensible object which is offered must be so removed from ordinary human use by his action as to be placed entirely at God's disposal. The external sacrifice thus always involves a kind of destruction of the thing offered, and in this way it truly signifies the interior, total surrender of self to God in recognition of his dominion over all things, especially over man himself. Thus of all man's external acts it best expresses the readiness and the completeness of dedication that is essential to the chief interior act of religion, devotion.

3) The primary purpose of sacrifice is to give this visible sign of our recognition of God's superiority and our submission to him. But it is also an act of thanksgiving, out of gratitude for the gifts God has given us, and of impetration, powerfully beseeching the gifts we have not yet received. Most important of all, in many ways, is the fact that it is an act which reconciles sinful man to God—an act of expiation for past sins which is pleasing to God because of the totality of man's surrender to him.

4) Sacrifice is, then, natural and necessary for man, an act of religious worship clamored for by his nature. But the private in-

dividual cannot satisfy this need, since it is basically a social need: man must protest before others his recognition of the relations between God and himself, and must act as a member of the human race and of human society. It is for this reason that the rite expressive of sacrifice must be external, signifying publicly his interior sentiments. In consequence, sacrifice is properly the work of the religious head of the community, the priest; he will, as the official mediator between themselves and God, make a sacrificial offering for all. **Sacrifice is the principal duty of the priest.**

(2) The Sacrifice of Christ

Under the former covenant, as the apostle Paul attests, there was no perfection, because of the powerlessness of the Levitical priesthood. Hence it was necessary—God the Father of mercies so ordaining—that another priest "according to the order of Melchisedech" (Gen. 14:18; Ps. 109:4; Heb. 1:11) should arise. This was our Lord Jesus Christ, who could perfect all who would be sanctified and lead them to perfection. He, therefore, our Lord and our God, was to offer himself to God the Father once and for all by his death on the altar of the cross, there to accomplish an everlasting redemption.[22]

The sacrifice of the new law is Christ's sacrifice of himself on the cross. This is the perfect act of sacrifice. The thing offered is the God-man, the victim without spot or blemish, the only perfect offering ever made in recognition of God's dominion and man's subjection. The devotion with which it is offered is the devotion of Christ who is both priest and victim.

This same sacrifice is renewed, re-presented, continued through the Mass, the sacrifice of Christ and his Mystical Body. It is thus, in the words of Pope Pius XII, "the culmination and center, as it were, of the Christian religion."[23] The Mass is not an empty commemoration, a human symbol of the passion and death of Christ; it is a true sacrifice, a sacred action by which Christ offers himself by an unbloody immolation as a most acceptable victim to the Father, as he did on

---

[22]Council of Trent, Sess. XXII, 1562, *Doctrine . . . concerning the Most Holy Sacrifice of the Mass,* Chap. 1; Denz. 938.

[23]Encyclical *Mediator Dei.*

the cross. "It is one and the same victim: he who now makes the offering through the ministry of priests and he who then offered himself on the cross; the only difference is in the manner of offering."[24]

With this in mind, the Christian can appreciate in terms of his own personal life the profound signficance of these words:

> The august sacrifice of the altar is, as it were, the supreme instrument whereby the merits won by the divine Redeemer upon the cross are distributed to the faithful: "as often as this commemorative sacrifice is offered, there is wrought the work of our redemption."[25] This, however, so far from lessening the dignity of the actual sacrifice on Calvary, rather proclaims and renders more manifest its greatness and its necessity, as the Council of Trent declares.[26] Its daily immolation reminds us that there is no salvation except in the cross of our Lord Jesus Christ (cf. Gal. 6:14), and that God himself wishes that there should be a continuation of this sacrifice "from the rising of the sun till the going down thereof" (Mal. 1:11), so that there may be no cessation of the hymn of praise and thanksgiving which man owes to God, seeing that he requires his help continually and has need of the blood of the Redeemer to remit sin which challenges God's justice.
>
> It is therefore desirable that all the faithful should be aware that to participate in the eucharistic sacrifice is their chief duty and supreme dignity, and that not in an inert and negligent fashion, giving way to distractions and day-dreaming, but with such earnestness and concentration that they may be united as closely as possible with the High Priest, according to the Apostle: "Let this mind be in you which was also in Christ Jesus" (Phil. 2:5). And together with him and through him let them make their oblation, and in union with him let them offer up themselves.[27]

(3) The Extended Meaning of Sacrifice

In a wide sense of the word anything *offered* to God may be called a sacrifice. St. Thomas distinguishes three classes of goods possessed by man which may be offered as sacrifices in this wide sense:

> The goods of man are threefold: First, the goods of his soul—and these he offers to God by devotion, prayer and other interior acts. Second, the goods of his body—and these he offers to God perfectly by the act of martyrdom and by the acts of many other virtues, such

---

[24]Council of Trent, *loc. cit.*, Chap. 2; Denz. 940.
[25]Secret for the Ninth Sunday after Pentecost.
[26]*Loc. cit.*
[27]Pope Pius XII, encyclical *Mediator Dei*.

as abstinence and continence. Third, external goods which he may offer to God either immediately, or mediately when he shares them for the love of God with his neighbor.[28]

This kind of sacrifice is the work of the virtue of religion in *commanding* the acts of all the other moral virtues and in *directing* them to the worship of God. It is recommended in the admonitions of the Apostle: "I exhort you therefore, brethren, to present your bodies as a sacrifice, living, holy, pleasing to God—your spiritual service" (Rom. 12:1); "and do not forget kindness and charity, for by such sacrifices God's favor is obtained" (Heb. 13:16).

C. Offerings

Many things are offered to God in a way which does not involve their destruction as does sacrifice but rather their use for some purpose connected with divine worship. They do represent a sacrifice on the part of the giver but are not sacrifices in the strict sense.

Some gifts may be used in divine worship, as would the gift of a chalice or of some church furnishing; others may be used for the support of God's ministers, like gifts to seminaries, monasteries, etc. Still others may be used to aid God's poor, like gifts to the St. Vincent de Paul Society, etc. All such gifts, if they are to pertain to the virtue of religion, *must be given freely for God's honor in recognition of God's generosity to us.*

D. Tithes

In the Old Testament, there were special gifts of money called "tithes" which represented a tenth part of men's revenues. All were obliged to pay tithes for the support of the Levites (Num. 18:21). In addition, men were obliged to offer a share in the crops for the sustenance of the priests of the Temple, and these gifts were called "first-fruits."[29]

[28]*Summa,* II-II, q. 85, a. 3, ad 2.
[29]Cf. Deut. 26:2-3; Num. 18:8.

It is a matter of divine command that gifts be made for the support of religion and of God's ministers. To the twelve, when sending them on their first mission, our Lord pointed out: "The laborer deserves his living" (Matt. 10:10).[30] Yet this precept does not change the fact that gifts must be freely given, because the kind and value of the gifts remain a matter of choice. In the first centuries of the Church's life the spontaneous offerings of the faithful were sufficient to care for the needs of the Church. Later on, the practice of giving tithes was introduced. Today there is among the laws of the Church the precept that the faithful must contribute to the support of their pastors (Can. 1502).

Exactly how and in what measure this is to be done is generally left to the prudence and generosity of the faithful, although some contributions are fixed by law. For the most part, these laws are established by the bishop for his diocese and regulate such things as the stipends for Masses, funerals, weddings, and the taxes levied for securing the services of the chancery office staff in obtaining dispensations, etc. In all these cases, the fees are very moderate, and provision is always made for those who could not afford even the smallest offering.

Here in the United States the vast undertakings of the Church in charitable and educational works, in supporting the missions, and in building churches is a great tribute to the zeal and generosity of priests, religious and the faithful. All of it was made possible by gifts. And the important thing about these gifts is that they were acts of religion.

E. Vows

(1) Their Nature

A vow is *a promise made to God of a greater and a possible good performed in worship of him*.[31] As man directs by command and by prayer what will be done for himself through others, so by vow he directs what he himself will do in the service of God. Hence a vow

---

[30]Cf. Luke 10:7; I Cor. 9:4 ff.
[31]By a "greater" good is meant one greater than its omission or its opposite.

is an act of reason directing, and because it is an act of worship it is made to God alone. The precise activity of a vow is to give stability and permanence to man's devotion: an attempt to fix his will immovably on the good which is profitable to him. By nature man is vacillating; by vow he tries to make lasting and permanent the readiness and complete dedication of the will to God that devotion requires.

For a vow to be valid, three things are required:

1) a true intention of obligating oneself to fulfill what is promised;

2) full deliberation and knowledge;

3) perfect freedom in making the promise.

A man should be faithful to every promise he makes. Because of God's dominion over him and because of the multitude of gifts he has received from God, there is a special reason for keeping his promises to God. A man who breaks a vow, therefore, is guilty of a special sin of faithlessness.

(2) The Excellence of Vows

Although there is no obligation to make a vow, *the same act performed under a vow is better and more meritorious.* This is true for several reasons:

1) A vow is an act of religion. Religion is a higher virtue and adds to the value and merit of the acts of the other moral virtues, such as fasting and continence.

2) A vow more perfectly subjects man to God. The vow offers to God not only the act itself but the power to act, since the vow obliges a man to use the power to fulfill the promise. E.g., one who vows to enter religious life not only performs a good act by entering but surrenders the will itself to God with regard to any other disposition of his life.

3) To act from a will fixed in good—which is the effect of a vow—is better, just as it is worse to act from a will fixed stubbornly in evil.

Every human act to be virtuous not only in itself but in view of all its circumstances must be ruled and regulated by the virtue of prudence. This is especially true of making a vow because its effects are serious and far-reaching. For this reason competent advice should be sought before a man binds himself by a vow. For once a vow is made it can be dispensed only by competent authority.

(3) The Kinds of Vows

Vows are **private** or **public.** A private vow does not involve any special recognition by the Church and is made privately. A public vow is made in the presence of official witnesses who represent the Church. The Church receives as public the vows of those entering Holy Orders and the vows of religious. Public vows are either *simple* or *solemn*, depending on how the Church receives and recognizes them. They differ in their effects even when simple vows are perpetual— e.g., a simple vow of chastity renders marriage unlawful, but the solemn vow of chastity makes marriage invalid.

(4) The Vows of Religion

The **vows of religion** presuppose devotion in a heroic degree. By the vows of religion—poverty, chastity and obedience—a human being is set apart in a way similar to the way a chalice or a church is set apart for divine worship. By these vows a person is *consecrated* or dedicated to God. The vows make possible to man a prompt and total giving of himself to God's service that is *permanent*.

By nature man is changeable. The clarity with which he sees his obligation to serve God and the generosity with which he wills it at one moment may desert him at the next. But the vows catch and stabilize his devotion, which is an *act* that comes and goes and, which in man's present state, is impossible to maintain constantly. While other acts of religion arouse his devotion or express it, only the vows have this special purpose with reference to devotion: they attempt—insofar as this is possible to man in his present state—to hold in actual existence and permanently the highest degree and perfection of human devotion.

The vows of religion promise a *totality* of giving in the service of God. It is possible to classify the things over which man has dominion or right of direction under three general headings: 1) over the material goods of this world insofar as they contribute to his goal; 2) over his own body with regard to those acts which are apt for generation; 3) over his will with regard to the choice of means to his goal. By the vows of religion man relinquishes his dominion over these three classes of goods. Since in some way they include all the things over which man has dominion, by the vows of religion he gives up all things in the service of God.

The vows are essentially promises of future giving, of giving which is done from moment to moment during years of religious life. The actual giving that is accomplished by the very pronouncing of the vows lies in the act of devotion. In fact, the essence of a religious vocation, whose public and official profession accepted by the Church is the making of vows, lies in the act of devotion. This is the totality of giving in God's service that dedication to him demands.

By devotion man consecrates and sets himself apart for the worship of God in a properly human manner, as an intelligent and free being. It is fitting that in every category of created things some individuals be set apart for the worship of God. This is accomplished among irrational creatures by such acts as sacrifice and oblations, by the consecration of chalices and churches. In the world of men, it is accomplished by devotion and the vows of religion.

F. Man's Use of the Divine Name

The internal acts of religion for whose sake the external exist are devotion and prayer. By external acts man offers to God his body, his material possessions and his future activity by promise. In order to worship God man also uses things that are not his but God's. These are two in number: the sacraments (to be treated in Volume Three) and God's holy name, the concern of this present section.

(1) Oaths

The purpose of an oath is very clearly set forth by St. Thomas.[32] Every human statement needs some kind of confirmation of its truth; man is not by nature or necessity truthful as is God. Statements of man which are deduced by necessity from naturally known principles are confirmed by reason itself. But very often man's statements are about particular contingent facts. In the ordinary circumstances of his everyday life his reputation for veracity will be sufficient confirmation of these statements. But there are certain occasions—e.g., when a man's life or freedom or property may be in jeopardy in a court of law, or when a man's freedom to enter into a marriage contract must be determined—when some greater confirmation is necessary. Only God can know the truth about secret thoughts or distant things or future events, and his witness is invoked by oaths.

An **oath** is *an act by which God is asked to witness the truth of a statement which is not subject to any other kind of confirmation.* It is an excellent kind of confirmation of a particular contingent fact, for it is impossible for God either to deceive or to be deceived. Some facts which need confirmation by an oath are past or present. Some are future. Oaths, then, are of two kinds: 1) *declaratory*—confirmatory of the past or present; 2) *promissory*—confirmation of the future.

An oath should be employed only when there is some kind of necessity, or at least great usefulness. It is not desirable for its own sake but only by reason of a defect in man's nature. If man were naturally truthful and had no need to develop the virtue of veracity, there would be no need for him to have recourse to an oath at any time: a man who is in perfect health has no need of medicine. The prudent man will take an oath only infrequently, and then with great caution and never for a trifling reason.

In taking an oath man *worships* God. An oath is an external act of religion which flows from devotion and which subjects man to God because it recognizes his infinite knowledge and truthfulness. It is only the taking of the oath itself which is an act of religion, however, not the statement made under oath. Hence a vow is a greater act

[32]Cf. *Summa*, II-II, q. 89, a. 1.

of religion because its effect is to make the very thing vowed an act of the virtue.

A prudent oath possesses three qualities:

1) **good judgment** or discretion, so that it is employed only when necessity demands;

2) **truthfulness**, so that God is not called upon to confirm a lie;

3) **justice**, so that what is promised in a promissory oath is lawful.

(2) Adjuration

The need for taking oaths rests on a defect of truthfulness in man. The need for adjuration rests on a defect in his ability to cause things. As by an oath man confirms his statements by the infinite knowledge and truthfulness of God, so by an adjuration he confirms his finite power to command his inferiors and beseech his equals or superiors by the infinite power of God. An adjuration is, then, an act of religion, because in recognizing man's defectiveness and God's superiority it subjects man to God. An **adjuration** is defined as *the invocation of the divine name in beseeching or commanding another.*

A common use of adjuration by the Church is the direction of her official prayers to God "through our Lord Jesus Christ." An example of adjuration by command is the Church's exorcism of the devil. Public exorcism requires special permission.[33]

(3) Praise of God

Praise of God by use of his name has an important place in the second internal act of religion, prayer, which has already been considered. As an external act of religion the use of God's name in praise is with the lips, or in chant and music. This act of religion is necessary not on God's account, who has no need of it, but for man's sake, because it arouses his devotion. Because the use of chant and music in the worship of God can easily become mere display or the seeking of pleasure rather than a help to devotion, the Church has always exercised a close supervision over it.

[33]Cf. Can. 1151.

5. THE LITURGY OF THE CHURCH

The divine Redeemer has so willed it that the priestly life begun with the supplication and sacrifice of his mortal body should continue without intermission down the ages in his Mystical Body which is the Church. That is why he established a visible priesthood to offer everywhere the clean oblation (Mal. 1:11) which would enable men from east to west, freed from the shackles of sin, to offer God that unconstrained and voluntary homage which their conscience dictates.

In obedience, therefore, to her founder's behest, the Church prolongs the priestly mission of Jesus Christ mainly by means of the sacred liturgy. She does this in the first place at the altar, where constantly the sacrifice of the cross is re-presented and, with a single difference in the manner of its offering, renewed.[34] She does it next by means of the sacraments, those special channels through which men are made partakers in the supernatural life. She does it finally by offering to God, all good and great, the daily tribute of her prayer of praise. "What a spectacle for heaven and earth," observes our predecessor of happy memory, Pius XI,[35] "is not the Church at prayer! For centuries without interruption, from midnight to midnight, the divine psalmody of the inspired canticles is repeated on earth; there is no hour of the day that is not hallowed by its special liturgy; there is no stage of human life that has not its part in the thanksgiving, praise, supplication and reparation of this common prayer of the Mystical Body of Christ which is his Church!"[36]

It is our purpose here to point out briefly something of the nature of the liturgy, its chief elements, the participation of the laity in these sacred functions, and the sanctification of feastdays.

A. The Nature of the Liturgy

Our word "liturgy" is a transliteration of the Greek word meaning "public work or service in the interest of the people," which was later restricted to religious affairs connected with worship. Hence its nominal definition is *divine service in the interests of the people—* a significant phrase which is the equivalent of "the divine worship of the Church." Pius XII gives the formal definition, which we will

[34]Council of Trent, Sess. XXII, Chap. 1 and 2; Denz. 938 and 940.
[35]Encyclical *Caritate Christi*, May 3, 1932.
[36]Pope Pius XII, encyclical *Mediator Dei*.

examine in some detail: "The sacred **liturgy** is the public worship which our Redeemer as Head of the Church renders to the Father, as well as the worship which the community renders to its founder, and through him to the heavenly Father. It is, in short, *the worship rendered by the Mystical Body of Christ in the entirety of its Head and members.*"[37]

In the first place, liturgy is **worship,** an expression through human action of the virtue of religion. But it is *communal* worship—"of the Mystical Body of Christ in the entirety of its Head and members"— a fulfillment of human duties toward God which falls, first of all, upon men as individuals, but likewise binds the whole community of mankind in the unity of mutual social relations, for the human race in its solidarity (natural and supernatural) depends also on the sovereign authority of God. From this fact flow certain consequences:

1) Since it is communal or social worship, the liturgy is necessarily *external* worship, expressed in forms (unlike private prayer, which may well be formless) that signify visibly or audibly the divine service which is the concern of all.

2) This means, further, that the liturgy must be *objective,* not the manifestation of private sentiment, private needs, private devotion (although it will usually well fulfill these personal interior responses when legitimate), but the expression of what belongs objectively and essentially to the virtue of religion itself, to man's reverence for God.

3) From these two characteristics of socialness and objectivity flows a third and more accidental one: the liturgy is *artistic*— that is, utilizing all material and human resources to clothe its expression in the noblest possible forms, both to stimulate interior devotion and provide a fitting external manifestation of the sentiments of the heart and mind.

Worship, then, may be called the *remote genus* of these human actions, and **communal worship,** with its accompanying *properties* of exteriority, objectivity and artistry, the *proximate genus.* What is it, then, which distinguishes the Church's liturgy from the expressions of

[37] *Ibid.*

natural religion, from the religious rites of Hindu or Protestant, Jew or Mohammedan? What is its *specific difference?*

The worship of Christ's Church is **supernatural,** "of the Mystical Body of Christ." God had established such a supernatural religion in the Old Testament, but this was only a shadowing and prefiguring, of its nature temporary, of the perfect worship of the Son of God made man, Jesus Christ. It is this worship, divine in its inspiration, its origins and its fulfillment, which is perpetuated and continued by the Church until that time when all of the elect will join in the liturgy of heaven to sing "to him who sits upon the throne, and to the Lamb, blessing and honor and glory and dominion, forever and ever" (Apoc. 5:13).

Hence the supernatural worship of the Church is an *official* worship, that offered by the Church, hierarchy and laity, in union with her bridegroom, spouse and Head, and not the private service of individual Christians. As such, then, it is performed by official ministers of God, divinely signed and divinely empowered to represent the person of Jesus Christ before the people and at the same time representatives of the people before God—the priests. Thus the organization of the liturgy, its regulation and its details are subject to the authority of the Church, and ultimately to the Sovereign Pontiff. In short, it is **Christian** worship.

All of this can be restated simply: the liturgy of the Church is the worship rendered by the Mystical Body of Christ in the entirety of its Head and members.

B. The Elements of the Liturgy

The official worship of the Church is a vast complexus of the exterior acts of religion, elaborated under divine guidance over the course of centuries, and embracing both divine components (divinely instituted, these are incapable of change) and human ones (subject, under ecclesiastical authorization, to modifications, as the needs of the times, particular circumstances and the good of souls makes necessary). For purposes of brief analysis, we may divide this religious whole into two parts: the structural elements of which it is composed; and the various functions by which the liturgy is carried out.

(1) The Structural Elements

Following the eminent liturgical scholar, J. A. Jungman, S.J.,[38] we may group the physical elements out of which the liturgy is composed—its *matter*, so to say—into the following categories:

1) **Readings.** Naturally enough, a prominent place in the various liturgical functions has been accorded to the sacred word of God. Excerpts from the various books of the Old and New Testaments, of smaller or greater length, will be found (at least by allusion) in almost all services, but chiefly in the Divine Office and in the Mass.

2) **Psalms.** From the beginning the Church has cherished the religious poems of the royal psalmist as an expression of genuine religious sentiment in fitting artistic form. Their use, sometimes in a very much curtailed form, is also most frequent.

3) **Hymns.** As manifestations of popular piety and devotion, contemporary in inspiration, hymns have always played an important role in the liturgy. The Church has incorporated the finest of these Latin works into her official worship, and encourages the formation of appropriate hymns in the vernacular, for use chiefly in less formal services.

4) **Church music.** "It is the mark of the lover to sing," remarked St. Augustine. Recognizing this fact, the "Mother of the arts" has especially fostered this means of human expression. Gregorian chant still remains her favorite for its soberness and beautiful simplicity, but she approves of the use of "sacred polyphony" and encourages the development of "modern sacred music."[39]

5) **The prayer of the people.** Liturgical prayer has been the business not only of the priest but also of the people—*liturgy*

[38]*Public Worship* (Collegeville, Minn.: The Liturgical Press, 1957), Chap. Four.

[39]Cf. the instruction of the Sacred Congregation of Rites concerning sacred music and the liturgy, Sept. 3, 1958, and the encyclical of Pope Pius XII, *Musicae Sacrae Disciplina,* Dec. 25, 1955.

implies that the Christian community is gathered under the hierarchical leadership of the priest to render due homage to God. Generally, liturgical prayers are in the plural, and in frequent cases the people are specifically invited to pray: *oremus*, a custom happily being revived today in greater measure.

6) **The prayer of the priest.** This is composed of official acts of thanksgiving (the eucharistic prayer of the Mass, for example) or of petition, spoken in the name of all. Thus before he begins, the priest invites the community to make his petition or thanksgiving their own, and the prayer is "approved" and its conclusion also, through the community's "Amen."

7) **The use of the body.** The use of expressive gesture and graceful bodily movements—mimesis, the art of dramaturgy and the dance—to signify interior attitudes is one of man's oldest and most common art forms. Standing, kneeling, bowing, sitting; the stretching out of hands or folding them; the orderly movements of celebrant and assistants—posture, gesture, bodily actions are all employed in the liturgy. A unique and most meaningful gesture is that of the sign of the cross.

Woven expertly into artistic unity in proper proportions, these divine and human components are placed by the Church in a fitting setting (the church and its appointments) and assisted by the necessary instruments (sacred vessels, vestments, etc.) for the due observance of divine service. Indeed, all the fine arts, and many servile arts as well, are called upon to lend their skills that the Church's worship may be as expressive and total as possible.

(2) Liturgical Functions

If the elements mentioned above may be considered the raw materials out of which the Church constructs her liturgy, the wonderfully varied rites of that liturgy may be considered the *forms* of divine worship. These **liturgical functions** have been defined as *"those sacred acts which, having been instituted by Jesus Christ and the Church, are performed by legitimately appointed persons according to the liturgical books approved by the Holy See for the giving of due* *worship to God, the saints, and the blessed* (cf. Can. 1256).[40] Broadly speaking, these various and multiple functions can be grouped in two classes:

1) *Those actions expressive of the interior act of devotion;* the **sacraments.** Instituted by Christ himself, the seven sacraments of the New Law culminate in the Eucharist, chief of them all, and in its celebration, the sacramental sacrifice which is the Mass. Directed toward man as purveyors of the grace of Christ, the sacraments are essentially **sacred signs,** *religious* in nature, and thus also oriented to the worship of God as vivid professions of faith in their very administration and reception.[41] Intimately connected with this sacramental worship is the adoration of the Eucharist in subsidiary ceremonies—processions, Benediction, Forty Hours, etc.—which is a feature of modern devotion. Also under this head would be grouped the **sacramentals,** including the rites accompanying, preparing for or implementing the various sacraments, as well as those of supplementary significance.

2) *Those actions expressive of the interior act of prayer:* the **Divine Office.** The chief and official prayer of the Church, its perennial paean of praise and petition, thanksgiving and supplication, is the Divine Office: "the prayer of the Mystical Body of Jesus Christ, offered to God in the name, and on behalf of all Christians, when recited by priests and other members of the Church and by religious who are deputed by the Church for this."[42] Other prayers—the litanies, for example—will be allied with this continuation of the great prayer of Christ, but private prayers (the Rosary, private litanies, etc.) are not included in the official worship of the Church.

More often than not, the liturgical celebrations of the Church will be comprised of both these forms of worship; the Mass, for example, besides its sacramental character, employs a great number of prayers.

---

[40]Instruction of the Sacred Congregation of Rites, Sept. 3, 1958. The instruction adds: "Other sacred acts performed either inside or outside the church, even if performed by the priest or in his presence, are called 'pious exercises.'"

[41]For detailed consideration of the sacraments, see *Christ, and His Sacraments,* 290-543.

[42]Pope Pius XII, encyclical *Mediator Dei.*

This is only natural (and supernatural), since man offers God in worship both his heart in devotion and his mind in prayer.

(3) The Liturgical Year

As the liturgy is concerned with space in its use of buildings and actions, so also it is concerned with time: it is not the present alone which concerns it, but it looks backward to the perfect worship of Christ and forward, in an eschatological view, to his Second Coming. Pope Pius XII offers some significant remarks on this aspect of the liturgy:

> Throughout the entire year, the Mass and the Divine Office center especially around the person of Jesus Christ: this arrangement is so suitably disposed that our Savior dominates the scene in the mysteries of his humiliation, of his redemption and triumph.
>
> While the sacred liturgy calls to mind the mysteries of Jesus Christ, it strives to make all believers take their part in them so that the divine Head of the Mystical Body may live in all the members with the fulness of his holiness. Let the souls of Christians be like altars on each one of which a different phase of the sacrifice, offered by the High Priest, comes to life again, as it were: pains and tears which wipe away and expiate sin; supplication to God which pierces heaven; dedication and even immolation of oneself made promptly, generously and earnestly; and finally that intimate union by which we commit ourselves and all we have to God, in whom we find our rest: "the perfection of religion is to imitate whom you adore."[43]
>
> . . . by these suitable ways and methods in which the liturgy at stated times proposes the life of Jesus Christ for our meditation, the Church gives us examples to imitate, points out treasures of sanctity for us to make our own; since it is fitting that the mind believe what the lips sing, and that what the mind believes should be practised in public and private life.
>
> Hence the liturgical year, devotedly fostered and accompanied by the Church, is not a cold and lifeless representation of the events of the past, or a simple and bare record of a former age. It is rather Christ himself who is ever living in his Church. Here he continues that journey of immense mercy which he lovingly began in his mortal life, going about doing good (Acts 10:38) with the design of bringing men to know his mysteries and in a way live by them. These mysteries are ever present and active, not in a vague and uncertain way as some modern writers hold, but in the way that Catholic doctrine teaches us. According to the Doctors of the Church, they are shining examples of Christian perfection, as well as sources of divine grace,

---

[43]St. Augustine, *The City of God*, Bk. VIII, Chap. 7.

due to the merit and prayers of Christ; they still influence us because each mystery brings its own special grace for our salvation. Moreover, our holy Mother the Church, while proposing for our contemplation the mysteries of our Redeemer, asks in her prayers for those gifts which would give her children the greatest possible share in the spirit of these mysteries through the merits of Christ. By means of his inspiration and help and through the co-operation of our wills, we can receive from him living vitality as branches do from the tree and members from the head; thus slowly and laboriously we can transform ourselves "unto the measure of the age of the fulness of Christ" Eph. 4:13).[44]

Besides this temporal cycle of feasts, the Church also honors the saints, Our Lady above all, in a cycle of feasts designed to furnish us with examples of Christian living, and to implore their intercession.

C. Participation of the Laity in the Liturgy

(1) General Recommendations

Since the time of St. Pius X modern pontiffs have repeatedly urged and encouraged the laity to take a more active part in the Church's celebration of the mysteries of Christ. This role, which the very nature of Christian liturgy demands, is not that of mere spectators but of actors, under the hierarchical direction of the priest, in the official prayers and ceremonies of the liturgy. It is principally exercised with respect to the Mass, as a modern instruction of the Sacred Congregation of Rites (Sept. 3, 1958) points out:

> Because of its nature, the Mass demands that all present should participate each in his own proper way. This participation must first of all be interior, undoubtedly exercised in the pious attention of the soul and in the affections of the heart. Through this, the faithful "closely join the Supreme Priest . . . and together with him and through him offer [the Sacrifice], and consecrate themselves together with him."[45]
>
> The participation of those present is more complete if exterior participation is joined to interior attention, and therefore manifested by external acts, such as by the position of the body (genuflecting, standing, sitting), by the ritual gesture, and, above all, by the responses, prayers and chants.

[44]Encyclical *Mediator Dei.*
[45]Pope Pius XII, encyclical *Mediator Dei.*

Regarding this participation, Pius XII used these general words of praise in the encyclical letter on the sacred liturgy, *Mediator Dei*: "And those also should be praised who strive to bring it about that the liturgy, in an external manner also, should be the holy action in which all who are present should take part. And this can be done in several ways: when all the people, according to the norms of the holy rubrics, either answer the words of the priest, preserving due order, or sing chants which are fitting to the various parts of the Sacrifice, or do both these things; or, finally, when in the holy solemnities they sing alternately liturgical chants."

The pontifical documents imply this harmonious participation when they refer to the "active participation" (*Mediator Dei*), the principal example of which is found in the priest celebrant and his ministers who, with due interior piety and accurately observing the rubrics and ceremonies, serve at the altar.

Finally, perfect active participation is achieved when one also adds sacramental participation, by means of which "the faithful present communicate, not only with spiritual affection, but also with reception of the sacrament of the Eucharist, so that they may derive greater fruit from this most blessed sacrifice."[46]

(2) *Specific Suggestions*

After these general remarks, the instruction continues with specific practical recommendations (to be carried out under the direction of the bishop) for increased active participation by the laity in the Mass. For, it points out, "the laity also exercises an active liturgical participation by force of their baptismal character. Because of this character, it is true that in the Holy Sacrifice of the Mass they offer in a certain manner, together with the priest, the divine victim to God the Father."[47] Of the many points suggested by the instruction, the most immediately practical and important can be summarized as follows:

1) **Participation at low ("read") Mass.** Three levels are distinguished:

a) that of individual initiative, interiorly by pious attention to the principal parts of the Mass, exteriorly according to approved customs; using a small missal, piously meditating on the

46Council of Trent, Sess. XXII, Chap. 6; Denz. 944.

47Cf. Pope Pius XII, encyclicals *Mystici Corporis* and *Mediator Dei;* see also *Christ, and His Sacraments*, 409-10, 428-29.

mysteries of Christ, or performing other pious exercises, reciting other suitable prayers, etc.;

b) taking part in the eucharistic sacrifice by offering up prayers and song in common.

c) most perfectly, by giving the liturgical responses and pronouncing the parts proper to them.

With respect to this last level of participation the instruction has several recommendations: recitation of the short responses (*Amen; et cum spiritu tuo;* etc.), extending gradually to all those given by the acolyte and ultimately to all the parts of the Ordinary which rightly belong to the laity (*Gloria; Credo; Sanctus; Agnus Dei*). The entire *Pater noster,* "a suitable and ancient prayer as a preparation for Communion," may be recited (in Latin) together with the priest. The lessons from Scripture may be read to the people in the vernacular while the celebrant reads them in Latin, but it is forbidden for the congregation (or a reader) to recite aloud, either in Latin or in a word-for-word translation, any prayers of the Mass except those mentioned, except that more advanced groups (religious communities, for example) may recite with the priest the Introit, Gradual, Offertory antiphon and Communion antiphon. The celebrant, of course, should read the prayers prescribed to be said aloud so that all can hear them (using a microphone if necessary), taking special care in the recitation of prayers that call for the people's response or that are to be said in unison by priest and people.

2) **Participation at high Mass (Solemn or *Missa cantata*).** All who attend high Mass should at least sing the simple responses. But the ultimate aim of this participation must be to enable the faithful to sing the easier Gregorian melodies: *Kyrie eleison, Sanctus-Benedictus* (to be sung together) and *Agnus Dei* according to Mass XVI of the Roman Gradual. The *Gloria* and *Deo gratias* (in response to *Ite, missa est*) from Mass XV should be used, and either *Credo I* or *Credo III*.

Besides active participation at Mass, the instruction also recommends attendance and participation in Sunday and feastday Vespers and

Benediction. All of this is no doubt an ambitious program, an ideal to be realized only gradually, patiently, prudently and co-operatively. But it has the high purpose of restoring the laity to their rightful role in the liturgy of the Church, so that the faithful will no longer be "outsiders or as silent spectators"[48] in the official worship of the Mystical Body of Christ.

D. Sanctification of Feastdays

From the natural law itself arises the obligation of setting aside certain specific days of the year to be dedicated especially to the worship of God, a phenomenon observable in all religious societies from the most primitive to the most complex. That this sanctification should include a rest one day each week from all servile work in order properly to give praise to the Creator is a strict obligation which seems to arise from divine positive law.

The Church herself has further specified these precepts by determining on what days God is to be worshipped. According to her present discipline, all Sundays of the year and, for the universal Church, ten feasts are days of obligation: the Nativity of our Lord and its Octave, the Epiphany, the Ascension, Corpus Christi, the Immaculate Conception, the Assumption of our Blessed Mother, the feast of St. Joseph, the feast of SS. Peter and Paul and the feast of All Saints. By local law some of these feasts are excluded and others may be added; in the United States, for example, by virtue of special indult, the Epiphany, Corpus Christi, the feast of St. Joseph and that of SS. Peter and Paul are not holydays of obligation.

All baptized persons who have reached the age of seven and have the use of reason—including heretics, who are, however, frequently excused from formal sin by ignorance—are bound by this ecclesiastical precept, and by its further determination that the worship of God should include, at a minimum, the hearing of Mass and resting from servile and public work.

[48]Apostolic constitution *Divini Cultus*, Dec. 20, 1928.

(1) The Precept of Hearing Mass

The precept to attend Mass on Sundays and holydays of obligation binds the faithful to hear Mass whole and entire. This means that *all* the parts of the liturgy of the Mass, from the beginning to the Last Gospel must be attended. It does not suffice to attend only the parts actually instituted by Christ (i.e., the two Consecrations and the Communion). The obligation to hear the entire Mass means that it does not suffice to attend parts of two Masses simultaneously; thus if Mass were begun at the main altar when another priest reached the Consecration at a side altar, a man would not fulfill his obligation if he left when the Mass at the main altar reached the Consecration, because parts of two sacrifices do not unite to form a single sacrifice. Nor is the precept satisfied by attending part of two Masses successively if the Consecration and Communion do not pertain to the same Mass. If one is present for the Consecration and Communion of one Mass, however, he can fulfill his obligation by supplying the other parts from a separate Mass that he hears later, because thus he attends what is substantially one entire sacrifice.

The precept to attend Mass binds gravely, but does admit of a venial infraction. Therefore:

1) To omit a principal part of the sacrifice, i.e., the Consecration or Communion, is mortally sinful.

2) To omit a relatively great portion of the whole Mass is mortally sinful, e.g., to arrive after the Offertory; to arrive at the Gospel and leave after the Communion; to leave at the Communion; to be absent from the Preface until the Consecraiton, or from after the Consecration until the *Pater Noster*.

3) Omissions less notable than those given above are venially sinful. When such lesser omissions occur, it is well to make them up at another Mass.

To fulfill the precept, one must be physically present in such a way that he is able to know what the celebrant is doing. Also, one must have an intention, at least implicit and virtual, of worshipping God, and the attention required to make the hearing of Mass a truly human act. Thus, one who sleeps or reads a novel throughout the sacrifice does not fulfill the precept. Voluntarily to entertain occasional distractions is a venial sin of irreverence. Deliberately to distract others is ordinarily venially sinful, although it can become mortal by reasons of serious scandal.

There are various causes which can excuse one from the obligation to assist at Mass. Sometimes a contrary obligation interferes, as is the case with soldiers, policemen, mothers who must care for children, etc. Sometimes reasons of health, inclement weather or the obligations of charity toward others will interfere. A good practical rule is to demand the same kind of reasons for missing Mass that one would require for missing work or an important social obligation. In cases of doubt about the obligation to attend Mass, a priest should be consulted.

(2) The Precept of Abstaining from Servile Work

The obligation of man to include his body in his worship of God is the foundation of his obligation to abstain from servile work on Sundays and other days specially consecrated to the service of God. The natural law obliges creatures to worship God, and the positive law determines the precise time and manner of this worship. Before the coming of Christ, the Old Testament made elaborate provisions for divine worship; now these determinations are made by Christ's Church.

The negative duty of sanctifying the Lord's Day and other feast-days is to abstain from those occupations which would interfere with divine worship. These are: servile work, public commerce, judicial proceedings.

1) **Servile work** is *that which is done principally by physical toil and is directed immediately to bodily needs,* such as the work formerly done by slaves and now by servants and workmen. Such work must be judged from its nature and its purpose, and not from the labor involved, the time consumed, or the fact that someone is paid for it.[49] The following are servile works: planting,

[49]Theologians and canonists in recent years have attempted to find a more "workable" definition, but the results are inconclusive and to date have not altered the traditional concept expressed here.

tilling, harvesting, tree-chopping, ditchdigging, road-building, tailoring, typsetting, house-painting, building, plumbing, commercial baking, sewing, dressmaking, etc.

The contrary are **free** (*liberal*) **works**, which are done chiefly by mental effort, or which immediately serve an intellectual or cultural end. Among free works are: reading, studying, teaching, writing, typing (even for pay), singing, playing musical instruments, artistic drawing or painting, traveling (and all that it requires), photography, fishing, hunting, playing games, performing in theatrical productions, boating, etc. All of these are lawful—not, thereby, recommended—on Sundays and holydays.

2) **Public commerce** includes the buying and selling which is usual in stores, at auctions, etc. It does not include such transactions as the private sale of a house or a car, nor the sale of such things as newspapers, flowers, refreshments, etc., by vendors on the highways.

3) **Judicial proceedings** comprise all transactions directed to the conduct of affairs in either civil or ecclesiastical courts.

The precept against such occupations on Sundays and holydays is a serious law binding all the faithful who have attained the use of reason. Through lightness of matter, breaking this law can be venially sinful. It would certainly be mortally sinful to engage in heavy servile work for a total of 2½ hours, or in lighter work for 3 hours, because this amount of work would seriously interfere with the obligation to keep the day holy.

There are several causes which excuse from the obligation to avoid servile work:

1) The requirements for divine worship make lawful those works which are directly and proximately necessary for it. E.g., the work of priests and servers in processions and other services; the decoration and preparation of altars; and, when such things cannot be done conveniently beforehand, the cleaning of churches and the erecting of outdoor altars, etc. It is not lawful to make or launder linens, to build churches, to repair chalices, etc.

2) Public necessity requires the work of transportation crews, policemen, those who are preparing for national celebrations, etc.

3) Personal needs require the labor expended in cooking meals, entertaining friends, cleaning the house, shaving, shoe-shining, etc.

4) Supporting a family may require working on Sunday to avoid losing needed employment, or to avoid missing a notable and exceptional gain in wages. Workmen who are habitually compelled to work on Sundays should try to get other employment. The extraordinary need of gathering harvests lest they be lost through bad weather will also justify servile work on Sundays.

5) The needs of others sometimes require that servile work be done on their behalf. E.g., to care for children or the sick, to donate labor to some people in grave need, to aid others in preparing for a journey, wedding or funeral, etc.

(3) Sanctification of Feastdays

Needless to say, these minimum essential requirements for worshipping God on feastdays do not constitute a recommendation for keeping the Sabbath holy; they are what is necessary to avoid sin, even serious sin. The Christian family will realize that the purpose of this day of rest is not primarily to offer opportunity for picnics, ball games, do-it-yourself projects, but principally to consecrate this day to God, a dedication not wholly absolved by the half-hour or hour spent at Mass. Attendance at Sunday Vespers and Benediction, private prayers in the home, some time devoted to spiritual reading and meditation—these and other means will be used by the devout (i.e, the religious) Christian to honor God in a fitting manner. Here, indeed, the inspiration of the Spirit will move the children of God through the gift of piety to a truly worshipful celebration of the days of the Lord.

6. Vices Opposed to Religion

From the analysis of the nature of religion and of its interior and exterior acts which has preceded, we should have attained a deeper appreciation of what it is. What the worship of God is not appears from a consideration of the vices opposed to religion. Religion is a moral virtue and hence must be active in a middle ground of reasonableness between excess and defect. The vices opposed to religion, then, will be either an excess of religion or a defect. These vices in outline are the following:

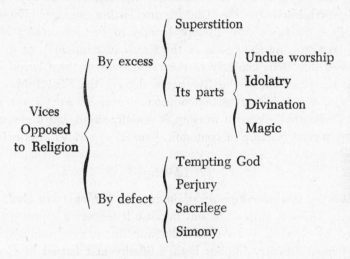

Vices Opposed to Religion
- By excess
  - Superstition
  - Its parts
    - Undue worship
    - Idolatry
    - Divination
    - Magic
- By defect
  - Tempting God
  - Perjury
  - Sacrilege
  - Simony

A. The Vices Opposed by Excess: Superstition

When it is said that superstition is an excess of divine worship, it does not mean that God is worshipped too much. It is not possible to worship God too much, any more than it is possible to love him too much. The excess of superstition is not one of quantity, but rather an excess in *direction* or *manner* of worship. **Superstition** is *a vice that pays divine worship either to someone who should not receive it, or to God himself, but in an unfitting manner.*

The following four vices are the principal kinds of superstition.

(1) Undue Worship

The worship of the true God may be undue or unsuitable either because it is false, or because it is excessive. **False worship** sometimes attributes something untrue to God, e.g., certain Jewish rituals indicate that the Messias is still to come. Sometimes the falsity of the worship arises from the fact that it is offered by an unauthorized minister, e.g., when a layman pretends to hear confessions. Ordinarily, false worship is mortally sinful.

Excessive worship does not attribute anything false to God, nor is it offered by unauthorized ministers; rather does it go beyond the limits established by the Church for divine worship. Excessive worship is found in any attempt to add to the ceremonies of the Mass (e.g., to sing the *Gloria* or the *Creed* in requiems), or to alter approved devotions contrary to the regulations of the Church (e.g., to change the form of the Rosary, to declare the First Fridays are holydays, to teach that certain novenas are necessary for salvation, etc.). Ordinarily, excessive worship is venially sinful, but it can easily become mortal because of contempt, scandal or serious disobedience.

(2) Idolatry

Idolatry is *the worshipping of images as if they were God.* This is among the very gravest of sins because it tenders a supreme insult to God by offering to a creature the worship reserved exclusively to the divinity. Idolatry implies both infidelity and hatred of God; it deprives God of his honor by striving to set up another god in the world.

(3) Divination

Those who claim to know and to foretell the future arrogate to themselves a power that is exclusively divine; hence, the methods by which they claim to do this are called divination. In its most proper sense, **divination** means *any unlawful inquiry into the future made with the aid of demons.* Divination is accomplished in many ways. Among the more common are: palm-reading, crystal-gazing, interpreting dreams, reading horoscopes, astrology, consulting spirits, etc. To be sure, few of these practices involve an explicit invocation of the devil; but only conjectural knowledge of future events can be gained by man's natural powers, nor will God, the angels or the blessed respond to such means, and hence these methods must of themselves derive their inspiration from the devil and necessarily involve an implicit invocation of his help.

Divination is ordinarily a mortal sin of supersitition, implying a willingness to receive information from devils, pretending to learn secrets known only to God, and thus offering insult to him. Knowingly and deliberately to consult diviners, fortune-tellers, etc., is seriously sinful, most especially so if there is explicit invocation of the devil, which usually involves other serious sins (blasphemy, sacrilege, etc.). To do so out of ignorance, curiosity or in jest could be venially sinful if it did not involve grave danger or scandal. At very best, trafficking with such people is extremely dangerous; at worst, it can be eternally tragic.

(4) Magic and Sorcery

In theological usage, the word "magic" does not refer to sleight of hand tricks done for amusement; it indicates rather *the use of anything to secure an effect which is beyond its natural power, or beyond the power imparted to it by divine or ecclesiastical authority.* Sometimes this is done with the invocation of demons, sometimes without.

Under the heading of magic are included: the use of charms for the cure of disease or the acquisition of knowledge; the enlistment of devils to do strange and wondrous deeds or to harm one's enemies; the attribution of false power to sacramentals or to peculiar devotions like "chain prayers," etc.

Like divination, the use of magic is ordinarily mortally sinful, although when there is no invocation of demons, and the power attributed to something is exaggerated rather than falsified, and there is no scandal or danger, it can become venially sinful.

B. Vices Opposed to Religion by Defeat: Irreligion

(1) Tempting God

All the vices which fall short of due worship of God are grouped together under the name of "irreligion." This and the following three subsections deal with the four kinds of irreligion.

To tempt God is *to seek a sign from him rashly and without any useful purpose*. Some examples are: to call upon God to strike one dead to show that he really exists; to pray Christ to appear in the Eucharist as a proof of its reality; to refuse human remedies to give God opportunity to prove his healing power.

There are times, however, when one may lawfully call for a sign from God, as when a missionary needs a sign from heaven to convince infidels, or when there is absolutely no other way to determine God's will in the face of mutually exclusive choices of what is good.

Ordinarily, to tempt God rashly is mortally sinful (cf. Deut. 6:16; Exod. 17:7; Matt. 4:7). Sometimes, however, it becomes venial due to lack of deliberation, or even because of the lightness of matter, as when someone expects to be cured of a cold without medicine and without miracles but by the power of God.

(2) Perjury

Perjury consists *in taking an oath to confirm a falsehood*. It is always *mortally* sinful because it implies a contempt for God, insofar as it suggests either that he ignores the truth or that he becomes party to a lie. Hence, the slightest lie becomes mortally sinful when confirmed by an oath.

God himself has promised the severest penalties for perjurers. (Cf. Lev. 19:12; Zach. 5:3, 4; Prov. 6:16-19; Matt. 5:33.)

(3) Sacrilege

Sacrilege is *any violation of a sacred person, place or thing*. Every sacrilege is contrary to religion because it implies an irreverence for God through the profanation of things dedicated to his service. Ordinarily, sacrilege is mortally sinful. The gravity of this sin increases both with the sanctity of what is violated and with the degree of profanation. The worst sacrileges of all are those committed against Christ himself in his eucharistic presence.

(4) Simony

The term "simony" is derived from the name of Simon the Magician who sought to buy spiritual power from the apostles (Acts 8:18).

Simony is *the deliberate intention to buy or to sell something spiritual for a temporal fee*. It is a sin opposed to religion because it bespeaks an irreverence for spiritual things by debasing them to the level of trade and commerce, by asserting falsely the power to dispose of them, and by opposing the source of spiritual things, which are all gifts of God. Simony is seriously sinful and is punishable by special penalties of the Church (Acts 8:20; Can. 2392).

Simony is always a true sale or purchase of something spiritual, e.g., to charge or to pay for absolution. It is not to be confused with gifts that may be offered for spiritual services to assist in the support of the ministers of the Church. For instance, the stipends offered for Masses are for the support of the priest, they are not a price paid for the Mass. Neither is it simony to give or to accept money for expenses incurred in spiritual ministrations, e.g., to pay the expenses of a priest who travels to officiate at a wedding.

7. Summary and Conclusion

Religion, the highest of the moral virtues, through its various acts offers to God in worship the rational creature in his entirety. Man's reasonable service to God is complete and eager subjection to him as his First Cause and ultimate perfection. So great is this creature of God that nothing less than union with infinite goodness can complete and fill him. By the gift of God such a union is possible to man and will fill him to overflowing. The gift can be his only if he subjects himself to God and the fulness of the gift is in proportion to his subjection. By the internal acts of religion especially, by devotion and by prayer, this subjection is accomplished. The external acts exist either to express the interior subjection or to arouse it.

Not a theological virtue, religion deals with the means to the end, human actions, rather than with the lofty end itself. But it is the highest of the virtues dealing with the means and as such has the right and indeed the obligation to organize and command all the moral virtues in the worship of God. In this capacity it has the special name of *sanctity* or *holiness,* and presupposes the moral cleansing of man that is the work of the other moral virtues in order that it may offer to God in worship an oblation that is in some sense worthy of the Creator.

Hence the following conclusions:

1. God's right to man's complete and dedicated service is based on a twofold title:

   1) God made man out of nothing and is the source of every perfection man has or can have.

   2) God redeemed man, purchased him from the slavery of sin and submission to the devil in the shedding of his blood, the perfect sacrifice.

2. "If the private and interior devotion of individuals were to neglect the august sacrifice of the altar and the sacraments, and to withdraw them from the stream of vital energy that flows from Head to members, it would indeed be sterile, and deserve to be condemned. But when devotional exercises, and pious practices in general not strictly connected with the sacred liturgy, confine themselves to merely human acts, with the express purpose of directing these latter to the Father in heaven, of rousing people to repentance and holy fear of God, of weaning them from seductions of the world and its vice, and leading them back to the difficult path of perfection—then certainly such practices are not only highly praiseworthy but absolutely indispensable. For they expose the dangers threatening the spiritual life; they promote the acquisition of virtue; and they increase the fervor and generosity with which we are bound to dedicate all that we are and all that we have to the service of Jesus Christ. Genuine and real piety, which the Angelic Doctor calls 'devotion,' and which is the principal act of the virtue of religion— that act which correctly relates and fitly directs men to God and by which they freely and spontaneously give themselves to the worship of God in its fullest sense—piety of this authentic sort needs meditation on the supernatural realities and spiritual exercises, if it is to be

nurtured, stimulated and sustained, and if it is to prompt us to lead a more perfect life."[50]

3. The prayers of the Mass form one integral prayer, i.e., they contain all the parts of prayer necessary to an integrally complete and perfect prayer.[51] These are:

1) *Supplications*, in which man addresses himself to God, reminding himself of God's sanctity and his own need and unworthiness. In the Mass these prayers precede the Consecration

2) *Orations* by which the mind of man is raised to God whom he addresses in prayer. These are found in the Consecration of the Mass, for then especially man's mind ought to be raised up to God.

3) *Petitions*, the essence of prayer by which man begs God for the things he needs. These follow the Consecration.

4) *Thanksgivings* by which the grateful man merits to receive greater benefits. These are found at the end of the Mass.[52]

4. "There are others who deny any impetratory power to our prayers, and would spread abroad the idea that prayers offered to God in private should not be considered worth very much. Public prayers, they say, prayers that are made in the name of the Church, are those which really count, as they come from the Mystical Body of Jesus Christ. Such an opinion is false; for the divine Redeemer maintains closest union not only with his Church, which is his beloved spouse, but also with each and every faithful soul in it, and he longs to speak with them heart to heart, especially after Holy Communion. It is true that public prayers—prayers, that is, that are offered by Mother Church—because of the dignity of the spouse of Christ, excel any other kind of prayer; but no prayer, even the most private, lacks its own dignity and power, and all prayer is immensely helpful to the Mystical Body.

"In that Body, thanks to the Communion of Saints, no good can be done, no virtue practiced by individual members without its contributing something also to the salvation of all. Similarly just because

[50]Pope Pius XII, encyclical *Mediator Dei.*
[51]Cf. I Tim. 2:1.
[52]Cf. St. Thomas, *Summa,* II-II, q. 83, a. 17.

a man is a member of this Body, he is not forbidden to ask for himself particular favors even for this life, provided he is always resigned to the divine will. The members do not lose their own personality, but remain subject to their own individual needs. Moreover, the common practice of the saints as well as ecclesiastical documents demonstrate how highly everyone should esteem mental prayer."[53]

5. "Our Redeemer showed his burning love for the Church particularly by praying for her to the heavenly Father. Imitating this example of Christ let us pray each day the Lord of the harvest to send laborers into his harvest. Let our united prayer rise daily to heaven for all the members of the Mystical Body of Jesus Christ, first for the bishops who are responsible in a particular way for their respective dioceses, then for the priests and religious men and women who have been called to the service of God, and are protecting, increasing, advancing the kingdom of the divine Redeemer at home and in the foreign missions. Let no member of this revered Body be forgotten in this common prayer; let there be a special memento for those who are burdened with the sorrows and afflictions of this earthly habitation and for the departed souls in purgatory. They, too, will be included who are being instructed in Christian doctrine, so that they may be able to receive baptism without delay.

"And oh how earnestly we desire that the immense charity of these common prayers embrace those also who, not yet perceiving the light of the Gospel's truth, are still outside the Church's safe fold, or because of the regrettable conflict of faith and unity are separated from us, who though unworthy bear the person of Jesus Christ on earth. Let us then re-echo that divine prayer of our Savior to the heavenly Father: 'That they all may be one, as thou Father in me and I in thee, that they also may be one in us; that the world may believe that thou hast sent me' (John 17:21). . . .

"And it is something more than commendable, in the present crisis above all it is imperative that fervent prayers rise to God for kings and princes and for all those who govern the nations and are thus in a position by their protecting power to help the Church, so that, the conflict ended, wearied man may see 'peace, the work of justice'

[53]Pope Pius XII, encyclical *Mystici Corporis*.

(Isa. 32:17) emerge under the gentle breeze of divine charity from out of these dread, tempestuous seas, and Holy Mother Church, 'may lead a quiet and peaceable life in all piety and chastity' (I Tim. 2:2)."[54]

6. "The worship [the Church] offers to God, all good and great, is a continuous profession of Catholic faith and a continuous exercise of hope and charity, as Augustine puts it tersely: 'God is to be worshipped,' he says, 'by faith, hope and charity.'[55] In the sacred liturgy we profess the Catholic faith explicitly and openly, not only by the celebration of the mysteries, and by offering the Holy Sacrifice and administering the sacraments, but also by saying or singing the Credo or Symbol of the faith—it is indeed the sign and badge, as it were, of the Christian—along with other texts, and likewise by the reading of Holy Scripture, written under the inspiration of the Holy Ghost. The entire liturgy, therefore, has the Catholic faith for its content, inasmuch as it bears public witness to the faith of the Church."[56]

7. "It is unquestionably the fundamental duty of man to orientate his person and his life towards God. 'For he it is to whom we must first be bound, as to an unfailing principle; to whom even our free choice must be directed as to an ultimate objective. It is he, too, whom we lose when carelessly we sin. It is he whom we must recover by our faith and trust.'[57] But man turns properly to God when he acknowledges his supreme majesty and supreme authority; when he accepts divinely revealed truths with a submissive mind; when he scrupulously obeys divine law, centering in God his every act and aspiration; when he accords, in short, due worship to the one true God by practicing the virtue of religion.

"This duty is incumbent, first of all, on men as individuals. But it also binds the whole community of human beings, grouped together by mutual social ties: mankind, too, depends on the sovereign authority of God. It should be noted, moreover, that men are bound by this obligation in a special way in virtue of the fact that God has raised them to the supernatural order. . . .

[54]Pope Pius XII, *ibid.*
[55]*Enchiridion*, Chap 3.
[56]Pope Pius XII, encyclical *Mediator Dei.*
[57]St. Thomas, *Summa*, II-II, q. 81, a. 1.

"The Church has, therefore, in common with the Word Incarnate, the aim, the obligation and the function of teaching all men the truth, of governing and directing them aright, of offering to God the pleasing and acceptable sacrifice; in this way the Church re-establishes between the Creator and his creatures that unity and harmony to which the Apostle of the Gentiles alludes in these words: 'Now, therefore, you are no more strangers and foreigners; but you are fellow citizens with the saints and domestics of God, built upon the foundation of the apostles and prophets, Jesus Christ himself being the chief corner stone: in whom all the building, being framed together, groweth up into a holy temple in the Lord, in whom you also are built together into a habitation of God in the Spirit' (Eph. 2:19-22). Thus the society founded by the divine Redeemer, whether in her doctrine and government, or in the sacrifice and sacraments instituted by him, or finally, in the ministry which he has confided to her charge with the outpouring of his prayer and the shedding of his blood has no other goal or purpose than to increase ever in strength and unity.

"This result is in fact achieved when Christ lives and thrives, as it were, in the hearts of men, and when men's hearts in turn are fashioned and expanded as though by Christ. This makes it possible for the sacred temple, where the divine majesty receives the acceptable worship which his law prescribes, to increase and prosper day by day in this land of exile on earth. Along with the Church, therefore, her divine founder is present at every liturgical function: Christ is present at the august sacrifice of the altar both in the person of his minister and above all under the eucharistic species. He is present in the sacraments, infusing into them the power which makes them ready instruments of sanctification. He is present finally in the prayer of praise and petition we direct to God, as it is written: 'Where there are two or three gathered together in my name, there am I in the midst of them' (Matt. 18:20). The sacred liturgy is consequently the public worship which our Redeemer as Head of the Church renders to the Father, as well as the worship which the community of the faithful renders to its founder, and through him to the heavenly Father."[58]

[58]Pope Pius XII, encyclical *Mediator Dei.*

BIBLIOGRAPHICAL NOTE

St. Thomas considers the virtue of religion in the *Summa*, II-II, Questions LXXXI-C. There is no work in English devoted specifically to the whole subject, but there are a great many works which treat one or another aspect. Among the works on prayer we may mention *Stages in Prayer* by J. G. Arintero, O.P. (St. Louis: Herder, 1958), *Prayer in Practice* by Romano Guardini (New York: Pantheon, 1957), *An Introduction to Contemplative Meditation* by F. D. Joret, O.P. (London: Blackfriars, 1955) and *The Craft of Prayer* by Vincent McNabb, O.P. (London: Burns, Oates and Washbourne, 1951), an excellent short work. Hubert Van Zeller, O.S.B., offers many practical suggestions for busy people in *Praying While You Work* (Springfield, Ill.: Templegate, 1951).

Of general works on the liturgy we may mention *Public Worship* by J. A. Jungmann, S.J. (Collegeville, Minn.: The Liturgical Press, 1957), *Catholic Liturgy* by Gaspar Lefebvre, O.S.B. (St. Louis: Herder, 1954), *Of Sacraments and Sacrifice* by Clifford Howell, S.J. (Collegeville, Minn.: The Liturgical Press, 1954), and, in more popular vein, *The Sacramental Way* by Mary Elizabeth Perkins (New York: Sheed and Ward, 1948). *Liturgical Piety* is discussed by Louis Bouyer, Orat. (Notre Dame: The University of Notre Dame Press, 1955) and *Sanctification of Sunday* is the subject of the 1949 Proceedings of the National Liturgical Week (Conception, Mo.: The Liturgical Conference, 1949). Pius Parsch has two specialized works of great interest: *The Church's Year of Grace* (Collegeville, Minn.: The Liturgical Press, 1953-1958) and *The Liturgy of the Mass* (St. Louis: Herder, 1958).

There are, besides, many excellent pamphlets and booklets on these subjects, and a great number of periodical articles in such magazines as *Worship, Cross and Crown, The Spiritual Life, The Life of the Spirit, The Grail, Altar and Home*, etc.

CHAPTER FOURTEEN

The Social Virtues

1. Introduction

Man is not alone. Like the grain of sand or the shining star he is part of a multitude, numbering among his companions on his journey through life both those of high and low estate. He comes *from God;* he lives *among men*—a situation giving rise to a number of relationships: man to God, man to man, man to society, society to man; relationships embracing the vast field of human activity subject to the influence of the two great virtues of justice and charity.

Grace and the virtues effect in man a transition "to perfect manhood, to the mature measure of the fulness of Christ" (Eph. 4:13). The present chapter presents but another phase of this maturing process: the share allotted to the allied virtues of justice in forming the image of Christ in each of us. Justice essentially regards others, renders to them their due, and strives for exact equality in its payment. Not every virtue related to justice bears these same three characteristics, although all do have one mark in common: *they deal with another.* They are, therefore, like justice itself, **social virtues.**

616

Virtue's goal is to put man in tune with all of reality; the function of justice is to put him in harmony with a particular part of that reality, that area of his operations dealing with debts owed to another, whether God or man.

Justice's perfection is reached in the virtues of commutative, legal and distributive justice, because a strict debt and the full measure of equality in the payment of debts is demanded by these. The other virtues of justice (its *potential parts*), those that are said to be related or annexed to the principal virtue, fail to measure up to the perfect virtue: either because no strict debt exists between the parts, or, granted a strict debt, because the debtor is unable to render the debt with exact equality. The virtues to be treated here will fall into these two general groupings.

With this distinction in mind we may give a brief outline of the virtues related to justice whose purpose is to help man cope with the myriad debts or obligations that fall to him as a member of society. To begin with, certain relationships give rise to truly strict debts, but debts which can never be paid in full: man's debt to God, to parents and country, to superiors and men of excelling virtue. Since society exists because of the good order established between superiors and inferiors, these virtues are needed to stabilize this order. The virtue of **religion** assists man in rendering his debt to God; the virtue of **piety** to parents and country; the virtue of **observance** to other earthly superiors. These three virtues are called **virtues of reverence,** for a debt of reverence, honor or esteem springs from the very nature of man's subordination to a superior, be that superior divine or human. If this debt is not paid, both society and the individual suffer.

But society also depends upon the good order established between its members who are equal. If a debt is a strict debt of justice and is capable of equal payment by the debtor, it is a job for the virtue of justice itself. But let us pause at this point to consider the notion of debt. A man who borrows five dollars immediately incurs the relationship of strict indebtedness to another. But if a man *gives* five dollars to another freely and spontaneously, certainly the recipient is neither bound to refuse this gift nor to return it. It is his to do with as he will, for the benefactor has freely surrendered his strict right to the object.

Although this is quite clear, it is also clear that the recipient of a gift "owes" something to his benefactor; fair play, common decency, moral integrity, social respectability, demand that a man react favorably to the action of a benefactor. St. Thomas called this a **moral debt** as opposed to strict **legal debt.** Refusal to pay a legal debt is punishable by the laws of society; but moral debt—the failure to manifest gratitude, for example—goes unpunished. The man who reneges on his moral debts, however, does harm himself in some way, for he is no longer considered a perfectly respectable member of society; his integrity and honor are shaken. Hence, man, the social animal, owes debts beyond the demands of strict justice to his fellows and needs special virtues to assist him in rendering these debts.

Man is indebted both to those who do him good and to those who do him evil. The virtues of **gratitude** and **revenge** help him pay these debts. The virtue of **truthfulness** also pertains to this area of moral debt, because (although frequently a strict obligation in justice demands that we speak the truth to legitimate authority) very often one deals only with social equals, not superiors, and as men of honor we "owe" the truth to our fellows. Thus, this is a debt both to society, lest its good order be impaired, and to man himself, lest his integrity be demeaned by falsehood.

Furthermore, man owes it to himself and to society to deal pleasantly with others. Since it is necessary that man live with others, it is fitting that he do it in a pleasant manner. The virtue of **affability** assures this mode of living. The virtue of **liberality** inspires man to give his external goods to others; for it is fitting to give others of one's surplus.

So we may add to the virtues of reverence another series of virtues concerned with man's moral debts to society: the **virtues of social conduct.**

All of these secondary virtues of justice are definitely social virtues. Charity and justice are certainly worthy of the name: charity influences the whole area of human activity and justice deals with the adequate satisfaction of strict rights. But to perfect the areas not governed by justice and to provide the proper climate for the exercise of charity, the related virtues of justice, the social virtues, are a necessity.

Consequently, the plan of our chapter will follow this schema:

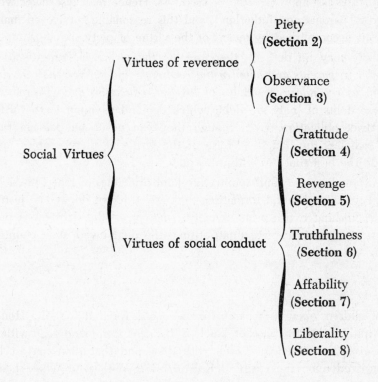

2. PIETY

God, as first cause and last end, as supreme and infinite excellence, has man in his everlasting debt, for man depends upon God for life, sustenance and direction to his ultimate goal. Although this debt will follow man to the grave and beyond, God is satisfied as long as man does what he is able. And man is able, by means of the virtue of religion, to satisfy the demands of divine justice by testifying to the superior excellence of the Godhead and by humbly acknowledging his submission and subjection to his Lord and Creator. In a word, man pays his debt with the coin of *worship*.

But secondary principles, one's parents and country, share in the divinely instigated work of providing life, nourishment and direction, thus assuming the role of creditors. Hence man also owes worship to parents and fatherland, and this reasonable service on man's part is accomplished by means of the virtue of piety.

Piety may be defined, therefore, as *the virtue inclining man to render to parents and country the reverence and service that are due them as secondary principles of his life, education and governance.* These debts of piety are debts which demand payment in the order of strict obligation. Even though they can never be paid in full, nevertheless the honest exercise of the virtue of piety enables man to do the best that lies within his power.

Although parents and country are joint principles of man's physical, intellectual and moral formation, they are different enough to justify distinguishing two aspects of piety: *filial* piety—the debt owed parents; and *patriotic* piety (patriotism)—the debt owed one's country.

A. Filial Piety

"Children, obey your parents in the Lord, for that is right. 'Honor thy father and thy mother'—such is the first commandment with a promise—'that it may be well with thee, and that thou mayest be long-lived upon the earth'" (Eph. 6:1-3). "With your whole heart honor your father; your mother's birthpangs forget not. Remember, of these parents you were born; what can you give them for all they gave you?" (Sir. 7:27-28).

The primary debt of filial piety is owed to one's parents; but in a secondary way it includes brothers, sisters, grandparents and even one's more distant relatives. All of those who share in the blood of one's father share in *his* right to honor and reverence. The obligations of filial piety, then, extend even further on this secondary plane, touching the relationships between husband and wife, parents and

children. For husband and wife see in each other the power of continuing the ancestral line; they honor this trace of ancestry in each
other, and by so doing exercise the virtue of filial piety. In the same
way they honor their children as representatives of their forebears,
carriers of the family honor and name.

Society's basic social unit, the family, is the field of operation for
filial piety. To this virtue belongs the task of seeing to it that the
natural rights of those living within the family circle suffer no harm
from others within that circle. Bearing this in mind, we shall consider
the obligations regulated by this virtue in the following order:
1) the obligations of children toward their parents; 2) of parents
toward their children; and 3) of man and wife to each other.

(1) Obligations of Children toward Parents

Piety imposes upon man four obligations of both natural and
divine law, due his parents precisely as they assume the parental
role: 1) *the service of love,* because they are closely united to him
by a most special relationship, for after God, parents are the source
of man's existence and his greatest benefactors; 2) *honor and
reverence,* because of their dignity and excellence as his superiors;
3) *obedience,* because they are his divinely appointed guides; and
at times when necessity urges, 4) *spiritual and material assistance.*

The first of these debts includes both natural love and the love
of charity. Nature and supernature demand that man love himself,
and parents are considered, in a sense, to be identified with their offspring by the powerful bond of blood. Piety itself presupposes this
debt of love and is built upon it. Honor and obedience, however, are
more properly the matter of filial piety, while the obligation to succor
one's parents in time of need arises equally from love and piety.

It follows from this that every venial sin of hatred, ill will and
contempt directed against those outside the family circle very easily
becomes mortal when directed against one's parents. Moreover, a
double sin is incurred, for to the basic malice of his bad action the
sinner adds the special evil of a sin against the special love of piety
owed to his parents.

Love, honor, obedience and assistance are the debts man owes his parents. Let us consider them in more detail.

1. **The obligation of love and assistance.** Children are bound to love their parents second only to God. A mere external show of love without the inner affection of the heart is insufficient. Besides an external display there must be an inner act of willing them their greatest good. Love must be forthcoming, therefore, at all times. Material and spiritual assistance, on the other hand, are due only when necessity demands.

Children sin gravely *through a lack of interior love* when they hate or despise their parents interiorly; when they rejoice in their adversity, or sorrow over their prosperity; and when they hope for the death of their parents in order to be free from their control. or enjoy an inheritance. Similarly, it would be seriously sinful if children *through a lack of exterior love* were to manifest hatred toward their parents by revealing their serious shortcomings, by insulting them seriously, or by causing them grave sorrow and worry (for example, associating with evil company, neglect of study, keeping late hours).

Children are bound to assist their parents when they are in need. So strict is this obligation that a son or daughter would be obliged to defer marriage or entrance into the religious life to come to their assistance. The possible needs that could arise defy cataloguing, ranging as they do from food and clothing to visiting them when ill or comforting their sorrow. Furthermore, children should come to the spiritual aid of their parents as well, e.g., by warning them of approaching death if they are seriously ill, by providing the necessary sacraments, and by praying for the repose of their souls in death.

2. **The obligation of reverence and honor.** Reverence toward parents demands that children not only give interior acknowledgment of the dignity and authority received by their parents from God, but that they must also manifest this attitude in their external deportment. Refusing to speak to one's father or mother, being ashamed to have them about when friends stop by, are examples of violations against this virtue.

3. **The obligation of obedience.** A corollary of the preceding obligation of reverence and honor, obedience, as well as fear and gratitude, are but marks of a child's respect for his parents' *command* (obedience), *authority* (fear) or *material, intellectual and moral assistance* (gratitude).

The obligation to love and honor one's parents never ceases; the obligation to assist one's parents ceases when their needs end. But the obligation to obey one's parents ceases when a child reaches his majority, when he undertakes to live independently, or when he marries. As long as a son or daughter remains in the home of his or her parents, however, he or she is obliged to submit to all the household directives of the parents, no matter what their age or condition might be.

Whenever parents seriously command a child in a serious matter, it is ordinarily mortally sinful to disobey. Serious matter means whatever might cause grave harm to either the child or the family, that is, disobedience which would result in immorality, grave danger to salvation, or notable danger to temporal goods or honor. To refuse to attend Mass or to receive the sacraments, to neglect study to the extent that one fails in school, to disgrace the family by associating with bad companions—these would be grave sins against obedience.

All that has been said here concerning obedience applies as well to permanent guardians or foster parents. The right of parents to obedience (respect and honor as well) is shared in a secondary manner by school administrators and teachers. To these, parents communicate a share of their own divinely given power to direct and govern. Consequently, classroom disturbances, insulting and insolent behaviour and discourtesy to instructors and disciplinarians, studied inattention in class, misuse of study time, all are highly offensive to piety.

(2) Obligations of Parents toward Children

Duties of parents toward children fall under the secondary acts of filial piety, and are binding by both natural and divine law. The very nature of the parent-child relationship demands payment of these obligations under threat of serious sin. Piety requires that parents provide for their children: 1) *a special love,* because of their oneness with them; 2) *physical and spiritual education,* because they are the first earthly principle of their children's existence and governance; and 3) *a certain paternal guidance* (providence, provision) for the purpose of forming or directing the child's life rightly, until that time when the child can do this for himself.

1. **The obligation of love.** Principally internal, but manifested outwardly for its full perfection, this love should be both natural (because the child, naturally speaking, is something of the parents), and supernatural (since the parents co-operate intimately with God in the work of sanctifying, as well as giving existence to their children).

The love of parents for their children must be sincere and it must be Christian. It must cause them to reject overly severe and unjust punishment, it must lead them to correct their children's faults and chastise their wrongdoings. No parent should idolize his children by granting all their wishes or by failing to correct their vices, for this, in the long run, is a cruel kindness; nor should parents display partiality in their affection for their children, for this proves a fertile source of domestic discord.

2. **The obligation of education.** Before we begin an analysis of the duties of parents in regard to education, certain basic premises concerning the nature and subject of education must be laid down. For this particular parental duty is meaningless until the precise nature of education has been determined.

The term "education" may be used to indicate two things: a perfection which an individual has or will attain (as when one speaks of the "well-educated man"); or the processes by which that perfection is attained (as when one says that another is "being subjected to a college education"). We are concerned with the particular perfection or good to be acquired. From this aspect a Catholic education (the only education perfectly attuned to reality) is the development of ". . . the supernatural man who thinks, judges and acts constantly and consistently in accordance with right reason illumined by the supernatural light of the example and teaching of Christ; in other words, to use the correct term, the true and finished man of character."[1]

Education, then, is a perfection to be realized in its subject, man: "The subject of Christian education is man whole and entire, soul united to body in unity of nature, with all his faculties, natural and supernatural, such as right reason and revelation show him to be."[2]

Hence, education is the progressive and harmonious development of human faculties, by means of which the infant is transformed into the perfect man. Consequently, education ought to be chiefly *spiritual*, so that it might destroy youth's evil inclinations by checking their untamed passions, and direct them to good by strengthening their good qualities and ordering them to human perfection. But education must extend also to the *corporeal*, so that the body may be well disposed to exercise its proper functions as an apt instrument of the soul. Hence the old adage: a sound mind in a sound body. In summary, education should be proportionate to the native abilities of the child, preparatory for his future state in life, and, most importantly, ordered to his supernatural goal.

Such must be the true conception of education. Among natural societies the primary rights and duties in regard to education belong to the parents. The source of these rights is divine: "God directly communicates fecundity to the family which is the principle of life in the natural order, and hence also the principle of education for life, together with authority which is the principle of order."[3] St. Thomas teaches: "The father is the principle of generation, of education and discipline, and of everything that bears on the perfecting of human life."[4] That this should be the case is evident because "nature intends not merely the generation of offspring, but also its development and advance to the perfection of man considered as man, that is, to the state of virtue."[5] In the Christian conception of

[1]Pius XI, encyclical *Divini Illius Magistri* (The Christian Education of Youth), Dec. 31, 1929.
[2]Pius XI, *ibid.*
[3]Pius XI, *ibid.*
[4]*Summa*, II-II, q. 102, a. 1.
[5]St. Thomas, *Summa*, III, q. 41, a. 1.

education, the parents have far-reaching responsibilities, for ". . . the obligation of the family to bring up children includes not only religious and moral education, but physical and civic education as well, principally insofar as it touches upon religion and morality."[6]

The duties of parents toward the corporeal education of their children embrace two principal points: provision for the material necessities of life, and, since nature intends that they care for the life they have brought into the world, care for the actual physical or bodily development of the child. Hence parents are seriously obliged to provide nourishment and other essentials—clothing, living quarters— until that time when their children can care for themselves; they must also see that their young develop their physical powers by exercise and other labors proportionate to their age, and acquire a condition of sound health that their bodies may always be fit to render apt service to their souls.

Of greater importance, however, is the responsibility for the spiritual education of the child. Spiritual education is a general term embracing particular parental responsibilities: religious instruction, character training and correction of their children. For the attainment of these ends good example and constant vigilance stand as invaluable adjuncts. Although these obligations fall primarily upon parents, they are fulfilled only by acknowledging the rights of the Church and accepting her magisterium. Consequently, the duty of parents to send their children to Catholic schools is not a light one. Non-Catholic, nondenominational and so-called mixed schools leave a child in religious ignorance; furthermore, their failure to teach religion minimizes its importance. Schools of this kind are considered dangerous occasions of sin and their attendance is prohibited by Church law (Can. 1374).

Of course, no one is held to the impossible. At present, because there are simply not enough Catholic schools, qualifications must be made. In such instances the bishop of the diocese must consider the circumstances, and decide what safeguards to take so that attendance at these schools by Catholics may be tolerated. Even so, the obligation

[6]Pius XI, *op. cit.*

of parents and Church to see to the religious formation of offspring and to obviate the evils involved in such attendance is a continuous one. Thus arises the pressing importance of "release time" religion classes on the primary and secondary school levels, and the Newman Club movement on the college plane.

3. **The obligation of parental guidance** (providence). Parents are obliged to provide for the future state of their children, helping them choose a way of life befitting their condition, natural abilities and inclinations, and insuring the successful pursuance of their chosen vocation. This obligation is satisfied: 1) by seeing to it that the child acquires sufficient mastery of those arts and sciences that will enable him to live as befits his condition; 2) by giving counsel and advice concerning the choice of a way of life which is in accord with his condition and circumstances; and 3) by supplying the materials required to attain the state of life that has been chosen.

(3) The Obligations of Spouses

Over and above the mutual duties arising between spouses from strict justice—the right administration of material goods and the rendering of the marriage debt—and in addition to the duty of observing conjugal fidelity, there are three obligations arising from piety: 1) *mutual love;* 2) *mutual help and comfort;* and 3) *cohabitation.*

1. **Mutual love.** Since husband and wife are as "one flesh" (Matt. 19:5), it is fitting that they be of one heart as well. And with this thought in mind, St. Paul has exhorted husbands to love their wives as Christ loved his Church (Eph. 5:25), and wives their husbands (Tit. 2:4; Col. 3:18; I Tim. 2:15). This love must be interior as well as exterior—the love of the heart overflowing into positive action. Negatively, it should act as a preventative, warding off inordinate egoism, hard and abusive words, and especially jealousy, which is truly the sepulcher of conjugal love.

2. **Mutual help and comfort.** Marriage is designed in such a way that the spouses complete one another, for the talents and gifts of the one are the complement of the other. Wherefore God has said:

"It is not good for man to be alone; let us make for him a help like unto himself" (Gen. 2:18). Marriage, therefore, implies not only a mere physical union of bodies, but a unity of minds and hearts as well. The result is an amicable social organism in which man and wife freely promise to render special service and help to each other.

3. **Cohabitation.** This obligation binds man and wife to common bed and board. A corollary of the preceding obligations of education and mutual help, it is necessary if these duties are to be fulfilled. "For this cause," therefore, "a man shall leave his father and mother, and cleave to his wife, and the two shall become one flesh" (Matt. 19:5).

Nature as well as Christian tradition places the husband as head of the wife and the family. "Let wives be subject to their husbands as to the Lord; because a husband is head of the wife, just as Christ is head of the Church" (Eph. 5:22, 23). Hence, it belongs to the husband to possess the primacy of rule not only over his children but also over his wife—mindful, however, that she is neither slave nor servant, but his worthy helpmate and associate. As head of the family, the husband is principally obliged to provide fitting support, assistance and protection for his wife; he is to see—prudently —that she fulfills her household functions; and he must take care to correct and admonish her should she become remiss in the execution of familial duties.

The wife ought to show respect for her spouse as head and ruler over the family, rendering him prompt and fitting obedience. She should be solicitous concerning her domestic duties, as her position in the family demands; she should subject herself to her husband in the matter of household management, and even more so in the matter of fitting moral conduct.

B. Patriotic Piety

Man has his beginnings from God, from parents and from the land of his birth, and therefore each lays claim in strict justice to his reverence, honor and subjection. The virtue of **patriotic** piety or **patriotism** is that virtue which inclines man to render this debt to his fatherland. Hence, preserving the proper proportions, all that was said of religion and filial piety regarding the matter of reverence and service must be said of patriotism.

The common good is not the object of patriotism; rather patriotism aims at the *recognition of the superiority of one's country* (in the limited field of its superiority) *and the subjection of man in that same limited field*. Hence, patriotism—and this must be carefully noted—is not primarily the love of one's country; its principal concern is that of rendering *service* to one's country, i.e., **worship**. Patriotism, then, demands of the citizen an *interior respect* for his country and its representatives. It requires *service* as well, the active work of sustaining, protecting and deepening the life of his country.

Service includes obedience, without which the machinery of government would soon cease to function; material aid through taxation (rendered not because of the common good but as an acknowledgment of one's dependence on his country as the source of one's being); a worship involving reverence, honor and subjection. Love of country certainly contributes to patriotism, as patriotism does to love of country, but they are distinct: patriotism is concerned with what is right and just, and not with one's emotions. Hence, it demands certain internal and external acts on the part of its citizens, acts which will add to the perfection of the individual as he is a part of the nation, and which will contribute to material life. Chief among these duties are *military service*, a debt paid from the same motive as material aid, and *voting*, the intelligent participation in the conservation and strengthening of one's governmental system.

The worship that patriotism directs to one's country includes the worship which is due to one's fellow citizens and even to all the friends of one's country. Respect and honor are due in these instances precisely and only insofar as this respect and honor redound to the fatherland itself; for citizens are united as parts to a whole, while friends are linked to one's country by the good they have bestowed, or shall bestow upon it.

Since a man's country is subordinate to God in the matter of authority, and to God and parents in the matter of earthly origins, there is no place for a philosophy of exaggerated nationalism. The state is not absolutely supreme, but is part of a greater hierarchical arrangement. "Our country! . . . may she always be in the right; but our country, right or wrong." This view voiced by Stephen Decatur, well-meaning as it no doubt was, gives expression to a complete upsetting of values. Nationalism, pushed to its extreme, allows the state to "put itself in the place of the Almighty and elevates the state or group into the last end of life, the supreme criterion of the moral and juridical order, and therefore forbids every appeal to the principles of natural reason and of the Christian conscience."[7] To consider one's country, therefore, as something ultimate to which everything else should be subordinated and directed cannot fail to harm the true and lasting prosperity of the state itself and its fellow nations, and is a far cry from true patriotism.

In addition to the dangers inherent in excessive nationalism, there is also a threat to patriotism in the doctrine that preaches the destruction of all national lines in favor of one great, all-inclusive supranational organization. Although such a possibility is extremely remote, a consideration of it does bring out two important truths: 1) Christianity provides many cogent arguments for the universal solidarity of mankind; but at the same time, 2) that solidarity is in no way to be construed as a false, supranational cure-all for world troubles which would deny all individuality to the cultures, traditions and ways of life of the nations involved.

Both of these ideas were voiced by Pius XII in his inaugural encyclical. Regarding the first point, the solidarity of all men, he wrote:

> The Apostle of the Gentiles makes himself the herald of this truth which associates men as brothers in one great family when he proclaims to the Greek world that God "hath made of one, all mankind, to dwell upon the whole face of the earth, determining appointed times, and the limits of their habitation: that they should seek God" (Acts 17:26-27). This is a marvelous vision, which makes us see the human race in the unity of one common origin in God . . . ; in the unity of nature which in every man is equally composed of material body and spiritual, immortal soul; in the unity of the immediate end and mission in the world; in the unity of dwelling-place, the earth, of whose resources all men can by natural right avail

[7]Pius XII, encyclical *Summi Pontificatus*, Oct. 20, 1939.

themselves, to sustain and develop life; in the unity of the supernatural end, God himself, to whom all should tend; in the unity of means to secure that end.

It is the same Apostle who portrays for us mankind in the unity of its relations with the Son of God . . . in the unity of its ransom, effected for all by Christ. . . .[8]

As to universal brotherhood being detrimental to the customs and traditions of individual peoples, Pius continued:

The Church of Christ . . . cannot and does not think of deprecating or disdaining the particular characteristics which each people with jealous and understandable pride cherishes and retains as a precious heritage. Her aim is a supernatural union in all-embracing love, deeply felt and practised, and not the unity which is exclusively external and superficial and by that very fact weak. The Church hails with joy and follows with her maternal blessing every method of guidance and care which aims at a wise and orderly evolution of particular forces and tendencies having their origin in the individual character of each race, provided that they are not opposed to the duties incumbent on men from their unity of origin and common destiny.

Nor is there any fear lest the consciousness of universal brotherhood aroused by the teaching of Christianity, and the spirit which it inspires, be in contrast with love of traditions or the glories of one's fatherland or impede the progress of prosperity or legitimate interests. For that same Christianity teaches that in the exercise of charity we follow a God-given order, yielding the place of honor in our affections and good works to those who are bound to us by special ties. . . .

Legitimate and well-ordered love of our native country, however, should not make us close our eyes to the all-embracing nature of Christian charity, which calls for consideration of others and of their interest in the pacifying light of love.[9]

One more distinction remains to be made before concluding the present discussion of patriotism. The concept of *fatherland,* in company with that of the *family,* denotes a natural social organism, as opposed to the artificial or juridicial unit which we might denominate as the *state* or *nation.* Historically, the fatherland and state were coterminous, but the vicissitudes of time and vagaries of mankind have produced a dichotomy between the two which is painfully evident in the case of the satellite countries under Communist domination.

[8]*Ibid.*
[9]*Ibid.*

Where fatherland and state are one and the same, there is no difficulty in determining the province of patriotism. But where there is conflict between the two, the opposition must be resolved—as far as patriotism is concerned—in favor of the fatherland, and this because of its close approximation as a principle of being to the natural unit which is the family. Latent in this truth, by way of corollary, is the reasoning which justifies any legitimate attempt at revolt against a tyrannical state.

3. OBSERVANCE

A. Observance in General

It is the special mark of justice to enable man to render to another his due. Hence, wherever there is a special aspect of something due to another, there is need for a special virtue. Therefore, since man owes a debt of reverence and submission to his parents because of their dignity as his source of familial rule, he owes a similar debt, in strict justice, to those of his fellow men who have been endowed by the state with authority to rule and govern outside the family circle. This is the area of human relationships governed by the virtue of observance, *the virtue which inclines man to render the debt of reverence and submission due to persons constituted in authority.*

The man thus established in authority shares in the principality and excellence of the state itself. But when service is rendered him in a personal fashion, for his own utility and glory, it comes under the virtue of observance. The debt, one also beyond man's power to pay, is owed to the excellence of the superior; it is an excellence shared either with parents (e.g., in the case of teachers and school officials) or with the state, depending upon the particular office and work of an individual superior. All that has been said, then, of religion, filial piety and patriotism—carefully preserving the proper proportion of steadily diminishing principality—must be said of the virtue of observance in regard to those established in authority.

In practice this means that *reverence* and *subjection* is owed to superiors: reverence because of their official position and dignity as superiors, subjection because of their office of government or direction. Consequently, the virtue of observance obliges the good citizen to give to his superiors in the state: **honor,** because of their official position; **fear,** because of their coercive power; **obedience,** because of their directive function; and **support,** because of the labor and losses sustained in their service of the common good.

B. Dulia

Dulia is a virtue concerned with giving honor to those who do not come under the honor rendered by the virtues of filial piety, patriotism and observance. Honor is owed to excellence, even though that excellence may fall short of that had by parents, country or legitimate authority.

The obligation to honor one's fellow man differs from the strict legal debt of honoring superiors who rank as principles of being or government, for dulia is owed to persons of excellence even though a man be not subject to them. The debt then is a *moral* one, rather than legal; it is a debt due by reason of a certain integrity, one fitting for the good of the man who renders it and for the good of society.

Dulia may be defined as *the virtue which inclines man to pay honor and reverence to any man because of some excellence of his virtue.* Thus dulia offers honor to all, save those confirmed in evil. For everyone possesses some excellence or superiority in virtue, learning or art. Indeed, the many types of excellence prove that the same kind and degree of honor will not be given to all. The excellence most deserving of honor among men is holiness, an honor increasing in proportion to one's progressive union with God. Therefore, men pay great honor to the saints and even greater honor to the Mother of God.

C. Obedience

Obedience, in its ordinary course, is designed to proceed from a subject's reverence and honor for a superior. In this general sense it is not the act of a special virtue but rather an act of religion or piety or observance, as the case may be. It is conceivable, however, that a subject might obey his superior for the precise motive *of fulfilling his command,* and not at all as a mark of respect or honor for the superior. This motive for human conduct may not be in itself the ideal—"obedience," St. Gregory points out,[10] "should be practiced, not out of servile fear but from a sense of charity, not through fear of punishment but through love of justice"—but because of its possibility there is a basis for maintaining the existence of another virtue, distinct because of its special motive and having its own material object. This virtue, **obedience,** may be defined as *that virtue which inclines man's will to comply promptly and willingly with the command of his superior, precisely because it is a command and obligatory.*

The attitude behind the phrase, "Orders are orders," expresses the moving spirit of this virtue quite well. Other virtues of reverence pay honor to *persons,* but obedience pays honor directly to the *command* of the superior. Although the object of obedience is less perfect than the object of the theological virtues and the moral virtue of religion, all of which are directed to God, if we consider what obedience renounces in order to adhere more closely to God, then it is the greatest of the moral virtues. For it is a greater good to contemn one's own will than to contemn lesser goods of the body and soul or of the external world, goods with which the other moral virtues are concerned. "Obedience is better than sacrifices: and to hearken rather than to offer the fat of rams" (I Kings 15:22).

Since obedience expresses respect for the commands of one's superiors, the extent of one's obedience will be measured by the extent of his superior's authority. The commands of God, since his authority is unlimited, are to be obeyed in all things. Human authority, however, is limited by divine and human law. Hence, a subject must not obey a command which goes contrary to natural or divine law: "We must obey God rather than men" (Acts 5:29). If a human superior should overstretch his competency but command nothing illicit, the subject *may,* but is not bound to obey. In case of doubt as to the liceity of

[10]*Book of Morals,* Bk. XXXV, Chap. 14, n. 10.

a particular commanded act, a doubt which cannot be removed, the presumption stands in favor of the superior and he must be obeyed.

Slavish or indiscreet obedience, which extends even to sinful matters, sins against true obedience **through excess**. One can also offend against obedience **by defect**, when he either materially or formally disobeys. By *material* disobedience one intends the satisfaction of a sinful desire contrary to the obligations of some other virtue; hence, there is only one sin formally committed, namely, that against the particular virtue violated and not against obedience. *Formal* disobedience, however, is a special sin, committed when the sinner refuses to obey because of actual contempt, either for the command itself or the person issuing the command. Consequently, although every sin involves at least material disobedience, only the presence of actual contempt directly violates the virtue of obedience.

Formal disobedience involving contempt of one's superior is always mortally sinful, admitting of no lightness of matter—a refusal of subjection which is directly opposed to God's law and his love, and the moral rights of our neighbor, our superior. Formal contempt of a particular command of a superior, however, though generally mortally sinful, does admit of lightness of matter.

St. Paul sums up this matter clearly:

> Let everyone be subject to the higher authorities, for there exists no authority except from God, and those who exist have been appointed by God. Therefore he who resists the authority resists the ordinance of God; and they that resist bring on themselves condemnation.[11]

D. Conclusion

Dulia and obedience have been treated in this section on observance for the sake of convenience: dulia, because it completes the treatment of the honor and reverence paid at the highest level to God by the virtue of religion, and at lower levels to parents, superiors and country through piety and observance; obedience, because of its importance as a service which men owe to God, parents and repre-

[11]Rom. 13:1-2.

sentatives of the state. Thus we conclude the consideration of the *virtues of reverence,* those allied virtues of justice regulating man's debts of honor, reverence and submission to those above him.

Next in line for consideration are those virtues governing man's operations in matters which involve only **moral debt**, which have for their purpose to bring man to the full perfection of his social being. The virtues treated up to now, in this and the preceding chapters on justice, serve to avert utter chaos in the social order; the virtues which follow are not as absolutely necessary, but they do contribute inestimably, in varying degrees, to the ultimate full-flowering of the perfection of social living.

4. GRATITUDE

A. The Virtue Itself

Not every act of gratitude is a matter of moral debt. Men are bound *in strict justice* by the virtues of religion, piety and observance to recognize the favors and benefits received from God, parents and lawful superiors, and the payment of these debts of gratitude requires no special virtue.

But the virtue of gratitude also has a special object: particular and private favors, distinct from those mentioned above. **Gratitude** is defined, then, as *the virtue inclining man to acknowledge and to make recompense for particular and private favors received.*

One's benefactor has no strict claim to an act of gratitude. But in giving he has already benefited: it is more blessed to give than to receive. The giver has grown in virtue, attained greater stature, has more fully perfected himself. Hence, the beneficiary does not incur a strict debt, because the giver has freely transferred his title to an object. But the beneficiary does "owe" it to himself to make some return for the kindness of his benefactor; by returning the favor, the beneficiary rises to the level of perfection gained by his benefactor, matching him, as it were, stride for stride.

Gratitude springs more from the affective part of the soul (i.e., from the thankful dispositions of the soul) than from the external giving of some material thing. Hence, even the poor, since they are able to cultivate at least the spirit of thankfulness, can show gratitude. In its perfection, however, gratitude imposes three duties: 1) to be mindful of and to acknowledge to oneself the receipt of a gift; 2) to express this attitude by words of thanks; 3) as far as possible, to make some concrete return for the gift received. The first two duties should be immediate, but the last, external payment, should await a fitting occasion, lest too speedy a return bespeak an unwillingness to remain in another's debt, and, consequently, make one appear ungrateful. Moreover, the return one makes should exceed in measure the original gift; for whenever one returns either less or exactly the same as the gift received, what is done does not seem to be gratuitous but smacks of an out-and-out simple return for what has been received. Consequently, gratitude's return always tends, according to one's capabilities, to surpass the gift of the original giver.

B. Sins against Gratitude

Opposed to gratitude are two vices: **excessive gratitude** and **ingratitude.**

1. **Excessive gratitude** either repays a real favor too abruptly, or gives thanks when it is not due, i.e., when one is grateful for things one should not desire, e.g., for co-operation in evil.

2. **Ingratitude** as a formal sin includes both the failure to render the debt of thankfulness and some element of contempt, either for the benefactor or for his gift. It admits of successive degrees each more serious than the one preceding:

1) deliberate failure to return a favor, which reaches its highest degree in returning evil for good;

2) deliberate failure to acknowledge an actual favor by disparaging the gift;

3) deliberate failure to recognize a favor that has been given, which reaches its highest degree in considering the favor as a positive injury.

By its nature formal ingratitude is mortally sinful, usually because of its element of contempt. Frequently, however, it is only venially sinful, either because of some imperfection in the act, or because light matter is involved.

5. REVENGE

One of the most powerful inclinations found in man is to avenge injuries. And because it is so easy for this natural urge to get out of hand, especially through excess, there is need of a virtue to assist man in confining his spirit of revenge within reasonable limits. This is the job for the virtue called **revenge** (or, variously, vengeance, vindication, punishment), which may be defined as *the virtue inclining man to employ lawful means for punishing private persons because of the evil they have voluntarily committed, in order to heal the disorder brought upon society and the rights of either self or others.*

There are two points especially to be noted regarding this virtue: first, it is a virtue of *private persons;* and, secondly, the obligation that it imposes is one of *moral debt only.* Therefore, the proper subjects of this virtue are private citizens; the *strict* obligations to punish malefactors belongs to those alone who have received official authorization. Consequently, no one is bound under strict obligation to exact vengeance for a purely personal injury. Indeed, the more perfect course is to pardon the wrong, for pardon may result in the conversion or amendment of the offender, or the edification of one's neighbor, or give reasons for a greater claim to the mercy of God. But when the injury done to an individual is tantamount to an injury to God, the Church or the civil society, there is a strict obligation for that individual to take action against the offender.

But what course of action does this virtue allow? Certainly not lynch law, vendetta, unlimited and unbridled private revenge, which are acts of sinful violence. The individual citizen may employ strong measures to defend himself when attacked, but once the attack has ceased, the matter of inflicting further punishment must be turned over to the civil authority. Rarely, then, and only in light matters, will the private citizen be obliged and permitted to seek private vengeance —for example to manhandle, though not too roughly, an unruly and undisciplined youth who is causing some harm. Parents may exercise this virtue when they properly chastise and correct their children. More often, however, the act of this virtue will consist in taking legal action to secure just punishment for the offender.

If one were to seek vengeance for the sole purpose of inflicting harm, it would be an instance of out-and-out hatred, rather than an act of virtue. If the aim is the correction or amendment of the offender, the act is one of fraternal correction, and hence of charity; if the motive is the public good, it is an act of legal justice; if the honor of God, then an act of religion. Only if the motive is the *reparation* of an injury and satisfaction for the injured party is the act *properly* an act of the virtue of revenge.

The vices opposed to this virtue tend either toward excess or defect. Punishment marked by **excessive cruelty** or **severity** clearly is offensive to this virtue. **Laxity** in punishment is a sin by defect: allowing offenses to go unpunished, administering poorly suited punishment, or, worse, actually rewarding the performance of evil.

6. TRUTHFULNESS

A. The Virtue Itself

Social life would become all but impossible unless men believed one another and told the truth to each other. Here, then, is a special aspect of goodness in human acts toward which man must be inclined by a special virtue. This virtue is **truthfulness,** which is defined as *the virtue inclining man to manifest himself, in his life and in his speech, according to the conviction of his mind.*

When one is questioned by lawful authority, e.g., under oath in court or by one's parents, a strict legal debt arises which demands the truth. This is a case for legal justice. The virtue of truthfulness, however, engenders only a **moral debt.** Society could survive without its payment, but not without the greatest difficulty.

He who speaks, or in any way expresses his mind to another, places himself under the obligation of not deceiving; this is a moral obligation *arising from the speaker himself.*

Truthfulness both manifests things just as they appear to one and reveals the truth opportunely. For although at times one can answer with a simple "Yes, yes" or "No, no" (cf. Matt. 5:37), there are also occasions when it is prudent and necessary not to reveal the truth. The contents of one's mind are not to be flung to the four winds nor revealed to just any inquirer; circumstances may arise which call for evasion, silence or other methods of protecting oneself either from violating secrets and confidences or from unjustified intrusions of one's privacy.

Consequently, two classes of sin oppose the virtue of truthfulness: **all indiscreet manifestations of the truth** (an excess), especially the *violation of secrets;* and **falsehood** (a defect), either by word, *lying,* or by action, *simulation* and *hypocrisy.*

B. Secrets

(1) Definition and Kinds

A **secret** is *the knowledge of some hidden fact with the obligation not to reveal it.* One who reveals a secret speaks truthfully, indeed, but his speech is offensive to truthfulness through a lack of discretion; he has spoken the truth, but inopportunely; he has sinned by excess.

There are three kinds of secrets:

1) *Natural secrets* arise from the very nature of certain things which cannot be revealed without causing injury or displeasure to someone who is, therefore, unwilling that they be disclosed. Thus, for example, a successful businessman who has served a prison term for a felony would be reasonably unwilling that this hidden fact be made public.

2) *Promised secrets* arise from an agreement—made spontaneously or by request—not to reveal something that is already

known; for example, to promise not to reveal another's where-abouts.

3) *Committed secrets* arise from the express or implied agreement to keep silent before one is entrusted with the secret. Such, for example, are the professional secrets of doctors, lawyers or priests. The seal of the confessional is a kind of committed secret; however, **absolutely no cause ever justifies disclosure of this secret.**

(2) *Morality of Violating Secrets*

Implicit in every obligation to keep a secret is the recognition that what is contained therein is another's property, to which he has a right in justice. Thus reading another's mail, eavesdropping on confidential discussions, disclosing and making use of secret knowledge is, or can be, seriously wrong. Strictly speaking, therefore, only *promised secrets* pertain directly to the virtue of truthfulness. The other two types bind primarily **in strict justice.**

To violate the confidence involved in a *committed secret* is most grave, and is followed in gravity by violation of the *natural secret.* In each instance, the obligation is a strict legal debt of justice: in the first case, both because of the antecedent contract, and because the revelation of professional secrets harms the community by shattering its faith in those in whom they need confidence; in the second case, because of the harm which might come about because of the disclosure. The *promised secret,* however, binds only in virtue of fidelity, i.e., that truthfulness which inclines man to manifest himself according to his pledged word. To break such a promise is generally a venial sin, unless the promise was meant to bind in justice or unless it protected a natural secret.

(3) *Revelation of Secrets*

In general, there are three causes justifying the revelation of a secret:

1) *The consent of the one whose secret it is.* In some cases this consent may be reasonably presumed; thus, for example, an

employee may criticize the work of a fellow worker to his boss, who in turn may manifest this criticism (though not the one criticizing) to the deficient worker.

2) *The disclosure of the secret from another source.* A lawyer, for example, might discuss a secret matter with a fellow lawyer who has discovered the secret from another source.

3) *The need to avert serious harm which cannot be avoided by any other means.* Such a necessity may arise in the following cases:

a) *When grave harm threatens Church or state.* For example, one could reveal the existence of a plot of rebellion or riot; a doctor could disclose a carrier of contagious disease; the identity of counterfeiters should be made known immediately.

b) *When grave harm threatens him whose secret it is.* In virtue of the law of self-preservation and the requirements of virtue, a person in this case cannot reasonably be unwilling that disclosure be made. This is one reason, then, why a Catholic knowing that a man proposing marriage is already married is obliged to reveal this to the pastor.

c) *When grave harm threatens an innocent party.* If the case concerns a committed secret, and particularly a professional secret, it may not be disclosed *unless the person who has committed the secret is the one inflicting the harm.* Hence a doctor who knew that a prospective husband had a serious infectious disease would be obligated to disclose this to the future bride if the man refused to do so himself; in this case the man himself is an unjust aggressor.

d) *When grave harm threatens one who keeps the secret.* Generally men do not obligate themselves to secrecy to the point of undergoing grave harm or, much less, death, nor may they be presumed to do so. Some secrets, however, must be preserved even unto death. Thus fear of personal harm *never* justifies the revelation of secrets gravely harmful to the good of the community—e.g., in the natural order, to reveal military plans to an enemy; or, on the supernatural plane, to break the seal of confession. In the case of a committed secret, one cannot make it known to avoid harm if thereby grave harm would come to the one who entrusted it, except when the one who committed the secret was also the one inflicting the harm.

C. Lying

(1) Definition and Kinds

The term "lying" is used frequently to embrace any defect against truthfulness, whether committed by word or deed. More properly, however, lying refers to those sins involving speech alone. Thus, lying may be defined as *the voluntary declaration of something contrary to what is in one's mind.*

A lie, then, is first of all a "declaration" of something either by the spoken or the written word or their equivalents, e.g., a nod, a wink, a movement of the hand, etc. It is, secondly, a declaration of something "false," at least as far as the judgment of the speaker is concerned. For lying is opposed to telling what is believed to be true, i.e., what is opposed to the conviction of one's mind. Hence a man may be in error about his information and tell an "untruth" without telling a lie. And, alternatively, one may still be guilty of lying if he speaks the truth, but did not think it was the truth.

Every lie of its nature is a sin, for every lie perverts the faculty of speech. Words are simply signs of ideas, and it is both unnatural and unbecoming to express by words something that is not in one's mind. Lying, then, suppresses the normal relationship that should exist between thought and word. Hence, a lie of its very nature deceives the listener. The consequence is that lies destroy confidence and trust; they cause a state of perpetual suspicion and aloofness; and, in general, they work serious harm to the common good.

The liar intends, therefore, to speak contrary to what he knows or thinks is true. This is the **immediate and necessary object** of the act.

An *implicit* intention of deceiving—the formal will to speak contrary to the truth—pertains to the essence of a lie; while an *explicit* intention of deceiving merely brings the lie to its full perfection. It follows that a lie is present even when a speaker foresees that his listener will not believe him.

If the implicit intention of deceiving is missing, on the other hand, no lie exists. For this reason a novelist cannot be accused of lying, nor are those cases of manifest hyperbole, irony and metaphor, which are never taken literally, called lies.

Lies fall into one of three categories: 1) *the jocose lie,* told for the purpose of amusement or humor, but presented as fact by one who certainly knows that it is false; 2) *the officious lie,* told for the sake of gaining some advantage for oneself or another, although no harm is intended, e.g., the lie of a child to avoid a parental scolding; 3) *the pernicious lie,* told with the intent of causing harm to another.

Pernicious lies, of their nature, are mortal sins, because they harm one's neighbor, and often their content is against faith and morals as well; but they admit of light matter. Jocose and officious lies are venially sinful because, ordinarily, they do no great harm to one's neighbor. They could become mortal, however, through scandal; moreover, by becoming accustomed to them a man prepares the way for telling pernicious lies.

Two other kinds of lies, ordinarily venially sinful but worthy of special note, are *boasting* and *self-depreciation.* Boasting, springing from vainglory, exaggerates the truth. Self-depreciation is a defect of truth. One who belittles himself either denies his own excellence or asserts something evil or derogatory of self.

(2) Concealing the Truth

At times it is prudent and even necessary to conceal the truth from unauthorized inquirers. "It is not permissible to speak a lie," wrote St. Thomas, "although it is permitted prudently to hide the truth";[12]

---

[12]*Summa,* II-II, q. 110, a. 3, ad 4.

and St. Augustine points out that "although everyone who lies intends to hide what is true, not everyone who intends to hide what is true is a liar."[13]

One is permitted to hide the truth in either a negative or positive way. *Negative* concealment of the truth is accomplished by silence or simple evasion, which is certainly lawful when there is no obligation to speak up directly to the questioner.

When, however, this method is impossible—for example, a refusal to answer or an evasive answer often reveals the gravity of a serious sin to curious inquirers—one may use *positive* concealment of the truth, by employing obscure language in his reply to a questioner. This is accomplished by the use of either equivocation or mental reservation.

1) **Equivocation** is *the use of words or entire phrases having a twofold meaning, the less obvious of which is meant by the speaker.* Thus Christ told the apostles that "Lazarus sleeps" (John 11:11), for "to sleep" can refer to physical sleep or the sleep of death.

2) **Mental reservation** is *an act of the mind by which a man, in speaking, restricts the meaning of the words he uses to a sense other than their obvious meaning.* When this restricted meaning can be detected because of the speaker, listener, time, place or from any other circumstance, the limitation is called a *broad* mental reservation. If the limitation can in no way be perceived either from the words used or from any of the above named circumstances, then the restriction is called a *strict* (pure) mental reservation. This latter type is a lie and is always wrong. For example to answer one's father with "I did not take your fifty dollars," meaning with one's right hand rather than the left, is simply telling a lie.

Broad mental reservation can, however, often enough be justified, and seems even to have been employed by Christ. For when his disciples asked him whether he was going up to the feast at Jerusalem, he answered, "As for you, go up to the feast, but I do not go up"

[13]*Against Lying*, Chap. 10.

(John 7:8). His meaning was that he would not go publicly and solemnly as his disciples had desired (cf. John 7:3 ff.), but rather privately. Similarly, a doctor, and more so a priest, may reply in professional matters to an importunate inquirer: "I know nothing of that matter." The circumstances of their position or office certainly indicate sufficiently the possible reservation behind their words.

But even if the questioner fails to perceive the reservation in a particular case, its use is not necessarily prohibited, for one may merely permit the evil of the deception, while at the same time positively intending some good end. The same must be said of equivocal answers. Since equivocation and mental reservation both permit an evil—the deception of another—the one employing either technique must observe the following conditions: 1) he must have *a sufficiently serious reason;* 2) he must be unable to use *other means of concealing the truth;* 3) he must have *a good intention;* and 4) the equivocation or reservation *must not be a purely mental restriction,* i.e., a reservation in no way discernible from the words used or from attendant circumstances. Furthermore, it must be remembered that equivocation or reservation can never be used when speaking with an authorized inquirer: one's confessor, a judge, a lawful superior.

D. Simulation

Simulation is lying, not by words, but by one's behavior, pretending to be other than one is; for example, to feign friendship for another, or to masquerade as a military officer, priest or sister in order to carry out evil pursuits. Judas was guilty of this sin in betraying Christ with a kiss.

There is a special kind of simulation called **hypocrisy,** *a pretense of sanctity,* used by those who have no real desire for true sanctity, but desire only its external appearance. When indulged in for a seriously evil intention (for example, the feigning of holiness in order to steal), hypocrisy is always mortally sinful. But hyprocisy which is not opposed to charity is only venially sinful. Such would be the case if one simply delights in his pretensions to virtue, or exaggerates rather than simulates holiness.

7. AFFABILITY

A. The Virtue Itself

Affability and liberality are the two virtues which incline man to give, respectively, himself and his material wealth for the pleasant and harmonious well-being of society.

The purpose of affability is to inject politeness into the ordinary dealings of men. Affability, therefore, may be defined as *the virtue inclining man to conduct himself agreeably and properly in his ordinary social dealings with other members of society.* At times however, for some necessary reason, one will displease another; hence, though affability ordinarily directs positive action (being agreeable in manner, speech and deeds), it may sometimes demand a negative approach, e.g., avoiding any show of friendliness that might seem to give approval of a sinful life.

Though sometimes called the virtue of friendliness, the "friendship" which it instills is not to be confused with the friendship of charity. As a lesser part of justice, affability does not concern itself with the internal love of neighbor, but rather with the externals of social order—signs of courtesy and politeness. The possessor of this virtue will always show consideration for everyone; he will not monopolize conversations, nor otherwise make himself a bore; he will speak well of others, avoiding words that might do them harm or injury; and seldom will he talk of himself.

B. Opposite Vices

There are two vices opposed to affability: flattery, which tends to excess: surliness, which fails by defect.

1. **Flattery** is *the vice which inclines man to please another, either by word or deed, in an excessive and inordinate manner, for the sake of gaining some favor.* The degrees and modes of flattery take on infinite variation, for there are unlimited ways a flatterer can please another: praise, applause, fawning, obsequiousness and so forth. The

only stable element in flattery is the driving motive of attaining personal advantage.

2. **Surliness** is *the vice inclining man to be difficult in the company of others, seldom agreeing, frequently opposing the words of others, motivated by the desire to be unpleasant.* Consequently, this vice should be distinguished from discord (disagreeableness through a lack of charity) and anger (a vice opposed to the virtue of meekness). The surly or ill-tempered man is always ready to contradict, to speak gruffly, to criticize and complain, or even to resort to sullen silence, if that course seems more apt to cause displeasure.

In itself, surliness is only venially sinful, since it is not necessarily opposed to charity; but circumstances, especially an evil intention, can make it mortal. Compared to flattery, surliness is more offensive because it is more opposed to the spirit of affability; for although flattery exaggerates courtesy, surliness contradicts it outright.

8. LIBERALITY

A. The Virtue Itself

In today's political jargon, a liberal is one with progressive views. He is "liberal," that is "free" from the long-established, the orthodox point of view. But for St. Thomas, a "liberal" person is one who has the virtue of liberality.

A great part of man's time and effort in this life is ordered to the acquisition, care and use both of money and those things money can buy. In his use of money, man is aided by the virtue of justice; but even after a man has paid what is *due* to others in strict right, he must still care for and use what remains. Liberality is *the virtue which regulates man's love for money and inclines him to use it well.*

Immediately, then, and directly, liberality moderates one's *affection* for wealth, curbing any love for it that is unfitting or improper. Secondarily and mediately it governs the use of riches, both directly by inclining one to bestow them upon others, and indirectly by removing the impediment to their use, namely, excessive attachment for riches. Hence this virtue is also called *generosity*.

Although giving to others is not the exclusive province of liberality, it has a distinct motive: justice causes one to give what is strictly due; charity is motivated by compassion or affection; but liberality proceeds from a well-ordered affection for money itself. It differs, too, from magnificence; for while the latter virtue deals with the fulfilling of great works, liberality deals with moderate gifts and donations. "Giving," therefore, pertains to the proper object of liberality. Its secondary acts, however, extend even to the actual acquiring and holding of one's money.

B. Vices Opposed to Liberality

Two vices offend against liberality. One is avarice, and the other is wastefulness (prodigality).

1. **Avarice** is *immoderate love of, and desire for money.* Naturally, this attitude affects one's external behavior in the acquisition, holding and spending of money. Undue preoccupation with money does not ordinarily exceed venial sin, but when money exerts such an attraction for men that they commit many sins for its sake, avarice becomes a **capital sin.** Sins committed on account of avarice are called its "daughters": treachery, fraud, falsehood, perjury, violence and insensibility to mercy.

2. **Wastefulness** is *unreasonable and unnecessary extravagance which results in wasteful expenditures of money.* The prodigal exceeds what is reasonable by giving too much, or to the wrong person, or at the wrong time, and he falls short of what is reasonable by not retaining what he ought.

He does give, however, though of course too much: wastefulness has at least the merit of aiding others, and is more easily cured than avarice, since the exercise of prodigality depletes funds so rapidly that poverty soon follows. Further, the wisdom of age usually checks waste. It is not as seriously defective as avarice, therefore, nor does it usually lead to such serious consequences.

9. Summary and Conclusion

The aim of this and the two preceding chapters has been to provide a plan for social morality. This plan is contained in the doctrine on justice and its allied virtues. No area of human commerce goes beyond the scope of these virtues. In effect, they enable man to follow —within the framework of the exigencies of his daily life—*the* universal blueprint of morality, the Decalogue.

The Ten Commandments contain the minimum requirements for proper social living, for the demands of justice are satisfied by adherence to them. The first three outline man's duties to God: the first two by removing the obstacles of superstition and irreligion, the third by giving him a positive plan for rendering his debt of worship to God. This is the area of operation for the virtue of religion. The fourth commandment provides the matter for the virtues of filial piety, patriotism and observance, for it guarantees the strict rights of parents, country and all legitimate authority over inferiors. The remaining six precepts turn to the domain of justice itself, embracing man's duties to all members of society in those matters pertaining to their rights to life, bodily integrity, physical properties and a good name. Man owes unswerving obedience to these divine laws.

But human law can never demand man's absolute obedience, for to follow exactly the letter of the law would sometimes cause man to sin against justice and the common good. The framers of human law, whether they legislate for nation, state, city, village or town, remain mere creatures. Hence their legislation takes into account only that which usually happens; they cannot possibly legislate for every individual instance when the literal interpretation of the law would result in real injustice. To mete out, and to preserve justice in these instances, yet another virtue, called **extra-legal justice** (good judgment, *epikeia*) is needed; a virtue which, like legal justice, considers the common good, but goes beyond legal justice, transcending the letter of the law and intending the good of the entire community and each of its members. Hence, this virtue subsumes the virtue of legal justice, bringing justice to its ultimate fulfillment.

The **gift of piety** unifies and perfects the entire content of justice; it pervades the entire order of man's social action, giving new meaning to the precepts and obligation of justice. For this gift so disposes man and enables him to be moved by the Holy Spirit as to look upon and to reverence God as his Father, and the Father of all men. God as Father, and all other men as brothers—this is the lofty view of this gift of the Spirit. Consequently, religion, the virtue of worshipping God as Creator, becomes piety, the supernatural godlike quality of giving reverence to God as Father. Moreover, piety influences the whole complexus of human social intercourse, for under its impulse all men are considered as of one family, of one common Father. Transformed by charity and piety, the Christian honors the rights of God and of his fellow men, never resting until the demands of justice are satisfied; for the Christian is possessed by a consuming "hunger and thirst for justice" (Matt. 5:6).

The Christian is a social being, both naturally and supernaturally speaking. For it is written that ". . . you are no longer strangers and foreigners, but you are citizens with the saints and members of God's household" (Eph. 2:19). Faith, hope and charity constitute the basic of this life, but the area of interaction among men, justice and its subordinate virtues are of the greatest importance.

BIBLIOGRAPHICAL NOTE

St. Thomas treats the matter of this chapter in the *Summa*, II-II, Questions CI-CXXII. Frank Sheed offers his insights, especially regarding family relationships, in *Society and Sanity* (New York: Sheed and Ward, 1953). Much excellent material concerning the duties of husband and wife toward each other and toward their family may be found in *Catholic Social Doctrine* (Westminster, Md.: The Newman Press, 1956) by Daniel A. O'Connor, C.S.V. Two chapters of *Cana Is Forever* (Tarrytown, N. Y.: The Nugent Press,

1949) by Charles H. Doyle offer many practical suggestions: Chapter 8—"Basic Requisites for Marital Happiness"—and Chapter 11—"The Important Role of Parents." Other practical works written in popular style are Mary Reed Newland's *We and Our Children* (New York: P. J. Kenedy and Sons, 1954), and Daniel A. Lord's *Some Notes for the Guidance of Parents* (St. Louis: The Queen's Work, 1944). *The Social Message of Jesus* (Paterson, N.J.: St. Anthony Guild Press, 1943) by Igino Giordani, is a detailed, historical work, which gives a commentary on our Lord's words concerning the subject. Antonin Sertillanges, O.P., in *Kinships* (New York: McMullen, Inc., 1952), 157-234, looks at family and neighbor relationships. For the Church on patriotism, consult J. J. Wright's *National Patriotism in Papal Teaching* (Westminster, Md.: The Newman Press, 1943).

Among the periodical articles on this subject, two excellent essays by Walter Farrell, O.P., may be consulted: "Virtues of the Household," in *The Thomist*, IX (1946), 337-78, and "Family Likeness," in *Cross and Crown*, III (1951), 5-25. The following articles provide valuable supplementary reading for some of the other virtues: "Obedience and Liberty," in *Theology Digest*, I (1953), 110-113, by A. S. Perret; "Affability—for Gracious Living," by B. Chapman in *Sursum Corda*, III (1957), 517-521; V. Long's "On Thanking the Hand That Feeds," in *Friar*, VI (1956), 45-52; W. C. Menninger on "How to Make and Keep Friends," in the *Catholic Digest*, IX (1955), 82-85; "The Virtue of Patriotism," by J. B. Sheerin in the *Homiletic and Pastoral Review*, LIV (1954), 1039-43; and "Observance," by N. Benedict Joseph, O.P., in *Cross and Crown*, IX (1957), 202-213.

CHAPTER FIFTEEN

Fortitude

1. INTRODUCTION

In the previous chapters we saw the need for a group of virtues which will regulate our actions with other people. Yet justice and its many allied virtues, for all the range of their activities, are not enough to regulate the complete moral life of man. Man requires other habits which will provide control over a vast area of activity which involves no one but himself; this is specifically the great wilderness of man's interior struggles, with its plains and peaks, its mountain torrents and arroyos, its level and high altitude living, the wilderness where the passions of his sensible appetites exercise the frontier and even Wild West expression of human possibility, for good or for ill.

Thus the need for other virtues in addition to justice is quite apparent, if we consider the moral life of man in the concrete—would you call a television hero who betrayed his wife a virtuous man, even if, by a quick draw and deadly shooting, he paid his debts? Or would you say theat a church-going man or the marshal of Tombstone was a good man, if he were a confirmed drunkard? Surely not, if you were Aristotle, or Cicero, or Thomas Aquinas, or anyone else who assessed the situation objectively. They did their duty: perhaps nobly, perhaps courageously, certainly with virility. But not virtuously, by any means, that is, not humanly.

In addition to justice, then, which many of our early law enforcers may have practiced to some degree, man needs other habits which will control himself, to put the order of reason in his passions so that other self-inspired obstacles to the establishment of reason's rule in human affairs will be removed.

These private sources of essential human disorder—man's passions or emotions—can offer an obstacle to the rule of reason in two ways. They can lead him *toward* some good contrary to reason, or they can lead him *away* from some good which reason says should be pursued. Because of the pleasure connected with drinking, for instance, the passions may lead a man to drink liquor in excess, or because of the difficulty connected with going to church on Sunday, man's passions may lead him to omit fulfilling the Sunday obligation of hearing Mass. But for each of these drives contrary to reason there is a correcting moral virtue. The first, fortitude, regulates the irascible appetite, which tends to make us retreat from the true good when it is difficult to obtain. The second virtue, temperance, rectifies the concupiscible appetite so that man is not led by compulsion to seek forbidden pleasure, howsoever powerful its attraction.

These two virtues, fortitude and temperance, complete the equipment which man must use, both on the natural and the supernatural planes of human activity, in his battle to lead a good moral life. Since these two virtues are concerned with the emotions of man, they do not signify a relationship to others, as justice does; they are called *individual* virtues, without suppressing the fact that what the human individual does has necessary repercusions in the natural social order and the supernatural fraternity of the Mystical Body of Christ. Not only is no man an island, he is a necessary part of the whole, whose private career may affect the whole body politic and the whole body of the Church. Yet directly these virtues rectify the moral life of the individual in regard to himself. Of these two virtues fortitude is the more perfect, dealing as it does with human greatness, and so therefore we will treat it first. As with the other proximate sources of human achievement, we will follow the sober and objective analysis of St. Thomas:

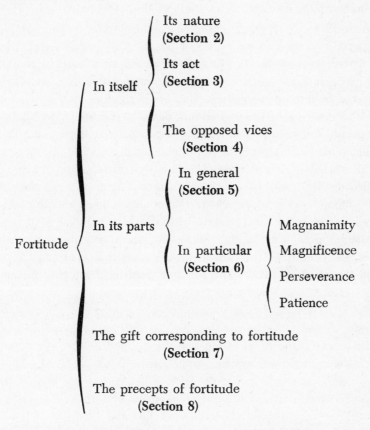

Fortitude
- In itself
  - Its nature (Section 2)
  - Its act (Section 3)
  - The opposed vices (Section 4)
- In its parts
  - In general (Section 5)
  - In particular (Section 6)
    - Magnanimity
    - Magnificence
    - Perseverance
    - Patience
- The gift corresponding to fortitude (Section 7)
- The precepts of fortitude (Section 8)

2. THE NATURE OF FORTITUDE

The term fortitude has two meanings in the context of moral theology. If we consider fortitude in the wide sense, then it means that firmness of soul (or what we might call strength of purpose) which is found in every virtue. Taken in this way, fortitude signifies a general virtue—more precisely, a quality which every virtue possesses. When considering the nature of moral virtue, we say that virtues are not easily lost and that they have a certain firmness which distinguishes them from a mere disposition. The firmness which is the natural possession and essential characteristic of all virtues corresponds to this concept of fortitude in the wide sense.

But fortitude in its strict sense has a more limited meaning: it does not pertain to all virtues; rather, it connotes a special virtue which has a definite function to perform in regard to a particular object. Yes, it still indicates a firmness of soul, but not that firmness of soul that is a quality of all virtues. Rather, it signifies that firmness of soul that is needed to repel or endure death, and similar grave dangers and perils of life, in a manner that is consonant with reason. Taken in this sense, then, fortitude has a much narrower signification and is concerned with a very special matter—danger of death from public or private war and other grave dangers. In this sense fortitude is the name for the moral virtue that makes a man and his actions morally good when he is faced with death or equivalent dangers; a more popular term for this virtue—not necessarily more accurate— might be courage. Throughout the rest of this chapter, we will adopt the word "fortitude" and use it in its strict theological meaning.

A. The Definition of Fortitude

The moral virtue of **fortitude** may be defined as *a cardinal virtue which stengthens the irascible appetite enabling it to continue to pursue difficult good even in the face of death or grave danger from battle.* Or, to put it another way, by means of fortitude a man will endure the dangers and difficulties of life and death in a manner that is reasonable. In order to obtain a clear and more concise concept of this virtue we will study some of the main elements which are included in this definition. That is, we will examine the subject, material object and formal object of fortitude.

B. The Subject of Fortitude

Where does fortitude reside? What is its subject? Since it is the purpose of fortitude to rectify and strengthen that part of man which might cause him to ignore the goods of reason because there is some difficulty connected in the pursuit of them, fortitude is concerned with the faculty that seeks the good that is difficult of attainment. This faculty is the irascible appetite; it is concerned with the strong or emergency emotions, such as fear, anger and daring, which tend to lead a man away from the virtuous and true good if they are not checked. The subject of fortitude, then, is the irascible appetite, for it is this faculty which, when aroused, will incline man to flee virtuous actions which reason says should be performed.

C. The Material Object

The **proximate material object,** or the matter with which fortitude is most immediately concerned, are those particular passions or emotions most likely to draw the will away from the true good when they are aroused. These emotions are fear and daring. If fear is left unchecked, we will turn away from everything that strikes our sense nature as evil, even though to bear this evil patiently might be morally good. If audacity is given free rein, then we will try to overcome everything which is viewed as evil, even though reason indicates that some conflicts should be avoided. Thus, if Christ had not controlled his human emotions when the Roman soldiers and Jews came after him in the Garden of Gethsemane, his fear might have led him to run and hide from them, or his audacity might have prompted him to lead his apostles in a counter-attack against his captors. But reason, enlightened by grace, told him that he must undergo the suffering and death that they were about to inflict so that he could redeem mankind.

All things that cause the movements of fear and daring in man are the **remote material** of fortitude. Hence, fortitude is concerned with all serious dangers, since it is these that give rise to the above emotions. Foremost among the dangers we encounter in this life is the danger of death. Experience shows that man's greatest movements of fear and audacity come at the time when he is threatened with death; at this time his irascible appetite makes its strongest bid to withdraw him from the virtuous acts he should perform. The danger of death, therefore, might be called the complete or perfect remote matter of fortitude. Only when he is in danger of death will a man really know if he can completely and perfectly control his emotions of fear and daring in a reasonable manner; only in the encounter with this danger will man have the chance to prove himself perfectly courageous.

Yet not just any danger of death or allied injuries calls forth the full and perfect expression of fortitude; it is a readiness to die, yes, but to die nobly, gloriously, in a manner which itself proves the valor and courage of the virtuous man.[1] Hence St. Thomas says:

> Fortitude strengthens a man's mind against the greatest danger, which is that of death. Fortitude is a virtue, however, and it is essential for virtue always to tend to good; thus it is in order to pursue some good that man does not fly from the danger of death. But the dangers of death which arise out of sickness, storms at sea, onslaughts from robbers, and so forth do not seem to come on a man through his pursuing some good. The dangers of death which occur in battle, on the other hand, directly come to man on account of some good—because he is defending the common good by a just fight.
>
> But a just fight is of two kinds. First, there is the general combat (for instance, those who fight in war); secondly, there is private combat, as when a judge or even a private individual does not refrain from giving a just judgment through fear of the sword or any other danger, even though it threatens death. It belongs to fortitude, therefore, to strengthen the mind against dangers of death, not only such as arise in war, but also such as occur in single combat, which may be called by the general name of battle. . . .
>
> Moreover, a brave man behaves well in face of danger from any other kind of death. This is particularly true since man may be in danger of death because of any virtue: thus a man will not fail to attend a sick friend through fear of deadly infection, nor refuse to undertake a voyage for some good purpose through fear of shipwreck or robbers.[2]

What about the other dangers of life? Are they subject to the control of fortitude? In facing the other dangers and perils of life in a reasonable manner, man will not be performing the perfect act of fortitude, but he will be disposing himself for the fulness of the virtue

---

[1]"He will properly, then, be called brave who is fearless in face of a noble death, and of all emergencies that involve death; and the emergencies of war are in the highest degree of this kind." Aristotle, *Nicomachean Ethics*, Bk. III, Chap. 6.

[2]*Summa*, II-II, q. 123, a. 5.

by overcoming the fear and daring that are caused by these less severe dangers. In order to perform the complete act well, therefore, a life spent in the practice of so-called "imperfect acts of fortitude" is necessary. The hero is not made the moment he leaps in front of a tank to protect his patrol's position. He is made in the long pains-taking period which precedes the heroic deed—every time he con-quers the fear or moderates the daring that come from lesser evils, the hero disposes himself for this one great act of courage.

Fortitude, although primarily concerned with the danger of death, extends also to lesser dangers. A man who is strong in the greatest peril will not be a weakling in the face of lesser assaults; he who can conquer the fear of death will not succumb to the fear of a lesser bodily harm. As a matter of fact, every truly courageous act is rooted in man's reasonable readiness to die, even though on the surface no such thought of death seems to enter into the performance of such an act.

Fortitude, then, is the bulwark and the safeguard of all the virtues. Every virtue, by nature, is stable in the face of difficulty. But an attack on a virtue may be a cause of fear, and fear must be conquered by fortitude. In the face of fear, faith or chastity or any virtue will fail unless supported by the strong arm of fortitude.

D. The Formal Object of Fortitude

In order to understand the function of fortitude in our moral life we must know not only the proximate and remote material object of this virtue but also the precise aspect under which the matter is treated. It is not enough to know that fortitude is concerned with the control of fear and daring—we must also know *how* to control them, the reason or motive which determines the right kind of control to be exercised. This last element contained in our definition is known as the **formal object**. In the case of fortitude, the formal object can be best expressed through the word **restraint**, that is, fortitude restrains the irascible appetite so as to limit fear and to moderate audacity. Hence, when fear impels us to withdraw from the thing that is causing our fear, reason examines the situation and decides whether such a withdrawal would be virtuous. Sometimes it decides that a retreat would be a good thing, but many times it decides that to take flight, while appealing to the passions, would be a moral evil. Then fortitude must enter in and control fear, so that it will not lead the will of man to forsake the reasonable course of action.

Much the same thing happens when danger causes in us the passion of daring. Daring prompts us to strike out at the evil facing us; rather than retreat, it says advance. But many times reason decides that daring must be moderated and that striking out at evil is not the wise course to follow. Then, as before, the task of fortitude is to control the passions; it must see to it that this tendency to attack is either moderated or repressed. The precise work of fortitude, therefore, is to restrain fear and daring—to keep them within the bounds set by reason.

This is equivalent to saying that there can be no fortitude without prudence. To charge heedlessly into the fray, or to flee at the slightest risk of danger—these are not the marks of a brave man. Fortitude, like all the moral virtues, must be governed by prudence. It strengthens the soul in the face of danger, to be sure, but strength without direction leads to disaster. When peril strikes, even suddenly, prudence must take command and direct the course of action that fortitude must take—either to attack and try to overcome the evil, or to cling tenaciously to the good while bearing the evil.

E. The Virtue of Fortitude

The reason for fortitude should now be clear; its purpose is to preserve the good of virtue at any cost, even at the cost of life. Fortitude is neither the swaggering bravado of the man who knows no fear, nor the passive surrender to suffering because there is nothing else to do; it is the courage to hold on to the good of virtue in the face of any evil. There is no fortitude where there is no good to defend. One is truly courageous only for the sake of a good that is threatened. The young man on the flying trapeze may be daring, but he is not truly brave. Maria Goretti, in defending her chastity to the death, performed a genuine act of fortitude.

Fortitude, like the other moral virtues, is either natural or supernatural. Natural fortitude is concerned with a natural good and directed to a natural end. Thus Socrates was courageous in the defense of natural truth. Supernatural fortitude proceeds from a supernatural motive and is ordered to a supernatural end. Although the acts of each, as death or suffering, may appear to be the same, they are in reality quite different. The act of natural fortitude is regulated by the good of human reason; the act of supernatural fortitude is measured by the good of divine faith.

3. The Acts of Fortitude

A. Aggression and Endurance

From the above discussion of the nature of fortitude, it is clear that fortitude has a twofold act and a double function: one active, which impels one to attack evil; and one passive, which strengthens one to endure evil. The endurance of evil is by far the more common act. This is clear from the fact that grave dangers, which cause fear and daring, tend by their very nature to check daring while they increase fear. The ordinary man faced with death in the battlefield, for example, has a tendency to hold back from the battle for fear that he will lose his life. Only the overly intrepid few have an eager impulse to rush out and join the battle against danger when their death is imminent. Therefore, the principal act of fortitude is endurance, that is, to stand immovable in the midst of danger rather than to attack it.

When fear arises, then, it is the function of fortitude to repress that fear and enable a man to endure the terrible danger in a manner that becomes a courageous man. On the other hand, when danger causes an audacity which is likely to get out of hand and lead one to rush headlong into the arms of peril, fortitude restrains this emotion so that virtuous courage, not passion, is the guiding force in our encounter with danger.

The act of endurance, as we have said above, is by far more common than the act of aggression. Is endurance also more difficult? Or is it harder to attack the danger causing that fear? At first glance, it may seem that attack is more difficult. It seems to be more difficult to strike out at the evil that is besieging us than to endure it patiently. The outnumbered cavalry charging against overwhelming odds seems to correspond more closely to our idea of courage than a man's dogged refusal to quit his post in the face of danger. But if we examine the matter more carefully, it becomes clear that enduring danger is more difficult than being audacious and attacking the evil which confronts us. In aggression we battle an evil which we have some hope of overcoming, and hence we attack a force which we regard as weaker than ourselves. In endurance, on the other hand, we submit to an evil stronger than ourselves, and it is certainly more difficult to contend with a stronger force than with a weaker one. From the standpoint of time, endurance is also more difficult. Aggression can remove danger in minutes, while endurance means that we must suffer evil for days, months or years. To sustain the prolonged siege is not so gallant as to launch a sudden attack, but it is certainly more difficult. Thus, both attack and endurance are necessary for the virtue of fortitude, but endurance is the principal and more difficult act of the virtue.

Endurance is not to be regarded as mere passive submission to bodily suffering; it involves, more importantly, a strong action of the soul holding steadfastly to the good and refusing to yield to the body's pain.[3]

B. Martyrdom, the Perfect Act of Fortitude

(1) In Itself

To endure danger is a more difficult and important part of fortitude than to attack danger. The act by which a man endures the greatest danger for the highest motive is the most perfect act of

---

[3]Cf. St. Thomas, *Summa*, II-II, q. 123, a. 6, ad 2.

fortitude. For the Christian, the most perfect act of courage is martyrdom: in this act a man dies bravely for love of God. A martyr freely gives up the greatest natural good, his life, in order to preserve or honor supernatural good. **Martyrdom,** then, is defined as *the endurance of death in witness to the truth of the Christianity.*

The Christian who dies a martyr performs one of the most perfect acts of virtue possible. The virtue of fortitude, which is the proximate principle of martyrdom, is not in itself greater than charity, for charity, we know, is the most perfect of the virtues. But if we consider true martyrdom in which the act of fortitude is prompted by love, it is clear that martyrdom bespeaks not only the highest act of fortitude, but also the highest act of charity. Man shows the amount of his love by what he is willing to suffer in order to protect and nourish the things or the persons that he loves. The man who is willing to suffer the loss of all natural good, even the loss of life, shows that he could not love more. "Greater love than this no one has, that one lay down his life for his friends" (John 15:13). The good which man gives up in martyrdom, and the motive he has in giving it up, indicate that martyrdom is one of the most perfect acts of virtue possible.

(2) *Effects of Martyrdom*

Because of the great love which prompts his heroic act of sacrifice, the martyr goes straight to heaven when he dies. All his sins, and all the punishment due to them, are forgiven, since he has made a perfect act of charity. This has always been the constant teaching of the Church; that is why she has always held martyrs in such esteem. Through one supreme act of love and courage the martyr leaps from this life into heaven. His imitation of the passion and death of Christ brings him the reward made possible through Christ's fortitude and God's mercy.

Even if the one who suffers death for the faith is not baptized with water, he can still win heaven and the martyr's crown. If the one who dies for the faith is sorry for his sins, at least because of the punishment they will bring, and he dies willingly, then he will automatically go to heaven, whether he is baptized or not. Just as the soul of an infant is cleansed from original sin *ex opere operato* through the waters of baptism, so martyrdom cleanses the soul of the martyr from all sin, whether original or actual. For this reason, martyrdom is sometimes called the "baptism of blood."

(3) Conditions Required for Martyrdom

How does one become a martyr, We can answer this question by considering the three conditions that are required for martyrdom.

1. First of all, **the one who suffers for the faith must actually die as a result of his wounds.** Grave injury from which death does not follow does not make a martyr. The martyr is one who shows he values supernatural good above all natural good. If he is not forced to die to show this disdain for worldly goods, then it cannot be said he gave up all natural good, since life is valued above all other natural goods, and to cling to life men will give up everything else— fortune, friends, honor. Death is the final convincing witness that man prefers God above all things. Not that the martyr is indifferent to life— he loves it as the greatest natural good. But he is willing to sacrifice it for a still greater good, the good of supernatural virtue. Thus while the one who suffers may have the desire to die for Christ, unless he actually does die, he is not a martyr in the strict sense of the word.

2. Death, however, is not enough to make a true martyr. **The death must be inflicted by an enemy because of hatred for Christianity or Christian virtue.** This is the second condition for martyrdom. Faith, then, might be called the cause of martyrdom—if there were no faith, there would be no martyrs. This does not mean, however, that the enemies of the faith will always put a martyr to death because he holds some particular truth of Catholic doctrine. The proximate cause for arousing the hatred of the enemies of God and virtue could be an action that the martyr has performed or wishes to perform in the future. Faith here is taken in the wide sense; therefore, when

we say it is the cause of martyrdom it includes those virtuous actions which are protestations of divine faith, as well as the confession of faith itself. St. Agnes, who refused to betray her vow of virginity, is just as much a martyr as St. John of Gorcum, who died in defense of the doctrine of the real presence of the body and blood of Christ in the Eucharist. Whether faith is expressed in words or deeds is not important so far as martyrdom is concerned; what does matter, however, is a willingness to die on the part of the martyr and a hatred of the Catholic faith or Christian virtue on the part of the persecutor.

In true martyrdom death must be inflicted by another person, as we said above. It follows, therefore, that those priests, sisters and brothers who have died as a result of their ministrations to the diseased and sick cannot be called martyrs in the strict sense. True, the motive that led these heroic souls to their death was the love of God, but their death was from natural causes.

Those who die for natural truth or for error cannot be called true martyrs either. Martyrs die for love of God in testimony to divine truth; natural motives do not suffice for this more perfect action. Since those who die for natural motives do not practice supernatural virtue, they cannot gain a supernatural reward. Socrates and others who died for natural truth displayed great natural courage; yet they did not die to show their love for God and therefore they are not martyrs.

The person who causes the martyr's death must act out of hatred for faith or virtue, but it is not necessary that this be his explicit motive. Nero undoubtedly was moved by hatred of the faith when he persecuted the early Christians; however, his alleged motive was to punish them for the burning of Rome. Nor need the one who puts the martyr to death be a pagan. St. Thomas of Canturbury was martyred by the lackeys of King Henry II of England, who was himself a Catholic.

3. The third condition for martyrdom is that **death must be accepted voluntarily.** The unwilling martyr would be a contradiction in terms. So would the sleeping martyr, or the unconscious martyr, unless he had a previous intention to die for the faith. The willingness

required for maryrdom does not mean that one must relish the thought of suffering and death. Oftentimes martyrs express the opinion that, given other circumstances, they would gladly go on living. Even Christ prayed, "Father, if it is possible, let this cup pass away from me; yet not as I will, but as thou willest" (Matt. 26:39). But when martyrs are faced with the choice in the concrete they choose to die, just as Christ did, rather than deny the faith.

4. Vices Opposed to Fortitude

Like all moral virtues, fortitude strives for the mean between excess and defect. Since fortitude is concerned with fear and daring, there will be vices opposed to each of these acts. The vices opposed to fear are excessive fear or **cowardice**, which sins against fear by defect, and **fearlessness**, which is opposed by excess. Contrary to daring is the vice of excessive daring or **foolhardiness**, which is an excess of daring. There is no vice opposed to daring by defect, for lack of daring is the same thing as cowardice.

A. Cowardice

Reason enlightened by faith indicates that certain dangers must be endured, others fled, and others overcome. The vice of cowardice occurs when one fears excessively and is led to fly dangers and difficulties he should endure or overcome. Thus when a man fears things which are not actually dangerous, or when he fears dangerous things too much, he allows himself to be drawn away from the course of action which right reason says he should pursue. To deny God for fear of death, for example, would be to fear a dangerous thing too greatly. Life is a precious good, and its loss should be feared; but when compared to the loss of God, loss of life is as nothing.

Regardless of how excessive fear or cowardice is manifested, it is sinful. In itself, it is a venial sin, but it can be a mortal sin if it causes man to do something seriously contrary to reason. Those who omit going to Mass on Sunday because they think a small rainstorm might ruin their clothes are allowing their fear to lead them into mortal sin. In some cases, however, as was pointed out in Chapter Two, excessive fear will destroy the voluntary action of man or diminish it, and then moral guilt is removed or mitigated.

B. Fearlessness

To fear danger is human. Therefore, not only the man who fears in excess, but also the one who does not fear at all, is acting contrary to virtue. The vice of fearlessness is not found as frequently as the vice of fear because it is more unnatural than cowardice. After all, things which are dangerous tend by their very nature to cause fear, and it is the rare man who apprehends these things as dangerous yet does not fear them.

Fearlessness can be caused by various states of mind. Love leads to fear since we automatically start to fear when it is obvious that we are in danger of losing something that we love. If a man does not love something as much as he should, he will not fear its loss as much as he should. Hence the man who does not love life, or does not realize that it is his greatest natural good (because without it he can have no other natural goods), will not fear to lose his life as much as he should. He will expose himself to unnecessary danger because reasonable fear will not hold him back.

Fearlessness is also caused through a miscalculation of the danger that faces one, or of the powers that one in danger possesses. The soldier who exposes himself to the enemy's fire may love life as much as he ought, but may not realize the range of the enemy guns; or he may think his equipment and experience are sufficient protection against the bullets of the enemy. If the miscalculations which bring about fearlessness are not culpable, then no formal sin will be committed by the man who acts under these misapprehensions.

C. Foolhardiness

Foolhardiness, the third vice contrary to fortitude, resembles fearlessness in its effect since both cause an unreasonable exposure to danger. The daring man, like the fearless man, also fails to take necessary precautions when faced with grave danger; yet his vice does not spring from a lack of fear but from an excess of audacity. Unlike the fearless man, the foolhardy man realizes that grave danger is present, and he may even fear it. But whether he fears it or not, he has a much stronger urge to overcome this danger—to attack it and drive it way. He wishes to make sure that the good he is trying to protect is not taken from him. If the bold man does this when reason tells him he should either flee or endure the danger without attacking it, then virtue is not served.

Foolhardiness can cause sins in another way, too. At times, when reason says that the evil causing danger should be attacked and overcome, excessive daring stirred up by anger may lead man to wage too violent an attack. Everyone has a right to defend his life against unjust aggressors; however, the defense must be reasonable. If an aggressor is using a cane or small stick, we would have no right to shoot him. Or if someone attacks us, we have no right to continue our counterattack after the person is unconscious, even though daring prompted by anger may desire that we do so. The gravity of this and the other forms of foolhardiness is reckoned in the same way as the other two vices opposed to fortitude. Since it is not directly contrary to charity it is not in itself a mortal sin, but it can easily lead to mortal sin when it causes the infraction of important laws.

5. THE INTEGRAL PARTS OF FORTITUDE

As we have seen, the division of the cardinal virtues into **subjective parts** is based on a division of the matter with which they are concerned. As a result, virtue is divided into various species of the same genus. For example, by dividing the matter of justice (i.e., the debt owed to another) three different species of justice may be enumerated: legal, distributive and commutative justice. Fortitude, however, is not divided in this way since its matter is already so limited that it does not admit of any division into species. Of course, we could divide the dangers of death into those that come from airplanes, those that come from automobiles, or those that come from firearms; but these dangers differ only materially, and cannot be the basis for specific difference. The danger of death is substantially the same no matter from what cause it proceeds. Fortitude, then, differs from the other cardinal virtues in that it is not divided into subjective parts. Like the other cardinal virtues, however, fortitude does have integral and potential parts.

The **integral parts** of fortitude, those functions of the soul which are necessary for the complete and perfect act of the virtue, are called magnanimity, magnificence, patience and perseverance. These parts are necessary because the twofold act of fortitude, daring and endurance, cannot be performed without them.

In order to perform the act of aggression, the soul must be prepared for it. The person must be ready to suffer the danger which will come when one seeks to overcome evil. For this, confidence or **magnanimity** ("assurance of the mind in great and honorable undertakings") is required. Lest the person falter once the difficult task of aggression has begun, another condition is required which will effect the accomplishment of so difficult a work. This second condition which must be present in the soul is called **magnificence** ("accomplishment of great and lofty undertakings with greatness of purpose").

The act of endurance also demands two conditions in the soul for its fulfillment. **Patience**—"the voluntary and prolonged endurance of arduous and difficult things for the sake of virtue or utility"—is necessary so that the soul will not be overcome by sorrow when it must endure evil. **Perseverance**—"the fixed and continued persistence in a well considered purpose"—takes care of the tedium which can easily arise from the fact that the battle of fortitude may be a prolonged one. Thus patience strengthens one so he can endure fear;

perseverance fights the weariness that comes from the prolonged enduring of evil.[4]

These four qualities are the integral parts of fortitude. They must be present when danger of death occurs if man is to perform the acts of fortitude and meet death in a courageous manner. They are not the act of fortitude itself, but they are conditions or qualities of soul which must run along side by side with the acts of courage if these acts are to achieve their proper perfection.

6. THE POTENTIAL PARTS OF FORTITUDE

These same four qualities of soul, when considered under a different aspect, are also the **potential parts** of fortitude. If we consider them in relation to the perfect matter of fortitude, danger of death, then, as we have seen, they are integral parts. But if we consider them in relation to any other danger, sorrow or hardship that man must suffer on earth, then these qualities are distinct from the cardinal virtue of fortitude and are annexed to it only in a secondary manner. Under this aspect the four qualities are separate moral virtues.

We might conceive of the relationship that magnanimity, magnificence, patience and perseverance have to fortitude in this manner: each difficulty of life can be considered as a fragment of the supreme danger which we face at the time of death. Thus in encountering each partial danger we will need a part of the courage that is necessary for facing the supreme danger. Hence, every time we act according to one of these potential parts, we will be performing an act of virtue in regard to the partial matter of fortitude, but we will also be disposing ourself for the perfect act which must be made at the time when death threatens. The same conditions of soul, then, are both the integral and potential parts of fortitude; they differ because they control different matters.

---

[4]These names and definitions of the integral parts of fortitude are borrowed and adapted by St. Thomas (*Summa*, II-II, q. 128) from the *Rhetoric* (*On Rhetorical Invention*) of the great Latin orator, statesman and man of letters, Marcus Tullius Cicero, Bk. II, Chap. 54.

A. Magnanimity

(1) The Nature of Magnanimity

Magnanimity, considered as a potential part of fortitude, is defined as *a moral virtue which inclines man to perform excellent works of virtue which are worthy of great honor.*

Other virtues, it is true, seek difficult goods, but not under the same aspect as magnanimity. When any other virtue seeks its act, no matter what it is, it does not seek it under the aspect of difficulty. Virginity, for example, is concerned with an action which is difficult—it is an arduous thing to preserve perfect and perpetual chastity throughout a lifetime—but when this virtue operates, it does not concern itself with the difficulty of the act. This is the function of magnanimity.

The difficult acts of justice, temperance and the other virtues which the magnanimous man will perform cannot help but bring him honor. But honor is not sought by magnanimous people for its own sake. When it comes, the magnanimous man takes it in stride; at times he may seek it, but only because of its connection with difficult acts of virtue.

Magnanimity has been rightly called a way of life, for the aspiration to greatness influences the whole pattern of a man's life. The preoccupation with great deeds of virtue is reflected in the lesser acts of virtue, for the expansive personality of the great man is stamped on all his actions.

Intent on great deeds, there is no room for pettiness in the life of the magnanimous man. In the presence of his equals he displays his greatness, but to others he is not condescending or patronizing. He is ready, indeed delighted, to bestow favors, but is reluctant to accept them. He is not like the irascible executive, but is quiet and slow to act; he does not engage in a variety of undertakings that dissipate his energies, but concentrates on a few worthwhile enterprises. He is slow to expose his needs, unwilling to be a burden to anyone. He suffers his setbacks and difficulties in silence, does not complain and murmur about "hard luck" or "misunderstanding" of others. He does not boast of his deeds nor speak much of himself; he speaks and acts openly and truthfully, and is not deterred from good deeds by fear of the opinion of others. He is a man of strong mind and strong will, free from the vacillating indecision, the timidity or the pettiness that can only end in failure.

Magnanimity, then, is concerned with honor, at least indirectly. But is this compatible with the Christian life? Does the humble Christian seek honors? Actually, magnanimity and humility may seem to differ, but they work hand in hand in the development of our spiritual life. Their matter is similar, but they treat it under different aspects. As St. Thomas points out:

> There is in man something great which he possesses through the goodness of God, and something defective which comes to him through the weakness of nature. Accordingly, magnanimity makes a man deem himself worthy of great things because of the gifts he has from God. . . . On the other hand, humility makes a man think little of himself in consideration of his own deficiency.[5]

St. Paul expressed this very succinctly: "I can do all things in him who strengthens me" (Phil. 4:13).

Humility, then, discerns that the very powers by which one is able to seek great works and honors are gifts of God, and for this reason it does not glory in honor but passes the credit for it on to God. Thus through the interworkings of magnanimity and humility honors are sought when they should be, but in the right manner.

Everyone does not have the same powers in regard to virtue, and therefore not everyone will be actually magnanimous. Virginity, for example, and other difficult virtues, will not be practiced by all. Yet we must remember that what is difficult for one will be comparatively easy for another because of his superior powers of nature and grace. Our Lenten fast, for example, may seem like a great work to us, but when compared to the asceticism of a St. Vincent Ferrer it is almost nothing. There is, then, a relative and absolute magnanimity. All of us must practice magnanimity in a relative way and not shy from works of virtue just because we consider them difficult. Only those with great talents, however, will be able to practice magnanimity in an absolute manner. Only a comparative

[5] *Summa*, II-II, q. 129, a. 3, ad 4.

few will be able to perform works of virtue which are worthy of great honor. But all Christians must attempt the greatest work of all, striving for Christian perfection. And for this great work the virtue of magnanimity is absolutely necessary.

(2) Vices Opposed to Magnanimity

Those who lack magnanimity manifest their vice in one of four ways. Three of these vices, presumption, ambition and vainglory, sin by excess; the fourth, pusillanimity, sins by defect. Each one of the vices that sins by excess leads a man to seek magnanimity in a manner contrary to reason. Presumption, for example, is concerned with the proximate matter of magnanimity, actions worthy of great honor. Ambition is concerned with the remote matter, honor itself; and vainglory seeks praise, the natural effect of honor. The pusillanimous person never seeks the matter of magnanimity, since he is afraid to.

1. **Presumption** is *a vice which leads a man to undertake great works of virtue that he does not have the ability to perform.* It is an overconfidence in one's own powers—the vice which leads politicians to seek offices for which they are not qualified, surgeons to perform operations for which they are not trained, scientists to attempt the solution of theological problems. Presumption is an excessive hope brought about by a culpable, erroneous opinion of our powers of knowledge and virtue, or of the works which make men worthy of honor. Thus, not only is the one who undertakes works for which he is not prepared presumptuous, but also the one who seeks to find honor in the wrong kind of work. Those who seek honor from wealth, beauty or fine clothing are victims of this vice.

It is worthy of note that it is impossible for a man to aim too high in the life of supernatural virtue. Here it is not a question of establishing a proportion between our capacities and the work we try to do; from the beginning there can be no proportion between the two because of the exalted nature of the supernatural. Yet there is always a proportion, a proportion that comes not from us but from the omnipotent, infallible grace of God.

The presumption which we are discussing is not the same as the presumption which is a sin against the Holy Spirit. This latter type of presumption is contrary to the theological virtue of hope; it is an unreasonable reliance upon the mercy of God, as when someone seeks pardon without being sorry, or expects to gain heaven without merit. The presumption which is contrary to magnanimity, however, is an unreasonable reliance on our own powers. It does not directly spurn the help of the Holy Spirit as does the other type of presumption.

Presumption against the Holy Spirit is, as we know, a very grave sin. Presumption contrary to magnanimity is also sinful, but not so gravely sinful as the aforementioned kind. It is less of a sin to rely too much upon one's own powers than to detract from the power of God. In itself, therefore, overconfidence or presumption is a venial sin, but it can be a mortal sin if it leads someone to have so much confidence in his own powers that he does things seriously contrary to the moral law.

2. Presumption aims too high; **ambition** aims at the wrong target. Through the vice of ambition man has *an inordinate desire for honor.* Instead of primarily intending the great works of virtue, and only secondarily the honor connected with them, the ambitious man desires only the honor. If possible, he will not perform the work of virtue if he can be sure of having the honor without it. If ambition prompts great works at all, it does so only as a means to the honor that they might bring. The ambitious man would rather gain the honor without the work, but if necessary he will do the good required.

Ambition can manifest itself in three ways. First, when a man desires recognition or honor for some quality which he does not have. Thus, when a dull person wishes to be reckoned as a brilliant conversationalist, or when a poor golfer passes himself off as an expert, the vice of ambition is at work.

The powers that man has which enable him to excel in some particular field of endeavor are *from God,* and they should be used *for the profit of others.* When man forgets this, he exposes himslf to the second and third type of ambition. Hence, when man does not ultimately refer the honor that comes to him to God, he is claiming rewards for himself which rightfully belong to God. Man need not deny that he has done great works of virtue if he has truly performed them, nor need he turn down all honors, but he must realize that the power to perform these great works came from God, and therefore the honor which they bring should be credited or referred to God. We must also remember that gifts and powers were given us by God for the good of other men. Man is a social animal and should use his powers to protect and foster the good of the social kingdom. The surgeon or preacher, therefore, who considers his skills and talents as means to honor, and not as things which should be used to serve others, is guilty of the third kind of ambition.

3. Glory or renown is the natural effect of honor. It consists in being well known and respected by other people. To desire glory is not wrong as long as the desire is reasonable. Christ himself told us that we should not hide our light under a bushel basket. To desire glory for its own sake, however, is wrong. Glory, like honor, is a means; like honor it should be desired only to show forth the glory of God, or as something which will help our neighbor. When the desire for glory is not controlled by reason, it leads to the vice of **vainglory**—*an inordinate desire for renown and the respect of other people.*

Desire for renown can be contrary to reason in three ways. We can seek glory in the wrong objects, from the wrong people or in the wrong manner. When we seek glory from things which cannot give it, we are acting sinfully. The racketeer, for example, wishes to be known as a ruthless person, and thinks that this gives him a standing in the community. But virtue, not ruthlessness, is the object which causes true honor, and so the racketeer can never win true glory. The same might be said of those who wish to have renown because of their physical beauty. The perfection of man consists in virtue, not beauty; so anyone seeking the esteem of men for the latter quality is guilty of a reversal of values.

Others seek glory in the right objects, but from people who are not capable of judging whether or not they are truly virtuous. The man who seeks honor from fools is as unreasonable as the opera singer who rejoices in the applause of her paid claque.

The third means of sinning in one's desire for glory concerns the manner in which glory is desired. Glory, as we said, is a means, not an end in itself. Thus those who perform truly good works but only for the glory they will bring are not truly virtuous but vainglorious frauds. This type of vainglory, since it results in good works, is often difficult to distinguish from true magnanimity.

Vainglory is not the most serious sin a man can commit; sins against charity, for example, are in themselves more serious. But since vainglory is *a capital sin*, it is dangerous in that it disposes one for several other serious sins. In seeking to manifest his own excellence, the vainglorious man is often led to actions which he thinks will enhance his reputation in the eyes of others. In truth, however, these actions are sinful. These sins are known as the "daughters" of vainglory and they are enumerated as follows: boasting, hypocrisy, love of novelty, quarreling, disobedience, stubborness and discord.

4. Magnanimity can also be sinned against by defect. This defect is known as the vice of **pusillanimity** and it is *a tendency to estimate that one's powers are not sufficient to attempt difficult works of virtue while in reality they are equal to the task*. This pettiness of soul may be caused by a culpable overestimation of the difficulty of the work facing a man, or the likewise culpable underestimation of the powers that one has at his disposal. When a man does not know his problem or himself, therefore, he is likely to fall victim to this vice. If pusillanimity leads one to neglect some action which he has a grave obligation to perform, then it is a mortal sin. Of itself, however, it is a venial sin.

Yet pusillanimity is usually a grave sin in those who are in positions of authority, since it does serious harm to the common good. If the leaders of any group, state or family are pusillanimous, then discipline and progress are almost impossible in that particular community. When pusillanimity extends to the individual's spiritual life it is also very serious. At this level it leads to the neglect of the works necessary for salvation and even to despair.

B. Magnificence

(1) *Its Nature*

The second potential part of fortitude, magnificence or munificence, is closely allied to magnanimity. Magnanimity is concerned with great works and deeds of all kinds. Included in these great works are the building of great edifices, such as churches, hospitals and schools, and the holding of great celebrations. In order to carry out these projects, large sums of money must be spent so that the work will be done in a fitting manner. Since the attraction of money is so strong, it presents a special difficulty when great amounts of it must be spent and therefore there must be a special virtue to regulate the desire for money. This is the work of magnificence. Through magnificence, man's desire for money is so regulated that when he must expend large amounts on buildings or celebrations he will do it graciously and according to right reason. Thus he will spend neither too much nor too little in the accomplishment of some necessary great work. **Magnificence** is defined as *the moral virtue which moderates the love of money so that man is ready to incur heavy expenses in order to execute great projects in a fitting manner.*

Since magnificence is concerned with great expenditures of money, the ordinary person has an opportunity to exercise this virtue only in a relative manner. That is, the average man will never spend an absolutely great sum of money—his usual expenditures will be small, and in this he will be governed by liberality. But now and then, when he builds a house or celebrates a wedding, the ordinary man will make a relatively great expenditure of money and then he must be guided by magnificence.

The spending of absolutely great sums of money, and therefore the practice of magnificence in an absolute manner, pertains nowadays to the civic official, the trustee of a fund and the great philanthropists.

(2) *Vices Opposed to Magnificence*

When the love of money leads anyone to spend too little on the project he has undertaken, then he is guilty of the vice of meanness or **stinginess**. On the other hand, if his wish for praise or disregard of money leads him to spend more than necessary on a project, then he is guilty of a sin of waste or **prodigality**. This vice is often seen in the conspicuous consumption of the *nouveaux riches*.

C. Patience

(1) Its Nature

The sorrow that man must endure in life can easily lead him to sin. When one is sad, one seeks something to relieve sadness. "Man cannot stay long in a state of sadness," said Aristotle, sagely if obviously. If what man seeks as a relief from sadness is not in accord with reason, then he falls into sin. To moderate sadness, which presents a special difficulty in our life, we have the moral virtue of patience. It is the task of patience to endure sorrow and to curb anguish so that man's basic drive for pleasure will not lead him into sin.

Patience is thus *the moral virtue which inclines man to suffer and endure present evils so that he may not be unreasonably sorrowful.* Since the principal act of patience is to endure, it has the same mode of action as fortitude, and therefore it is numbered among the potential parts of fortitude. Unlike the other potential parts of fortitude, however, unlike fortitude itself, patience does not have the irascible appetite for its subject. The emotion which patience moderates, sorrow, is not in the irascible but the concupiscible appetite. Therefore, patience is in this appetite as in a subject. The fact that patience is reckoned as a part of fortitude even though it has a different subject serves to illustrate that the criterion for the annexation of virtues to cardinal virtues is not a material one. Rather, the formal aspect—the mode of acting—determines to which virtue the secondary virtue will be annexed. If the material aspect, the concupiscible appetite, were the determining factor, then patience would be annexed to temperance as a secondary virtue.

Patience is a virtue which everyone must exercise frequently. Unlike magnanimity and magnificence, it is a virtue of the average man. If we reflect upon the number of times each day that we are confronted with situations, persons or things that displease us and make us sad, we can see how often patience must be used. Patience does not have the special splendor of soul that characterizes magnanimity, but in its own way it is important because it prepares the way for the practice of all the other virtues. Virtuous action is usually difficult and likely to cause sorrow on the sense level. Patience, by moderating the emotion of sorrow, removes one of the serious obstacles to the practice of other virtues. If the passion of sorrow were given free rein, works of virtue would be much more difficult than they are now. The sadness that would come with every work of virtue would make it unpleasant to do even the least good work. In a very real sense, then, all the virtues owe something to patience, and no one can long follow in the path of virtue without it.

All sorrow deprives man of some good—if a man does not hope to gain a greater good than the one of which he is being deprived, he will not endure sorrow, he will flee from it or try to overcome it whenever he encounters it. On the natural level, therefore, patience is a very difficult virtue to cultivate, since it is not easy for a man without faith to see what advantage there is in tolerating sorrow. Even the Catholic, who sees in the bearing of sorrow a means of imitating Christ and atoning for sin, does not have an easy time practicing this virtue. To the pagan, the silent suffering Christian has always been a stumbling block. But the Christian has always seen in patience a way to express love of God—to show our love for him, we suffer for him. As St. Paul said, "Charity is patient." As love for God grows so does patience. At first it may be difficult to be patient, but as love grows the Christian finds that he can accept suffering and sorrow with an absolute joy.

(2) Vices Opposed to Patience

Opposed to patience are the vices of insensibility and impatience. The former vice, a lack of feeling which leaves a man unmoved by his own suffering or the suffering of another, puts man in the same class as brute animals. It is contrary to human nature and to the concern that man should have for his fellow human beings to be unmoved by danger and difficulty which may come to them. People who are not saddened to some extent by the death of children in school fires, or by the persecution of Christians behind the Iron Curtain, are truly to be pitied, since their ignorance or self-concern has cut them off from the human community. Since it is so inhuman a vice, **insensibility** is not common.

Impatience, on the other hand, is a very common vice in our fast-paced society. Anyone who does not wish to practice patience can always find excuses for not doing so in the slogans of our times. We disguise our inability to put up with sorrow by saying we only wish to be "efficient," or we joke about our impatience, thinking that the impatient man typifies the aggressive "go-getter." But this is subterfuge. Impatience is still a sin, no matter how we disguise it, for through impatience we neglect, because of sorrow, some good work that we should perform. If man does not make an effort to root out the impatience from his soul, he will soon decide that there is no joy in virtue or loving God. The next step is to turn away from God and seek joy in material things.

D. Perseverance

(1) Its Nature

It is not too difficult to perform one small act of kindness, but it is not easy to spend a whole lifetime being kind to others. It is not hard to pass up one piece of candy but to give it up for Lent is difficult. From the fact that human beings must practice some acts of virtue over a prolonged period of time, a special difficulty arises. This difficulty, a fatigue or tedium which arises in the passions, tends to make man withdraw from the practice of good works. The person who offers up to God abstinence from alcohol for one year may have an easy time of it for the first few days, but after that, the man starts to think of the long period that he must abstain, and the sorrow which this causes inclines him to break the pledge and have "just one drink." In order to counteract this tendency, man must develop the fourth potential part of fortitude, perseverance. Just as fortitude endures the dangers of death, perseverance endures the tedium that comes from prolonged human action. **Perseverence** is defined, therefore, as *the moral virtue which inclines man to continue in the practice of virtue notwithstanding the tedium which results from this action when it is prolonged over a period of time.*

The perseverance which we are treating here is not the same as the perseverance which enables man to stay in the state of grace up to and including the time of death. The latter form of perseverance is not a moral virtue but an essentially gratuitous gift of God, as we saw in the chapter on grace. Both types of perseverance have an important task to play in the spiritual life of man, but they must not be confused since their natures and functions are totally different.

The virtues of perseverance and patience have much in common. They are a co-ordinated defense that protects the other virtues, and a united front which encourages their activities by removing some of the difficulty connected with their practice. Patience helps overcome the initial reluctance to the practice of virtue, and perseverance gives that strength which is needed to carry on when emotional fatigue sets in and inclines one to find something more pleasing to the senses. Patience and perseverance, however, do not have the same object; since perseverance moderates one of the emergency passions, it is in the irascible appetite.

(2) Vices Opposed to Perseverance

Just as man can reasonably endure the tedium of prolonged action, so he can endure it too long, or not long enough. When one does not endure as long as reason says he should, he is guilty of the vice of **inconstancy.** The Latin word for this vice, *mollities,* is even more descriptive, since it signifies a "softness of soul." Because of this vice, a virtuous action is never begun, or if begun, is soon abandoned because of the emotional fatigue connected with it. One who yields to the pressure of time in this manner is "soft"—instead of standing fast in the face of this tedium because of the greater good which he will gain through virtuous action, the "soft man" gives in to his passions, forgets about virtue, and seeks pleasure in actions which are not so emotionally strenuous. Unfortunately, this vice is very common today. It seems that our society, which caters so much to convenience and comfort, saps our moral courage at the same time. This is a vivid illustration, if we need it, that grace builds upon nature.

At the other extreme of the human scale is the hard, pertinacious individual who will not give up a course of action no matter what happens. Even though reason tells him that the fatigue he will suffer from continuing along the present path is not worth the goal he seeks, the pertinacious man will persist in his endeavor, since he does not wish to admit that anyone or anything can defeat him. The man with this vice of **pertinacity** is the type who will not abandon actions which are in themselves good, even in order to avoid scandalizing the weak, or in order to help another. For example, the man who goes to Mass on Sunday when he should stay home and nurse his sick children is being too pertinacious in the practice of what would ordinarily be a good work.

It is obvious that the vice of pertinacity has its roots in vainglory. Vainglory seeks to display the excellence of a man, and many misguided souls feel that there is no better way to do this than to show how well they can persevere, even when others have given up. Whether or not the others were more reasonable when they gave up makes no difference. Aristotle signified another characteristic of people with this vice when he used the term "self-opinionated" to describe them. Thus, the pertinacious strive to show that they are not in error by continuing a course of action long after the reasonable man would have admitted that he was wrong.

7. THE GIFT OF FORTITUDE

The crowning glory of courage is that fortitude which is the gift of the Holy Spirit. The natural and supernatural virtues of fortitude equip man with powerful weapons to combat the onslaught of evil— but they do not make him invincible. Human invincibility can be realized only through the power of God, which is placed, as it were, at man's disposal through the gift of fortitude.

The virtues of themselves are insufficient to insure final victory, for they operate in a completely human way. But it is not always within man's power to carry out every difficult undertaking to its conclusion, or to avoid all dangers that may threaten him. His whole effort may crumble to pieces in the face of death. By the gift of fortitude, man acts under the special motion of the Holy Spirit, which inspires in him a sublime confidence of overcoming all obstacles in his struggle for ultimate triumph. This is a confidence that even the strength of the supernatural virtue of fortitude cannot give—it is the work of God.

Operating through the gift of fortitude, man is wholly assured that no power on earth or in hell can defeat him. He forgets the sufferings, the violence, the blandishments, the puny rewards that the world can offer, and turns wholly and irrevocably to God. He severs all ties that bind him to earth; eagerly, joyfully, he is ready to die for God, for the faith. He becomes, in the finest sense of the word, a hero.

Corresponding to the gift of fortitude is the fourth beatitude: "Blessed are they who hunger and thirst for justice, for they shall be satisfied." Justice is taken here in a general sense, signifying the works of all the virtues. Hunger and thirst denote an insatiable desire. But to tend to the virtuous life with such a desire involves great difficulty. This beatitude, therefore, fittingly corresponds to the gift of fortitude.

8. THE PRECEPTS OF FORTITUDE

Enemies of the Christian, some of whom attack his body while others attempt to destroy his living soul, close in on him from every side. Hence, in order to keep the human mind on the difficult path toward the vision of the divine essence, God has given certain precepts to him concerning fortitude, just as he gave them with regard to other virtues. The Old Law is filled with commands to forget fear in the face of bodily injury or death: "Hear, O Israel, you join battle this day against your enemies. Let not your heart be dismayed, be not afraid, do not give back, fear ye them not: because the Lord your God is in the midst of you and will fight for you against your enemies" (Deut. 20:3-4). To this courage the New Law adds fearlessness before spiritual foes: "And do not be afraid of those who kill the body but cannot kill the soul" (Matt. 10:28), rather, ". . . resist the devil, and he will flee from you" (Jas. 4:7), "fight the good fight of the faith, lay hold of life eternal, to which thou hast been called" (I Tim. 6:12).

Besides commands being attached to the principal act of fortitude (martyrdom), precepts are given to the acts of certain of its annexed or secondary virtues. And these precepts of divine law are both suitable and necessary, because perfect instruction from God is needed for perfect Christian living. Thus, the Lord commands **patience** in times of persecution: ". . . you will be delivered up by your parents and brothers and relatives and friends; and some of you they will put to death. And you will be hated by all for my name's sake; yet not a hair of your head shall perish. By your patience you will win your souls" (Luke 21:16-19). And he commands **perseverance:** in sorrow—"take all that shall be brought upon thee and in thy sorrow endure" (Sir. 2:4); in the labors of life—"be steadfast and immovable, always abounding in the work of the Lord, knowing that your labor is not in vain in the Lord" (I Cor. 15:58), for "he who has persevered to the end will be saved" (Matt. 10:22); and in the yoke of discipline—"my son, neglect not the discipline of the Lord, neither be thou weary when thou art rebuked by him. For whom the Lord loves, he chastises" (Prov. 3:11).

Divine precepts are not given for magnificence and magnanimity because they pertain to excellence, and virtues which concern excellence fall under the counsels of perfection rather than under obligatory precepts. Thus Christ counseled greatness of soul when he said: "You therefore are to be perfect, even as your heavenly Father is perfect" (Matt. 5:48), and he recommended munificence in his eulogy of Mary Magdalene who anointed him with a perfume of great value: "Amen I say to you, wherever in the whole world this gospel is preached, this also that she has done shall be told in memory of her" (Mark 14:9).

Secondary virtues, therefore, are counselled when they tend toward that which is excellent or superabundant, and they are commanded when the normal hardships and labors of earthly existence demand them.

9. SUMMARY AND CONCLUSION

The Christian life, as St. Paul so often points out, is a warfare. There is the warfare within us, the struggle of the spirit against the flesh, the reason against the passions; and warfare without, a genuine and often fierce battle with the enemies of the faith who surround us on all sides, Satan and his angels at their head.

The follower of Christ must be truly a valiant soldier, an unyielding foe of everything that imperils his faith or the life of virtue. Weakness has no place in the Christian life. The moral coward who calls himself Christian is deceived; to shrink from the difficulties of the virtuous life is not to live at all, but to sneak off from trial to trial to despicable and dishonorable death.

Fortitude and magnanimity must be part of daily living. Not all are called to be martyrs or to perform outstanding deeds, but the readiness to do and the readiness to die will give the stamp of true courage and greatness to all our virtuous actions.

The doctrine proposed in this chapter leads to the following conclusions.

1. Fortitude must be exercised constantly throughout the Christian life. "I assert that an imperfect human being needs more fortitude to pursue the way of perfection than suddenly to become a martyr," observes St. Theresa of Avila (*Autobiography*, Chap. 31, 18). To make progress into the higher realms of the spiritual life, one must abandon reliance upon creatures and cleave wholly to God. Such a prospect engenders fear, as Francis Thompson says in "The Hound of Heaven,"

"For though I knew His love who followèd,
Yet was I sore adread
Lest, having Him, I must have naught beside."

A special exercise of fortitude is necessary to overcome this fear of the consequences of self-abandonment.

2. The contemporary Christian living in and among the complex societies of today is in special need of the gift of fortitude. For hopelessness often stalks the unwary Christian who finds his initiative trapped by the evils of social dissensions and differences. The utter lack of unity in thought and action among the nations of the world may force him to one of two tragic decisions: either despair, or a withdrawal into the shell of self-complacency where, without compassion, he can watch the world destroy itself. And yet our Lord said that the fields are ripe for the harvest. Hence the Christian needs fortitude to enable him to avoid either of the easy ways out; to keep him from shirking social issues by recognizing the truth without flinching; and to help him in the sphere of action, impelling him to choose difficult rather than easy means and to persevere in his work for the glory of God—in spite of unsympathetic and unsupporting companions who load opprobrium and misunderstanding upon him.

3. "Clarity of vision, devotion, courage, inventive genius—and the sense of brotherly love in all upright and honest men determine the measure and extent to which Christian thought will succeed in maintaining and supporting the gigantic work of restoration in social, economic and international life through a plan that does not conflict with the religious and moral content of Christian civilization."[6]

4. "You must practice the little virtues. This is sometimes difficult, but God never refuses the first grace—*courage for self-conquest*; and if the soul corresponds to that grace, she at once finds herself in the sunlight of God. The praise given to Judith has always struck me: 'Thou hast done manfully, and thy heart has been strengthened' (Judith 15:11). In this battle we must act with courage: by so doing the heart gains strength, and victory follows victory."[7]

---

[6]Pope Pius XII, radio address, Sept. 1, 1944.

[7]Taken from the reminiscences of a sister religious of St. Thérèse of Lisieux. Cf. *Saint Thérèse of Lisieux* by Thomas N. Taylor (New York: P. J. Kenedy and Sons, 1927), 298.

5. "Embolden thy heart, and speak to it with the Holy One and say: 'Act manfully, and let thy heart take courage, and wait thou for the Lord.' Imitate David and with one stone prostrate thy adversary. The angels stand beside thee as spectators of thy courage, for 'we have been made a spectacle to the world, and to angels, and to men' (I Cor. 4:9). Should they behold you victor in a good work, they will rejoice. And if they behold you overcome, they depart unhappy, since they cannot endure this. But the demons will rejoice over thee."[8]

BIBLIOGRAPHICAL NOTE

St. Thomas' highly technical treatment of fortitude and its annexed virtues is taken up in the *Summa*, II-II, Questions CXXIII-CXL. Not much material is available in English on the virtue itself, although we can name *The Courageous Shall Conquer* by Henry Brenner, O.S.B. (St. Meinrad, Ind.: The Grail, 1943) as a popular treatment of fortitude which gives practical hints on ways of heightening one's courage. Another work, semi-popular in style, can be highly recommended: *Fortitude and Temperance* by Josef Pieper (New York: Pantheon, 1954)—a book which will be useful for the study of temperance also, because it shows the nature and worth of both virtues, and particularly their breadth of meaning which makes them worthy of being hinges of man's life.

Several periodicals yield articles on fortitude or its allied virtues. Among them are: "Call to Fortitude," by Dorothy Dohen in *Cross and Crown*, VIII (1956), 22-29; "Fortitude and Temperance," by J. W. O'Brien in *Journal of Religious Instruction*, IX (1939), 677-681; "Virtue of Fortitude," by F. J. Connell, C.SS.R., in *Journal of Religious Instruction*, XI (1941), 505-510; N. Kinsella's "Humility and Some Allied Virtues," in *Sursum Corda*, III (1957), 629-634; "Meaning of Martyrdom," by Columba Ryan, O.P., in *Blackfriars*, XXXIV (1953), 164-171; and "On Patience," by Irene Marinoff in *Blackfriars*, XXV sup. (1944), 3-8.

[8]St. Ephraem, *Homily on the First Sunday of Advent*.

CHAPTER SIXTEEN

Temperance

1. Introduction

Up to this point, all the virtues which have been studied are concerned in some way with something outside the individual who possesses them. The theological virtues are directed to God; prudence relates man to the whole reality of his environment; justice is directed to the rights of others, whether of men or of God; fortitude looks to the dangers and fears arising from forces extrinsic to the individual.

With the consideration of the virtue of temperance, all of that changes. Now, extrinsic things assume a secondary role; they are considered precisely in relation to the individual. This does not imply that temperance is the virtue of selfish personal concern. In truth, temperance is the virtue of stewardship exercised over one's own person; it is man's effort to conform his appetites to reason in imitation of God, who exemplifies temperance by "turning the divine gaze on himself,"[1] where exists the supreme internal harmony that is the perfect pattern of human temperance.

[1]St. Thomas, *Summa*, I-II, q. 61, a. 5.

Our investigation of this vital and necessary realm of human activity will unfold according to this plan:

In itself
(Section 2)

Its opposed vices
(Section 3)

Its integral parts
(Section 4)

Temperance

Its subjective parts

Concerning pleasures of food
(Section 5)

Concerning pleasures of sex
(Sections 6 and 7)

Its potential parts
(Section 8)

The precepts of temperance
(Section 9)

2. TEMPERANCE IN ITSELF

A. The Meaning of Temperance

The word "temperance," which signifies moderation, has gradually acquired in common usage a restricted meaning which robs it of the richness and profundity of its earlier signification. Today, temperance generally means restraint or moderation chiefly in regard to the use of alcohol. Indeed, in some quarters temperance has been made to mean something quite negative—total abstinence from alcoholic drink. Temperance, then, was first made into a quantitative measure of alcoholic consumption; it was reduced to a number. Later it was made synonymous with complete abstinence; it was reduced to a zero.

Such restricted usages belie the true nature of temperance and give rise to many serious and even anti-Christian misconceptions of the virtue.

A consideration of the etymology of the word gives some inkling of its full and proper meaning. In the Greek *sophrosyne* and the Latin *temperantia,* which are the antecedents of our English "temperance," there is implied an interjection of reasonable equilibrium or moderation into man's actions. The Latin *temperantia* is akin to *temperies,* which suggests a cooling breeze dispelling the oppressive heat of summer, or the tempering of strong wine through the addition of water. These usages evolved into the idea of self-restraint and moderation, achieved by tempering the forces and instincts of nature by ordering and restraining them under the governance of reason. Hence, in its primary and essential signification, "temperance" came to mean the disposition of man's sensual powers by reason, which orders and unifies them harmoniously.

The flavor of this original meaning is evident in St. Paul's expression: "God has so tempered the body together in due portion as to give more abundant honor where it was lacking" (I Cor. 12:24).[2] This use of the word denotes a harmonious unification of the diverse parts of the body in a definite order. Very significantly, it connotes the fact that temperance moderates vital, active entities like the parts of the body rather than static, inanimate things. We would not use the word temperate in reference to a stack of bricks.

Temperance causes a certain tranquillity or serenity in man's interior life. This results from the fact that his vital forces and inclinations operate in a harmonious order, and he is free of the turmoil resulting from the dominion of his passions. How unrealistic to confine temperance to the regulation of alcoholic drink! The range of temperance is as wide as the rule of reason over all the passions that drive man to self-preservation and self-realization. This can be

---

[2]The Vulgate has: "*Deus temperavit corpus,*" which could be rendered, "God has established a harmony in the body." The Greek text says, "God has combined the body in due proportion." All of these renditions indicate the bringing forth of harmony among diverse parts.

seen from the many parts of temperance listed in the rest of this chapter. Each of these virtues moderates some basic human instinct or passion, and all of them must function if the individual is to know the interior serenity that marks the temperate man.

B. The Virtue of Temperance

Moral virtues make both their possessor and his deeds good. This goodness results from living and acting in accord with reason. Hence, it is the proper function of moral virtue to accustom man to live according to reason. This is exactly what is done by temperance, which functions to moderate man's inclinations according to reason.

Not every temperate act is an infallible sign of the presence of the perfect virtue of temperance. There are some people who have natural or acquired dispositions toward temperance in some matters. For instance, some people of a placid disposition never get angry; others have poor appetites and are not inclined to gluttony; some are raised in a puritanical atmosphere that cultivates a horror of alcohol; etc. These and similar manifestations are not necessarily the result of true temperance. The perfect virtue exists only in conjunction with prudence, and extends to all of man's inclinations toward pleasure and self-assertiveness.

There is a sense in which every virtue bears a stamp of temperance, because every virtue achieves a balance between excess and defect in its object. This general spirit of moderation is not the virtue of temperance, but rather a general condition present in every moral virtue.

The virtue of temperance exists independently of other virtues because it has a specific and distinct object. Man has very strong natural desires for pleasure, especially for the pleasures of the senses, and these desires are particularly capable of drawing him away from the rule of reason and from the divine law. It is the role of temperance to moderate, control and "temper" these desires for pleasure so that man will not forsake reason or break the divine law in order to satisfy them. Temperance, then, is directly concerned with desires and pleasures of the senses; indirectly it is concerned with the sorrows that arise from the absence of those pleasures. Because the desires and pleasures of the senses are primarily the object of the concupiscible passions, it is the task of temperance to moderate these passions. The irascible appetites come under the moderation of temperance only insofar as they are conjoined with the concupiscible passions in particular instances.

Indirect, too, is the influence of temperance upon external deeds. Man's actions flow from his internal passions, and it is these passions that are directly controlled by temperance.

(1) The Specific Object of Temperance

Fortitude strengthens man against the greatest evil which is death: *a fortiori*, it enables him to face all lesser dangers. In the same way, temperance primarily controls man's desire for the greatest pleasures, and consequently for all desires for lesser delights.

Pleasure results from a natural function, and pleasure is greater in proportion as the function is more natural. In animal natures, the most natural functions are those which preserve the individual by food and drink, and those which preserve the species by the union of the sexes. The pleasures resulting from these functions result from the sense of touch, and they are the greatest and most alluring that can be experienced by animal nature. Hence, *temperance is principally concerned with moderating the desires for the pleasures of touch that accompany eating, drinking, and sexual union.* A virtue which can moderate the desires for these greatest pleasures will also temper the inclinations toward lesser delights.

It is admitted that spiritual delights are by their nature greater than bodily pleasures, but they are not so vehement because they do not directly affect the senses or stir up the passions. Spiritual pleasures are subject to the indirect control of prudence, but bodily delights so excite the passions to tear man from the rule of reason and the divine law that they must be controlled directly by a special virtue.

(2) The Sense of Touch

Since the sense of touch is the seat of the pleasures moderated by temperance, it is important to have some appreciation of St. Thomas' estimation of the importance of this sense.

The sense of touch is essential to animal life; the most rudimentary forms of animal life are endowed with this sense, even though they may have no other. The very existence of animal life depends upon the sense of touch.

Touch apprehends tangible bodily qualities through physical contact. The organs of touch are not localized like those of sight, hearing, etc.; they are rather spread throughout the entire organism in the skin, muscles and vital organs. A vast network of sensory cells and free nerve endings transmits the sensations of pressure, pain, temperature, balance, muscular movement, bodily needs, satisfactions, illnesses, fatigues, well-being, etc. Because of the vast scope of this sense, "touch" is really too restricted to describe it. It is more accurately called **body sense** or *somesthesis*.[3]

The sense of touch is most highly developed in human beings. Other animals may be endowed with keener sight, a more discriminating sense of smell, or more acute hearing, but man excels them all in the acuteness of his sense of touch.

Furthermore, there is generally a proportion between the acuity of touch and keenness of intellect in individual men. This follows from the fact that the senses are the gateway to intellectual knowledge. All the other external senses are grounded in somesthesis, because they depend upon some kind of physical contact for their sensations. Thus, a more acute sense of touch perceives the sensible world more perfectly and is better able to garner the sense impressions upon which the intellect bases its knowledge. It is quite true to say that a man is as thick as his skin.

Finally, the sense of touch is most closely allied to the nutritive and reproductive faculties, which rely mainly on tactile sensations.

---

[3]This term comes from the Greek: *soma*, meaning "body," and *aisthesis*, meaning "sense."

It is through the somesthetic sense that the pleasures of these powers are experienced, and for this reason, temperance is especially concerned with regulating the pleasures of touch or *somesthesis*.[4]

(3) *The Rule and Measure of Temperance*

The pleasures of the sense of touch are essentially good. "It is not contrary to human nature to enjoy natural pleasures, but it would be against human nature to enjoy pleasure beyond the rule of reason."[5] The rule of reason is particularly difficult to achieve in matters of temperance, because it involves the moderation of pleasures so basic to the very essence of the animal side of human nature that they can most easily disturb the mind. The rule of reason for temperance, then, must be clearly determined by prudence, because a vague notion of this rule can easily be upset by the vehemence of the passions.

Basic to the formulation of a rule of temperance is the fact that all the pleasurable objects at man's disposal are related to some necessity of life as to their goal. The pleasures of eating and drinking are related to the preservation of one's life; the pleasures of sexuality have to do with the preservation of the race. It is from the necessities of this life, then, that the rule of temperance is derived.

The "necessities of life" in this context are not limited to the things without which man would die or the race would perish. A far broader concept must be used. The needs of spiritual progress, of cultural and intellectual growth, of custom and good manners, of social standing, and of physical and mental well-being—all these and more must be considered in determining what is temperate and what is not.

Hence the rule and measure of temperance is not exclusively determined by the generic needs of human nature, but also by the individual needs of each man as he exists in the concrete circumstances of his life. This means that, for the Christian, the "rule of reason" embraces the truths of faith. This is because reason is man's bond

---

[4] A highly interesting and eminently readable brief account of this subject is available in R. E. Brennan, O.P., *The Image of His Maker* (Milwaukee: Bruce, 1948), 115-26.

[5] St. Thomas, *Summa*, II-II, q. 141, a. 5.

with all the reality he knows, and divine faith establishes contact with supernatural reality. It is true that the natural and supernatural orders are distinct, but as a practical rule of action, faith and reason act in concert, embracing the totality of reality that is known to a man endowed with faith.

(4) The Definition of Temperance

Temperance is *a moral virtue which moderates man's appetite for the greatest pleasures of the sense of touch according to the needs of his station in life as judged by right reason and the divine law.*

The full meaning of this definition is evident through an examination of its terms:

1) As **a moral virtue,** temperance may be either natural and acquired, or supernatural and infused, depending on its origin.

2) **Appetite** here refers to the concupiscible appetite which is *the proper subject* of temperance. Thus it differs from prudence, which is found in the intellect.

3) **Moderation** of the concupiscible appetite is *the proper act* of temperance, which must curb this appetite lest it carry man away. Thus temperance is distinguished from fortitude, which must spur the irascible appetite lest it give way before fear of death.

4) The **desire for the greatest pleasures of the sense of touch** is the *material object* of temperance. Thus temperance is distinguished from its own subordinate virtues which regulate lesser desires, and also from justice which regulates external deeds.

5) The *formal object* or proximate motive of temperance is **the needs of man's station in life.** In the case of acquired temperance, these needs are judged according to reason; in infused temperance they are judged according to reason and the divine law.

C. The Gift of Fear

It can hardly be surprising that special divine assistance is given the Christian to enable him properly to control this most difficult area of human operation, of vehement sense action and reaction. Through the gift of the Holy Spirit which is fear (whose primary workings we have previously examined in the chapter on hope), man will, in a suprahuman way, flee those carnal pleasures whose enjoyment would displease his Father in heaven and separate him from God's love. This gift, then, creates in the Christian a special sensitivity with respect to the powerful urges of the flesh; it enables him, for the love of God, to avoid offending even when most strongly enticed to unreasonable sense pleasures.

3. THE VICES OPPOSED TO TEMPERANCE

We have already stated that nature intended man's enjoyment of the pleasures attached to the various faculties and their operations, and that the virtue of temperance comes into play in the control or reasonable moderation of these pleasures. Now the temperate control of these things is, as we have explained, according to the needs of the present life (for the acquired virtue of temperance) and the needs of the spiritual life in a given person (for the infused virtue of temperance). Hence, when we come to treat of the vices which are opposed to temperance, it should be immediately evident that they will be such by reason of unreasonable deficiency or unreasonable excess. In other words, the standard or norm for temperance is a need of human life: if one without sufficient cause does not provide for the need, he is guilty of the vice of insensibility; if he goes beyond the need, he may be guilty of the vice of intemperance.

A. Insensibility

Insensibility is *a vice whereby man rejects pleasure to the extent that he omits things necessary for life as judged by reason and the divine law.* Since the pleasures of food, drink and sex readily lead a person to excess, it is logical to expect that the vice of insensibility will be comparatively rare, and when it does occur, it will, as often as not, be due to a faulty judgment concerning the liceity of the pleasures of the flesh. We must insist vigorously that when the necessity of life in given circumstances requires the satisfaction of the bodily instincts, it would be unlawful to refuse to satisfy the needs of life. We mean to imply in the word "necessity," of course, that in the given circumstances there is some kind of moral obligation involved. The insensible person is not only far from the virtue of temperance, but his attitude is an outrage to nature.

In certain circumstances, however, it is perfectly lawful to make a voluntary renunciation of sense gratifications. This is true on both the natural and supernatural planes. As a prelude to any such renunciations, it is imperative to be free of erroneous attitudes that could vitiate the self-denial. Among such false notions are: the condemnation of pleasure as evil in itself; renunciation for its own sake; and the avoidance of all sense pleasures because of unreasonable repressive fear.

In the purely natural order the body itself, once its needs have been supplied, can become insensible to any further sense pleasure. This is nature's method of warning the individual against excess. Indeed, if the pleasures of the sense of touch are intensified beyond their normal threshold, they are changed into pain. In the matter of food and drink excessive consumption may lead the body to reject any further intake until it has digested that which has already been consumed.

Again, in the purely natural order, there may be any number of justifying factors for renouncing food, drink and sex without falling into the vice of insensibility. Thus the athlete may abstain from these things for the greater perfection of his bodily faculties; an individual may follow a rigid diet for reasons of health; a student may eat sparingly in order to have greater intellectual acumen; or a professional person may forego marriage in view of a particular type of work and a more complete dedication to that work.

With even greater reason it would be lawful, and even a mark of greater virtue, to renounce the satisfaction of bodily needs (either partially in regard to food and drink or totally in regard to the legitimate sex act) for a supernatural motive, which elevates the natural virtue of temperance to the supernatural level.[6] Thus, the works of

---

[6]The acquired natural virtue of temperance is specifically distinct from the infused supernatural virtue, but the point of emphasis here is that the supernatural virtue operates through the acquired virtue as regards facility in operation, and through the natural faculties in any case (*modo humano*).

penance, which are directed to atonement for sin; the voluntary ascetical practices which aim at restricting excessive inclinations; the consecrated celibacy in view of the ministry, the apostolate or the contemplative life; or the search for renunciation in order to imitate Christ in his sufferings: all these are both lawful and virtuous. But here these renunciations must be justified by a sufficient reason, for there is all the difference in the world among a supernaturally motivated penance or mortification, the vice of insensibility, and the psychosomatic disorder of frigidity.[7]

B. Intemperance

The second vice, **intemperance** or **immoderation,** is truly the corruption of the virtue of temperance, for it is directly contrary to the moderate and controlled use of the instincts for self-preservation and procreation. This vice is much more serious than insensibility, and for several reasons:

1) intemperance is less likely to be involuntary because the sensible good of pleasure is intensely alluring and, for that reason, the acts which produce it are more strongly willed;

2) intemperance is less likely to result from uncontrollable passion, such as motivates those insensible persons who may be under the domination of fear—even when the passion for sense pleasure antecedes any act of the will, the awareness of the situation and the subsequent moral judgment;[8]

3) intemperance is markedly contrary to the rule of reason and is especially degrading to human dignity.

St. Thomas remarks that the sin of intemperance is a childish sin,[9] not because children generally commit it, but because it has the characteristics generally found in children: 1) like a child, intemperance pays no heed to the dictates of reason; 2) as it has its own way

---

[7] It is not in the domain of theology to discuss the psychosomatic disorders as such, for that belongs to the field of abnormal psychology. Nevertheless, it is necessary that one be aware of the fact that such disorders are possible in the human personality.

[8] It is possible, however, that certain persons afflicted with emotional and mental unbalance may reach a point at which their compulsive acts of sense pleasure are beyond the control of reason and will.

[9] Cf. *Summa,* II-II, q. 142, a. 2.

more and more, it becomes more self-willed and more demanding; 3) the only way it can be checked is by restraint. This is perfectly in keeping with the psychological fact that, as a given action is more delightful, there is a stronger urge to do it again and a stronger demand on the part of the delight to be experienced again.

It is therefore evident that the sins of intemperance easily lead to a strongly rooted vice. And since the passions cause a profound reverberation in the entire organism, one can readily see the great difficulty involved in ridding oneself of any habit of intemperance. It is more difficult to resist the desire for pleasure than it is to resist any other passion, except the fear of death. For that reason, educators sometimes are forced to resort to fear as a last measure for turning individuals away from the pursuit of sense pleasure.

It is bad enough that the vice of intemperance dulls the intellect and obstructs the rule of reason. The intemperate person can quickly lose his taste for spiritual things and thus become more and more disposed to a deeper radication of the vice. He may even reach the point of compulsive behavior, and then for all intents and purposes he is incapable of helping himself.

4. The Integral Parts of Temperance

A. The Parts of Temperance in General

With temperance, as with the other cardinal and general virtues, it is necessary to descend from the general to the particular and from the universal to the concrete order of human action. Virtue is a good operative habit and operations are concerned with particulars. Hence, having seen what is involved in the virtue of temperance as such, we logically ask how this virtue operates in the concrete order of reality. This leads us to a consideration of the parts of the virtue of temperance, and it is well to note that not each and every part enumerated is a virtue in its own right, but may be merely an extrinsic quality of virtue. This will become evident, however, as we proceed along the lines of the traditional division of a cardinal virtue into its integral, subjective and potential parts, as indicated in this outline:

The Parts of Temperance
- Integral parts of temperance
  - Sense of shame
  - Sense of honor
- Subjective parts of temperance

VIRTUE	VICE
Abstinence	gluttony
Sobriety	drunkenness
Chastity	lust

- Potential parts of temperance

VIRTUE	VICE
Continence	incontinence
Meekness	anger
Clemency	cruelty
Modesty { Humility	pride
Studiousness	curiosity
Modesty of action and dress	immodesty

B. The Integral Parts

The integral parts of a virtue are those conditions which are necessary for the virtue, although they do not constitute the essence of the virtue. Thus of the parts assigned to temperance, two are designated as integral parts: a sense of shame and a sense of honor.

(1) The Sense of Shame

As commonly understood, the sense of shame refers to a feeling which one experiences after performing a disgraceful action. It is not in this sense that we speak of shame as it is an integral part of the virtue of temperance, although it is certain that the temperate person would feel shame if he were to have the misfortune of falling into an intemperate action. But the **sense of shame** to which we here refer is *a fear of something base,* and since the sins of intemperance are especially degrading and base, it is evident why the sense of shame belongs in a special way to the virtue of temperance.

It should be noted that this sense of shame is a fear of a base action and not the fear of the loss of one's reputation. It is true that many persons refrain from intemperate actions out of fear of being discovered by others and that this is effective in keeping them from certain sins. It does not follow, however, that such persons have a high degree of the virtue of temperance, for it may happen that their mental attitude is such that if they would not be discovered their intemperate appetite would lead them to sin. The sense of shame as an integral part of temperance refers *to the shamefulness of the sin itself* and constitutes one of the motivating factors for refraining from sin and moderating one's appetite for sense pleasure.

While the sense of shame has its roots in nature, it is greatly influenced by custom and education. This is evident in the various customs of clothing that obtain among people of different cultures. This is not to imply that the entire matter is relative, but rather to indicate that circumstances exert considerable influence in the matter. Shamelessness is a reality, and it is the threshold of utter degradation.

The sense of shame which is an integral part of temperance is a natural and virtuous quality and should never be confused with that distortion of reality which is found in those persons who identify all sensual pleasure with moral evil and guilt. Rather, it is a God-given inclination, placed in human nature to prevent or deter men from going to excess in those matters that are particularly alluring. It is not, we repeat, a complete virtue; it is not a free act, but something anterior to the free act, an instinct which has as its object the fear of the dishonor caused by a base act. In other words, the virtue of temperance tends to a good which is the moderation of the appetite for sense pleasure; shame fears the dishonor which follows upon the excessive use and satisfaction of that pleasure.

St. Thomas asks the interesting question, "Whether a person experiences greater shame in regard to those who are closer to him?"[10] It is a fact of experience that we are more ashamed in front of those whose opinion we value, whose knowledge and virtue we esteem, or with whom we are more intimately associated, such as members of our own family. On the other hand, those who sin habitually in disgraceful matters do not usually condemn such action, and strangers do not usually arouse in us any special feelings of shame. Hence, one of the greatest safeguards in the matters of temperance, and one of the strongest incentives to a cultivation of a sense of shame, is association with one's own family and virtuous friends. One can readily see the importance of cultivating this natural instinct of shame in children before they reach the age of puberty.

(2) The Sense of Honor

It is difficult to find an equivalent English word for the Latin term *honestas*. To translate it simply as "honesty" would be misleading, for in common usage the word honesty refers to the virtue of justice. The **sense of honor** which constitutes the second integral part of temperance refers to *a certain honorableness and integrity whereby a person has a positive appreciation and reverence for the virtue*

---

[10]Cf. *Summa*, II-II, q. 144, a. 3.

of temperance. It is a much more positive quality than the sense of shame, which is based on fear.

A human act is honorable when it possesses a certain degree of perfection and splendor which arouses respect and praise. Therefore, the state or quality of honor designates the excellence of virtue and the splendor of moral beauty which are proper to the integrity of good actions.

One important point must be emphasized here. Since sense pleasures so readily lead to excess and to disgraceful acts, the sense of fear will usually be predominant in human experience. Not only that, but it may become so pronounced that a person can lose sight of the positive beauty of temperance, and what positive sense of honor remains may be associated only with virginity. While it is true that virginity is a most excellent state, it must also be insisted that the proper enjoyment of the sex act in marriage is the virtue of temperance in action, and that it therefore requires the functioning of the sense of honor. The sense of honor does not outlaw the satisfaction of the instincts; it moderates them and enables a human being to enjoy them in a manner which is in keeping with his dignity both as a man and as a child of God through grace. As St. Thomas states it: "A thing is said to be honorable insofar as it has a certain beauty through being regulated by reason. But whatever is regulated by reason is naturally becoming to man. And it is natural for a thing to take pleasure in that which is becoming to it. Therefore anything honorable is naturally pleasing to man."[11]

5. The Subjective Parts of Temperance concerning Pleasures of Food and Drink

The subjective parts of a virtue are the species into which a virtue can be divided, and the division itself is based upon the various objects to which the operations or acts of the virtue will tend. In regard to temperance this is the extremely practical consideration of

[11]Cf. *Summa*, II-II, q. 145, a. 3.

the virtue as it operates in the concrete order of reality. And since temperance is concerned with the desire and enjoyment of the basic human instincts for nourishment and procreation, its subjective parts will be listed accordingly: abstinence, sobriety, chastity and purity. All of these virtues possess the essential notion of temperance, which is the moderation of the sense appetite in reference to the satisfaction and delight of the instincts for self-preservation and procreation. The first two will be treated in this section, the others in the section to follow.

A. Abstinence

(1) Abstinence as a Virtue

As a specific virtue under the general virtue of temperance, **abstinence** *regulates the appetite for food and drink*. It is not to be confused with the abstinence of which canon law speaks when it legislates abstinence from meat on Friday. The virtue of abstinence, like temperance generally, has as its rule the needs of this life. Hence, abstinence is not so much a question of *depriving* oneself of food and drink as of *taking* the nutrition that is required for the well-being of the body.

Considered in itself, to eat certain foods or to abstain from them is neither virtuous nor vicious. On the other hand, when regulated by the rule of reason and the needs of the body, it may be virtuous to eat and virtuous to abstain from eating. But no special virtue is required to assure that a person will take nourishment, for this is one of the bodily instincts and God has attached a special pleasure to this function so that men would eat. This very pleasure is such, however, that it may be desired simply and solely for itself and to excess. Hence, a special virtue is required so that men will observe the moderation demanded by reason.

When operating as a purely natural virtue, abstinence will take that nourishment which is reasonably necessary. It should be noted that it is not merely a mechanistic approach to food that is demanded by the virtue, like filling the tank of an automobile with fuel, but that man should take food in view of his personal needs, the duties of his state in life and as a social being. Thus the natural requirements of a given person in regard to nutrition will demand that he take those things that are conducive to good health and abstain from those others that are injurious or which cause physical discomfort. Again, the duties of one's state in life or one's work may require more nourishment in one case than in another. The person engaged in heavy manual labor will have a need for more food than does the individual whose daily work is predominantly intellectual.

Finally, man is a social being, and eating is a focal point of his social activities, whether at the family table, the banquet-hall or the picnic grove. Hence, man is able to enjoy virtuously not only the taste of what he eats and drinks, but also the entire setting: the decor of the surroundings, the attractiveness of carefully prepared and graciously served meals, the bouquet of fine wine, the evident satisfaction of his fellow diners, their conversation, and whatever other elements may enter into the atmosphere.

The virtue of abstinence can also be practiced as a supernatural virtue, either through one's own volition or through obedience to the positive laws of the Church. In regard to the latter, it should again be noted that the Church herself, in imposing laws of abstinence, does so for a supernatural reason, and these laws bind in conscience, although they admit of dispensation for a justifying cause. In itself it is not wrong to eat meat on a Friday; it is wrong because to do so is to violate a positive law. Neither is it virtuous in itself to abstain from meat on Friday; it is virtuous because such an act consists in obedience to the law, which is to follow reason enlightened by faith.

(2) The Act of Abstinence Which Is Fasting

The virtue of abstinence, as we have said, regulates the nourishment of an individual according to the rule of reason in view of his well-being and the duties of his state in life. **Fasting** is *a special act of the virtue of abstinence by which a person abstains, either totally or partially, from food.* It is the negative aspect of temperance, i.e., refraining from food and drink.

We can distinguish various types of fasting. Natural fasting signifies nothing more than not taking any nourishment; it is neither a virtue nor a vice, because it is a pure negation: during sleep or between meals a person is fasting simply because he is not actually taking nourishment. Fasting, considered morally, is voluntary self-denial assumed under the rule of reason. If this is done solely in view of one's physical well-being it is an act of natural virtue. If it is done for a motive of faith, such as the calming of the passions, the raising of the mind more readily to divine things, or for performing a penance, it is an act of supernatural virtue. The eucharistic fast is imposed by the law of the Church as a preparation for the reception of Communion. The ecclesiastical fast is imposed by Church law for penance and mortification, and its fulfillment is at once an act of the supernatural virtue of abstinence and an act of obedience.

(3) The Church Law on Fast and Abstinence

The law of the Church imposes the obligation to fast and abstain either at certain times for all the faithful or on particular occasions for those preparing to receive certain sacraments, e.g., Holy Communion, or to join in special religious solemnities, e.g., on the day before the consecration of a church. These laws are self-explanatory, and are set forth here in summarized form for personal guidance.

1. **Uniform norms for fast and abstinence** in the United States were adopted at the meeting of the bishops in November, 1956. The regulations now in force are as follows:

> To foster the spirit of penance and of reparation for sin, to encourage self-denial and mortification, and to guide her children in the footsteps of our divine Savior, Holy Mother Church imposes by law the observance of fast and abstinence.
>
> In accordance with the provisions of canon law, as modified through the use of special faculties granted by the Holy See, we herewith publish the following regulations:

On Abstinence

> Everyone over seven years of age is bound to observe the law of abstinence.
>
> Complete abstinence is to be observed on Fridays, Ash Wednesday and the Vigils of the Immaculate Conception and Christmas. On days of complete abstinence meat and soup or gravy made from meat may not be used at all.

Partial abstinence is to be observed on Ember Wednesdays and Saturdays and on the Vigil of Pentecost. On days of partial abstinence meat and soup or gravy made from meat may be taken once a day at the principal meal.

On Fast

Everyone over 21 and under 59 years of age is also bound to observe the law of fast.

The days of fast are the weekdays of Lent, including Holy Saturday, Ember Days, the Vigils of Pentecost, the Immaculate Conception and Christmas.

On days of fast only one full meal is allowed. Two other meals, sufficient to maintain strength, may be taken according to each one's needs; but together they should not equal another full meal. Meat may be taken at the principal meal on a day of fast except on Fridays, Ash Wednesday and the Vigils of the Immaculate Conception and Christmas.

Eating between meals is not permitted but liquids, including milk and fruit juices, are allowed.

Where health or ability to work would be seriously affected, the law does not oblige. In doubt concerning fast or abstinence, a parish priest or confessor should be consulted.

We earnestly exhort the faithful during the periods of fast and abstinence to attend daily Mass; to receive Holy Communion often; to take part more frequently in exercises of piety; to give generously to works of religion and charity; to perform acts of kindness toward the sick, the aged and the poor; to practice voluntary self-denial, especially regarding alcoholic drink and worldly amusements; and to pray more fervently, particularly for the intentions of the Holy Father.[12]

The law of fasting binds under pain of serious sin,[13] but it is commonly taught by moralists that the law of fasting admits of slight matter, and that to break it in this way is venially sinful. A venial offense against the law is committed when the quantity of extra food eaten amounts to less than another full meal. The law of abstinence from meat also binds under grave sin and, similarly, is considered to admit of slight matter, so that to eat a very small amount of meat on a day of abstinence would constitute the matter of a venial sin.

An important difference between the laws of fast and of abstinence is this: the law of abstinence is broken as often as meat is eaten on

[12]These rules are generally published in all diocesan papers around the beginning of Lent.

[13]This is clear from the condemnation of a contrary proposition in a decree of Pope Alexander VII, Sept. 24, 1665; Denz. 1123.

a day of abstinence, but the law of fast can be broken only once, no matter how often one eats over and above the established limitation of a single full meal. The reason is that the essence of fasting consists in eating only a single full meal on a fast day. If more than a single full meal is eaten, a condition essential to fasting ceases to exist for that day. Hence, the law of fasting, once broken, cannot be re-applied on that day, because a condition necessary for its application (i.e., that only one full meal be taken) has ceased to exist.[14] On the other hand, the law of abstinence prohibits meat absolutely, and not simply as a condition for the fulfillment of the law. Hence, the law is broken as often as meat is eaten.

2. **The eucharistic fast** imposes a grave obligation on the faithful to fast entirely from solid food and alcoholic beverages for at least three hours, and from all other liquids (except plain water which never breaks the fast) for at least one hour before receiving Communion.[15]

(4) Gluttony

As a vice opposed to the virtue of abstinence, **gluttony** is *an inordinate desire for eating and drinking.* The desire for food and drink is not only natural and virtuous, it must be satisfied; this is a dictate of the natural law for self-preservation, and this dictate is made known to man by the instinct which periodically clamors for the satisfaction of this bodily need. Man must eat or die.

But in view of the fact that there is a special pleasure attached to the use of food and drink (which is a God-given pleasure and perfectly lawful when used reasonably), there exists a special moral danger in the enjoyment of this pleasure. It becomes morally evil whenever a person is inordinate in his desire for, or his enjoyment of food and drink. This may be manifested in various ways: e.g.,

[14]There is a difference of opinion about this matter, and it is treated at length in various works on moral theology. The more benign view here presented is founded on the opinion of Cardinal Cajetan. Cf. *Commentary on the Summa,* II-II, q. 147, a. 8.

[15]This is the law ordinarily applicable to the laity. Provisions for the sick and others in special circumstances are explained in the *Motu Proprio* of Pope Pius XII, *On the Laws of Fasting and the Evening Mass* (Washington: N.C.W.C., 1957).

by excessive use of exotic and delicate foods which deprive the body of proper nourishment and a balanced diet; by the consumption of quantities of food far in excess of bodily requirements, which can easily cause sickness; or by eating too greedily or too frequently.

Gluttony is listed as a capital sin because of the evil effects which it causes in the glutton, and because it is the origin or source of other sins. Thus, it is not uncommon to find one or another of the following defects in persons who are inordinate in food and drink: dullness of intellect, unrestrained passions, excessive talking and unrestrained behavior.

B. Sobriety

(1) The Virtue Itself

Following the principle that wherever there is special danger of sin there is need of a special virtue, we come to the question of the use of intoxicating drinks. When nonintoxicants are used, the drink in question is controlled by the virtue of abstinence and an excess would constitute gluttony. Intoxicating drinks, however, are in a special class because of the rapidity with which they may cause the loss of the use of reason and the ease with which one can form the habit of drinking to excess. The virtue of **sobriety** *controls the use of intoxicating drinks.*

As moderated by the virtue of temperance, the use of intoxicating beverages is not only lawful but virtuous: for example, for the health of the body, for lifting one's spirits, or for contributing to greater sociability at a gathering. Therefore, the use of intoxicating beverages is not evil nor is it unlawful, but it may become evil by reason of some special circumstances; e.g., if a person is easily influenced by intoxicating drinks, if one drinks to excess, or if one gives scandal to others by drinking.

The cardinal principle in regard to the use of these drinks is to know both one's needs and capacity, and then to observe that measure. Some people are capable of drinking greater quantities than others without showing any evil effects. Again, it may happen that because of physical weariness, emotional fatigue or excessive hilarity, a person is the more quickly affected by intoxicants. The individual must always be aware of his condition at any given time so that he will be able to apply the rule of reason and moderation. Temperance requires that an individual observe moderation and self-control before, during and after partaking of intoxicating drinks.

(2) The Vice of Drunkenness

As a vice opposed to sobriety, **drunkenness** is *any deliberate excess in the use of intoxicating drinks which leads to the loss of reason.* It must be deliberate to be sinful, for a sinful act must be a human act, and a human act requires both knowledge and freedom. Hence, it may happen that a person becomes intoxicated either because he did not realize the strength of the drink, or he did not know from experience the amount of drink he could reasonably consume. We specify the use of intoxicating drinks because, although a man may lose the control of reason as a result of hypnotism or drugs, this is not classified as drunkenness.[16]

A special problem is posed in regard to the guilt of those who drink to excess. Drunkenness is by its nature a mortal sin because it involves the loss of reason. If the drunkenness is foreseen and willed, the individual is guilty of mortal sin. If the effects of drink are less than the loss of reason, the sin is generally considered to be venial. But if one knows from experience that the use of intoxicating drinks arouses lust, anger or some other passion which easily leads to sin, even moderate drinking could be seriously wrong for such a person. And even if a person completely loses reason as a result of drink, he is responsible for any ensuing evil acts of whatever kind in the measure that he could foresee the likelihood that he would commit them.

---

[16]The same principle will be brought into play, however, when determining the moral guilt of persons who use hypnosis or drugs. If the loss of reason was deliberately sought and without a justifying cause, the act is morally evil. On the other hand, the use of hypnosis, drugs, anesthesia or intoxicating drinks with the resulting loss of control of reason could, if used as medicinal measures, be morally justifiable.

Yet in this matter, as in the matter of sex gratification, a person could possibly reach the stage of compulsive behavior and become an alcoholic. Such a person, while having a stronger inclination to use drink to excess, has a weaker will in regard to self-control, with the result that the particular act of excess may no longer be a perfect human act but the result of compulsion. Nevertheless, the person will most likely be responsible for having allowed himself to cultivate such a strong inclination to drink and will, therefore, be responsible in cause for that which follows the compulsion. It is not uncommon to find that alcoholics and chronic drunkards seek intoxicants, not for any pleasure in the drinks themselves, but as an escape from some circumstance in life which they lack the fortitude to bear; and with some, in truth, alcoholism is a disease and not a moral fault. But again, the general characteristic of the virtue of temperance must be emphasized as an urgent necessity for all: self-control and self-restraint according to the dictates of reason and faith.

6. The Subjective Parts of Temperance concerning Pleasures of Sex

We next study the virtues which moderate the desire for the pleasures arising from the exercise of the procreative faculties. These passions are commonly called "venereal," a term derived from the name of Venus, the goddess of love in Roman mythology. Venereal pleasures arise from the very source of the transmission of life; they are associated with important and sacred functions; they are vehement, all-absorbing, strongly alluring and difficult to control. For these reasons, special parts of temperance are needed to regulate the desire for these pleasures. We will consider successively the virtues of chastity, purity and virginity, and the vices and sins opposed to them.

A. Chastity

Chastity is *the moral virtue which moderates the desire for venereal pleasures according to the necessities of life judged by right reason* *and the divine law.* Chastity deals proximately with desires for venereal pleasure and remotely with the acts—such as sexual intercourse, touches, embraces and kisses—which give rise to these pleasures.

It is imperative to understand that the use and enjoyment of sexuality in keeping with the needs of one's station in life is both lawful and virtuous. While this truth has been obscured by such errors as Manicheism and Puritanism, the intrinsic goodness of sexual functions and pleasures has always been defended in authentic Christian teaching. The very real dangers of excess in these matters and the consequent moral havoc should not be allowed to obscure the basic truth that is involved. This truth is clearly expressed in the following passage of St. Thomas:

> A sin in human acts is that which is against the order of reason. Now the order of reason consists in ordaining everything to its end in the proper manner. Therefore it is no sin if a person, by the dictate of reason, uses certain things in the proper manner and order for the end for which they are adapted, provided the end itself be truly good.
>
> But just as the preservation of the bodily nature of an individual is a true good, so also is the preservation of the nature of the human species a great good. And just as the use of food is directed to the preservation of life in the individual, so is the use of venereal acts directed to the preservation of the whole human race. . . . Therefore just as the use of food can be without sin if taken in due manner and order, as required for the well-being of the body, so the use of venereal actions can be without sin if performed in due manner and order, in keeping with the end of human procreation.[17]

In this area of the sexual functions, perhaps more than in any other, we must remind ourselves of the scriptural statement to the effect that God looked upon that which he had made and saw that it was good.[18] Nothing evil comes from the hands of God; surely, nothing morally evil. But the instinct for human procreation, the pleasures concomitant with the sex act, and the passions that are aroused at the prospect

---

[17]*Summa*, II-II, q. 153, a. 2.

[18]It is worthy of remark that the account of creation in the Book of Genesis is punctuated with, "And God saw that it was good," as each day's work is completed. But after the sixth day's work added man and woman to the universe, Genesis says, "And God saw all the things that he had made, and they were *very* good" (Gen. 1:31).

of such pleasure—all these are in themselves physically good. Not only that, but the marriage contract has been raised to the order of a sacrament by Christ and thus made a channel of grace. No unclean thing could be used as a vessel of sanctification.

We have stressed repeatedly that the proper order of a virtue is the order of reason, and that the order of reason is determined by the ends to which functions and operations are ordained. This ontological basis is especially necessary in delineating the area of the virtue of chastity and in determining what is the reasonable and moderate use and enjoyment of venereal pleasure.

The sexual instinct is social, directed to the good of the race, rather than personal. The sexual difference between men and women is in view of the ultimate sexual union of man and woman; and the sexual union is for the purpose of the offspring. Consequently, the natural vocation of man and woman is to marriage.

St. Thomas explains this doctrine in terms that are at once realistic and well-balanced:

> Human nature rebels against an indeterminate union of the sexes and demands that a man should be united to a determinate woman and should abide with her for a long time or even for a whole lifetime. . . . This union with a certain definite woman is called matrimony, which for the above reason is said to belong to the natural law. Since, however, the union of the sexes is directed to the common good of the whole human race, and common goods depend on the law for their determination, it follows that this union of man and woman, which is called matrimony, is determined by some law.[19]

Marriage is governed by many laws, natural, divine and human.[20] It is clear from this body of laws that marriage is a permanent state, the primary object of which is the procreation *and* education of children. Consequently, chastity, the norm for which is determined by the needs of one's station in life as judged by right reason and faith, will be modified according to the needs of this particular state of life.

With a view to the primary end of marriage, marital chastity moderates the actual use and enjoyment of sexuality as well as the desires for the pleasures that arise therefrom. For the unmarried,

[19]*Summa*, II-II, q. 154, a. 2.
[20]Cf. Donlan, *et al.*, *Toward Marriage in Christ*, Chaps. One, Three and Four.

whatever their state in life, *there can be no virtuous use of the generative powers,* simply because the unmarried state is not proper for the generation and education of children. Chastity for the unmarried begins with total abstinence from any deliberate desire for, and enjoyment of the pleasures deriving from venereal acts.

In addition to the needs of the state of marriage, marital chastity must also be governed by the needs of the partners in each individual marriage. The judgments necessary in each case require the exercise of many virtues. Basically, of course, there are the demands of justice, because marriage is essentially a contract. But there must be a generous measure of charity which looks to another's needs rather than to one's own rights. Patience and fortitude must enter in as well. And it is prudence which ultimately determines the norm for chastity in the concrete situation of each marriage.

Such an array of virtues cannot be expected to come to full bloom overnight. It is clear, then, that the best promise of happiness in marriage is to be found in the practice of virtue, and particularly of premarital chastity—which is a novitiate, as it were, for what is often the more difficult chastity of marriage.[21]

B. Purity

Besides the act of generation, there are accessory venereal acts which, by the purposes inherent in nature itself, prepare for and lead to sexual union. These external acts naturally excite venereal pleasure, and hence must be controlled by chastity. This is accomplished by purity, which is not a special virtue distinct from chastity itself but rather a special circumstance, an essential safeguard for that virtue whose immediate and primary object is the act of which these related and accessory acts are signs. It may be defined: *the moderation of the external acts which of their nature lead to sexual union, according to the needs of one's state of life as judged by reason and faith.*

[21]Divine grace plays an indispensable part in the formation of this virtue. Cf. Donlan, *et al., op. cit.,* 157 ff.

(1) Purity and the Married

Married people have the *right* to employ whatever expressions of affection are calculated to promote their mutual love and their marital relations. But this does not mean that purity has no place in marriage; like marital chastity, purity must be an integral element of the married state. Purity demands that married people be guided by the rule of reason and faith, lest carelessness about purity lead to unchastity, and requires mutual respect for the sensibilities and the needs of both partners, or else the expression of love may become a mask for self-indulgence. In this matter, as in many others, Christians do well to recall St. Paul's admonition that everything lawful is not expedient.[22]

(2) Purity and the Single

Purity for the unmarried is also governed by the needs of their state in life as measured by reason and faith. Having no right to sexual relations, the unmarried have no right to those mutual exchanges, caresses, kisses or words which *of their nature* lead to the desire for venereal pleasure or to sexual relations. The deliberate seeking of sexual delight is restricted to the married state, and to desire it or achieve it deliberately outside of marriage is sinful.

Among the acts and thoughts moderated by purity, some are more proximately related to sexual union than others. Then, too, different individuals react differently than others, and the same person may react differently at different times. All of this gives rise to some difficulty in applying the norm of purity in concrete situations. But the problem is far from insoluble if it is approached with honesty, coupled with the sincere desire to practice purity. There can be no purity for those who either feign ignorance or cultivate it, or for those who are not willing to make the sacrifices that purity demands.

Practical guidance can be found by analyzing problematical matters in terms of the elements of a human act. This can be done quite easily by facing these questions:

[22]On this topic of marital purity, two short readings are highly recommended: the Book of Tobias, and St. Francis de Sales, *Philothea: An Introduction to the Devout Life*, Chap. 18.

1) *What am I doing or planning to do?* This determines the **object of the act.** Certain acts, such as intimate embracing and prolonged passionate kissing, are so closely related to sexual union and so stimulating of venereal pleasures that they are of their nature impure and seriously sinful for the unmmarried. The person who is not aroused by such intimacies would seem to be a victim of the vice of insensibility or of some psychic or physical disorder. *But note well*: other acts, such as a modest kiss or dance, cannot be judged impure in terms of their object.

2) *Why am I doing or planning to do this?* This reveals the **intention of the agent.** If the object of an act is itself impure, no good intention can make it pure. But if the act itself be either pure or at least morally indifferent, a bad intention can make it sinful. Thus, if something as innocuous as holding hands or modest dancing were made part of an approach to impurity, these very actions would themselves become sinful because of the evil intention. And it does not alter morality of the case if one party should repudiate the advances of the other and thus prevent the actual indulgence of impurity; impurity, like all intemperance, arises from immoderate *desires,* and external acts are simply aggravating circumstances. This is clearly taught by Christ. "Whosoever shall look upon a woman to lust after her, hath already committed adultery with her in his heart" (Matt. 5:28).

3) *What results will this have for myself and others?* This question reveals the **moral circumstances** of the act. Experience teaches that good or indifferent actions undertaken for good motives sometimes arouse venereal desires in certain people. When one is faced with such dangers to purity, several factors must be weighed in making a prudent decision about accepting or rejecting the risk.

a) The supreme law of charity obliges the Christian to value divine friendship above everything else. The body is the temple of the Holy Spirit. It is contrary to the love of

God to embrace any pleasure that would turn one's heart away from him. It is contrary to the love of neighbor to lead another to turn from God through impurity.

b) Personal experience must be recalled. For example, if one has previously consented to impure desires excited by reading a book containing occasional suggestive passages, it would be certainly a sin of imprudence, and possibly a sin of impurity, to read a similar book; if a couple has frequently fallen into serious sin that began with modest kissing and embracing, then such kissing and embracing must be avoided as proximate occasions of serious sin; if association with certain persons or frequentation of particular places has generally led to serious sin, then such persons and places must be avoided.

c) The sufficiency of one's reasons for taking risks must be honestly weighed according to prudence. Medical students have better reasons for reading scientific works that may have a stimulating effect than those who read out of curiosity. Teachers and research scholars have better reasons for dangerous reading (within the limitations established by law as previously explained) than students. Engaged couples have better reason for modest displays of affection than casual companions or those for whom marriage is not a real possibility. Those engaged in legitimate business or discharging official duties have better reason to enter places featuring dangerous amusements than mere curiosity-seekers. "He who loves danger shall perish in it" (Sir. 3:27).

C. Virginity

Virginity is popularly conceived in a completely negative and materialistic way as a physical integrity that everyone is born with and that some preserve by avoiding sexual intercourse. This barren idea is completely alien to the lofty and ennobling ideal of virginity that is one of the greatest treasures of our Christian heritage.

Virginity surpasses chastity somewhat as magnificence excels generosity. Temperance is a kind of stewardship over the intensely personal divine gifts that make a man what he is. "You are not your own," St. Paul reminds us (I Cor. 6:19). Through chastity and purity man becomes a trustworthy steward of the gifts of life by which he imitates the divine paternity, wherefrom all fatherhood derives its name (Eph. 3:15). But by espousing virginity the Christian declares by his very life that the supernatural totally surpasses the natural, that the spiritual is infinitely superior to the physical, and that marriage is a good both naturally and supernaturally.[23]

Virginity is not simply happenstance; it is not just the lack of conjugal experience; it is not merely a life-long freedom from deliberate carnal desire. **Virginity** is *a virtue whereby one completely free of all deliberate venereal experience of mind or body firmly resolves to abstain perpetually from every voluntary venereal pleasure in order to follow the divine will more freely and completely.*

The definition makes clear that virginity is not a common privilege. It is reserved to those who wish to dedicate their lives to divine service by a perpetual vow.[24] In this it differs from perfect chastity, which is found in those unsullied by deliberate venereal indulgence but who make no vow to preserve this perfect chastity throughout life. It also differs from the chastity of the sinner converted from unchastity, for virginity is a stranger to any willful venery. It is also clear that to apply the term "virgin" to one who has deliberately experienced venereal acts short of intercourse is as spiritually meaningless as to apply it to woolen material that is unmixed with cotton.

It is the constant teaching of the Church that the state of virginity is superior to that of matrimony.[25] The reason is that viriginity is

[23]The relationship between virginity and the goods of marriage is clear in the prayer of the *Pontificale Romanum*, "On the blessing and consecration of Virgins," where virgins are described as aspiring to the spirituality represented in marriage. This refers especially to the "sacramentality" of marriage whereby it represents the union of Christ with his Church. Cf. Eph. 5:32; *Christ, and His Sacraments*, 517 f.

[24]This need not be a vow in a religious community. There are, and have always been, Christians who make private vows of virginity without entering religious life.

[25]Cf. I Cor. 8:34; Council of Trent, Sess. XXIV, Can. 10 (Denz. 980); Pope Pius XII, encyclical *Sacra Virginitas*, March 25, 1954.

directed to the things of God, things of a higher nature than the things of the world that must claim the attention of married people. It would be false to reason from the superiority of the *state* of virginity to the superiority of *people* who espouse virginity.[26] Spiritual excellence is measured only in terms of charity, of the intimacy of divine friendship. The value of all else in life, marriage and virginity included, must be computed in terms of its effects in hindering or fostering the soul's advance in love. Virginity is the seal on the heart of those who aspire to give themselves to God in undivided love.

7. LUST: THE VICE OPPOSED TO CHASTITY

A. In General

(1) Its Nature

Lust is *an inordinate desire for venereal pleasure.* Since lust is directly opposed to chastity, it is measured by the same norm, i.e., the needs of one's station in life as judged by right reason and faith. The malice of lust consists in an excessive attachment to venereal pleasure for the married, or the deliberate indulgence of venereal acts and pleasures for those who are unmarried. It is forbidden repeatedly in Sacred Scripture, notably in the sixth and ninth precepts of the Decalogue.

Lust is among the capital vices because its object, venereal pleasure, is so alluring that men will commit a wide variety of sins because of it. These sins are called the "daughters" of lust. These "daughters of lust" are often observed in those who abandon themselves to venery. When the concupiscible appetite is drawn vehemently to a pleasurable object, there arise disorders in the intellect and will.

    1) In the intellect, the following sins arise: the understanding, which functions to apprehend the end as a good, is afflicted by *blindness* which closes the mind to every good except venereal

[26]Cf. St. Thomas, *Summa*, II-II, q. 154, a. 4, ad 2.

pleasure; the act of counsel, by which means are weighed in view of the end, is disordered by *rashness* in the pursuit of this pleasure; the act of judgment is upset by *thoughtlessness* excluding all means except those which lead to venereal pleasures; and the act of command is vitiated by *inconstancy*, flitting from one means of gratification to another.

2) In the will there are two evil effects of lust: *self-love*, which results from catering to one's disordered passions and which tends toward hatred of God, who is regarded as an obstacle to self-gratification; and *excessive attachment to this world*, which often leads to despair of the world to come.[27]

This enumeration makes clear why lust destroys man's humanity: it most effectively destroys the virtue of prudence which perfects man's distinctive faculty of reason, and thus reduces him to the level of the brute.

(2) The Kinds of Lust

We have seen that a special virtue is needed wherever there is a special difficulty in regulating human affairs according to reason and faith. Conversely, a special sin exists wherever there is a special repugnance to reason or faith in human acts. These byways of lust are enumerated and condemned in various places in the Scriptures. To begin with, our Lord equates the malice of internal thoughts and desires of lust with the external deeds they represent: "Whosoever shall look upon a woman to lust after her, has already committed adultery with her in his heart" (Matt. 5:28). Then St. Paul enumerates and condemns as mortal the various external sins of lust: "Do not be deceived; neither fornicators nor idolaters not adulterers nor the effeminiate nor sodomites . . . shall inherit the kingdom of God" (I Cor. 6:9 f.).

These various kinds of lust are divided technically by theologians for a clearer understanding of the malice involved in each. **Internal acts** of lust are thoughts or desires which are not carried out in act; these internal sins are forbidden by the ninth commandment. External

[27]Cf. St. Thomas, *Summa*, II-II, q. 153, a. 5.

acts of lust are unchaste or impure deeds and words; these external sins are forbidden by the sixth commandment. External sins of lust may be either *completed*, if complete sexual gratification is attained, or *incomplete*, if venereal pleasure is obtained by anything short of complete sexual gratification. Completed sins of lust are *natural* if the venereal pleasure results from natural intercourse; they are *unnatural* if the pleasure is derived from venereal acts which of their nature could not possibly result in the conception of a child.

(3) The Gravity of Lust

Any lustful act is of its very nature a mortal sin, as is evident from the teaching of St. Paul and the fact that the sixth and ninth commandments directly forbid such actions. This applies not only to completed acts of sexual gratification by those to whom this gratification is forbidden, but also to incompleted actions. The reason for this is that the sexual instinct is so vehement that a person is easily placed in the proximate occasion of sin by any impurity, and it is a mortal sin deliberately to place oneself in such danger. Thus, Pope Alexander VII condemned as false the proposition which stated that it could be held as a probable opinion that it would be only a venial sin to kiss for the sake of (venereal) pleasure as long as one did not consent to anything further.[28]

In practice it may sometimes be difficult to judge concerning one's guilt in such matters. It is helpful to recognize the distinction between indeliberate venereal sensation and the deliberate enjoyment of venereal pleasure. It is also well to remember that certain actions which are not of themselves evil may easily cause venereal sensations and that the moral danger involved will vary with different persons or different circumstances. Nevertheless, the basic rule will always remain in effect, namely, that any willful enjoyment of venereal pleasure which is against reason or the natural and divine law is illicit and sinful.

We shall now discuss in detail the various species of lust.

[28]Decree of Mar. 18, 1666, 40th error; Denz. 1140.

B. Internal Acts of Lust

First, as regards the **internal acts of lust,** there are three types of sin: *lingering delectation, lustful desire* and *delight in the remembrance of past acts of lust.*

1. **Lingering delectation** consists in the enjoyment of sexual actions as represented in one's imagination but without the intention of performing those actions. The gravity and species of sin will depend upon the type of sexual act which is represented; this sin is usually known as an "impure thought."

2. **Lustful desire** signifies the wish or intention to perform some sexual act or to enjoy venereal pleasure. It too will be specified by the type of action involved. It is usually known as an "impure desire."

3. The **delight in one's past sins of lust** is also described generally as impure thought, although it differs from lingering delectation in the fact that the latter is a delight in something represented in the imagination (as happens when one reads an obscene book), while the former refers to a specific lustful act which was actually performed and now recalled and relived, so to speak. Note, however, that persons who have a lawful right to the marital act do not sin by thoughts or desires concerning these matters unless 1) they lead to solitary sins, or 2) the thoughts or desires are about a type of venereal pleasure which is unlawful for them.

C. External, Incomplete Acts of Lust

We now come to the sins of lust which are **external acts** but *incomplete,* that is, the sexual action is not carried through to its termination. These actions are either accompanied by some degree of venereal pleasure or are performed with that end in mind. Although it is sometimes difficult in practice to distinguish between a simple venereal sensation and a deliberate venereal pleasure, the general norm to be followed in this matter is the following: *any sexual excitation or venereal pleasure which is directly willed is gravely sinful for those who have no right to such satisfaction.* On the other hand, the awareness of a veneral sensation which is in no way willed is not sinful. But if a venereal sensation caused by natural factors is accepted and enjoyed, it enters the classification of a deliberate venereal delight.

Another type of incompleted external acts is called by the general name of **impure actions**. The reason for this is that the virtue of purity controls those actions which are secondary or concomitant to the venereal pleasure itself. The general rule is that *any kind of action which is performed for the venereal pleasure which accompanies it, or in view of venereal pleasure to follow, is seriously sinful for those who have no right to the venereal pleasure in question.* It should be noted that some of these actions are not of themselves evil, or are not proximate dangers of sin; therefore the individual must judge for himself whether or not he is morally justified in indulging in such actions and, if so, to what extent. Hence, kissing, embracing, dancing and looking at another's body will be seriously sinful if they are accompanied by deliberate venereal pleasure or if they are done with the intent of obtaining venereal satisfaction. Other actions, such as reading obscene books or looking at photographs of nudes, are generally considered to be so inflammatory for the average person that they are listed as dangers for all, and therefore prohibited under pain of serious sin. One can easily determine the danger to himself in these matters by asking the reason or motive for performing the action in question. It is also helpful to remember that not all things that are lawful are prudent for a given person at a given time.[29]

D. Completed Acts of Lust

The *completed* and *natural* **acts of lust** comprise all unlawful sexual intercourse between a man and a woman. It is a *completed act*, in the sense that the action is carried through to its termination; it is

---

[29]Sometimes a distinction is necessary between the intrinsic morality of certain actions and the obligations of prudence and obedience to positive law. Since one cannot know, for example, whether a given book or movie is an occasion of sin unless he expose himself to them, general prohibitions are sometimes formulated by the Church to warn the faithful to avoid certain books or movies. The rule used is that what would be harmful to the average person is to be considered as harmful to all. The same norm is used in warning the faithful about kissing, dating, etc.

a *natural* act in the sense that the sexual act is performed in such a way that procreation could possibly follow. There are various types of consummated natural acts of venereal pleasure but they all involve sexual intercourse.

1. **Fornication** is sexual intercourse between unmarried persons indulged in by mutual consent. It is morally evil—not only because it is prohibited by law, but from the very nature of the act. The reason for this is that since the sexual act is by nature ordained to procreation, and since the upbringing of a child requires the care of parents in the secure atmosphere of a home, fornication is opposed to the good of the child.[30]

The sin of fornication can be aggravated by certain circumstances; these circumstances do not, however, change its species and make it another kind of sin. For example, *prostitution* is commercialized fornication (or adultery, as the case may be); *concubinage* is habitual fornication (or adultery) between a couple who associate as if they were married, and is referred to as a companionate or a "free love" marriage; *seduction* is the initiation of a maiden to sexual relations; *rape* is intercourse forced upon an unwilling woman.

2. **Adultery** is unlawful sexual intercourse between two persons, at least one of whom is married. Adultery is specifically different from fornication because it involves a violation of justice, i.e., of the marital rights of the partner's spouse. Impure acts or desires involving another's spouse partake of the malice of adultery. Even if impurity or unchastity is not involved, it is seriously sinful to have dates with married people because of scandal, danger to chastity and the alienation of affection from the rightful spouse.

3. **Incest** is sexual intercourse between persons who are related within the degrees of kindred that make marriage invalid. For Christians, the prohibition against marriage extends to all blood relations in the direct line, to blood relations up to and including

---

[30]The argument against fornication based on the natural law is objectively valid, but not very compelling. For Christians, the compelling arguments against this sin are to be found in Scripture. Cf. Deut. 23:17; I Cor. 6-9; Rom. 1; Heb. 13; Gal. 5.

the third degree in the collateral line, and to the second degree between those related by affinity.

4. **Carnal sacrilege** is the violation, by means of impurity or unchastity, of any sacred person, place or thing.

E. Unnatural Completed Sins of Lust

Every sinful act is contrary to nature because sin is against the order of reason which is natural to man. But the term "unnatural sin" is reserved to those acts of lust which are contrary to man's physical nature as well. Because of their compounded unnaturalness, such sins are the gravest of all lustful acts; they are all intrinsically evil and mortally sinful.

Unnatural consummated sins of lust are those sins which lead to complete sexual satisfaction by acts which are either contrary to the physical process of generation, or which, preserving the order of normal relations, are prevented from resulting in conception.

A simple enumeration of these sins will suffice to impart adequate knowledge of these offensive practices.

1. **Masturbation** is solitary sexual gratification. If this is deliberate, it is mortally sinful. If it should occur accidentally through exercise or similar innocuous causes, or indeliberately during sleep, it is not sinful.

2. **Onanism** is any interruption of, or interference with sexual relations which allows complete gratification while making conception impossible. This practice is known by a variety of names: birth control; contraception; withdrawal; wasting the seed; etc.

3. **Homosexuality** (from the Greek *homos*, "the same," and the Latin *sexus*, "sex") is carnal gratification obtained between members of the same sex.

4. **Bestiality** is sexual gratification involving an animal.

F. Conclusion

"The debasement of noblest things is worst," goes the familiar apothegm. It is nowhere more applicable than to matters of chastity and unchastity.

In his goodness, God shares his dominion over life with men and women. In his wisdom, God appoints a unique pleasure to the exercise of generative faculties to attract his children to undertake the married life which brings many cares and responsibilities. In his omnipotence, God enables men and women to grow in divine friendship through the exchanges of marital love under the influence of the special grace of matrimony.

As man was created, all the forces of his nature were obedient to his reason, just as he was himself obedient to God. But man disobeyed God in the primal sin, and man's passions rebelled against him in turn. Thus, through sin, man became adept at separating the pleasures of sex from the purpose of sex, and the plan for human reproduction based on the goodness, wisdom and omnipotence of God was attacked by the very creature for whose benefit it was designed. That attack takes many forms, as we have seen. But all the forms of impurity and unchastity add up to the means whereby man debases the sacred powers, instincts and acts that were designed to make him a sharer in the creativeness of God himself. These powers were not given to men as playthings; they were entrusted to his care to be used virtuously in raising up citizens for the kingdom of heaven. This is among the foremost of man's responsibilities, and if he rejects it by impurity and unchastity, he destroys humanity along with its creativeness.

Chastity is a positive virtue, a watchfulness without end, a custody of self without interruption, a stewardship over the forces of life itself. Zealously practiced, purity and chastity make a man more human; offered as an act of divine friendship, they make man more divine. "O how beautiful is the chaste generation in glory; the memory thereof is immortal, for it is known both by God and men" (Wisd. 4:1).

8. THE POTENTIAL PARTS OF TEMPERANCE

As we have already seen, the virtue of temperance is divided into four specifically distinct virtues, namely, abstinence, sobriety, chastity and virginity. Abstinence moderates the pleasures of food and drink; sobriety moderates the use of intoxicating drink; chastity moderates the use of enjoyment of sexual functions; and virginity abstains from all venereal pleasure, even that which is lawful in marriage.

In addition to these *species* of temperance, there are numerous other virtues which are related in some way to the virtue of temperance and called the *potential parts* of the virtue. They are generally enumerated as continence, meekness, clemency and modesty.

A. Continence

(1) In Itself

Continence is *a disposition of the will, inclining it to resist the vehemence of passions;* and since the most vehement passions are those concerning sexual pleasure, *continence has to do with the resistance of sexual pleasure.* At first glance it would seem that continence is merely another name for chastity, but such is not the case. Indeed, continence is not even a perfect virtue, but a *disposition* of the will. This will be evident if we note the differences between chastity and continence.

Chastity dominates and controls the concupiscible passions, which tend with vehemence toward sexual delight. This control is exercised to such an extent that when the virtue of chastity is sufficiently perfect the passions do not tend toward the pleasures of sex against the control of reason. Indeed, that is what is meant by saying that the virtue of chastity is localized or radicated in the concupiscible appetite in relation to sexual pleasure.[31]

---

[31]Note again the distinction between the body need or instinct for sex, which is not subject directly to control by reason, and the inclination of passion to the recognized sensible good of sexual pleasure, which must be subjected to the rule of reason and as such is the subject of the virtue of chastity.

Continence, on the other hand, resists the inclination of passion when it arises, and is therefore a *disposition* of the will and not a *habit* in the concupiscible appetite. Hence the continent man may be subject to violent attacks of passion, but he resists them; the perfectly chaste man will not have the vehement surge of passion toward sexual delight.[32]

(2) *Its Opposite Vice: Incontinence*

If continence is a firmness of will which resists the vehemence of the concupiscible passions, **incontinence** signifies *a weakness of the will in the face of the same passions*. Incontinence is not, therefore, caused by the concupiscible passions, however vehement they may be, for any man can always resist passion if reason and will are brought into play. Indeed, if the passion is antecedent to any act of the will or if the vehemence of the passion destroys the use of reason altogether, there can no longer be any question of continence or incontinence, for the judgment of reason and the subsequent act of the will are no longer present. In other words, the movement of passion merely offers an *occasion* for continence or incontinence, as long as the use of reason remains.

At this point it should be evident why a distinction is made between incontinence and intemperance. While the intemperate man will always be incontinent, it does not follow that the incontinent man will have the habit of intemperance. But without continence it is impossible to have the virtue of temperance perfectly, for while a man may practice continence in regard to milder movements of passions, he would falter in the case of vehement passions. Hence the importance of the counsel to resist the first impulses of unlawful passion.

[32]Note again that the chaste man may be a man of strong sexual instinct, which is something quite different from the vehement movement of passion toward a sensible good. The movement of passion presupposes a judgment of the good in terms of self and then the strong inclination arises. The chaste man does not make such a judgment regarding sexual pleasure in terms of self.

B. Meekness and Clemency

We have explained that the potential parts of a virtue are those virtues or virtuous dispositions which in some way are related to a principal virtue. They do not in every case fulfill all the requisites for a complete virtue (as in the case of continence related to temperance) and the precise point of relationship is the restraint and self-control which they require.

(1) Meekness

Meekness has been extolled frequently in Sacred Scripture[33] and Jesus himself commands us "to be meek and humble of heart" (Matt. 11:29).

Meekness may be defined as *the moral virtue which moderates anger and restrains the desire for vengeance.* Since it is concerned with anger, it is a virtue which resides in the irascible appetite. Now it is the nature of anger to want to strike back, to retaliate, to seek revenge. As a passion, anger is in itself neither good nor evil; it is indifferent. Consequently, there is such a thing as a just anger, and the virtue of meekness does not repress or restrain this type of anger. The virtue enables a man to use anger according to the rule of right reason.

It is to caricature virtue and betray virtue itself to consider meekness as a form of timidity or cowardice. The meek man does not cease to be meek when aroused to a just anger any more than Jesus ceased to be meek and humble of heart when in justifiable anger he drove the money-changers from the Temple. The beauty of meekness as a virtue consists in a certain evenness, sweetness and gentleness of disposition whereby a person is able to live in peace and equanimity. In its perfection, it leans heavily on the virtue of fortitude (in its passive aspect of bearing with evil) and on the virtue of humility (which enables a person to prefer others to self).

(2) Clemency

Closely associated with the virtue of meekness is the virtue of **clemency,** which is *a moral virtue by which one diminishes the*

[33]Cf. Ps. 4:5, 36:11; Eccles. 10:31; Jer. 11:19; Matt. 5:4, 21:5.

punishment of faults so far as right reason permits. We say "so far as right reason permits," because there are times when reason commands that punishment be affixed with due severity, which is the mean between cruelty and laxity. Nevertheless, it is more virtuous, and especially for those in positions of authority, to incline more to mercy than to severity.

The difference between meekness and clemency is readily apparent. Meekness is in the irascible appetite; clemency is in the will. Meekness is concerned with the passion of anger; clemency is concerned with external actions of punishment. At the same time, these two virtues may be closely interrelated, as when meekness restrains the anger which would otherwise impel one to punish more severely than reason demands.

In its general lines, the virtue of clemency bears a great resemblance to the virtue of equity, which enables one to apply or interpret a law with benignity. In both cases there is required an ability to judge a particular case in view of a general law. In both cases likewise there is a great dependence on the virtues of justice and prudence.

(3) The Vice of Anger

The word anger (*ira*) gives the name to the irascible passions, those concerned with some difficulty related to good or evil. Although anger is commonly considered to be evil by its very nature, such is not the case, for anger is a passion and the passions are in themselves morally indifferent. St. Thomas specifically states that the only evil to be found in anger is by reason of excess or defect.[34] Here, as with all the moral virtues, the norm is to be guided by the dictates of right reason. It is easy to see that excessive anger or misdirected anger would be contrary to reason; it should likewise be emphasized that it would be against the dictate of reason and therefore morally evil *not* to be angry when circumstances reasonably demand it.

As a vice opposed to meekness, therefore, **anger** is *the inordinate desire for revenge.* This brings the will and reason into play, for just as there can be no virtue without the function of intellect and

[34]Cf. *Summa*, II-II, q. 158, a. 1.

will, so neither can there be any vice without the functioning of those faculties. And this enables us to see why anger is classified as a vice against a potential part of temperance rather than being a vice against the virtue of fortitude, which controls the irascible passions in general. Temperance consists in self-restraint and moderation, and this is precisely what is lacking in the person who sins through excessive anger. This does not mean, however, that every vehement movement of anger is sinful, for anger may arise suddenly, antecedent to the act of reason and will, and then it would not be a human act. Even when it is ordinate, anger may interrupt the deliberation of reason and still be a virtuous anger. Anger is sinful only when it is opposed to the dictates of reason; for example, to be angry at one who is undeserving of anger or to be angry out of proportion to the occasion of anger, or if the anger is manifested internally or externally in a fierce and immoderate manner.

Anger is likewise listed as a **capital vice** because it can be the origin from which other sins flow. Thus, anger sometimes leads to *indignation,* which is a feeling of hurt pride at suffering injury from another, or it may lead to an *inordinate plotting* and *scheming* for revenge. Again, anger may lead to vices of speech, and this in three ways: by *inordinate and confused speech or cries of rage,* by *blasphemous expressions,* or by *insults* and *derisive speech* against one's neighbor. Lastly, anger may occasion all manner of external acts such as *quarreling, fighting,* etc.

(4) The Sin of Cruelty

That which is characteristic of **cruelty** is *to inflict punishment beyond the demands of reason and the law.* It designates a hardness of heart and an inflexibility which are untouched by the demands of clemency and equity. The external act of punishment very often violates justice itself, but it is the mental attitude in the inflicting of the punishment that constitutes cruelty. Hence, a person is guilty of cruelty not only when he punishes in excess of that which is due to a fault, but when he deliberately refuses to remit or lessen the punishment as prudence demands.

But it would be equally vicious of a person to remit or lessen punishment for crime when the common good and reason demand that an evil be punished. This excessive laxity is sometimes found in the dealings of the courts with criminals. It is not only an evil for the criminal (since it encourages further crime), but it is an injustice to society and the common good.

C. Modesty

We now come to a set of virtues which, for the most part, are further removed from the essence of temperance, and yet they are connected with temperance because they still retain the notion of moderation and self-control. We have already explained that the virtue of temperance is concerned with the most vehement pleasures, and especially the pleasures related to the sense of touch; we then demonstrated how the virtue is divided into integral parts and species. The virtues which we shall now discuss are concerned with acts which present some difficulty, but the difficulty is as a rule much more readily brought under the control of reason. The general name given by St. Thomas and the ancients to this class of virtue is **modesty**, and it is divided into various particular virtues:[35] humility, studiousness, modesty of action and dress. We shall consider these virtues and their contrary vices in what follows.

(1) Humility

It may seem strange at first glance that the virtue of humility, which is so highly extolled in Sacred Scripture and is so highly emphasized by preachers and spiritual writers as the foundation of Christian living,[36] should be given such a seemingly inferior position

---

[35]Cf. *Summa*, II-II, q. 160, a. 2. It is evident that the word "modesty" as used by St. Thomas does not have the same meaning as in modern usage.

[36]"Just as the orderly assembly of virtues is, by a certain likeness, compared to a building, so that which is the first step in the acquisition of virtue is compared to the foundation . . . The first step in the acquisition of virtue may be understood in two ways. First, by way of removing obstacles, and thus humility holds the first place, inasmuch as it expels pride. . . . In this sense humility is said to be the foundation of the spiritual edifice. Secondly, a thing is said to be first among virtues directly, inasmuch as it is the first step toward God. But the first step toward God is by faith. . . . In this sense faith is the foundation in a more excellent way than humility." St. Thomas, *Summa*, II-II, q. 161, a. 5, ad 2.

as an annexed virtue related to temperance. Nevertheless, when we examine the psychological operation of the virtue of humility it will be evident that it is properly related to temperance even though it surpasses temperance in excellence.

Both the concupiscible and irascible passions are characterized by a double movement: attraction and repulsion. If the stimulus of the passions is judged to be a difficult or arduous good, there is yet another double movement: the good attracts, but the difficulty discourages the individual. Now, there is present here a twofold danger to the rule of reason: one may tend inordinately to a given difficult good and not pay sufficient attention to the obstacles involved, or one may concentrate on the difficulties and give up before he starts. For the former dangerous excess there is required a special virtue, and that virtue is humility. For the latter, there is also required a special virtue, and that virtue is magnanimity. Thus humility restrains one from striving for lofty things against the dictates of reason; magnanimity, on the other hand, impels one to attempt great things according to reason and thus to avoid despair. The two virtues counterbalance each other, although magnanimity is presupposed to humility.

It should be evident from the foregoing why the virtue of humility is annexed to temperance. Located in the irascible appetite (to suppress presumptuous hope), its primary function is to control, restrain or moderate—and this is the very mode of temperance. Magnanimity, on the other hand, which is annexed to the virtue of fortitude, restrains unreasonable daring and strengthens the soul against fear. Hence the excess of daring is less opposed to the virtue of fortitude than is a defect in daring, and excess of self-confidence or hope is more opposed to humility than is a lack of self-confidence.

In view of this, we may define **humility** as *a moral virtue which restrains the inordinate desire for one's own excellence.* Humility does not prevent erroneous judgments, for that is the work of prudence, working through the cognitive powers, but since it is a virtue radicated in the irascible appetite and concerned with the passion of hope, it relies on and presupposes the prudent judgment concerning one's powers and strength. Thus it may happen that a person attempts great works which are above his strength and is accused of lacking humility; but such may not actually be the case, for what is at fault is the lack of prudence which would have saved him from the erroneous judgment concerning his abilities.

True humility, then, is not at all to be confused with timidity, self-disparagement and the self-effacing mimicry of a Uriah Heep. It is true that great saints have written or spoken of themselves in most degrading terms, but that was based on the judgment they had made when they compared themselves to the perfection and power of God. Moreover, those were the manifestations of perfect and even heroic humility, and for a beginner or even a pious Christian to go through the external motions of heroic virtue is to act a part and to bring discredit on the true virtue.

Nevertheless, the basis of humility is self-knowledge. The goal is to see oneself as God sees him. This means a recognition of one's God-given talents as well as an acknowledgment of one's sins and defects. It is no glory to God if a man denies the gifts that God gave him to use for his greater perfection. And yet, the true knowledge of oneself can be had only in relation to God, for we are all creatures of God. Therefore, humility in its highest sense, as a supernatural virtue, always implies man's subjection to God.

But this awareness of one's subjection to God must always be coupled with a kind of "high-mindedness" or a sense of man's innate dignity as a creature of God and a child of God. When these two values are properly balanced, a man can virtuously acknowledge his talents, use them for the greater glory of God, and at the same time confess his faults and ask God to supply for his defects.

(2) Its Opposite Vice: Pride

Wherever we find singularity, surpassing excellence or a super-abundance of perfection, we may speak of pride. But not every singularity or excellence is to be considered in an evil sense; hence there is a good pride and an evil pride. Even in ordinary speech we advise a person to take pride in himself or his work, and the individual himself may rightly have a sense of superiority in one respect or another. It is fully in accord with the virtue of humility, based as it is on self-knowledge and a recognition of one's subjection to God, to acknowledge one's talents and one's superiority in a given area and then to develop those talents to the greatest possible perfection. Grace perfects nature and does not destroy it; it could never be defended as true humility if one were to annihilate oneself and bury his talents.

But if one uses his talents for selfish motives, if he seeks his perfection by trampling upon the rights of others with a disdain for his neighbor, and if he acts as if his abilities were not gifts from God, then his pride is vicious and sinful. This is what is known as the sin of **pride** and it is defined as *the inordinate desire for one's own excellence*. What makes pride vicious, therefore, is the element of inordinateness, the failure to observe the rule of right reason which would make the proper practical judgment concerning the relation between a man's abilities and the difficult good which he desires. The proud man does not observe this rule of reason, but, because of an inordinate desire for his own excellence, judges himself to be greater than he is. A person readily believes anything that he desires very much.

Like the virtue of humility, the vice of pride is localized in the irascible appetite because the object to which it tends is something arduous and difficult. And since one may seek to exalt oneself unreasonably through both sensible and spiritual things, the subject of pride is both the intellectual appetite or the will, and the sensitive appetite which is the source of the passion of hope.

The proud man is consumed with a vehement desire for his own excellence and he will utilize every possible means to further his end. And it is for this reason that pride must be considered not only as a specific sin but as **a general sin and "the beginning of all evil."** In this latter sense, the proud man uses every means to promote his own excellence, and thus pride induces him to perform any other sinful act in view of his goal, or even to perform good acts for the same vicious end. It is in this sense that St. Augustine warned that pride creeps in to destroy even good works. Moreover, pride as a general sin or vehement impulse removes the last vestige of restraint through fear of offending God, for it makes a man disdain the laws of God. From there it is but a short step to the loss of faith and the denial of God's existence.[37]

The gravity of the sin of pride can easily be deduced from the foregoing. If humility is the basic and fundamental virtue of the Christian life, its opposite vice must surely be among the most serious of sins. We cannot say that the sin of pride is absolutely the most grievous, however, because there is no sin more serious than direct hatred of God. There is in every sin a twofold element: aversion from God and inordinate conversion to some good that is not God. The good to which the proud man tends inordinately is his own self-excellence, and this is surely not the worst of all sins—self-excellence is not the most incompatible thing with virtue. But as an aversion from God, pride constitutes truly grave sin because this turning away constitutes the very essence of pride. The proud man disdains subjection to God because he knows full well that it is a necessary corrective of his inordinate desire for his own excellence. In other sins, on the other hand, it may easily happen that the aversion from God is a consequence of the attraction to some good and therefore allows for an element of ignorance or weakness. We conclude, therefore, that pride is in its nature a most grave sin and considered from the aspect of aversion from God it is the gravest of all sins.[38]

Precisely because the formality of pride is aversion from God, pride has been called the first sin and the beginning of all sin and has also been listed as a capital sin.[39] This does not mean that pride is

[37] St. Gregory assigns four species of pride: 1) to boast about having what one does not have; 2) to claim to have from oneself what one has received from God; 3) to believe that what is from God is due to one's own merits; and 4) to disdain others and wish to be the exclusive possessors of that which they have.

[38] This does not nullify the statement that hatred of God is the most serious of all sins. Pride is the most grave from the point of view of aversion from God, but not from the point of view of conversion to one's own excellence. Hatred of God is the worst sin by way of a positive act of hatred of God and without any necessary direct conversion to any created thing.

[39] While pride may also be called the first sin in the sense that it constituted the sin of the fallen angels and the original sin of Adam and Eve, it is not in this sense that we are speaking of the first sin.

the first sin or the beginning of sin in the sense that every sin committed by man is commanded by pride, for we have already seen that there can also be sins of weakness and ignorance. Neither does it mean that pride is first chronologically. But in any series of sins in which pride is involved, pride will usually be the source, and this for two reasons: 1) pride causes a disdain for the laws of God, and when this occurs a man is liable to commit any sin; 2) the desire for one's own excellence, which pertains to the essence of pride, explains how a man can withdraw his love from God and give it inordinately to a created good in view of his own self-exaltation.

Since pride is, as explained above, the first sin and the beginning of all possible sin, it follows that pride is also *a capital sin,* for a capital sin is that from which others arise. Indeed, pride is more than a capital sin, as St. Gregory points out: it is the queen and mother of all vices and sins. Nevertheless, certain sins can be singled out as "daughters" of pride: *sinful ambition,* which is the inordinate desire for honor and office or position; *presumption,* which is the inordinate desire to achieve something beyond one's powers; *vainglory,* which is the inordinate desire of demonstrating one's excellence and which, in turn, leads to other vices, such as *ostentation, hypocrisy, disobedience, contention,* etc.[40]

(3) Studiousness

The material of the virtue of studiosity or studiousness is the knowledge of the truth, which is in itself good and needs no virtue to regulate it. But the *desire* for knowledge admits of good or evil—this is the area in which a virtue is required. The rule of reason must be

---

[40]"Pride is directly opposed to the virtue of humility, which is in a way concerned about the same matter as magnanimity. Hence the vice opposed to pride by defect is similar to the vice of pusillanimity, which is opposed to magnanimity by defect. For just as it belongs to magnanimity to urge the mind to great things, against despair, so it belongs to humility to restrain the mind from the inordinate desire for great things, against presumption. If we consider pusillanimity as a defect in the pursuit of great things, it is opposed to magnanimity by defect; if we consider it as the mind's attachment to things that are beneath that which is becoming a man, it is opposed to humility by defect, but in either case it proceeds from smallness of mind." St. Thomas, *Summa,* II-II, q. 162, a. 1, ad 3.

followed lest one have too great or too little a desire for knowledge and, consequently, is too intent or too slothful in the pursuit of knowledge. The actual *pursuit* of study in spite of difficulties and natural distaste is related to the virtue of fortitude, but the *moderation* of the desire for knowledge, keeping it within reasonable bounds, is a potential part of the virtue of temperance. It belongs to temperance to restrain the inordinate appetite and hence the virtue of studiosity may operate either in the will or in the concupiscible appetite. The virtue of studiosity is therefore defined as *the moderation of the desire for knowledge within the bounds of reason.*

But what are the bounds of reason in regard to the acquisition of knowledge? As to the *content* of knowledge, an individual has an obligation to acquire a knowledge of those things that are necessary for leading a moral life, for eternal salvation and for performing the duties of one's state in life. As regards the *manner* or mode of aspiring to this knowledge, the virtue of studiosity enables one to avoid studying merely for the selfish satisfaction of knowing or to neglect the necessary study because of sloth or fatigue or difficulty.

The reasonable pursuit of knowledge under the virtue of studiousness is sufficiently indicated by considering the two vices which may result from excess or defect. In itself, knowledge is not evil, but the desire for certain types of knowledge will be either good or evil. Therefore, there is a large area of knowledge which for most people could be considered a matter of personal selection, depending upon circumstances. There may be no moral obligation to acquire the knowledge, and yet the knowledge may be useful or lawfully desired for some other reason.

Normally in the pursuit of any study that is voluntarily undertaken there will be a double tendency on the part of the student. The mind may be eager for the knowledge and need no impulse from outside to urge the pursuit, but the body may become weary and become a weight upon the mind. If the latter situation prevails and it is a question of necessary knowledge to be acquired, the individual may fall into the vice of **negligence,** which is a defect in the command of the will and is opposed to prudence as well as studiousness.[41] At the other extreme, by way of excess, is the vice of **curiosity.**

Sinful curiosity may be committed in a variety of ways, and it is always indicative of an inordinate desire for knowledge:

1) Superstitious curiosity is sinful because it involves the attempt to know hidden things from sources that are unlawful, as in fortune-telling, demonology, etc.

2) It is inordinate to study to acquire knowledge merely to be able to take pride in one's knowledge.

3) It is sinful to take the time required for the study of necessary knowledge in order to study material that is unnecessary.

4) It is sinful to study created things without in any way referring this study and knowledge to God, as happens in cases of idle curiosity about the affairs or faults of others, the search for new experiences and thrills, or the morbid curiosity about matters that may easily become an occasion of sin or temptation.

5) It is sinful curiosity to attempt to acquire a knowledge of those things which surpass one's mental capacity, as happens with those persons who are attracted by the novel, the seemingly miraculous, or the occult.

On the other hand, whenever there is a reasonable cause for the pursuit of any study, and the knowledge itself is not spiritually harmful in itself or as a deterrent from obligatory study, and there is no extrinsic factor which is evil (such as motives of pride or an occasion of sin)—then the study is itself morally right.

(4) Modesty of Action and Dress

We come finally to the consideration of what are generally known as the virtues of good manners—virtues which are related to temperance and govern the individual in his life as a member of society. It is a subject which should be based on solid principles of theology and which yet must be flexible enough for adaptations according to

[41]Cf. St. Thomas, *Summa,* II-II, q. 54, a. 2.

legitimate customs and manners. These virtues have been the subject of many articles and discussions and they will always be so, because in their secondary aspects they are constantly undergoing adaptation and change. The mere enumeration and definition of each of the virtues involved will suffice to demonstrate this fact.

1. **Modesty of external behavior** is *a virtue which regulates one's actions according to reason, so that proper decorum will always be observed.* The material of this virtue consists in any external action or movement of the body, such as one's posture, walk, sitting, facial expressions, movements of the head or hands, etc. It may seem that these are too trivial to be discussed as material for virtue, and yet they need a regulating virtue precisely because they are matters which are not determined by nature but by the control of one's own reason. The two extremes to be avoided are effeminacy or affectation and rusticity or rudeness. As applied to external actions, modesty should regulate man in serious matters and in his recreation.

As regards his serious actions, a man should observe modesty or self-control in regard to his own person and in regard to his dealings with others. The particular virtue which regulates one's *personal behavior* according to reason may be called by various names: decency, composure, dignity, etc. The virtue which regulates *one's external actions toward others* may be called courtesy, etiquette, social grace, good manners, etc. But insofar as man should by his outward actions reveal his inward dispositions, these actions should also be regulated by the virtue of **veracity** (to which hypocrisy and simulation are opposed as vices). In order that a man may restrain himself from giving pain or offense by his actions, the virtue of **affability** is necessary (to which the defect of unfriendliness or antipathy is opposed).

2. As regards man's **recreation,** *a virtue* is required *to moderate this exercise lest a person go to excess or be defective.* It has the strange name of *eutrapelia,* but in modern speech it may be simply called "recreation"—a very good word since the whole purpose of the virtue is to "re-create" man for the further pursuit of happiness. Constant work and application cause weariness of mind and body.

The need for relaxation and recreation is a body need and should be supplied. But a virtue is required lest one go beyond the dictates of reason, which will require that the recreation should not involve anything morally wrong, that it should not cause the participant to lose self-control altogether, and that prudence govern the time, persons and other circumstances. It is a practice of the virtue of recreation, therefore, to attend social gatherings, the theater, sports events, etc., as long as the recreation itself and surrounding circumstances are in accord with right reason and morality. On the other hand, it is a vice to take too little recreation and to be boorish or excessively austere, or to be excessive in recreation by taking too much delight in relaxation or by neglecting the serious matters of one's life.[42]

3. **Modesty of dress** is another matter which is constantly disputed and subject to adaptation; therefore *a virtue is required so that one may follow the dictates of reason in view of particular circumstances in the matter of attire.* Clothing is worn for protection against the weather, for reasons of decency, for reasons of one's position, or for beauty and adornment. But when it comes to a question of the type of clothing and the style, various factors must be taken into consideration if one wishes to follow the dictates of reason. Thus, one should reasonably respect the customs of the country in which he is; one should use clothing for one of the reasons given above and not seek attention through one's manner of dress nor be too much attached to clothing and styles. On the other hand, it would be a defect against the required modesty of dress if one were to be careless and slovenly, or if one were to be deliberately negligent in this matter in order to attract attention.

Although men as a rule are less concerned about clothing and styles and are consequently more simple and conservative in their tastes, women often fall into fastidiousness, vanity and excessive attachment to clothing and bodily adornments. But while it is difficult to determine in detail what is the line of demarcation in this matter, if a woman's apparel provokes lust in men or if the woman knows

---

[42]Some socially important moral problems relating to recreation in the schools are discussed in: T. C. Donlan, "The Moral Price of Interschool Athletics," *The American Ecclesiastical Review*, CXXVI (1952), 351-365.

that she dresses for reasons of vanity, then there is a lack of the virtue of modesty in dress. Modest dress may not always be the fashion, but it will always be in good taste.

These same principles will govern the use of jewels and other bodily ornaments and the employment of perfumes, cosmetics, etc.

9. The Precepts of Temperance

The precepts of the Decalogue are universal principles of divine law, and hence they command that which is common to many men or to mankind as a whole; they are like first self-evident principles of the moral life. Since temperance is so intensely a personal matter, despite its social repercussions, its virtuous practice will differ widely, not only among individuals, but also according to different times and according to different human laws and customs. The attire which would have shocked and scandalized a Victorian can today be an example of modesty in dress (which is not to deny the unfortunate fact that many modern customs in dress seriously offend modesty). Because of this fact, which flows from the nature of the virtue of temperance, no affirmative precepts concerning it were given by God.

But the end of the law was love—the love of friendship which is charity, embracing love of God and love of neighbor. Hence the Ten Commandments contain those precepts which tend more directly to this charity. And of all the vices against temperance that which appears as most opposed to love of our neighbor is that of adultery, the abuse of one's neighbor's wife. For this reason the Decalogue contains a special prohibition of this vice, not only as committed in deed but also as desired in thought.

The inordinateness of the other vices opposed to temperance, however, is more interior and inward, and therefore less directly injurious to love of neighbor. The Decalogue prohibits these vices, then, not in themselves (for so they have little or no direct connection with God or neighbor), but in their effects. Thus the effect of the vice of anger may be murder, which is specifically forbidden; the effect of pride will be contempt for God and parents, violations of other commandments.

10. Summary and Conclusion

This chapter began with the idea that the virtue of temperance is the quality that makes a man a good steward over the personal gifts he has received from God. The extent of that stewardship has been traced as the doctrine of the chapter was developed. All that has been said can be summarized from the same point of view.

Man enters this life endowed with the seeds of many powers, and these seeds develop as he matures. As the mainspring of these powers, man is endowed with love, the force which sets all other human forces in motion. Because man is a body-spirit, all the knowledge which excites his desires begins in the senses. Man reacts to the stimuli of the sense by movements called passions, and these passions are the beginnings of human behavior. Some passions are specialized and reserved for emergency situations when man is confronted with difficulty in getting what is good or in avoiding what is evil. But such reactions are transitory—the irascible passions cannot be the ordinary climate of anyone's life. The ordinary or concupiscible passions are awakened at the beginning of every human reaction, and it is in these same passions that human rest is found. All human endeavor seeks rest, and the natural terminus of all man's striving is to be found in the joy of possession or in the sorrow of loss. These are not, of course, simply passions of the sense appetite; they are emotions in the will too. But the importance of the passions cannot be denied.

In man, the passions are designed to be subject to reason. Because they are passions, they are man's touchstone with the animal kingdom; because they are capable of being subject to reason, they are at the threshold of man's spirituality. These passions are precious forces in human life. Man is steward over them: he can be a wastrel through intemperance or a miser through insensitivity. Best of all, of course, he can be a good steward through the moderation of temperance. This is no easy task; yet it is one which must be done. Not to strive is the same as to lose, and what is lost for lack of temperance is man's very humanity, and ultimately his eternal salvation.

The Christian enjoys a great advantage. He receives infused temperance with the supernatural organism in sanctifying grace; he re-

ceives actual graces that impel him to acts of temperance. But all
this does not absolve him from personal effort in guarding the
treasures of his own human powers. Exercise is necessary. The infant
is born with the power to make noise, but he must harness that
power by learning to talk. Some harness the power to make noise
more perfectly than others; they go on to become singers or orators.
So, too, with temperance. A natural virtue must be built up to accustom the human organism to the pattern of moderation; man must
become prompt to moderate his desires; he must do it with ease;
he must find satisfaction in moderation. In other words, he must
be at home with his own humanness.

The rule of temperance is determined by man's needs as these are
judged by reason and faith. It is a flexible and intensely personal
rule, and its application comes under the judgment of prudence. Sometimes temperance must undergo radical changes in application, as
when one passes from the single to the married life. In matters of
temperance, it is literally true that one man's drink is another's poison.

This norm based on personal and social necessity destroys anything smacking of a mathematical approach to temperance. Whereas
a temperance measured exclusively by natural standards may generally
find its norm in a nicety of proportion, a temperance enlightened by
supernatural faith will often find that moderation consists in total
self-denial. The legitimate goods of the flesh and the advantages of
this world assume a different value when judged according to the
standards of the kingdom of God. The temperate Christian is steward
over himself not simply for time but for eternity.

The following brief passages will serve to encourage further thoughts
about the meaning of Christian temperance and its allied virtues.

1. The *positive approach* to temperance, which is especially important in the formation of the young, consists in a recognition of
the dignity of man and the ontological purpose of his instincts (for
the virtuous control from a natural point of view) and a deep appreciation for man's supernatural vocation to sanctification and salvation (for the functioning of the infused virtue). And thus it is evident
that for the perfection of the acquired virtue of temperance a person

needs an intellectual awareness of the nature and purpose of man accompanied by the will to be humanly perfect.

The infused virtue of temperance will, over and above this, require a knowledge of the truths of faith which touch upon man's eternal and supernatural destiny, a high degree of infused prudence which will enable the individual to make supernatural judgments in given circumstances in view of the supernatural end, and—not least in importance—a charity which will prompt the individual to practice the virtue of temperance in daily life. Then indeed will the Christian be truly temperate, so that he can take the advice of St. Paul and put it into everyday practice: "Therefore whether you eat or drink, or do anything else, do all for the glory of God" (I Cor. 10:31).

2. "The formal element in a virtue can be restored by repentance, but not the material. For example, if a free-spending man were to squander his wealth, it would not be restored to him through repentance. And likewise, whoever loses virginity by sinning does not recover through repentance the material element of virginity, but rather the intention of virginity. There is, indeed, something of the material element of virginity that could be restored miraculously by divine power, and that is the bodily integrity which is only accidental to the virtue. But there is something else which could not be restored even miraculously, namely, that someone who had experienced venereal pleasure should be made not to have experienced it. God can not cause things which have been done to be as if they were not."[43]

3. "The Apostle of the Gentiles, divinely inspired, tells in the following passage why celibacy is a liberation. 'And I would have you free from concern. . . . The married man is concerned with the world's claim, asking how he is to please his wife; and thus he is at issue with himself' (I Cor. 7:32 f.). But here it must be noted that the Apostle is not blaming husbands because they are concerned with their wives. Nor is he taking wives to task for trying to please their husbands. He is merely pointing out that their hearts are divided between love of their partner and love of God, that they are too distracted by the anxieties and obligations of the married state to be able readily to give

[43]St. Thomas, *Summa*, II-II, q. 152, a. 3, ad 3.

their minds to the affairs of God. They are subject to the duty of wedlock, which clearly commands that 'the two become one flesh' (Gen. 2:24). Man and wife are yoked to one another in all the gladdening and saddening circumstances of their lives (cf. I Cor. 7:39). Hence it will be readily appreciated why those who wish to give themselves to the service of God embrace the state of virginity as a state of emancipation, which enables them to serve God more completely and to devote their undivided energies to the welfare of their fellow-men."[44]

4. "Whereas other vices are practiced by doing evil, pride enters by stealth to destroy even good deeds."[45]

5. No one is ever so exalted that he can dispense with humility. When the Blessed Virgin heard from the Archangel Gabriel that she was to become the Mother of God, she had such a lowly opinion of herself that she marvelled greatly that she should be exalted to such an eminent dignity. "To a humble soul nothing is more wondrous than to hear of its own excellence. Thus to Mary's saying, 'How shall this be?' the angel brings forward a proof, not to take away her belief, but rather to dispel her wonder."[46]

6. St. Augustine has said: "Love God and do what you will; you will not sin." This is verified in those who, although beset by temptations against temperance or naturally constituted to be especially vehement in the body instincts and passions, nevertheless resist temptation and control themselves primarily because they fear to offend the good God whom they love. Theirs is that "fear of the Lord" which is the beginning of wisdom—the fear which is the gift of the Holy Spirit, so perfecting acquired and infused temperance as to enable man to act, even on the plane of his too human passions, *in a divine manner.*

They see as evil, not the instincts or passions or delight as such, but the sinful use and enjoyment of such things. And since they love God, they hate all sin; since they love God, they are fearful of of-

---

[44]Pope Pius XII, encyclical *Sacra Virginitas.*
[45]*The Rule of St. Augustine.*
[46]St. Thomas, *Summa,* III, q. 30, a. 4.

fending him whom they love. Few Christians have so perfectly exemplified how the gift of fear of the Lord preserves chastity as did St. Maria Goretti, who would not yield to temptation because she feared to offend God by sinful action.

BIBLIOGRAPHICAL NOTE

St. Thomas treats the virtue of temperance in his *Summa*, II-II, Questions CXLI-CLXX. Another saint, Francis de Sales, has written a short spiritual classic which shows great discernment in the area of temperance, *Introduction to a Devout Life* (Garden City, N.Y.: Doubleday [Image Books]). A rather technical but worthwhile consideration of temperance in relation to the emotions is Kenneth F. Slattery's *The Thomistic Concept of the Virtue of Temperance* (Washington: Catholic University of America Press, 1952). Josef Pieper's *Fortitude and Temperance* (New York: Pantheon, 1954) will be a valuable aid in understanding the true nature and worth of temperance. Other books worthy of note for their treatment of one or more of the parts of temperance are: *The Virtue of Humility* by Sebastian Carlson, O.P. (Dubuque: Wm. C. Brown Co., 1952), a profound though fascinating account of this virtue; *Humility* by Father Canice, O.F.M.Cap. (Westminster, Md.: The Newman Press, 1951), a synthesis of the teachings of the Doctors of the Church in simple and direct language; *Virginity* by Joseph Marie Perrin, O.P. (Westminster, Md.: The Newman Press, 1956), which shows the difficulties of the religious vocation and its potential grandeur; *Accent on Purity* by Joseph E. Haley, C.S.C. (Chicago: Fides Publishers Association, 1948), a practical guide to sex education; *Innocence and Ignorance* by Martin S. Gillet, O.P. (New York: Devin-Adair, 1917), which treats some effective means for acquiring purity; and *The Intellectual Life* by A. D. Sertillanges, O.P. (Westminster, Md.: The Newman Press, 1947), a consideration of the virtue of studiosity and the relation of the intellectual life to other aspects of temperance.

Of the many available books and booklets on chastity, the following are suggested for particular excellences. *The Christian Design for Sex* by J. Buckley, S.M., (Chicago: Fides, 1952); *Modern Youth and Chastity* by Gerald L. Kelly, S.J., *et al.* (St. Louis: The Queen's Work, 1944); *In Defence of Purity* by Dietrich von Hildebrand (New York: Sheed and Ward, 1935). For works on marriage and marital chastity see the extensive bibliography of the short college text *Toward Marriage in Christ* by T. C. Donlan, O.P., F. L. B. Cunningham, O.P., and Augustine Rock, O.P. (Dubuque: The Priory Press, 1957).

Essays on the particular parts of temperance can also be found in various periodicals. Those especially worthy of mention are: J. I. O'Connor, S.J., "Virginity and Chastity" in *American Ecclesiastical Review*, CXL (1959), 17-26; "Chastity and Marriage," by J. R. Connery, S.J., in *Theological Studies*, XVII (1956), 576-583; "Virtue of Chastity," by A. Plé, O.P., in *Theology Digest*, V (1957), 13-17; Père Lallemant's "Perfection," a study of the virtue of humility, in *Life of the Spirit*, XIII (1958), 130-132; and "Victory over Self," by Melchior Cano, O.P., a series of articles on the capital sins in *Cross and Crown*, VIII (1956).

CHAPTER SEVENTEEN

Christian Specialization and Perfection

1. INTRODUCTION

The last chapter terminated an extensive section of the theology which pertains to all men in general: every man's relation to God, his end, the divine call to supernatural beatitude and the essential means for its realization. Everyone must have grace and live virtuously on the theological and moral level in order to reach God and attain everlasting happiness. But while there are no exceptions to this divine requirement, God has given special helps on occasion. And he has also permitted the development, in the use of the ordinary means, of special tendencies, emphases and methods.

Specialization, in varying degrees, has always characterized human society. Not everyone does exactly the same things, nor are all capable of doing the same activities; indeed, there is no need for all men to be engaged in exactly the same activities. Special circumstances and the variety of talents and limitations of men cause a multitude of differences in human action.

Within the framework of the Church there is also a wide variety of human activity: there are married and single people, priests, broth-

749

ers and sisters, religious engaged in external activities and others cloistered from the world. This variety is not an accident; it is brought about by the provident designs of God.

Actually, in God's providence *everyone* has a special dignity and a special job to do. The failure to appreciate this is due to ignorance of the fact that God is constantly interested in all of us, whether our lives appear to be drab or spectacular.

God has, at times, raised some to fill spectacular roles in his care of the world. In the Old Testament we read of leaders like Abraham and Moses to whom were revealed divine truths and who were gifted with the power of performing miracles. These gifts were not given to these specially selected leaders for their benefit but for the sake of the people, in order to instruct them in the knowledge of God and teach them how to act in a way pleasing to God. The miracles were worked to strengthen the people to accept the truths thus made known as truths coming from God.

When Christ was on earth, he selected a group of men, the apostles, to carry on his work. Although it was a special blessing for them to be chosen, yet their rise from a simple life to the special public one of an apostle was for the sake of others. They were instructed by Christ, enlightened by the Holy Ghost, made suddenly capable of being understood in a variety of foreign languages and of performing miracles. None of these gifts was personal; all were special aids for bringing the word of salvation to the people.

These more spectacular displays of God's power which showed forth in the lives of the prophets and apostles were due to special circumstances. Moses had the difficult task of leading the Hebrew people to a new land and to a purification of their knowledge of the true God, for the chosen people had grievously weakened in faith and morals during their captivity among the pagan Egyptians. The apostles had the gigantic task of establishing the kingdom of Christ in their own land, which was hostile, and in the rest of the world, which was pagan. In his mercy, God was not wanting in generosity in enhancing the powers of these special agents whose work it was to lead others to eternal salvation.

God's interest in the salvation of men has never ceased, and the history of the Church since the time of Christ contains a continuous line of holy men and women who were raised up to help others.[1]

The spectacular lives of those given special tasks by God may mislead us into thinking that only the spectacular and extraordinary marks a thing as special. In God's plan everyone is special: he has a reason for the existence of every human being, he sent his dearly beloved Son to die for each one of us. Each one has a role to fulfill to which he has been called by God; it is his vocation. It is these various special vocations in the kingdom of Christ which cause the differences in emphasis and method in the exercise of the basic virtues that lead to eternal happiness. A husband and wife, among other things, should be characterized by a special marital justice; a priest should stand out with the virtues that stamp him as another Christ; a religious, among his array of virtues, should be known for his love of the virtue of obedience.

Although each one has his own special vocation from God, these vocations are not so individualistic as not to admit of being grouped in general classifications. An educated person should not only understand his own vocation but should also have an intellectual appreciation of the roles that others fill in God's overall plan.

By way of concluding our study of man's relationship to God, we shall consider this matter according to the outline on the next page.

2. The Broad Classification of Virtuous Living

A. The Contemplative and Active Life

Psychology teaches us that the soul is the principle of life and the ultimate source of the activities of a living organism. This fundamental meaning of the relationship of life and activity is applied to

---

[1]St. Thomas' penetrating and detailed analysis of these special and extraordinary gifts of God (*gratiae gratis datae*) will be found in the *Summa*, II-II, qq. 171-178.

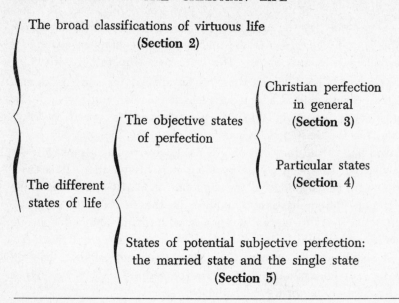

The broad classifications of virtuous life
(Section 2)

The different states of life

The objective states of perfection

Christian perfection in general
(Section 3)

Particular states
(Section 4)

States of potential subjective perfection:
the married state and the single state
(Section 5)

various kinds of activities in order to sum them up under the title of "life." We talk about campus life, married life, a dull life, an exciting life.

Since the exercise of virtue is an activity, it is customary, in and outside the Church, to talk about "the life of virtue." A virtuous life is most compatible with the intellectual nature of man, even at the level of natural reason, for virtuous acts are indications that man is acting according to his reason. Reason is the faculty which elevates man's nature and activities above other living organisms. An apple tree laden with delicious fruit or a well-trained hunting dog is never called virtuous, despite the good produced, because they lack the power of intelligence. Likewise, when a man pursues a life of pleasure he is not known as virtuous; he has failed to use his reason effectively, he has descended from the distinguishing intellectual level of human nature to that of the animals. Even the pagan Aristotle called such a way of life "the life of a beast."[2]

The life of virtue, as an expression of man's intellectual nature, has two general objects which it pursues; in practice, the virtuous

2*Nicomachean Ethics*, Bk. I, Chap. 5.

person gives special emphasis to one or the other of these objects. Either he predominantly seeks the knowledge of truth, or he is especially concerned with external actions of the virtuous life, such, for example, as are necessary for the married life, a teaching career, or caring for the sick.

The seeker after truth is said to live **the contemplative life; the one** engaged in external virtuous actions lives **the active life.** This is the classic division of virtuous life among philosophers and theologians. All members of the Mystical Body of Christ who pursue a life of virtue have title to one or the other of these categories. You may never have thought about it in these terms, but your virtuous general specialty is, or will be, either contemplative or active.

B. The Contemplative Life

(1) Its Dignity

American life is known for its absorption in external activities and its production and acquisition of useful goods. The habitué of the river bank, fishing pole in hand, sitting alone and absorbed in his thoughts, is not exactly an American ideal. At best, he may be the object of a fleeting envy. Even when he is imitated, his emulators demand more external action. Lack of noticeable activity is linked up with oddity of character, or physical impairment, or old age and retirement.

The study of man's nature reveals a variety of gradation of the powers that are the sources of human activity: the laboring man uses the power of his body; the athlete has dexterity in muscular co-ordination and sharpness of external sense; the successful business man shows practical intelligence in planning the use of apt means to further his business; the artist executes externally his internal images endowed with signs of his intellectual intuition of beauty; the true scientist often is engaged in abstract thought and exhibits his thought in a formula just as abstract: $e = mc^2$.[3]

[3]Einstein's mass-energy equation which led to the development of nuclear fission.

Man's activities range from those exclusively of the body to those of the mind. If we admit that man is distinguished from other earthly things by his intellectual powers, then intellectual activities are man's most honorable, for they are the express indications of the superiority of his nature. A Kentucky Derby winner would not be impressed—if one could impress a horse—with the news that a few athletes have run the mile in a little under four minutes; at such a distance, he could beat any human being with a two-minute advantage. Only when man uses the products of his intelligence, e.g., the jet plane, the radio telescope, does he surpass, at the physical level, the bodily endowments of animals. Man is truly a man when he uses his intellectual powers.

Since faith teaches us that man's perfect happiness is his union with God in heaven, it is reasonable for man, while on earth, to concentrate on this goal. God, being spiritual and immaterial, is possible of attainment only by those human faculties that are spiritual and immaterial, the intellect and will. Man's realization of union with God, consequently, will consist in the internal activities of his powers of greatest dignity, the intellect and will; to aid these faculties of man in this task, God endows them with special graces and gifts—faith, hope, charity, wisdom, understanding, counsel.

Among men there are some who so clearly understand and appreciate that God is their greatest good that they keep all other activities at a minimum in order to increase and intensify the intellectual activities that bring them to God. At the human level they are very much alive, and they are more perfectly human because their activities are on the plane of the divine: and these we call "contemplatives." Such a way of life is not only becoming to the dignity of the human person; it has divine approbation and praise.

The gospels record a visit of Christ to Mary and Martha:

> Now it came to pass as they were on their journey that he entered a certain village; and a woman named Martha welcomed him to her house. And she had a sister called Mary, who seated herself at the Lord's feet, and listened to his word. But Martha was worried about much serving. And she came up and said, "Lord, is it no concern of thine that my sister has left me to serve alone? Tell her therefore to help me."

But the Lord answered and said to her, "Martha, Martha, thou art anxious and troubled about many things; and yet only one thing is needful. Mary has chosen the best part, and it will not be taken away from her."[4]

In the theology of the life of the spirit, Mary is the symbol of the contemplative.

(2) The Nature of the Contemplative Life

The contemplative seeks the truth—the ultimate truth which is God. Like anyone who takes up the difficult human task of exploring the depths of unyielding reality, he needs motivation. The contemplative gets his motivation from his love of God. And the rewards for this labor are great: delight follows from the possession of the thing loved; so the life of contemplation is filled with delight and joy as a consequence of the possession of God, for of divine wisdom it is written: "association with her involves no bitterness and living with her no grief, but rather joy and gladness" (Wisd. 8:16). Has not God himself extended the invitation to this great joy? "Taste and see how good the Lord is; happy the man who takes refuge in him" (Ps. 33:9).

The cycle of the act of contemplation starts in the will. With the act of supernatural love as the motivating cause, the Christian seeks a deeper, more meaningful knowledge of the triune God, and from this more intimate union with his beloved arises in the will the delight and intensity of fervent charity.

Charity must enter every human act, to be sure, if it is to have any eternal value; it is the directive spiritual force that links all our virtuous actions to God. But the contemplative is not a disinterested spectator glancing at God like a sports-minded husband dutifully accompanying his wife to an art exhibit. The contemplative is inflamed with a love of God. Charity starts the contemplative on his way to God and joins him to God as his greatest good.

The essence of the act of contemplation, however, is not an act of charity, for contemplation is essentially concerned with truth, the

4Luke 10:38-42.

object of the intellect. The contemplative wants to know God as perfectly as possible; he is seeking the intellectual vision of the divine essence. This is the beginning of heaven on earth, for the goal of our existence is the vision of God: "Now this is everlasting life, that they may know thee, the only true God, and him whom thou hast sent, Jesus Christ" (John 17:3).

The act of contemplation is a far more perfect act than the acts of the human intellect usually are. Man's intellect is a *rational* one. This makes his acquisition of knowledge a step-by-step affair whereby he uses what he already knows to arrive at additional knowledge. The contemplative does not escape the natural workings of his intellect, but he does, at times, rise above the limitations of rational processes. The bodily senses, the imagination, the lower functions of discoursing from one truth to a new truth, are laid aside, and the intellectual gaze on God in the act of contemplation becomes fixed because it is simple, direct and intuitive. This is contemplation at its highest peak, as in the ecstasies of a St. Thomas, a St. John of the Cross, a St. Theresa of Avila, or a St. Catherine of Siena, and hence it is difficult to maintain it for a long time.

Although the contemplative reaches a perfection in the knowledge of God, this is not to be confused with the beatific vision of the essence of God enjoyed by those in heaven. "As long as we live in this mortal flesh," St. Gregory the Great points out, "no one reaches such a height of contemplation as to fix the eyes of his mind on the very ray of incomprehensible light."[5] The contemplative is a wayfarer, and the graces he receives are commensurate with his condition; the blessed in heaven have arrived at their ultimate state of perfection, and the light of glory produces for them the heavenly vision of the divine essence, a beatifying vision which is of its nature permanent. St. Paul, by an extraordinary grace of contemplation called rapture,[6] was raised, most probably, to a vision of the divine essence.[7] This is a height beyond what is normal for an act of contemplation,

---

[5]*Homilies on Ezechiel*, Bk. II, Hom. 2, n. 14.
[6]II Cor. 12:1-7.
[7]Cf. St. Thomas, *Summa*, II-II, q. 175, a. 3.

but, close as it came to the gift enjoyed by the blessed in heaven, it was only for that occasion, not a permanent gift.

Truly, the true contemplative must be a happy man, and the acts of his way of life a source of delight and joy to him. He is concerned with acts most becoming to the dignity of his nature and supernature, and with the goal of his existence. He has evaluated things other than God and found them wanting; in detaching himself from these he gains immeasurably in the things that matter, for, as St. Gregory says, "the contemplative life tramples on all cares and longs to see the face of its creator."[8] Of all men, the contemplative most closely approaches the perfect happiness of our heavenly home.

(3) The Genesis of the Contemplative Life

How does one become a contemplative? God does most in the formation of a contemplative. His grace makes it possible for man to attain a more perfect knowledge of the Godhead than one could ever attain by natural reason;[9] the theological virtues of faith, hope and charity, which are so active in the contemplative life, are his direct gifts; the gifts of the Holy Ghost—especially those which pertain to the intellect: wisdom, understanding, knowledge and counsel—dispose man to avoid the complication of reasoning and to accept the intellectual promptings inspired by the Holy Ghost. This is what removes the difficulty and adds swiftness and assuredness to the act of contemplation.

Although God does most of the work, man has his share to do; without his co-operation, God's gifts will be wasted or hindered. To arrive at the perfection of contemplation man must start at the more imperfect levels. Since the motivating cause of contemplation is charity, whatever would dispose to charity must be developed and whatever would impede it must be removed. On the side of truth man must use his knowing powers on the things more easily known to him, the things of this world, before he can rise to a knowledge

[8]Op. cit., n. 8.
[9]Cf. St. Thomas, Summa, I, q. 12, a. 13.

of the invisible God; as St. Paul says, "since the creation of the world his invisible attributes are clearly seen . . . being understood by the things that are made" (Rom. 1:20).

A boxer, baseball player or football player must either be in proper physical condition or put himself in good condition; hence, athletes have an intensive training period before a fight or before their playing season begins, and remain in training during the season. The lover of God must be in good spiritual condition and well disposed in order to perform the acts of love which lead one into the contemplative life. The love of God which motivates a contemplative cannot be a mere spark but must be a warm and bright flame. Familiar to us all in terms of personal experience is the case of Peter, who, having said he would give his life for Christ, at the crucial moment would not even admit he was a friend of Christ. Due to his love of this world, his fear of the opinion of others, he was not in good enough condition to express the necessary love for God. Would that his were a singular instance among Christians!

The fearful man lacks the courage to love God; the intemperate man, e.g., one habitually guilty of sins of impurity, is so busy fulfilling his fleshly desires that he finds spiritual things distasteful; the unjust man cannot even give to others what they have a right to, much less enjoy the freedom of divine love. The whole array of the moral virtues disposes a man for the higher life of charity and contemplation. These virtues do not enter directly into the life of contemplation but only indirectly, by removing those things which would impede contemplation. For by disciplining the passions, and their unreasonable desires, fears, loves and joys, and by quelling outward disturbances occasioned by injustices, internal peace and quiet result in the moral order; then man can rise, undisturbed, to spiritual things. Christ taught this in his beatitudes: "Blessed are the pure of heart, for they shall see God" (Matt. 5:8). By pure of heart, he meant not only those possessing the virtue of purity but those who have achieved the entire purification and disciplining of their wayward nature. The result and reward is the seeing of God, which is the life of the contemplative.

Besides the moral virtues, man's knowing powers must be used and developed. Before God can be known as lovable, his existence must be known or believed. Although the gift of faith, and consequently the power to believe, is from God, ordinarily the truths to be believed do not come immediately to man from God. In some written or spoken way, truths must be proposed to man: "Faith then depends on hearing" (Rom. 10:17). A good Christian mother, instructing her child about God in heaven, his love, his care of us, his kindness, is implanting the first seeds of contemplation. Christians must listen to instruction about God and also read and study. Even the study of the material world can be a stepping stone to God, for the world is an effect of God, its creator and cause, and every effect contains some knowledge of its cause. Modern discoveries about the atom, for example, are testament to the wisdom and power of God. St. Augustine advises us that "in the study of created things we must not exercise an empty and futile curiosity, but should make them the stepping stones to things imperishable and everlasting."[10] Hence, in a true and complete system of education, the science of theology orders and uses the other sciences and arts, not so as to destroy their integrity and immediate goals, but additionally, as stepping stones to the everlasting and imperishable things of God.

Study and reading should include God's revelation about himself as contained in the Sacred Scriptures, and especially the New Testament, wherein God reveals himself concretely through the human nature of Christ in his life and death. As an aid to an understanding of the Scriptures, the approved writers, teachers and preachers of the Church, both ancient and modern, should be consulted.

All this acquired knowledge is material to think about and to meditate on. Meditation is nothing more than the process of reason's combing over truth already possessed in order to arrive at new practical conclusions, resolutions to correct self and to practice virtue, or the acquisition of new knowledge about God that leads to greater appreciation and love of him. Although ordinary prayer has not been mentioned, it should be understood that, since prayer raises the hu-

[10]*On the True Religion,* Chap. 29.

man mind and heart to God, it belongs to the formation of a contemplative.

(4) Conclusion

There are degrees of perfection within the various professions that human beings pursue. A young man just admitted to a law firm after the completion of his studies and the successful passing of his bar examination has a right to be called a lawyer. He is not, however, as perfect a lawyer as one who has had the experience of many years in the profession.

There are degrees in the contemplative life. The beginner sets his goal at the perfection of true contemplation, but begins working on the lower levels. The acquisition of moral virtue, instruction, study, reading, prayer, meditation help prepare him for the more perfect degree. These lower activities give one a right to the name of contemplative, not by reason of themselves, but by reason of the goal they tend to: true contemplation. The true contemplative is not formed overnight but must patiently follow the grace of God through many steps before arriving at the heights.

C. The Active Life

(1) What It Is

The active life is the virtuous activity of man with his fellow man in a manner which befits the rational and supernatural dignity of a human person called to union with God. A bank-robber leads an active life but quite obviously it is not virtuous. A child is usually full of activity, but its source is found in the exuberance of the bodily side of his nature; such activity is not that of the active life.

The active life is one in which the moral virtues predominate. Since these moral actions are to be linked to man's final end, the eternal happiness of heaven, then charity must also be a virtue of the active life. Unlike the charity of the contemplative life which deals almost exclusively with God, the charity of the active life must be an expression of love of neighbor for the sake of God. In this way, charity leads one into the active life of the moral virtues.

(2) *The Genesis of the Active Life*

The success of human relations depends on the moral character of the individuals involved. Each individual must be aware of the dignity that rational nature and sanctifying grace confer on him and others in order to direct himself according to right reason enlightened by faith. Virtuous action is fittingly human because it is reasonable.

After the infusion of grace and the virtues, the moral structure of man begins with the development of the virtues of temperance and fortitude. These virtues, together with their allied ones, foster the emotional maturity so necessary in human relations. They change the child into a man, channel his desires to fitting things, control his animalistic tendencies, impel him to face the arduous facts of life and to bring the better goods to society.

The emotionally mature and controlled man is ready to live justly with his fellow men. Justice is the special virtue that regulates the interrelations of human society. Together with charity, it gives man the moral power that fosters a sense of personal responsibility and obligation toward others. Justice itself guarantees that others will receive what is rightly due them, so that true social life, worthily called human, is possible only when the virtue of justice abounds.

The intellectual overlord of the active life is the virtue of prudence. It regulates, directs and puts into action the other moral virtues. It assures that the acts of justice, fortitude and temperance will be reasonable and befitting the eternal destiny of human nature. Prudence is right reason made practical, applied to action. With time and experience the knowledge of how to act virtuously accumulates and is applied to further action.

The moral virtues have been previously mentioned as necessary for the contemplative life and quite obviously they are essential virtues of the active life. There is this difference: in the contemplative life they are dispositions that assist in attaining the goal of contemplation through the removal of those things which would impede it; in the

762 THE CHRISTIAN LIFE

active life they are developed for their own sakes and exercised for the good that comes from them, for man himself and for their impact on his relations with others.

D. Comparison of the Active and Contemplative Life

It is easy to make comparisons in the abstract; in the concrete there is greater difficulty. Circumstances can change the value of goods. A very hungry man would have little trouble in choosing between a meal now and a gift of one thousand dollars promised for next month. There is a greater relative value of a meal now to a hungry man.

When we compare goods, we can consider them in themselves (*absolutely*), or we can consider their relationship to various circumstances (*relatively*). The comparison of the two generic modes of the Christian life will be made in both ways.

(1) Absolute Comparison

In an *absolute* sense, there can be no debate about whether the contemplative life is better than the active life. That which is concerned with the greater object is better than that which has some lower object. Quite obviously the man with a million dollars has a greater sum than the man with ten dollars.

The contemplative life is directly concerned with God, who is the greatest good man can seek; the active life is concerned directly with the love of neighbor and the problems connected thereto. Mary was content with Christ, the Son of God, and she asked for no more, for she was completely satisfied; Martha had less satisfaction and more trouble because her direct interests, although good, left much to be desired.

(2) Relative Comparison

Could all Christians desert the world and enter the cloister to live a contemplative life? They could, but human life would soon disappear. Under God's providence it seems that he wants the world to continue and that he will command when it will cease. God gave a general command to the human race to enter the state of matrimony when he said to Adam and Eve, "Increase and multiply and fill the earth . . ." (Gen. 1:28). Any exceptions to this general command God provides for by special vocations.

The call to the active life of the moral virtues, which is love of neighbor in action, is according to God's designs and therefore good. Absolutely, it will rank below the contemplative life, but *relatively* its perfection will depend on the intention of him who enters it and how well he fulfills its obligations. An individual who has considered his own particular temperament, talents and graces and chooses the active life should do so because he deems it a better way of life for him to save his soul. What is absolutely better would not be better in this individual case.

Concretely, married life, although a special state of life, belongs to the active life. Every good career in the world can be an expression of the active life. The men and women of the medical profession who justly fulfill their obligations to their patients can add up merit in heaven. The teacher who leads his students along the path of knowledge can, by the same actions, be stepping along the road to heaven. The labor leader who honestly serves the men of his union can be working out his salvation by such service. The clerk in the store, the TV repairman, the stenographer—all perform services for others, and for them they can be rewarded by God in heaven.

The point so often missed in life is that all of man's daily actions are moving him to or away from his final goal. It does not matter whether these actions belong to the professional world, the classroom, the labor union, the supermarket, the neighborhood, the home. All such actions are worthy of merit or blame before God. Our Lord illustrated this in one of his parables:

> Lord, when did we see thee hungry, and fed thee; or thirsty, and give thee drink? And when did we see thee a stranger, and take thee in; or naked, and clothe thee? Or when did we see thee sick, or in prison, and come to thee? And answering the king will say to them, "Amen, I say to thee, as long as you did it for one of these, the least of my brethren, you did it for me."[11]

[11]Matt. 25:37-40.

Our Lord here mentions some of the extremes in social action but he does not intend to exclude those of immediate responsibility as also being done for him. He has said elsewhere, "If you love me, keep my commandments" (John 14:15). The fourth to the tenth commandments deal with personal discipline and immediate social responsibility. These commandments encompass the active life of parental responsibility and childhood's obligations, respect for the fundamental rights and goods of others, and the rational control of sexual appetites. No social or personal action escapes accountability to God.

The dignity and importance of the active life can be judged from the contrast afforded by the predominant troubles affecting American life today. Divorces, broken homes, neglected children, the variety of crimes, even among the young, corruption in persons of responsibility, all give testimony of what happens when the active life of virtue is abandoned.

The comparison between the contemplative and the active life is mainly academic; it is helpful information previous to one's final choice of a way of life. Those who seek the active life are intended by God to use it as a method to reach heaven. Perfection of virtue and love of God can and should be developed by it.

E. Summary and Conclusion

We have called these two general ways of the Christian life "specialties," for those who follow the one or the other have been called to such by God. God does not look on the mass of human beings in a blurred and confused manner. He has a clear conception of each one and how each fits, individually, into the scheme of his providence. Although you will find many men similarly selected, even for some particular way of the active life, that does not take away from the fact that it is a specialty. God is the one who has made it special for the individual concerned.

The division of these two ways of life is based on the predominance of the type of virtues that are practiced. The active life is not without a degree of contemplation and the contemplative may be called to works of the active life. In fact (although not mentioned in this section, because they will be treated later), there are religious orders which lead a mixed life of contemplation and activity. Every Christian will find the true motivation for his other virtuous activities in his knowledge and love of God. The sacrifices of the married life, for instance, need the motivation of the love of God in order to be sustained.

Natural reasons can be found for the practice of moral virtues, but they are not sufficient to lead one to heaven. Hence, the need of sufficient knowledge and love of God as the motivating forces of the active life.

It should be understood that the contemplative is not drawn to God in any way because he hates mankind, nor is he negatively escaping from the world. As St. Gregory says, "Those who wish to hold the fortress of contemplation must first of all train in the camp of action. Thus after careful study they will learn whether they no longer wrong their neighbor, whether they bear with equanimity the wrongs their neighbors do them. . . ."[12] The contemplative cannot succeed in loving God if he fails to love his neighbor. The perfection of charity consists in the two great commandments, the love of God and the love of neighbor. This is according to the teaching of Christ, who said: "Therefore, if thou art offering thy gift at the altar, and there thou rememberest that thy brother has anything against thee, leave thy gift before the altar and go first to be reconciled to thy brother, and then come and offer thy gift" (Matt. 5:23-24). God asks that one's relationship with his fellow man be rectified before one makes a gift of himself in the contemplative life.

St. Thomas makes the comment that the contemplative who is so filled with the knowledge and love of God that it overflows in the form of preaching and teaching to bring others to this knowledge and love is living a more perfect life than one who only contemplates.[13] This way of life, he says, is an imitation of the life and ministry of Christ.

The purpose of this section is not to engage in academic debate, but rather to show how God provides for all things in his kingdom

[12]*Book of Morals*, Bk. VI, Chap. 37.
[13]*Summa*, III, q. 40, a. 1, ad 2.

on earth. The two ways are not opposed as rivals but are complementary to the Christian way of life. One can lead into the other, one can overflow into the other. If it is chiefly the *seeds* of contemplation that we find in a predominantly active life, and its *fruits* in the predominantly contemplative life, both have their place in the garden of Christian virtue.

3. THE STATE OF PERFECTION

A. Introduction

After considering the virtues which pertain to men in every condition of life, and placing emphasis upon certain virtues which divide the virtuous life into the contemplative and active, we proceed to a consideration of the status of certain members of the Church.

Before proceeding we must explain an omission. In a treatment of the different classes of members in the Church, there is no need to bring it to too great a refinement. Among the laity there are professional people, laborers, farmers, clerks, mechanics and a long list of others. These are natural pursuits and are so ranked by human society but they have no special standing as such in the life of the Church. Some may have special ethical problems, like the members of the medical profession, but the special problems do not give one a special status in the Church. The teacher, the nurse, the bricklayer, the salesman have various responsibilities in their careers and jobs, but all of these responsibilities have reference to the keeping of the commandments and the exercise of appropriate virtues. As the lawyer leaves his office and forgets his legal cases for the day, or the electrician closes his tool-kit after a day's work, they do not step out into another way of the virtuous life; basically it is the same pursuit of the goal of everlasting happiness. The members of the laity, all day—at home, at work, at recreation—follow the way of the commandments and of virtue. This does not give one special status in the Church. This is the fundamental way for all.

The division of the activities of its members into active and contemplative does not place these members in different states. Active or contemplative members may be found in any of the special states of life in the Church.

To have status in the Church, that is, to be in a special state of life, is, by its very definition, something different from being active or contemplative. The state of a person is *a condition which is connatural, not easily movable and which begets certain obligations which bind him.*

To be in a state of life demands an immobility and stability based on its very nature. Thus matters that easily change or are extrinsic to man do not constitute a state among men. To be well or sick is more a temporary condition than a state, for it can change. To be elected a senator of the United States is an honor, but it does not place the senator in a special state of life, since it is an honor extrinsic to a man and in the following election the title may pass to another. Up to about one hundred years ago in our country ways of life were followed which are examples of different states of life: the state of freedom and the state of slavery, wherein one was his own master, and the other subject to a master. The free man was bound by his condition to the obligations of liberty, the slave to the obligations of servitude.

In the Church there are states differing in degrees of perfection with correspondingly different duties, but this diversity in no way affects the unity of the Church. It is a variety which serves to make known the perfection, the beauty and the activities of the Church, the Mystical Body of Christ unified by the bonds of faith, charity and mutual service. These diversified states will be considered in general in this section, in particular in the section to follow.

B. The State of Perfection in General

Our Lord said to all who follow him: "You therefore are to be perfect, even as your heavenly Father is perfect" (Matt. 5:48). The theologians of the Church teach that bishops and religious are perfect, but it is quite obvious, both from the present condition of the Church and from its past history, that not everyone is called to be a bishop or a religious in order to achieve the perfection of which Christ spoke.

The directive to be perfect given by our Lord to his followers was not limited; it was given to all, to you and me. This directive does not differentiate one group from another; hence it does not constitute a special objective state in the Church. Christian perfection will be the internal, subjective condition of a man in relation to God, and how perfect he is only God can judge.

(1) The Primacy of Charity

This subjective perfection consists in being united to God who is the ultimate end of man, for a thing is perfect when it attains its end or goal and lacks nothing it should have. When Picasso laid aside his brush on the completion of his painting, he had brought to perfection his work of art. It was not that he had no more work to do, only that he had put into his painting all he wanted to, and nothing was lacking that he intended. The goal of his work had been attained, and in that sense he was finished; the end, the *finis*, had been reached, perfection had been attained.

When a man attains God there is no greater good left for him. He has attained that for which he has been created; in beatitude achieved he gives that glory to God for which he was brought forth from nothingness and redeemed from the abyss of sin by the blood of Jesus Christ. This is his highest perfection.

On the journey to everlasting life in heaven, the union with God comes from charity or love of God. The Scriptures teach us that "God is love, and he who abides in love abides in God, and God in him" (I John 4:16). St. Paul adds the information that "above all these things have charity, which is the bond of perfection" (Gal. 3:14). The principal virtue of the Christian life is charity, the root of perfection. This does not destroy the importance of the other virtues, it merely properly subordinates them to the primary virtue of love of God in the work of perfection.

If there should arise any doubt as to how one is to exercise charity, the problem has been clarified by our Lord: "If you love me, keep my commandments" (John 14:15). Christ summed up all the commandments in two, the love of God and the love of neighbor.[14] The commandments other than the precepts of charity are directed by charity to its end. They remove things incompatible with charity.

The keeping of the commandments is the means by which we express our love for God; thus it is the basic element of Christian perfection. It is important that this be noted well, for there can be no true perfection in the Christian life without the essential element of charity.

(2) Degrees of Perfection

Although charity is perfection because it prefers God above all else (and so there is only one *kind* of charity), it nonetheless admits of degrees. The lowest degree is present when nothing is loved more than God, or contrary to God, or equally with God. This lowest degree of charity is a matter of grave precept for all Christians—indeed, for all men—without exception. But charity is love, perfect love, and love can grow and increase, deepen and intensify; and man's love of God can burn higher and higher, even to the extent of directing all of his energies so exclusively to love of God as to abandon everything, even lawful goods, that would hold one back from union with him. Between this perfect degree of charity and the minimum level on which beginners in the life of the spirit operate, lies the middle state of those lovers of God who are progressing in the school of divine love, through the increasing illumination of God's grace, to perfect union with him. All—beginners, proficients, the perfect—enjoy the freedom of the children of God from the slavery of sin: "where the spirit of the Lord is, there is freedom" (II Cor. 3:17).

The perfection of charity is the way of Christian life for all, for then one's love for God and neighbor will remove his affections from all that is contrary to charity, such as mortal sin—and this is necessary for salvation. Through the powerful workings of the grace of Christ, the Christian has been freed from the inclination to sin so as to serve exclusively the justice of God. This is a state of true freedom, as contrasted with the state of the sinner, slave of his pas-

[14]Cf. Matt. 22:36-40; Mark 12:28-34; Luke 10:25-28.

sions, his habits, his evil acts, and the distorted inclination of his will toward sin.

But the spiritual freedom of Christian perfection does not constitute a *state* of perfection as understood by the Church. This fact in no way takes away from the primary importance of the general state of the perfection of charity; but by definition it is subjective and internal, whereas the states of the Church must have elements which are objective and external.

4. THE STATES OF PERFECTION IN THE CHURCH

State has been defined as a condition of a person which is connatural and not easily movable and begets certain obligations which bind him. To be in a state in the Church the condition must be *externally recognizable,* so that the Christian's relation to the Church can be known. In order to be connatural it must be *something that pertains to perfection,* i.e., to the works of Christian charity. It must not be easily movable, it must have stability and permanence; this note will be indicated *by a certain solemnity on one's entrance into a state.* Finally, one is bound by strict obligation to that which pertains to his state. An ecclesiastical state, therefore, is one in which a person binds himself with external solemnity, in perpetuity and under obligation to certain works of perfection in the Church.

The conditions of this definition are fulfilled in two groups of the Church, bishops and religious. By publicly professing their vows religious bind themselves to refrain from worldly affairs (which otherwise would be lawful for them), in order to give themselves more completely to God, for perfection consists in union with God. Likewise bishops bind themselves to things pertaining to perfection when they take up the pastoral duty of their dioceses; this is externally indicated by the public, solemn ceremonies of their consecration. Both states will be considered more fully below.

One final thing to note: when a distinction is made between being perfect but not in a state of perfection (or, conversely, of being in a state of perfection but not being perfect), the distinction is between the perfection produced by charity, which is personal, and the state of perfection, which is objective and external, i.e., being a bishop or a religious. A lay person who has supernatural charity and is keeping the commandments has personal perfection but is not in a state of perfection.

A. The Episcopacy

There is a certain amount of awe awakened in people when a bishop is present in a parish to confer confirmation, or at the time of graduation. His right to be present is sensed; he is not considered an intruder. For by the perfection of his state and office he is the pastor or chief shepherd of his entire diocese, subject only to the pope. His is the lofty but heavy responsibility of bringing the flock entrusted to him by Christ to the perfection of charity: "Feed my lambs," our Lord commands him, as he once commanded Peter (John 21:15-17). To bring others to perfection one must already possess a perfection of love of God and of man like that of St. Peter.

Bishops are the successors of the apostles and by divine institution are placed over particular churches, e.g., dioceses, which they govern *with ordinary jurisdiction* under the authority of the pope. Their appointment comes from the Holy See.

"Ordinary jurisdiction" may appear to be a rather weak phrase because of the modern meaning given to the term "ordinary." In the Church's positive legislation, however, it has an important significance: it defines the gauge of authority which is attached to an office in a strict sense, and attached to that office by law.[15] The bishop, by reason of his office, has full and complete authority within his diocese in those matters set down by ecclesiastical law and is subject to no one save the pope. So restricted and specific is the legal meaning of the term "ordinary jurisdiction," that the bishop is often referred to as the Ordinary of the diocese, indicating the one who has power of office and law.

(1) The Power of the Episcopacy

The bishop has the right and duty to govern his diocese both in temporal and spiritual matters, with legislative, judicial and coercive

[15]Canons 329-450 of the Code of Canon Law deal with bishops and the government of dioceses.

power. In governing his diocese he must see to the observance of the laws of the Church, prevent abuses, safeguard the purity of faith and morals and promote Catholic education. He is the official preacher of the diocese; frequently he will exercise this office of the apostles by means of his letters, read in church or printed in the diocesan paper. No one has more right to communicate with the people by word, whether written or spoken, than the bishop; so properly and exclusively is his right and power in preaching that no one of the secular or religious clergy (except the pastors he has appointed) may preach publicly in his diocese without his permission.

As guardian of faith and morals in his diocese, he is first teacher of these matters, and although infallibility belongs to the pope, he teaches with the full authority of his office, in dependence, of course, on the supreme *magisterium* of the Church. He is, by office, the guardian of education in his diocese. Parochial schools and diocesan high schools and colleges are under his complete authority. In schools established by religious groups (e.g., high schools and colleges), he has the duty of seeing that nothing is taught or done which is contrary to faith and morals. He may make canonical visitation of all schools and institutions concerned with doctrinal and moral training, with the exception of a few exempted by law or custom.

The sacramental life of his diocese is completely in his hands. This does not take away from a pastor the ordinary power he has within his own parish to baptize, hear confessions, witness marriages, anoint the dying, and (under special circumstances) to confirm. The appointment of the pastor has come from the bishop in order to carry on these sacramental functions. Other priests who hear the confessions of the laity or of sisters do so in virtue of faculties granted by the bishop.

The bishop alone is the ordinary minister of the sacrament of holy orders. It is his special concern to provide priests for his diocese by founding a seminary, by collecting money in his diocese for its support, by appointing priests to direct and teach in the seminary, and by providing for the special education of those who undertake such responsibilities. His concern does not stop with the preparation of candidates for the priesthood but continues after their ordination. For the bishop is not pastor only of the laity but of the diocesan clergy as well. He is the shepherd of all.

(2) The Perfection of the Episcopacy

The state of perfection of the bishop is without equal in the Mystical Body. With the full solemnity of the Church he is consecrated to fulfill his role as a shepherd of his diocese, to guide all in the path of salvation. By his office he has power to exercise a complete variety of sacred duties, and by his elevation to the bishopric he has been raised to the highest rank of sacred orders. Raised up by God to watch over the others, he enters a *state*: here perfection of life is not something to be achieved but a necessary prerequisite.[16] For out of the abundance of the bishops' love for God arises the proof of that love, their pastoral care for the spiritual welfare of their flock.

This is a state, then, worthy of all respect. For those who are selected for it, a state weighted with heavy responsibilities, accepted with humility at the command of one's superior out of love for one's neighbor. The bishops are the modern apostles and, like the apostles, they are by their state closest to Christ in the work of salvation of the people. "Let the presbyters who rule well," St. Paul admonishes, "be held worthy of double honors" (I Tim. 5:17).

B. The Priesthood

(1) Its Nature

We take up the consideration of the priesthood in this section in order to determine whether it is a state of perfection or not, what perfection belongs to it, and to analyze the vocation to the priesthood. We have already pointed out that the two states of perfection in the Church are the episcopacy and the religious state; the priesthood, as such, is not a state of perfection. Yet because of the relationship of the priest in his dignity and ministry to the bishop, it seems proper

[16]Cf. St. Thomas, *Summa*, II-II, q. 185, a. 1, ad 2.

to consider the priesthood here. As St. Thomas says, "We should say that [priests] have an office pertaining to perfection rather than that they attain the state of perfection."[17]

Although the priesthood is eliminated as a state *of perfection*, this does not in any way derogate from the holiness and dignity of the priesthood. These qualities can be considered under three aspects, as the priesthood is a **state**, an **order** and an **office**.

1. **The priesthood as a state.** As a state, the priesthood must be divided into diocesan clergy and religious clergy. The priesthood of both is the same, for both receive the same sacrament. (This is evidenced by the fact that, on many occasions, the bishop ordains together the candidates of his diocese and members of religious orders.) While their priesthood is exactly the same, the priest of a diocese does not belong to a state of perfection; but a priest who is also a religious by his state makes a pledge of his whole life, by reason of his vows, to the quest of perfection. The diocesan priest does not have the same technical obligation by reason of vow. As long as they are members of a diocese, to be sure, diocesan clergy must promise obedience to their bishop and, in the Western Church, must take a solemn vow of chastity when they are ordained to the subdeaconate. But the *state* of a diocesan priest, in an objective sense, is "secular" and that of a priest with vows is "religious." Yet while not obliged by divine law to observe the evangelical counsels, it would be erroneous to think—as the present pontiff has pointed out—"that the secular priest might be called to a perfection less than that of the religious."[18]

2. **The priesthood as an order.** The above does not essentially touch the dignity of the priesthood; it is extrinsic to the priesthood that it be diocesan or religious. The dignity of the priesthood comes from the reception of the sacrament by which one receives this sacred order. The effects this sacrament produces in its recipient are what give this sacred order its dignity.

The priesthood of the Catholic Church is a share in the priesthood of Christ, who is the priest, in a pre-eminent degree, of the Church

[17]*Summa*, II-II, q. 184, a. 6, ad 3.
[18]Pope John XXIII, encyclical *Sacerdotii Nostri Primordia* (From the Beginning of Our Priesthood), July, 1959.

that he founded. Pope Pius XI, in his encyclical on the priesthood, wrote:

> The Apostle of the Gentiles thus perfectly sums up what may be said of the greatness, the dignity and the duty of the Christian priesthood: "*Sic nos existimet homo ut ministros Christi et mysteriorum Dei* —let a man so account us as the servants of Christ and the stewards of the mysteries of God" (I Cor. 4:1). The priest is the minister of Christ, an instrument, that is to say, in the hands of the divine Redeemer. He continues the work of redemption in all its world-embracing universality and divine efficacy, that work that wrought so marvelous a transformation in the world. Thus the priest, as is said with good reasons, is "another Christ"; for in some way, he is himself a continuation of Christ. "As the Father has sent me, I also send you" (John 20:21), is spoken to the priest, and hence the priest, like Christ, continues to give "glory to God in the highest; and on earth peace among men of good will" (Luke 2:14).[19]

Because the priesthood conforms a man to Christ in a special way and obliges him to the ministry of Christ, the priest must be holy at the time of his reception of the priesthood and strive for still greater holiness: to do the work of Christ he must be Christlike. For the priest is "appointed for men in the things pertaining to God" (Heb. 5:1).

The holiness and perfection of a priest is not that of a state of perfection but that of the personal and internal perfection which is of the essence of the Christian life. His degree of this Christian perfection, however, must be high and ever tend to be higher. Holy orders places the priest on a grade higher than the laity and a corresponding perfection is expected.[20]

A contrast can be made concerning the demand for perfection between a man about to be ordained to the priesthood and one about to enter the religious life. St. Thomas points out that a man who receives a sacred order must have inward perfection in order to exercise the acts of his order worthily. A religious, on the other hand, may have been a serious sinner before entering the religious life; his entrance does not demand perfection, but his state of life obliges

[19]Encyclical *Ad Catholici Sacerdotii* (On the Catholic Priesthood), December 20, 1935.

[20]Cf. encyclical of Pope St. Pius X, *Haerent Animo* (Exhortation to the Catholic Clergy); encyclical of Pius XI, *Ad Catholici Sacerdotii;* St. Thomas, *Supplement*, q. 35, a. 1, ad 3; Canon 124.

him henceforth to strive to be more perfect: the goal of his religious perfection is to tend toward ever greater perfection. St. Thomas states: "Holy orders demands holiness as a prerequisite, whereas the religious state is a school for the attainment of holiness. Hence the burden of orders should be laid on [men] when they are already seasoned with holiness, whereas the burden of religion seasons [men] by drawing out the damp of vice."[21]

He explains this further:

> The pre-eminence of order is more excellent from the point of view of dignity, since by holy orders a man is appointed to the most august ministry of serving Christ himself in the sacrament of the altar. For this requires a greater inward holiness than that which is necessary for the religious state. Hence, other things being equal, a cleric who is in holy orders sins more grievously if he does something contrary to holiness than a religious who is not in holy orders.[22]

3. The office of the priesthood. The sacred order of the priesthood has a relationship to an office or ministry. Each of the minor and major orders brings the recipient a grade of the sacred powers of the Church. The grade and office of the priesthood is not primarily concerned with the advantage of the one who receives it; it is an office for the sake of others. St. Paul says, "For every high priest taken from among men is appointed for men in the things pertaining to God, that he may offer gifts and sacrifices for sins" (Heb. 5:1).

The activity or ministry of the priest demands holiness both in an objective and subjective sense. The means and methods by which a priest is to help people save their souls are according to the way of Christ, the Son of God. Christ set the objective pattern of the ministry of the priest and because of that it is a holy ministry. By his death on the cross he obtained salvation for all men, and the graces sufficient for mankind. The priest is to be the instrument through whom the priesthood of Christ continuously works. As Christ in his priesthood was a mediator between God and man, so is the human priest. Like Christ, especially when offering Mass, the priest from his middle position brings God to the people and the people to God;

[21]*Summa*, II-II, q. 189, a. 1, ad 3.
[22]*Ibid.*, q. 184, a. 8.

this is accomplished in union with Christ, to whom his priesthood conjoins him as an instrument. In the other sacraments also the priest becomes the instrument of Christ in dispensing other spiritual gifts. In his teaching and instruction to the people it should be the word of God and the teaching and example of Christ that he is imparting to the people to bring them to eternal salvation.

The ministry of the priesthood has a holy objectivity which comes from Christ himself independently of the priest's personal qualities. Even serious sin on the part of the priest cannot destroy the efficacy of the priestly ministry; he can offer a true sacrifice to God, absolutely absolve someone from his sins, prepare the dying for their appearance before God, and administer all the other sacraments he is capable of performing by his office. If he is in serious sin, however, he sullies his sacred ministry, his priesthood and himself. He mocks Christ, the priest.

In a subjective sense, the ministry of the priest should flow from his personal holiness, from his love of God, from a high degree of charity. For a priest, as an instrument of Christ, is an intelligent and voluntary instrument; his ministry should flow from the graces that perfect those special human powers. Since a priest deals with the things that pertain to God, then, personally, he should first be filled with a knowledge and love of God himself, so that his ministry becomes not a mechanical fulfillment of an office, but an overflow of that knowledge and love. Since his ministry in the care of souls is an activity, he must be classed with that group in the Church which leads an active life; but for his personal sanctity as a priest, he must also live, to the degree possible to him, the contemplative life.

Pope St. Pius X points out that the master and exemplar of all sanctity is Christ, and that since even the laity are to follow his virtuous example, it is more incumbent on the priest to do so. He urges the priest to be filled with a spirit of self-abnegation so that he will not fall victim to the various emotional desires and weaknesses that beset men; to cultivate sanctity of life and morals, which he equates with the supereminent knowledge of Jesus Christ; to cultivate a habit of prayer and to devote a certain period of time each day to meditation upon things eternal; to be faithful to spiritual reading.[23] What St. Pius X recommends are those preparatory steps which lead to a more perfect degree of contemplation, the indispensable source of the priest's apostolic activities.

The priest, then, is not a member of an objective state of perfection, but he does pertain to the state of the bishop, under whom he exercises and shares his ministry. His ministry is holy and dignified for it is a continuation of the ministry of Christ. The holy orders he receives places him on an elevated plane. His ministry demands personal perfection, and his elevated place over the laity demands a greater grade of the perfection of charity. The priest must be holy and exercise that holiness in the fulfillment of his office.

(2) The Vocation to the Priesthood

An appreciation of the vocation and office of the priest—both on the part of young men who are capable of being called to this life and on the part of the laity for whom the priesthood was established—requires a revival of the true Christian spirit. The eternal spirit of Christ will show up the errors and weaknesses of the modern day, so inimical to his sacred priesthood.

Since the priesthood is concerned with the things that pertain to God, a just estimate of its value and significance is dependent upon a revivification of the dynamic theological virtues of faith, hope and charity. They help us to share in the truth, strength and love of God, and to live accordingly, and thus to appreciate the redemptive sacrifice of Christ, the Son of God, our dependence on that sacrifice, and our opportunity to avail ourselves of the continuing effects of that sacrifice through the priesthood established by Christ. A weakness in the appreciation of the priesthood is always and equally a sign of a weakness in man's relationship with God and his divine Son.

As faith enlightens us to the fact that man's final end is God, so it also informs us that original and personal sin prevent man's arrival at that goal. Although Christ by his death on the cross destroyed sin, he did not destroy man's ability to commit sin; his sacrifice obtains the graces by which man can avoid sin, or, if he unfortunately falls,

[23]Cf. the encyclical *Haerent Animo* (Exhortation to the Catholic Clergy).

graces by which to arise again. By his teaching and example the Son of man showed that a program of self-discipline is the best remedy for the weakness of will and the unruliness of emotion left in us as effects of original sin. To all who wished to follow him to the goal of eternal happiness Christ gave this directive: "If anyone wishes to come after me, let him deny himself" (Matt. 16:24).

This program of self-denial to strengthen man to overcome his weakness of will and the unruliness of his emotions is especially expressed in the development of the moral virtues of fortitude and temperance. These two virtues effect the emotional maturity so necessary for man to live according to reason, the key-note of his nature, the substructure of his supernatural perfection. Those who have the responsibility to train and educate children, under God's providence, must prudently guide the souls entrusted to their care in the development of these two virtues. Parents must exercise the guidance of reason for children too immature to be morally self-determining; to permit them to satisfy their every desire, to have their way in most of the things they want—this is an abdication of responsibility which justly bears the appellation of adult delinquency: it is to educate intemperate, selfish and emotionally stunted human beings. On the contrary, those parents who overprotect their children from the normal problems and difficulties that beset their early and teen years are rearing unto adult life offspring devoid of the virtue of fortitude. Study and homework, no doubt difficult for a child (to say nothing of the college student), can be the matter of fortitude when a child is encouraged to face the difficulty, even when his parents must help. Or it can become matter for the viciousness of softness in the face of difficulty, when a child out of human sympathy is permitted to avoid it. In the foreseeable future, yours, as parents or grown-ups, may be the choice.

Many a vocation to the priesthood is not offered by God because a child in his formative years was permitted to grow up with an ever-engulfing wave of vices—of selfishness, unreasonable self-gratification, softness, lack of courage. Even if the vocation is offered the recipient may be too wrapped up in himself to answer it; or, if he does answer it, often too weak to persevere. What nobility is there

in this situation? And where does the fault lie? With the unrespon-
sive adolescent? With God?

A great perfection of virtue, complete eradication of every human
weakness, is not demanded of the candidate for the priesthood. The
normal candidate as he starts on his career leading to ordination
must be one who has sufficiently exercised the theological virtues
of faith, hope and charity. His ambition, as he looks about at the
legitimate goods offered by the world, must be a life dedicated to
God, his greatest good; he must know and love God so much that he
prefers him to other things. This, to be sure, in the face of the values
of this world, demands a spirit of generosity and self-sacrifice. The
emotional discipline of temperance helps make this possible; in the
discipline of his desires and consequent joys, he can ignore lower
for higher goods, and find greater satisfaction in them. Above this,
however, those called by God must have courage and its companions
of patience and perseverance, for the task of preparation is long and
the goal is high, and the future is filled with difficulties, the normal
difficulties of human achievement of a goal so far beyond merely
human means.

The vocation to the priesthood comes only from God. St. Paul
tells us: "No man takes the honor to himself; he takes it who is
called by God, as Aaron was" (Heb. 5:4). The call is not spectacular
in most cases: no angel descends with flaming sword, no vision or
revelation takes place. But God does not ordinarily call those who are
deficient in love of him; the absence of normal Christian virtues is almost a certain sign of divine disapproval, not of the predilection which
would select one for so lofty a ministry of God's love. Sometimes
the presence of this divine invitation may not be perceived by the
one whom God has chosen; but it may be noticed, and clearly so, by
the priest who has charge of him, his parish priest, the spiritual director of his school, a personal friend, or anyone sensitive to the inspirations of the spirit. It should not be forgotten that no one is a
good judge in his own cause.

The vocation to the priesthood is a holy one. It is a call to be a
continuation of the redemptive work of Christ, to be a minister in

helping others to the final goal of life. Future candidates best develop in an atmosphere that results from the vigorous presence of the activities of the virtuous gifts of God, principal among them the theological virtues of faith, hope and charity. The future candidate from early boyhood must be encouraged and directed to a prudent and reasonable degree of self-discipline of his emotional life, so that he does not grow up self-centered and soft. This is not, however, a special training for the priesthood; this is the normal development for every Christian. With this normal development, then God can offer the grace of the priesthood to those whom he chooses. Then the chances are more than good that God's call will be heard, that this Christian young man will heed the gentle inspiration of the Spirit, and in charity consider generously the plight of the rest of us. Like Samuel, he must say, in humble obedience: "Here am I: for thou didst call me" (I Kings 3:1-14). If he does not, it is not the fault of God.

Pope John XXIII has pointed out our conclusion:

> Today, Christians expect much of the priest. They wish to see in him— in a world where power of money, seduction of the senses and prestige of technical knowledge triumph—a testimony of the invisible God, a man of faith forgetful of himself and full of charity.
>
> May such Christians know that they can have great influence on the loyalty of their priests to this ideal, by means of religious respect for their priestly character, by a more accurate understanding of their pastoral duties and their difficulties, and by a more active collaboration in their apostolate.[24]

C. The Religious Life

(1) Its Nature

The **religious state** is *a fixed or stable manner of life in which the members live a common life together, observing not only the commandments but also the evangelical counsels. To this common life of perfection in the observance of the counsels recommended by Christ they bind themselves by the vows of poverty, chastity and*

[24]Encyclical *Sacerdotii Nostri Primordia.*

obedience.[25] A religious society, congregation or order is one in which this special evangelical life of the counsels is realized under the guide of a rule and constitutions and the approval of the legitimate ecclesiastical authority.[26]

The religious state is a state of perfection because with the steadfastness assured by vow it aims at the perfection of charity. The vows are taken in a solemn, public manner to God through a superior designated by the rule of the society, so that the whole Church can affirm the candidate's consecration to the pursuit of perfection.[27]

The vows are the distinguishing mark of the religious life, for they embrace the total giving of one's self to God—truly a holocaust, an offering which wholly consumes the victim offered—in which religious perfection consists. Between Christian perfection and the perfection of religious, therefore, there is a significant difference. The religious is striving for Christian perfection, to be sure: the love of God. His is the aim of all who are seeking the eternal happiness of heaven, his also are the basic means of observing the commandments, by which we fulfill the general precept of the love of God and of neighbor. Keeping the commandments is necessary for all Christians, for their violation is a direct offense against almighty God; by mortal sin, one chooses a finite thing to replace God as the greatest good. With mortal sin Christian perfection is utterly incompatible: loss of the divine life which is grace necessarily involves the loss of the divine love which is charity, principle of union with God. All Christians must maintain this essential element of perfection, the love which is exercised in the keeping of the commandments.

The religious by freely taking his vows binds himself to further obligations to insure his love for God. He solemnly makes profession to follow the counsels of our Lord, which he offered as means to a greater perfection and love of God. When a certain young man came to our Lord to get his advice about how to gain eternal life, he was told to keep the commandments. The young man replied, "All these I

[25]This is the official definition of the religious life given by the Code of Canon Law, Can. 487.

[26]Cf. Can. 488.

[27]It should be recalled that vows are acts of the virtue of religion, a means of offering worship to God; cf. *supra*, 584-587.

have kept; what is yet wanting to me?" Jesus said to him, "If thou wilt be perfect, go, sell what thou hast, and give to the poor, and thou shalt have treasure in heaven; and come follow me" (Matt. 19:20-22). But when the young man heard the saying, he went away sad, for he had great possessions.

Our Lord did not condemn the young man because he had great material wealth; he pointed out that if he wanted to be more perfect he should free himself of it, so that he could follow Christ without the encumbrance of material concern. A religious does this. He gives up his right to legitimate things which may interfere and be a hindrance to the greater love of God.

(2) The Vows of Religion

A religious follows the counsels of our Lord by taking the vows of poverty, chastity and obedience. This poverty is voluntary; in itself poverty is an evil. In the religious life the vow of poverty is taken to free one from the natural inclination to possess material things as one's own or to use as one's own, in order that one may have God as his greatest possession. Marriage is itself a good, but its obligations are absorbing of one's time, energy, interest and love. In order to free himself of the restrictions of earthly love, the religious takes the vow of chastity so that his time and energies may be absorbed exclusively in the love of God, and thence may flow unrestrictedly to love of neighbor.

Freedom of the will is a special privilege from God; yet the religious gives it up by the vow of obedience, to free himself from the dangers that arise from the abuse of free will.

Earthly possessions are necessary especially for the active life, but they also can be troublesome; their care is time-consuming, the desire to possess them can increase without limitation, and for some, earthly riches become a means to commit other sins. St. Matthew said in his gospel: "But the care of this world and the deceitfulness of riches choke the word [of God] and it is made fruitless" (Matt. 13:22). The religious voluntarily vows poverty to be free of material cares so that, in keeping nothing for himself, he can find his satisfaction in God.

Marriage is good and Christ raised it to the dignity of a sacrament. But it is a state which hinders the more perfect love of God. The very sexual acts of marriage, although good and according to the designs of God, by their nature diminish the use of reason and so withdraw one's mind from the intellectual plane of God. The care of a home, the providing of necessities, and human love are immediate concerns of the married state and thus prevent the direct absorption in the love of God. As St. Paul says: "He who is unmarried is concerned about the things of the Lord, how he may please God: whereas he who is married is concerned about the things of the world, how he may please his wife; and he is divided. And the unmarried woman and virgin thinks about the things of the Lord, that she may be holy in body and spirit" (I Cor. 7:32-34). For this reason the religious takes the vow of chastity, to give up a lesser love for the greater love of God.

(3) The Way of Obedience

The gift of free will which God so generously gave to man is a gift that man, particularly in the state of fallen nature, can abuse. God's intention is that man should always seek a true good, which is the object of his will. Man, due to ignorance or to the strength of his passions or the tendency to evil arising from sin, can allow his will, already weakened by original sin, to become further weakened.

The will is the power which we use when we obey or disobey. The need for obedience does not find its origin in the religious life; it is one of the most important virtues of the Christian life, a virtue for all. The example and teaching of Christ can well be summed up, not only as an act of love, but also of obedience: "And appearing in the form of man, he humbled himself, becoming obedient to death, even to the death of the cross" (Phil. 2:8). Christ said of his mission, "My food is to do the will of him who sent me, to accomplish his work" (John 4:34). To do the will of a superior is to obey. This is the way that leads to eternal salvation, a fact that our Lord laid particular stress on: "He who does the will of my Father in heaven shall enter the kingdom of heaven" (Matt. 7:21).

The necessity of obedience knows no exception in the Christian life; all are to obey God, and from this arises the primary obligation of children to obey their parents, of subjects to obey their proper superiors. Such an arrangement of authority and its subjects is not intended as the enslavement of the subject and the arbitrary exaltation of authority. Those who have a right to be obeyed have the grave obligation to use their authority to guide those subject to them to the goal for which their authority exists. For example, we obey the pope, the vicar of Christ, because his directives lead us to eternal salvation. Parents' commands should be thoughtful directives for their children to supply for their lack of developed reason and controlled passions, and their limited experience.

In the light of the rebelliousness of man's will, and the importance of obedience in the way of salvation, the vow of obedience becomes a bulwark against man's weakness and a stabilizing influence in preserving him in the path of doing the will of God. True, the religious extends the area of obedience to include many things not embraced by the obligations of the ordinary Christian; but the greater exercise of the virtue demanded by the vow guarantees a more ready obedience to the commands of God.

The final reason for the vow of obedience—and this the most important reason for the one who dedicates himself to God in the religious life—is the completion of the sacrifice of self that the religious makes to God. By poverty he makes a sacrifice of earthly goods which are outside himself; by chastity he makes a sacrifice of something that pertains to the body; there remains the last part of the sacrifice, a sacrifice of something that pertains to his higher nature, and this is the sacrifice of his own will, which completes and perfects his offering of self. Because the vow of obedience is a sacrifice of will, it is the most important of the vows and most in conformity with the perfection of Christ.

(4) The Value of Vows

Finally, an error about the vows that has cropped up intermittently throughout the history of religious life must be corrected.

The error is that it is better and more perfect to do something for God without a vow than with one, because one does it freely. First of all, the vows do not destroy man's freedom; if they did they would destroy a property of his will, and reduce him from the dignity of human nature to the level of an animal without freedom. The vows, on the contrary, actually add merit to man's acts. The necessity that results from a vow has itself been willed by the religious, and every time he obeys he freely wills to do so.

There are three points which make an act more praiseworthy under a vow than without a vow: 1) the vow is an act of the virtue of religion, the chief of the moral virtues; 2) he that vows something and does it, offers to God not only a good act but also the power from which the good act came, while without the vow one offers only the good act (it is like an act of generosity, when two men with equal amounts in their wallets offer a gift: one offers something from his wallet, but the more generous offers the wallet with all its contents, which takes care of now and the future); and 3) the man with vows fixes his will on a good immovably, and this stability belongs to the perfection of virtue; the one without vows always retains his will to do and act when and if he pleases.

(5) Vocation to the Religious Life

Unlike the priesthood, the religious life, although a state of perfection, does not require personal perfection on entrance. It is *a school of perfection,* and its aim, like that of all schools, is gradual movement toward the goal of the school. Those who have been living a good life and those whose past life has been marked by sin, provided other requirements are met, are both possible candidates for the religious life.

This does not mean that proper remote preparation is unnecessary. Those who have lived a life of innocence must have a spirit of generosity in order to offer their lives to God and to seek the greater perfection that the religious life offers. The reformed sinner must be truly reformed and have been making sincere efforts to remain in the love of God.

As regards entering the religious life, St. Thomas points out that three things should be considered:

First, it is a certainty that entrance into the religious life is a greater good, and to doubt this is to disparage Christ who gave this counsel. One who enters the religious life must have this intellectual conviction, for a right intention must be based on this consideration. To seek something other than this greater good is a wrong understanding of the life of the vows.

Secondly, one entering must consider his spiritual and physical and emotional strength. As regards spiritual strength, the one entering should not trust in his own power but in the assistance almighty God can give him; this is the virtue of hope. As regards his physical and emotional strength, his superiors will make the judgment.

Lastly, one should investigate the type of religious community that suits his abilities and the immediate aim he has in mind in dedicating his life to God.[28]

Once the candidate enters, he should look on his dedication to God as an extraordinary good for him, and not look back to the allurements of the things he has left, his home, his friends, his material goods and worldly possibilities. To the young man who said, "I will follow thee, Lord; but let me first bid farewell to those at home," our Lord gave the admonition: "No one, having put his hand to the plow and looking back, is fit for the kingdom of God" (Luke 9:62). This does not mean that some, even those who enter with the greatest sincerity and with the best intention, may not find sufficient reason for leaving. After sufficient trial and on the scrutiny of their superiors, there may be some who are discovered to lack the qualities —whether physical, emotional, intellectual or moral—necessary for that type of religious life or for the religious life in general. There are others who discover that they are not strong enough for the invitation of our Lord, "Let him accept it who can" (Matt. 19:12); for them the serious advice of St. Paul may be far more to the point: "It is better to marry than to burn" (I Cor. 7:9).

---

[28]Cf. *Summa,* II-II, q. 189, a. 10.

The true failures are those who enter religion but do not give themselves completely to God. They are the split personalities of the religious life who keep one foot in the world of material goods, bodily goods and self-will, while the other foot is in the religious life. If they do not leave completely but remain half in the life, they are its unhappy members, unhappy in seeing the things of the world they do not possess, but more unhappy in realizing that they do not possess the total dedication to God which is proper to a religious.

(6) The Kinds of Religious Life

God in his providence has provided a variety of religious ways of life. The variety comes from the aim, and not from the vows, for all religious must be bound by the evangelical cousels of poverty, chastity and obedience. Some religious groups have risen only for a time to meet some particular need in the Church, and when the need disappeared the institute disappeared too. With new needs, new groups arise.

Although God reserves the priesthood for the male sex, he offers the religious life to both sexes. Among both, you will find some in a completely contemplative life and others in a primarily active life, and still others combining both ways. Some take what the Church designates as solemn vows and others take simple vows. Some ways are stricter and others more lenient.

Among religious men, some are in holy orders, others are not. The priest religious usually are concerned with preaching, teaching, writing, hearing confessions and directing souls, social work, foreign and home missions, and so forth; but they are available for any special work the Holy Father may request them to do. Priests of a strictly contemplative order, however, do not engage in activities outside their communities.

Religious men without sacred orders may be found working in all fields that a religious priest would engage in, except the administration of the sacraments and preaching. Some engage in various manual labors to assist the priest, and others teach in schools, run and staff hospitals, engage in social work, etc.

Religious women, with the exception of the strictly contemplative, are engaged in every manner of the spiritual and corporal works of mercy. They teach not only the normal student at all levels, but also the handicapped child and the mentally retarded. They have general hospitals, and special hospitals in which they care for particular human afflictions, like cancer and leprosy. They go as nurses to the homes of the poor. You will find them working in poor areas as skilled Christlike social workers, teaching catechism on the home missions, tackling every manner of task on foreign missions. So long is the list of the works of the active life that sisters engage in, that almost any religious ideal a young woman could have can be found in a community already established. The self-sacrifice of women religious has been one of the great glories of the Church, the variety of works they do for their fellowmen out of love for God a sign of its vitality and Christlike fervor.

D. Secular Institutes

As indicated in the Code of Canon Law (Canon 487) the religious life by definition includes life in common, the vows, a specific rule of life, and the approval of proper ecclesiastical authority. Under God's providence a new type of institute has developed in the Church during the past forty years, although the seeds of it have appeared at various times, even as far back as the latter part of the 18th century. This new type of institute is not a religious institute, for it does not fulfill the definition of the religious life; hence it is called a secular institute.

Secular institutes belong to the state of perfection because their members follow the evangelical perfections of poverty, chastity and obedience, although their vows are private, not public. They are secular rather than religious for they do not live in communities; they live in the world, work in the world in the factories, in the schools, or as members of different professions, and they wear no distinctive garb. Their apostolic aim is to restore Christ to all things in the world by being part of it themselves. Unlike a religious who returns to his community after his apostolic work, the member of a secular institute does not return to a community home. His or her house is an ordinary dwelling. The latest papal directives, however, indicate that there should be one or more common houses in an institute. In the common house the supreme or regional superiors should live, members be received and trained, the sick cared for, and spiritual exercises offered at certain times for the members of the institute. These institutes exist both for men and women, for lay people and members of the clergy.

These secular institutes are defined as societies, whether clerical or lay, whose members profess the evangelical counsels in the world as their aim, in order to attain Christian perfection and the full exercise of the apostolate.[29]

5. THE STATES OF POTENTIAL SUBJECTIVE PERFECTION

A. The Married Life

Marriage, as a sacrament, will be treated in another volume of this series;[30] here our emphasis will be placed upon the married state as it is a way of life for Christians.

Marriage can and should be a school of holiness for those who enter it. It gives an increase of sanctifying grace and the special sacramental grace to insure its success. The beautiful instruction read before the marriage ceremony points out the faith, hope and love of God which must be in the hearts and minds of those about to be joined in this sacrament, and the sacrifices of love which the spouses must be prepared to make for each other and their future children.

St. Paul instructs, "Let marriage be held in honor with all" (Heb. 13:4). Unfortunately modern concepts of marriage have produced, in theory and in practice, an erroneous defilement which has robbed it of its sacredness in the minds of many.

[29]Cf. *De Institutis Saecularibus*, Vol. I, containing the official documents of Pius XII, *Provida Mater Ecclesia* (1947) and *Primo Feliciter* (1948).

[30]Cf. *Christ, and His Sacraments*, Chapter 15; a more detailed study by the same authors is available in *Toward Marriage in Christ* (Dubuque: The Priory Press, 1960).

Success in marriage demands a sufficient progression in the virtues of the active life; but there must also be present at least the seeds of the contemplative life, i.e., the knowledge and love of God that will help the married couple carry on in sickness and in health, for richer or for poorer, for better or for worse, until death. Modern blindness to the fact of the divine institution of marriage, plus the ignoring of even fundamental precepts of the natural law, have led to a more or less total disregard of the obligations of husband and wife, and their combined obligations as parents to their children. The problems which have resulted from the weakness or total lack of virtue in the family present a dire warning of what can happen to the entire life of virtue in the Church. From the family come the future parents, the religious, the priests, the hierarchy of the Church. If this fertile garden of virtue is untilled by its custodians, how can its seedlings bring forth in due season the blossoms and fruits of Christian life?

The ideals of virtue must start in the family from the example and direction of the parents. In the blessing for mothers after childbirth (commonly called "the churching of women"), the mother is reminded of her task to bring her children to the pathway to heaven. This as a primary obligation for the father also, which he fulfills together with his wife by directing and instructing their children in the way of salvation. The work of direction includes the exercise of authority over their children to assure the practice of virtue and the rooting out of vice. The exercise of this authority is an act of virtue on the part of the parents, of a virtue which makes them like to God in their family sphere; it is with God and under God that they hold and exercise this authority. When parents fail to use their God-given authority, the home becomes a disordered and chaotic unit of society, going nowhere so far as eternal happiness and the common good is concerned.

If the young couple entering marriage do so with a spirit which is according to God's law, then there is hope that that spirit will, with God's grace, continue and strengthen as the years go by. A good beginning is a promise of success, and modern movements, like the pre-Cana and Cana conferences, are intended to insure just such a good beginning and later to help the married couple persevere in the good so auspiciously begun. They start well who appreciate the dignity of the sacrament they are to receive and the goodness of the life they are to enter. Their love one for another will not be purely carnal, but the love of charity; they will look on each other with that proper respect which is an act of the virtue of justice; their marital relations will not be understood only, nor even chiefly, as a relief from the weakness of concupiscence, but intended primarily for the begetting of children in obedience to God's command. To enter matrimony otherwise is to leave themselves open to the punishment of which the Book of Tobias (6:17) warns: "For they who in such manner receive matrimony, as to shut God from themselves, and from their minds, and to give themselves to their lust, as the horse and mule, which have not understanding, over them the devil hath power."

Marriage is a *potential* state of perfection because within it exist the means of producing perfection. It is *subjective* because, like the priesthood, the exercise of virtue must be developed personally by the married people themselves, according to the general norms of virtue and with emphasis on those virtues which pertain to the married state. Those who live a virtuous married life are the bulwark of society and the Church.

Of such is the kingdom of heaven.

B. The Single State

Some do not marry because they do not care for responsiblities or are afraid of them. There is no virtue in that attitude. Others do not marry because God has, mysteriously, planned that they remain single in the world to fill a role that is part of his scheme. The lives of those so chosen by God are marked by a spirit of self-sacrifice, often for other members of their families, by the good works they perform for the Church, by prayerful and sacramental activity, and by the dedication of their virginity to God. The life of virginity in the world, according to the mind of God, is not without honor. St. Paul writes of the duty of a father toward his unmarried daughter: "But he who . . . has decided to keep his virgin—he does well. Therefore, both he who gives his virgin in marriage does well, and he who does not give her does better" (I Cor. 7:37-38).

The single life in the world, both for men and women, provided the motive is good, is a way of perfection in the Christian life. The virtues required of it are the basic theological and moral virtues. It does not require a special sacramental grace as does marriage, nor the vows of religion, although its state of virginity is a favorable condition for the higher contemplation of God.

Such a life cannot be a negative one; it should be one in which the freedom afforded is used for freer exercise of the love of neighbor and the love of God. The unmarried recluse who withdraws from God and neighbor withdraws from the dignity of his nature, degrades his humanity, denies his vocation to eternal life. The virtues either of the active life or the contemplative life must be developed, for the single life dedicated to God, like the dedicated life in marriage, in religion or in the priesthood, is a way to the eternal happiness of heaven, a way which must be travelled by means of the acts of Christian virtue.

6. Conclusion

This chapter has considered the special aspects of the virtuous life that arise from the differences among the members of the Church, and their connection with Christian perfection. A priest and married man could meet on the street and exchange similar queries about striving for the same charity, and then indicate their differences as one would hurry to work to support his family and the other would be on his way to church in order to offer the holy sacrifice of the Mass.

These differences lead to specialization along the road to man's final goal, the happiness of heaven. Specialization comes from God who orders all men to a special part in his overall scheme. Only those who have ambitions for this world fail to appreciate their special place as offered to them by God. Those who are interested in God do value the fact that he orders all things according to his power, wisdom and love.

The different states and duties within the Church today are not an obstacle to its unity, but a guarantee of preserving it and maintaining the virtues that belong to all members of whatever condition or state. As nature itself does not use many means where one suffices, neither does it confine itself to one when many are required. The needs of virtue in the society of the Church which is the Mystical Body of Christ are varied; so there are many special duties, states and grades in the Church.

These differences among the members are directed to three things, the perfection, action and beauty of the Church. The various states with their degrees of perfection line up, one above the other, rising to the ultimate perfection of heaven. The various grades within the same states add beauty to the structure of the Church. The actions that flow from the various states and grades are directed to maintain that vast field of virtue which pertains to all men, and to stifle the vices which may touch all kinds. From the Old Testament, with its men of special vocations in their prophecies, miracles, gifts of wisdom and tongues, to the hierarchy of the Church today, there has been one special purpose: the use of their gifts or office to lead the people to the knowledge and love of God in the practice of the virtues common to all. The priests are the extension of the hands of the bishops in this work. The religious, by the complete dedication of their lives to God by the use of more sacrificial methods, point out the more strongly the importance of the virtues which all must practice. The married life should be a way of following these virtues and the method by which new generations of childen of God are first taught and directed in this way of virtue. The unmmaried state presents yet another method of following the same virtues.

The division into the active and contemplative life is merely a degree of emphasis on the virtues that predominate, without, however, abandoning any of those that pertain to men of all conditions and states.

The variety and specialties within the Christian life are God's way of maintaining the unity of one faith, one hope, one charity and one set of disciplinary virtues that are the means to the end. On the one road to the same goal of the everlasting happiness with God in heaven there are various parts to fill. This variety within unity which causes wonderment is just a hint of what is to be attained at the arrival of the final goal, God, who is infinitely wonderful.

Thus we complete our study of man's relationship to God. One major area of theology remains to be investigated: the study of him who is both God and man, of our Savior, the Lord Jesus Christ, who "showed unto us in his very person the way of truth, whereby by rising again we may reach the beatitude of immortal life."[31] This will be the work of the final volume of this series, *Christ, and His Sacraments.*

BIBLIOGRAPHICAL NOTE

St. Thomas gives his significant and profound doctrine on gratuitous graces in the *Summa*, II-II, Questions CLXXI-CLXXVIII; he considers the state of life from Question CLXXIX to CLXXXIX. So much has been written on these subjects that we can give only a sampling of materials which will be useful for outside reading and study. Among the general works we can list *Christ Our Brother* (New York: The Macmillan Co., 1939) by Karl Adam; *The Soul of the Apostolate* (Gethsemani, Ky., 1946) by J. B. Chautard, O.C.S.O.; St. Francis de Sales' *Introduction to the Devout Life; This Tremendous Lover* (Westminster, Md.: The Newman Press, 1947) by Eugene Boylan, O.Cist.R.; *The Three Ages of the Interior Life* by Reginald Garrigou-Lagrange, O.P. (St. Louis: B. Herder Book Co., 1947); Thomas Merton's *The Waters of Siloe* (New York: Harcourt, Brace and Co., 1949); *The Mystery of Godliness* (Chicago: Fides, 1954) by Ceslaus Spicq, O.P.; and the *"Cross and Crown* Series of Spirituality," a series of books put out under the editorship of John L. Callahan, O.P. (St. Louis: B. Herder Book Co.).

Besides the many books written on Christian perfection in general, numerous articles have appeared in contemporary Catholic periodicals. Among these articles the following should be of special in-

[31]St. Thomas, *Summa*, III, Prologue.

terest: "Nature of Sanctity," by J. Cartmell in *Life of the Spirit,* VIII (1953), 87-96; "Increase of Charity," by A. Condit in *The Thomist,* XVII (1954), 367-386; "One Commandment," by A. D'Amato, O.P., in *Cross and Crown,* IV (1952), 405-420; "Perfection and Imperfection," by A. Farrell, O.P., in *Life of the Spirit,* IX (1954), 63-67; "Destiny's Master," by Walter Farrell, O.P., in *Cross and Crown,* VI (1954), 16-26; Dominic Hughes' "Dynamics of Christian Perfection" in *The Thomist,* XV (1952), 247-288; "Christian Holiness," by M. Matthijs, O.P., in *Cross and Crown,* IV (1952), 209-221; and "Spiritual Life of the Average Man," by Luigi Sturzo in *Spiritual Life,* I (1955), 201-209.

Those interested in more information on the particular states of life should consult the following books and essays. A treatment of modern secular institutes and lay developments in general can be found in *Our Time Is Now* by Mary F. M. O'Leary (Westminster, Md.: The Newman Press, 1956), and *Secular Institutes,* a symposium (London: Blackfriars Publications, 1959). A consideration of the religious life is taken up in Oliver J. Kapsner's *Catholic Religious Orders* (Collegeville, Minn.: St. John's Abbey Press, 1957); *The Religious Vocation* by Jacques Leclercq (New York: P. J. Kenedy and Sons, 1955); *The Meaning of the Religious Life* by Benoit Lavaud, O. P. (London: Blackfriars Publications, 1955); *The Silent Life* by Thomas Merton, O.C.S.O.; and, particularly for women, *A Right to Be Merry* by Sr. Mary Francis, P.C. (New York: Sheed and Ward, 1956). The glories of the priesthood are presented in the following books: *Vocation to the Priesthood* by Aidan Carr, O.F.M.Conv. (Washington: Catholic University Press, 1950); *The Defence of the Priesthood* by St. John, Cardinal Fisher (London: Burns, Oates and Washbourne, Ltd., 1935); *The Popes and the Priesthood,* a collection of papal writings on the priesthood (St. Meinrad, Ind: Grail Publications, 1953); and *The Greatest Calling,* a presentation of the priesthood by famous Catholics, edited by Rawley Myers (1956). An extensive bibliography on marriage can be found in *Toward Marriage in Christ* by Thomas C. Donlan, O.P., Francis L. B. Cunningham, O.P., and Augustine Rock, O.P. (Dubuque: The Priory Press, 2nd ed., 1960). And, finally, for those who embrace the single state, we can recommend *The Mystery of Love for the Single* by Dominic J. Unger, O.F.M. Cap. (Franciscan Herald Press, 1958).

INDEX

Abortion, 510 f.
Abstinence,
  act of, 705 f.
  Church law on, 706 ff.
  virtue of, 704 f.
Accession,
  as title to ownership, 537
Accident,
  and grace, 282
  and habit, 114 f.
Accidents,
  kinds of, 115
Accusations, 528
Act, Action
  commanded, 50 f.
    and violence, 34, 35
  elicited, 50
    and violence, 34, 35
  end of, 64
  exterior,
    extension of, 68
    intensity of, 68
    morality of, 66 ff.
    multiplication of, 68
    nature of, 67
    subject to command, 54
  good and evil
    See Morality
  human
    analysis of, 50 ff.
      chart of, 55
    and end, 2
    and grace, 28
    and reason, 1
    and the will, 1
    circumstances of,
      See Circumstances
    complexity of, 3
    division of, 29
    freedom of, 39 ff.
      See Freedom
    mastery of, 2

morality of, 29, 55 ff.
object of,
  as source of morality, 61 f.
principle of, 2
psychology of, 29 ff.
substance of, 48
impure, 722 f.
indifference of,
  moral, 3, 65
interior
  morality of, 66 f.
involuntary,
  See Involuntary
object of,
  integral, 66
of will,
  See Will, act of,
voluntary,
  See Voluntary
Adam,
  and impassibility, 192
  and original justice, 191
  fault of, 193 f.
  immortality of, 192
  integrity of, 191 f.
  sin of, 191 f.
Adjuration, 589
  definition of, 589
Adoration, 578 f.
  definition of, 579
Adultery, 724
Affability, 647, 740
  vices opposed to, 647 f.
Agent,
  end of, 64
Aggression,
  as act of fortitude, 661 f.
  unjust, 511 f.
Agility,
  of glorified body, 19
Agony, 106